Library of Congress Catalog Card Number:
93-84336
ISBN 0-87529-751-X

© 1998 Clara Johnson Scroggins

© 1998 Hallmark Cards, Inc.

Author:	Clara Johnson Scroggins
Publisher:	Rachel Perkal
Editorial Director:	Karla Schiller
Editor:	Barbara Hall Palar
Contributing Editor:	Nancy Fandel
Art Director:	Faith Berven
Contributing Designer:	Nancy Wiles
Editor-in-Chief:	Douglas Holthaus
Executive Editor:	Don Johnson
Design Director:	Deetra Polito
Production Director:	Ivan McDonald
Marketing Director:	Hugh Kennedy

Contents

DEDICATION
CLARA JOHNSON SCROGGINS

To my family—all of the Johnsons, and to Joe, Michael, Kathy, Michelle, Alexzandra, Terrence, and my new grandson, Chaise, and in memory of Rose and Joe Scroggins, Sr., who both passed away in 1991.

To Rachel Perkal and the Hallmark Keepsake Ornament Collector's Club staff; all the ornament collectors I've met; the special group of show promoters and those who strive to publish accurate and up-to-date information for collectors; store owners who tirelessly work to help collectors; the talented Keepsake Ornaments artists who provide us with a never-ending stream of beautiful ornament designs.

To "my" clubs—the NASA Noelers and the Tampa Bay Tree Trimmers.

A special memorial dedication to my brother, Charles Johnson, and my nephew, Billy Johnson, both lost since the last issue of the *Hallmark Keepsake Ornament Collector's Guide.*

NOTE TO THE COLLECTOR:
The *Hallmark Keepsake Ornament Collector's Guide* provides a way for you to keep a record of your ornaments. You will find a small shaded box beside each ornament description. Use the boxes to check off the ornaments in your collection.

To show detail, some ornaments are shown larger than actual size.

ABOUT THE AUTHOR
Clara Johnson Scroggins

During the holiday season of 1972, Clara Johnson Scroggins grieved the death of her husband. Inspired by a close friend to "get out of the house," she went shopping. That's when she spotted the sterling reflections of Reed and Barton's second-edition Silver Cross ornament through a jewelry store window. It captivated Clara, creating for her a comforting sense of spiritual unity with her husband and God.

After purchasing the silver cross, Clara began a nationwide search for Reed and Barton's first edition, produced in 1971. Her quest, which was successful, introduced her to many beautiful, contemporary Christmas ornaments. By this time, Clara had developed a passion for collecting ornaments. When Hallmark introduced its Keepsake Ornaments in 1973, she added those to her rapidly growing treasure trove of collectible ornaments.

With over 200,000 in her possession today, Clara is said to have the world's largest array of tree ornaments. Still, her collection continues to grow as she carefully selects approximately 2,000 new additions each year.

What began as Clara's hobby is now her career. She travels extensively to speak, conduct seminars, and appear at shows and exhibitions. She has written several books, including a collector's guide on silver ornaments and six editions of the *Hallmark Keepsake Ornament Collector's Guide*.

During December 1992, Clara was featured in stories for *USA Today* and a *Better Homes and Gardens®* Christmas ornament publication, as well as on a CNN news segment. She has been interviewed by hundreds of newspapers and has appeared on television talk shows throughout the nation and beyond.

Clara, who lives in Tampa, Florida, is now married to Joe Scroggins, Jr., who, Clara says, offers unyielding patience and understanding of her hobby. She shares her love of contemporary tree ornaments with her family, which includes her son, Michael, her daughter-in-law, Kathy, and three grandchildren.

In addition, Clara says she has a second family: "That's the wonderful extended family of collectors. We share an unbelievable camaraderie, even the very first time we meet."

Dear Collecting Friends,

If I were to list history's most inspiring
events, I'd begin with a quiet birth in Bethlehem
nearly two centuries ago. Millions of people
today celebrate that birthday and enjoy it as
a time to gather families, thank friends and
revisit memories.

Helping us do that was what Hallmark had
in mind 25 years ago when it introduced 18
ornaments. The rest, as they say, is history!

This sixth edition of *Hallmark Keepsake
Ornaments: A Collector's Guide* (1973-93)—
itself a part of Hallmark collecting history—has
been reprinted as part of the 25th Anniversary
Celebration of Hallmark Keepsake Ornaments.
Pair this volume with the seventh edition of
*Hallmark Keepsake Ornaments: A Collector's
Guide* (1994-98), and you'll enjoy a
comprehensive look at 25 years of beautiful,
meaningful ornaments.

I know you've discovered, as I have, that the
Hallmark Keepsake Ornament line gets better and
better every year. And, as I wrote in these pages
five years ago, my wish for you is that the magic
and wonder of the holiday season always will be
present in your life, and that your Christmas tree
will be heavily laden with the ornaments of your
dreams on Christmas morning.

Now, that's worth celebrating!

Happy Anniversary, Hallmark Keepsake
Ornaments! And happy collecting to us all!

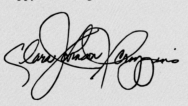

GALLERY OF ARTISTS

Patricia Andrews

When Patricia Andrews began her Hallmark career 16 years ago, she did everything backward. Fortunately, she was an engraver, and this was a necessary talent.

"As an engraver, you take the design from the artist and interpret that shape in metal. It's done backward and inside out so it embosses an image on paper. When it's printed it creates a copy that's identical to the original," Patricia says.

Six years ago, she made the transition to Keepsake Ornament artist. Her designs have a special spark of life, including such favorites as the 1990 Limited Edition Collector's Club Ornament *Sugar Plum Fairy* and the 1992 Keepsake Magic Ornament *Lighting the Way.*

John Francis (Collin)

When it comes to his animal ornaments, John Francis (Collin) doesn't like to be pigeonholed. "Some artists make all their animals cute. Others only want realism in their figures. I like to do both," John says. His wide-ranging tastes and talents are evident in such designs as *Baby Partridge,* Keepsake Miniature Ornament *Black-Capped Chickadee,* and Keepsake Magic design *The Animals Speak.*

When he aims for cuteness in his animals, John enlarges their heads and eyes.

"It's a matter of exaggerating certain features. You always make the head bigger than the body and give the animal large eyes. Also, you have to give them a slight smile by sculpting upturned mouths. All these things give animals a more animated look," the artist says.

Diana McGehee

Diana, a native of Kansas City, has been with Hallmark for 15 years. Besides designing such ornaments as *Gift of Joy,* and the Keepsake Magic Ornament *Festive Brass Church,* she is a technical artist. In that capacity, she prepares detailed descriptions of each ornament before it is released for production. By spelling out which materials to use, sizes, colors, and assembly instructions, she makes certain the artist's vision is reproduced accurately. If her other jobs aren't enough, Diana also uses her computer skills to generate the lettering seen on Keepsake Ornaments.

Dill Rhodus

The smaller the project, the more Dill Rhodus tries to flesh out the details. A Keepsake Ornament designer for the last six of his 26 years at Hallmark, Dill enjoys making miniatures. But he finds they take even more attention than their larger counterparts.

His Keepsake Miniature Ornaments have included *Bright Boxers* and *Busy Bear*. Other projects include work on the "PEANUTS®" Keepsake Magic Collectible Series and Keepsake Magic Ornament *Unicorn Fantasy*, still his favorite ornament.

"I especially enjoyed *Bright Boxers*, a 1991 Keepsake Miniature Ornament showing Santa Claus in his underwear. It took some doing to get that design accepted into the line, but people really got a kick out of it," Dill says.

Ed Seale

The ornaments created by Keepsake Ornament artist Ed Seale have a recurring element: mice. Ed depicted mice busily working with needle and thread in *Sew, Sew Tiny*, and they were featured creatures in his *Mouseboat, Tiny Tea Party*, and *Merry "Swiss" Mouse*.

Ed has been with Hallmark since 1968 and has created Keepsake Ornaments since 1980. Among his highly prized Collectible Series are his contributions to "Frosty Friends," "Fabulous Decade," and "Heart of Christmas."

Anita Marra Rogers

Though she once viewed herself as an artist who would tackle only "serious" subject matter, Anita Marra Rogers visited Hallmark and discovered the joy of whimsy. "Before my first visit here, I couldn't have imagined myself doing sculptures of little children, flowers, or animals. But then I found out that Hallmark was completely different from what I had thought. I saw the studios and, wow, I wanted to work here," she says.

Since 1987, the Missourian has been a full-time Hallmark artist. Look for her 1993 Artists' Favorites Ornament portraying Santa in a country music setting, *Howling Good Time*. Also, watch for her basset hound, Lulu, to pop up in her designs.

Ken Crow

Working on a deadline was not a new concept for Ken Crow when he started with Hallmark in 1979. His previous job was as a cartoonist and artist at a newspaper—a business where deadlines are a way of life. Though he still lives on deadlines, the subject matter is much more pleasing.

"I love animation and working with the lighted mechanical ornaments we sometimes make. Hallmark has brought back the little boy in me. I come to work every day and I think about toys," he says.

In 1992, Ken had the opportunity to create *Santa Maria*, an ornament celebrating the 500th anniversary of Christopher Columbus' voyage.

LaDene Votruba

For some people, art is a hobby. For others it is a job. But for LaDene Votruba it's her life. Growing up on a farm near Wilson, Kansas, she dug clay from surrounding hillsides so she could sculpt. Later, she pursued art at Fort Hays State University in Kansas.

The fruits of her talent can be seen throughout a long Hallmark career. Her 1992 "Greatest Story" design was the final edition in an exquisite collectible series. Other standouts are *Sweet Holiday Harmony*, the sixth and final edition in the "Collector's Plate" Series, and the Keepsake Magic Ornament *The Dancing Nutcracker*, one of her favorites.

Don Palmiter

Although he has been sculpting Keepsake Ornaments full-time for only three years, Don Palmiter is already steering collectors in a whole new direction. In 1991 Don introduced his "Classic American Cars" Collectible Series with a *1957 Corvette*, which rode to the top of the sales charts. He has followed up with a *1966 Mustang* and, for 1993, a *1956 Ford Thunderbird*.

"It's been a big hit with people from the baby-boom generation. Someday, when we finish with the American classics, I'd even like to move into foreign classics, like the old MGs and Jaguars," Don says.

Sharon Pike

If you want to shower artist Sharon Pike with compliments, laugh at her designs. Since joining the Keepsake Ornament design staff in 1983, she has reaped a bounty of chortles, guffaws, and belly laughs with such work as *Nutty Squirrel, Owliday Greetings*, and *Meow Mart*. Inspiring much of her artistic vision are the antics of her three house cats.

"They're unpredictable, and that's a quality I seek in my art—unpredictability. My characters are always just a little bit off the wall, just off center. You'll know they're mine because the characters are always posed so they are looking right at you," she says.

Julia Lee

Any artist who sculpts an ornament called *Turtle Dreams* must be an avid nature lover—an apt description of Julia Lee. Inspired by nature, Julia creates a whimsical peek inside a turtle's shell as an Artists' Favorites Keepsake Ornament in 1992.

Julia grew up in the Missouri countryside with pets as diverse as snakes and horses. She continues to pursue outdoor pleasures, such as camping, skiing, fishing, and hiking. These activities fill her storehouse of inspiration. Some of Julia's other designs include *Hooked on Santa*—wherein poor Mr. Claus snags his own trousers with his fishing hook—*Ski Lift Bunny*, and the Keepsake Magic Ornament *Jingle Bears*.

Robert Chad

Whether he is sculpting a couple sitting in front of a flickering fire or a character from a Dickens story, Robert Chad strives for realism. "I try to put life into these sculptures in a way that implies movement. I think the nicest compliment would be for someone to look at my ornaments and say they look as if they could come alive," he says.

Robert joined the Keepsake Ornament studio in 1987 after stints as a printmaker and animator following art institute studies at both Dayton and Kansas City. His penchant for realism can be seen in *Lord Chadwick*, the third in the "Dickens Caroler Bell" Collection, or in *Elfin Marionette*, which features an elf with hinged legs and arms.

Lynn Norton

For his first journey into the world of Keepsake Ornament design, Lynn Norton took a starship. When Hallmark was looking for the right artist to capture the soul of the much-beloved *Starship Enterprise*™ of STAR TREK® fame, Lynn was the obvious recruit for the assignment. Not only is he an admirer of the television and cinema's space saga, but he is also a longtime technical artist at Hallmark. In that position, he crafts duplicate prototypes of other artists' ornaments. His replicas then are used in the production process. Boosted by the popularity of the *Starship Enterprise*™, more familiar and exotic space hardware is expected to be landing in stores soon.

Joyce Lyle

During the past decade, Joyce has been a Keepsake Ornament designer. It has proved a delightful way to express her joys, her love of family, and her faith.

Joyce captured her position with a portfolio composed of posters and projects created for her church and friends. During her years at Hallmark, she has launched the "Heavenly Angels" Collectible Series and designed such inspiring designs as the Keepsake Miniature Ornaments *Little Star Bringer* and *Angelic Harpist*.

Two of her favorite works were the 1990 *Holiday Cardinals* and the Keepsake Miniature Ornament *Cardinal Cameo* from 1991.

Duane Unruh

In 1969, while visiting a local crafts show in his hometown, Duane Unruh discovered the art of woodcarving. But he never dreamed he'd carve and sculpt for a living. Instead, he followed in his father's footsteps and became a high school coach. As time allowed, he continued his artistic pursuits, eventually joining Hallmark after his retirement from coaching.

As a Keepsake Ornament artist, Duane has incorporated his love for sports into such ornaments as the handpainted porcelain Limited Edition *Victorian Skater,* created for Keepsake Ornament Collector's Club members. Some of his memorable Keepsake Magic Ornaments include 1991's *Bringing Home the Tree* and *Salvation Army Band.*

Bob Siedler

Designer Bob Siedler spends much of his time these days with a boy, an owl, and a "bear of very little brain." He has been sculpting Winnie the Pooh ornaments since 1991. Bob's mastery of his craft can be seen in new Pooh ornaments for Christmas 1993. These join more than 125 other favorites produced by Bob since joining Hallmark in 1979. The Iowa native's ornaments include *Chris Mouse Mail,* a Keepsake Ornament Collector's Club Ornament called *Beary Artistic,* and a group of six 1990 ornaments portraying whimsical penguins.

Donna Lee

Longtime Keepsake Ornament artist Donna Lee, recently retired, had been designing Keepsake Ornaments since they were launched in 1973. During her tenure, she created such memorable Collectible Series as "Nostalgic Houses and Shops" and "Windows of the World." Two Artists' Favorites from recent years, *Donder's Diner* and the *Santa's Streetcar* Miniature Ornament, have received well-deserved accolades.

Donna attributes her success at Hallmark to the support of colleagues and the late Jed Beck, her supervisor for many years. "Jed encouraged his artists to express themselves and not just do things that were safe. It was what I needed to hear," Donna says.

THE ART OF MAKING MEMORIES

When Linda Sickman recalls the Christmases of her childhood, her memories are filled with the excitement of her family's annual 30-mile train ride into the Missouri countryside to visit her grandparents' home.

"It seemed like such an adventure. This was when I was not even 6 years old, and our family didn't have a car. So we took the train. Well, at only 4 or 5 years of age, you can imagine the impression made on me by those enormous, noisy trains," says Linda, now a senior designer of Hallmark Keepsake Ornaments.

For most of us, such recollections—sweet as they may be—have little to do with the present. But Linda is an artist, and the reservoirs of her creativity are fed by such long-ago experiences. Her train stories have jelled into her designs for the

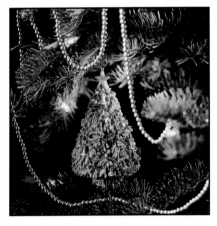

Linda Sickman's *Trimmed With Memories* ornament is a Members Only, 20th Anniversary celebration for the Keepsake Ornament Collector's Club.

"Tin Locomotive" Keepsake Ornament Collectible Series, which first appeared in 1982.

This ability to blend fragments of one's own life into art is the expression of an artist's gift. Like the other Keepsake Ornament artists, Linda is an interpreter of the heart who transforms her own memories into glorious objects, which become, in turn, a whole new set of wonderful memories for others around the world.

"The artists here really inspire each other," Linda explains. "It's amazing to me to see so many talented artists working under one roof."

Each member of the studio has a unique story to tell about becoming an artist. Linda's artistic bent surfaced during childhood in the small town of Clinton, Missouri. Though she has always enjoyed taking up a brush for painting or a pen to draw, she discovered early that her real interests lay in building and sculpting

projects rather than in flat, two-dimensional presentations.

Linda began her career at Hallmark 30 years ago. Her first assignment was in the process art department where she helped prepare color plates for greeting cards. Through the years, she moved to other departments, working on hand lettering, gift wrap design, and party goods.

Then, 11 years ago, Linda developed proposals for a few Christmas ornaments. It wasn't too long before she was receiving congratulatory greetings on her new position as a Keepsake Ornament designer.

Linda remains an artist whether she's pursuing information about 18th-century soldier uniforms at the library, visiting a horse farm to study the graceful movements of a thoroughbred, experiencing a revelation while meditating on the reds and blues of a church's stained glass, or capturing an unexpected inspiration while watching hummingbirds zip around the feeder at her back door.

Does Linda have an all-time

Trimmed With Memories is conceived on paper.

To create details on her wax model, Linda uses knives and dental tools.

Using water-soluble acrylic paints, Linda puts the finishing touches on the piece.

favorite ornament? "I'd have to say a 1986 design called _Gentle Blessings,_" she says.

The Keepsake Lighted Ornament was a simple Nativity scene with the Baby Jesus in the manger surrounded by the stable's animals. The ornament has an understated grace.

Linda feels blessed to be able to share her work with a wide audience. She expressed much of this feeling with a Members Only ornament, _Trimmed With Memories,_ for the Keepsake Ornament Collector's Club. It was released as part of the 20th Anniversary of Keepsake Ornaments.

The ornament is a blue spruce decorated with favorite Keepsake Ornaments from years past. Some are Linda's designs and others are popular ornaments from her Hallmark colleagues. She knows, as with all of the collection, it will find an appreciative audience. She says, "It's very satisfying for me, and for the other artists here, to work for people who really enjoy what we do. It's the excitement and enthusiasm of the public for Hallmark Keepsake Ornaments that makes this such a great place to be."

A NEW TRADITION

COLLECTING HALLMARK KEEPSAKE ORNAMENTS

I t's a Saturday afternoon at Baker's Cafeteria in suburban Des Moines, and the tables are filling up quickly. School teachers, shopkeepers, homemakers, and business professionals—some traveling more than 100 miles to be here—are greeting each other like old friends. It's not the restaurant's daily special that draws them together, or the chocolate pie. This is a quarterly meeting of the Hawkeye Hallmark Collector's Club, and these folks have one subject on their collective mind: Hallmark Keepsake Ornaments.

"We started out with 16 members and have more than 60 now," says Linda Depue, who sponsors the club through her retail store, Linda's Hallmark. The group started meeting casually, she says, once she noticed an unusually strong interest in Hallmark Keepsake Ornaments among local collectors—an interest that pushed ornament sales at her store far above the national average.

Indeed, the common bond among the members gathered together for their three-hour session of Hallmark is clear: Everyone here is hopelessly addicted to collecting Keepsake Ornaments and

happy to share their stories with others.

"I've gone into attics in 100-degree heat looking for ornaments," says Meredith DeGood, one of the club's founding members. "The most important part of collecting for me is the search."

Tales of the hunt are always points of pride discussed at meetings; sharing one's personal collection is another. "If people look at my collection they can understand what's important to me," says club president Nola Ryan. "I have all the kids ornaments—all the Sons, all the Daughters, and all the Baby's Firsts, Seconds, and Thirds. The hearts are very special to me, too."

Although the club members describe themselves as an easygoing bunch—they don't take attendance and they don't charge formal dues—they're undeniably committed to collecting Keepsake Ornaments and to sharing their passion with others.

"One of the things we particularly enjoy doing is speculating on which ornaments are going to be hot sellers," Nola says.

Other items on the meeting's agenda might include watching a slide presentation on decorating tips, seeing a parade of members' favorite ornaments, or poring over the latest Hallmark catalogs. Some local clubs even have been treated to a visit from an artist on the Keepsake

Members of the Hawkeye Hallmark Collector's Club enjoy a lively discussion with Rachel Perkal, *seated at right*, manager of the Hallmark Keepsake Ornament Collector's Club. Hawkeye Club members are, *left to right*, Larry Turbot, Ellen Turbot, Linda Depue and Joe Pendergast.

Ornament staff, through Hallmark's Artist Appearance program.

The Hawkeye Hallmark Collector's Club, like dozens of others across the country and throughout the world, also plans community service projects, particularly at Christmastime. This year the club will donate a decorated Christmas tree to the local Festival of Trees, an annual holiday event at which trees are sold to raise money for a children's hospital. Other clubs nationwide have decorated trees at retirement homes, donated ornaments to shelters for battered women, and brought Keepsake Ornament magic to a local Ronald McDonald House.

"One of the things that warms my heart the most," says Rachel Perkal, manager of Hallmark's Keepsake Ornament Collector's Club with a following of more than 100,000 members throughout the world, "are the philanthropic pursuits that these local clubs take on. It demonstrates that, in addition to the passion and love they have for Keepsake Ornaments, they don't really lose sight of the real meaning of Christmas."

Undoubtedly, the holiday season is the most rewarding time of year for club members, second, perhaps, only to the times when they can meet as a group and reveal their passion for Keepsake Ornament collecting to people who understand it best.

COLLECTING MEMORIES

THROUGH THE YEARS

For some, the spirit of Christmas arrives each year in the lilting strains of a familiar carol or is caught in the scent of fresh-cut pine. For others, it's crystallized by a single image— the angel at the top of the tree, a string of colored lights burning against the nighttime sky, or a child perched on Santa's knee. But for Karen Barksdale of Kansas City, Missouri, all the warm memories of Christmases past, and the happy hopes for those to come, are captured in the hundreds of Hallmark Keepsake Ornaments she has collected for the past 20 years.

At her suburban home in the cradle of America's heartland, the first mark of the season often is a sloshy layer of sleet and ice followed by a soft blanket of Santa

Karen Barksdale relaxes with some of her favorite Keepsake Ornaments.

Claus snow. But whatever the weather, Karen and her husband, Buddy, stoke the fires of friendship and hospitality in anticipation of holiday visitors and the homecoming of their three sons, Matthew, 26, Adam, 24, and Ethan, 22.

At Christmastime Karen's home—trimmed almost exclusively in Keepsake Ornaments—is like the magnetic pole of holiday magic: to it all family and friends are drawn.

"You just have to see Karen's house at Christmas," exclaims longtime friend Glynda Jacobson, who lived next door to the Barksdales for 14 years and first introduced Karen to Hallmark Keepsake Ornaments in 1973. Theirs was a friendship forged as young mothers who discovered, in the delicate and charming Keepsake Ornaments they bought faithfully each year, tangible evidence of the love and affection they felt for their growing families.

The good times for Karen begin in early summer with the release of the Hallmark Keepsake Ornaments Dream Book. She eagerly pores over the pages, marking the new ornaments in each Collectible Series and picking out special ones for friends and family. At the same time, she's saving up her pennies for the day when she and Glynda will hit the Hallmark store for the first shopping trip of the season. It's a happy ritual the two friends still share, even though they're no longer next-door neighbors and their children have long since left for college and beyond.

There's no telling how many ornaments will tumble out of Karen's shopping bags once she gets home ("She won't tell me, and I don't really want to know," Buddy says). But she'll return to the store shelves throughout the months leading up to Christmas, until she satisfies every name on her gift list.

Karen doesn't know for sure exactly how many Keepsake Ornaments she owns. During the holidays, the ornaments in her collection fill one miniature and two full-size Christmas trees, adorn the ropes of garland that hang on every window, and are scattered in various Christmas displays around the house— and that doesn't include a container full of ornaments for which there's no room left in the house.

In the beginning, Karen says she

Some of Karen Barksdale's most treasured Keepsake Ornaments hold an honored place in the center of her holiday mantel.

collected whatever Keepsake Ornaments caught her fancy, which often turned out to be boylike figurines that reminded her of the personalities and interests of her husband and sons. Her technique now honed, Karen is a shrewd collector who understands the value of buying the Keepsake Collectible Series Ornaments, and who knows it's best to nab the first in a series because those often are the hardest to fill in later. In the "off-season," Karen scours flea markets and antique stores in search of treasures that have eluded her in years past, such as those from the "Tin Locomotive" series— her personal favorites.

By making records of her collection, Karen has noticed that many of the series ornaments she's missing are from years when money most probably was spent instead on the people who needed it at home—times, maybe, when one of the boys wanted a new skateboard, or when she and Buddy decided to put an addition on the house. But these inconsistencies in the collection are markers in themselves— reminders of life's passages and of the give-and-take that defines a family.

Karen's son Matthew explains it best: "This is not about collecting the ornaments," he says. "For her, the ornaments are an extension of the Christmas spirit and the spirit of gift giving. A lot of people say it's better to give than to receive, and that's become sort of a trite expression. But to Mom, it's real."

CLARA'S
COLLECTOR'S
CALENDAR

JANUARY

While decorations are still on the tree, take stock of which ornaments are missing from your collection. Now is the time to buy—prices of Christmas collectibles will never be better. Make a chronological list of your collection. Future generations will appreciate your efforts. Plus, an easy-to-scan inventory will simplify shopping for pieces still missing.

Before storing your ornaments for the year, clean them with a soft, damp cloth to eliminate any accumulation of dust and dirt. Be sure to dry them thoroughly before repacking them in their original boxes. I then store my boxed ornaments in hard plastic containers that can be easily stacked on closet shelves or stored away under a bed.

FEBRUARY

A heart-shaped grapevine wreath is an ideal canvas for expressing your feelings on Valentine's Day. Heart-shaped ornaments from the Keepsake Ornament Collection will touch the tender feelings of those you love when showcased in this warm display of affection.

MARCH

Usher in springtime or celebrate a March birthday with a centerpiece of festive "Rocking Horses." Suggestive of outdoor fun, these charming steeds evoke playful childhood memories. Each rocking horse in this colorful arrangement invites you to take an imaginative springtime ride.

APRIL

There's more to an Easter basket than eggs. Decorated with whimsical creations from Hallmark's Keepsake Easter Collection, an Easter basket becomes the stuff of dreams, rich with wonderment and sweetness that long outlasts the edible Easter goodies.

MAY

Honor Mother on her special day with a breakfast-in-bed tray, complete with an elegant pillow ornamented with favorite Keepsake Ornament tributes and lacy finery. These personally selected gifts announce the love and caring only a mother can inspire.

JUNE

If you aren't actually attending a wedding this June, you may very well be commemorating the anniversary of someone close to you. Give the newlywed or not-so-newly married something to build on in the future. Decorate your gift package with ribbon accented with an anniversary or wedding ornament that can be the beginning of an ornament collection marking the couple's years together.

JULY

Celebrate Independence Day family style, with an old-fashioned picnic. Embellish an outdoor setting with red, white, and blue decorations interspersed with patriotic ornaments. No Fourth of July would be complete without the homage to Uncle Sam and our founding fathers that you'll find in a variety of Keepsake Ornament designs.

AUGUST

It won't be long before the days get shorter and summer fades into a warm memory. While the outdoor season is still here, seize the remaining days and celebrate. Adorn a protected screen door in your home or vacation home with a grapevine wreath bearing ornamental tributes to fun in the sun—everything from baseball and bicycle ornaments to Santa engaged in his favorite sports.

SEPTEMBER

September signals back to school for children and teachers alike. Help your child welcome the teacher back to the classroom with a desk centerpiece decorated with favorite teacher ornaments. This special gift beats an apple a day anytime.

OCTOBER

A transitional month, October is a time for reflecting upon nature, including our feathered friends who are departing for warmer climes. Bring the bird-watching season indoors with a Victorian birdcage that cleverly displays an outstanding array of birds from the Keepsake Ornament line.

NOVEMBER

Holiday gift giving is just around the corner, so plan now for creative ways to present your friends and family with seasonal collectibles. Try sewing Keepsake Miniature Ornaments to hats and jewelry for a dramatic presentation that's as much fun to give as it is to receive.

DECEMBER

This is the month we've all been waiting for. If your Christmas collection has grown as much as mine has, you may want to select a theme for your tree, rather than decorating it with everything in your collection. The Keepsake Ornaments on this rustic tree all depict small animals seen in winter. Because some of them are whimsically engaged in outdoor situations, I added lots of natural items like raffia and ornaments made of twigs.

Hallmark

ANGELS ON HIGH
A HEAVENLY HALLMARK DISPLAY

For most of the year, your bannister may be the domain of real live cherubs looking for a fast descent down the stairs. But at holiday time, it's a perfect site for your collection of Keepsake Ornament angels, and divine inspiration for this little angel all dressed and ready for the annual Christmas pageant.

The Keepsake Ornaments in this display are complemented by fresh greenery and airy clouds of netting. We added ornaments that portray Mary and the Baby Jesus to the porcelain, brass, and acrylic "crystal" angels.

To re-create the ethereal setting pictured, you'll need garland the length of the bannister and twice as much tulle fabric. Wrap covered florist's wire in a spiral around the bannister, the garland, and the tulle, gathering the tulle into "clouds" as you go. Use additional florist's wire to fasten the ornaments to the garland. If your angel collection isn't extensive enough for a full bannister, fill any gaps with velvet roses or ornamental brass horns. Or, display the collection on a table or piano.

If you have a host of whimsical cherub Keepsake Ornaments, they also would be right at home ascending your stair rail in this setting. Or, turn your imagination loose in the fabric store: Wind your bannister with red and green lamé in a spiral, drape scallops of a colorful Christmas print, or tie on oversized holiday plaid taffeta bows.

Visions Of Sugarplums
HALLMARK KEEPSAKE ORNAMENTS BRING THIS SPLENDID CONFECTIONARY CREATION TO LIFE

*'T*was the night before Christmas, when all through the house, not a creature was stirring—not even a mouse.

When Clement Moore penned his immortal poem, he became a beloved part of the era from which many of our most cherished Christmas customs evolved. That period, roughly coinciding with the reign of Queen Victoria in England, presented us the image of a jolly and benevolent Santa Claus, Christmas trees with ornaments, and Charles Dickens' *A Christmas Carol*.

Though Moore wrote the poem merely for the amusement of his own six children, it inspired the political cartoonist Thomas Nast to create his first visual image of "the right jolly old elf" in 1863. It was Nast's depictions that originated the idea that Santa lived at the North Pole.

Meantime, events in Germany were establishing Christmas-tree customs. Trees had been associated with Christmas for many

Create a Christmas village with "Nostalgic Houses and Shops" (top) and the "Dickens Caroler Bell" ornaments (lower photo).

years—they were used in seasonal pageants all over Europe during the Middle Ages. By 1600 Germans probably had begun bringing evergreens into their homes and decorating them with paper roses, apples, nuts, and cookies. It wasn't until the mid-1800s, however, that trees became firmly rooted in Christmas traditions. At that time, in the German village of Lauscha, a downturn in the glass bead trade led glassblowers to develop the glass ball ornament for Christmas trees as a source of income. These sparkly decorations were quickly adopted in their homeland.

To bring back the magic of a Victorian Christmas, display the Keepsake Ornament Collection "A Christmas Carol" from 1991 or the "Dickens Caroler Bell" ornaments in front of a delicious-looking gingerbread house, complete with ice cream cone Christmas trees.

Continue the turn-of-the-century holiday magic by attaching "Nostalgic Houses and Shops" Keepsake Ornaments to a wreath. Baby's breath tucked into the branches of your wreath creates the illusion of fluffy snowflakes *(see photograph, above left)*.

Feliz Navidad
A SOUTHWESTERN WAY TO CELEBRATE CHRISTMAS AND KEEPSAKE ORNAMENTS

Tex-Mex is more than a cuisine: It's an exciting style that's becoming popular in all areas of the country. More generally referred to as "Southwest," the elements of this fresh approach to holiday decor include brightly colored woven rugs, pottery, citrus fruit, candles, and almost anything that looks like straw.

This motif offers a prime opportunity to show off your Southwestern-themed Keepsake

Hallmark Keepsake Ornaments help set a fiesta mood for your holiday decor.

Ornaments. Carry the authentic feeling into gift wrap with papers that resemble tooled silver and gold. Under the tree, include a few packages wrapped in brown paper and accented with raffia or brightly colored ribbons. Finish each with one of the many Keepsake Ornaments that carries the traditional Mexican Christmas greeting, "Feliz Navidad."

A warm welcome for your holiday visitors, as shown on the pages here, can be arranged on a tabletop near the front entrance. Attach a few peppers along with *Cactus Cowboy* and the *Feliz Navidad* burro ornaments on a straw mat. Surround them with additional ornaments, limes and kumquats for color, tooled silver boxes, and candles for added warmth.

CHRISTMAS MEMORIES
WITH KEEPSAKE MINIATURE ORNAMENTS

Keepsake Miniature Ornaments can take center stage at your Christmas dinner when you display them on your holiday table.

These miniature designs are created with the same craftsmanship and detail as their full-sized Keepsake Ornament counterparts, yet they measure only about 1 to 1½ inches tall. The intimacy of the dinner table means all diners will have a chance to admire the delicate features of these remarkable ornaments.

For an elegant centerpiece, group two or three tiny trees in the center of the table and adorn them with Keepsake Miniature Ornaments and petite glass balls. Whether you use heirloom Victorian feather trees or reproductions from your Hallmark store, they add a luxurious touch to your holiday decor and display small ornaments at their glittering best.

For a more playful look, Hallmark offers the Holiday Express Revolving Tree Base complete with a miniature tree. The tiny old-time train that

Above, specially selected Keepsake Ornaments are perfect party favors for your holiday table. Below, start a tradition in Miniature.

circles the tree has the same amazing detail as the rest of the Keepsake Miniature Ornament Collection.

To complete the festive look of your holiday table, use Miniature and full-sized Keepsake Ornaments to mark each place setting. Spark conversation and add personality to your table by attaching a Keepsake Miniature Ornament to each napkin ring for a take-home favor. Or, select Keepsake Ornaments that reflect the special interest of each guest (*see top inset photo*). Use ornaments on the table in lieu of place cards and let guests try to guess which ornament is theirs. Of course, the ornament is a gift they may take with them.

You also can create a new holiday tradition celebrating your children or grandchildren with Keepsake Miniature Ornaments. Begin with a purchased stocking decorated with tiny bows of yarn or ribbon (*see lower photo*). Each year, remove one of the bows and replace it with a Keepsake Miniature Ornament reflecting the child's personality or a milestone achieved during that year. This stocking will become a treasured tribute to your child's special occasions.

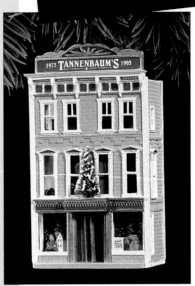

Frosty Friends

1993

Tannenbaum's Dept. Store

Glowing Pewter Wreath

F our special edition designs were created in 1993 to commemorate the 20th anniversary of the Keepsake Ornament line. Three favorite on-going series are complemented by the special editions: "Frosty Friends," "Nostalgic Houses and Shops," and "Here Comes Santa." A beautifully sculpted pewter wreath helps us all remember 20 years of Christmas memories. Several new property characters also came on the scene this year, including "Sylvester and Tweety," "Superman," and "The Pink Panther."

Personalized Keepsake Ornaments made their debut in 1993, with an entire line of designs that could be personalized for the collector with a special message or dedication.

And, a sophisticated group of ornaments called the "Keepsake Ornament Showcase" introduced four distinctive, highly stylized collections. Although they do not look like "typical" Keepsake Ornaments, they demonstrate the same dedication to detail and quality that distinguishes every Keepsake Ornament design.

Shopping With Santa

20th Anniversary Editions

To commemorate the appearance of the first Keepsake Ornaments in 1973, four designs have been created as 20th Anniversary Editions. Three of the ornaments complement, but are not part of, official, numbered Collectible Series. "1973" and "1993" appear on each ornament, and all except the "Glowing Pewter Wreath" bear the inscription: "Anniversary Edition, 20 Years of Keepsake Ornaments."

Frosty Friends
One of the original Keepsake artists, Ed Seale sculpted this ornament in which a penguin and his Eskimo friend decorate an igloo. The dates "1973" and "1993" appear on two blocks, one on each side of the igloo. Inside, above the fireplace hangs a plaque that reads: "Dome Sweet Dome." (Complements the "Frosty Friends" series.)
◼ Handcrafted, Acrylic, 2½" tall
2000QX568-2, $20.00
Artist: Ed Seale

Tannenbaum's Dept. Store
The toy-filled windows of Tannenbaum's invite passing children to stop and stare. The "Visit Santa" sign has already lured many inside. Above the revolving door is a snowy bottle-brush tree, and at the top of the building, a sign identifies "Tannenbaum's 1973 1993." This nostalgic design is the creation of Donna Lee, one of the original Keepsake Ornament artists.

Glowing Pewter Wreath
Fine pewter is known as the sculptor's metal because it lends itself to detailed designing. Duane Unruh created this graceful, hollow wreath using many popular Christmas motifs including Santa faces and a star and large bow. The dates "1993" and "1973" appear on stockings on the front and back, respectively.
◼ Fine Pewter, 3¹¹⁄₁₆" tall
1875QX530-2, $18.75
Artist: Duane Unruh

Shopping With Santa
Santa and Mrs. Claus ride in a classic red car with golden trim, wheels that turn, and doors that open. Sculpted by Linda Sickman, one of the original Keepsake artists, this delightfully detailed ornament features the two anniversary dates on its license plates—"1973" in back and "1993" in front. (Complements the "Here Comes Santa" series.)
◼ Handcrafted, 3½" tall
2400QX567-5, $24.00
Artist: Linda Sickman

(Complements the "Nostalgic Houses and Shops" series.)
◼ Handcrafted, 4¹⁵⁄₁₆" tall
2600QX561-2, $26.00
Artist: Donna Lee

Commemoratives

Baby's First Christmas

Snug in a nutshell swing, this bright-eyed squirrel celebrates the holidays with a shiny red rattle. Caption: "93 Baby's First Christmas."
▉ Handcrafted, 3³⁄₁₆" tall
1075QX551-5, $10.75
Artist: Patricia Andrews

Baby's First Christmas

Antiquing adds an heirloom quality to this silver-plated ornament dated "1993" and captioned: "Baby's First Christmas." A jewelry clasp holds a silver tag that can be removed for engraving.
▉ Silver-plated, 3¹⁄₁₆" tall
1875QX551-2, $18.75
Artist: Don Palmiter

Baby's First Christmas Photoholder

This photoholder wreath has a quilted look. Front: "Baby's First Christmas 1993." Back: "Christmas and babies fill a home with special joys."
▉ Handcrafted, Lace, 4¼" diam.
775QX552-2, $7.75
Artist: Anita Marra Rogers

Baby's First Christmas—Baby Girl

Toy animals encircle the ornament, holding Christmas symbols—a star (dated 1993), tree, and holly. Captions: "Baby's First Christmas" and "A Baby Girl is a bundle of delight."
▉ Pink Glass, 2⅞" diam.
475QX209-2, $4.75
Artist: LaDene Votruba

Baby's First Christmas—Baby Boy

Toy animals encircle the ornament which holds a star, tree, and holly. Captions: "Baby's First Christmas," and "A Baby Boy is a bundle of delight."
▉ Blue Glass, 2⅞" diam.
475QX210-5, $4.75
Artist: LaDene Votruba

Grandchild's First Christmas

A sweet expression adds to this baby raccoon's appeal. The bib says "Grandchild's First Christmas" and the acorn-shaped rattle is dated "93."
▉ Handcrafted, 1⅞" tall
675QX555-2, $6.75
Artist: John Francis (Collin)

A Child's Christmas

This fuzzy, flocked bear is a lovable gift. A lavish bow tops the box, and the "1993" tag can be personalized for: "Niece, Nephew, Granddaughter, Grandson, Great-Grandchild," or "A Child's Christmas."
▉ Handcrafted, 2⁵⁄₁₆" tall
975QX588-2, $9.75
Artist: John Francis (Collin)

Baby's First Christmas

Baby's First Christmas

Baby's First Christmas Photoholder

Baby's First Christmas—Baby Girl

Baby's First Christmas—Baby Boy

Grandchild's First Christmas

A Child's Christmas

Baby's First Christmas

Baby's Second Christmas

Child's Third Christmas

Child's Fourth Christmas

Child's Fifth Christmas

Mom-to-Be

Dad-to-Be

Children's Age Collection

The Teddy Bear Years

This endearing group commemorates a child's first five Christmases. (See the 1989 Annual Collection for design details.)

Baby's First Christmas

Introducing a new theme for the collection, Teddy holds a sugar cookie with the number "1" and a "Baby's 1st Christmas" stocking dated "93."

■ Handcrafted, 2³⁄₁₆" tall
775QX552-5, $7.75
Artist: Ken Crow

Baby's Second Christmas

Caption: "Baby's 2nd Christmas '93."

■ Handcrafted, 2³⁄₁₆" tall
675QX599-2, $ 6.75
Artist: John Francis (Collin)

Child's Third Christmas

Caption: "My 3rd Christmas '93"

■ Handcrafted, 2½" tall
675QX599-5, $6.75
Artist: John Francis (Collin)

Child's Fourth Christmas

Caption: "My 4th Christmas '93"

■ Handcrafted, 3" tall
675QX521-5, $6.75
Artist: John Francis (Collin)

Child's Fifth Christmas

Caption: "My 5th Christmas '93"

■ Handcrafted, 2⅜" tall
675QX522-2, $6.75
Artist: Dill Rhodus

Mom-to-Be

This "MOM-TO-BEE" with frosted acrylic wings holds a jar labeled "HONEY," and wears a bow dated "93."

■ Handcrafted, 2⅛" tall
675QX553-5, $6.75
Artist: Julia Lee

Dad-to-Be

Waiting "in the wings" is "DAD-TO-BEE." One of the daisies in his bouquet is dated "93."

■ Handcrafted, 2⅛" tall
675QX553-2, $6.75
Artist: Julia Lee

Mom

A happy shopper holds the fabric cord handle of her holiday gift bag labeled "Mom 1993."

■ Handcrafted, 2⅝" tall
775QX585-2, $7.75
Artist: Julia Lee

Dad

Papa bear can handle any job in his shirt that reads "Dad's Workshop." He holds a shiny foil saw and wears a tool belt dated "93."

■ Handcrafted, 2⅝" tall
775QX585-5, $7.75
Artist: Julia Lee

Mom and Dad

Foxy parents wear reindeer footwear from a box labeled "His 'N' Hers Slippers." Hers have little pink bows, while the sole of one of Dad's is inscribed "93." "Mom" and "Dad" are written on the pockets of their bathrobes.

■ Handcrafted, 2¹¹⁄₁₆" tall
975QX584-5, $9.75
Artist: Don Palmiter

Daughter

"Daughter 1993" is so flexible she can bend into different poses. She wears a red bow, ruffled collar and socks, and pom-poms on her skates.

■ Handcrafted, 4⁷⁄₁₆" tall
675QX587-2, $6.75
Artist: LaDene Votruba

Mom

Son

Head and shoulders above the other skaters, this flexible fellow sports a bright red turtle neck that says "Son 1993."

■ Handcrafted, 4⁷⁄₁₆" tall
675QX586-5, $6.75
Artist: LaDene Votruba

Sister

Cheerleader kitty roots for her brother in a sweater with "Super Sister" on the front and "93" on the back.

■ Handcrafted, 2¼" tall
675QX554-5, $6.75
Artist: Anita Marra Rogers

Brother

"All-Pro Brother 93" looks like a real team logo on both sides of this puppy's helmet. A metal face-guard adds a realistic touch.

■ Handcrafted, 2⅜" tall
675QX554-2, $6.75
Artist: Anita Marra Rogers

Dad

Mom and Dad

Daughter

Son

Sister

Brother

Sister to Sister

Grandmother

Grandparents

Granddaughter

Grandson

Sister to Sister

For this new commemorative, two mice sit on their powder puff. Behind them is the tube of lipstick with which they've written "Sisters are forever friends!" across the mirror. "1993" is printed on the lid of the compact.

■ Handcrafted, 2⁵⁄₁₆" tall
975QX588-5, $9.75
Artist: Ed Seale

Grandmother

Filled with poinsettias, this woven-textured basket carries holiday wishes to "Grandmother 1993." A tag on the back says "Merry Christmas" and "Love," with space for a signature.

■ Handcrafted, 2⁵⁄₁₆" tall
675QX566-5, $6.75
Artist: Patricia Andrews

Grandparents

Bright poinsettia blossoms cluster on either side of a warm message, "The Christmas traditions of loving and giving are kept by Grandparents all year." The ball is dated "1993."

■ Gold Glass, 2⅞" diam.
475QX208-5, $4.75
Artist: LaDene Votruba

To My Grandma Photoholder

The front of this photoholder, designed to look like a child's writing tablet, says, "To My Grandma XOXO 1993 XOXO." The back says, "I May Be Little, But I Love You Great Big! From" and provides a space for a signature to be added.

■ Handcrafted, 3⁵⁄₁₆" tall
775QX555-5, $7.75
Artist: Donna Lee

Granddaughter

A little girl koala stands on a bright red phone receiver that says, "Only a call away!" and "Granddaughter." The date, "93," appears as "holes" in the mouthpiece.

■ Handcrafted, 3⅝" tall
675QX563-5, $6.75
Artist: Robert Chad

Grandson

This little boy koala has his ear pressed to the receiver. "Holes" in the mouthpiece form the "93" date. Captions on the receiver read: "Grandson" and "Only a call away!"

■ Handcrafted, 3¹¹⁄₁₆" tall
675QX563-2, $6.75
Artist: Robert Chad

Niece

This pony-tailed young woman goes western in her big cowgirl hat labeled "NIECE." Her star badge is dated "93."

■ Handcrafted, 2½" tall
675QX573-2, $6.75
Artist: Anita Marra Rogers

Nephew

Cowpoke "NEPHEW" tips his hat as one boot scoots over the other. He wears a sheriff's badge with the year "93."

■ Handcrafted, 2½" tall
675QX573-5, $6.75
Artist: Anita Marra Rogers

To My Grandma Photoholder

Niece

Nephew

Godchild

Our Family Photoholder

Our First Christmas Together

Godchild
A little sleepyhead kneels next to a bear that joins in with folded paws for bedtime prayers. The pillow says: "Bless You, Godchild 1993."
▣ Handcrafted, 2" tall
875QX587-5, $8.75
Artist: Robert Chad

Our Family Photoholder
Santa waves from the roof where "Our Family" is written in pearly snow. The picture window frames a photo. On the back of this new commemorative is the caption: "Happy Holidays 1993."
▣ Handcrafted, 4⁹⁄₁₆" tall
775QX589-2, $7.75
Artist: Duane Unruh

Our First Christmas Together
This couple hangs a banner proudly proclaiming "Our First Christmas Together." Shiny red ornaments decorate the tree, and a gift beneath it is dated "1993."
▣ Handcrafted, 2⁵⁄₁₆" tall
975QX564-2, $9.75
Artist: Joyce Lyle

Our First Christmas Together
A heart-shaped wreath, sculpted on both sides with leaves and wrapped ribbon, frames this pair of swans. Their graceful necks create another heart shape, and "Our 1st Christmas Together 1993" is stamped below.
▣ Acrylic, 3⅜" tall
675QX301-5, $6.75
Artist: Patricia Andrews

Our First Christmas Together
This dancing couple of antiqued silver-plate twirl as they celebrate "Our First Christmas." Holly leaves are etched on both sides of the brass heart, which is dated "1993."
▣ Brass, Silver-plated, 3¼" tall
1875QX595-5, $18.75
Artist: Anita Marra Rogers

Our First Christmas Together Photoholder
Hearts and holly leaves encircle a treasured photo of "Our First Christmas Together." The date "1993" is embossed on a heart and the back reads: "Love is the heart's most cherished treasure."
▣ Handcrafted, 3⅜" tall
875QX595-2, $8.75
Artist: Duane Unruh

Our Christmas Together
Two cats cuddle on a realistic porch swing that hangs from silvery chains. The front of this new commemorative is captioned: "Our Christmas Together 1993."
▣ Handcrafted, 4¹³⁄₁₆" tall
1075QX594-2, $10.75
Artist: Donna Lee

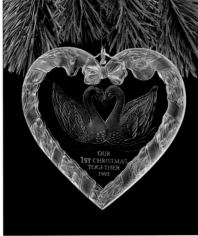

Our First Christmas Together

Our First Christmas Together

Our First Christmas Together Photoholder

Our Christmas Together

Anniversary Year Photoholder

Warm and Special Friends

Perfect Pooch 1993

Special Dog Photoholder

Special Cat Photoholder

Across the Miles

New Home

Anniversary Year Photoholder

This frame can be personalized to commemorate anniversaries number 5, 10, 25, 30, 35, 40, 50 and, for the first time, 60. "Years Together" and Christmas 1993" encircle the space for a photograph, and the back reads, "Loving moments together... Loving memories forever."

▪ Brass, Chrome, 3¹³⁄₁₆" tall
975QX597-2, $9.75
Artist: Joyce Lyle

Warm and Special Friends

Two mice sip cocoa atop a "Hershey's Cocoa™" can look-alike. The realistic-looking can has this message on the back: "The warmest Christmas memories are the ones we make together" and the date, "1993."

▪ Handcrafted, Stamped Metal, 3⁵⁄₁₆" tall
1075QX589-5, $10.75
Artist: Linda Sickman

Special Dog Photoholder

Stars and bones ring this collar-shaped ornament designed to hold a favorite canine's picture. A brass fire hydrant tag says, "Perfect Pooch 1993."

▪ Handcrafted, Brass, 4¹³⁄₁₆" tall
775QX596-2, $7.75
Artist: LaDene Votruba

Special Cat Photoholder

Display your cat's photo in this collar-shaped ornament decked with fish and simulated jewels. A brass bell dangles from the buckle, and the caption reads, "Classy Cat 1993."

▪ Handcrafted, Brass, 4⅛" tall
775QX523-5, $7.75
Artist: LaDene Votruba

Across the Miles

A polar bear cub looks at a memory book. The cover reads "Across the Miles 1993" and inside is a quote: "Happy memories make the miles disappear!"

▪ Handcrafted, 1¹¹⁄₁₆" tall
875QX591-2, $8.75
Artist: John Francis (Collin)

New Home

This sturdy metal "house key" is a wonderful way to commemorate a new home, year after year. Wreaths and bows decorate the cozy cottage dated "1993," and the back reads: "A new home opens the door to memories and love."

▪ Enamel on Die-cast Metal, 3⁵⁄₁₆" tall
775QX590-5, $7.75
Artist: Don Palmiter

Apple for Teacher

An apple opens to reveal a scene of two mouse pupils. "1993" is carved in the floorboards. The other inside panel reads, "A is for apple A+ is for teacher!" Personalization after the words "For:" and "From:" can be written using a ball-point pen.

⬜ Handcrafted, 2⅜" tall
775QX590-2, $7.75
Artist: Ed Seale

Star Teacher Photoholder

A bear holds a star with the date, "1993," and the caption, "For a Star Teacher." A photo can be displayed in the center of the star. The back is captioned "Have a beary Merry Christmas! From:" and it has space for a signature.

⬜ Handcrafted, 2¹⁵⁄₁₆" tall
575QX564-5, $5.75
Artist: Patricia Andrews

Coach

This versatile coach is a new commemorative. He sports a silvery whistle on a real string, a hat dated "93," and a clipboard that says "Cool Coach."

⬜ Handcrafted, 2½" tall
675QX593-5, $6.75
Artist: Don Palmiter

People Friendly

This little fellow strings lights on a rubber cord across his computer dated "1993." Personalized messages saying "Secretary Friendly," "Student Friendly," or "VIP Friendly" slide into the screen. A blank insert provides space for an original message.

⬜ Handcrafted, 2⁷⁄₁₆" tall
875QX593-2, $8.75
Artist: Ed Seale

Top Banana

A merry monkey perches atop a bunch of bananas wearing a Santa suit and a hat that says: "Top Banana." The date, "93," is etched into the banana.

⬜ Handcrafted, 2⁷⁄₁₆" tall
775QX592-5, $7.75
Artist: Anita Marra Rogers

Strange and Wonderful Love

A porcupine grasps a cactus in a warm-hearted embrace. A star, dated "93," tops the cactus, and the plant's pot announces: "Ours is a Strange and Wonderful Relationship."

⬜ Handcrafted, 2¹³⁄₁₆" tall
875QX596-5, $8.75
Artist: Linda Sickman

Apple for Teacher

Star Teacher Photoholder   Coach

People Friendly

Top Banana

Strange and Wonderful Love

Look for the Wonder

He Is Born

Little Drummer Boy

Silvery Noel

Holiday Traditions

Look for the Wonder

At the 1991 Keepsake Ornament Collector's Club Convention, the costume contest winner was Joanne Pawelek, of Edmonton, Alberta. Her prize was to have her fondest Christmas memories used as the inspiration for a Keepsake Ornament. "My family is Ukrainian," says Joanne, "so we observed many Ukrainian customs. The design portrays the preparation for a Ukrainian Christmas Eve supper." The view shown through the ornament's "window" is similar to the one Joanne's grandmother had in the Ukraine. Joanne also recalls using an advent wreath to count the days until Christmas. The window frame of this ornament serves the same purpose. The front of the ornament reads, "Look for the Wonder" and the back, "Christmas...season of wonder and joy." Also on the back are Joanne Pawelek's signature and the date, "1993."

■ Handcrafted, 3½" tall
1275QX568-5, $12.75
Artist: Donna Lee

He Is Born

The beautiful detail of the holly border around this nativity scene extends to the back, which also bears the golden inscription "For unto us a child is born...Isaiah 9:6" and the date, "Christmas 1993."

■ Handcrafted, Handpainted, 3⁹⁄₁₆" tall
975QX536-2, $9.75
Artist: Joyce Lyle

Little Drummer Boy

Playing on his drum dated "1993," this drummer boy marches merrily. His drumsticks, molded from real ones, are especially authentic-looking.

■ Handcrafted, 2¾" tall
875QX537-2, $8.75
Artist: Don Palmiter

Silvery Noel

This ornate, silver-plated box features sculpted holly on the top and bottom, and on each side, one letter of the word "NOEL." The lid of the box, which is hinged and actually opens, bears the date, "1993."

■ Silver-plated, 2" tall
1275QX530-5, $12.75
Artist: Joyce Lyle

Star of Wonder

In this bas-relief scene, the Christmas Star shines down on four animals. On the front of the ornament is "1993," and on the back is this message: "May the Star of Wonder shine brightly for you."

■ Handcrafted, 3¼" tall
675QX598-2, $6.75
Artist: Joyce Lyle

Snowy Hideaway

Beneath glittery evergreen boughs, a fox sits in his cozy hideaway. The scene is fully sculpted front and back and is reminiscent of the early Keepsake "Nostalgia" ornaments. "1993" appears on the front of the ornament.

■ Handcrafted, 3" diam.
975QX531-2, $9.75
Artist: John Francis (Collin)

Star of Wonder

Snowy Hideaway

Mary Engelbreit

PEANUTS®

Feliz Navidad

Playful Pals

Mary Engelbreit

A parade of children carrying new toys on "Christmas Morning 1993" is the subject of this ornament by popular artist Mary Engelbreit.

▥ Red Glass, 2⅛" diam.
500QX207-5, $5.00

PEANUTS®

SNOOPY and WOODSTOCK appear wearing Santa hats and beards under a banner which

reads, "Merry Christmas 1993." Other members of the PEANUTS® gang are shown with "Merry Christmas" greetings in four other languages: German, Italian, Spanish, and French.

▥ Chrome Glass, 2⅞" diam.
500QX207-2, $5.00

Feliz Navidad

A smiling *padre* stands beside the door of a mission church.

Above the door is a banner with the caption, "Feliz Navidad 1993," and a shiny brass bell. The back of the ornament is fully decorated.

▥ Handcrafted, Brass, 2¹⁵⁄₁₆" tall
875QX536-5, $8.75
Artist: Donna Lee

Playful Pals

Haddon Sundblom's illustrations inspired this nostalgic design of jolly old "Coca-Cola" Santa.

Fabric ribbon wraps around the "1993" doghouse.

▥ Handcrafted, 3⅜" tall
1475QX574-2, $14.75
Artist: Anita Marra Rogers

Bugs Bunny

New Attractions

Looney Tunes Collection

In their Keepsake Ornaments debut, five of the most popular members of the Looney Tunes family bring a touch of animated humor to any Christmas tree.

Sylvester and Tweety

Bugs Bunny

It looks as if Bugs is already munching one of his favorite holiday treats—carrots, of course!

▥ Handcrafted, 4⅛" tall
875QX541-2, $8.75
Artist: Linda Sickman

Sylvester and Tweety

Sylvester's in his reindeer get-up of antlers and jingle bells. Tweety has the last laugh, using

Porky Pig

mistletoe to plant a big kiss on his arch rival's cheek.

▥ Handcrafted, 3⁹⁄₁₆" tall
975QX540-5, $9.75
Artist: Don Palmiter

Porky Pig

Dressed in his nightshirt, cap, and slippers, Porky Pig puts out a plate of cookies marked "For Santa."

▥ Handcrafted, 2⁹⁄₁₆" tall
875QX565-2, $8.75
Artist: Patricia Andrews

Elmer Fudd

Elmer Fudd

In his red Santa suit and white beard, there's really no one jollier than Elmer Fudd.

▥ Handcrafted, 2⅞" tall
875QX549-5, $8.75
Artist: Joyce Lyle

Winnie the Pooh

Kanga and Roo

Eeyore

Owl

Tigger and Piglet

Rabbit

Winnie the Pooh Collection

This appealing collection features lovable Winnie the Pooh and his friends as they share in wintertime fun.

Winnie the Pooh
The "Silly Old Bear" is gleefully skiing downhill right toward a pot of honey!
▨ Handcrafted, 3⅝" tall
975QX571-5, $9.75
Artist: Bob Siedler

Kanga and Roo
Kanga and Roo hop, skip, and ski cross-country, taking in the sights and looking for adventure.
▨ Handcrafted, 3¼" tall
975QX567-2, $9.75
Artist: Bob Siedler

Eeyore
With his mane and tail blowing, gloomy Eeyore toboggans into his favorite thistle patch!
▨ Handcrafted, 2" tall
975QX571-2, $9.75
Artist: Bob Siedler

Owl
When frosty weather comes to the Hundred Acre Wood, Owl keeps warm by flapping his beak with an endless stream of talk!
▨ Handcrafted, 3⅝" tall
975QX569-5, $9.75
Artist: Bob Siedler

Tigger and Piglet
With help from Piglet, Tigger does some bouncy figure eights in skates with real metal blades.
▨ Handcrafted, 3¼" tall
975QX570-5, $9.75
Artist: Bob Siedler

Rabbit
Rabbit makes some mighty big tracks in his snowshoes!
▨ Handcrafted, 3½" tall
975QX570-2, $9.75
Artist: Bob Siedler

The Pink Panther

With one foot in the chimney, Pink Panther Santa pauses to look before leaping. The date, "93," is etched in the snow at one corner of the chimney.
▪ Handcrafted, 3" tall
1275QX575-5, $12.75
Artist: Don Palmiter

Maxine

Maxine is a favorite character in Hallmark's SHOEBOX GREETINGS offering. Wearing her characteristic bunny slippers, "shades," and Santa disguise, Maxine brings her own unique holiday message: "Ho-Ho-Ho, Yourself!"
▪ Handcrafted, 3⁷⁄₁₆" tall
875QX538-5, $8.75
Artist: Linda Sickman

Superman™

Sculpted in one of his classic in-flight poses, Superman™ lends strength to any Christmas tree. The famous "S" logo appears on Superman™'s chest and red cape.
▪ Handcrafted, 2" tall
1275QX575-2, $12.75
Artist: Robert Chad

The Pink Panther

Maxine

Superman™

Holiday Fliers

Although sold separately, these three pressed tin ornaments make a charming trio. Each ornament has a revolving propeller and is initialed by the artist, Linda Sickman.

Tin Hot Air Balloon

"Merry Christmas 1993" decorates this pressed tin hot air balloon, which bears Santa and a load of gifts in its basket.
▪ Pressed Tin, 2⅜" tall
775QX561-5, $7.75
Artist: Linda Sickman

Tin Airplane

Santa takes off with a load of gifts in a tin airplane which brings "Season's Greetings" to all. The detail on the plane extends to the underside. The date, "93," appears on the tail.
▪ Pressed Tin, 1⁵⁄₁₆" tall
775QX562-2, $7.75
Artist: Linda Sickman

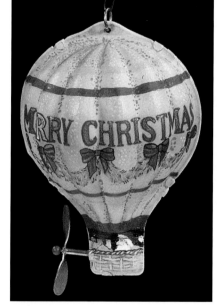
Tin Hot Air Balloon

Tin Airplane

Tin Blimp

Santa's spirits are lighter than air as he peeks out from the observation deck of this gift-laden tin blimp. The blimp features the inscription, "Happy Holidays 1993," on its side.
▪ Pressed Tin, 1¹¹⁄₁₆" tall
775QX562-5, $7.75
Artist: Linda Sickman

Tin Blimp

Caring Nurse

Faithful Fire Fighter

Quick as a Fox

Making Waves

Icicle Bicycle

Putt-Putt Penguin

Occupations

A new group of ornaments debuts with the following three characters.

Caring Nurse
Nurse uses a silvery stethoscope to check out a little bear. She has "TLC" on her cap, "93" on her pocket, and a big supply of warm bear-hugs!
▪ Handcrafted, 1¼ tall
675QX578-5, $6.75
Artist: John Francis (Collin)

Faithful Fire Fighter
Where there's smoke...this Dalmatian "spots" it! He wears an over-sized helmet dated "93" and a yellow slicker.
▪ Handcrafted, 2¾" tall
775QX578-2, $7.75
Artist: LaDene Votruba

Quick as a Fox
The quick brown fox zips along on his sled to deliver a "RUSH" package. He wears a blue cap dated "93."
▪ Handcrafted, 2⅝" tall
875QX579-2, $8.75
Artist: Ken Crow

Making Waves
Santa takes his motorboat out for a cruise with one of his reindeer. "Kringle Craft" appears on both sides of this clip-on ornament, and "93" is etched in the stern.
▪ Handcrafted, 2½" tall
975QX577-5, $9.75
Artist: Don Palmiter

Icicle Bicycle
This glittery snowman pedals energetically along, his fabric neck scarf fluttering behind him. The revolving wheels of his bike feature snowflake designs, and his helmet is dated "93."
▪ Handcrafted, 2¹⁵⁄₁₆" tall
975QX583-5, $9.75
Artist: Julia Lee

Putt-Putt Penguin
Wearing realistic-looking golf shoes and a dapper hat, the happy penguin rides in a red golf cart with "93" on the front, and "Putt-Putt" on either side.
▪ Handcrafted, 3" tall
975QX579-5, $9.75
Artist: Julia Lee

Big on Gardening
With a trowel in one hand and a pot of fabric flowers in the other, this elephant is happy to be out in the garden. A red and green apron features a "93" date on the pocket.
▪ Handcrafted, 2½" tall
975QX584-2, $9.75
Artist: LaDene Votruba

Fills the Bill
The first pelican to appear as a Keepsake Ornament sits on a post marked "Pier 93" and engages in a favorite pastime. The fishing pole has real string, a bobber, and a sculpted hook and worm.
▪ Handcrafted, 3⅛" tall
875QX557-2, $8.75
Artist: Bob Siedler

Big on Gardening

Fills the Bill

Perfect Match

A mouse pushes a tennis ball out of a plastic container. Like real tennis balls, these are covered with fuzzy yellow flocking. The container says, "Perfect Match Tennis Balls" and is dated "93."
■ Handcrafted, 3½" tall
775QX577-2, $8.75
Artist: Bob Siedler

Home for Christmas

Sliding in to home plate, a bunny ballplayer scores a run. His festive red cap has a snowflake on the front and "93" on the back. A clip attaches the ornament to a tree branch.
■ Handcrafted, 1¼" tall
775QX556-2, $7.75
Artist: Bob Siedler

Bowling for ZZZs

A little mouse snoozes in the pocket of a bowling bag, under a towel from "Santa Claus Lanes." The bag features a "1993" I.D. tag.
■ Handcrafted, 1¹³⁄₁₆" tall
775QX556-5, $7.75
Artist: John Francis (Collin)

Dunkin' Roo

On the front and back of this kangaroo's shirt is the "Holiday Roos" team name and number "93." His red sneakers have a realistic tread design.
■ Handcrafted, 3⅞" tall
775QX557-5, $7.75
Artist: Bob Siedler

Beary Gifted

This little artist "pictures" himself in a gold-painted frame that says, "Masterpiece." On his palette is the date, "93."
■ Handcrafted, 2⅜" tall
775QX576-2, $7.75
Artist: Ken Crow

Room for One More

It looks a little crowded in this snow-covered phone booth, now that Santa and all eight reindeer have squeezed inside! Above the door of the booth is: "TELE-PHONE." Below: "1993."
■ Handcrafted, 3³⁄₁₆" tall
875QX538-2, $8.75
Artist: Ken Crow

Christmas Break

Santa's cast is signed with the date " '93" and "XOX," for kisses and a hug. This ornament can be personalized by signing a name on Santa's cast with a ball-point pen.
■ Handcrafted, 3¹⁄₁₆" tall
775QX582-5, $7.75
Artist: Ed Seale

Peep Inside

A mother chickadee perches at a birdhouse with a red roof that sparkles with snow. Above the door, "1993" appears. When the house swings open, three baby birds and speckled eggs are revealed!
■ Handcrafted, 2⁷⁄₁₆" tall
1375QX532-2, $13.75
Artist: Donna Lee

Home for Christmas

Perfect Match

Bowling for ZZZs

Dunkin' Roo

Beary Gifted

Room for One More

Christmas Break

Peep Inside

Ready for Fun

Clever Cookie

Ready for Fun
Here's an ornament that looks good enough to eat—a smiling gingerbread boy just stepping out of his tin cookie cutter. "1993" appears on his pocket.
■ Handcrafted, Tin, 3⅛" tall
775QX512-4, $7.75
Artist: Joyce Lyle

Clever Cookie
This gingerbread girl is coming out of her tin mold just in time for some Christmas fun. Her pearly green purse says "1993."
■ Handcrafted, Tin, 3⅛" tall
775QX566-2, $7.75
Artist: Linda Sickman

Makin' Music
A mouse cellist sits atop a brass music staff. Gold-colored paint brightens the strings and tuning keys of his cello.
■ Handcrafted, Brass, 2" tall
975QX532-5, $9.75
Artist: Ed Seale

Curly 'n' Kingly
A lion and lamb dangle from red and green cord bell ropes. When the lion's rope is pulled, the brass bell rings merrily. The arch above the bell features "1993."
■ Handcrafted, Brass, 4⅛" tall
1075QX528-5, $10.75
Artist: Ken Crow

That's Entertainment
Santa is dressed in a bow tie and fancy red coattails. Pulling the cord makes the rabbit pop out of a top hat dated "93."
■ Handcrafted, 2¹⁵⁄₁₆" tall
875QX534-5, $8.75
Artist: Bob Siedler

High Top-purr
What a fun place for a playful kitty—a high-topped sneaker with a real shoelace! The "93" date appears in a pine tree "logo" on one side of the shoe.
■ Handcrafted, 2³⁄₁₆" tall
875QX533-2, $8.75
Artist: Ed Seale

One-Elf Marching Band
A pull on the red cord makes this elf's drum beat and his brass cymbals clash. Both sides of the drum read: "One-Elf Marching Band" and "93."
■ Handcrafted, Brass, 2⅞" tall
1275QX534-2, $12.75
Artist: Robert Chad

Smile! It's Christmas Photoholder
A mouse photographer poses beside a roll of "film" which has spaces to display two photos. The film canister reads, "Develop by December 25th, 35mm Merry Memories (Double Exposure), CHRISTMAS COLOR, ASA 93." Back caption: "Smile! It's Christmas!"
■ Handcrafted, 4" tall
975QX533-5, $9.75
Artist: Ed Seale

Makin' Music

Curly 'n' Kingly

That's Entertainment

High Top-purr

One-Elf Marching Band

Smile! It's Christmas Photoholder

Snowbird

This snowbird is wearing dark glasses, sensible walking shoes, and a camera for capturing memories. The camera bag is dated "93."
- ▨ Handcrafted, 2⅝" tall
775QX576-5, $7.75
Artist: Julia Lee

Lou Rankin Polar Bear

Adapted from one of Lou Rankin's original collectible sculptures, this wistful-eyed bear has "Rankin" on its underside.
- ▨ Handcrafted, 3¹⁵⁄₁₆" tall
975QX574-5, $9.75
Artist: Dill Rhodus

Water Bed Snooze

This polar bear naps on a "Polar Water Bed" with a "93"-dated ice cube for a pillow. A clip on the bottom of the ornament makes it easy to attach to a tree branch.
- ▨ Handcrafted, 1¾" tall
975QX537-5, $9.75
Artist: Julia Lee

Snow Bear Angel

Just pull the snowball at the end of the red cord and watch the

Snowbird

bear's arms and legs trace angel patterns in the pearly white snow. "1993" is printed on the back of the ornament, along with a verse: "This little bear has Christmas fun by making angels, one by one!"
- ▨ Handcrafted, 2¼" diam.
775QX535-5, $7.75
Artist: Julia Lee

Big Roller

A happy hamster jogs along in a nickel-plated wheel that actually spins. "1993" is imprinted on each side.
- ▨ Handcrafted, Nickel-plated, 3¹⁄₁₆" tall
875QX535-2, $8.75
Artist: Bob Siedler

Lou Rankin Polar Bear

Water Bed Snooze

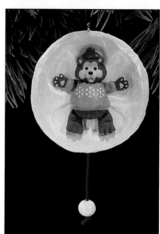

Snow Bear Angel

Big Roller

Great Connections

Popping Good Times

The Swat Team

Hang-Togethers

For the second year, sets of ornaments meant to be hung together add an element of fun and ingenuity to decorating.

Great Connections

Two happy redbirds make a Christmas chain out of vinyl strips. One bird has a bottle marked "GLUE" and the other holds the "1993"-dated chain.
- ▨ Handcrafted
Bird with chain, 3⅝" tall
Bird with glue, 1¼" tall
1075QX540-2, $10.75
Artist: Anita Marra Rogers

Popping Good Times

These two adorable mice are popping corn. The blonde mouse holds an old-fashioned popcorn popper, and her buddy pours "cheese popcorn" into the popper. The bag bears the date "1993."
- ▨ Handcrafted, both 2" tall
1475QX539-2, $14.75
Artist: Robert Chad

The Swat Team

These two kittens play with a ball of red yarn. Just clip the cat with the yarn on a branch above the one who is reaching up to play. The kitty reaching upward is dated "93."
- ▨ Handcrafted, Yarn
Cat with yarn, 1⁹⁄₁₆" tall
Cat with paw up, 1¾" tall
1275QX539-5, $12.75
Artist: Patricia Andrews

Wake-Up Call

Howling Good Time

On Her Toes

Peek-a-Boo Tree

Artists' Favorites

Wake-Up Call

Artist Duane Unruh remembers the Christmas mornings when his children nudged him awake, just as this puppy is trying to rouse his Dad. The basket bears the inscription, "Wake up, Dad, it's Christmas!" The blanket bears the date, "93." The artist's signature is on the bottom.

■ Handcrafted, 1⁷⁄₁₆" tall
875QX526-2, $8.75
Artist: Duane Unruh

Howling Good Time

This Santa in his ten-gallon hat is no match for his howling side-kick. Artist Anita Marra Rogers' love of country music shows in the joy on Santa's face. "93" appears on his belt buckle. Anita's signature is on the underside.

■ Handcrafted, 3" tall
975QX525-5, $9.75
Artist: Anita Marra Rogers

On Her Toes

A deep love of dance, shared by Patricia Andrews and her daughter, inspired the creation of this ornament. The ballerina wears a pearly pink tutu and slippers, and on the sole of her left slipper is the signature, "Patricia."

■ Handcrafted, 3¹⁵⁄₁₆" tall
875QX526-5, $8.75
Artist: Patricia Andrews

Peek-a-Boo Tree

When he designed this ornament, Ken Crow was thinking about playing peek-a-boo with his children. Turn the pine cone at the bottom and make the owl's head twirl and the other animals peek out of their hiding places. The star on top is dated "93." On the base are the words "Peek-a-Boo! We See You!" and the signature, "Ken Crow."

■ Handcrafted, 4 ³⁄₁₆" tall
1075QX524-5, $10.75
Artist: Ken Crow

Bird-Watcher

A bluebird peers through binoculars at Santa and his reindeer. Artist Julia Lee likes to hike and watch birds. That's why her bird-watcher wears boots and earmuffs and carries a camera. The signature, "Julia Lee," is on the bird's tail, and "1993" is on the camera strap.

■ Handcrafted, 2⁷⁄₁₆" tall
975QX525-2, $9.75
Artist: Julia Lee

Bird-Watcher

Julianne and Teddy

Dickens Caroler Bell

Special Editions

Julianne and Teddy

Two best friends share an affectionate moment. The doll wears her holiday best, a satiny bonnet and fabric dress with a tiny rosette on the collar. Her old-fashioned bear is softly flocked and his fabric ribbon holds a brass "93" tag.

■ Handcrafted, 2¾" tall
2175QX529-5, $21.75
Artist: Duane Unruh

Dickens Caroler Bell— Fourth and Final in Collection

The fourth member of this collection of handpainted, fine porcelain bells is "Lady Daphne." Wearing an authentic Victorian outfit, she holds a songbook that has musical staffs inside and a "1993" date on the cover. Caption inside bell: "Lady Daphne, Fine Porcelain."

■ Handpainted Fine Porcelain, 4¼" tall
2175QX550-5, $21.75
Artist: Robert Chad

Collectible Series

Mother Goose

The PEANUTS® Gang

U.S. Christmas Stamps

Mother Goose—First Edition

Childhood nursery rhymes are the focus of this appealing new series. On the front of this year's ornament, Humpty-Dumpty prepares to ascend a ladder to the top of the wall. The cover says, "Mother Goose Nursery Rhymes" and the spine, "Christmas 1993." Inside, Humpty-Dumpty appears in bas-relief, opposite the verse: "Humpty-Dumpty sat on a wall, Humpty-Dumpty had a great fall; All the king's horses and all the king's men, Couldn't put Humpty together again."
- Handcrafted, 2½" tall
  1375QX528-2, $13.75
  Cover Art: LaDene Votruba
  Sculpture: Ed Seale

The PEANUTS® Gang—First Edition

In this new PEANUTS® Gang series CHARLIE BROWN seems quite proud of his creation, a snowman who wears a "93" date on the back of his scarf.
- Handcrafted, 2⅜" tall
  975QX531-5, $9.75
  Artist: Dill Rhodus

U.S. Christmas Stamps—First Edition

This new series features reproductions of designs selected over the years by the U.S. Postal Service for its commemorative Christmas stamps. Each ornament has a fabric ribbon and comes with an acrylic stand. A design from 1983 appears on this first edition. The front reads, "Season's Greetings USA 20c" and the back, "Christmas 1993, Santa Claus, Designer: John Berkey, Date of Issue: October 28, 1983, Place of Issue: Santa Claus, Indiana."
- Enamel on Copper, 2⅖₁₆" tall
  1075QX529-2, $10.75
  Artist: Linda Sickman

Tobin Fraley Carousel—Second Edition

Turn-of-the-century fantasy comes to life in this second in a series of carousel horses designed by Tobin Fraley. The brass pole serves as a hanger or may be inserted into the brass display stand dated "1993," with the artist's signature, "Tobin Fraley."
- Fine Porcelain, Brass, 5¼" tall
  2800QX550-2, $28.00
  Artist: Tobin Fraley

Owliver—Second Edition

While Owliver snoozes in his red stocking cap and green blanket, a squirrel brings him a holiday gift. "93" is carved on the trunk of Owliver's tree.
- Handcrafted, 2⅞" tall
  775QX542-5, $7.75
  Artist: Bob Siedler

Betsey's Country Christmas—Second Edition

Betsey and her friends are engaged in outdoor holiday activities, including caroling from music dated "1993." Caption: "Happy is the memory of bringing home the Christmas tree!"
- White Iridescent Glass, 2⅞" diam.
  500QX206-2, $5.00

Puppy Love—Third Edition

Decked out in a red fabric ribbon and "93"-dated brass tag, this golden retriever puppy takes a downhill ride.
- Handcrafted, 1⅞₁₆" tall
  775QX504-5, $7.75
  Artist: Anita Marra Rogers

Classic American Cars—Third Edition

This cool blue classic T-Bird from 1956 features white sidewall tires that turn, and a replica of what was originally a removable hardtop. Under the car is captioned: "1956 Ford Thunderbird." The front license plate is dated "1956" and the back one "1993."
- Handcrafted, 2⅖₁₆" tall
  1275QX527-5, $12.75
  Artist: Don Palmiter

Tobin Fraley Carousel

Owliver

Betsey's Country Christmas

Puppy Love

Classic American Cars

Peace on Earth

Heavenly Angels

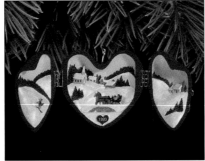

Fabulous Decade

Heart of Christmas

Merry Olde Santa

CRAYOLA® Crayon

Mary's Angels

The Gift Bringers

Peace on Earth—
Third and Final Edition

Poland is highlighted on the globe between two children. Above them, a banner proclaims, "Pokój Ludziom Dobrej Woli," whose translation, "Peace on Earth," is on the opposite side. Below the children's feet is the date, "1993." The Polish flag, an olive branch, and "Poland" are on the back of the ornament.

◼ Handcrafted, 3" diam.
  1175QX524-2, $11.75
  Artist: Linda Sickman

Heavenly Angels—
Third and Final Edition

A delicately sculpted angel appears in a bas-relief scene, holding the dove of peace. Caption on back: "Heavenly Angels Christmas 1993."

◼ Handcrafted, Hand-antiqued, 3" tall
  775QX494-5, $7.75
  Artist: Joyce Lyle

Fabulous Decade—
Fourth Edition

This little skunk wears a green fabric bow and holds the brass numerals "1993" in the curl of his very graceful tail.

◼ Handcrafted, Brass, 1¹³⁄₁₆" tall
  775QX447-5, $7.75
  Artist: Sharon Pike

Heart of Christmas—
Fourth Edition

A charming village scene appears inside this three-panel ornament, which can be displayed open or closed. "1993" is found on the center inside panel, and on the back: "Christmas brings a gentle peace that enters every heart."

◼ Handcrafted, 2" tall
  1475QX448-2, $14.75
  Artist: Ed Seale

Merry Olde Santa—
Fourth Edition

With a full pack on his back and a brass bell in one hand, this traditional Santa embodies the Christmas spirit. At his belt is a pouch dated "1993." Dangling from one side of his pack is a pair of skates with silvery blades.

◼ Handcrafted, 4⁵⁄₁₆" tall
  1475QX484-2, $14.75
  Artist: Anita Marra Rogers

CRAYOLA® Crayon—
Fifth Edition

A bear blows a fanfare at the gate of a castle made of a CRAYOLA® box and crayons. The "CRAYOLA® Crayon" logo appears on the box front, back, and bottom flap, as well as on two crayons at the sides of the castle. On the back is "Bright Shining Castle," with a bar code, "Christmas," and the "Binney & Smith®" trademark. Above the castle ramparts is "1993."

◼ Handcrafted, 3⅜" tall
  1075QX442-2, $10.75
  Artist: Ken Crow

The Gift Bringers—
Fifth and Final Edition

The last ornament in this series features the best-known gift bringers of all, the Three Kings. They are shown at the door of the stable, surrounded by animals and watched over by the guiding star. Caption: "The Gift Bringers, The Magi, Christmas 1993."

◼ Frosted White Glass, 2⅞" diam.
  500QX206-5, $5.00
  Artist: LaDene Votruba

Mary's Angels—
Sixth Edition

Perched on a cloud of frosted acrylic, this little angel reads stories of Christmas. Her green dress inspired her name, "Ivy." The designer's signature, "Mary," appears on the back of the cloud.

◼ Handcrafted, 2⅜" tall
  675QX428-2, $6.75
  Artist: Robert Chad

Reindeer Champs—Eighth and Final Edition

In a skillful play, "Blitzen" sprints toward the end zone. On the back of his jersey, the name "Blitzen" and the number "93" appear.

■ Handcrafted, 3⅛" tall
875QX433-1, $8.75
Artist: Bob Siedler

Mr. and Mrs. Claus—Eighth Edition

Santa wonders why his coat no longer fits, as Mrs. Claus uses a yellow vinyl tape measure to see the damage. She'll have to work fast since the calendar page Santa holds behind his back shows that it's "1993 Dec. 24."

■ Handcrafted, 3⅛" tall
1475QX420-2, $14.75
Artist: John Francis (Collin)

Nostalgic Houses and Shops—Tenth Edition

The two-story "Cozy Home" at the "1993" address boasts verandas on both levels, a side door, and a shingled roof. The living room contains a bottle-brush tree ready for decorating.

■ Handcrafted, 3¹³⁄₁₆" tall
1475QX417-5, $14.75
Artist: Donna Lee

Twelve Days of Christmas—Tenth Edition

Surrounded by a holly motif, a lord in 18th-century dress comes "a-leaping." The gold foil lettering on this beveled, heart-shaped ornament reads, "The Twelve Days of Christmas 1993" and "…ten lords a-leaping…"

■ Acrylic, 3" tall
675QX301-2, $6.75
Artist: Robert Chad

Rocking Horse—Thirteenth Edition

Glossy black rockers with red trim and "1993" lend a classic look to this gray steed. A multi-colored saddle and red bridle feature golden accents.

■ Handcrafted, 4" wide
1075QX416-2, $10.75
Artist: Linda Sickman

Reindeer Champs

Mr. and Mrs. Claus

Nostalgic Houses and Shops

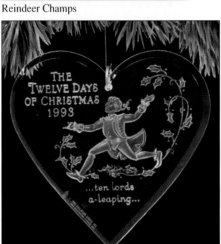

Twelve Days of Christmas

Rocking Horse

Frosty Friends—Fourteenth Edition

An eager little husky comes out of his acrylic igloo doghouse to get a Christmas treat from his friend. The bright red food dish is dated "1993."

■ Handcrafted, 2⅛⁄₁₆" tall
975QX414-2, $9.75
Artist: Julia Lee

Here Comes Santa—Fifteenth Edition

Waving "Happy Haul-idays," Santa drives a truck with a flatbed that tips up and wheels that really turn. The hood ornament is a snowman, the front license plate says "SANTA," and the back reads "1993."

■ Handcrafted, 2⅞" tall
1475QX410-2, $14.75
Artist: Linda Sickman

Frosty Friends

Here Comes Santa

Special Issue

Holiday Barbie™— First Edition

Barbie™ is dressed in her dazzling holiday best as she celebrates the beginning of the new Holiday Barbie™ Collectible Series. The date, "1993," appears on the underside of the ornament.
■ Handcrafted,
3½" tall
1475QX572-5,
$14.75
Artist: Patricia Andrews

Personalized Keepsake Ornaments

These twelve special designs make up Hallmark's first collection of "Personalized Keepsake Ornaments." To help create one-of-a-kind gifts, Hallmark adds the names of friends and family or your personal messages to the ornaments.

Baby Block Photoholder

A charming teddy bear holding a rattle sits atop a block that can be personalized with a message and photo.
■ Handcrafted, 2¹³⁄₁₆" tall
1475QP603-5, $14.75
Artist: John Francis (Collin)

Baby Block Photoholder

Festive Album Photoholder

This album, which can be personalized on the cover, opens to reveal a special photo.
■ Handcrafted, 5 ⁷⁄₁₆" tall
1275QP602-5, $12.75
Artist: LaDene Votruba

Playing Ball

This little slugger has his eye on the ball—and a holiday message on his oversized bat.
■ Handcrafted, 3¹¹⁄₁₆" tall
1275QP603-2, $12.75
Artist: John Francis (Collin)

Mailbox Delivery

Open this merry mailbox and a friendly raccoon pops out—with a personal "Merry

Christmas" note. The outside of the mailbox can be printed with a name or message.
■ Handcrafted, 1⅞" tall
1475QP601-5, $14.75
Artist: Ken Crow

Filled With Cookies

A variety of happy messages can be printed on the front of this lucky little squirrel's acorn-shaped cookie jar.
■ Handcrafted, 2⅛" tall
1275QP604-2, $12.75
Artist: Anita Marra Rogers

On the Billboard

Advertise your holiday greetings on this miniature billboard which proudly bears the "Santa Sign Co." name.
■ Handcrafted, 2⅛" tall
1275QP602-2, $12.75
Artist: Ken Crow

Festive Album Photoholder

Playing Ball

Mailbox Delivery

Filled With Cookies

On the Billboard

Santa Says

Pull the cord to reveal a message direct from Santa—and you.

■ Handcrafted, 2¹⁵⁄₁₆” tall
1475QP600-5, $14.75
Artist: Ed Seale

Going Golfin’

This golfing beaver is happy to top any message that's chosen for the front of his golf ball seat.

■ Handcrafted, 2¹³⁄₁₆” tall
1275QP601-2, $12.75
Artist: Don Palmiter

Here's Your Fortune

It could be your lucky day when you read the personalized fortune contained in this realistic-looking fortune cookie.

■ Handcrafted, 1¹³⁄₁₆” tall
1075QP600-2, $10.75
Artist: Ed Seale

PEANUTS®

Those delightful PEANUTS® characters help announce a greeting by holding up a banner that can be personalized.

■ Frosted White Glass, 2⅞” diam.
900QP604-5, $9.00

Cool Snowman

Sending a "Cool Yule" message to a special someone is easy with this happy snowman. You can personalize the balloon in the center panel.

■ Frosted White Glass, 2⅞” diam.
875QP605-2, $8.75

Reindeer in the Sky

Two of Santa's reindeer have something to say—and you decide what it is! The cartoon balloons above the reindeer can be imprinted with a personal message.

■ Frosted White Glass, 2⅞” diam.
875QP605-5, $8.75

Santa Says

Going Golfin’

Here's Your Fortune

PEANUTS®

Cool Snowman

Reindeer in the Sky

Joy of Sharing

Keepsake Ornament Showcase

This special collection of four unique groups of ornaments was inspired by designs from the Old World and America. Each ornament was carefully crafted using only the finest materials. The collection is a "showcase" for the craftsmanship and enduring quality that have always made Keepsake Ornaments cherished and collectible.

Portraits in Bisque Collection

Inspired by the work of Norman Rockwell and artwork reminiscent of the Victorian Age, favorite holiday scenes are captured in fine bisque porcelain. Each ornament is fully designed in bas-relief on both sides, includes the year date on the back, and features a fabric ribbon hanger.

Joy of Sharing

Two happy children in Victorian-era clothing are on their way to deliver gifts. Sprigs of holly adorn the circular portion of the ornament, and "1993" is etched on the back.

■ Fine Bisque Porcelain, 3¼" tall
1575QK114-2, $15.75
Artist: Joyce Lyle

Mistletoe Kiss

A young man holds mistletoe above his sweetheart's head as they stand cheek-to-cheek. Mistletoe garlands appear on the circular disk, which is dated on the back: "1993."

■ Fine Bisque Porcelain, 3⅝" tall
1575QK114-5, $15.75
Artist: Sharon Pike

Christmas Feast

Two young girls watch in wonder as their mother carries a holly-decked turkey to the Christmas table. All three wear dresses and hairstyles of the Victorian period. The date, "1993," appears on the back.

■ Fine Bisque Porcelain, 3½" tall
1575QK115-2, $15.75
Artist: Sharon Pike

Norman Rockwell— Jolly Postman

Loaded with holiday packages and letters, a postman is escorted on his route by two excited boys and a dog. A popular painting by Norman Rockwell was the inspiration for this ornament, which is dated "1993."

■ Fine Bisque Porcelain, 3¼" tall
1575QK116-2, $15.75
Artist: Peter Dutkin

Norman Rockwell— Filling the Stockings

Inspired by a Norman Rockwell painting, this portrait of Santa captures his delighted look as he discovers the tiny new stocking that has been hung up for him. The ornament is dated "1993."

■ Fine Bisque Porcelain, 3⁹⁄₁₆" tall
1575QK115-5, $15.75
Artist: Peter Dutkin

Mistletoe Kiss

Christmas Feast

Norman Rockwell—Jolly Postman

Norman Rockwell—Filling the Stockings

Old-World Silver Collection

The exquisite designs in this group are created in the likeness of early European Christmas ornaments using detailed engraving. Every ornament is individually cast and silver-plated. Each one includes a dated, silver-plated tag and a fabric ribbon hanger.

Silver Stars and Holly

The graceful shape of this ornament, which carries the "1993" date, is enhanced by engraved and sculpted holly leaves and berries, plus sparkling stars.
▨ Silver-plated, 3⁵⁄₁₆" tall
2475QK108-5, $24.75
Artist: Don Palmiter

Silver Santa

Sculpted faces of Santa alternate with panels of delicate filigree mesh in which engraved toys and candy treats appear. The ornament is dated "1993."
▨ Silver-plated, 3³⁄₁₆" tall
2475QK109-2, $24.75
Artist: Duane Unruh

Silver Sleigh

Two "one-horse open sleighs" appear silhouetted amid elegant silver mesh, one on each side of the ornament, which is dated "1993." Above the mesh is a garland of evergreen and holly.
▨ Silver-plated, 3⅛" tall
2475QK108-2, $24.75
Artist: Don Palmiter

Silver Dove of Peace

The caption, "Peace on Earth," is featured in script on one side and the dove of peace on the other, both framed with intricate filigree. A band of sculpted holly encircles the ornament, which also has a "1993" date.
▨ Silver-plated, 3⁵⁄₁₆" tall
2475QK107-5, $24.75
Artist: Don Palmiter

Silver Stars and Holly

Silver Santa

Silver Sleigh

Silver Dove of Peace

Riding in the Woods

Folk Art Americana Collection

Honoring a folk tradition that goes back many centuries, artist Linda Sickman has created this group of ornaments with the charm of handcarved wood. Each handcrafted and dated design is individually cast and painted to preserve every angle and cut made by the artist. Every ornament features the artist's initials and year date.

Riding in the Woods
Mounted on a red fox, a fisherman brings home three fish. Twine serves as reins and an ornament hanger.
- Handcrafted, Handpainted, 2¹³⁄₁₆" tall
  1575QK106-5, $15.75
  Artist: Linda Sickman

Santa Claus
Santa carries a teddy bear in one arm and a pack of colorful toys on his back. A ship and horse pull-toy are attached with twine and dangle from his hand.
- Handcrafted, Handpainted, 4⅝" tall
  1675QK107-2, $16.75
  Artist: Linda Sickman

Angel in Flight
With her wings and arms spread wide, this angel makes her heavenly flight. A bag of golden stars is tied to the twine belt around her waist.
- Handcrafted, Handpainted, 3¼" tall
  1575QK105-2, $15.75
  Artist: Linda Sickman

Polar Bear Adventure
This little fellow brings home the Christmas tree on the back of a polar bear. The twine reins pass through the rider's hands, and twine is tied around the bear and his cargo.
- Handcrafted, Handpainted, 2¹⁵⁄₁₆" tall
  1500QK105-5, $15.00
  Artist: Linda Sickman

Riding the Wind
Looking like a character straight from folklore, this little bearded man takes a ride on a flying goose. On his back is a purple pack and in his hand a rein made of real twine.
- Handcrafted, Handpainted, 2¹⁄₁₆" tall
  1575QK104-5, $15.75
  Artist: Linda Sickman

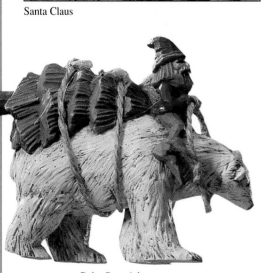
Santa Claus

Angel in Flight

Riding the Wind

Polar Bear Adventure

Holiday Enchantment Collection

These beautifully embellished ornaments have been created by carefully firing the art to fine porcelain. Each ornament has a golden cord hanger, the year date, and a quotation on the back.

Journey to the Forest
Santa pays a special visit to the forest in this peaceful scene. The quotation on the back reads, "All is peaceful in the forest, where a kindly old visitor brings joy to earth's gentle creatures. 1993."
▦ Fine Porcelain, 4½" tall
1375QK101-2, $13.75

The Magi
Following the guiding star, the three wise men journey toward Bethlehem. On the back is "1993" and the words: "We three Kings of Orient are, Bearing gifts we traverse afar, Field and fountain, moor and mountain, Following yonder star."
▦ Fine Porcelain, 3¾" tall
1375QK102-5, $13.75

Visions of Sugarplums
A young child dreams of treats on Christmas Eve. On the back are "1993" and "The children were nestled all snug in their beds, While visions of sugarplums danced in their heads... Clement Clarke Moore."
▦ Fine Porcelain, 3½" diam.
1375QK100-5, $13.75

Bringing Home the Tree
A couple brings their Christmas tree home on a sled. The ornament back reads: "As frosty winds blow, and gentle snowflakes fall, Christmas warms the hearts of all. 1993."
▦ Fine Porcelain, 2¹³⁄₁₆" tall
1375QK104-2, $13.75
Artist: Robert Chad

Angelic Messengers
In the star-bright sky over Bethlehem, three angels proclaim glad tidings. On the back are "1993" and "Christmas is a song sung by angels, heard by all the earth."
▦ Fine Porcelain, 4⅜" tall
1375QK103-2, $13.75
Artist: LaDene Votruba

Journey to the Forest

The Magi

Visions of Sugarplums

Bringing Home the Tree

Angelic Messengers

1992

Baby's First Christmas

Baby's First Christmas Photoholder

Commemorating special people and relationships is an important aspect of Keepsake Ornaments. In 1992, collectors were given the opportunity to commemorate their special relationships with their pets. Cats and dogs were honored and celebrated in two popular new commemoratives, "Special Dog" and "Special Cat."

Memories of carefree childhood days came to life in the stunning debut of the "Tobin Fraley Carousel Horse" series. Its rich treatment in brass and porcelain caught the fancy of collectors everywhere, making this a highly sought after debut ornament.

Another important first was the introduction of "Cheerful Santa," celebrating the rich African-American culture and tradition as it relates to the celebration of Christmas.

The "Spirit of Christmas Stress" ornament is a humorous portrayal of the feelings many people have during the busy holiday season. This is the first ornament adapted from Hallmark's own cast of SHOEBOX GREETINGS characters.

Commemoratives

Baby's First Christmas—Baby Boy
Toys and friendly woodland animals welcome the new baby. Captions: "Baby's First Christmas 1992" and "To love, spoil, Play with, adore—That's what Baby Boys are for!"
- ■ Blue Satin, 2⅞" diam.
  475QX219-1, $4.75
  Artist: LaDene Votruba

Baby's First Christmas— Baby Girl
Forest friends and toys celebrate the new baby's arrival. Captions: "Baby's First Christmas 1992" and "To love, spoil, Play with, adore—That's what Baby Girls are for!"
- ■ Pink Satin, 2⅞" diam.
  475QX220-4, $4.75
  Artist: LaDene Votruba

Baby's First Christmas
Baby slumbers in a basket of fine porcelain. A blanket, dated "1992," and a fabric ribbon wrap up this dreamy scene. Caption: "Baby's First Christmas."
- ■ Handpainted Fine Porcelain, 3½" tall
  1875QX458-1, $18.75
  Artist: Patricia Andrews

Baby's First Christmas Photoholder
This heart-shaped fabric ornament, trimmed in white lace, frames a favorite photo and commemorates: "Baby's First Christmas 1992." Caption: "With every small discovery, Baby makes a merry memory!"
- ■ Fabric, 3³⁄₁₆" tall
  775QX464-1, $7.75
  Artist: LaDene Votruba

Baby's First Christmas – Baby Boy   Baby's First Christmas – Baby Girl

Children's Age Collection

The Teddy Bear Years

This unique collection celebrates a child's first five Christmases. (See the 1989 Annual Collection for design details.)

Baby's First Christmas

This bear cub hugs a green blanket and a candy cane to mark number "1" in Baby's Christmas celebrations. The cap says "Baby's First Christmas" on the trim and " '92" on the pompom.
▨ Handcrafted, 2⅛" tall
775QX464-4, $7.75
   Artist: John Francis (Collin)

Baby's Second Christmas

Caption: "Baby's 2nd Christmas '92"
▨ Handcrafted, 2³⁄₁₆" tall
675QX465-1, $6.75
   Artist: John Francis (Collin)

Child's Third Christmas

Caption: "My 3rd Christmas '92"
▨ Handcrafted, 2½" tall
675QX465-4, $6.75
   Artist: John Francis (Collin)

Child's Fourth Christmas

Caption: "My 4th Christmas '92"
▨ Handcrafted, 3" tall
675QX466-1, $6.75
   Artist: John Francis (Collin)

Child's Fifth Christmas

Caption: "My 5th Christmas '92"
▨ Handcrafted, 2⅛" tall
675QX466-4, $6.75
   Artist: Dill Rhodus

Baby's First Christmas

Baby's Second Christmas

Child's Third Christmas

Grandmother

Antique toys from Grandmother's attic frame the caption: "A Grandmother's world…a world of love and cherished memories. Christmas 1992."
▨ Peach Glass, 2⅞" diam.
475QX201-1, $4.75

Grandparents

The luster of chrome shines through a wreath and Christmas tree on this tribute. Caption: "Grandparents have a special way of brightening up the holiday! Christmas 1992."
▨ Chrome Glass, 2⅞" diam.
475QX200-4, $4.75

A Child's Christmas

Personalize this teddy bear and rocking lamb design with: "A Child's Christmas," "Grandson," "Granddaughter," "Niece," "Nephew," or "Great-Grandchild."
▨ Handcrafted, 2¾" tall
975QX457-4, $9.75
   Artist: John Francis (Collin)

Child's Fourth Christmas

Child's Fifth Christmas

Granddaughter's First Christmas

A baby bear wears a sculpted ribbon and opens a sack of toys that holds an ice skate, ball, and block. Caption: "Granddaughter's 1st Christmas 1992."
▨ Handcrafted, 2³⁄₁₆" tall
675QX463-4, $6.75
   Artist: Bob Siedler

Granddaughter's First Christmas

Grandmother

Grandparents

A Child's Christmas

Grandson's First Christmas   Mom and Dad

Dad   Mom   For My Grandma Photoholder

Grandson's First Christmas

A baby bear discovers a jack-in-the-box, car, and ball in his toy sack. Caption: "Grandson's 1st Christmas 1992."
■ Handcrafted, 2¼" tall
675QX462-1, $6.75
Artist: Bob Siedler

Mom and Dad

Mom and Dad chipmunk string colorful lights from a box labeled, "Christmas 1992." Their sweaters display "MOM" and "DAD."
■ Handcrafted, 1¹⁵⁄₁₆" tall
975QX467-1, $9.75
Artist: Bob Siedler

Dad

Dad naps in his recliner while the "Sports" page headlines declare, "Dad's a Winner!" and the back page reads, "1992 Banner Year for Dad!"
■ Handcrafted, 2⁵⁄₁₆" tall
775QX467-4, $7.75
Artist: Bob Siedler

Mom

Mom savors the quiet in her overstuffed chair, reflecting on the photo album titled, "Mom's Christmas Memories 1992."
■ Handcrafted, 2⅜" tall
775QX516-4, $7.75
Artist: Anita Marra Rogers

For My Grandma Photoholder

This new commemorative features embroidered hearts and holly, lace trim, and a red fabric ribbon. Caption: "For My Grandma 1992." Back caption: "Merry Christmas with Love and Kisses from _____ XOXO."
■ Fabric, 3⅛" tall
775QX518-4, $7.75

Dad-to-Be

Dad has something to crow about this year! He's preparing for the big event, carrying a striped pillow dated "1992" and wearing a sweatshirt captioned, "DAD TO BE."
■ Handcrafted, 2⅜" tall
675QX461-1, $6.75
Artist: Julia Lee

Dad-to-Be   Mom-to-Be

Mom-to-Be

Wrapped with a ribbon and dated "1992," this egg is kept warm by Mother hen. Her pinafore proclaims: "MOM TO BE."
■ Handcrafted, 2⁵⁄₁₆" tall
675QX461-4, $6.75
Artist: Julia Lee

Godchild

These loving lambs snuggle close. A green ribbon carries the caption: "Godchild 1992."
■ Handcrafted, 1⅝" tall
675QX594-1, $6.75
Artist: Duane Unruh

Godchild

Son

Daughter

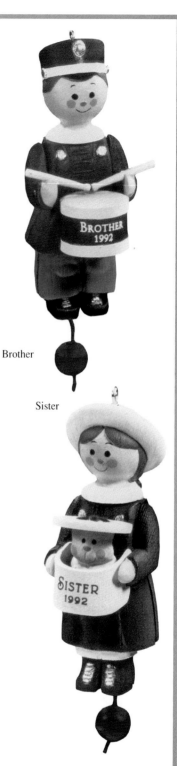

Brother

Sister

Grandson

Granddaughter

Son

Outfitted with goggles, flyer's cap, and pearly white scarf, this squirrel proudly sits in his shiny aircraft, inscribed with: "Son" and "Christmas 1992."
▧ Handcrafted, 2" tall
675QX502-4, $6.75
Artist: John Francis (Collin)

Daughter

Daughter climbs into the cockpit of a shiny plane. She's dressed for flying, with goggles, aviator scarf, and flier's cap with a pink bow. Captions: "Daughter" and "Christmas 1992."
▧ Handcrafted, 2⅛" tall
675QX503-1, $6.75
Artist: John Francis (Collin)

Brother

Pull the dangling ball below the handsome drummer, and he'll play the drum captioned: "Brother 1992."
▧ Handcrafted, 4⅛" tall
675QX468-4, $6.75
Artist: Ken Crow

Sister

This girl wears a festive green coat and has long braided hair tied with a bow. When you pull the ball hanging below her basket captioned "Sister 1992," a kitten peeks out.
▧ Handcrafted, 4" tall
675QX468-1, $6.75
Artist: Ken Crow

Grandson

A slumbering mouse nestles in an apple core carrying the compliment: "Grandson, you're the apple of my eye." "1992" appears on a leaf on top.
▧ Handcrafted, 1¾" tall
675QX561-1, $6.75
Artist: Ed Seale

Granddaughter

Napping in an apple core, this mouse dreams of the treats waiting in her stocking. The caption reads: "Granddaughter, you're the apple of my eye. 1992."
▧ Handcrafted, 1¾" tall
675QX560-4, $6.75
Artist: Ed Seale

Loving Shepherd

Jesus Loves Me

Our First Christmas Together

For the One I Love

Our First Christmas Together

Our First Christmas Together
Photoholder

Anniversary Year Photoholder

Loving Shepherd
This shepherd boy has a lamb nestled at his feet. His outfit includes a brass staff and a pouch dated "1992."
- Handcrafted, Brass, 2¹³⁄₁₆" tall
  775QX515-1, $7.75
  Artist: Patricia Andrews

Jesus Loves Me
Sitting in his rocker with his teddy bear, this child bows his head in prayer. The cameo is framed in brass. Back caption: "Jesus Loves Me. Christmas 1992."
- Cameo, 2⅞" diam.
  775QX302-4, $7.75
  Artist: Patricia Andrews

Our First Christmas Together
Two mice snuggle in a silvery sugar bowl engraved with the message: "Our First Christmas Together 1992." They hold a sparkling "sugar" heart.
- Handcrafted, 2⅞" tall
  975QX506-1, $9.75
  Artist: Julia Lee

For the One I Love
This handpainted heart is a new commemorative inscribed, "For the One I Love." Caption: "Having your love makes Christmas perfect. 1992."
- Handpainted Fine Porcelain, 2⅜" tall
  975QX484-4, $9.75
  Artist: Joyce Lyle

Our First Christmas Together
Shimmering red hearts dance on this acrylic heart. Caption: "Our First Christmas Together 1992."
- Acrylic, 3" tall
  675QX301-1, $6.75
  Artist: LaDene Votruba

Our First Christmas Together Photoholder
This Alpine window frame holds a photo of a special couple to mark: "Our First Christmas Together 1992." Back caption: "Home is where the heart is."
- Handcrafted, 3½" tall
  875QX469-4, $8.75
  Artist: Ed Seale

Anniversary Year Photoholder
This new commemorative can be personalized to celebrate "5, 10, 25, 30, 35, 40, and 50 Years Together." "Christmas 1992" is engraved below the photo. Back caption: "Loving moments together…Loving memories forever."
- Chrome, Brass, 3¹¹⁄₁₆" tall
  975QX485-1, $9.75
  Artist: Duane Unruh

Love to Skate

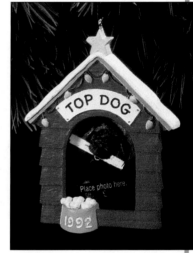

World-Class Teacher

Love to Skate

A bear couple glides across the ice on skates with real metal blades. Her white sweater carries the message: "Christmas 1992."
▧ Handcrafted, 2⅝" tall
875QX484-1, $8.75
Artist: Anita Marra Rogers

World-Class Teacher

This squirrel tells the world about his "World-Class Teacher 1992." He's outfitted in a festive sweater with a tiny knapsack. On the back of the map, there's space for personalization of teacher and student names: "FOR:" and "FROM:"
▧ Handcrafted, 3¼" tall
775QX505-4, $7.75
Artist: Bob Siedler

Teacher

Designed by Mary Engelbreit, this scene depicts the delight of "THE CHRISTMAS PAGEANT" with "Christams" creatively spelled. Costumed children perform in front of one blackboard dated: "Dec. 25, 1992." Another blackboard carries the caption: "For Teacher—Thanks for Making Learning Lots of Fun!"
▧ Red Glass, 2⅞" diam.
475QX226-4, $4.75

Special Dog Photoholder

A dog house trimmed with Christmas lights and a gold star makes it clear who's "Top Dog." This new commemorative has a bone-filled dog dish dated "1992."
▧ Handcrafted, 4" tall
775QX542-1, $7.75
Artist: Robert Chad

Special Cat Photoholder

A special cat's photo will look adorable under the caption, "Favorite Feline," on this new commemorative. A mouse unwraps a package of cheese tagged "92."
▧ Handcrafted, 3¾" tall
775QX541-4, $7.75
Artist: Robert Chad

Secret Pal

Introducing a new commemorative, this postal carrier cheerfully delivers a gift-wrapped Christmas package captioned, "From Your Secret Pal." The raccoon tips a "Special Delivery" hat dated "92."
▧ Handcrafted, 2¾" tall
775QX542-4, $7.75
Artist: Anita Marra Rogers

Teacher

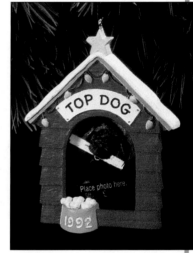

Special Dog Photoholder

Special Cat Photoholder

Secret Pal

V.P. of Important Stuff

From Our Home to Yours

Holiday Memo

Across the Miles

Friendly Greetings

Friendship Line

V.P. of Important Stuff

This penguin nibbles on a frosted doughnut while perching in a coffee mug imprinted with: "V.P. of Important Stuff." Back caption: "Christmas 1992."

◼ Handcrafted, 2⁷⁄₁₆" tall
675QX505-1, $6.75
Artist: Bob Siedler

From Our Home to Yours

A gingerbread snowman sends the warmest Christmas wishes from his snowy village: "From Our Home To Yours." Caption on the sign reads: "Christmas 1992."

◼ White Glass, 2⅞" diam.
475QX213-1, $4.75
Artist: LaDene Votruba

Holiday Memo

Santa's chipmunk assistant is decked out in a Santa hat with a sculpted bell at the tip. He sits atop a stapler dated "1992," holding a stapled memo cover that reads, "MEMO: Have a very Merry Christmas!" Inside: "And a terrific New Year!"

◼ Handcrafted, 2⁷⁄₁₆" tall
775QX504-4, $7.75
Artist: Anita Marra Rogers

Across the Miles

This unique acrylic ornament offers the message, "Merry Christmas Across the Miles," in gold foil. A Christmas wreath frames an engraved, snowy scene dated: "1992."

◼ Acrylic, 3⅜" diam.
675QX304-4, $6.75
Artist: Dill Rhodus

Friendly Greetings

A kitten invites you to personalize the message inside this Hallmark card. "A Friendly Christmas Greeting 1992" is printed on the cover. Inside: "Friendship—'Tis the reason to be jolly!"

◼ Handcrafted, 2⁵⁄₁₆" tall
775QX504-1, $7.75
Artist: Robert Chad

Friendship Line

The "Friendship Line '92" is filled with chatter from these delightful chipmunks. With real brass jingle bells on their collars, they ring up holiday greetings.

◼ Handcrafted, 4½" tall
975QX503-4, $9.75
Artist: Ed Seale

New Home

A chocolate cupcake with whipped cream and a cherry repeats the phrase "Home Sweet Home" in the frosting. Rolling out a "New Home" welcome mat, a mouse opens the door to his house with a "1992" address.

◼ Handcrafted, 2½" tall
875QX519-1, $8.75
Artist: Sharon Pike

New Home

Holiday Traditions

SNOOPY and WOODSTOCK

The ever-popular PEANUTS® characters take to the ice. WOODSTOCK hangs onto SNOOPY's cap which is dated "92." SNOOPY glides on racing skates with real metal blades.
- Handcrafted, 2¼" tall
  875QX595-4, $8.75
  Artist: Anita Marra Rogers

GARFIELD

This mischief-maker is ready for a long winter's nap. Carrying a book titled "Stories" and a blanket dated "92," he ambles along in reindeer slippers and a red Santa cap.
- Handcrafted, 2⁷⁄₁₆" tall
  775QX537-4, $7.75
  Artist: Don Palmiter

Please Pause Here

Inspired by the illustrations of Haddon Sundblom, this clip-on Santa finds refreshment in a "Coca-Cola" and a plate of cookies. The message from a fan says, "Dear SANTA, Please Pause Here. Your PAL." Santa's back pocket is dated "92."
- Handcrafted, 4" tall
  1475QX529-1, $14.75
  Artist: Donna Lee

Cheerful Santa

This cheerful Santa carries a sack dated "1992." Though African-American characters have appeared on ball ornaments as early as 1974, this is Hallmark's first African-American hand-crafted Santa.
- Handcrafted, 3⅛" tall
  975QX515-4, $9.75
  Artist: Duane Unruh

Norman Rockwell Art

This familiar scene of holiday carolers titled, "Christmas…Sing Merrilie" by Norman Rockwell, repeats twice on this ornament.

Captions: "*Post* Cover: Dec. 8, 1923," and "A Famous Holiday Cover From *The Saturday Evening Post*." Sentiment: "In each of our hearts lives an ideal Christmas…a season of snow-covered trees, smiling carolers, and Santa Claus, a season of memories and dreams. 1992."
- Light Blue Glass, 2⅞" diam.
  500QX222-4, $5.00
  Artist: Joyce Lyle

PEANUTS®

The popular PEANUTS® gang performs a Christmas pageant. LINUS narrates, "…Behold, I bring you good tidings of great joy, which shall be to all people." Caption: "Christmas 1992."
- Chrome Glass, 2⅞" diam.
  500QX224-4, $5.00

Memories to Cherish Photoholder

A favorite photo, framed in this porcelain photoholder, reminds us of all the Christmas memories we cherish. Caption: "Merry Christmas 1992."
- Handpainted Fine Porcelain, 3⅝" tall
  1075QX516-1, $10.75
  Artist: Patricia Andrews

SNOOPY and WOODSTOCK

GARFIELD

Please Pause Here

Cheerful Santa

Norman Rockwell Art

PEANUTS®

Memories to Cherish Photoholder

Max the Tailor

Otto the Carpenter

Frieda the Animals' Friend

Eric the Baker

North Pole Nutcrackers

These six fanciful North Pole Nutcrackers feature furry hair and movable parts. All are dated "1992," with each nutcracker's name and title on the bottom of the ornament.

Max the Tailor

In addition to expert stitching of teddy bears and other childhood friends, Max the tailor completes the final stitch with loving care and a real needle and thread.

■ Handcrafted, 4⅜" tall
875QX525-1, $8.75
Artist: Linda Sickman

Otto the Carpenter

Using his trusty hammer, Otto puts the finishing touches on a bird house. He wears a real fabric carpenter's apron.

■ Handcrafted, 4⅜" tall
875QX525-4, $8.75
Artist: Linda Sickman

Frieda the Animals' Friend

With her gentle nature, Frieda attracts many animal friends.

She's dressed in a real fabric apron with a blue bow.

■ Handcrafted, 4⅛" tall
875QX526-4, $8.75
Artist: Linda Sickman

Eric the Baker

Eric's fabric apron keeps his uniform clean as he holds a tray of freshly baked cakes.

■ Handcrafted, 4⅛" tall
875QX524-4, $8.75
Artist: Linda Sickman

Franz the Artist

Franz has a flair for fun. Using his painter's palette and real paint brush, he adds smiles and bright colors to Santa's toys.

■ Handcrafted, 4⅝" tall
875QX526-1, $8.75
Artist: Linda Sickman

Ludwig the Musician

As Santa's master musician, Ludwig wears a tuxedo bib and carries a golden horn and the score to "Dance of the Sugarplum Fairies" from Tchaikovsky's *Nutcracker Suite*.

■ Handcrafted, 4⅞" tall
875QX528-1, $8.75
Artist: Linda Sickman

Franz the Artist

Ludwig the Musician

Tasty Christmas

A Santa-Full!

New Attractions

Tasty Christmas

"It's beginning to taste a lot like Christmas" is inscribed on the body and tail of this shark. Twist his tail and his jaws open to reveal a gift-wrapped package tied with a real fabric bow. Twist his tail again, and his jaws close.
▨ Handcrafted, 2⁵⁄₁₆" tall
975QX599-4, $9.75
Artist: Julia Lee

A Santa-Full!

The see-through tummy helps us peek inside this jolly, well-fed Santa toting a surprise-filled bundle dated "1992."
▨ Handcrafted, 3" tall
975QX599-1, $9.75
Artist: Julia Lee

Golf's a Ball

This snowman's golf ball-textured base reads: "Golf's a Ball 1992." The snowman sports a red cap, golf club arms, and real fabric ribbon.
▨ Handcrafted, 3½" tall
675QX598-4, $6.75
Artist: Lee Schuler

Partridge IN a Pear Tree

Open this clever ornament, and a bewildered partridge looks embarrassed that you've discovered him in his boxer shorts. The pear tree

is "rooted" in a gift captioned: "Partridge IN a Pear Tree." The tree trunk is dated "92."
▨ Handcrafted, 4⅛" tall
875QX523-4, $8.75
Artist: Bob Siedler

Spirit of Christmas Stress

Mrs. Lundquist, a popular character from Hallmark's Shoebox Greetings, colorfully captures "The Spirit of Christmas STRESS," as the message on her shopping bag declares.
▨ Handcrafted, 3½" tall
875QX523-1, $8.75
Artist: Robert Chad

Skiing 'Round

Outfitted with reflective shades, neon ski poles, and skis, this "pro" flips around a brass hanger inserted in a sparkling snowball. Both skis are dated "92."
▨ Handcrafted, 3⅝" tall
875QX521-4, $8.75
Artist: Julia Lee

Golf's a Ball

Partridge IN a Pear Tree

Spirit of Christmas Stress

Skiing 'Round

Deck the Hogs   Gone Wishin'

Egg Nog Nest

Merry "Swiss" Mouse

Deck the Hogs
This pig is wrapped in a festive red wreath inscribed, "Deck the Hogs with Boughs of Holly!" His stocking is dated "1992."
▪ Handcrafted, 3⅛" tall
875QX520-4, $8.75
Artist: John Francis
(Collin)

Gone Wishin'
On this clip-on ornament, Santa props up his feet in a rowboat captioned: "Gone Wishin' 1992," holds a brass fishing pole with real fishing line, and dangles a gift-wrapped package as bait.
▪ Handcrafted, 1¹¹⁄₁₆" tall
875QX517-1, $8.75
Artist: Donna Lee

Egg Nog Nest
A blue bird hangs a Christmas stocking on this egg nog house. Dated with the message, "Enjoy by 12-25-92," the rooftop is trimmed with Christmas lights. The carton reads: "Fresh Egg Nog, Vitamins and

Cheer Added, One Quart."
▪ Handcrafted, 2½" tall
775QX512-1, $7.75

Merry "Swiss" Mouse
Nibbling on cheese from a wedge stamped "Merry 'Swiss' Mouse 1992," this hungry mouse is ready for the holidays.
▪ Handcrafted, 1¹³⁄₁₆" tall
775QX511-4, $7.75
Artist: Ed Seale

North Pole Fire Fighter
Outfitted in a fireman's boots, slicker, and a hat labeled "NPFD," Santa is an honorary member of the North Pole Fire Department. Wearing an "S" on his belt buckle, he slides down a brass "North Pole." His sack full of toys is dated "1992."
▪ Handcrafted, Brass, 3¾" tall
975QX510-4, $9.75
Artist: Ed Seale

Green Thumb Santa
Dressed for gardening with apron and sun visor, Santa helps a tiny seedling grow into a handsome bottle-brush Christmas tree. The watering can is dated "92."
▪ Handcrafted, 2⁵⁄₁₆" tall
775QX510-1, $7.75
Artist: Don Palmiter

North Pole Fire Fighter   Green Thumb Santa

Tread Bear

This bear has added his own paw print signature to the tire swing. Made of flexible rubbery material, the swing is imprinted with the message: "BEAR PAWS 1992 ROAD GRIPPER." Real twine serves as the ornament hanger.

■ Handcrafted, 2¼" tall
875QX509-1, $8.75
Artist: Ed Seale

Santa's Roundup

From the real pompom on his cowboy hat dated "92" to his reindeer belt buckle and silver star spurs, this buckaroo's outfit doesn't miss a trick.

■ Handcrafted, 3¾" tall
875QX508-4, $8.75
Artist: Julia Lee

Down-Under Holiday

A kangaroo hops on high-top tennis shoes that enable the ornament to rock back and forth. He wears a reindeer hat and a bandana captioned, "Down Under Holiday." The boomerang is dated "92."

■ Handcrafted, 2⅞" tall
775QX514-4, $7.75
Artist: Ken Crow

Rapid Delivery

To make sure his cargo arrives safely, this elf wears a life vest as he maneuvers through the rapids. Made of a flexible rubbery material, the raft is dated "1992."

■ Handcrafted, 1⅞" tall
875QX509-4, $8.75
Artist: Don Palmiter

Fun on a Big Scale

This plump fellow is the first hamster in the Keepsake Ornament Collection. Gently push on the dish of Christmas candy and tip the scales the other way. The dial is dated "1992," and the back caption reads: "Fun on a Big Scale!"

■ Handcrafted, 3³⁄₁₆" tall
1075QX513-4, $10.75
Artist: Ken Crow

Hello-Ho-Ho

When you gently pull the dangling ball on this ornament, the windows open so Santa can wish you, "Hello-Ho-Ho! Merry Christmas!" "1992" appears in gold on the rooftop.

■ Handcrafted, 3¹⁵⁄₁₆" tall
975QX514-1, $9.75
Artist: Ken Crow

Tread Bear

Santa's Roundup

Down-Under Holiday

Rapid Delivery

Fun on a Big Scale

Hello-Ho-Ho

Holiday Wishes

Feliz Navidad

Genius at Work

Honest George

Holiday Wishes

Two kittens tug on a wishbone captioned: "Holiday Wishes." One wears a red bandana dated "92," and the other, a green bandana with white polka dots.
■ Handcrafted, 2¹⁄₁₆" tall
775QX513-1, $7.75
Artist: Sharon Pike

Feliz Navidad

This merry mouse strums Christmas songs on a guitar captioned: "Feliz Navidad 1992." The mouse wears a complete South-of-the-Border outfit.
■ Handcrafted, 2⅞" tall
675QX518-1, $6.75
Artist: Patricia Andrews

Genius at Work

One of Santa's elves is busy making toys to meet the Christmas Eve deadline. Gently pulling the brass paint bucket starts him working. The front of the workbench is captioned: "Christmas 1992."
■ Handcrafted, 2⅜" tall
1075QX537-1, $10.75
Artist: Ken Crow

Honest George

In a patriotic uniform, George Washington reminds us 1992 was an election year. He carries a bottle-brush Christmas tree on his shoulder and a silver ax imprinted with "George Washington." His vest pocket is dated "92."
■ Handcrafted, 2½" tall
775QX506-4, $7.75
Artist: Julia Lee

Bear Bell Champ

This sporting champ rings in holiday cheer as he lifts his brass jingle bell barbells. His muscle shirt is captioned "Bear Bell Champ" on the front and "92" on the back.
■ Handcrafted, Brass, 2³⁄₁₆" tall
775QX507-1, $7.75
Artist: Ed Seale

Owl

Known for his frequent and long-winded lectures, Owl joins his friends in the Winnie-the-Pooh Collection offered in 1991. His pals have invited Owl to string the Christmas lights.
■ Handcrafted, 2⅞" tall
975QX561-4, $9.75
Artist: Bob Siedler

Bear Bell Champ

Owl

Hang-Togethers

Introduced in 1992, these three sets of interacting ornaments add a new dimension of fun to holiday displays.

Holiday Teatime

These charming mice re-create that wonderful holiday tradition—tea for two. Designed to be clipped on different branches of your tree, one mouse holds the tea bag while the other holds the teacup dated "1992."

■ Handcrafted, 1⅛" tall
(Mouse with Tea Bag)
Handcrafted, 1⁷⁄₁₆" tall
(Mouse with Cup)
1475QX543-1, $14.75
Artist: Anita Marra Rogers

Cool Fliers

Flying through the air with the greatest of ease, these snow people connect with interlocking hands. This daring couple's holiday act features real string on both trapezes. Her outfit includes a Santa cap, and he wears a holly-adorned top hat and a scarf dated "92."

■ Handcrafted, 3½" tall (both)
1075QX547-4, $10.75
Artist: Julia Lee

Santa's Hook Shot

Santa demonstrates his hook shot in this combination of ornaments. Clip the hoop onto one branch of the tree, and hook Santa onto a branch below. The backboard is captioned: "Hooked on Christmas." Santa's jersey is dated "92."

■ Handcrafted, 2⁷⁄₁₆" tall (Santa)
Handcrafted, 2" tall (Backboard)
1275QX543-4, $12.75
Artist: Ed Seale

Toboggan Tail

These beavers whiz gleefully down the slopes on a toboggan built for two. The beaver's tail forms the toboggan. The larger beaver wears a scarf dated "1992."

■ Handcrafted, 2½" tall
775QX545-9, $7.75
Artist: Patricia Andrews

Holiday Teatime

Cool Fliers

Santa's Hook Shot

Toboggan Tail

Sky Line Locomotive

Sky Line Coal Car

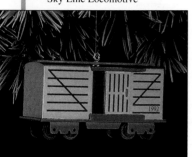

Sky Line Stock Car

Sky Line Caboose

Silver Star Train Set

Christmas Sky Line Collection

This collection of four brightly painted, die-cast metal train cars chugs along on revolving wheels. Each is dated "1992" on both sides and can be displayed hanging or standing.

Sky Line Locomotive
This sturdy teal engine with golden trim is complete with a cowcatcher in front and an engineer's window in back.
- Die-Cast Metal, 1¾" tall
  975QX531-1, $9.75
  Artist: Linda Sickman

Sky Line Coal Car
The name of the collection appears on both sides of this ornament in bright red letters: "Christmas Sky Line."
- Die-Cast Metal, 1⅞" tall
  975QX540-1, $9.75
  Artist: Linda Sickman

Sky Line Stock Car
This striking yellow and black stock car has doors that slide open on both sides.
- Die-Cast Metal, 1⅞" tall
  975QX531-4, $9.75
  Artist: Linda Sickman

Sky Line Caboose
The bright red caboose has bright blue railings on both front and back.
- Die-Cast Metal, 2" tall
  975QX532-1, $9.75
  Artist: Linda Sickman

Silver Star Train Set
The Silver Star is the Keepsake Ornament Collection's first streamliner. To be displayed hanging or standing, this three-piece set includes a "Locomotive," "Luggage Car" and "Dome Car." Each car has revolving wheels and "Silver Star" painted on both sides. The locomotive features a star on the front and "1992."
- Die-Cast Metal, 1½" tall (All Cars)
  2800QX532-4, $28.00
  Artist: Linda Sickman

Artists' Favorites

Elfin Marionette
Robert Chad captured his fascination with old-fashioned toys in this marionette that looks like carved wood. The artist's signature and the date, "Chad 1992," appear on the crossbars.
- Handcrafted, 3¹⁵⁄₁₆" tall
  1175QX593-1, $11.75
  Artist: Robert Chad

Stocked With Joy
Linda Sickman filled this tin stocking with "playthings that people might have enjoyed as children." She's included a surprise gift tagged "1992." Her initials, "LS," appear on one of the checkerboard's red squares.
- Pressed Tin, 4¾" tall
  775QX593-4, $7.75
  Artist: Linda Sickman

Elfin Marionette

Stocked With Joy

Special Edition Dickens Caroler Bell— Third in Collection

"Lord Chadwick" adds his voice to the other carolers in the Special Edition Victorian Bell Collection. Sculpted in authentic Victorian attire, this gentleman sings from a songbook with musical notes on the pages. The cover is dated "1992." Caption: "Lord Chadwick, Fine Porcelain."

▪ Handpainted Fine Porcelain, 4⅝" tall
2175QX455-4, $21.75
Artist: Robert Chad

Polar Post

Artists' Favorites

Polar Post

Ed Seale equipped this furry mail carrier with a real working compass. Filled with cards and a letter addressed, "To Santa," the mailbag is captioned "Polar Post 1992" and carries the artist's signature: "Ed Seale."

▪ Handcrafted, 2⅞" tall
875QX491-4, $8.75
Artist: Ed Seale

Turtle Dreams

This turtle is "never far from home, no matter where he travels," says artist Julia Lee. His metallic green turtle shell, which opens and closes, is tagged "DON'T OPEN TILL CHRIST-MAS" and is dated "1992." The artist's signature, "Julia," appears on the bright red ribbon underneath the shell.

▪ Handcrafted, 1¹³⁄₁₆" tall
875QX499-1, $8.75
Artist: Julia Lee

Mother Goose

Ken Crow created this fanciful goose, whose wings, head, and tail move up and down when you gently swing the ornament back and forth. Mother Goose reads "Christmas Stories." The front of the swing is captioned: "Mother Goose 1992." The back carries a sculpted scene along with the artist's signature, "Ken Crow."

▪ Handcrafted, 3½" tall
1375QX498-4, $13.75
Artist: Ken Crow

Turtle Dreams

Mother Goose

Uncle Art's Ice Cream

Remembering homemade ice cream at family gatherings, Bob Siedler enlisted the help of this little mouse to turn the crank. Modeled after his Uncle Art's ice cream maker, the wood-look bucket holds clear "ice" and is captioned, "Uncle Art's Ice Cream 1992." Tip the bucket to find the artist's signature, "Bob."

▪ Handcrafted, 3¼" tall
875QX500-1, $8.75
Artist: Bob Siedler

Uncle Art's Ice Cream

Special Issues

Santa Maria
With his ship, "Santa Maria," Captain Santa helped commemorate the 500th anniversary of Christopher Columbus' arrival in America. A cheerful crow is perched in his nest above the front sail, captioned: "500 Years 1492-1992."
■ Handcrafted, 3⅛" tall
1275QX507-4, $12.75
Artist: Ken Crow

Elvis
This Special Issue brass-plated ornament pays tribute to the "King of Rock and Roll." Elvis Presley is captured in a pose millions of fans remember. The date, "1992," is inscribed in the bottom of his guitar.
■ Brass-plated, 4½" tall
1475QX562-4, $14.75
Artists: Dill Rhodus
Joyce Lyle

Tobin Fraley Carousel

Owliver

Collectible Series

Tobin Fraley Carousel— First Edition
Dreams of childhood are reflected in this fanciful carousel horse, the first in a series designed by Tobin Fraley, renowned authority on carousels. The brass pole pulls out of a brass display stand dated "1992" and signed: "Tobin Fraley."
■ Handpainted Fine Porcelain, Brass, 5¼" tall
2800QX489-1, $28.00
Artist: Tobin Fraley

Owliver—First Edition
Engrossed in the "1992" edition of *Owliday Tales,* this little owl makes his debut. Owliver delights in sharing a story with his little rabbit friend.
■ Handcrafted, 2¹⁄₁₆" tall
775QX454-4, $7.75
Artist: Bob Siedler

Betsey's Country Christmas—First Edition
Betsey and friends enjoy square dancing to the party theme: "Christmas Sets Our Hearts A-Dancing!" The barn door is dated "1992." This is the third Betsey Clark ball ornament series, the first teardrop-shaped ball series.
■ Blue-Green Glass, 2⅞" diam.
500QX210-4, $5.00

Puppy Love— Second Edition
This friendly gray and white schnauzer puppy is sure to steal your heart away. An identifying characteristic of this series is the pup's heart-shaped tag, dated "92."
■ Handcrafted, Brass, 2⅝" tall
775QX448-4, $7.75
Artist: Anita Marra Rogers

Betsey's Country Christmas

Puppy Love

Classic American Cars—Second Edition

This white 1966 Mustang convertible makes its holiday rounds on wheels that really move. The front license plate is dated "1966," the back plate, "1992." Underneath the chassis: "1966 Mustang."

◼ Handcrafted, 1¼" tall
1275QX428-4, $12.75
Artist: Don Palmiter

Heavenly Angels — Second Edition

A bas-relief design is sculpted in the baroque style of old-world masters, and extends beyond the quadrafoil-shaped borders of this exquisite scene. "Heavenly Angels Christmas 1992" is scripted in golden letters on the back.

◼ Handcrafted, Hand-antiqued, 3" tall
775QX445-4, $7.75
Artist: Joyce Lyle

Heart of Christmas— Third Edition

This three-panel, locket-style ornament illustrates some favorite Christmas traditions: hanging stockings, trimming the tree, and bringing gifts. Captions: "Christmas traditions warm every heart" and "1992." This design can be displayed open or closed.

◼ Handcrafted, 2" tall
1375QX441-1, $13.75
Artist: Ed Seale

Peace on Earth— Second Edition

While her beau plays his guitar, a lovely maiden cradles a globe with Spain highlighted in gold. "1992" and the words "Pax Sobre La Tierra" complete the front design. The translation, "Peace on Earth," appears on the back.

◼ Handcrafted, 3" diam.
1175QX517-4, $11.75
Artist: Linda Sickman

Classic American Cars

Heavenly Angels

Heart of Christmas

Peace on Earth

Merry Olde Santa

Merry Olde Santa— Third Edition

Old-world Santa brings delight to children on Christmas morning with traditional favorites. Santa slips a gleaming brass horn into a special stocking, along with a doll tucked in a dangling pouch dated "1992."

◼ Handcrafted, 4⅛" tall
1475QX441-4, $14.75
Artist: Duane Unruh

Greatest Story— Third and Final Edition

A brass snowflake frames the nativity scene. The bas-relief design, crafted in fine porcelain, is displayed on both sides of the medallion. "1992" is printed on the snowflake.

◼ Fine Porcelain, Brass, 3¾" tall
1275QX425-1, $12.75
Artist: LaDene Votruba

Greatest Story

Winter Surprise— Fourth and Final Edition

Three penguins put finishing touches on their snow penguin, who wears a green top hat dated "1992." Inside this see-through egg world is a bottle-brush tree on glittery snow.

◼ Handcrafted, 3¼" tall
1175QX427-1, $11.75
Artist: John Francis (Collin)

Winter Surprise

Fabulous Decade

The Gift Bringers

Hark! It's Herald

CRAYOLA® Crayon

Mary's Angels

Collector's Plate

Mr. and Mrs. Claus

Fabulous Decade— Third Edition

This clever bear joins a parade of animals celebrating the '90s. He wears a fabric red ribbon and proudly holds the gleaming brass numerals: "1992."
■ Handcrafted, Brass, 1⅛" tall
775QX424-4, $7.75
Artist: Ed Seale

The Gift Bringers— Fourth Edition

Depicting the legend of the elf-maiden "Kolyada," this scene illustrates her traveling through Russia on Christmas Eve, visiting each family in her sleigh. Caption: "The Gift Bringers Kolyada Christmas 1992."
■ White Glass, 2⅞" diam.
500QX212-4, $5.00
Artist: LaDene Votruba

Hark! It's Herald— Fourth and Final Edition

Herald's repertoire is now complete. The tuba carries "1992."
■ Handcrafted, 2¹⁄₁₆" tall
775QX446-4, $7.75
Artist: Julia Lee

CRAYOLA® Crayon— Fourth Edition

This dalmatian steers a fire truck constructed of a CRAYOLA® box and four crayons with the "CRAYOLA® Crayon" logo. "1992" appears on the front flap of the crayon box, and "Bright

Blazing Colors" and the Binney & Smith® trademark are on the bed of the truck. The UPC code and "Christmas" are located underneath the chassis.
■ Handcrafted, 2⅛" tall
975QX426-4, $9.75
Artist: Ken Crow

Mary's Angels— Fifth Edition

Our tawny-haired angel wears a "Lily" white gown that inspired her name. Designed by artist Mary Hamilton, the ornament carries her signature, "Mary," on the bottom.
■ Handcrafted, 2⁷⁄₁₆" tall
675QX427-4, $6.75
Artist: Robert Chad

Collector's Plate— Sixth and Final Edition

Gathered around the piano, a boy and girl harmonize. The caption on the back reads: "Sweet Holiday Harmony 1992." An acrylic plate stand is included.
■ Fine Porcelain, 3¼" diam.
875QX446-1, $8.75
Artist: LaDene Votruba

Mr. and Mrs. Claus— Seventh Edition

Santa and Mrs. Claus exchange presents. Their affection is evident in the loving expressions on their faces. Santa's gift is dated "1992."
■ Handcrafted, 3⅛" tall
1475QX429-4, $14.75
Artist: Duane Unruh

Reindeer Champs

Nostalgic Houses and Shops

Rocking Horse

Reindeer Champs—
Seventh Edition
Winding up for a pitch, "Donder" shows us he's a star pitcher. His jersey reads: "Donder 92."
▨ Handcrafted, 3¹⁄₁₆" tall
875QX528-4, $8.75
Artist: Bob Siedler

Nostalgic Houses and
Shops—Ninth Edition
The classic "Five and Ten Cent Store" is the centerpiece of small town business. Upstairs is the "Meeting Hall," home for the "Order of the Buffalo." "1992" is on the cornice of the store.
▨ Handcrafted, 3⅝" tall
1475QX425-4, $14.75
Artist: Donna Lee

Rocking Horse—
Twelfth Edition
This spotted brown horse displays a bright green saddle with dangling chrome stirrups, red, blue, gold and silver trappings, white socks, a chocolate brown mane, and yarn tail. The date, "1992," is printed on the blue and silver rockers.
▨ Handcrafted, 4" wide
1075QX426-1, $10.75
Artist: Linda Sickman

Frosty Friends—
Thirteenth Edition
A baby whale jumps through the ice for candy canes our little Eskimo is happy to share. The date, "1992," appears in blue numerals on top of the ice.
▨ Handcrafted, 2¹¹⁄₁₆" tall
975QX429-1, $9.75
Artist: Julia Lee

Here Comes Santa—
Fourteenth Edition
"Kringle Tours" is a 15-passenger tour bus, equipped with a stairway to the top deck and wheels that really move. It carries "1992" on the front license plate.
▨ Handcrafted, 2⅝" tall
1475QX434-1, $14.75
Artist: Linda Sickman

Twelve Days of
Christmas—
Ninth Edition
This pretty lady has petticoats swirling. The quadrafoil acrylic has a beveled edge and gold foil lettering that reads: "The Twelve Days of Christmas 1992…nine ladies dancing…"
▨ Acrylic, 3" tall
675QX303-1, $6.75
Artist: Michele Pyda-Sevcik

Frosty Friends

Here Comes Santa

Twelve Days of Christmas

1991

Collectors have long enjoyed selecting and creating displays of ornaments that depict favorite traditions or rekindle cherished memories. In 1991, three special groups offered collectors an opportunity to choose ornaments that have special meaning for them. "A Christmas Carol Collection," fashioned of fine porcelain, includes "Ebenezer Scrooge" and the Cratchit family from Dickens' classic holiday story. The "Winnie-the-Pooh Collection" stars the lovable little bear and his friends, and the "Tender Touches Collection" portrays charming little woodland animals engaged in holiday activities.

Collectors were treated to three theme groups: the "Jolly Wollies," tin ornaments that are containers as well; "Matchbox Memories," miniature scenes of holiday destinations; and designs reminiscent of the "Nostalgia" ornaments of past years.

A new caption, "A Child's Christmas," commemorates the year 1991 for preschool children, while "Baby's First Christmas" appears in a silver-plated format. Four commemoratives have a handcrafted format for the first time: "Grandson's First Christmas," "Granddaughter's First Christmas," "Godchild," and "Sister." "Mother" features a fine porcelain pendant and delicate tin embellishments. Commemorative photoholders for the first, twenty-fifth, and fiftieth year celebrations feature a choice of a chrome or brass frame with a sculpted, handcrafted banner.

Commemoratives

Baby's First Christmas

Elegant and intricately sculpted, this appealing bear in a bootie is all the more precious because it is the first silver-plated commemorative ornament in the Keepsake line. A silver tag that can be detached for engraving and personalization is suspended from a ribbon around the bear's neck. The shimmering "Baby's 1st Christmas" design is delicately antiqued to highlight the careful detailing and carries the year "1991."

■ Silver-plated, 2⅝" tall
1775QX510-7, $17.75
Artist: John Francis (Collin)

Baby's First Christmas Photoholder

The sentiment on the back of the wreath-shaped photoholder says: "The cutest grins, the brightest eyes, always come in baby size." The padded ecru-colored fabric wreath is embroidered with teddy bears and sprigs of holly and trimmed with matching lace and red ribbon. Front caption: "Baby's First Christmas 1991."

■ Fabric, 4⅛" diam.
775QX486-9, $7.75
Artist: LaDene Votruba

Baby's First Christmas: Silver-Plated, Photoholder

Baby's First Christmas—Baby Girl

The "Baby Girl" and "Baby Boy" ball ornaments were created by Hallmark artist Mary Hamilton, and her signature, "Mary," appears on both designs. Soft pastel flowers surround her charming portrait of a rosy-faced baby girl with a cuddly teddy bear and bunny. The caption reads: "A Baby Girl's World...soft with lullabies, sweet with hugs, bright with wonder, warm with love. Baby's First Christmas 1991."
■ Pink Satin, 2⅞" diam.
 475QX222-7, $4.75

Baby's First Christmas—Baby Boy

All smiles for the holidays, this lovable little boy is shown with his favorite toys—a teddy bear, duck, train, and drum. Caption: "A Baby Boy's World...soft with lullabies, sweet with hugs, bright with wonder, warm with love. Baby's First Christmas 1991."
■ Blue Satin, 2⅞" diam.
 475QX221-7, $4.75
 Artist: Mary Hamilton

Grandson's First Christmas

This commemorative, as well as "Granddaughter's First Christ-mas," makes its first appearance in a handcrafted format. For grandson, the bright-eyed teddy bear holds a chain of raised letters highlighted with shiny blue foil. Caption: "Grandson, My First Christmas 1991." The bear design is repeated on the back of the ornament.
■ Handcrafted, 4¼" tall
 675QX511-7, $6.75
 Artist: Robert Chad

Granddaughter's First Christmas

Pearly accents glisten on the lacy collar, cuffs, and hair-bow of this bear. Pink foil makes the raised letters, "Granddaughter," sparkle in the holiday lights. The reverse side of the ornament repeats the bear design. Caption: "My First Christmas 1991."
■ Handcrafted, 4¼" tall
 675QX511-9, $6.75
 Artist: Robert Chad

Baby's First Christmas: Baby Girl, Baby Boy

A Child's Christmas

A preschool child looks up from Christmas play. Old-fashioned wood-style blocks are decorated with raised designs, including a star, tree, and holly leaves. The child is seated on a braided rug captioned, "A Child's Christmas 1991." The commemorative is new to the Keepsake line.
■ Handcrafted, 2⅜" tall
 975QX488-7, $9.75
 Artist: John Francis (Collin)

Grandson's First Christmas,
Granddaughter's First Christmas,
A Child's Christmas

Mom-to-Be, Dad-to-Be

Children's Age Collection

The Teddy Bear Years: This special group of ornaments commemorates a child's first five Christmases. (See the 1989 Annual Collection for design details.)

Baby's First Christmas

This teddy gives a bear hug to a pearly candy cane, number "1." His flocked Santa cap reads: "Baby's 1st Christmas '91."
- Handcrafted, 2½" tall
  775QX488-9 $7.75
  Artist: John Francis (Collin)

Baby's Second Christmas

Caption: "Baby's 2nd Christmas '91."
- Handcrafted, 2³⁄₁₆" tall
  675QX489-7, $6.75
  Artist: John Francis (Collin)

Child's Third Christmas

Caption: "My 3rd Christmas '91."
- Handcrafted, 2½" tall
  675QX489-9, $6.75
  Artist: John Francis (Collin)

Child's Fourth Christmas

Caption: "My 4th Christmas '91."
- Handcrafted, 3" tall
  675QX490-7, $6.75
  Artist: John Francis (Collin)

Child's Fifth Christmas

Caption: "My 5th Christmas '91."
- Handcrafted, 2⅛" tall
  675QX490-9, $6.75
  Artist: Dill Rhodus

Mother

Mom-to-Be

A great start for Mom's collection! This kangaroo carries a special gift-wrapped package in her pouch and wears a sweatshirt that announces she's a "MOM TO BE." Back caption: "Christmas 1991."
- Handcrafted, 2⅝"tall
  575QX487-7, $5.75
  Artist: Julia Lee

Dad-to-Be

This proud fella wants the world to know Baby's coming. Front caption: "DAD TO BE." Back caption: "Christmas 1991."
- Handcrafted, 2⅝" tall
  575QX487-9, $5.75
  Artist: Julia Lee

Mother

Designed with the elegance of fine jewelry, this lovely porcelain pendant is suspended from a cluster of holly leaves and a curling ribbon fashioned of tin. Front caption: "Mother, Christmas 1991." Back caption: "Having you for a mother is the nicest gift of all."
- Fine Porcelain, Handformed Tin, 3⅛" tall
  975QX545-7, $9.75

The Children's Age Collection: First, Second, Third, Fourth, and Fifth Christmas

Dad, Mom and Dad

Dad

This white, polar bear dad is up against a holiday deadline. He has a wrench in one paw and a page labeled "Instruction Sheet" and "Easy to Assemble!" in the other. But the directions on the reverse side look pretty complex, and our hero has yet to cope with an impressive array of gears and parts. His sweater reads, "Dad 1991."

▪ Handcrafted, 2¼" tall
775QX512-7, $7.75
Artist: Julia Lee

Mom and Dad

Two raccoons spend the holiday snuggled in a real knit stocking. The extra-large stocking (one size fits two) carries the caption: "Mom & Dad 1991." Mom's pink outfit is trimmed with a lacy collar. Dad dresses up his favorite blue shirt with a vest and tie.

▪ Handcrafted, 3⅝" tall
975QX546-7, $9.75
Artist: Nina Aubé

Daughter

A white mouse, as sweet as she can be, is sound asleep inside a flocked pink slipper. Wearing a red hairbow, she naps on a green pillow and dreams of Christmas. The slipper is captioned: "Daughter 1991."

▪ Handcrafted, 3 1/16'' tall
575QX547-7, $5.75
Artist: Bob Siedler

Son

Not even a mouse was stirring on Christmas Eve, certainly not the little white mouse tucked inside this flocked red slipper. The caption, "Son 1991," appears above the mouse's head, which rests on a green pillow.

▪ Handcrafted, 3 3/16" tall
575QX546-9, $5.75
Artist: Bob Siedler

Sister

A gingerbread angel serves up a holiday treat—a gingerbread star captioned, "Sister." The angel has a sparkling halo, pretty pearly wings and pearly "icing" decorations on her robe and gown. The ornament is dated "1991." Its fanciful styling is reminiscent of the 1988 "Daughter" and "Son" ornaments favored by collectors.

▪ Handcrafted, 3¼" tall
675QX548-7, $6.75
Artist: Joyce Lyle

Brother

Designed for every boy who's ever bounced a basketball beneath a hoop, this Keepsake Ornament will win extra points with Brother. A puppy holds onto the rim of the hoop, and the net is made of real string. The backboard displays the caption, "Superstar Brother 1991."

▪ Handcrafted, 2¼" tall
675QX547-9, $6.75
Artist: Bob Siedler

Daughter, Son

Sister, Brother

Commemorative
Photoholders: First Christmas
Together, 25 Years Together,
50 Years Together

Commemorative Photoholders

A beautiful format, new in 1991, combines two materials and displays a favorite photograph in a heart-shaped window.

First Christmas Together Photoholder

Glowing doves carry an ivory-colored banner: "1st Christmas Together." Back: "Of life's many treasures, the most beautiful is love." Front: "1991."

■ Handcrafted, Brass, 3¼" diam.
875QX491-7, $8.75
Artist: LaDene Votruba

Twenty-Five Years Together Photoholder

Graceful swans float gently on blue waves above a silvery photoholder. Front captions: "25 Years Together" and "1991." Back caption: "Silver Christmas memories...Silver years of love."

■ Handcrafted, Chrome, 3¼" diam.
875QX493-7, $8.75
Artist: LaDene Votruba

Fifty Years Together Photoholder

Bouquets of pearly white roses adorn the ivory-colored banner. The golden lettering and frame emphasize the messages: "50 Years Together" and "Golden Christmas memories...Golden years of love." Front: "1991."

■ Handcrafted, Brass, 3¼" diam.
875QX494-7, $8.75
Artist: LaDene Votruba

Grandmother

A traditional design of poinsettias, pinecones, and holly forms a graceful frame for the tribute on a lustrous, gold teardrop ball: "A Grandmother grows ever more loving...ever more loved. Christmas 1991."

■ Light Gold Glass, 2⅞" diam.
475QX230-7, $4.75

Grandparents

From a sleigh ride to bringing home the Christmas tree, holiday activities dot the landscape in this Americana scene. Caption: "Grandparents add so many beautiful pages to your album of memories. Christmas 1991."

■ White Glass, 2⅞" diam.
475QX230-9, $4.75
Artist: Michele Pyda-Sevcik

Granddaughter

White bunnies wearing Christmas scarves form a design with a cross-stitch influence. Caption: "A Granddaughter is a special joy! Christmas 1991."

■ Porcelain White Glass, 2⅞" diam.
475QX229-9, $4.75
Artist: Michele Pyda-Sevcik

Grandson

Prancing reindeer form a design reminiscent of patterns on hand-knit holiday sweaters. Caption: "A Grandson makes Christmas even more wonderful! 1991."

■ Porcelain White Glass, 2⅞" diam.
475QX229-7, $4.75
Artist: Michele Pyda-Sevcik

Grandmother, Grandparents

Granddaughter, Grandson, Godchild

First Christmas Together: Acrylic, White Glass

Godchild

Suspended from a golden banner, an angel trumpets holiday greetings to someone special. The angel has pearly wings, and her halo and trumpet are painted gold. Caption: "Merry Christmas, Godchild."

◼ Handcrafted, 2¹/₁₆" tall
675QX548-9, $6.75
Artist: Ron Bishop

First Christmas Together

Symbolizing true love, a pair of sculpted doves adorns a heart-shaped wreath. The gold foil caption reads, "Our First Christmas Together 1991."

◼ Acrylic, 3³/₁₆" tall
675QX313-9, $6.75
Artist: Sharon Pike

First Christmas Together

A pair of romantic skaters is depicted twice on this nostalgic teardrop ball. A close-up view appears near the captions: "Our First Christmas Together" and "1991." The couple is seen in the distance above the message: "Christmas is for sharing with the special one you love."

◼ White Glass, 2⅞" diam.
475QX222-9, $4.75

Sweetheart

An old-fashioned sleigh ride sets the scene for winter romance. The nostalgic design is beautifully reproduced on a heart-shaped fine porcelain ornament, which uses a red ribbon for its hanger. Captions: "Merry Christmas, Sweetheart" and "Gently comes the season of Love. 1991."

◼ Fine Porcelain, 2½" tall
975QX495-7, $9.75

First Christmas Together

In this Twirl-About design, the dancing couple turns in the center of their heart-shaped world. Caption: "Our First Christmas Together 1991."

◼ Handcrafted, 3⅛" tall
875QX491-9, $8.75
Artist: Linda Sickman

Sweetheart, First Christmas Together: Twirl-About

Commemorative Glass Hearts

Designed to reflect holiday lights, this group of ornaments was patterned after 1990 hearts celebrating 25, 40, and 50 years together. The faceted hearts are captioned in red lettering.

Five Years Together
Caption: "5 Years Together, Christmas 1991."
- Faceted Glass, 2⁹⁄₁₆" tall
775QX492-7, $7.75

Ten Years Together
Caption: "10 Years Together, Christmas 1991."
- Faceted Glass, 2⁹⁄₁₆" tall
775QX492-9, $7.75

Forty Years Together
Caption: "40 Years Together, Christmas 1991."
- Faceted Glass, 2⁹⁄₁₆" tall
775QX493-9, $7.75

Under the Mistletoe
The little tan rabbit holds a sprig of mistletoe over his sweetie's head—a perfect excuse to steal a holiday kiss. The bunnies' cottontails are made of real pom-poms. Caption: "1991."
- Handcrafted, 2⅜" tall
875QX494-9, $8.75
Artist: Sharon Pike

Jesus Loves Me
A sweet baby squirrel kneels to say his bedtime prayers. His Christmas stocking hangs from a bedpost. Framed in chrome, the ornament has silvery lettering on the back: "Jesus Loves Me, Christmas 1991."
- Cameo, 2¼" diam.
775QX314-7, $7.75
Artist: Dill Rhodus

Friends Are Fun
Two bunny buddies demonstrate what fun a teeter-totter can be. Give one bunny a gentle down-ward push to start the action. The teeter-totter moves up and down, a gift-wrapped package slides back and forth, and the brass bell rings. Captions: "Friends are for fun!" and "Christmas 1991."
- Handcrafted, 2¹⁵⁄₁₆" tall
975QX528-9, $9.75
Artist: Ken Crow

Commemorative Glass Hearts: 5 Years Together, 10 Years Together, 40 Years Together

Under the Mistletoe, Jesus Loves Me, Friends Are Fun, Extra-Special Friends

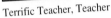

Terrific Teacher, Teacher

Gift of Joy, The Big Cheese

Extra-Special Friends

A mouse and rabbit go sledding, as a squirrel and raccoon ski. The caption, "Special Friends Make Christmas Extra Special," appears three times in a line, signifying friendship that never ends. Caption: "1991."

■ White Glass, 2⅞" diam.
475QX227-9, $4.75
Artist: Nina Aubé

Terrific Teacher

This wise little owl knows a "Terrific Teacher" when he sees one! The special rubbery material on the bottom of the ornament repeats the caption in raised, reversed letters. The back reads, "Christmas 1991." The design looks so realistic that the box

advises consumers that the ornament is for decorating and not for stamping papers.

■ Handcrafted, 2¼" tall
675QX530-9, $6.75
Artist: Linda Sickman

Teacher

Gift packages, a tree, and a wreath symbolize the season on this brightly colored ornament, designed to look like a child's drawing. Front caption: "For My Teacher." Back caption: "Christmas 1991."

■ Porcelain White Glass, 2⅞" diam.
475QX228-9, $4.75
Artist: Anita Marra Rogers

Gift of Joy

Ideal for business use, a die-cut design spells "JOY" on all four sides. Each letter revolves and has a different metallic finish: "J" is finished in brass, "O" in chrome, and "Y" in copper. Caption: "Christmas 1991."

■ Brass, Chrome, Copper, 4" tall
875QX531-9, $8.75
Artist: Diana McGehee

The Big Cheese

This ornament is designed "For the Big Cheese" at work or home. A mouse is curled up in a large hole in a tempting wedge of Swiss, topped with a red fabric bow. Back caption: "Merry Christmas 1991."

■ Handcrafted, 1⅞" tall
675QX532-7, $6.75
Artist: Bob Siedler

Across the Miles

An exquisite engraving of holly leaves, ribbons, and bow decorates a sparkling acrylic, framed in brass. The gold foil message: "There's no such thing as far away when Christmas draws us close. 1991."

■ Acrylic, 2⅝" tall
675QX315-7, $6.75
Artist: Joyce Lyle

From Our Home to Yours

A cardinal flies an air mail "JOY" to a family of mice from a neighboring pair of bears. Caption: "From Our Home to Yours, Christmas 1991."

■ Midnight Blue and White Glass, 2⅞" diam.
475QX228-7, $4.75
Artist: LaDene Votruba

New Home

A cheerful cardinal poses by a chalet-style birdhouse with a "1991" address. Front caption: "New Home." Back caption: "Home...the place where happiness lives!"

■ Handcrafted, 2¼" tall
675QX544-9, $6.75
Artist: Ron Bishop

Across the Miles, From Our Home to Yours, New Home

Joyous Memories Photoholder

Folk Art Reindeer

Nutshell Nativity

This is the sixth Keepsake Ornament to utilize the unique nutshell format since its introduction in 1987. Molded from a real walnut, the ornament presents a scene from the Christmas story. The three kings bearing gifts appear on the left side. The right side portrays the Christ Child in the manger, with a lamb at his side and the Star of Bethlehem shining in the night sky. The ornament is hinged, so it can be displayed open or closed for storing.

- Handcrafted, 1⁷⁄₁₆" tall
  675QX517-6, $6.75
  Artist: Anita Marra Rogers

Cuddly Lamb

Careful texturing and soft, white flocking give this little lamb a coat with the look and feel of fleecy wool. Fabric was used for the red neck ribbon and bow, as well as the green holly leaves.

- Handcrafted, 1⁷⁄₈" tall
  675QX519-9, $6.75
  Artist: Anita Marra Rogers

Snowy Owl

This impressive bird, perched in the fork of a snow-capped tree, is ever-alert to his surroundings. The artist's interpretation captures the beauty of the "Snowy Owl" and reflects its distinctive markings. The tree branch was molded from a branch found in the artist's yard.

- Handcrafted, 3" tall
  775QX526-9, $7.75
  Artist: Linda Sickman

Holiday Traditions

Joyous Memories Photoholder

A sculpted holly wreath forms a white-on-white bas-relief. A soft pastel banner at the top of the wreath displays the year "1991," and a pink ribbon and bow appear beneath the photo. The ornament is carefully handpainted, and the caption is silkscreened on the reverse side: "Each joy of Christmas becomes a precious memory."

- Handpainted, Handcrafted, 3⅛" diam.
  675QX536-9, $6.75
  Artist: LaDene Votruba

Folk Art Reindeer

No two of these reindeer ornaments look exactly alike, because each one is carefully handcarved out of wood and handpainted in soft, washed colors. The reindeer is posed in a graceful kneeling position, yet he seems to sense holiday excitement in the air. The brass medallion on his collar displays the year "1991."

- Handpainted Wood, Brass, 2⁵⁄₁₆" tall
  875QX535-9, $8.75
  Artist: LaDene Votruba

Snowy Owl, Nutshell Nativity, Cuddly Lamb

Feliz Navidad

Santa's adapting his customary attire to a sunnier climate. He's substituted a *sombrero* for his red cap, and added a colorful *serape* made of real fabric. His *sombrero* displays the traditional Spanish holiday greeting and the date: "Feliz Navidad 1991."

◼ Handcrafted, 2" tall
675QX527-9, $6.75
Artist: Julia Lee

SNOOPY and WOODSTOCK

The pals are ready for a non-traditional holiday feast. The pepperoni on their pizza forms the date "1991." SNOOPY holds a foamy mug of root beer, and WOODSTOCK has one, too.

◼ Handcrafted, 2⅛" tall
675QX519-7, $6.75
Artist: Dill Rhodus

GARFIELD®

Wearing a golden halo and white angel's wings, GARFIELD® sits on a star and tries to look angel-ic.This is his first appearance in a handcrafted design. The date "'91" is embossed on the star.

◼ Handcrafted, 3¼" tall
775QX517-7, $7.75
Artist: Dill Rhodus

PEANUTS®

CHARLIE BROWN and all the gang are rallying 'round to deco-rate SNOOPY's doghouse for the holidays. Caption: "It's the time of the year for sharing good cheer!" The year "1991" appears on the doghouse roof.

◼ Chrome Glass, 2⅞" diam.
500QX225-7, $5.00

Norman Rockwell Art

While Santa catches 40 winks, a bevy of elves takes over. The original painting by this beloved American artist is part of the Hallmark Historical Collection. The captions on the ornament read, "Santa's wee helpers work all through the year, but they're specially busy as Christmas draws near with last minute touches to finish the toys and make them all ready for good girls and boys!" and "Santa and His Helpers, From The Norman Rockwell Collection, Christmas 1991."

◼ Light Gold Glass, 2⅞" diam
500QX225-9, $5.00
Artist: Joyce Lyle

Feliz Navidad, SNOOPY and WOODSTOCK, GARFIELD®

Mary Engelbreit

Carrying a lantern on a staff that's peppermint-striped, Santa leads an impromptu parade that includes three elves, a dove, a little bunny, and a reindeer pulling a sled topped with a Christmas tree. This fanciful design is by contemporary American artist Mary Engelbreit. Caption: "Christmas 1991."

◼ Porcelain White Glass, 2⅞" diam.
475QX223-7, $4.75

PEANUTS®, Norman Rockwell, Mary Engelbreit

Sweet Talk

The love of a little girl for her pony is beautifully expressed in this highly detailed ornament. Much to the delight of the curious colt, the girl is offering to share her bright red-and-white striped candy cane. She's already given the pony a red ribbon to match her own red cap.

▧ Handcrafted, 2⅛" tall
875QX536-7, $8.75
Artist: Duane Unruh

Old-Fashioned Sled

Authentically detailed, this nostalgic design captures the style and spirit of antique sleds. Graceful bentwood-style runners rise at the front, encircling tiny golden bells. A wintry scene on the bed of the sled features the current year, "1991," and adds to the beauty of the design.

▧ Handcrafted, 1⁵⁄₁₆" tall
875QX431-7, $8.75
Artist: Linda Sickman

Basket Bell Players

Two Christmas kittens are taking turns batting at the shiny brass bell that swings from the handle of their wicker basket. While they play, they keep warm under a cozy knit blanket. The basket is topped with a red fabric ribbon and displays a gift tag with the year "1991."

▧ Handcrafted, Wicker, 2" tall
775QX537-7, $7.75
Artist: Ed Seale

Old-Fashioned Sled, Sweet Talk,
Basket Bell Players

New Attractions

On a Roll

Designed to swing merrily from a branch of your tree, this little mouse is really something of a cut-up. Scissors in hand, he's holding onto a strand of green fabric ribbon that's attached to a red spool. A wishbone hanger enables the spool to roll gently back and forth. Both sides of the spool display the message, "Merry Christmas 1991."

▧ Handcrafted, 5" tall
675QX534-7, $6.75
Artist: Ken Crow

Up 'N' Down Journey

Hold the ornament by the banner and tap the sleigh gently. You'll see Santa rocking back and forth, waving to all, while his reindeer prances through the sky. Santa holds tight to the reins made of real fabric ribbon. The caption on the golden banner proclaims, "Merry Christmas 1991." The reverse side of the banner repeats the year "1991" and includes a sculpted design of a Christmas tree surrounded by toys.

▧ Handcrafted, 3⅜" tall
975QX504-7, $9.75
Artist: Ken Crow

On a Roll, Up 'N' Down Journey (two views show movement)

Notes of Cheer

A softly flocked brown bear plays a holiday concert. His "1991" keyboard has sculpted keys and silvery controls and matches the red fabric bow behind his neck.

▨ Handcrafted, 1¾" tall
575QX535-7, $5.75
Artist: Bob Siedler

Nutty Squirrel

Collectors who like squirrels will find it difficult to locate one with a fancier tail! This stylish little fellow is bringing a gift—an acorn tied with a red hand-crafted bow.

▨ Handcrafted, 1¾" tall
575QX483-3, $5.75
Artist: Sharon Pike

Dinoclaus

A smiling dinosaur delivers toys to good little cave-boys and cave-girls. He covers the continents with giant strides, toting a home-stitched "1991" sack of toys. His tunic is labeled "Dinoclaus."

▨ Handcrafted, 2⅜" tall
775QX527-7, $7.75
Artist: Robert Chad

Polar Classic

Sporting a visor cap that reads "Polar Classic 91," a snow-white bear demonstrates what every golfer wants for Christmas—a perfect, classic swing. The shaft of the club is made of metal.

▨ Handcrafted, 3" tall
675QX528-7, $6.75
Artist: Bob Siedler

All-Star

A two-toned turtle carries his own catcher's mitt. He wears his cap with the bill in back—just like his major league heroes do. Fans in the stands can read the coveted title on the cap: "All-Star 91."

▨ Handcrafted, 2⅛" tall
675QX532-9, $6.75
Artist: Bob Siedler

Ski Lift Bunny

A snow bunny enjoys going up and down the mountain. He wears a "1991" sweater and has a white pompom tail.

▨ Handcrafted, 2¾" tall
675QX544-7, $6.75
Artist: Julia Lee

Chilly Chap

This glistening vanilla snowman is a double-dip delight. His ice-cream cone was patterned after a real one, his pearly buttons look like candy drops, and a holly leaf dated "1991" decorates his sparkly hat.

▨ Handcrafted, 3¾" tall
675QX533-9, $6.75
Artist: Donna Lee

Notes of Cheer,
Nutty Squirrel, Dinoclaus

Polar Classic, All-Star, Ski Lift Bunny

Chilly Chap

Tiny Tim, Mrs. Cratchit, Bob Cratchit

Mrs. Cratchit

Mrs.Cratchit has prepared a traditional holiday feast for her family. Her long dress is ruffled and trimmed in satiny white, and pearly buttons accent the front and back of her bodice. Caption: "Mrs. Cratchit 1991."

◾ Handpainted Fine Porcelain, 3⅞" tall
1375QX499-9, $13.75

Bob Cratchit

The loyal bookkeeper is shown with the Victorian-era tools of his trade. He holds a quill pen for making entries in a book that bears a golden inscription, "Ledger." He wears a shirt with a wing collar and a tie, vest, and cutaway jacket. Caption: "Bob Cratchit 1991."

◾ Handpainted Fine Porcelain, 3¹⁵⁄₁₆" tall
1375QX499-7, $13.75

Merry Carolers

This elegantly dressed pair holds a book entitled "Christmas Carols." The inside pages display musical notes and the words: "Joy to the World! The Lord is come." Caption: "Merry Carolers 1991."

◾ Handpainted Fine Porcelain, 4⅛" tall
2975QX479-9, $29.75

Ebenezer Scrooge

This portrayal of Scrooge depicts him striding confidently through the snow, his golden-tipped walking cane behind his back and a rosy scarf wrapped 'round the neck of his coat. He is a man of wealth who has found a new treasure in the warmth of the Cratchit family circle. Caption: "Ebenezer Scrooge 1991."

◾ Handpainted Fine Porcelain, 4¹⁄₁₆" tall
1375QX498-9, $13.75

"A Christmas Carol" Collection

Charles Dickens' classic holiday story reminds all that the greatest riches are to be found in the closeness we share with family and friends. In this special Keepsake collection sculpted by Duane Unruh, Dickens' memorable characters have been interpreted as fine porcelain works of art to grace your home. Each ornament is carefully handpainted in soft, delicate colors, and a touch of gloss on the eyes enhances and softens the expression. The caption appears on the bottom of each ornament.

Tiny Tim

Smiling as if he's ready to repeat his familiar quotation, "God bless us, every one," Tiny Tim represents the faith and hope of Christmas best. He's sitting on a bench and holding his crutch. His leg brace is a silvery color. Caption: "Tiny Tim 1991."

◾ Handpainted Fine Porcelain, 2⅛" tall
1075QX503-7, $10.75

Merry Carolers, Ebenezer Scrooge

Winnie-the-Pooh Collection

This special collection of six Keepsake Ornaments was designed by Bob Siedler to decorate your tree with fun. It's based on characters created by A. A. Milne and enjoyed by children and adults alike. There's "Christopher Robin," his special friend "Winnie-the-Pooh," and other pals who like to go adventuring in the Hundred Acre Wood (also known as Christopher Robin's backyard).

Christopher Robin

A boy with a wonderful imagination, Christopher Robin explores the world around him with the help of a unique menagerie of friends. He's wearing a red fabric scarf and red shoes as he brings home the Christmas tree.
■ Handcrafted, 4¾" tall
975QX557-9, $9.75

Winnie-the-Pooh

Affectionately known as "Silly Old Bear" and "the bear with very little brain," Pooh follows his curiosity into many happy adventures. He proudly holds a bear's idea of the perfect gift—a big jar of "HUNNY" with a red fabric bow.
■ Handcrafted, 3" tall
975QX556-9, $9.75

Piglet and Eeyore

He thinks of himself as a very small animal, but "Piglet" is always brave enough to tag along with his pals. He feels taller today, because he's riding on the back of his good friend "Eeyore," the group's independent thinker. "Piglet" holds a red ornament.
■ Handcrafted, 2¾" tall
975QX557-7, $9.75

Kanga and Roo, Tigger, Rabbit

Kanga and Roo

Patient mother "Kanga" is showing her baby "Roo" how to make decorations for the tree. Their strand of red beads looks very much like a string of cranberries.
■ Handcrafted, 3¼" tall
975QX561-7, $9.75

Tigger

A bit over-enthusiastic, "Tigger," the striped dynamo, has lots of fun running circles around his friends. He's bouncing into the holiday season carrying a festive red package, topped with a green fabric bow.
■ Handcrafted, 3½" tall
975QX560-9, $9.75

Rabbit

A born organizer who wants to have everything "just so," "Rabbit" is holding a bright translucent star. He's sure it belongs at the very top of the tree.
■ Handcrafted, 3" tall
975QX560-7, $9.75

Christopher Robin, Winnie-the-Pooh, Piglet and Eeyore

Plum Delightful, Look Out Below, Loving Stitches, Fanfare Bear

Tender Touches Collection

Charming woodland creatures created by Ed Seale make an enchanting holiday world. Their distinctive characteristic—a tiny heart—may appear anywhere on the design. Collectors will recognize the name "Tender Touches" as a figurine group from Hallmark Collections.

Plum Delightful

A raccoon hostess serves up her famous plum pudding. Her lacy apron is decorated with a heart and dated "1991."
■ Handpainted, Handcrafted, 2¼" tall
875QX497-7, $8.75

Look Out Below

Waving merrily to friends, a little mouse takes a ride on a new sled. A real green cord serves as his steering rope. A heart and the year "1991" are carved into the sled.
■ Handpainted, Handcrafted, 1¾" tall
875QX495-9, $8.75

Loving Stitches

Rocking in an old-fashioned, high-back chair, a chipmunk uses real thread to create a gift. The year "1991" and a heart are carved into the chair.
■ Handpainted, Handcrafted, 2¼" tall
875QX498-7, $8.75

Fanfare Bear

Holding real wooden drumsticks, this little bear welcomes the holidays with a drum roll. The head of the drum features the year "1991" and the "Tender Touches" heart.
■ Handpainted, Handcrafted, 2⁷⁄₁₆" tall
875QX533-7, $8.75

Snow Twins

This snowman has long white ears, a carrot nose, and a "Tender Touches" heart dated "91."
■ Handpainted, Handcrafted, 2⅛" tall
875QX497-9, $8.75

Glee Club Bears

Three bears carol from a songbook captioned "Deck the Halls" and "1991." A heart appears on their satiny white robes.
■ Handpainted, Handcrafted, 2" tall
875QX496-9, $8.75

Yule Logger

This proud beaver has found the "perfect" Christmas tree. His cozy sweater displays a "Tender Touches" heart dated " '91."
■ Handpainted, Handcrafted, 2" tall
875QX496-7, $8.75

Snow Twins, Glee Club Bears, Yule Logger

Matchbox Memories

Each ornament slides open to reveal an imaginary holiday destination. The format includes a textured, make-believe "striking strip" on the side of each ornament. The caption, "Matchbox Memories" is on the back of each one.

Evergreen Inn

One of the joys of staying in this country inn is being greeted by a gentleman who looks quite a bit like St. Nick! Front caption: "Evergreen Inn 1991."
◻ Handcrafted, 1⁷⁄₁₆" tall
875QX538-9, $8.75
Artist: Ed Seale

Santa's Studio

Silver hammer and chisel in hand, the Jolly Old Elf enjoys being a sculptor while his elfin subject poses patiently. The statue has the pearly appearance of marble. Front caption: "Santa's Studio 1991."
◻ Handcrafted, 1⁷⁄₁₆" tall
875QX539-7, $8.75
Artist: Ed Seale

Holiday Cafe

Holding hands at a table for two, a happy couple spends some quiet moments at the "Holiday Cafe." Lettering on the window is reversed so that it can be read from the street. Front caption: "Holiday Cafe 1991."
◻ Handcrafted, 1⁷⁄₁₆" tall
875QX539-9, $8.75
Artist: Ed Seale

Wood Look

Christmas Welcome

This ornament is one of three 1991 designs created in the style of "Nostalgia" ornaments, which entered the Keepsake line in 1975. The fruit basket symbolizes holiday giving. Front caption: "Christmas Welcome." Back caption: "1991."
◻ Handcrafted, 3⅛" tall
975QX529-9, $9.75
Artist: Linda Sickman

Night Before Christmas

In this Twirl-About design, Santa stands on a chimney top and turns in a full circle, deciding which house to visit next! The village scene appears on both sides of the ornament.
Front caption: "Night Before Christmas 1991."
◻ Handcrafted, 3¼" tall
975QX530-7, $9.75
Artist: Linda Sickman

Partridge in a Pear Tree

The traditional carol inspired this elaborate and colorful design, which is repeated on the back of the ornament. Front caption: "Partridge in a Pear Tree 1991."
◻ Handcrafted, 3³⁄₁₆" tall
975QX529-7, $9.75
Artist: Linda Sickman

Evergreen Inn,
Santa's Studio,
Holiday Cafe

Christmas Welcome, Night Before Christmas, Partridge in a Pear Tree

Jolly Wolly Santa, Jolly Wolly Snowman, Jolly Wolly Soldier

Jolly Wollies

Jolly Wollies bring an extra measure of fun to the holidays. You can enjoy them as whimsical ornaments and tuck a surprise inside. The styling is reminiscent of antique tobacco tins. To open the container, just twist off the top. All three designs by artist Linda Sickman were lithographed on pressed tin.

Jolly Wolly Santa
True to legend, this kindly Father Claus is round as round can be. His sack of toys includes a strand of "1991" jingle bells.
■ Pressed Tin, 3¾" tall
775QX541-9, $7.75

Jolly Wolly Snowman
Round as a snowball, this wintry friend has a bluebird on his arm to keep him company. Back caption: "1991."
■ Pressed Tin, 3¾" tall
775QX542-7, $7.75

Jolly Wolly Soldier
This whimsical shape gives the traditional tin soldier a bright, new look. He's the pride of the holiday parade in his elaborate blue and red uniform. His drum is dated "1991."
■ Pressed Tin, 3¾" tall
775QX542-9, $7.75

Artists' Favorites

Noah's Ark
Artist Ken Crow says the opportunity to create the first wind-up Keepsake Ornament was "a dream come true." The design incorporates a variety of movements. When you turn the knob on the side of the boat clockwise, the ark slides forward and back, and rocks from side to side. Three different animals move their heads, and Noah raises his arm, ready to release a dove. The artist's signature appears on the hull of the boat. Captions: "Noah's Ark, " "1991," and "Joy, Love, Hope, Peace."
■ Handcrafted, 3" tall
1375QX486-7, $13.75
Artist: Ken Crow

Polar Circus Wagon
Linda Sickman loves the excitement of the circus, and she's also fascinated with antique pull-toys. She combined the two interests in one design, noting that "the polar bear in this wagon relates to Santa's North Pole neighborhood." The wagon's wheels revolve, and its bars are gleaming brass. The artist's initials appear on top of the wagon. Caption: "1991."
■ Handcrafted, 2⅞" tall
1375QX439-9, $13.75
Artist: Linda Sickman

Noah's Ark, Polar Circus Wagon

Special Edition

Dickens Caroler Bell
—Second in Collection

Dressed in Victorian fashion, "Mrs. Beaumont" joins the 1990 Special Edition, "Mr. Ashbourne," in a group of ornaments whose graceful shape combines both the qualities of a bell and those of a figurine. Beautifully detailed and carefully painted by hand, this lovely lady holds an open songbook with musical notes printed on the pages. The cover is dated "1991." Caption: "Mrs. Beaumont, Fine Porcelain."
▪ Handpainted Fine Porcelain, 4¼" tall
2175QX503-9, $21.75
Artist: Robert Chad

Santa Sailor

Sailing is a favorite pastime for Ed Seale, so he's given Santa a nautical look. Decked out in dress blues, "Santa Sailor" stands on a hefty anchor cast of real metal. The back of the crossbar carries the artist's signature and the year "91."
▪ Handcrafted, Metal, 3⅜" tall
975QX438-9, $9.75
Artist: Ed Seale

Tramp and Laddie

Sculptor John Francis (Collin)'s collie, "Laddie," adopted a stray kitten and would carry it to safety if another dog came into the yard. Here, "Tramp" rides in a basket decorated with a green fabric bow. The artist's signature, "Collin," which is his middle name, appears on the bottom of the ornament.
▪ Handcrafted, 2¹¹⁄₁₆" tall
775QX439-7, $7.75
Artist: John Francis (Collin)

Fiddlin' Around

A bear dances a jig while playing holiday tunes on his fiddle. Sculptor LaDene Votruba imagines that he's the star performer at a Christmas concert. His outfit includes golden buttons on his vest and jacket. The artist's signature, "LaDene," appears on the back of the jacket.
▪ Handcrafted, 2⅞" tall
775QX438-7, $7.75
Artist: LaDene Votruba

Hooked on Santa

Fishing is Julia Lee's hobby, and she decided to sculpt Santa in a humorous situation—"at the moment when he thinks he's caught something big!" Santa's silver fishing rod is arched all the way back to the point where it snags his bright green waders! The artist signed her name, "Julia," on the waders.
▪ Handcrafted, 4" tall
775QX410-9, $7.75
Artist: Julia Lee

Santa Sailor, Tramp and Laddie, Fiddlin' Around, Hooked on Santa

Collectible Series

Classic American Cars
—First Edition

The "1957 Corvette" set the pace for a motorcade of dream cars from the past. A different memorable model drives into the series each year. The lead-off car rolls in on wheels that really turn. License plates read "1957" in front and "1991" in back. Caption underneath the car: "1957 Corvette."

◼ Handcrafted, 1⁵⁄₁₆" tall
1275QX431-9, $12.75
Artist: Don Palmiter

Peace on Earth—
First Edition

Children, scenes, and symbols of a different country each year is featured in this "international series." In this first edition, two children hold a globe that highlights "Italy." The year "1991" and the message "Pace al Mondo" (Peace on Earth) appear on the front, along with bas-relief scenes of St. Peter's Basilica, a gondola, the Coliseum, and the leaning tower of Pisa. "Peace on Earth" with bas-relief olive branches and the Italian flag are on the back.

◼ Handcrafted, 3" tall
1175QX512-9, $11.75
Artist: Linda Sickman

Classic American Cars, Peace on Earth, Heavenly Angels, Puppy Love

Heavenly Angels—
First Edition

Carefully sculpted in the baroque style of old-world masters, this bas-relief angel graces a lovely quadrafoil. Light antiquing by hand brings out the exquisite detailing on the angel's robe and wings. Back caption, in golden letters: "Heavenly Angels, Christmas 1991."

◼ Hand-antiqued, Handcrafted, 3¹⁄₁₆" tall
775QX436-7, $7.75
Artist: Joyce Lyle

Merry Olde Santa

Puppy Love—
First Edition

A friendly little cocker spaniel introduced a new series that features a different lovable puppy each year. Each puppy has its own heart-shaped, year-dated brass identification tag. This year's pup wears it on a red fabric ribbon that ties in a bow behind his head. Caption: "91."

◼ Handcrafted, Brass, 3⅛" tall
775QX537-9, $7.75
Artist: Anita Marra Rogers

Merry Olde Santa—
Second Edition

Representing the spirit of Christmas, this old-world Santa strides into the season wearing a long red coat that swirls above his boot-tops. A golden trumpet swings from a clip on his belt, and a bright brass bell is attached to his staff. A gift package in his sack is dated "1991."

◼ Handcrafted, 4" tall
1475QX435-9, $14.75
Artist: Julia Lee

Heart of Christmas —
Second Edition

This three-panel locket-style ornament can be displayed open or closed. Center panel: A father and child, accompanied by their little Scottie dog, carry their treasure home. Left: Their mother stands in the doorway. Right: A neighbor's home. The center panel is dated "1991." Back caption: "The heart always has room for beautiful memories."

◼ Handcrafted, 2" tall
1375QX435-7, $13.75
Artist: Ed Seale

Greatest Story—
Second Edition

The glowing brass snowflake, dated "1991," frames a beautiful fine porcelain bas-relief medallion, which portrays three shepherds gazing at the Star of Bethlehem.

◼ Bisque Fine Porcelain, Brass, 3¾" tall
1275QX412-9, $12.75
Artist: LaDene Votruba

Fabulous Decade—
Second Edition

A raccoon proudly presents a set of sparkling brass numerals that form the year "1991." This series is designed especially to commemorate the 1990s.

◻ Handcrafted, Brass, 1¼" tall
775QX411-9, $7.75
Artist: Ed Seale

Christmas Kitty—Third
and Final Edition

The last kitty in the series carries a pair of peppermint candy canes, gifts for two friends from the previous editions. Her ruffled gown has tiny buttons on the back of the bodice.

◻ Handpainted Fine Porcelain, 3⅟₁₆" tall
1475QX437-7, $14.75
Artist: Anita Marra Rogers

Winter Surprise—
Third Edition

Standing beside a snow-covered bottlebrush tree, a trio of penguins sing from the book, "Polar Carols 1991." The pearly, peek-through egg world has a glittery carpet of snow and a sparkling light blue sky.

◻ Handcrafted, 3¼" tall
1075QX427-7, $10.75
Artist: Joyce Lyle

CRAYOLA® Crayon—
Third Edition

Seated at a pipe organ composed of a box of CRAYOLA® Crayons, a talented teddy plays "Bright Vibrant Carols"—a tune whose lyrics read, "Jingle Bears! Jingle Bears!" The identification "CRAYOLA® Crayons" appears on the box front, sides and bottom flap. On the back is the UPC code for "Christmas" and: "1991 CRAYOLA® Crayons, Binney & Smith®."

◻ Handcrafted, 3¼" tall
975QX421-9, $9.75
Artist: Ken Crow

Heart of Christmas, Greatest Story, Fabulous Decade

Christmas Kitty, Winter Surprise, CRAYOLA® Crayon

Hark! It's Herald—
Third Edition

The sprightly little elf adds yet another musical instrument to his repertoire. This year he's playing a golden fife. His flowing white scarf is dated "1991," and a real pompom decorates his red hat.

■ Handcrafted, 2" tall
675QX437-9, $6.75
Artist: Anita Marra Rogers

Mary's Angels—
Fourth Edition

Sweet dreams are surely in store for "Iris," as she settles down for a nap on her frosted acrylic cloud. The little angel has pearly wings, and her lavender dress recalls the delicate shades of the blossoms that share her name. The signature of Hallmark artist Mary Hamilton, who designed each angel in the series, appears on the bottom of the cloud: "Mary."

■ Handcrafted, Acrylic, 2" tall
675QX427-9, $6.75
Artist: Robert Chad

The Gift Bringers—
Third Edition

Traveling through the country-side on a tiny deer, "Christkindl" delivers gifts of toys and sweets on Christmas Eve. Dressed in white and symbolizing the Christ Child, the angel is shown arriv-ing in a snow-covered town in Germany or Switzerland, where the legend originated. Caption: "The Gift Bringers, Christkindl, Christmas 1991."

■ White Glass, 2⅞" diam.
500QX211-7, $5.00
Artist: LaDene Votruba

Collector's Plate—
Fifth Edition

Two children discover how much fun a snowy day can be. One child adds a Santa hat to a just-built snowman, while the other makes snowballs. Their dog bounces playfully in the snow. The caption on the back reads: "Let It Snow! 1991." Plate stand included.

■ Fine Porcelain, 3¼" diam.
875QX436-9, $8.75
Artist: LaDene Votruba

Mr. and Mrs. Claus—
Sixth Edition

When it comes to "Checking His List," the happy couple believes that two Clauses are better than one. Mrs. Claus holds the list, which is dated "1991" on one side. Santa reads the second side, "LIST, Doll, Soldier, Horn." All three toys are accounted for, in and around his sack.

■ Handcrafted, 3" tall
1375QX433-9, $13.75
Artist: Duane Unruh

Reindeer Champs—
Sixth Edition

"Cupid" has found her true love in sports – it's volleyball! And of course, she's noted for her arrow-swift serves. The reindeer's name and number, "Cupid 91," appears on the back of her shirt.

■ Handcrafted, 3⅛" tall
775QX434-7, $7.75
Artist: Bob Siedler

Hark! It's Herald, Mary's Angels, The Gift Bringers

Collector's Plate, Mr. and Mrs. Claus, Reindeer Champs

Betsey Clark: Home for Christmas—Sixth and Final Edition

Betsey and her friends deliver gifts by sled, build a snowman, ice skate and ski. A yard sign is dated "1991," and the caption reads: "Getting favorite friends together is extra fun in frosty weather!" Although this design concludes the current series, a note on the ornament box reveals that a new Betsey Clark series would begin in 1992.
◼ Light Blue Glass, 2⅞" diam.
500QX210-9, $5.00

Nostalgic Houses and Shops—Eighth Edition

Golden letters atop the red brick "Fire Station" identify it as the home of "FIRE CO. 1991." Inside, there's an old-time fire engine, a bottle-brush Christmas tree, and two dalmations who await the return of their firefighter friends.
◼ Handcrafted, 4" tall
1475QX413-9, $14.75
Artist: Donna Lee

Twelve Days of Christmas—Eighth Edition

A pretty lass sits by a cow that's been outfitted with a festive garland and bell. The design is etched into a diamond-shaped acrylic with a beveled edge. Gold foil caption: "The Twelve Days of Christmas 1991...eight maids a-milking..."
◼ Acrylic, 3⅛" tall
675QX308-9, $6.75

Betsey Clark: Home for Christmas, Nostalgic Houses and Shops, Twelve Days of Christmas

Rocking Horse—Eleventh Edition

This proud buckskin was the first in the series to wear a patterned saddle. It resembles hand-tooled leather, and has shiny brass stirrups. The pony's mane, hooves, and yarn tail are black. His slate blue rockers are dated "1991."
◼ Handcrafted, 4" wide
1075QX414-7, $10.75
Artist: Linda Sickman

Here Comes Santa—Thirteenth Edition

Santa wants everyone to recognize his nostalgic red roadster – so he's added a hood ornament that looks like reindeer antlers! The license plates on "Santa's Antique Car" say "SANTA" and "1991," and its white sidewall tires really turn.
◼ Handcrafted, 2¼" tall
1475QX434-9, $14.75
Artist: Linda Sickman

Frosty Friends—Twelfth Edition

A frozen lake is the perfect place to play ice hockey! The red netting on the goal was molded from a net woven of real string. The year "1991," etched into the bottom of the clear acrylic ice, can be seen from above.
◼ Handcrafted, Acrylic, 1⅞" tall
975QX432-7, $9.75
Artist: Sharon Pike

Rocking Horse, Here Comes Santa, Frosty Friends

1990

H umor was a key feature in the 1990 Keepsake Ornament collection. Collectors enjoyed non-traditional Santas and a parade of newcomers, such as the first Keepsake Ornament cow, crocodile, and coyotes.

Prospective parents were honored for the first time, with "Mom-to-Be" and "Dad-to-Be" handcrafted ornaments. Three other new commemoratives entered the line in acrylic formats: "Across the Miles," "Child Care Giver," and "Jesus Loves Me."

For the third consecutive year, lifestyle designs were offered. This year, a group of six "Polar Penguin" ornaments depicted contemporary activities such as jogging and using a portable telephone. GARFIELD® made his first appearance, ice skating his way around a glass ball. The "SNOOPY and WOODSTOCK" and "PEANUTS®" designs commemorated the 40th anniversary of the PEANUTS® gang, and their boxes carried the special PEANUTS® 40th anniversary logo.

Four new Collectible Series debuted: "Merry Olde Santa," "Greatest Story," "Heart of Christmas," and "Fabulous Decade." Two series retired this year: "Porcelain Bear" and "Windows of the World." The Special Edition fine porcelain "Dickens Caroler Bell," the first in an ongoing collection, also was introduced.

Children's Age Collection: First, Second, Third, Fourth, and Fifth Christmas

Children's Age Collection

The Teddy Bear Years: This group of playful bears was created to enable a child's family and friends to build a unique kind of collection. In 1990, the "Baby's First Christmas" bear was a new design. The other four designs were reissues of 1989 ornaments updated to display the year "1990." For their full descriptions, see the 1989 Annual Collection. They are:

Baby's First Christmas

Napping on a holly leaf, Baby Bear holds the candy-cane number "1" in plump paws and smiles sweetly in his sleep. The red flocked cap says "Baby's 1st Christmas" on the trim and "'90" on the pompom.
◼ Handcrafted, 2⅜" tall
775QX485-6, $7.75
Artist: John Francis (Collin)

Baby's Second Christmas

Caption: "Baby's 2nd Christmas '90."
◼ Handcrafted, 2³⁄₁₆" tall
675QX486-3, $6.75
Artist: John Francis (Collin)

Child's Third Christmas

Caption: "My 3rd Christmas '90."
◼ Handcrafted, 2½" tall
675QX486-6, $6.75
Artist: John Francis (Collin)

Child's Fourth Christmas

Caption: "My 4th Christmas '90."
◼ Handcrafted, 3" tall
675QX487-3, $6.75
Artist: John Francis (Collin)

Child's Fifth Christmas

Caption: "My 5th Christmas '90."
◼ Handcrafted, 2⅜" tall
675QX487-6, $6.75
Artist: Dill Rhodus

Baby's First Christmas

A puppy takes a ride in the basket of a hot air balloon dated "1990." Clear and frosted acrylic are combined in this design, highlighted by the gold foil caption: "Baby's 1st Christmas."
◼ Acrylic, 4⅛" tall
675QX303-6, $6.75
Artist: Anita Marra Rogers

Grandson's First Christmas

Blue foil lettering enhances the caption: "Grandson's First Christmas." A woolly lamb of frosted acrylic nestles in a clear box tied with a "1990" ribbon.
◼ Acrylic, 3²¹⁄₃₂" tall
675QX306-3, $6.75
Artist: John Francis (Collin)

Granddaughter's First Christmas

This acrylic ornament is the first to feature pink foil lettering. Frosted and textured fur adds to the charm of the little mouse sitting in a hatbox. Caption: "Granddaughter's First Christmas 1990."

◾ Acrylic, 3⁵⁄₁₆" tall
675QX310-6, $6.75
Artist: John Francis (Collin)

Baby's First Christmas

In a baby-walker, this little one wears a "1990" bib. Caption on bumper ring: "Baby's 1st Christmas."

◾ Handcrafted, 3⅛" tall
975QX485-3, $9.75
Artist: John Francis (Collin)

Baby's First Christmas Photoholder

Delicately embroidered bunnies, holly, and "Baby's First Christmas 1990" decorate an ecru-colored fabric wreath. Back Caption: "There are so many moments to cherish with a beautiful Baby to love."

◾ Fabric, 3½" diam.
775QX484-3, $7.75

Baby's First Christmas—Baby Boy

Little woodland friends watch over Baby as he naps. Captions: "Baby's First Christmas 1990" and "Joy comes into your heart when a Baby Boy comes into your world."

◾ Blue Satin, 2⅞" diam.
475QX206-3, $4.75

Baby's First Christmas—Baby Girl

A sweet baby girl sleeps beneath her cozy quilt. Captions: "Baby's First Christmas 1990" and "Joy comes into your heart when a Baby Girl comes into your world."

◾ Pink Satin, 2⅞" diam.
475QX206-6, $4.75

Baby's First Christmas, Grandson's First Christmas, Granddaughter's First Christmas

Baby's First Christmas: Handcrafted, Photoholder, Baby Boy, Baby Girl

Mom-to-Be, Dad-to-Be

Mother

Filigree script affirms what all of us learned early in life, that "Mother is Love." The circular border encloses sprigs of holly and the date "1990." A fabric ribbon is the hanger.

▨ Ceramic with Bisque Finish, 2⅞" diam.
875QX453-6, $8.75
Artist: LaDene Votruba

Dad

In an oversized sweater, this papa lion is ready for the holidays. Detailed sculpting makes this first lion "Dad" truly appealing. Caption: "Dad 1990."

▨ Handcrafted, 2½" tall
675QX453-3, $6.75
Artist: Julia Lee

Mom and Dad

Bears mail a Christmas card dated "1990." It's a Hallmark card, of course—you can tell by the embossed crown on the envelope! The mailbox, captioned "Mom and Dad," is mounted on a tree stump. You can count the rings in the stump on the bottom of the ornament.

▨ Handcrafted, 2½" tall
875QX459-3, $8.75
Artist: Robert Chad

Mom-to-Be

Here's a new commemorative that pays tribute to prospective parents. This expectant bunny-mom is happily anticipating the joys of motherhood. She's comfy in slippers and a pink nightshirt that reads "MOM TO BE" on the front and "Christmas 1990" on the back.

▨ Handcrafted, 2⅞" tall
575QX491-6, $5.75
Artist: Bob Siedler

Dad-to-Be

Celebrating parents-to-be, this proud bunny is ready to hop into the role of fatherhood. He wears a "DAD TO BE" button, holds a book titled "Tips for Dads," and carries a suitcase labeled "Christmas 1990."

▨ Handcrafted, 3" tall
575QX491-3, $5.75
Artist: Bob Siedler

Son

With bright black eyes and a carrot nose, this hockey player made of snow is poised on silvery skates, ready to make a goal. His sporty cap reads, "Son," his jersey back, "90."

▨ Handcrafted, 1⅞" tall
575QX451-6, $5.75
Artist: Bob Siedler

Daughter

As graceful as can be, this little skater made of snow practices her figure eights. The word "Daughter" appears on her tam, and "1990" is on her muffler.

▨ Handcrafted, 2¼" tall
575QX449-6, $5.75
Artist: Bob Siedler

Son, Daughter

Mother, Dad, Mom and Dad

Sister, Brother

Grandmother, Grandparents

Grandson, Granddaughter, Godchild

Sister

Poinsettias lend festive charm to this classic teardrop ball. The sentiment reads: "A Sister adds her own special touch to the beauty and joy of Christmas. 1990."
◻ Porcelain White Glass 2⅞" diam.
   475QX227-3, $4.75

Brother

Sitting in a baseball glove dated "1990," this perky puppy catches the Christmas spirit. Detailed stitching on the glove creates an authentic look. Caption: "M.V.B. Most Valuable Brother."
◻ Handcrafted, 2³⁄₁₆" tall
   575QX449-3, $5.75
   Artist: Bob Siedler

Grandmother

A loving little mouse has painted "Grandmother… You're Wonderful!" and "Christmas 1990" on a tall wood fence. This is Hallmark's first cute Grandmother ornament. The design is enhanced by a technique that allows two colors of glass to be used on this ball.
◻ Blue and White Glass, 2⅞" diam.
   475QX223-6, $4.75
   Artist: LaDene Votruba

Grandparents

Traditional garlands of evergreen, holly, candy canes, poinsettia, and ribbon encircle two messages: "Grandparents and Christmas…Two beautiful ways to say 'Love.'" and "Season's Greetings 1990."
◻ Kelly Green Glass, 2⅞" diam.
   475QX225-3, $4.75

Grandson

Five furry white bears are busy skating, sledding, delivering gifts, and decorating the tree with a "1990" star. One of the gift tags says "For You," and the caption is so "beary" true: "A Grandson fills Christmas with cheer!"
◻ Porcelain White Glass, 2⅞" diam.
   475QX229-3, $4.75
   Artist: LaDene Votruba

Granddaughter

A little old-fashioned girl carrying a wreath is silhouetted against a rich, cranberry-colored background. She is followed by ten Christmas geese decked out in bows and holly. The caption reads: "—Granddaughter—Happiness happens wherever she goes! Christmas 1990."
◻ Pink Glass, 2⅞" diam.
   475QX228-6, $4.75
   Artist: Joyce Lyle

Godchild

Wearing a scarf dated "1990," a merry little koala goes sliding down the hill on his toboggan. This frosted acrylic features sculpted detail on both sides. Gold foil caption: "Merry Christmas, Godchild."
◻ Acrylic, 2⅞" tall
   675QX317-6, $6.75
   Artist: John Francis (Collin)

Sweetheart

A wishing well, filled with acrylic "water," provides a romantic meeting place "For Sweethearts." Its brass-handled bucket, dated "1990," swings beneath a crosspiece captioned: "Merry Christmas."

■ Handcrafted, 3⅛" tall
1175QX489-3, $11.75
Artist: Dill Rhodus

First Christmas Together

Snug under the blanket of pearly white snow that tops their cozy home, two foxes are framed by a wreath dated "1990." Captions: "Our First Christmas Together" and "Isn't love wonderful!"

■ Handcrafted, 1⁹⁄₁₆" tall
975QX488-3, $9.75
Artist: Michele Pyda-Sevcik

Sweetheart, First Christmas Together: Handcrafted

First Christmas Together Photoholder

Embroidered poinsettias and snow-white lace decorate this heart-shaped fabric frame, designed to hold a favorite photo. Front caption: "First Christmas Together 1990." Back caption: "Loving memories are celebrations of the heart."

■ Fabric, 3¼ " tall
775QX488-6, $7.75
Artist: LaDene Votruba

First Christmas Together

Two doves and a heart-shaped holly wreath symbolize both Christmas and the love that makes it so special. The design is etched and frosted, and the gold foil caption reads: "Our First Christmas Together 1990."

■ Acrylic, 2¼" diam.
675QX314-6, $6.75
Artist: LaDene Votruba

First Christmas Together: Photoholder, Acrylic

First Christmas Together

It's their first Christmas together, and this happy raccoon couple is busy stringing lights on the tree. The words, "Our First Christmas Together 1990" are framed above the mantel. Back caption: "Love decorates our lives with joy!"

■ Light Gold Glass, 2⅞" diam.
475QX213-6, $4.75
Artist: LaDene Votruba

Five Years Together

Two deer wearing Christmas wreaths frolic through a winter scene on this classic teardrop ball. The captions read: "Love makes you Happy!" and "5 Years Together Christmas 1990."

■ Light Silver Glass, 2⅞" diam.
475QX210-3, $4.75
Artist: LaDene Votruba

Ten Years Together

In front of a cozy house, a pair of redbirds are cavorting in an early winter snowfall. Caption: "Love wraps the world in wonder. Christmas 1990, 10 Years Together."

■ White Glass, 2⅞" diam.
475QX215-3, $4.75
Artist: Joyce Lyle

First Christmas Together: Glass Ball, Five Years Together, Ten Years Together

Commemorative Hearts

These three heart-shaped glass ornaments are designed to commemorate special milestone Christmases in a couple's life. The faceted border of each heart reflects the warm glowing lights of the holiday season. Each heart displays a foil caption and holly leaf design.

Twenty-Five Years Together

The joyful tradition of the Silver Anniversary celebration is represented in the silver foil caption which reads, "25 Years Together Christmas 1990." There is a silvery metal ring for attaching the ornament to the tree.

■ Faceted Glass, 2⁹⁄₁₆" tall
975QX489-6, $9.75
Artist: Joyce Pattee

Forty Years Together

Ruby is the color for the fortieth anniversary, and the glowing caption on this heart keeps with this tradition. It reads "40 Years Together Christmas 1990," and there is a gold colored metal ring for hanging the ornament.

■ Faceted Glass, 2⁹⁄₁₆" tall
975QX490-3, $9.75
Artist: Joyce Pattee

Fifty Years Together

The warm and special glow of the Golden Anniversary is captured in the gold foil caption: "50 Years Together Christmas 1990." A gold-colored metal ring is the ornament's hanger.

■ Faceted Glass, 2⁹⁄₁₆" tall
975QX490-6, $9.75
Artist: Joyce Pattee

Time for Love

Evergreen and holly branches serve as a perch for a pair of cardinals. The caption below them reads: "Christmas is a beautiful time to be in love. 1990." On the back, snow blankets a house and the surrounding countryside in gentle white.

■ Light Gold Glass, 2⅞" diam.
475QX213-3, $4.75
Artist: Joyce Lyle

Commemorative Hearts: 25 Years Together, 40 Years Together, 50 Years Together

Time for Love, Peaceful Kingdom, Jesus Loves Me

Peaceful Kingdom

A sweet little lamb and a lion cub snuggle together on this ornament which bears the words, "And peace will reign in the kingdom—the lion will lie down with the lamb. Christmas 1990." A border of evergreens completes the peaceful scene.

■ Light Gold Glass, 2⅞" diam.
475QX210-6, $4.75

Jesus Loves Me

This bunny shows how happy he is to be loved. Charming detail in the bunny's face, fur, and whiskers is captured in etched and frosted acrylic. The caption, "Jesus Loves Me," is stamped in gold foil.

■ Acrylic, 2¾" diam.
675QX315-6, $6.75
Artist: Joyce Pattee

New Home

A layered, three-dimensional scene, in a checkerboard heart, bears "1990" and the caption: "There's no place like…A New Home!" On the back of the ornament is a space for personalization: "For:" and "From:"
■ Handcrafted, 2¹¹⁄₁₆" tall
675QX434-3, $6.75
Artist: Michele Pyda-Sevcik

New Home, From Our Home to Yours

From Our Home to Yours

A warmly nostalgic petit point scene features two neighboring homes and a white picket fence. Captions: "From Our Home to Yours" and "Christmas 1990."
■ Periwinkle Blue Glass, 2⅞" diam.
475QX216-6, $4.75

Copy of Cheer

Perched atop a "1990" model "Cranberry Copier," this little mouse makes copies of cheery holiday greetings that say, "Merry Christmas!" The words "For:" and "From:" appear on the bottom, with space for personalization.
■ Handcrafted, 2¹⁄₁₆" tall
775QX448-6, $7.75
Artist: Bob Siedler

Friendship Kitten

Wearing a bright red bow, this pretty kitty licks an envelope printed with a crown and "Hallmark" logo. Addressed "To a Special Friend," the envelope bears a "1990" stamp and adds a warm "Merry Christmas."
■ Handcrafted, 2⅜" tall
675QX414-3, $6.75
Artist: Dill Rhodus

Across the Miles

A raccoon delivers a poinsettia in this new commemorative. Caption: "Christmas Smiles Across the Miles."
■ Acrylic, 3½" tall
675QX317-3, $6.75
Artist: LaDene Votruba

Copy of Cheer, Friendship Kitten, Across the Miles

Teacher

An educated chipmunk points to the message on a green chalk-board: "Dec. 25, 1990," "We (heart) Teacher" and "(acorn) + (acorn) =." On the floor is a paper airplane that was molded from a real one. The bottom of the ornament is labeled "For:" and "From:" for personalization.
■ Handcrafted, 2⅜" tall
775QX448-3, $7.75
Artist: Ed Seale

Child Care Giver

A teddy bear hugs a small bunny. Gold foil caption: "A Special Person like you is every child's dream. Christmas 1990."
■ Acrylic, 3" tall
675QX316-6, $6.75

Teacher, Child Care Giver

Stocking Pals, Baby Unicorn, Bearback Rider

Holiday Traditions

Stocking Pals
A pair of koalas team up to form a stringer ornament that can be hung on one or two branches of your tree. Their colorful stocking, knit from real yarn, holds a gift-wrapped package labeled "1990."
▨ Handcrafted, 3¼" tall
1075QX549-3, $10.75
Artist: Ed Seale

Baby Unicorn
This iridescent unicorn peers from his magical world with gentle, dark eyes. The shiny bow of real fabric gracing his neck complements his horn and hooves, which are painted with 18-karat gold.
▨ Fine Porcelain, 2" tall
975QX548-6, $9.75
Artist: Anita Marra Rogers

Bearback Rider
This jaunty penguin jockey gallops on "bearback" in search of some Christmas fun. A real brass jingle bell hangs from the bear's neck, and the reins are made of fabric ribbon. The date "1990" appears on the rocker on each side of the ornament.
▨ Handcrafted, 3¼" tall
975QX548-3, $9.75
Artist: Ken Crow

Spoon Rider
A teaspoon full of Christmas elf adds cheer to any tree. Santa's happy little helpers, suspended from a chrome wishbone hanger, just need a pinch of snow to try some "spoon sledding."
▨ Handcrafted, 2¼" tall
975QX549-6, $9.75
Artist: Patricia Andrews

Meow Mart
Don't let the cat out of the bag...he's having too much fun! The grocery sack, labeled "Meow Mart" on both sides, was molded from a real paper bag so the artist could achieve a realistic look. The kitten's bright red ball is made of real string.
▨ Handcrafted, 1¼" tall
775QX444-6, $7.75
Artist: Sharon Pike

Lovable Dears
This sweet little girl, in her bright red coat and her button-up boots, looks as if she might have grown up in the 1940s. She's happy to be sharing the loving spirit of the season with her gentle pet fawn.
▨ Handcrafted, 2⁵⁄₁₆" tall
875QX547-6, $8.75
Artist: Duane Unruh

Spoon Rider, Meow Mart, Lovable Dears

Perfect Catch

Jolly Old Saint Nick is a real sport. He catches the spirit of the season and a fly ball in one great play! His shirt has the team name, "North Pole Nicks," and his number, "90."

■ Handcrafted, 3¹³⁄₁₆" tall
775QX469-3, $7.75
Artist: Bob Siedler

Stitches of Joy

Seated on a stool, this bunny is cross-stitching "JOY" with a real needle and thread. Her toes peek out from under her aqua dress, and her sash is tied in a bright red bow behind her.

■ Handcrafted, 2½'' tall
775QX518-6, $7.75
Artist: Julia Lee

Little Drummer Boy

His clothes may be ragged and patched, but there's a happy look on this drummer boy's face as he plays a tune. The date "1990" is printed on the drum in golden numerals.

■ Handcrafted, 2⅜" tall
775QX523-3, $7.75
Artist: Duane Unruh

Goose Cart

This pretty Christmas goose is nestled in a bed of straw. With revolving wheels and a "Welcome, Christmas" caption on one side, the goose cart is reminiscent of old-fashioned pull toys. The pull-rope is made of real string.

■ Handcrafted, 1¼" tall
775QX523-6, $7.75

Joy is in the Air

What a surprise to see Santa, with his pearly white beard and bulging pack, floating gently as a snowflake through holiday skies in a parachute captioned "Joy is in the Air! 1990."

■ Handcrafted, 2⅝" tall
775QX550-3, $7.75
Artist: Ken Crow

Jolly Dolphin

The first dolphin in the Keepsake line poses in a wreath of sparkling foil and satiny red ribbon. The design complements the "Jolly Walrus" from the 1988 line.

■ Handcrafted, 3" tall
675QX468-3, $6.75
Artist: Anita Marra Rogers

Beary Good Deal

This bear plays to win your heart. Don't worry, he's a real softie, all covered with flocking! The cards in the bear's paw have Santa's picture on the backs. The card faces reveal a flush that includes a "10, 5, 9, 4, 8" of hearts—a sure bet for a warm, loving Christmas.

■ Handcrafted, 2" tall
675QX473-3, $6.75
Artist: Bob Siedler

Perfect Catch, Stitches of Joy, Little Drummer Boy, Goose Cart

Joy is in the Air, Jolly Dolphin, Beary Good Deal

Long Winter's Nap,
Hang In There,
Feliz Navidad,
Kitty's Best Pal

Long Winter's Nap
A sleepy dachshund wears a
Santa cap dated "1990," and
is partially "wrapped" in a
gift box with pearly white tissue
paper and a golden bow. A special clip will fasten this "package" to your tree.
◼ Handcrafted, 1⅜" tall
675QX470-3, $6.75
Artist: Anita Marra Rogers

Hang in There
This little raccoon in his perky
green cap is determined not to
miss a single minute of
Christmas fun. That's why
you'll see him "hanging in
there" on your tree until all the
festivities are over.
◼ Handcrafted, 2¼" tall
675QX471-3, $6.75
Artist: Ed Seale

Feliz Navidad
A little mouse peeks out from
his bright red chili pepper. His
sombrero says, "Feliz Navidad,"
and he's wearing a *serape* with
the date "1990." The curling
stem of the chili pepper serves
as the ornament's hanger.
◼ Handcrafted, 3" tall
675QX517-3, $6.75

Kitty's Best Pal
Snuggled cheek-to-cheek with
the jolly old elf, this kitten looks
purr-fectly content. Santa's little
friend is cozy in a Christmas
stocking dated "1990."
◼ Handcrafted, 2⅜" tall
675QX471-6, $6.75
Artist: John Francis (Collin)

Home for the Owlidays
This little owl is on his way
home for Christmas. His suitcase, which reads, "Home for the
Owlidays!" is tucked safely
beneath his wing. Handcrafted
owls like this one are popular
with collectors and have been
included in the Keepsake offer
since 1980.
◼ Handcrafted, 2¼" tall
675QX518-3, $6.75

Nutshell Chat
Molded from a real walnut, this
ornament opens on a small hinge
to reveal a charming scene. A
child is talking on the phone to
Santa, who listens from the comfort of his easy chair in the other
half of the nutshell. The ornament can be closed for storage.
◼ Handcrafted, 1⁷⁄₁₆" tall
675QX519-3, $6.75

Gingerbread Elf
Decked out in a sparkling chef's
hat and festive "1990" apron,
this pearly bearded, rosy-
cheeked baker carries a silvery
tray. It holds two sugar cookies
in the shape of reindeer.
◼ Handcrafted, 3¹¹⁄₁₆" tall
575QX503-3, $5.75

Home for the Owlidays, Nutshell Chat, Gingerbread Elf

SNOOPY and WOODSTOCK, PEANUTS®, Norman Rockwell Art

Holiday Cardinals, Christmas Partridge, Happy Voices

riding on his father's shoulder. "'God Bless us everyone,' said Tiny Tim" is the first part of the caption, followed by "*Post* Cover: Dec. 15, 1934." In the third scene, a couple does a lively dance beneath the mistletoe. Caption: "Merrie Christmas, *Post* Cover: Dec. 8, 1928."
■ Light Gold Glass, 2⅞" diam.
475QX229-6, $4.75
Artist: Joyce Lyle

Holiday Cardinals
A pair of shiny cardinals perch among the holly branches and poinsettias. Two separate layers of brass create the dimensional effect of this ornament, while detail is achieved through delicate etching. Caption: "1990."
■ Dimensional Brass, 2¹³⁄₁₆" tall
775QX524-3, $7.75
Artist: Joyce Lyle

Christmas Partridge
A dimensional partridge, fashioned of etched brass, dangles from a slender chain in the center of a pear. The leaves and stem of the pear are also etched, an attractive contrast to the smooth, shiny pear shape.
■ Dimensional Brass, 3¼" tall
775QX524-6, $7.75
Artist: Linda Sickman

Happy Voices
Two carolers and their dog harmonize in the foreground of this dimensional wood shadow box. A fabric ribbon serves as the hanger. Back caption: "Happy voices fill the air!"
■ Wood, 3⅛" tall
675QX464-5, $6.75
Artist: LaDene Votruba

Claus Construction
This is a reissue from 1989. (See 1989 Annual Collection.)
■ Handcrafted, 4¼" tall
775QX488-5, $7.75
Artist: Ed Seale

Stocking Kitten
This is a reissue from 1989. (See 1989 Annual Collection.)
■ Handcrafted, 2¼" tall
675QX456-5, $6.75
Artist: Sharon Pike

SNOOPY and WOODSTOCK
SNOOPY gives WOODSTOCK a holiday hug. The PEANUTS® anniversary slogan, "40 Years of Happiness," is printed on the ornament box.
■ Handcrafted, 2¼" tall
675QX472-3, $6.75
Artist: Dill Rhodus

PEANUTS®
The entire PEANUTS® gang dances around this chrome ball dated "1990." Caption: "Christmas is the merriest, lightest, jolliest, brightest, happiest time of the year!" The PEANUTS® anniversary logo appears on the ornament's box with the words, "40 Years of Happiness."
■ Chrome Glass, 2⅞" diam.
475QX223-3, $4.75

Norman Rockwell Art
Three delightful Victorian Christmas scenes decorate this ball, which reads, "Christmas 1990, Norman Rockwell, Famous Holiday Covers From *The Saturday Evening Post*." A portrait of a gentleman with a carpetbag and market basket reads, "Merrie Christmas, *Post* Cover: Dec. 17, 1938." In another painting, Tiny Tim is shown

Spencer® Sparrow, Esq.

This is a reissue from 1989. (See 1989 Annual Collection.)
- Handcrafted, 1¼" tall
675QX431-2, $6.75
Artist: Sharon Pike

Nutshell Holiday

This is a reissue from 1989. (See 1989 Annual Collection.)
- Handcrafted, 1½" tall
575QX465-2, $5.75
Artist: Anita Marra Rogers

New Attractions

S. Claus Taxi

Santa's taxi business is rolling right along, and he's awfully proud of his new cab! It says, "S. Claus Taxi," on the driver's door and "S. Claus" on the roof light. The cab's wheels revolve, and the underside features molded detail. A teddy bear rides in the front seat, and there's a bottle-brush tree in back. Front license plate: "SANTA." Back plate: "12-25-90."
- Handcrafted, 2" tall
1175QX468-6, $11.75
Artist: Peter Dutkin

Coyote Carols

These two coyotes are having a howling good time singing Christmas carols! Take a peek inside their "Coyote Carols" songbook, and you will see a real music staff with notes. The back of the book displays a single coyote footprint.
- Handcrafted, 3" tall
875QX499-3, $8.75
Artist: Julia Lee

King Klaus

Perched high atop the Empire State Building, a daring Santa waves his Merry Christmas greeting to the whole world.
- Handcrafted, 4⅛" tall
775QX410-6, $7.75
Artist: Ed Seale

Poolside Walrus

There's nothing this walrus likes to do more than bask in the sun on his reindeer float. He's wearing a red walrus-size swimming suit, and his float is made of a special rubbery material.
- Handcrafted, 1¼" tall
775QX498-6, $7.75
Artist: Julia Lee

Three Little Piggies

Pudgy, rosy-cheeked piggies, all cozy in their nightcaps, snuggle down for a long winter's nap. They look blissfully content in their colorful five-toed stocking.
- Handcrafted, 2⅜" tall
775QX499-6, $7.75
Artist: Ken Crow

Hot Dogger

Wearing shiny, reflective goggles to look cool and a stocking cap to keep warm, this plump "Hot Dogger" is ready to swoosh down the slopes. Slowpokes behind him will see the number "90" on the back of the lightly toasted bun.
- Handcrafted, 2⅞" tall
775QX497-6, $7.75
Artist: Ken Crow

Golf's My Bag

Come Dec. 26, Santa likes to relax on the links! Custom covers, designed as reindeer heads, add the perfect touch to his set of clubs. The bag is inscribed: "Golf's my bag! Santa."
- Handcrafted, 3¾" tall
775QX496-3, $7.75
Artist: Julia Lee

S. Claus Taxi, Coyote Carols, King Klaus

Poolside Walrus, Three Little Piggies, Hot Dogger, Golf's My Bag

Billboard Bunny, Mooy Christmas, Pepperoni Mouse

Chiming In, Born to Dance, GARFIELD®

Billboard Bunny

This bunny holds a basket of eggs for the best season of all! He's wearing a bright red sandwich board to help him make his point. Front caption: "BAH HUM BUG." Back caption: "BAN FRUIT CAKE."

Handcrafted, 2⅜" tall
775QX519-6, $7.75
Artist: Julia Lee

Mooy Christmas

The first Keepsake cow ever is all decked out for Christmas. The caption on her bright red scarf reads: "Mooy Christmas."

Handcrafted, 2¹⁄₁₆" tall
675QX493-3, $6.75

Pepperoni Mouse

This pizza-eating mouse has little pink pads on his feet and big pink ears. White mice have long been favorites with collectors, but this is the first ornament to feature pizza.

Handcrafted, 1¾" tall
675QX497-3, $6.75
Artist: Bob Siedler

Chiming In

These jingly brass chimes add a cheery note to any Christmas tree. On top, a little squirrel is poised to ring the chimes with a candy-cane mallet. All it takes is a tap of the small brass acorn, dated "1990," to make it chime.

Handcrafted, Brass, 5" tall
975QX436-6, $9.75
Artist: Sharon Pike

Born to Dance

This limber ballerina mouse is always on her toes! She's made from a special rubbery material that lets you bend her arms, legs, and tail into different dance positions. Her pink tutu is made of fabric lace.

Handcrafted, 2⁵⁄₁₆" tall
775QX504-3, $7.75
Artist: Sharon Pike

GARFIELD®

Here's GARFIELD® in his Keepsake debut. GARFIELD® writes "Merry Christmas 1990" with his skates, but then falls through the ice! "Oh yeah— Happy New Year, too!" he adds.
■ Blue Chrome Glass, 2⅞" diam.
475QX230-3, $4.75

Cozy Goose

What's good for the goose is good for the vest, too! This fellow wears a goose-down vest and carries a brightly wrapped gift under his wing.
■ Handcrafted, 3⅛" tall
575QX496-6, $5.75
Artist: Sharon Pike

Two Peas in a Pod

Everyone loves peas like these! This whimsical pair looks happy in its little green pod topped by a satiny red fabric bow.
■ Handcrafted, 3¾" tall
475QX492-6, $4.75
Artist: Patricia Andrews

Polar Penguins

Dressed in their Polar best, this flock of six little penguins created by artist Bob Siedler represents a variety of contemporary activities and lifestyles.

Polar Sport

A penguin driver braves the wintry air in a snazzy red convertible with the license plate "POLAR 1."
■ Handcrafted, 1¼" tall
775QX515-6, $7.75

Cozy Goose

Two Peas in a Pod

Polar TV

Relaxing on a pearly white iceberg chaise, this penguin watches the "Polar News." A curly straw in the penguin's cool drink serves as the ornament hanger.
■ Handcrafted, 1⅜" tall
775QX516-6, $7.75

Polar Pair

It's a package deal! Wherever the parent penguin goes, the baby penguin goes, too.
■ Handcrafted, 2" tall
575QX462-6, $5.75

Polar Video

This feathered photographer is recording a bird's-eye view of holiday fun. Picture all those black-and-white memories! The camera has shiny silver accents.
■ Handcrafted, 2" tall
575QX463-3, $5.75

Polar V.I.P.

This bird means business…and carries a cordless phone, complete with a real metal pin for the antenna. The briefcase is initialed "V.I.P." for a very important penguin.
■ Handcrafted, 2" tall
575QX466-3, $5.75

Polar Jogger

Not just a fair-weather fitness fan, this pudgy penguin sports a "Polar College" sweatshirt to help ward off the cold while working off calories.
■ Handcrafted, 1⅛" tall
575QX466-6, $5.75

Polar Sport, Polar TV, Polar Pair

Polar Video, Polar V.I.P., Polar Jogger

Christmas Croc

It's fun to dress up for Christmas, and no one looks more stylish than this crocodile in his knit fabric, polka-dot red muffler. Just give the tip of his tail a twist, and he'll open his bright pink mouth for you.
■ Handcrafted, 1⅛" tall
775QX437-3, $7.75
Artist: Michele Pyda-Sevcik

Santa Schnoz

It looks like Santa is trying to hide his identity with a nose-and-glasses disguise! But the gift he's holding behind his back lets us know that, as usual, he's just up to something nice. Santa's glasses and "schnoz" (a fun word for nose) are made of a special flexible material.
■ Handcrafted, 2½" tall
675QX498-3, $6.75
Artist: Ken Crow

Artists' Favorites

Donder's Diner

Artist Donna Lee got the idea for this ornament from memories of the old diners she used to see as a kid. Like those diners, this one appears to be a converted streetcar. A peek into the interior of "Donder's Diner" reveals the proprietor himself serving a hamburger to Santa. Wall signs advertise "Blitzen Burgers 19¢" and "Home Made Pie 5¢." The front door has a festive wreath and "1990." Donna's signature is on the back of the sign.
■ Handcrafted, 2⅛" tall
1375QX482-3, $13.75
Artist: Donna Lee

Welcome, Santa

Ken Crow says Christmas brings out the child in him. Since kids love surprises, he added mechanical movement to this fireplace. It's patterned after one in his home. When the candle on the mantel is pressed, Santa starts up the chimney! A homey sign says, "Welcome, Santa."

The artist's signature appears on the bottom of the ornament. Back: "With a wink and a grin and a 'Ho Ho Ho,' Santa drops in with a Christmas hello!"
■ Handcrafted, 2⅝" tall
1175QX477-3, $11.75
Artist: Ken Crow

Happy Woodcutter

Julia Lee loves wildlife, especially beavers, and grows trees

Christmas Croc

for a hobby. She gave this busy beaver a chain-saw like the one she uses at cutting time. "It's fun," she says, "and much speedier than teeth!" The artist's signature, "Julia," is printed on the saw's silvery blade. The beaver wears a red sweatshirt dated "1990," and he carries a bottle-brush tree.
■ Handcrafted, 2" tall
975QX476-3, $9.75
Artist: Julia Lee

Santa Schnoz

Donder's Diner; Welcome, Santa; Happy Woodcutter

Angel Kitty, Mouseboat, Gentle Dreamers

Gentle Dreamers

Nestled together on a bed of poinsettia leaves, two flocked bunnies dream about Christmas. This clip-on ornament was designed by John Francis, who has had a special fondness for rabbits and other animals ever since his childhood in Wyoming. The signature "Collin," which is the artist's middle name, appears on the back of one of the poinsettia leaves.

◼ Handcrafted, 1⁷⁄₁₆" tall
875QX475-6, $8.75
Artist: John Francis (Collin)

Angel Kitty

Her own cat, "Half-Pint," was the model for Michele Pyda-Sevcik's ornament. She says he acts like an innocent little angel, too cute to scold for his playful antics. The kitten-angel has sheer net wings with silvery sparkles, a brass halo and a wand with a star dated "'90." The artist's signature, "Michele," appears on the kitty's petticoat.

◼ Handcrafted, 2⁹⁄₁₆" tall
875QX474-6, $8.75
Artist: Michele Pyda-Sevcik

Mouseboat

Ed Seale likes to make puns and go sailing. That combination resulted in this whimsical boat, molded from a real walnut shell. It carries his signature, "Seale," and "1990" on the sail. The sailor-mouse holds a real string rope in one hand and waves with the other. He uses his tail to guide the rudder, which is debossed with the craft's name, "Mouseboat."

◼ Handcrafted, 3" tall
775QX475-3, $7.75
Artist: Ed Seale

Special Edition

Dickens Caroler Bell
—First in Collection

"Mr. Ashbourne" is the first Special Edition in the "Dickens Caroler Bell" collection. Handpainting and carefully sculpted details help create the special charm of this Victorian-era figure. The unique shape combines both the qualities of a bell and those of a figurine. Gold paint accents enhance the caroler's green coat and songbook, which contains actual musical notes. The date "1990" is painted on the cover of the book. In following years, "Mr. Ashbourne" will be joined by other Special Edition caroler bells.

◼ Handpainted Fine Porcelain, 4¼" tall
2175QX505-6, $21.75
Artist: Robert Chad

Fabulous Decade—
First Edition

This series is specifically designed to commemorate the 1990s. The first ornament features a playful squirrel holding a large brass "1990." Each year a different animal will be added until the collection is complete.

▢ Handcrafted, Brass, 1⅜" tall
775QX446-6, $7.75
Artist: Ed Seale

Greatest Story—
First Edition

This new series depicts some of the wondrous events which took place during that first Christmas season long ago. The brass snowflake dated "1990" frames a fine bisque porcelain bas-relief scene of the holy couple's journey to Bethlehem. Mary rides a small donkey led by Joseph.

▢ Fine Bisque, Porcelain, Brass, 3¼" tall
1275QX465-6, $12.75
Artist: LaDene Votruba

Christmas Kitty—
Second Edition

With her dainty muff and fancy blue coat, this little kitty is looking pretty for the holidays. Sprigs of holly on her cap and muff add to the hand-painted charm of this fine porcelain ornament.

▢ Handpainted Fine Porcelain, 3" tall
1475QX450-6, $14.75
Artist: Anita Marra Rogers

Merry Olde Santa,
Heart of Christmas

Collectible Series

Merry Olde Santa—
First Edition

Reminiscent of the Father Christmas of German folklore, this Santa wears the traditional red suit and black boots. He holds a small Christmas tree, which is trimmed with a golden cord. A brass jingle bell is attached to the tip of Santa's cap, and a drum dated "1990" dangles from his belt. Tucked in Santa's pocket is a little teddy bear for some lucky boy or girl. Future editions in the series will portray Santa as he appears in other cultures and traditions.

▢ Handcrafted, 4¼" tall
1475QX473-6, $14.75
Artist: Ed Seale

Heart of Christmas—
First Edition

A three-part, heart-shaped shadow box depicts a Christmas scene. Center: The date "1990" is on a tiny gold heart and Santa fills stockings at the fireplace. Left: A girl peeks around the tree. Right: A boy watches from the staircase. Designed to be displayed opened or closed, the heart features brass hinges and clasp. Back: "Keep the magic of Christmas in your heart."

▢ Handcrafted, 2" tall
1375QX472-6, $13.75
Artist: Ed Seale

Fabulous Decade, Greatest Story, Christmas Kitty

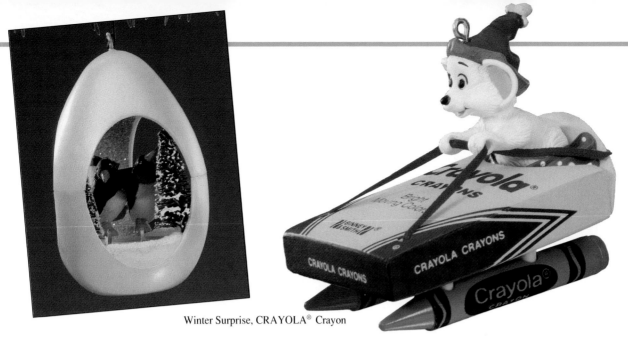

Winter Surprise, CRAYOLA® Crayon

Winter Surprise—
Second Edition

With bright scarves flying, two penguins on silvery skates glide across a frozen lake dated "1990." The sky inside the pearly peek-a-boo egg glitters with pale blue sparkles, and two bottle-brush trees frame the whimsical scene.

■ Handcrafted, 3¼" tall
1075QX444-3, $10.75
Artist: John Francis (Collin)

CRAYOLA® Crayon
—Second Edition

Entitled "Bright Moving Colors," this second ornament in the series depicts a little white mouse on a downhill run in his colorful sled. He's steering by means of a red fabric ribbon, and the runners are made of blue and red crayons featuring the "CRAYOLA® Crayon" logo. The box, which forms the body of the sled, reads "CRAYOLA® Crayons" on three sides and "1990" on the flap. On the front and back of the box it says, "CRAYOLA® Crayons," and the back says, "Christmas." The words "Bright Moving Colors, Binney & Smith®" also appear on the front of the box.

■ Handcrafted, 2¼" tall
875QX458-6, $8.75
Artist: Ken Crow

Hark! It's Herald—
Second Edition

The musical elf returns for an encore performance. He's beating a bass drum with "1990" on one side and "Hark! It's Herald" on the other. A white yarn pom-pom tops his bright red hat.

■ Handcrafted, 2⅛" tall
675QX446-3, $6.75
Artist: Ken Crow

The Gift Bringers—
Second Edition

The legend of St. Lucia, whose name means light, is celebrated by young Swedish girls. Wearing white robes and crowns of candles, they wake their families with song and food to welcome the Christmas season. The candlelight scene portrays St. Lucia and carolers in a snowy Scandinavian village. Caption: "The Gift Bringers, St. Lucia, Christmas 1990."

■ White Glass, 2⅞" diam.
500QX280-3, $5.00
Artist: LaDene Votruba

Mary's Angels—
Third Edition

High atop her frosted acrylic cloud, little "Rosebud" spreads her pearly wings and holds a Christmas candle for all the world to see. The signature of Hallmark artist Mary Hamilton, who designed each angel in this series, appears on the bottom of the cloud: "Mary."

■ Handcrafted, Acrylic, 3⅛" tall
575QX442-3, $5.75
Artist: Robert Chad

Hark! It's Herald, The Gift Bringers, Mary's Angels

Windows of the World, Betsey Clark:
Home for Christmas

Reindeer Champs—
Fifth Edition
This fellow wears a uniform
of green knee-socks and a red
jersey. The jersey carries his
name "Comet" and the num-
ber "90" on the back.
◼ Handcrafted, 3³⁄₁₆" tall
775QX443-3, $7.75
Artist: Bob Siedler

Betsey Clark: Home
for Christmas —
Fifth Edition
Christmas is a time for making music. Two girls sing a
Christmas carol, while a third
plays a piano bearing the date
"1990." On the wall near a
decorated tree, a sampler says

"Merry Christmas." A drummer
boy marches across the room,
while his kitten plays with a
crumpled piece of music. The
holly-framed caption reads,
"'Tis the season when hearts
are singing!"
◼ Pink Glass, 2⅞" diam.
500QX203-3, $5.00

Windows of the World—
Sixth and Final Edition
A sweet Irish lass finds a lep-
rechaun holding a Christmas
present outside her window.
There's a basket of potatoes
behind the wall of her stone cottage, and the date "1990"
appears on the chimney atop the
thatched roof. The Gaelic caption "Nollaig Shona" means
Merry Christmas.
◼ Handcrafted, 3" tall
1075QX463-6, $10.75
Artist: Donna Lee

Collector's Plate—
Fourth Edition
Two children prepare for Santa's
visit by putting out a plate of
cookies and writing a note that
says, "For Santa." Their kitty
naps on the window-sill. Caption:
"Cookies for Santa 1990." The
plate stand is included.
◼ Fine Porcelain, 3¼" diam.
875QX443-6, $8.75
Artist: LaDene Votruba

Mr. and Mrs. Claus—
Fifth Edition
At their private "Popcorn Party,"
the jolly couple holds a string of
popcorn on real thread that
swings between them. The hanger is brass, and the copper bowl
at their feet is dated "1990."
◼ Handcrafted, 3" tall
1375QX439-3, $13.75
Artist: Duane Unruh

Collector's Plate, Mr. and Mrs. Claus, Reindeer Champs

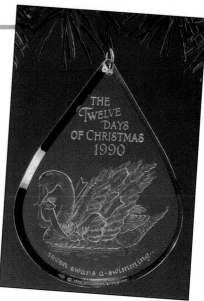

Porcelain Bear—Eighth and Final Edition

A golden brown "Cinnamon Bear" ends this series. He places a pearly star atop a Christmas tree, hiding its little belly "button" so familiar to his collectors.
◾ Handpainted Fine Porcelain, 1⅟₁₆" tall
875QX442-6, $8.75

Nostalgic Houses and Shops—Seventh Edition

This "Holiday Home" at the "1990" address has a decorated bottle-brush tree in its front window. A sofa and small table complete the living room furnishings. The upstairs bedroom contains a dresser, bed, and trunk. A staircase leads to the attic, where a dress form and box are found.
◾ Handcrafted, 3⅞" tall
1475QX469-6, $14.75
Artist: Donna Lee

Twelve Days of Christmas—Seventh Edition

Within this beveled acrylic teardrop, a swan is swimming, symbolic of the gift given on the seventh day of Christmas. Gold foil caption: "The Twelve Days of Christmas 1990…seven swans a-swimming..."
◾ Acrylic, 3⅜" tall
675QX303-3, $6.75

Porcelain Bear,
Nostalgic Houses and Shops,
Twelve Days of Christmas

Rocking Horse—Tenth Edition

This dainty appaloosa looks especially festive with a red and green saddle and rockers bearing the date "1990." The gold-painted trim on the saddle is matched with a gold cord rein, and the pony's tail is made of cream-colored yarn.
◾ Handcrafted, 4" wide
1075QX464-6, $10.75
Artist: Linda Sickman

Frosty Friends—Eleventh Edition

Sliding on the ice is lots of fun for this little flocked seal and his Eskimo friend. The ice is made of crystal clear acrylic and is engraved with the date "1990."
◾ Handcrafted, Acrylic, 2½" tall
975QX439-6, $9.75
Artist: Ed Seale

Here Comes Santa — Twelfth Edition

Santa rides merrily along in his "Festive Surrey" with silvery wheels that actually revolve. The wreath on the back of the seat is trimmed with a red satin bow. The date "1990" appears on both side panels and a bag full of toys rests at Santa's feet.
◾ Handcrafted, 3⅛" tall
1475QX492-3, $14.75
Artist: Linda Sickman

Rocking Horse, Frosty Friends, Here Comes Santa

1989

Attention focused on the Collectible Series in 1989, as five new series made their debut. They were "The Gift Bringers," "Hark! It's Herald," "Christmas Kitty," "Winter Surprise," and "CRAYOLA® Crayon." Especially notable was "The Gift Bringers." Not only was it the first new ball series since 1986, but Hallmark announced at the outset that a total of five editions would be offered. Four series were retired this year: "Thimble," "Wood Childhood Ornaments," "Tin Locomotive," and "Miniature Crèche."

For many people who enjoy collecting ornaments for children, the 1989 Keepsake offering introduced an appealing group of bear ornaments that commemorates a child's first five Christmases. The group included two new captions: "Child's Fourth Christmas" and "Child's Fifth Christmas."

Continuing the Keepsake tradition of commemorating events of historical or popular interest, "George Washington Bicentennial" honors the 200th anniversary of the first presidential inauguration.

Commemoratives

Baby's First Christmas Photoholder
The sentiment on the back of this star-shaped photoholder announces that Baby is "A new star on the family tree!" Decorated with toys, the ornament holds a favorite photo and carries the caption: "Baby's First Christmas 1989."
◾ Handcrafted, 3¾" tall
625QX468-2, $6.25
Artist: LaDene Votruba

Baby's First Christmas—Baby Boy
The Baby Boy on this blue satin ball is fast asleep on his first Christmas Eve. Santa motions for quiet while he watches the little one slumber. Caption: "A New Baby Boy To Love. Baby's First Christmas 1989."
◾ Blue Satin, 2⅞" diam.
475QX272-5, $4.75
Artist: LaDene Votruba

Baby's First Christmas—Baby Girl
Sleeping sweetly through her first Christmas Eve, the Baby Girl on this pink satin ball doesn't see Santa standing by her cradle. Caption: "A New Baby Girl To Love. Baby's First Christmas 1989."
◾ Pink Satin, 2⅞" diam.
475QX272-2, $4.75
Artist: LaDene Votruba

Baby's First Christmas
An acrylic reindeer brings gifts for Baby. The stocking holds etched toys and the gold-foil caption, "Baby's First Christmas." The collar is dated "89."
◾ Acrylic, 3⁷⁄₁₆" tall
675QX381-5, $6.75
Artist: John Francis (Collin)

Grandson's First Christmas
A puppy finds a hideaway inside an acrylic stocking. This holds a new commemorative caption, stamped in gold foil: "Grandson's First Christmas 1989."
◾ Acrylic, 4¼" tall
675QX382-5, $6.75
Artist: John Francis (Collin)

Baby's First Christmas: Photoholder, Baby Boy, Baby Girl

Granddaughter's First Christmas

An acrylic stocking is the perfect place for a kitty to play, especially when it carries the gold-foil caption, "Granddaughter's First Christmas 1989." This ornament is a new commemorative caption.

▨ Acrylic, 4¼" tall
675QX382-2, $6.75
Artist: John Francis (Collin)

Children's Age Collection

These bear ornaments commemorate a child's first five Christmases. Each bear wears a flocked hat and has a pearly candy cane number.

Baby's First Christmas

A bear in a green bow holds a big candy cane number "1" dated "1989." Caption: "Baby's 1st Christmas."

▨ Handcrafted, 2⅜" tall
725QX449-2, $7.25
Artist: Robert Chad

Baby's Second Christmas

A polar bear holds a candy cane "2" and waves "hello." Caption: "Baby's 2nd Christmas '89."

▨ Handcrafted, 2¹³⁄₁₆" tall
675QX449-5, $6.75
Artist: John Francis (Collin)

Child's Third Christmas

A honey bear hugs a candy cane number "3." Caption: "My 3rd Christmas '89."

▨ Handcrafted, 2½" tall
675QX469-5, $6.75
Artist: John Francis (Collin)

Child's Fourth Christmas

A marching panda has a candy cane "4." Caption: "My 4th Christmas '89."

▨ Handcrafted, 3" tall
675QX543-2, $6.75
Artist: John Francis (Collin)

Child's Fifth Christmas

A smiling koala holds a candy cane "5." Caption: "My 5th Christmas '89."

▨ Handcrafted, 2⅜" tall
675QX543-5, $6.75
Artist: Dill Rhodus

Baby's First Christmas, Grandson's First Christmas, Granddaughter's First Christmas

Children's Age Collection: First, Second, Third, Fourth, and Fifth Christmas

Brother, Sister

Grandparents, Grandmother

Daughter,
Son

Brother

This commemorative caption made its first appearance in 1989. The high-top shoe, tied with a real shoelace, is captioned for "BROTHER." Two snowflake insignia are dated "1989," and the bottom of the shoe carries a warm compliment: "No one else can fill your shoes!"

■ Handcrafted, 3¼" tall
725QX445-2, $7.25
Artist: Joyce Lyle

Sister

Reminiscent of American folk-art designs, a trio of large Christmas hearts appears on a white porcelain ball for Sister. The caption is divided into three parts—one under each heart: "Having a Sister means happiness. Loving a Sister means joy. Christmas 1989."

■ White Porcelain Glass, 2⅞" diam.
475QX279-2, $4.75

Grandparents

A delicately painted winter scene on a pearly glass ball evokes memories of home, Christmas, and grandparents. The caption is a loving compliment: "Grandparents make Christmas welcome in their home and in their hearts. 1989."

■ Peach Glass, 2⅞" diam.
475QX277-2, $4.75
Artist: Joyce Lyle

Grandmother

This teardrop ball is decorated with a garland of poinsettias, pinecones, and holiday greenery. The stencil-look design frames the caption: "A Grandmother is thought about often…and always with love. Christmas 1989."

■ Tan Glass, 2⅞" diam.
475QX277-5, $4.75
Artist: Joyce Lyle

Daughter

This rosy-cheeked girl just purchased a new bonnet. She's bringing it home in a hatbox captioned: "Daughter Christmas 1989." Her colorful attire reflects American folk art.

■ Handcrafted, 3" tall
625QX443-2, $6.25
Artist: Linda Sickman

Son

Dressed for frosty weather, this boy is carrying home a gift that bears the caption: "SON Christmas 1989." His knickers and hose give him an appealing, old-fashioned look.

■ Handcrafted, 3" tall
625QX444-5, $6.25
Artist: Linda Sickman

Mother, Dad, Mom and Dad

Mother

Christmas flowers frame a loving sentiment on the front of a fine porcelain heart. Caption: "Mother is the heart of the family. 1989." The ornament is tied with a red fabric ribbon.

■ Fine Porcelain, 2½" tall
975QX440-5, $9.75

Dad

Designer shorts are a bit too big for this polar bear dad. Painted a pearly white, the shorts look like silk. Caption: "For Dad 1989."

■ Handcrafted, 2⅞" tall
725QX441-2, $7.25
Artist: Julia Lee

Mom and Dad

This penguin duo loves skating and honoring two very special people! "MOM" and "DAD" appear on their shirts, and "1989" is printed on Dad's scarf.

■ Handcrafted, 2⅜" tall
975QX442-5, $9.75
Artist: Sharon Pike

Granddaughter

Forest animals happily skate around this two-toned glass ball. The "star skater" bunny etches "1989" in the ice. Caption: "A Granddaughter makes Christmas-time one of the best times of all!"

■ White and Green Glass, 2⅞" diam.
475QX278-2, $4.75

Godchild

Etched onto an acrylic oval, a little angel delivers a big star with a very special wish: "Merry Christmas, Godchild 1989." The stars, caption, and angel's halo are stamped in gold foil.

■ Acrylic, 2¾" tall
625QX311-2, $6.25
Artist: John Francis (Collin)

Grandson

The stylized design on this glass ball shows Santa climbing into a chimney. He's bringing gifts to the children of the house. The caption on Santa's bag reflects a similar idea: "A Grandson brings joy to everyone…just like Christmas!" One of the reindeer wears a blanket dated "1989."

■ Periwinkle Blue Glass, 2⅞" diam.
475QX278-5, $4.75

Granddaughter, Godchild, Grandson

Sweetheart

A bicycle built for two takes Sweethearts on a holiday ride. The wheels turn, and a package in the basket carries the caption: "Merry Christmas, Sweetheart." The license plate reads "1989."
■ Handcrafted, 4⅝" wide
975QX486-5, $9.75
Artist: Linda Sickman

First Christmas Together

Real branches were used to mold the heart-shaped wreath in this romantic ornament. Attached with red cord is a swing with two chipmunks. Caption: Our First Christmas Together 1989."
■ Handcrafted, 3½" tall
975QX485-2, $9.75
Artist: Anita Marra Rogers

First Christmas Together

Two deer stand in a wintry forest. This acrylic commemorative is engraved on front and back to enhance the dimension of the design. The gold foil caption reads: "Our First Christmas Together 1989."
■ Acrylic, 2¹¹⁄₁₆" tall
675QX383-2, $6.75
Artist: Dill Rhodus

First Christmas Together

Mr. Polar Bear holds a sprig of mistletoe above his sweetie! The back of this ball presents a whimsical back view of the same couple. Front caption: "Our First Christmas Together." Back caption: " 'Tis the season to be cuddly." The year "1989" appears on a log.
■ White Glass, 2⅞" diam.
475QX273-2, $4.75

Five Years Together

Two lovely swans symbolize a couple celebrating their fifth Christmas. The sentiment on the back of the teardrop ball reflects the mood: "Love makes the world a beautiful place to be." Front caption: "Five Years Together Christmas 1989."
■ Blue-Green Glass, 2⅞" diam.
475QX273-5, $4.75

Ten Years Together

What could be more romantic than sharing your tenth Christmas together in a one-horse open sleigh? This nostalgic scene appears on a white teardrop ball with the caption: "Ten Years Together Christmas 1989." Back: "There's joy in each season when there's love in our hearts."
■ White Glass, 2⅞" diam.
475QX274-2, $4.75
Artist: Joyce Lyle

Sweetheart, First Christmas Together: Handcrafted, Acrylic

First Christmas Together, Five Years Together, Ten Years Together

Commemorative Photoholders: 25 Years Together, 40 Years Together, 50 Years Together

Language of Love, World of Love

Commemorative Photoholders

Three lovely photoholders offer a unique way to preserve a memory forever. Fashioned in snow-white fine porcelain, each ornament is a bas-relief wreath decorated with a handpainted green and red holly design. The photoholders have captions on the front and back and are tied with fabric ribbons.

Twenty-Five Years Together Photoholder

Printed in silver, the front caption reads: "25 Years Together." The back caption, printed in red, says: "Christmas 1989." The photoholder is tied with a red ribbon.
■ Handpainted Fine Porcelain, 3¾" tall
  875QX485-5, $8.75
  Artist: Anita Marra Rogers

Forty Years Together Photoholder

Both the captions on this new commemorative are printed in red. The ornament is tied with a green ribbon. Front: "40 Years Together." Back: "Christmas 1989."
■ Handpainted Fine Porcelain, 3¾" tall
  875QX545-2, $8.75
  Artist: Anita Marra Rogers

Fifty Years Together Photoholder

Suspended from a white fabric ribbon, this photoholder has the gold front caption: "50 Years Together." The reverse side caption, in red, says: "Christmas 1989."
■ Handpainted Fine Porcelain, 3¾" tall
  875QX486-2, $8.75
  Artist: Anita Marra Rogers

Language of Love

Just as Christmas goes with love, the poinsettia complements the romantic sentiment on this acrylic ornament. Beneath the etched flower, the gold foil caption reads, "Together…the most caring word in the language of love. 1989."
■ Acrylic, 3" tall
  625QX383-5, $6.25

World of Love

"Christmas is here, and the sound of love echoes all over the world." This sentiment, and the artwork on this glass ball, reflect the loving spirit of brotherhood. The design shows children from countries throughout the world enjoying the season together. A sleigh carries the date "1989."
■ Silver Blue Glass, 2⅞" diam.
  475QX274-5, $4.75

Friendship Time

Like special friends everywhere, the two charmingly gowned mice in this teacup enjoy a holiday chat. The cup carries a warm message: "…Always time for friendship." Back: "Christmas 1989."
■ Handcrafted, 2½" tall
975QX413-2, $9.75
Artist: Julia Lee

New Home

Pearlized lavender and white provide the background for a nostalgic winter scene. The home and tree glow with light, illustrating the words of the caption: "Love is the light in the window of your new home. Christmas 1989."
■ Lavender-and-White Glass, 2⅞" diam.
475QX275-5, $4.75
Artist: LaDene Votruba

Teacher

This student has a leather tail and is writing in his book: "For a Nice Teacher." The other books are titled: "Christmas" and "1989." "From" is on the bottom of the ornament, for personalization.
■ Handcrafted, 2¼" tall
575QX412-5, $5.75
Artist: Bob Siedler

Festive Year

The combination of silver foil and glowing color gives this acrylic ornament the appearance of stained glass. Specially designed for business use, the ornament is bezeled in chrome and carries a silver foil "1989."
■ Acrylic, 2¹³⁄₁₆" tall
775QX384-2, $7.75
Artist: LaDene Votruba

From Our Home to Yours

Etched onto an acrylic oval, the design on this ornament reminds us of home and friends we hold dear. Two cardinals perch atop a mailbox filled with gifts. Below, an old-fashioned milk can and festive packages complete the scene. Stamped in gold foil, the caption reads, "From Our Home to Yours at Christmas." The address on the mailbox reads, "1989."
■ Acrylic, 3½" tall
625QX384-5, $6.25

Gratitude

Bezeled in brass, this acrylic ornament evokes feelings of warmth and friendship. A finely-etched design of holly tied with flowing ribbons accents the graceful calligraphy of the sentiment. The gold-foil caption reads: "Thankful feelings flow from heart to heart at Christmas. 1989."
■ Acrylic, 2¾" diam.
675QX385-2, $6.75
Artist: LaDene Votruba

Friendship Time, New Home, Teacher

Festive Year, From Our Home to Yours, Gratitude

Gentle Fawn, SNOOPY and WOODSTOCK, Spencer® Sparrow, Esq.

Joyful Trio, Old-World Gnome, Hoppy Holidays, The First Christmas

Holiday Traditions

Gentle Fawn
This fawn's softly flocked coat empha-sizes his large shiny eyes. He wears a real fabric ribbon and a sprig of fabric holly.
- Handcrafted, 2⁵⁄₁₆" tall
  775QX548-5, $7.75
  Artist: Anita Marra Rogers

SNOOPY and WOODSTOCK
These two dapper pals perform a snappy soft-shoe routine for the holidays. Coordinated from head to toe, their cos-tumes include shiny hats and bow ties.
- Handcrafted, 3" tall
  675QX433-2, $6.75
  Artist: Dill Rhodus

Spencer® Sparrow, Esq.
This sesame "treat" carries Spencer® Sparrow. His logo is on the underside.
- Handcrafted, 1¾" tall
  675QX431-2, $6.75
  Artist: Sharon Pike

Joyful Trio
A whimsical trio of angels sings in perfect harmony even though one of the three is having a little bit of halo trouble! Wear-ing pearly white, the angels symbolize Christmas love and brotherhood. Caption: "Joy To You."
- Handcrafted, 2¼" tall
  975QX437-2, $9.75
  Artist: John Francis (Collin)

Old-World Gnome
Special care, equated with old-world craftsmanship, went into the creation of this appealing gnome. Dressed like Santa, he has been sculpted and painted to resemble a fine European woodcarving.
- Handcrafted, 3¼" tall
  775QX434-5, $7.75

Hoppy Holidays
Christmas shopping can be fun when you ride through the store like this flocked bunny. He's selected two gifts, captioned "Hoppy Holidays!" and "1989."
- Handcrafted, 2¾" tall
  775QX469-2, $7.75
  Artist: Bob Siedler

The First Christmas
This sculpted cameo design is framed in brass. The nativity scene is ivory, with subtle shadings against a blue back-ground. Caption: "For unto you is born this day in the city of David a Saviour, which is Christ the Lord. LUKE 2:11"
- Cameo, 3⅛" tall
  775QX547-5, $7.75

Sweet Memories Photoholder, George Washington Bicentennial, Stocking Kitten

Feliz Navidad, Cranberry Bunny, Deer Disguise, Paddington™ Bear

Sweet Memories Photoholder

Designed to look like peppermint candy, this hand-crafted wreath will hold a treasured photograph. The wreath is trimmed with a handcrafted bow and holly. Back caption: "Christmas is the perfect time for making sweet memories. 1989."

■ Handcrafted, 3¹⁄₁₆" tall
675QX438-5, $6.75

George Washington Bicentennial

An engraved acrylic commemorates the bicentennial of the first American presidential inauguration. The likeness of Washington, designed to resemble his most famous portrait, is framed by a stamped, gold foil caption. Top caption: "1789-1989 American Bicentennial." Bottom caption: "George Washington First Presidential Inauguration."

■ Acrylic, 3⁹⁄₁₆" tall
625QX386-2, $6.25

Stocking Kitten

The fluffy pompom on the toe of the brightly flocked stocking is irresistible to this playful kitten. He'll soon discover it's a real pompom.

■ Handcrafted, 2¾" tall
675QX456-5, $6.75
Artist: Sharon Pike

Feliz Navidad

Elaborately textured to look like a real piñata, this colorful bull carries a cheery message on both sides of his fringed blanket: "Feliz Navidad." This phrase is the traditional Christmas greeting in Spanish. The bull's tail is made of red yarn.

■ Handcrafted, 2" tall
675QX439-2, $6.75
Artist: Michele Pyda-Sevcik

Cranberry Bunny

This flocked bunny likes cranberries almost as much as carrots! He strings a garland of cranberry beads with a real metal needle and fabric thread.

■ Handcrafted, 2⅝" tall
575QX426-2, $5.75
Artist: Anita Marra Rogers

Deer Disguise

Two children peek out of their reindeer costume to decide which way they're going. The costume has antlers and a tail and a little patch at the back.

■ Handcrafted, 1¾" tall
575QX426-5, $5.75
Artist: Bob Siedler

Paddington™ Bear

Paddington™ likes to play his drum almost as much as he likes to eat honey! His name, "Paddington™ Bear," appears on his hat, and his familiar tag is attached with a red fabric ribbon. Tag: "Please look after this Bear Thank You."

■ Handcrafted, 4¼" tall
575QX429-2, $5.75
Artist: John Francis (Collin)

Snowplow Santa

The North Pole is the ideal place for skiing. Wearing a shirt that carries the caption, "I (heart) Skiing," Santa executes a smooth snowplow stop.

■ Handcrafted, 2³⁄₁₆" tall
575QX420-5, $5.75
Artist: Bob Siedler

Kristy Claus

A vision on ice, Mrs. Claus wears green earmuffs and a sweater with her name: "Kristy Claus."

■ Handcrafted, 2¹⁵⁄₁₆" tall
575QX424-5, $5.75
Artist: Bob Siedler

Here's the Pitch

It's the ninth inning, and Santa is only one strike away from a perfect game! His major league outfit includes a red baseball cap, cleated shoes, and a uniform printed with his name and number: "SANTA 1."

■ Handcrafted, 2⅜" tall
575QX545-5, $5.75
Artist: Bob Siedler

North Pole Jogger

The race is on, and Santa leads the pack! He listens to his favorite North Pole radio station as he nears the finish line. His red jogging suit carries the caption: "North Pole 1K."

■ Handcrafted, 2¼" tall
575QX546-2, $5.75
Artist: Bob Siedler

Camera Claus

Santa carries his camera and camera case. He plans to fill an entire album with top-notch snapshots.

■ Handcrafted, 2⅜" tall
575QX546-5, $5.75
Artist: Bob Siedler

Sea Santa

Santa is ready to scuba-dive with flippers, goggles, and a silvery tank of air. Perhaps he's bringing gifts to his pals beneath the ocean. Caption: "Sea Santa."

■ Handcrafted, 2½" tall
575QX415-2, $5.75
Artist: Bob Siedler

Gym Dandy

A member of "Kringle's Gym," Santa stays in shape by exercising with small weights.

■ Handcrafted, 2½" tall
575QX418-5, $5.75
Artist: Bob Siedler

On the Links

Practicing his golf swing, Santa's fashionably attired in matching slacks and sunshade, a diamond-patterned shirt, and white golf shoes.

■ Handcrafted, 2½" tall
575QX419-2, $5.75
Artist: Bob Siedler

Snowplow Santa, Kristy Claus, Here's the Pitch, North Pole Jogger

Camera Claus, Sea Santa, Gym Dandy, On the Links

PEANUTS®—A Charlie Brown Christmas   Norman Rockwell

Special Delivery, Hang in There, Owliday Greetings

PEANUTS®—A Charlie Brown Christmas

The entire PEANUTS® gang appears on this sky blue ball to commemorate their TV special. The ball shows scenes from the program, including a picture of Charlie Brown's thin little Christmas tree. Captions: " 'A Charlie Brown Christmas' Television Special, Happy 25th Anniversary 1965-1989" and "Christmas. . .Season of Love."
◼ Blue Glass, 2⅞" diam.
475QX276-5, $4.75

Norman Rockwell

Two *Saturday Evening Post* covers are reproduced. Santa with globe caption: "*Post* Cover: December 4, 1926." Santa at desk caption: "*Post* Cover December 21, 1935." The ornament also carries the captions: "Norman Rockwell Famous Holiday Covers From *The Saturday Evening Post*" and "Santa's seen in the smiles the whole world is sharing, he's found where there's friendship and loving and caring. 1989."
◼ Gold Glass, 2⅞" diam.
475QX276-2, $4.75
Artist: Joyce Lyle

Special Delivery

A flocked seal couldn't wait till Christmas to pop out of his box. Decorated with a fancy hand-crafted red bow, the box carries the pun: "Signed, Sealed, & Delivered." The ornament displays the words "For:" and "From:" on the bottom, indicating a place for personalization.
◼ Handcrafted, 2" tall
525QX432-5, $5.25
Artist: Anita Marra Rogers

Hang in There

This mouse wears a green fabric bow on his leather tail. The loop at the top of his hat provides a place for your ornament hook.
◼ Handcrafted, 3" tall
525QX430-5, $5.25
Artist: Ken Crow

Owliday Greetings

Holding a bright red banner, an owl spreads cheer. He's covered with carefully textured feathers. Caption: "Owliday Greetings!"
◼ Handcrafted, 1½" tall
400QX436-5, $4.00
Artist: Sharon Pike

Party Line

This is a reissue from 1988. (See 1988 Annual Collection.)
◼ Handcrafted, 1¾" tall
875QX476-1, $8.75
Artist: Sharon Pike

Peek-a-Boo Kitties

This is a reissue from 1988. (See 1988 Annual Collection.)
◼ Handcrafted, 5" tall
750QX487-1, $7.50
Artist: Ken Crow

Polar Bowler

This is a reissue from 1988. (See 1988 Annual Collection.)
◼ Handcrafted, 2¼" tall
575QX478-4, $5.75
Artist: Bob Siedler

Gone Fishing

This is reissue from 1988. (See 1988 Annual Collection.)
◼ Handcrafted, 2½" tall
575QX479-4, $5.75
Artist: Bob Siedler

Teeny Taster

This is reissue from 1988. (See 1988 Collection.)
◼ Handcrafted, 4⅜" tall
475QX418-1, $4.75
Artist: Ed Seale

A KISS™ From Santa

This is a reissue from 1988. (See 1988 Annual Collection.)
◼ Handcrafted, 3¼" tall
450QX482-1, $4.50
Artist: Duane Unruh

OREO® Chocolate Sandwich Cookies

This a reissue from 1988. (See 1988 Annual Collection.)
◼ Handcrafted, 1⅜" diam.
400QX481-4, $4.00
Artist: Duane Unruh

Sparkling Snowflake, Festive Angel, Graceful Swan

Nostalgic Lamb, Horse Weathervane, Rooster Weathervane, Country Cat

New Attractions

Sparkling Snowflake
Separate layers of brass, etched with a lacy design, form a shimmery snowflake. The year "1989" is etched in the center.
▪ Brass, 3⅜" tall
775QX547-2, $7.75
Artist: Joyce Lyle

Festive Angel
To create a dimensional design, this glowing angel is fashioned from etched layers of brass. Her wings are formed by pieces of brass that arch together, giving the ornament added depth and beauty.
▪ Dimensional Brass, 3⁵⁄₁₆" tall
675QX463-5, $6.75

Graceful Swan
Elaborately etched and detailed, this dimensional brass swan is a vision of elegance. The gleaming wings are created with layers of brass that come together in a graceful curve.
▪ Dimensional Brass, 2¼" tall
675QX464-2, $6.75

Nostalgic Lamb
Sculpted to show detail, the lamb's curly coat keeps him warm as he rides in his bright red cart. The cart is fitted with revolving wheels.
▪ Handcrafted, 1¾" tall
675QX466-5, $6.75
Artist: Michele Pyda-Sevcik

Horse Weathervane
The craft of creating weathervanes has existed for many centuries throughout Europe. However, it was in America that the weathervane became appreciated as a unique art form. This steed, galloping into the wind, is fashioned to resemble handcarved wood.
▪ Handcrafted, 3" tall
575QX463-2, $5.75
Artist: Linda Sickman

Rooster Weathervane
This colorful rooster was designed to resemble American folk art.
▪ Handcrafted, 3½" tall
575QX467-5, $5.75
Artist: Linda Sickman

Country Cat
Wearing a polka dot scarf and resting on a real fabric pillow, a cat rides in an old-fashioned cart that has revolving wheels and is designed to look like wood.
▪ Handcrafted, 2¼" tall
625QX467-2, $6.25
Artist: Michele Pyda-Sevcik

Nutshell Holiday, Nutshell Dreams, Nutshell Workshop

Claus Construction, Rodney Reindeer, Cactus Cowboy

Nutshell Trio

The 1989 Keepsake line offered three nutshell ornaments. Each of the shells was molded from a real walnut and designed with hinges. The ornaments can be displayed open and stored closed.

Nutshell Holiday
Two tiny stockings hang from the mantel of the fireplace inside a cozy nutshell. A sampler on the wall says the shell is "Home Sweet Home." The sleepy kitten catches a quick nap before Santa arrives.
◾ Handcrafted, 1½" tall
575QX465-2, $5.75
Artist: Anita Marra Rogers

Nutshell Dreams
Inside his nutshell bedroom, a child dreams of Christmas toys. He doesn't know that Santa is in the other room. The jolly old elf motions for quiet.
◾ Handcrafted, 1½" tall
575QX465-5, $5.75
Artist: Robert Chad

Nutshell Workshop
A nutshell is transformed into Santa's workshop. Two industrious elves work as snow falls gently past the windows. One elf fashions a little wooden horse while the other finishes a wagon.
◾ Handcrafted, 1½" tall
575QX487-2, $5.75
Artist: Robert Chad

Claus Construction
Wearing a belt engraved with "NICK" and a shiny hard hat, Santa oversees the progress of his workshop. Four cords hold the big beam displaying the company name, "Claus Construction."
◾ Handcrafted, 4¾" tall
775QX488-5, $7.75
Artist: Ed Seale

Rodney Reindeer
You can bend Rodney's arms and legs to point in any direction. Rodney's map is titled "Reindeer Route 89," and his shirt says "Rodney."
◾ Handcrafted, 5" tall
675QX407-2, $6.75
Artist: Bob Siedler

Cactus Cowboy
Trimmed with strings of tiny "cranberry" beads, a colorful cactus is ready for a western-style Christmas. He has a sprig of holly on his cowboy hat and holds a golden star dated "1989."
◾ Handcrafted, 3½" tall
675QX411-2, $6.75
Artist: Peter Dutkin

Let's Play, TV Break, Balancing Elf, Wiggly Snowman

Cool Swing, Goin' South

Peppermint Clown

Let's Play

When you tap this ornament, the pup will wiggle his head up and down, and the kitten will waggle her tail side to side! Their house is decorated with garland. On the roof, two little paw prints and a "1989" trail are visible in the pearly snow.

■ Handcrafted, 2¾" tall
725QX488-2, $7.25
Artist: Ken Crow

TV Break

Santa watches "All My Reindeer" every afternoon as he relaxes in the sun. His hammock was molded from a piece of cloth woven out of string. Suspended from hooks on each end, the ornament can hang from one branch or between two.

■ Handcrafted, 3" tall
625QX409-2, $6.25
Artist: Donna Lee

Balancing Elf

Standing in the center of a big brass ring, one of Santa's elves is ready to perform a circus act. The two brass bells will jingle when you tap them gently.

■ Handcrafted, 4⅛" tall
675QX489-5, $6.75
Artist: Robert Chad

Wiggly Snowman

Tap this pearly snowman gently, and he'll wiggle and jiggle his head. He's wearing a great big smile, because he thinks nodding to friends is lots of fun!

■ Handcrafted, 4¾" tall
675QX489-2, $6.75
Artist: Dill Rhodus

Cool Swing

Wearing a warm winter hat, a penguin sits in his icy swing. When you tap the acrylic ice cube gently, it swings back and forth. Caption: "Have a Cool Christmas!"

■ Handcrafted, Acrylic, 3½" tall
625QX487-5, $6.25
Artist: Ken Crow

Goin' South

The suitcase this little mouse carries says he's "Goin' South." He's ready for sun and fun, wearing shiny green sunglasses as he rides on the Redbird Express.

■ Handcrafted, 1⅞" tall
425QX410-5, $4.25
Artist: Ken Crow

Peppermint Clown

This clown rides a peppermint unicycle! He was painted by hand and fashioned in the finest porcelain.

■ Handpainted Fine Porcelain, 5½₂" tall
2475QX450-5, $24.75
Artist: Peter Dutkin

Merry-Go-Round Unicorn, Carousel Zebra

Mail Call, Baby Partridge, Playful Angel

Artists' Favorites

Merry-Go-Round Unicorn

Fine porcelain is the ideal medium for portraying a unicorn, says artist Anita Marra Rogers. The smooth material captures the subtle lines and grace of the mythical creature. The candy cane pole adds a bright touch of color to the handpainted design.

■ Handpainted Fine Porcelain, 2¹¹⁄₁₆" tall
 1075QX447-2, $10.75
 Artist: Anita Marra Rogers

Carousel Zebra

Artist Linda Sickman relates that she's always been fascinated with animals, especially the unusual ones. It follows that her vision of a carousel would include a colorful zebra. The saddle is decorated with roses and dated "1989" on both sides.

■ Handcrafted, 2¾" tall
 925QX451-5, $9.25
 Artist: Linda Sickman

Mail Call

A raccoon mail carrier delivers a letter at his own "Branch Office." The whimsical pun and sculpted ornament are the works of artist Ed Seale. He says he enjoys sculpting designs of animals displaying human traits, and then creating an original pun to match! The word "MAIL" is carved in the branch.

■ Handcrafted, 3" tall
 875QX452-2, $8.75
 Artist: Ed Seale

Baby Partridge

Watching the birds who visit his front yard at home is one of artist John Francis' favorite pastimes. Although he hasn't seen a "Baby Partridge" recently, he enjoyed sculpting one for the Keepsake line. The ornament attaches to your tree with a special clip.

■ Handcrafted, 2¾" tall
 675QX452-5, $6.75
 Artist: John Francis (Collin)

Playful Angel

The angels that artist Donna Lee creates often act and look like real children, sometimes even getting into mischief! This angel wears a brass halo, and her swing attaches to the frosted acrylic cloud with a red cord.

▨ Handcrafted, Acrylic, 3⅛" tall
675QX453-5, $6.75
Artist: Donna Lee

Cherry Jubilee

This mouse is having a very sweet Christmas. The cherry is bigger than he is—a whimsical size relationship that artist Linda Sickman enjoyed portraying in her cherry tart design. The ornament attaches to your tree from the cherry's stem.

▨ Handcrafted, 2¼" tall
500QX453-2, $5.00
Artist: Linda Sickman

Bear-i-Tone

Artist Bob Siedler says he pays careful attention to the poses and expressions of the animals he sculpts so that each will have its own personality. This flocked bear plays a real metal triangle.

▨ Handcrafted, 2¼" tall
475QX454-2, $4.75
Artist: Bob Siedler

Cherry Jubilee, Bear-i-Tone

Special Edition

The Ornament Express

There's a load of excitement at the North Pole Station because this year's Special Edition is a train set featuring three different ornaments. Each is a distinctive collectible that can be displayed separately or with the other two. All of the designs have revolving wheels and carry a caption. Dated "1989," the colorful "Locomotive" has a silvery cowcatcher and a gold colored whistle. The "Coal Car" is captioned "Ornament Express" and holds a bag of tiny reproductions of past years' Keepsake Ornaments: the 1983 "Tin Locomotive," 1986 "Porcelain Bear," and 1985 "Old-Fashioned Toy Shop." The 1987 "Goldfinch" perches on top of the bag. The "Caboose," designed with a bright red roof, completes the set and carries a wish for the holiday: "Merry Christmas."

▨ Handcrafted, Locomotive 2¼" tall,
Coal Car 1¾" tall, Caboose 2⅛" tall
2200QX580-5, $22.00
Artist: Linda Sickman

Collectible Series

Christmas Kitty— First Edition

This new Keepsake Ornament series was the first to feature a cat. Each year, the "Christmas Kitty" series will offer a different fine porcelain kitten, festively dressed for the season. Painted by hand, the 1989 edition wears a soft green frock and a crisp white apron. She carries a basket of holiday poinsettias.

◼ Handpainted Fine Porcelain, 3³⁄₁₆" tall
  1475QX544-5, $14.75
  Artist: Anita Marra Rogers

Winter Surprise— First Edition

A sparkling winter world appears inside each peek-through ornament in this new series. In the first edition, two penguins decorate their Christmas tree. The bottle-brush evergreen is covered with fluffy snow and tiny ornaments. One of the gifts under the tree carries a "1989" tag. The penguins return each year, bringing new winter surprises inside their egg-shaped universe.

◼ Handcrafted, 3¼" tall
  1075QX427-2, $10.75
  Artist: John Francis (Collin)

CRAYOLA® Crayon — First Edition

This series got off to a great start with a "Bright Journey" on a CRAYOLA® Crayon raft. Crayons bring back childhood memories of merry hours spent coloring and drawing at Christmas and all through the year. The animals in this series show how inventive they can be with CRAYOLA® Crayons and often with the box as well. Each crayon is labeled "CRAYOLA® CRAYON," and the sail, dated "1989," duplicates a portion of the box design.

◼ Handcrafted, 3" tall
  875QX435-2, $8.75
  Artist: Linda Sickman

Hark! It's Herald— First Edition

The whimsical name of this series, which was new in 1989, is a word play on the famous carol. It is especially significant because Herald is a musician. He plays a different instrument each year. Wearing a hat topped with a real pompom, the elf plays golden chimes dated "1989."

◼ Handcrafted, 2" tall
  675QX455-5, $6.75
  Artist: Ken Crow

The Gift Bringers— First Edition

The myriad traditions of the Christmas "Gift Bringer" have captured the hearts of young and old throughout the world. This new ball series, new in 1989, brings a beautifully painted interpretation of a different gift bringer each year. This first edition of five features one of the most famous, identified in the caption: "The Gift Bringers, St. Nicholas, Christmas 1989."

◼ White Glass, 2⅞" diam.
  500QX279-5, $5.00
  Artist: LaDene Votruba

Christmas Kitty, Winter Surprise

CRAYOLA® Crayon, Hark! It's Herald, The Gift Bringers

Mary's Angels, Collector's Plate, Mr. and Mrs. Claus

Reindeer Champs, Betsey Clark: Home for Christmas

Mary's Angels— Second Edition

Pretty "Bluebell" says a Christmas prayer as she kneels on a frosted acrylic cloud. Designed by Mary Hamilton, the angel has pearly wings and wears a light blue gown that inspired her flower name. The artist's signature, "Mary," appears on the bottom of the cloud.

■ Handcrafted, Acrylic, 3" tall
575QX454-5, $5.75
Artist: Robert Chad

Collector's Plate— Third Edition

Christmas morning is a thrilling time for the two children pictured on this fine porcelain miniature plate. Even their little dog is excited about all the toys Santa has delivered. Caption: "Morning of Wonder 1989." Plate stand included.

■ Fine Porcelain, 3¼" diam.
825QX461-2, $8.25
Artist: LaDene Votruba

Mr. and Mrs. Claus— Fourth Edition

The North Pole's most famous couple performs a "Holiday Duet." Brightly dressed in Christmas red and green, they join voices to sing a favorite carol identified on the front of the songbook: "We Wish You a Merry Christmas 1989." The caption continues inside: "…And a Happy New Year!"

■ Handcrafted, 3¼" tall
1325QX457-5, $13.25
Artist: Duane Unruh

Reindeer Champs— Fourth Edition

When it comes to tennis, there's no match for this reindeer! Wearing a sporty tennis shirt printed with her name, "Vixen" wins the North Pole Cup every season. Her racket is dated "89."

■ Handcrafted, 3¼" tall
775QX456-2, $7.75
Artist: Bob Siedler

Betsey Clark: Home for Christmas—Fourth Edition

Winter is a favorite time for Betsey and her friends. One girl ties a scarf around her dog's neck, while others build a snowman and feed the birds. Caption: "Fun and friendship are the things the Christmas season always brings!" The doghouse has a "1989" address.

■ Blue-Green Glass, 2⅞" diam.
500QX230-2, $5.00

Windows of the World, Miniature Crèche

Nostalgic Houses and Shops, Wood Childhood Ornaments, Twelve Days of Christmas

Windows of the World—Fifth Edition

Inside his cozy Alpine cottage, a little German boy plays carols on his concertina. A brightly decorated tree fills the room with holiday cheer. The year "1989" appears on the back of the ornament, and a Christmas greeting in German appears on the front: "Fröhliche Weihnachten."
■ Handcrafted, 3¾" tall
1075QX462-5, $10.75
Artist: Donna Lee

Miniature Crèche— Fifth and Final Edition

Standing on the rooftop, an angel watches over this final edition. The double-doored design is called a *retablo*. Original *retablos* were miniatures of full-sized altar pieces and were brought to the Americas by the Spanish in the 16th century. This nativity can be displayed open or closed.
■ Handcrafted, 3" tall
925QX459-2, $9.25
Artist: Anita Marra Rogers

Nostalgic Houses and Shops—Sixth Edition

Christmas is a busy time at the "U.S. Post Office." The main branch is located downstairs. There, behind an old-fashioned counter, packages and letters are ready to be sorted into the correct compartments and pigeon holes. Upstairs, an office is furnished with files, a desk and a telephone for the mysterious occupant identified on the window: "Investigator Private." The front door carries the address "1989."
■ Handcrafted, 4¼" tall
1425QX458-2, $14.25
Artist: Donna Lee

Wood Childhood Ornaments— Sixth and Final Edition

The "Wooden Truck" hauls a load of bottle-brush Christmas trees. Fashioned with movable wheels and a yarn pull-string, this truck is the final ornament in this series. A license plate on the back reads "1989."
■ Wood, 2" tall
775QX459-5, $7.75

Twelve Days of Christmas—Sixth Edition

A graceful design of six geese is etched onto an acrylic heart to illustrate the sixth day of the beloved Christmas carol. The gold foil-stamped caption reads, "The Twelve Days of Christmas 1989…six geese a-laying…"
■ Acrylic, 3" tall
675QX381-2, $6.75

Porcelain Bear, Tin Locomotive, Rocking Horse

Frosty Friends, Here Comes Santa, Thimble

Porcelain Bear— Seventh Edition

Santa has delivered a big bag of peppermint candy to "Cinnamon Bear." He'll eat one piece now and save the rest for later. Carefully painted by hand, the bear is fashioned of fine porcelain.

■ Handpainted Fine Porcelain, 2" tall
875QX461-5, $8.75
Artist: Sharon Pike

Tin Locomotive— Eighth and Final Edition

This last "Tin Locomotive" is one of the most complex designs in the series. As the train's wheels turn, the brass bell jingles merrily, signaling that it's been a great journey for all! Caption: "1989."

■ Pressed Tin, 3³⁄₁₆" tall
1475QX460-2, $14.75
Artist: Linda Sickman

Rocking Horse—Ninth Edition

The pony's black yarn tail flies in the wind as he gallops on his gray and aqua rockers dated "1989." The russet and black bay is fitted with shiny brass stirrups and a red yarn rein.

■ Handcrafted, 4" wide
1075QX462-2, $10.75
Artist: Linda Sickman

Frosty Friends—Tenth Edition

The little husky puppy and his Eskimo pal are rushing to a Christmas party. They hope their sled glides quickly over the sloping acrylic ice, because they're carrying a gift captioned "1989."

■ Handcrafted, Acrylic, 2½" tall
925QX457-2, $9.25
Artist: Ed Seale

Here Comes Santa— Eleventh Edition

Santa waves from his "Christmas Caboose." A stocking hangs in the window on the opposite side of the car. There's a teddy bear inside and a toy soldier on the roof. A ball rests on the back platform. The caboose has movable wheels and is dated "1989."

■ Handcrafted, 3¼" tall
1475QX458-5, $14.75
Artist: Ken Crow

Thimble—Twelfth and Final Edition

This "Thimble Puppy," with his soulful eyes, melts hearts wherever he goes. Wearing a red handcrafted bow, he sits inside a silvery thimble in this last ornament of the series.

■ Handcrafted, 1¾" tall
575QX455-2, $5.75
Artist: Anita Marra Rogers

1988

The 1988 Keepsake Ornament line provided collectors with eight "lifestyle" Santas enjoying contemporary pastimes and wearing different outfits for each one.

One of Hallmark's early logos was featured for the first time on "Hall Bro's Card Shop," the fifth edition of "Nostalgic Houses and Shops." A new Collectible Series, "Mary's Angels," premiered with "Buttercup." This new series was based on drawings by Hallmark artist Mary Hamilton. Two series were retired this year: "Norman Rockwell Cameo" and "Holiday Wildlife."

"Five Years Together" made its first appearance, and "Americana Drum" and "Uncle Sam Nutcracker" were issued in observance of the 1988 election year.

Colors were embedded in acrylic on "Our First Christmas Together," and a new rubbery material added to the fun of "Child's Third Christmas." Artists created new characters with "Jolly Walrus" and "Santa Flamingo" and food for thought with "Party Line," "OREO® Chocolate Sandwich Cookies," and "A KISS™ From Santa."

Limited edition ornaments were offered exclusively to Hallmark Keepsake Ornament Collector's Club members for the first time in 1988.

Commemoratives

Baby's First Christmas

All bundled up in a softly flocked, snow-white bunting, Baby enjoys a gentle ride in a beautifully detailed rocking horse suspended from a wishbone hanger. The green fabric blanket is edged with real lace. Caption: "Baby's First Christmas 1988."
- Handcrafted, 3⅝" tall
  975QX470-1, $9.75
  Artist: Ken Crow

Baby's First Christmas Photoholder

A padded fabric heart, embroidered with golden-haired angels and sprigs of holly, frames a treasured photograph. The eggshell-colored fabric is trimmed with matching lace. Front caption: "Baby's First Christmas 1988." Back caption: "A Baby is a gift of joy, a gift of love at Christmas."
- Fabric, 5" tall
  750QX470-4, $7.50

Baby's First Christmas

A bunny holds a heart fashioned from two candy canes. Stamped in gold foil, the caption reads: "Baby's 1st Christmas 1988." The acrylic is carefully etched to suggest the bunny's soft fur.
- Acrylic, 4" tall
  600QX372-1, $6.00
  Artist: Sharon Pike

Baby's First Christmas—Baby Boy

Peering out from his sky blue blanket and cap, this little boy is being delivered by a flying white stork. Caption: "From the moment a new Baby Boy arrives, he's the love of your heart, the light in your eyes. Baby's First Christmas 1988."
- White Satin, 2⅞" diam.
  475QX272-1, $4.75

Baby's First Christmas: Handcrafted, Photoholder

Baby's First Christmas: Acrylic, Baby Boy, Baby Girl

Baby's Second Christmas, Daughter, Child's Third Christmas, Son

Baby's First Christmas—Baby Girl

Safe and snug in her pink blanket, this little girl is arriving by stork express. The caption reads: "A sweet Baby Girl, so tiny and new, is a bundle of joy and a dream come true. Baby's First Christmas 1988."

■ White Satin, 2⅞" diam.
475QX272-4, $4.75

Baby's Second Christmas

A softly flocked bear with a hammer discovers the fun of a classic childhood toy, the pounding bench. The captions "1988" and "Baby's 2nd Christmas" are printed on the ends of the bench.

■ Handcrafted, 1¾" tall
600QX471-1, $6.00
Artist: Sharon Pike

Daughter

The gingerbread girl presents a tray with four tiny gingerbread girls. The caption, "Daughter," is in pink icing. There's a pink bow on her sparkly white cap, and pink flowers border her skirt. The year "1988" decorates her frosty white apron.

■ Handcrafted, 3⅝" tall
575QX415-1, $5.75
Artist: Joyce Pattee

Child's Third Christmas

This little one rides a reindeer bouncy-ball made of a flexible new material that makes it feel like rubber. The commemorative caption printed on the side of the bright red ball reads: "My Third Christmas 1988."

■ Handcrafted, 2½" tall
600QX471-4, $6.00
Artist: Robert Chad

Son

All set to satisfy a Christmas sweet tooth, the gingerbread boy holds a cookie sheet with four small gingerbread boys and the icing caption: "Son." He's donned a sparkly white baker's cap, a white neckerchief, and an apron with "1988."

■ Handcrafted, 3⅝" tall
575QX415-4, $5.75
Artist: Joyce Pattee

Mother, Mother and Dad, Dad

Sister

Grandmother, Grandparents

Mother

This delicate filigree design is of a heart tied with a bow. The gold foil design and calligraphy sentiment are embedded in clear acrylic. Captions: "Mother puts love inside each moment of Christmas" and "1988."

■ Acrylic, 3¾" tall
650QX375-1 $6.50

Mother and Dad

Accents of gold give this traditional holly and glowing red candle the look of cloisonné. The white, fine porcelain bell is tied with a red satin ribbon. Captions: "Mother and Dad 1988" and "You give Christmas a special warmth and glow."

■ Fine Porcelain, 3" tall
800QX414-4, $8.00
Artist: Joyce Lyle

Dad

A polar bear dons bright red-and-green argyle socks to keep his paws warm. The gift box reads: "For Dad 1988."

■ Handcrafted, 2¾" tall
700QX414-1, $7.00
Artist: Bob Siedler

Sister

Wearing a candy-apple red pinafore dress and a ruffled white bonnet, this little girl puts a gold star atop a Christmas tree that's just her size. The white bell is tied with a lacy red ribbon. Caption: "Sisters know so many ways to brighten up the holidays! 1988."

■ Fine Porcelain, 3" tall
800QX499-4, $8.00
Artist: LaDene Votruba

Grandmother

A partridge-in-a-pear-tree design looks like crewel work. The caption on the teardrop-shaped ball reads: "Grandmother makes love a Christmas tradition. 1988."

■ Gold Glass, 2⅞" diam.
475QX276-4, $4.75

Grandparents

The caption on this teardrop ball reads: "Grandparents are the heart of so many treasured memories. Christmas 1988."An old-fashioned tree and a napping kitty are on the other side.

■ Red Glass, 2⅞" diam.
475QX277-1, $4.75
Artist: Joyce Pattee

Granddaughter

For the first time, a Keepsake glass ball ornament has been painted in two contrasting background colors that softly blend. An angel reaches for a star in a sunset-colored sky. Caption: "A Granddaughter is a delight to love! Christmas 1988."

▪ Red and White Glass, 2⅞" diam.
475QX277-4, $4.75
Artist: LaDene Votruba

Grandson

Santa's catching snowflakes! The caption reads: "A Grandson makes Christmas merry! 1988." Background colors of green and white gradually blend, the result of a new design technique.

▪ Green and White Glass, 2⅞" diam.
475QX278-1, $4.75
Artist: LaDene Votruba

Godchild

Carrying an old-fashioned lamp, a bell, and a songbook, these three children go a-caroling with their little dog. This charming scene celebrates a special relationship: "A Godchild brings joy to the world…especially at Christmas. 1988."

▪ Gold Glass, 2⅞" diam.
475QX278-4, $4.75
Artist: Sue Tague

Sweetheart

A romantic swan sleigh features pearly colors that shimmer in the light. Inside the sleigh, a single rose signifies true love. On the sleigh's underside is a place for personalization: "For (name), Love (name)." Front caption: "Sweetheart." Back caption: "Christmas 1988."

▪ Handcrafted, 3⅜" tall
975QX490-1, $9.75
Artist: Duane Unruh

First Christmas Together

Two bears hide heart-shaped gifts behind their backs. They stand on a braided rug inside a heart-shaped frame that looks like wood. Front: "First Christmas Together." Back: "1988."

▪ Handcrafted, 3¼" tall
900QX489-4, $9.00
Artist: Sharon Pike

First Christmas Together

Subtle colors embedded in acrylic add depth to holiday greenery. The oval ornament has a beveled edge and is framed in brass. The gold foil caption reads: "Our First Christmas Together 1988."

▪ Acrylic, 4" tall
675QX373-1, $6.75
Artist: LaDene Votruba

First Christmas Together

Two cardinals symbolize lasting love in this wintry scene featuring snow-covered evergreens and a sparkling sky. Caption: "Beauty is found in many things, but most of all in love. Our First Christmas Together 1988."

▪ Sparkling Glass, 2⅞" diam.
475QX274-1, $4.75
Artist: Sue Tague

Granddaughter, Grandson, Godchild

Sweetheart; First Christmas Together: Handcrafted, Acrylic, Ball

Five Years Together

This new commemorative features five trees composed of green hearts. Each tree contains from one to five red hearts, celebrating the passing years. Caption: "5 Years Together. Christmas 1988."

◻ White Glass, 2⅞" diam.
475QX274-4, $4.75
Artist: Diana McGehee

Ten Years Together

Two deer stand on a hill overlooking a quiet village where snow is falling. Caption: "Love warms every moment, brightens every day. Ten Years Together Christmas 1988."

◻ White Glass, 2⅞" diam.
475QX275-1, $4.75

Twenty-Five Years Together

Stamped in silver foil to commemorate a Silver Anniversary, this lovely acrylic ornament is beveled to catch the light. It is framed in chrome. Caption: "25 Years Together Christmas 1988."

◻ Acrylic, 3⅛" tall
675QX373-4, $6.75
Artist: Joyce Pattee

Fifty Years Together

To celebrate a Golden Anniversary celebration, "50 Years Together Christmas 1988" appears in gold foil. A beveled edge and brass frame further enrich the design.

◻ Acrylic, 3⅛" tall
675QX374-1, $6.75

Love Fills the Heart

A holly and berries pattern repeats the silhouette of this finely etched acrylic heart. Two birds and a gold-foil sentiment complete the design. Caption: "Love fills the heart forever."

◻ Acrylic, 3" tall
600QX374-4, $6.00
Artist: LaDene Votruba

Love Grows

Flowers in full bloom are accented with pale green leaves against black for a rich, lacquered look. The caption on this chrome teardrop ornament reads, "Patiently, joyfully, beautifully, Love grows. Christmas 1988."

◻ Chrome Glass, 2⅞" diam.
475QX275-4, $4.75
Artist: LaDene Votruba

Spirit of Christmas

Dressed in native costumes, children hold hands around the ball. Caption: "Love begins changing the world by awakening one heart at a time. Christmas 1988."

◻ Chrome Glass, 2⅞" diam.
475QX276-1, $4.75
Artist: Joyce Lyle

Five Years Together, Ten Years Together

Twenty-Five Years Together, Fifty Years Together, Love Fills the Heart

Love Grows, Spirit of Christmas

Year to Remember, New Home, Gratitude

Year to Remember
Designed for business use, this filigree ornament commemorates the year. Fashioned in ivory ceramic, the motif incorporates holly and "1988" in an oval frame. A slender, red satin ribbon and bow complete the design.
- ◼ Ceramic, 3¾" tall
700QX416-4, $7.00

New Home
Santa and his reindeer fly over a house nestled among the trees. The frosted bas-relief design is on the front, and gold foil stars and the caption are stamped on the back. Caption: "A new home makes Christmas merry and bright." "1988" is etched into the design.
- ◼ Acrylic, 2½" tall
600QX376-1, $6.00
Artist: LaDene Votruba

Gratitude
Snowflakes and a graceful evergreen tree highlight this etched acrylic teardrop. The sparkling silver foil caption reads: "Christmas fills our hearts with thoughts of those who care. 1988."
- ◼ Acrylic, 3⅜" tall
600QX375-4, $6.00
Artist: Joyce Pattee

From Our Home to Yours
Scenes of playful snowpeople alternate with homes decorated for the holidays. Caption: "Merry Christmas From Our Home to Yours. 1988."
- ◼ Sparkling Glass, 2⅞" diam.
475QX279-4, $4.75
Artist: Joyce Pattee

Babysitter
Building a snowman, throwing snowballs, and sledding are depicted in childlike drawings. The green glass ball is speckled with white to suggest a gentle snowfall. The snowman holds a sign that reads: "May the love you show children return to you this holiday. 1988."
- ◼ Green Glass, 2⅞" diam.
475QX279-1, $4.75
Artist: Linda Sickman

PEANUTS®
Flying across the sky, WOODSTOCK and pals pull SNOOPY on a gift-laden sled. The caption on the blue teardrop ball explains: "Where friendship goes, happiness follows! Christmas 1988."
- ◼ Blue Glass, 2⅞" diam.
475QX280-1, $4.75

From Our Home to Yours, Babysitter, PEANUTS®

Teacher

Teacher

This flocked bunny creates a special card "For Teacher." He's drawn a carrot inside, and now he's using his favorite CRAYOLA® crayon to add "Merry Christmas 1988."

There's a place for your name on the back side of the card, where it reads: "From:"
- Handcrafted, 2¼" tall
625QX417-1, $6.25
Artist: Sharon Pike

Holiday Traditions

Jingle Bell Clown

This musical ornament plays "Jingle Bells." Riding in a wood-look reindeer sleigh, a clown holds a brass bell. "1988" appears on the license plate.
- Handcrafted, Musical, 3" tall
1500QX477-4, $15.00

Travels with Santa

Mr. and Mrs. Claus travel in a trailer with movable wheels and the license plate: "B MERRY."
- Handcrafted, 2" tall
1000QX477-1, $10.00
Artist: Donna Lee

Party Line

Two chatty little raccoons have recycled cans of "Campbell's Chicken Noodle Soup" to start their own phone company. It's a local call or long distance, depending on whether you place the pals close together or on separate branches of your tree.
- Handcrafted, 1¼" tall
875QX476-1, $8.75
Artist: Sharon Pike

Goin' Cross Country

Now that he's mastered those bright red skis, this confident bear would rather glide than walk. His warm white coat is accented with a jaunty muffler of ribbon, and there's a real pompom on his cap.
- Handcrafted, 3¼" tall
850QX476-4, $8.50
Artist: Linda Sickman

Winter Fun

It's a wide-eyed ride for a happy, three-kid crew on a brand-new toboggan. Two face forward, one's riding backwards. The design includes a real rope for controlling the sled.
- Handcrafted, 2" tall
850QX478-1, $8.50
Artist: Robert Chad

Go for the Gold

An exuberant Santa dashes by, celebrating an exciting year in sports. Outfitted in a red, white, and blue jogging suit, he carries a golden torch with a translucent flame. Number "88" is on Santa's jacket.
- Handcrafted, 3½" tall
800QX417-4, $8.00
Artist: Bob Siedler

Jingle Bell Clown

Travels with Santa, Party Line, Goin' Cross Country, Winter Fun

Go for the Gold, Soft Landing, Feliz Navidad, Squeaky Clean

Soft Landing

Santa beams as he glides on ice skates. From the back, you can see his secret— a real fabric pillow in holiday green and white, tied around his waist with a green fabric ribbon.

■ Handcrafted, 3" tall
700QX475-1, $7.00
Artist: Robert Chad

Feliz Navidad

This gray burro wears a *sombrero* and carries two saddlebags. One holds a green bottle-brush tree; the other has a holiday package with the caption, "Feliz Navidad," Spanish for Merry Christmas.

■ Handcrafted, 2⅞" tall
675QX416-1, $6.75
Artist: Duane Unruh

Squeaky Clean

'Twas the night before Christmas…time for this little mouse to relax in a bubble-filled tub, molded from a walnut shell. The tub stands on four golden feet, and there's a tiny shower head.

■ Handcrafted, 2⅜" tall
675QX475-4, $6.75
Artist: Sharon Pike

Christmas Memories Photoholder

Silver foil snowflakes encircle an acrylic wreath. The year "1988" is shown on the front. The silvery caption on the back reads: "Christmas is more than a day in December…it's the magic and love we'll always remember."

■ Acrylic, 3¾" tall
650QX372-4, $6.50
Artist: Joyce Pattee

SNOOPY and WOODSTOCK

These two friends have tucked themselves inside a real knit stocking to decorate your tree. They even brought along a bow-tied gift bone.

■ Handcrafted, 2⅜" tall
600QX474-1, $6.00
Artist: Duane Unruh

Purrfect Snuggle

This gray-and-white striped kitten is purring his way into the heart of a new friend—a teddy bear, decked out for Christmas.

■ Handcrafted, 2" tall
625QX474-4, $6.25
Artist: Anita Marra Rogers

Christmas Memories Photoholder, SNOOPY and WOODSTOCK, Purrfect Snuggle

The Town Crier, Norman Rockwell: Christmas Scenes

Jolly Walrus, Slipper Spaniel, Arctic Tenor

The Town Crier
Dressed in Colonial clothing, a rabbit rings a bell and reads the proclamation: "Hear Ye! Hear Ye! Christmas time has come to cheer ye!" Front caption: "Hear Ye! Hear Ye! Christmas joy is always near ye!"
▪ Handcrafted, 2¼" tall
550QX473-4, $5.50
Artist: Ed Seale

Norman Rockwell: Christmas Scenes
These portrayals of children were carefully reproduced to reflect the original paintings. A child saying bedtime prayers is captioned: "Christmas...the sea-son that blesses the world. 1988." The scene with two children dressed for a holiday pageant says: "Christmas... the season that touches the heart. From the Norman Rockwell Collection."
▪ White Glass, 2⅞" diam.
475QX273-1, $4.75
Artist: Joyce Lyle

Jolly Walrus
The first Keepsake walrus, this fellow flashes a toothy smile. He's donned a wreath of shiny green foil and bright red satin ribbon to celebrate the occasion.
▪ Handcrafted, 1⅞" tall
450QX473-1, $4.50
Artist: Anita Marra Rogers

Slipper Spaniel
A cute, brown and white puppy sleeps in a flocked red slipper. His tail peeks out the bottom.
▪ Handcrafted, 3" tall
425QX472-4, $4.25
Artist: Ken Crow

Arctic Tenor
This penguin is wearing a green bow tie and colorful spats to per-form his holiday program. Musical notes are printed on the pages of his open songbook, titled "Arctic Arias."
▪ Handcrafted, 1¾" tall
400QX472-1, $4.00
Artist: Bob Siedler

St. Louie Nick
This is a reissue from 1987. (See 1987 Annual Collection.)
▪ Handcrafted, 3½" tall
775QX453-9, $7.75
Artist: Peter Dutkin

Mistletoad
This is a reissue from 1987. (See 1987 Annual Collection.)
▪ Handcrafted, 3¾" tall
700QX468-7, $7.00
Artist: Ken Crow

Treetop Dreams
This is a reissue from 1987. (See 1987 Annual Collection.)
▪ Handcrafted, 3" tall
675QX459-7, $6.75
Artist: Ed Seale

Night Before Christmas
This is a reissue from 1987. (See 1987 Annual Collection.)
▪ Handcrafted, 2¾" tall
650QX451-7, $6.50
Artist: Ken Crow

Owliday Wish
This is a reissue from 1987. (See 1987 Annual Collection.)
▪ Handcrafted, 2" tall
650QX455-9, $6.50
Artist: Sharon Pike

Happy Holidata
This is a reissue from 1987. (See 1987 Annual Collection.)
▪ Handcrafted, 1½" tall
650QX471-7, $6.50
Artist: Bob Siedler

Reindoggy
This is a reissue from 1987. (See 1987 Annual Collection.)
▪ Handcrafted, 2¾" tall
575QX452-7, $5.75
Artist: Bob Siedler

In a Nutshell
This is a reissue from 1987. (See 1987 Annual Collection.)
▪ Handcrafted, 1½" tall
550QX469-7, $5.50
Artist: Duane Unruh

New Attractions

Christmas Cuckoo
Hold the clock, and tap the pen-dulum. The door opens, reveal-ing a blue bird inside, and the clock's face turns from 12:00 to 3:00.
▪ Handcrafted, 4⅞" tall
800QX480-1, $8.00
Artist: Ken Crow

Special Edition

The Wonderful Santacycle

Santa really rolls along on this fanciful three-wheeler. It's reminiscent of that childhood favorite—a rocking horse—but this one sits atop golden-spoked wheels that turn. Special details include a brass bell on Santa's cap.

■ Handcrafted, 4¼" tall
2250QX411-4, $22.50
Artist: Ed Seale

Cool Juggler

Hold this snowman by the base and gently tap the snowball below. The snowman's arms move up and down, while three sparkling snowballs glide from hand to hand.

■ Handcrafted, 4¾" tall
650QX487-4, $6.50
Artist: Ken Crow

Peek-a-Boo Kitties

If you hold this basket and gently tap the kitten swinging on the ball of yarn, the lid of the basket will open on one side and then the other, displaying two more kittens hiding inside.

■ Handcrafted, 5" tall
750QX487-1, $7.50
Artist: Ken Crow

Santa Flamingo

This whimsical flamingo wears a red fabric Santa hat with fluffy white trim and a real pompom. His long, stilt-like legs really move, enabling him to take the holidays in stride.

■ Handcrafted, 5½" tall
475QX483-4, $4.75
Artist: Michele Pyda-Sevcik

Christmas Cuckoo, Cool Juggler, Peek-a-Boo Kitties, Santa Flamingo

Par for Santa

This group of lifestyle ornaments shows what Santa does for fun! In this design, he's playing golf. Holding a scorecard for the "St. Nick Open," he waits to tee off with his favorite wood.

■ Handcrafted, 2⅜" tall
500QX479-1, $5.00
Artist: Bob Siedler

Hoe-Hoe-Hoe!

Santa likes to tend his garden. He orders his gardening clothes in Christmas colors—a red visor and green overalls.

■ Handcrafted, 2⅜" tall
500QX422-1, $5.00
Artist: Bob Siedler

Nick the Kick

Santa's keeping pace with soccer. His team's emblem, a snowflake, is emblazoned on the front of his sweater. The team name, "Blizzard," as well as Santa's number, "00," appear on the back.

■ Handcrafted, 2¼" tall
500QX422-4, $5.00
Artist: Bob Siedler

Holiday Hero

Quarterback Claus steps back to pass the football for a touchdown. He's very sure-footed, thanks to the tiny cleats on the soles of his shoes. The back of his shirt carries his name, "S. Claus," and also makes it official—he's number "1."

■ Handcrafted, 2⅝" tall
500QX423-1, $5.00
Artist: Bob Siedler

Polar Bowler

Santa practices bowling with a polished green bowling ball, and there's a green towel in his hip pocket. The back of his shirt reads: "North Pole Bowl."

■ Handcrafted, 2¼" tall
500QX478-4, $5.00
Artist: Bob Siedler

Gone Fishing

Santa's equipped for fishing success. A rare bluefish swings from the nylon line connected to his flexible rod. He carries a creel to hold the fish he catches.

■ Handcrafted, 2½" tall
500QX479-4, $5.00
Artist: Bob Siedler

Love Santa

Santa skillfully returns a serve. The soft pompom ball is attached to his silvery racket. His attire for the courts includes a green headband and matching wristbands.

■ Handcrafted, 2½" tall
500QX486-4, $5.00
Artist: Bob Siedler

Par for Santa, Hoe-Hoe-Hoe!, Nick the Kick, Holiday Hero

Polar Bowler, Gone Fishing, Love Santa, Kiss the Claus

Sweet Star, Teeny Taster, Filled With Fudge

A KISS™ From Santa, OREO® Chocolate Sandwich Cookies (shown open and closed)

Kiss the Claus

Santa will be happy to serve his specialty —a cheeseburger on a bun. Be sure to dress casually, Santa's wearing thongs. His apron reads, "Kiss the Claus."

▧ Handcrafted, 2¾" tall
500QX486-1, $5.00
Artist: Bob Siedler

Sweet Star

Chocolate lovers find several 1988 Keepsake Ornaments especially tempting. Claiming this chocolate-rimmed sugar cookie for his very own, a mischievous squirrel begins nibbling on the maraschino cherry he found on top. The cookie clips onto a branch of your tree.

▧ Handcrafted, 1¾" tall
500QX418-4, $5.00
Artist: Ed Seale

Teeny Taster

This chipmunk taster is careful not to spill on his green fabric neck-ribbon and bow.

▧ Handcrafted, 4⅜" tall
475QX418-1, $4.75
Artist: Ed Seale

Filled With Fudge

This little mouse found his favorite dessert and jumped right in. Now he's holding out a spoon for a second helping. The mouse's red fabric ribbon is tied in a bow in back.

▧ Handcrafted, 3⅜" tall
475QX419-1, $4.75
Artist: Ed Seale

A KISS™ From Santa

Looking just like chocolate, this Keepsake Ornament is a treat that can be enjoyed season after season. The sculpted Santa wears a bright red hat with silver trim, and he's holding a silver likeness of the popular candy. The attached plume reads, "HERSHEY'S® KISSES."

▧ Handcrafted, 3¼" tall
450QX482-1, $4.50
Artist: Duane Unruh

OREO® Chocolate Sandwich Cookies

This life-size cookie is hinged and can be displayed closed or open. Inside, Santa's smiling face appears in the creamy filling. Caption: "ho ho ho!"

▧ Handcrafted, 1⅞" diam.
400QX481-4, $4.00
Artist: Duane Unruh

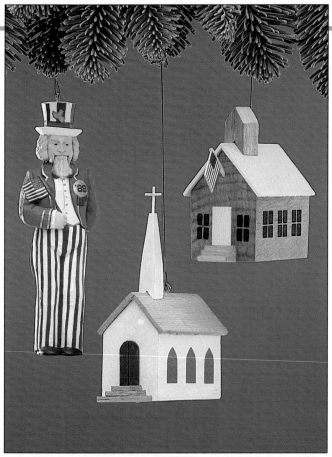

Uncle Sam Nutcracker, Old-Fashioned Church, Old-Fashioned Schoolhouse

Sailing! Sailing!, Noah's Ark, Americana Drum

Kringle Portrait, Kringle Tree, Kringle Moon

Glowing Wreath, Sparkling Tree, Shiny Sleigh

Uncle Sam Nutcracker

This traditional American figure wears his hair pulled back in a ponytail. Lift it, and his mouth moves in true Nutcracker fashion. Uncle Sam has a soft plush beard and wears a campaign button dated "1988."

■ Handcrafted, 5¼" tall
700QX488-4, $7.00
Artist: Donna Lee

Old-Fashioned Church

The village church was the hub of the holiday celebration in American country life. Classic lines include an arched doorway and windows and a tall steeple.

■ Wood, 4½" tall
400QX498-1, $4.00
Artist: Linda Sickman

Old-Fashioned Schoolhouse

The little red schoolhouse is made of wood. It represents the handmade villages that were favorite folk art decorations. An American flag is above the door, and a tower on the roof houses the school bell.

■ Wood, 3" tall
400QX497-1, $4.00
Artist: Linda Sickman

Sailing! Sailing!

This year's second nautical pressed tin ornament also features a nostalgic pull-toy design. Here, a sailor enjoys a breezy day. Water laps against the sides of his boat, and fish jump over the waves. Pull the metallic cord and the sailboat rolls along.

■ Pressed Tin, 2⅞" tall
850QX491-1, $8.50
Artist: Linda Sickman

Noah's Ark

Reminiscent of antique pull-toys, this colorful and highly detailed craft is filled with passengers from stem to stern. It is one of two nautical pressed tin designs in the 1988 Keepsake Ornament line. The wheels on the ark really turn, and there's a metallic pull-cord.

■ Pressed Tin, 2⅛" tall
850QX490-4, $8.50
Artist: Linda Sickman

Americana Drum

The sides of this colorful tin drum are decorated with a holiday version of a traditional American eagle and banner design. The eagle holds evergreen branches and holly. The caption, "Merry Christmas U.S.A. 1988," appears on both drumheads. Gold metallic cord forms the bindings, and a set of drumsticks is attached.

■ Tin, 2" diam.
775QX488-1, $7.75
Artist: Linda Sickman

Kringle Portrait

Santa's face and flowing beard are encircled by a wreath. Santa's sleigh, complete with Christmas tree and teddy bear, is on the back.

■ Handcrafted, 3¼" tall
750QX496-1, $7.50

Kringle Tree

Two favorite symbols of Christmas—Santa and a tree—are combined in one ornament, carefully sculpted to give the appearance of an old-world carving. The antiqued finish lends a timeless quality to the design.

■ Handcrafted, 3⅜" tall
650QX495-4, $6.50

Kringle Moon

The man in the moon is Santa himself, and he's catching 40 winks. There's a tiny brass jingle bell at the tip of his cap. The carving appears on both sides of the ornament.

■ Handcrafted, 3⅜" tall
550QX495-1, $5.50
Artist: Anita Marra Rogers

Glowing Wreath

This year's trio of multi-dimensional brass ornaments is a tribute to early-American artisans who created their decorations from simple metal shapes.

Loving Bear, Christmas Cardinal, Starry Angel

gleaming brass wreath begins with a circle and the silhouettes of a house and heart. Nine additional silhouettes extend from the wreath at various levels, effecting a layered appearance.

■ Dimensional Brass, 3½" tall
600QX492-1, $6.00
Artist: Joyce Pattee

Sparkling Tree

The brass silhouette of a Christmas tree is layered with additional brass silhouettes of a home, a reindeer, two doves of peace, a heart, and a star. Tiny cut-outs in the tree allow light to shine through.

■ Dimensional Brass, 3⅜" tall
600QX493-1, $6.00
Artist: Joyce Pattee

Shiny Sleigh

Fashioned from one continuous piece of metal, this multi-dimensional design is created by careful bending and shaping. The red cord in Santa's hand is the hanger for the ornament and the reins for the reindeer.

■ Dimensional Brass, 1⅛" tall
575QX492-4, $5.75
Artist: Joyce Pattee

Loving Bear

"Twirl-Abouts," ornaments with rotating center designs, were introduced in 1976. Three new ornaments similar to Twirl-Abouts appeared in 1988. This teddy bear twirls inside a holiday wreath decorated with folk-art shapes of hearts and holly.

■ Handcrafted, 3¼" tall
475QX493-4, $4.75
Artist: Anita Marra Rogers

Christmas Cardinal

A cheerful cardinal twirls inside the silhouette of an evergreen tree. The folk art flavor of the design is emphasized by a pattern that suggests pine branches accented with white ornaments.

■ Handcrafted, 2⅞" tall
475QX494-1, $4.75
Artist: Anita Marra Rogers

Starry Angel

In a white robe trimmed in red and green, this angel twirls inside the silhouette of a star. The star's stencil-like design shows a Scandinavian influence.

■ Handcrafted, 2⅞" tall
475QX494-4, $4.75
Artist: Anita Marra Rogers

Artists' Favorites

Merry-Mint Unicorn

As a child, artist Anita Marra Rogers loved to draw pictures of unicorns with big doe-eyes and curly manes. Here, she's created a unicorn that appears to be balancing on a piece of peppermint candy.
- Handpainted Fine Porcelain, 3¾" tall
  850QX423-4, $8.50
  Artist: Anita Marra Rogers

Midnight Snack

This whimsical white mouse enjoys a treat, thanks to artist Bob Siedler. The handcrafted doughnut is topped with make-believe icing and red sparkles. The mouse wears a green fabric bow.
- Handcrafted, 2½" tall
  600QX410-4, $6.00
  Artist: Bob Siedler

Little Jack Horner

Artist Bob Siedler thinks this nursery rhyme is especially appropriate for the holiday season, so he's sculpted his vision of the well-known lad pulling a plum out of his Christmas pie. The boy's hat, adorned with a handcrafted yellow feather, is captioned: "Little Jack Horner."
- Handcrafted, 2½" tall
  800QX408-1, $8.00
  Artist: Bob Siedler

Cymbals of Christmas

Artist Donna Lee explains that this playful angel wants everyone to know she's there. So she's pulled two golden stars out of the sky to make a big ka-boom! Her halo is brass, and her frosted acrylic cloud is decorated with holly and stars.
- Handcrafted, Acrylic, 2⅛" tall
  550QX411-1, $5.50
  Artist: Donna Lee

Baby Redbird

This cheerful fellow reminds artist Robert Chad of cardinals who feast on sunflower seeds at feeding stations, then rest like lovely decorations in nearby trees. "Baby Redbird" clips onto your tree.
- Handcrafted, 2⅝" tall
  500QX410-1, $5.00
  Artist: Robert Chad

Very Strawbeary

Artist Peter Dutkin remembers waiting for the ice-cream truck as a boy, so he's given this flocked teddy bear a treat. The decorated cone carries the artist's initials, "PDII." Sparkling red acrylic ice crystals add a holiday flavor.
- Handcrafted, 2¼" tall
  475QX409-1, $4.75
  Artist: Peter Dutkin

Merry-Mint Unicorn, Midnight Snack, Little Jack Horner

Cymbals of Christmas, Baby Redbird, Very Strawbeary

Mary's Angels, Collector's Plate, Mr. and Mrs. Claus

Collectible Series

Mary's Angels—First Edition

"Buttercup" is the first angel in a series of new designs by Mary Hamilton. This little angel has a pastel-yellow dress and pearly wings. She naps on a frosted acrylic cloud that displays "Mary" on the bottom.
■ Handcrafted, 2¼" tall
500QX407-4, $5.00
Artist: Robert Chad

Collector's Plate —Second Edition

The tree is decorated, stockings are hung, and there's a plate of cookies on the table. Brother and sister nap, and puppy peers up the fireplace. Caption: "Waiting for Santa 1988." Plate stand included.
■ Fine Porcelain, 3¼" diam.
800QX406-1, $8.00
Artist: LaDene Votruba

Mr. and Mrs. Claus —Third Edition

Santa and Mrs. Claus dance, but Santa still carries a gift list, dated "1988," in his pocket. The wishbone hanger enhances the design, titled "Shall We Dance."
■ Handcrafted, 4¼ " tall
1300QX401-1, $13.00
Artist: Duane Unruh

Reindeer Champs —Third Edition

Prancer bounces a basketball, preparing to shoot. The back of his shirt shows his name and number, "Prancer 88."
■ Handcrafted, 3½" tall
750QX405-1, $7.50
Artist: Bob Seidler

Windows of the World —Fourth Edition

A poodle and his master wait for Santa in front of the fireplace. Overhead, red bows hold a banner with the French greeting: "Joyeux Noel." "1988" is on the yule logs.
■ Handcrafted, 3½" tall
1000QX402-1, $10.00
Artist: Donna Lee

Betsey Clark: Home for Christmas—Third Edition

Betsy and her friends are baking cookies, stitching a quilt, and pressing a red stocking captioned "Noel." The wall poster says: "A homemade touch can do so much to make each Christmas special!" The wall clock reads: "1988."
■ Light-Blue Glass, 2⅞" diam.
500QX271-4, $5.00
Artist: Sharon Pike

Reindeer Champs, Windows of the World, Betsey Clark: Home for Christmas

Miniature Crèche
—Fourth Edition

This crèche is frosted acrylic, silhouetted within a clear acrylic star. Sides of the star are gold and faceted to reflect the light. A golden, star-shaped finding covers the top.
■ Acrylic, 2¾" tall
   850QX403-4, $8.50
   Artist: Duane Unruh

Nostalgic Houses
and Shops—Fifth Edition

Inside this replica of "Hall Bro's" is an old-fashioned cash register and a greeting card display. The second floor holds an artist's studio. "Hall Bro's Card Shop" enjoys a prime corner location with a "1988" address.
■ Handcrafted, 4¼" tall
   1450QX401-4, $14.50
   Artist: Donna Lee

Wood Childhood
Ornaments—Fifth Edition

The propeller spins, and the wheels really roll on this nostalgic "Wooden Airplane." Handpainted details and a green yarn pull-cord help bring back warm memories. The design is dated "1988."
■ Wood, 1⅜" tall
   750QX404-1, $7.50
   Artist: Peter Dutkin

The Twelve Days
of Christmas—Fifth Edition

This quadrafoil ornament has five differently styled rings linked with a ribbon and bow. The design is etched into clear acrylic, and the caption is stamped in gold foil: "The Twelve Days of Christmas 1988…five golden rings…"
■ Acrylic, 3" tall
   650QX371-4, $6.50
   Artist: Sharon Pike

Tin Locomotive—
Seventh Edition

This colorful "Tin Locomotive" has a distinctive, pierced-tin cowcatcher. The wheels are decorated with bright embossed patterns, which add to the sense of motion as the wheels turn. The year "1988" appears on the boiler.
■ Pressed Tin, 3" tall
   1475QX400-4, $14.75
   Artist: Linda Sickman

Porcelain Bear—Sixth Edition

Cinnamon Bear has wrapped up a heart full of memories. This fine porcelain bear is handpainted.
■ Handpainted Fine Porcelain, 2¼" tall
   800QX404-4, $8.00
   Artist: Sharon Pike

Miniature Crèche, Nostalgic Houses and Shops, Wood Childhood Ornaments

The Twelve Days of Christmas, Tin Locomotive, Porcelain Bear

Holiday Wildlife, Frosty Friends, Rocking Horse

Norman Rockwell, Here Comes Santa, Thimble

Holiday Wildlife—
Seventh and Final Edition

Perched on a pine branch, a pair of purple finches is realistically depicted on this porcelain-look inset framed in wood. Caption: "Purple Finch, CARPODACUS PURPUREUS, Seventh in a Series, Wildlife Collection, Christmas 1988."
■ Wood, 2½" diam.
775QX371-1, $7.75

Frosty Friends—Ninth Edition

A polar-bear cub holds one end of a real fabric ribbon while an Eskimo wraps the "North Pole" in holiday style. They stand on an icy base of acrylic, dated "1988."
■ Handcrafted, 3⅜" tall
875QX403-1, $8.75
Artist: Ed Seale

Rocking Horse—Eighth Edition

Hurrying to the festivities, this dapple-gray pony brings happy memories of childhood. His red-and-green trappings are accented with gold, and the red-and-green rockers read: "1988." The pony's mane and fore-lock are dark gray, and he boasts the first two-tone yarn tail in the series.
■ Handcrafted, 3¼" wide
1075QX402-4, $10.75
Artist: Linda Sickman

Norman Rockwell—
Ninth and Final Edition

Santa relaxes in his chair, holding the "Dec 24" calendar page in his hand. The wall calendar reads "Dec 25." This white bas-relief cameo is on a red background framed in brass. Back caption: "And to All a Good Night, Ninth in a Series, Christmas 1988, The Norman Rockwell Collection."
■ Cameo, 3¼" diam.
775QX370-4, $7.75

Here Comes Santa—
Tenth Edition

Santa drives a stagecoach with gifts atop and a bottle-brush tree in the boot. A teddy bear waves from inside. The door next to the bear opens and carries the caption: "Kringle Koach 1988." The opposite door reads: "Kringle Koach."
■ Handcrafted, 3¼" tall
1400QX400-1, $14.00
Artist: Ken Crow

Thimble—Eleventh Edition

"Thimble Snowman" wears a silver thim-ble for a hat. The pearly snowman's attire includes a red muffler and green mittens.
■ Handcrafted, 2⅜" tall
575QX405-4, $5.75
Artist: Bob Siedler

1987

Three limited edition ornaments highlighted the 1987 Keepsake line. "Christmas Time Mime" is a combination of fantasy and tradition, limited to an edition size of 24,700. Introducing new formats and new kinds of design markings were "Christmas is Gentle," an individually numbered, bone china basket holding two lambs, also limited to 24,700, and "Holiday Heirloom," a lead crystal bell framed by a sculpted silver-plated wreath, limited to 34,600.

The new "Collector's Plate" series premiered a miniature porcelain plate decorated with artwork of children trimming the tree. The "Clothespin Soldier" series came to an end with the sixth edition—a sailor.

Three new collections appeared in 1987. "Artists' Favorites" feature popular subjects, such as bears and mice. Favorites of Hallmark artists *and* collectors, the ornaments carry the artists' signature or initials. "Christmas Pizzazz" offers a lighthearted, contemporary look at the season. And "Old-Fashioned Christmas" consists of traditional designs that look handcarved or homemade. New Property ornaments in 1987 included "Jammie Pies™," "Crayola,®" and "Dr. Seuss."

Commemoratives

Baby's First Christmas
Holding onto a tiny rattle, Baby has fun in the real spring seat-swing. The ornament carries the caption, "Baby's First Christmas 1987," on the back of the seat.
- Handcrafted, 4¼" tall
  975QX411-3, $9.75
  Artist: Donna Lee

Baby's First Christmas Photoholder
An ecru fabric wreath, trimmed in lace and ribbon and embroidered with toys and holly, frames a favorite photo of Baby. "Baby's First Christmas 1987" is embroidered on the front, and a sentiment is silk-screened on the flocked back: "Welcome to Christmas, Baby dear. Everyone is glad you're here."
- Fabric, 3¼" diam.
  750QX461-9, $7.50

Baby's First Christmas
Baby's acrylic booties are decorated with etched jingle bells and holly. The caption, "Baby's First Christmas 1987," is stamped on the bow in gold foil.
- Acrylic, 3½" tall
  600QX372-9, $6.00

Baby's First Christmas—Baby Girl
Dressed in rosy pink, the rag doll on this white satin ball spells "BABY GIRL" with her blocks. Caption: "A Baby Girl, so dear and sweet, makes your Christmas joy complete. Baby's First Christmas 1987."
- White Satin, 2⅞" diam.
  475QX274-7, $4.75
  Artist: Joyce Pattee

Baby's First Christmas: Handcrafted, Photoholder, Acrylic

Baby's First Christmas—Baby Boy

A cuddly blue bear and a train carrying holly keep Baby's blocks from tumbling down. The blocks spell "BABY BOY," and the caption on this white satin ball reads, "A Baby Boy, so darling and dear, makes Christmas extra special this year. Baby's First Christmas 1987."
▨ White Satin, 2⅞" diam.
475QX274-9, $4.75
Artist: Joyce Pattee

Grandchild's First Christmas

A teddy bear plays with his blocks inside a Jenny Lind style playpen lined with a green and red quilt sprinkled with stars. The fabric blanket carries the caption: "Grandchild's First Christmas 1987." The ornament has room for personalization on the bottom.
▨ Handcrafted, 1¾" tall
900QX460-9, $9.00
Artist: Ed Seale

Baby's Second Christmas

A cheery clown-in-the-box bounces on a real spring as he wishes Baby a happy holiday. Caption: "Baby's 2nd Christmas 1987." The ornament attaches to your tree with a special clip.
▨ Handcrafted, 2¾" tall
575QX460-7, $5.75
Artist: Donna Lee

Child's Third Christmas

Dressed in bright red with a real pompom on his cap, the child enjoys a ride. The reindeer makes a galloping motion when it is tapped gently. Caption: "My 3rd Christmas 1987."
▨ Handcrafted, 3" tall
575QX459-9, $5.75
Artist: Ken Crow

Baby Locket

Baby's photo will look festive inside this special locket that has the shimmery look of silver. Embossed on the front is the word "Baby" and on the back, "1987." The locket has a special insert for personalization and comes with a wishbone hanger.
▨ Textured Metal, 2¼" diam.
1500QX461-7, $15.00

Baby's First Christmas: Baby Girl, Baby Boy; Grandchild's First Christmas

Baby's Second Christmas, Child's Third Christmas, Baby Locket

Mother and Dad, Mother, Dad

Granddaughter
Filled with toys, the antique sleigh on this padded satin ornament offers a nostalgic look at the joys of the holiday. The ornament is bezeled in brass and carries the caption, "A Granddaughter makes each day a holiday in the heart. Christmas 1987."
■ Bezeled Satin, 2¾" diam.
600QX374-7, $6.00
Artist: LaDene Votruba

Godchild
This blue ball looks as if it were sprinkled with snow. The brightly lit holiday tree on the front, designed to resemble torn paper, symbolizes the warmth of the season and reflects the caption: "A God-child makes Christmas glow a little brighter. 1987."
■ Blue Glass, 2⅞" diam.
475QX276-7, $4.75
Artist: Michele Pyda-Sevcik

Grandmother
The caption on this frosted pink teardrop ball is illustrated with delicately painted roses and carnations. Caption: Grand-mothers, like flowers, fill the world with beauty, the heart with joy. Christmas 1987."
■ Pink Glass, 3" diam.
475QX277-9, $4.75

Grandparents
Building a snowman, skating on a frozen stream, and riding in a horse-drawn sleigh are just some of the activities depicted in this country portrait. The scene, reminiscent of American folk art, captures the warmth of the holiday and echoes the special message: "Grandparents...so warm, so loving, so like the Christmas season. 1987."
■ Porcelain White Glass, 2⅞" diam.
475QX277-7, $4.75
Artist: Sharon Pike

Mother and Dad
Tied with a red satin ribbon, this deep blue porcelain bell carries the tribute: "For a Mother and Dad who give the gift of love. Christmas 1987." The tree on the front has a sponged stencil look.
■ Fine Porcelain, 4¾" tall
700QX462-7, $7.00
Artist: Sharon Pike

Mother
This brass-framed, acrylic oval's intricately cut beveled edge, a design seen for the first time in the Keepsake line, gives the ornament the look of cut glass. An etched sprig of holly accents the gold foil-stamped caption: "Mother is another word for love. Christmas 1987."
■ Acrylic, 3½" tall
650QX373-7, $6.50
Artist: Sharon Pike

Dad
What does Dad want for Christmas? Another tie, of course! This polar bear has some special favorites—even one with a bright Hawaiian motif. Caption: "For Dad Christmas 1987."
■ Handcrafted, 3" tall
600QX462-9, $6.00
Artist: Bob Siedler

Husband
The sentiment and design on this ornament remind us that Christmas is the season of love and sharing. Against a sky blue background, the ivory cameo sleigh has delicate bas-relief detailing. Front Caption: "For My Husband." Back caption: "The nicest part of Christmas is sharing it with you. 1987."
■ Cameo, 3¼" diam.
700QX373-9, $7.00
Artist: LaDene Votruba

Sister
A lovely basket of poinsettias has been tied with a bright green bow. The design, a bright stencil-look printed on wood, reflects the back message: "A Sister brings happiness wrapped in love. Christmas 1987."
■ Wood, 2¾" tall
600QX474-7, $6.00
Artist: Linda Sickman

Daughter
A pair of prancing reindeer pull a graceful swan sleigh, just like the ones seen in carousels. Fashioned to look like wood, the ornament carries the caption: "Daughter Christmas 1987."
■ Handcrafted, 1¼" tall
575QX463-7, $5.75
Artist: Linda Sickman

Son
This colorful train races across the tree to wish Son a happy holiday. It looks like an old-fashioned toy. Caption: "For Son Christmas 1987."
■ Handcrafted, 1" tall
575QX463-9, $5.75
Artist: Linda Sickman

Niece
Accented with touches of red, a flock of snow-white lambs frolic around a turquoise blue teardrop ball. The caption, printed in the lower border, reflects a cheery look: "Christmas is happier...merrier...cheerier...because of a Niece's love. 1987."
■ Turquoise Blue Glass, 3" diam.
475QX275-9, $4.75

Grandson
Dressed in holiday uniforms, a musical marching band parades around this sky blue teardrop ball, carrying a banner with a special message: "Grandsons have a talent for making wonderful memories." The drum reads: "Christmas 1987."
■ Sky Blue Glass, 3" diam.
475QX276-9, $4.75
Artist: LaDene Votruba

Husband, Sister

Daughter, Son, Niece

Grandson, Granddaughter, Godchild

Grandmother, Grandparents

First Christmas Together

Displayed open or closed, this heart-shaped brass locket is a loving memento of the season. Embossed lovebirds decorate the back, and the embossed caption, "First Christmas Together 1987," adorns the front. The ornament comes with a wishbone hanger.

▦ Textured Brass, 2¼" tall
1500QX446-9, $15.00

First Christmas Together

Home is where the heart is in this Alpine cottage captioned: "First Christmas Together 1987." The room inside holds a bottle-brush tree and a sampler with, "Love Sweet Love."

▦ Handcrafted, 3" tall
950QX446-7, $9.50
Artist: Donna Lee

First Christmas Together

Two raccoons snuggle inside a fabric sweatshirt with "First Christmas Together" silk-screened on the front. The date, "1987," appears on the back, inside a heart.

▦ Handcrafted, 2½" tall
800QX445-9, $8.00

First Christmas Together

Two exquisitely etched swans float across an acrylic oval framed in brass. The caption, stamped in gold foil, says "First Christmas Together 1987."

▦ Acrylic, 2½" tall
650QX371-9, $6.50

First Christmas Together

A garden of pastel poinsettias, touched with silver, decorates this frosted white glass ball. Two lovebirds appear on the front with the caption: "First Christmas Together 1987." On the back is: "To all who love, love is all the world."

▦ White Glass, 2⅞" diam.
475QX272-9, $4.75
Artist: Joyce Lyle

Ten Years Together

A heart-shaped floral wreath frames the caption, "Ten Years Together," on this snow-white porcelain bell with a red satin ribbon. Back: "Christmas 1987."

▦ Fine Porcelain, 4¾" tall
700QX444-7, $7.00
Artist: LaDene Votruba

Twenty-Five Years Together

A crisply painted pair of cardinals enjoys the holiday season on a miniature porcelain collector's plate that celebrates a life of sharing. The lettering is printed in traditional silver. Front: "25 Years Together Christmas 1987." Back: "Love is for always." Plate stand's included.

▦ Fine Porcelain, 3¼" diam.
750QX443-9, $7.50

Fifty Years Together

The velvety bisque finish of this lovely porcelain bell contrasts nicely with the glazed finish of the bas-relief poinsettia design and sculpted handle. "Fifty Years Together" and "Christmas 1987" are printed in gold.

▦ Fine Porcelain, 5" tall
800QX443-7, $8.00
Artist: Ed Seale

Word of Love

There's no other word that means so much. This bisque fine porcelain ornament is accented with touches of gold and a tiny red dangling heart. Caption: "Christmas 1987."

▦ Fine Porcelain, 2⅛" tall
800QX447-7, $8.00

Heart in Blossom

A single rose is a timeless symbol of love. It has been carefully etched into this heart-shaped acrylic ornament to reflect the message stamped in gold foil: "Love is the heart in blossom. Christmas 1987."

▦ Acrylic, 2¼" tall
600QX372-7, $6.00
Artist: LaDene Votruba

Sweetheart

A package labeled "For My Sweetheart" is about to be delivered in this surrey with the fabric fringe on top. Beautifully detailed, the vehicle has wheels that turn and room for personalization underneath. "Christmas 1987" is printed in gold on the front of the surrey, and "Sweet," printed above two entwined hearts, appears on the back.

▦ Handcrafted, 3⅛" tall
1100QX447-9, $11.00
Artist: Linda Sickman

Love Is Everywhere

A winter landscape echoes the peace and serenity of the holiday season. A pair of cardinals brings a bright splash of color to the silvery sky. Caption: "Beautifully, peacefully, Christmas touches our lives... love is everywhere. 1987."

▦ Chrome and Frosted Blue Glass, 2⅞" diam.
475QX278-7, $4.75
Artist: Joyce Lyle

First Christmas Together: Textured Brass, Handcrafted, Handcrafted, Acrylic

First Christmas Together White Glass

Ten Years Together, Twenty-Five Years Together, Fifty Years Together

Word of Love, Heart in Blossom

Sweetheart, Love is Everywhere

Holiday Greetings, Warmth of Friendship, Time for Friends

From Our Home to Yours, New Home, Babysitter

Holiday Greetings

This elegant ornament features a graphic silver Christmas tree and lettering against a shimmery blue and violet foil background. Bezeled in chrome, the ornament has been designed to be especially appropriate for business use. The ornament box provides room for personalization. Front caption: "Season's Greetings." Back caption: "Wishing you happiness at this beautiful time of year. 1987."

■ Bezeled Foil, 2¾" diam.
  600QX375-7 $6.00

Warmth of Friendship

The gold foil caption stamped on this acrylic ornament displays the classic beauty of calligraphy. Caption: "As Christmas warms the world friendship warms our hearts. 1987."

■ Acrylic, 3¾" tall
  600QX375-9, $6.00

Time for Friends

Two white mice hang garland around a red glass teardrop ball. They're hurrying to meet one another because: "When good friends meet, good times are complete! Christmas 1987."

■ Red Glass, 3" diam.
  475QX280-7, $4.75
  Artist: LaDene Votruba

From Our Home to Yours

A friendly welcome awaits you at every door in this neighborhood. Decorated for the holidays, the doors circle a frosted white glass teardrop ball that carries the caption: "From Our Home...To Yours... At Christmas 1987."

■ White Glass, 3" diam.
  475QX279-9, $4.75
  Artist: Michele Pyda-Sevcik

New Home

The scene on this ornament brings back memories of holidays long ago, but the format was new to the Keepsake line during this year. Printed in white on a mirrored acrylic background is a snug and cozy cottage. Caption: "A New Home is a wonderful beginning to wonderful memories. Christmas 1987."

■ Mirrored Acrylic, 2¾" diam.
  600QX376-7 $6.00
  Artist: Joyce Pattee

Babysitter

The scenes on this porcelain-white teardrop ball symbolize the love given to children by those special people who take care of them. One bunny is reading a book titled "Bunny Tales," and a calendar on the wall says it's "1987." Caption: "For bringing children such special gifts...gentleness, caring, and love. Merry Christmas."

■ Porcelain-White Glass, 3" diam.
  475QX279-7, $4.75
  Artist: Sharon Pike

Teacher

This "beary" good student has a message for teacher and room for personalization on his slate: "Merry Christmas, Teacher From (name)." The bear has carved "1987" into the desk.
■ Handcrafted, 2" tall
  575QX466-7, $5.75
  Artist: Bob Siedler

Holiday Humor

SNOOPY and WOODSTOCK

SNOOPY and WOODSTOCK have decorated a bottle-brush tree for the holiday. WOODSTOCK perches on top—the perfect angel. On the dish is: "SNOOPY."
■ Handcrafted, 2½" tall
  725QX472-9, $7.25
  Artist: Bob Siedler

Bright Christmas Dreams

Wearing colorful nightcaps, four mice dream of a bright Christmas in an authentic Crayola® box made of varnished paper. Front of box: "Crayola® Crayons, Bright Christmas Dreams, Binney & Smith®." Back, sides, and bottom of box: "Crayola® Crayons." The back of the box also carries the caption, "Christmas 1987," designed to look like part of a store code.
■ Handcrafted, 4" tall
  725QX473-7, $7.25
  Artist: Bob Siedler

Joy Ride

Santa and a reindeer take a holiday ride on a motorcycle. The wheels really do spin, and the reindeer wears a fabric muffler. Caption on front fender: "Joy Ride." On license plate: "1987."
■ Handcrafted, 3½" tall
  1150QX440-7, $11.50
  Artist: Ed Seale

Pretty Kitty

This little kitten is all tangled up in some red beads. He has to hold on tight because he's the clapper inside the clear glass bell.
■ Handcrafted, Glass, 3½" tall
  1100QX448-9, $11.00
  Artist: Ken Crow

Santa at the Bat

Santa is the star of the team as his signature "Santa Claus" bat hits a pearlized snowball. His uniform reads: "North Pole Nicks 87."
■ Handcrafted, 3¼" tall
  775QX457-9, $7.75
  Artist: Bob Siedler

Jogging Through the Snow

Carrying his radio and wearing headphones, this rabbit listens to Christmas music. His shirt carries his number, "87," and "Holiday Run."
■ Handcrafted, 3" tall
  725QX457-7, $7.25
  Artist: Peter Dutkin

Teacher

SNOOPY, Bright Christmas Dreams

Joy Ride, Pretty Kitty, Santa at the Bat, Jogging Through the Snow

Jack Frosting, Raccoon Biker, Treetop Dreams, Night Before Christmas

Jack Frosting

Jack dips his brush into an acorn filled with sparkling frost and brushes the glitter onto each leaf. This ornament attaches with a special clip.
◼ Handcrafted, 2½" tall
700QX449-9, $7.00
Artist: Ed Seale

Raccoon Biker

This spunky raccoon rides his dirt bike, delivering a Christmas gift. The bike's front is marked "87."
◼ Handcrafted, 3" tall
700QX458-7, $7.00
Artist: Bob Siedler

Treetop Dreams

The squirrel was nestled all snug in his bed while visions of acorns danced in his head! His blanket is polka-dot fabric, and a matching fabric ribbon decorates the wreath. To achieve an especially authentic look, real sticks were used to mold this design.
◼ Handcrafted, 3" tall
675QX459-7, $6.75
Artist: Ed Seale

Night Before Christmas

It's the night before Christmas, and this mouse isn't stirring. He'd much rather be sleeping on Santa's hat. The flocked hat has furry trim and a pompom at the top. A tiny chunk of cheese is tucked into the trim at the back.
◼ Handcrafted, 2¾" tall
650QX451-7, $6.50
Artist: Ken Crow

"Owliday" Wish

Wearing brass spectacles, this owl helps us all get a clear vision of his "owliday" wish on the eyechart: "SEASONS GREETINGS TO YOU." Real sticks were used to mold his perch and pointer.
◼ Handcrafted, 2" tall
650QX455-9, $6.50
Artist: Sharon Pike

Let It Snow

Wearing a knitted cap, muffler, and real pompom earmuffs, this tyke is dressed for cold weather.
◼ Handcrafted, 3" tall
650QX458-9, $6.50

Hot Dogger

Santa is king of the hill, a champion skier and, as his ski jacket says, a "Hot Dogger" on the slopes! His ski outfit is decorated with snowflake patches.
◼ Handcrafted, 2½" tall
650QX471-9, $6.50
Artist: Duane Unruh

Spots 'n Stripes

Santa has left a gift in a Dalmatian pup's Christmas stocking—a candy cane in his favorite shape.
◼ Handcrafted, 2¼" tall
550QX452-9, $5.50

"Owliday" Wish, Let It Snow, Hot Dogger, Spots 'n Stripes

Seasoned Greetings

This elf has a very important job to do— placing salt on all the holiday pretzels. He uses a silvery shaker that he fills from his salt bag labeled, "Seasoned Greetings SALT."

◾ Handcrafted, 2" tall
625QX454-9, $6.25
Artist: Ed Seale

Chocolate Chipmunk

This chipmunk's dressed for winter in a knitted red muffler. A real cookie was used to mold the design. The ornament attaches with a special clip.

◾ Handcrafted, 2" tall
600QX456-7, $6.00
Artist: Ed Seale

Fudge Forever

Sitting in a dark blue spatterware ladle, this little mouse is so full of fudge he can hardly budge! But that doesn't stop him from scooping up just a little bit more with his own mouse-sized spoon.

◾ Handcrafted, 3" tall
500QX449-7, $5.00
Artist: Peter Dutkin

Sleepy Santa

If there's one person who deserves a nap after Christmas, it's Santa. He lounges in his favorite chair, soaking his feet. The chair is flocked, and the calendar page reads: "DEC. 26."

◾ Handcrafted, 2¾" tall
625QX450-7, $6.25
Artist: Ken Crow

Reindoggy

This little puppy may be wearing antlers, but his expression shows he isn't ready to pull Santa's sleigh. The antlers were molded from real sticks and tied to the puppy's head with a red satin bow.

◾ Handcrafted, 2¾" tall
575QX452-7, $5.75
Artist: Bob Siedler

Christmas Cuddle

Wearing matching Santa hats in honor of the holiday, two buddies enjoy a warm Christmas hug. The kitten's hat is topped with a real pompom.

◾ Handcrafted, 2¾" tall
575QX453-7 $5.75

Paddington™ Bear

Paddington™ likes to eat what he bakes! Perhaps he's flavored the cookies with his favorite food— honey. He wears a red apron marked, "Paddington™ Bear," and a chef's hat tagged: "Please look after this Bear Thank You."

◾ Handcrafted, 3" tall
550QX472-7, $5.50
Artist: Sharon Pike

Seasoned Greetings, Chocolate Chipmunk, Fudge Forever

Sleepy Santa, Reindoggy, Christmas Cuddle, Paddington™ Bear

Nature's Decorations, Dr. Seuss: The Grinch's Christmas, Jammie Pies™

PEANUTS®, Happy Santa, Icy Treat

Nature's Decorations
The painted animals and birds on this light blue glass ball are Mother Nature's way of decorating her wintry world. Caption: "The nicest Christmas decorations start with Nature's own creations. 1987."
▢ Blue Glass, 2⅞" diam.
475QX273-9, $4.75
Artist: LaDene Votruba

Dr. Seuss:
The Grinch's Christmas
Framed by a colorful Christmas wreath, the Grinch is smiling at last. He and a chorus of Whos from Who-ville celebrate the holiday on a blue glass ball. Caption: "A very merry wish for a merry, merry Christmas."
▢ Blue Glass, 2⅞" diam.
475QX278-3, $4.75

Jammie Pies™
A new Hallmark property, Jammie Pies,™ made its Keepsake debut on this porcelain-white glass ball. The swan from the "Land of Sweet Dreams," brings a Jammie Pie friend to tell the child stories. Caption: "When Jammie Pies are close to you, all your Christmas dreams come true. 1987."
▢ Porcelain-White Glass, 2⅞" diam.
475QX283-9, $4.75

PEANUTS®
SNOOPY, WOODSTOCK, and his friends show that: "Everyone's cool at Christmastime!" The supper dish carries "1987."
▢ Chrome Glass, 3" diam.
475QX281-9, $4.75

Happy Santa
Santa carries a brass bell and uses his candy cane to hang from your tree.
▢ Handcrafted, 2½" tall
475QX456-9, $4.75
Artist: Ken Crow

Icy Treat
This penguin's shimmery cherry treat is just the thing for a frosty afternoon snack.
▢ Handcrafted, 2¼" tall
450QX450-9, $4.50
Artist: Bob Siedler

Mouse in the Moon
This is a reissue from 1986. (See 1986 Annual Collection.)
▢ Handcrafted, 2¾" tall
550QX416-6, $5.50
Artist: Ed Seale

L'il Jingler
This is a reissue from 1986. (See 1986 Annual Collection.)
▢ Handcrafted, 2" tall
675QX419-3, $6.75
Artist: Ed Seale

Walnut Shell Rider
This is a reissue from 1986. (See 1986 Annual Collection.)
▢ Handcrafted, 1¼" tall
600QX419-6, $6.00
Artist: Ed Seale

Treetop Trio
This is a reissue from 1986. (See 1986 Annual Collection.)
▢ Handcrafted, 2" tall
1100QX425-6, $11.00
Artist: Donna Lee

Jolly Hiker
This is a reissue from 1986. (See 1986 Annual Collection.)
▢ Handcrafted, 2" tall
500QX483-2, $5.00
Artist: Bob Siedler

Merry Koala
This is a reissue from 1986. (See 1986 Annual Collection.)
▢ Handcrafted, 2" tall
500QX415-3, $5.00
Artist: Linda Sickman

The Constitution

An acrylic oval, framed in brass, commemorates the 200th anniversary of the signing of the Constitution. Stamped in silver foil, the quill design complements the gold-foil caption: "We the People, The Constitution of the United States, 200 Years, 1787-1987."

■ Acrylic, 2½" tall
  650QX377-7, $6.50
  Artist: Joyce Pattee

Old-Fashioned Christmas Collection

Nostalgic Rocker

Looking as if it were crafted by hand, this subtly painted pony was fashioned in wood and has fabric ears. The clean lines and simple design reflect an American country styling.

■ Wood, 2½" tall
  650QX468-9, $6.50
  Artist: Linda Sickman

Little Whittler

The little carver smiles at the reindeer toy he is carving. This ornament was sculpted and painted to resemble carved wood with a bit of whimsy.

■ Handcrafted, 3" tall
  600QX469-9, $6.00
  Artist: Peter Dutkin

Country Wreath

The warm, old-fashioned design of this straw wreath reflects Christmas in the country. Tied with burgundy yarn, it is decorated with tiny wooden hearts, trees, and a wooden house.

■ Wood, Straw, 4¾" tall
  575QX470-9, $5.75
  Artist: Michele Pyda-Sevcik

In a Nutshell

There's a world of Christmas inside this nutshell. Two intricately detailed scenes show a teddy bear beneath a Christmas tree and a fireplace with two tiny stockings. Molded from a real walnut, the ornament is hinged so it can be displayed open and stored closed.

■ Handcrafted, 1½" tall
  550QX469-7, $5.50
  Artist: Duane Unruh

Folk Art Santa

Carefully painted and antiqued, this old-world Santa reflects the rich tradition of folk art. His deeply sculpted face and beard, and the details of his clothing, give him the appearance of hand-carved wood. Carrying a bottle-brush tree, he wears a long coat accented with touches of gold.

■ Handcrafted, 4" tall
  525QX474-9, $5.25
  Artist: Linda Sickman

The Constitution

Nostalgic Rocker, Little Whittler

Country Wreath, In a Nutshell, Folk Art Santa

Christmas Pizzazz Collection

Doc Holiday

Santa rides a spring-powered mechanical reindeer. When you set the ornament on a mantel or table and gently tap it, Santa gets a bouncy ride. His cowboy shirt carries the name: "Doc Holiday."
- Handcrafted, 4" tall
  800QX467-7, $8.00
  Artist: Ed Seale

Christmas Fun Puzzle

A favorite childhood puzzle is updated in a whimsical ball ornament. Divided horizontally into three movable sections, this blue ball is decorated with three bas-relief figures—Santa, mouse, and reindeer. Turning the sections will mix the top, middle, and bottom parts of the figures, creating new characters such as a rein-mouse or a Santa-deer.
- Handcrafted, 2½" diam.
  800QX467-9, $8.00
  Artist: Donna Lee

Jolly Follies

Dressed in tuxes and tails, three dapper penguins actually kick up their heels and dance each time the string is pulled. The sparkling acrylic stage carries the name of their act: "Jolly Follies."
- Handcrafted, 2" tall
  850QX466-9, $8.50
  Artist: Ken Crow

St. Louie Nick

He's cool, he's hot, he's a jazzy dresser from his beret to his spats. Santa blows the sweetest horn this side of the North Pole and wears a vest with his stage name: "St. Louie Nick."
- Handcrafted, 3½" tall
  775QX453-9, $7.75
  Artist: Peter Dutkin

Holiday Hourglass

Designed to be displayed in two different ways, this realistic hourglass celebrates both Christmas and the New Year. Through Christmas Day, the ornament can be displayed so that the "Merry Christmas" and a snowman in Santa's cap appear. After Christmas, the hourglass can be flipped to display the snowman in a top hat and "Happy New Year."
- Handcrafted, 3" tall
  800QX470-7, $8.00
  Artist: Duane Unruh

Doc Holiday, Christmas Fun Puzzle

Jolly Follies, St. Louie Nick, Holiday Hourglass

Mistletoad

You don't have to kiss this whimsical fellow to get a special Christmas surprise. When you pull the cord, he gives you a wide holiday grin and a loud greeting in a very froggy voice. His hat is decorated with a pompom and "Mistletoad."
■ Handcrafted, 3¾" tall
700QX468-7, $7.00
Artist: Ken Crow

Happy Holidata

Two little programmers watch the message, "Happy Holidata," flash onto the computer screen in alternating colors of green and red. On the back of the terminal, the name "Cranberry Computer" tells you this ornament is a high-tech edition.
■ Handcrafted, 1½" tall
650QX471-7, $6.50
Artist: Bob Siedler

Traditional Ornaments

Goldfinch

This Goldfinch looks as if he has paused in flight to admire the scenery below. Fashioned of fine porcelain, he has been painted by hand to accentuate detail. Unlike the previous porcelain birds in the Keepsake line, this ornament attaches to your tree with a traditional hook, instead of a clip.
■ Handpainted Fine Porcelain, 2½" tall
700QX464-9, $7.00
Artist: Linda Sickman

Heavenly Harmony

This little angel brings Christmas music for all the world to hear. Reminiscent of an old-world Spanish belltower, the ornament plays "Joy to the World." The music is started by a key at the back.
■ Musical, Handcrafted, 4¼" tall
1500QX465-9, $15.00
Artist: Ken Crow

Special Memories Photoholder

Both needlepoint and embroidery decorate the front of this bright holiday wreath. Trimmed in lace, it will display one of your cherished photographs. The wreath hangs from a green satin ribbon, accented with a red satin rosette. Caption on back: "Every Christmas brings special moments to remember. 1987."
■ Fabric, 3¼" diam.
675QX464-7, $6.75

Joyous Angels

Three intricately sculpted angels join hands and dance their joy beneath a brass star. Their halos and the trim on their snowy white dresses are touched with gold.
■ Handcrafted, 4" tall
775QX465-7, $7.75
Artist: Ed Seale

Mistletoad, Happy Holidata

Goldfinch, Heavenly Harmony, Special Memories Photoholder, Joyous Angels

Promise of Peace, Christmas Keys

I Remember Santa, Norman Rockwell, Currier & Ives

happy times spent caroling with family and friends. The music is captioned: "Carols."
◼ Handcrafted, 2" tall
575QX473-9, $5.75
Artist: Duane Unruh

I Remember Santa

Taken from the Hallmark Historical Collection, three antique postcard paintings are reproduced on this porcelain-white glass ball. They offer a vision of Santa Claus that brings back memories of Christmas long ago. Caption: "At Christmastime, especially, those magic memories start...those memories of yesterday that so delight the heart. 1987."
◼ Porcelain White Glass, 2⅞" diam.
475QX278-9, $4.75
Artist: Joyce Lyle

Norman Rockwell: Christmas Scenes

A hearty toast, a joyful dance, a stolen kiss under the mistletoe— all of these are depicted with warmth and gentle humor in the Norman Rockwell paintings on this gold glass ball. The three "Christmas Scenes" come from the Hallmark Collection of Norman Rockwell originals. Caption: "O gather friends, at Christmastime, to sing a song of cheer, to reminisce the days gone by, to toast the bright new year. From the Norman Rockwell Collection 1987."
◼ Gold Glass, 2⅞" diam.
475QX282-7, $4.75
Artist: Joyce Lyle

Currier & Ives: American Farm Scene

Porcelain-white glass is the perfect setting for this nostalgic portrait of a wintry morning on the farm. The caption is decorated with painted holly and ribbon. Caption: "Christmas 1987, American Farm Scene, Currier & Ives."
◼ Porcelain-White Glass, 2⅞" diam.
475QX282-9, $4.75
Artist: Joyce Lyle

Promise of Peace

Carrying a gold foil olive branch, the Christmas dove spreads a timeless seasonal message. To enhance the dimension of the design, the dove was etched into the back of the acrylic piece and the caption into the front, along the bevel. The ornament is framed in brass.

Caption: "A season of hope, a reminder of miracles, a promise of peace."
◼ Acrylic, 2¾" diam.
650QX374-9, $6.50
Artist: Sharon Pike

Christmas Keys

A miniature upright piano, decorated with festive green-and-red holly, brings to mind those

Special Edition

Favorite Santa

Like previous Special Edition ornaments, this one is designed for display on table or mantel, as well as the tree. Fashioned of fine porcelain and painted by hand, Santa carries a long, long stocking, which is the subject of the following legend printed on a card tucked into the ornament box:

One day Old St. Nick found a stocking—
It was threadbare, and tattered, and torn,
But his elves fixed it up with their magic,
And a new Christmas legend was born.
They say that it's loaded with presents
That are tied up with ribbons and bows;
For each gift he gives, a new one appears,
How it works—only Santa Claus knows!

■ Handpainted Fine Porcelain, 5½" tall
2250QX445-7, $22.50
Artist: Peter Dutkin

Limited Editions

Christmas Time Mime

Wearing a Santa hat and beard, the mime shares a moment of Christmas with a friend. His bag, tied with a golden chain, is filled with stars and magic. This ornament, made of fine porcelain and painted by hand, is limited to an edition size of 24,700 pieces. A wooden display stand is included in the box as well as the following poem that tells a charming story about the design:

The Mime looks deep in the teddy bear's eyes.
The teddy bear looks at the Mime,
And they feel they have known each other
From some other place and time.
There's a magical bond between them
From the silent world they share,
And now they know, wherever one goes,
The other will always be there.

■ Handpainted Fine Porcelain, 2½" tall
2750QX442-9, $27.50
Artist: Duane Unruh

Christmas is Gentle

Two lambs embody this gentle season. This ornament was limited to 24,700 pieces and was the first in the Keepsake line individually numbered by hand. It is made of white bone china, accented with gold and subtle touches of color. Caption on the bottom: "Christmas is Gentle, Bone China, Limited Edition of 24,700 Max., Number: (handwritten number)."

■ Handpainted Bone China, 3" tall
1750QX444-9, $17.50
Artist: Ed Seale

Christmas Time Mime, Christmas is Gentle

Three Men in a Tub, Wee Chimney Sweep

December Showers

Beary Special

Holiday Heirloom

Artists' Favorites

Three Men in a Tub

Inside the tub, the famous trio—butcher, baker, and candlestick maker—hold sausages, a cake with holly icing, and a Christmas candle. Donna Lee, the sculptor of this ornament, likes to bring classic nursery rhymes to life with a contemporary look that is often whimsical. The tub looks like wood and carries the caption: "Rub-A-Dub-Dub."

■ Handcrafted, 3" tall
800QX454-7, $8.00
Artist: Donna Lee

Wee Chimney Sweep

Artist Ed Seale's mouse sweeps the chimney so Santa will stay neat and clean on Christmas Eve. A hard worker, the mouse carries a real brush. Seale commented that his design reflects the increased use of fireplaces and woodburning stoves to keep homes warm in the winter.

■ Handcrafted, 3" tall
625QX451-9, $6.25
Artist: Ed Seale

December Showers

Sitting on an acrylic cloud, this angel stays dry under her holly-trimmed umbrella. She checks to see if the shower has stopped because she wants to play. Artist Donna Lee designed the angel to resemble a real child—full of fun and mischief.

■ Handcrafted, 2½" tall
550QX448-7, $5.50
Artist: Donna Lee

Beary Special

This cuddly, flocked bear reaches up to put his ornament on your tree. It's a tiny green ball decorated with his own likeness. Artist Bob Siedler explained that he likes sculpting bears because they are his daughter's favorite and part of everyone's childhood memories.

■ Handcrafted, 2½" tall
475QX455-7, $4.75
Artist: Bob Siedler

Collectible Series

Holiday Heirloom—First Edition/Limited Edition

This elegant new series introduces lead crystal and a precious metal into the Keepsake line. The intricately sculpted wreath has been plated in silver and frames a bell made of 24 percent lead crystal with a silver-plated holly clapper inside. The series also is the first to be offered in a limited edition. The date "1987" is embossed on the front of the wreath, and the edition size is embossed on the back: "Limited Edition 34,600."

■ Lead Crystal, Silver Plating, 3¼" tall
2500QX485-7, $25.00
Artist: Duane Unruh

Collector's Plate— First Edition

The first collector's plate, issued in the late 1800s, offered a beautiful Christmas scene. This new ornament continues that meaningful tradition in miniature plates fashioned of fine porcelain. Each edition will bring a vision of children celebrating the season and a message on the back. The first plate shows children decorating the tree. Caption: "Light Shines at Christmas. 1987." Plate stand included.

■ Fine Porcelain, 3¼" diam.
800QX481-7, $8.00
Artist: LaDene Votruba

Reindeer Champs— Second Edition

Warmly dressed in a skating sweater monogrammed with "Dancer" and "87," this reindeer is a star on ice. She whirls and twirls on skates trimmed with real pompoms.

■ Handcrafted, 3½" tall
750QX480-9, $7.50
Artist: Bob Siedler

Mr. and Mrs. Claus—
Second Edition

Mrs. Claus baked her spouse a plate of cookies to give him energy for his Christmas Eve ride. His calendar reads, "1987 Dec. 24," so it's almost time to go. But Santa won't leave without his snack. There's nothing better than "Home Cooking."

■ Handcrafted, 3" tall
1325QX483-7, $13.25
Artist: Duane Unruh

Betsey Clark:
Home for Christmas—
Second Edition

While Santa peers around the porch of the house addressed "1987," Betsey and her friends trim the outdoor trees and paint holiday messages on the windows. One says: "There's no place like Christmas." The other reads: "Noel."

■ Gold Glass, 2⅞" diam.
500QX272-7, $5.00
Artist: Sharon Pike

Windows of the
World—Third Edition

Sitting by the sea, a little Polynesian child strums a holiday tune on her ukulele. She has written "1987" in the sand and hung her stocking out for Santa. Her thatched window seat carries the Christmas greeting, "Mele Kalikimaka."

■ Handcrafted, 3" tall
1000QX482-7, $10.00
Artist: Donna Lee

Miniature Crèche—
Third Edition

Multiple layers of delicately etched brass, washed in gold, nickel, and copper, create a stunning three-dimensional nativity. Gold wire starbeams shine on the Holy Family from a Christmas star above the stable.

■ Multi-plated Brass, 3½" tall
900QX481-9, $9.00
Artist: Ed Seale

Collector's Plate, Reindeer Champs, Mr. and Mrs. Claus

Betsey Clark: Home for Christmas, Windows of the World, Miniature Crèche

Nostalgic Houses and Shops, Twelve Days of Christmas, Wood Childhood Ornaments

Nostalgic Houses and Shops—Fourth Edition

The Victorian "House on Main St." has an exclusive "1987" address. Its spacious upstairs bedroom is decorated in shades of lavender and mauve, the downstairs parlor has a blue chair, matching drapes, and a tiny bottle-brush Christmas tree.
- Handcrafted, 4¼" tall
  1400QX483-9, $14.00
  Artist: Donna Lee

Twelve Days of Christmas—Fourth Edition

Four etched colly birds gather in the center of a beveled, acrylic diamond because it's the fourth day of Christmas. The gold foil-stamped caption reads: "The Twelve Days of Christmas 1987...four colly birds..." The four classic acrylic shapes used in this series—quadrafoil, heart, teardrop, and diamond—will be repeated three times.
- Acrylic, 4" tall
  650QX370-9, $6.50
  Artist: Sharon Pike

Wood Childhood Ornaments—Fourth Edition

Saddled in festive green and red and carefully groomed from his plush mane to his yarn tail, this "Wooden Horse" is ready to lead the Christmas parade. His cart has wheels that turn as he is pulled along. He is dated "1987."
- Wood, 2¼" tall
  750QX441-7, $7.50
  Artist: Bob Siedler

Porcelain Bear—Fifth Edition

What is "Cinnamon Bear" searching for inside his Christmas stocking? Maybe some honey! Made of fine porcelain, the ornament is handpainted.
- Handpainted Fine Porcelain, 2⅛" tall
  775QX442-7, $7.75

Tin Locomotive—Sixth Edition

Ringing its brass bell and chugging along on wheels that actually roll, this tin locomotive arrives at the North Pole station. The spoke pattern of the large rear wheels resembles a circle of cut-out hearts. The train is dated "1987."
- Pressed Tin, 3½" tall
  1475QX484-9, $14.75
  Artist: Linda Sickman

Holiday Wildlife—Sixth Edition

Framed in wood, two snow geese fly across the starry Christmas sky, creating a picture of beauty and grace. The caption on the back reads, "Snow Goose, CHEN HYPERBOREA, Sixth in a Series, Wildlife Collection, Christmas 1987."
- Wood, 2½" diam.
  750QX371-7, $7.50
  Artist: LaDene Votruba

Porcelain Bear, Tin Locomotive, Holiday Wildlife

Clothespin Soldier—
Sixth and Final Edition

Fashioned with movable arms, this "Sailor" in a crisp white uniform signals all hands on deck to bid farewell to the Clothespin series. His signals are easy to see because his flags display bright green trees against a red background.

■ Handcrafted, 2¼" tall
550QX480-7, $5.50
Artist: Linda Sickman

Frosty Friends—Eighth Edition

This little flocked seal has jumped up through a hole in the ice to deliver a gift to his Eskimo friend. He's carrying the package the best way he can—balancing it ever so carefully on his nose. The ice is made of clear acrylic, and the package is dated "1987."

■ Handcrafted, 2" tall
850QX440-9, $8.50
Artist: Ed Seale

Rocking Horse—Seventh Edition

A fitting steed for any prince or princess, this white charger is saddled in red, blue, and gold and rides on royal purple rockers dated "1987." His mane and graceful yarn tail are the color of cream.

■ Handcrafted, 3¾" wide
1075QX482-9, $10.75
Artist: Linda Sickman

Norman Rockwell—Eighth Edition

Norman Rockwell is one of America's most beloved artists. His delightful painting of a little girl dancing with her dog while a man plays a bass fiddle, was transformed into a bas-relief cameo against a light blue background. The chrome-framed ornament reads: "The Christmas Dance, Eighth in a Series, Christmas 1987, The Norman Rockwell Collection."

■ Cameo, 3¼" diam.
775QX370-7, $7.75
Artist: Don Palmiter

Here Comes Santa—Ninth Edition

All the toys are packed, and Santa is driving through town in his sporty new car. "Santa's Woody" has whitewalls that turn, custom paneling, and two personalized license plates. The rear plate carries the date "1987," and the front one conveys Santa's special wish: "JOY-2-U."

■ Handcrafted, 2" tall
1400QX484-7, $14.00
Artist: Ken Crow

Thimble—Tenth Edition

A bunny plays his silvery thimble drum to celebrate the tenth year of this series. The "Thimble Drummer" has a fluffy pompom tail, and the strap around his drum is made of striped fabric ribbon.

■ Handcrafted, 2" tall
575QX441-9, $5.75
Artist: Bob Siedler

Clothespin Soldier, Frosty Friends, Rocking Horse

Norman Rockwell, Here Comes Santa, Thimble

1986

The year 1986 saw the immense popularity of the limited edition "Magical Unicorn." Four months after it was offered, the ornament became virtually impossible to find and the most sought after piece of the year. Another 1986 ornament also appeared at the top of the collectors' "must-have" list, commemorating the birthday of the most beloved "Lady" of the land, the acrylic "Statue of Liberty," of course.

Three Collectible Series debuted in 1986: The "Betsey Clark: Home for Christmas" ball series, "Mr. and Mrs. Claus," and "Reindeer Champs." One series, "Art Masterpiece," came to an end with a third classic work of art.

New formats jingled, squeaked, and tap-tap-tapped in 1986. "L'il Jingler" has a chain dotted with jingle bells, "Chatty Penguin" makes a squeaking noise, and "Little Drummers" tap their tiny drums.

"Heathcliff" and "Paddington™ Bear" made their premiere appearance as did "Husband," "Nephew," and "Sweetheart." Collectors of country items were pleased to see the "American Country" collection of four coordinated glass balls by Mary Emmerling and the "Country Treasures" collection of handcrafted and porcelain ornaments.

Commemoratives

Baby's First Christmas
Painted in soft pastels, this realistic miniature mobile has four of Baby's favorite things. A toy duck, Santa, teddy bear, and stocking dangle from an acrylic cloud topped with a star bearing the caption "Baby's First Christmas 1986."
- Handcrafted, 3½" tall
  900QX412-6, $9.00
  Artist: Linda Sickman

Baby's First Christmas
An acrylic lamb, with an etched coat that looks like curly wool, brings Baby a holiday stocking captioned "1986 Baby's First Christmas" stamped in gold foil.
- Acrylic, 3¼" tall
  600QX380-3, $6.00
  Artist: Don Palmiter

Baby's First Christmas Photoholder
As sweet as Baby's picture, this heartshaped gingham photoholder is decorated with white lace and delicate embroidery. Front caption: "Baby's First Christmas." Back caption: "A Baby puts special magic in holiday moments. 1986."
- Fabric, 3¾" tall
  800QX379-2, $8.00
  Artist: Joyce Pattee

Baby's First Christmas
Baby loves to ride his rocking horse and so does Teddy Bear on this ecru satin ball topped with a handcrafted bear. The rockers carry the caption, "Baby's First Christmas 1986." The message, "A Baby's a bundle of hope and joy," is on a bright red heart.
- Ecru Satin, 2⅞" diam.
  550QX271-3, $5.50
  Artist: Joyce Pattee

Baby's First Christmas: Handcrafted, Acrylic, Photoholder

Baby's First Christmas: Satin Ball; Grandchild's First Christmas

Baby's Second Christmas, Child's Third Christmas, Baby Locket

Husband, Sister

Grandchild's First Christmas

A beary sleepy flocked bear dreams of Christmas on a lace-trimmed fabric pillow nestled in a straw basket. "Grandchild's First Christmas 1986" appears on the tag.
■ Handcrafted, 2¼" tall
1000QX411-6, $10.00

Baby's Second Christmas

His diaper is slipping, but that won't stop this adorable mouse from delivering a little toy mouse snuggled inside a stocking. Caption: "Baby's 2nd Christmas 1986."
■ Handcrafted, 1¼" tall
650QX413-3, $6.50
Artist: Bob Siedler

Child's Third Christmas

Dressed in soft fabric sleepers and cap, this flocked panda is trying to wait up for Santa. His bib reads, "My Third Christmas 1986."
■ Fabric, 2¹¹⁄₃₂" tall
650QX413-6, $6.50
Artist: LaDene Votruba

Baby Locket

Embossed lettering and baby toys decorate this textured brass locket. Inside is space for Baby's photograph and for personalization. "Baby" appears on the front and "1986" on the back. The ornament has a wishbone hanger and may be displayed open or closed.
■ Textured Brass, 2¼" diam.
1600QX412-3, $16.00
Artist: Diana McGehee

Husband

The "Husband" ornament was a new caption in 1986. Accented with touches of color, the intricately detailed, bas-relief duck decoy design is a traditional favorite. The sentiment on the reverse reads, "A Husband is a forever friend. Christmas 1986."
■ Cameo, 2¾" diam.
800QX383-6, $8.00
Artist: Sharon Pike

Sister

Printed on red padded satin, the cuddly teddy bear sitting inside a country grapevine wreath eagerly awaits Christmas. The ornament is framed in brass and carries the caption: "With every Christmas, every year, a Sister grows more loved...more dear. 1986."
■ Bezeled Satin, 2¾" diam.
675QX380-6, $6.75
Artist: LaDene Votruba

Daughter, Son

Mother and Dad, Father, Mother

Grandmother, Grandparents

Niece, Nephew

Daughter
Fashioned to look like wood, the little girl in this knit stocking captures the nostalgia of an old-world European toy. Caption: "For Daughter 1986."
◼ Handcrafted, 3½" tall
575QX430-6, $5.75
Artist: Ed Seale

Son
Similar to the girl in the "Daughter" ornament, the little boy in this knitted stocking is designed to look like a wooden European toy of years past. Caption: "For Son 1986."
◼ Handcrafted, 4" tall
575QX430-3, $5.75
Artist: Ed Seale

Mother and Dad
Vivid holiday candles, symbolizing the warmth a family shares, decorate a snowy-white porcelain bell tied with a red ribbon. Caption: "For a Mother and Dad who are warmly loved. Christmas 1986."
◼ Fine Porcelain, 5½" tall
750QX431-6, $7.50
Artist: Michele Pyda-Sevcik

Father
A festive French horn, printed in silver, decorates the front of this wooden ornament for Father. On the reverse, the caption reads: "Nothing can ever replace the wisdom, guidance and love of a Father. Christmas 1986."
◼ Wood, 3¼" diam.
650QX431-3, $6.50
Artist: LaDene Votruba

Mother
The etched and frosted background of this bezeled acrylic ornament provides an attractive contrast to the clear heart in the center. The heart holds the gold foil caption: "A Mother's love reflects the warmth of Christmas all year through. 1986."
◼ Acrylic, 2¾" diam.
700QX382-6, $7.00

Granddaughter, Grandson, Godchild

Grandmother
A country quilt design of Christmas trees decorates the center of an ivory satin ball capped with a golden crown. "A Grandmother's love is for always" and "Christmas 1986" appear on two of the trees located on opposite sides of the ball.
◼ Ivory Satin, 2⅞" diam.
475QX274-3, $4.75
Artist: Joyce Pattee

Grandparents
A stitchery design in holiday green and red, accented with gold, decorates a white porcelain bell for Grandparents. Two colorful doves appear on the front with: "Christmas 1986." The back says: "Grandparents are never far from thought...ever near in love."
◼ Fine Porcelain, 5½" tall
750QX432-3, $7.50
Artist: Joyce Pattee

Niece
The white cat and interesting shapes and patterns in this silk-screened design give the ornament a fresh, contemporary look. A red feather-edge satin ribbon circles the wood embroidery hoop. Caption: "Nieces give the nicest gifts...beauty, joy and love. Christmas 1986."
◼ Fabric and Wood, 4½" tall
600QX426-6, $6.00

Nephew
A crisp white snowman, accented with bright touches of red, stands out vividly against a dark blue sky in this graphic design. Bezeled in chrome, this ornament carries the sentiment: "To wish a special Nephew a happy holiday season! 1986."
◼ Bezeled Lacquer-Look, 2¾" diam.
625QX381-3, $6.25

Granddaughter
Antique scenes of children enjoying the holiday are accented with gold on a frosted glass ball fashioned to appeal to Granddaughters of all ages. Caption: "Season after season, a Granddaughter grows dearer and dearer. Christmas 1986."
◼ White Glass, 2⅞" diam.
475QX273-6, $4.75
Artist: Joyce Lyle

Grandson
A sign in the forest proclaims it's "Christmas 1986." As a jolly beaver brings a tree home for the animals on this teardrop ball, a bunny carries a banner that says, "A Grandson is a bringer of a very special kind of love."
◼ Blue Glass, 3" diam.
475QX273-3, $4.75
Artist: LaDene Votruba

Godchild
Brightly dressed, appliqued teddy bears circle a white satin ball capped with a golden crown. Two bears hold a banner that reads: "Christmas 1986." Caption: "A Godchild is a very special someone."
◼ White Satin, 2⅞" diam.
475QX271-6, $4.75

First Christmas Together: Textured Brass, Handcrafted, Acrylic, Green Glass

First Christmas Together

This romantic brass locket holds two photographs. The embossed caption, "First Christmas Together 1986," decorates the front, and embossed ribbon and doves appear on the back. The locket comes with a wishbone hanger.

■ Textured Brass, 2¼" tall
1600QX400-3, $16.00

First Christmas Together

Two turtledoves appear in a miniature birdcage captioned "First Christmas Together 1986." The water and seed dishes are frosted acrylic, and the bars are polished brass.

■ Handcrafted, 4" tall
1200QX409-6, $12.00
Artist: Linda Sickman

First Christmas Together

A contemporary design of etched, entwined hearts marks this acrylic teardrop, framed in chrome. The silver foil caption says: "First Christmas Together 1986."

■ Acrylic, 3¹¹⁄₃₂" tall
700QX379-3, $7.00
Artist: Diana McGehee

First Christmas Together

The artist used a torn-paper design technique to create the wintry landscape on this light green glass ball. Two redbirds appear next to the words: "First Christmas Together 1986." On the other side is the sentiment: "How beautiful the season when it's filled with love."

■ Light Green Glass, 2⅞" diam.
475QX270-3, $4.75

Ten Years Together

Accented with gold, the roses and holly on this porcelain bell look like cloisonné. Front: "Ten Years Together Christmas 1986." Back: "More than yesterday...less than tomorrow."

■ Fine Porcelain, 3" tall
750QX401-3, $7.50

Twenty-Five Years Together

Made of fine porcelain, this miniature collector's plate ornament commemorates enduring love. The front features blue holiday bells accented with silver. Front: "Twenty-Five Years Together Christmas 1986." Back: "Love lights all the seasons of our years." Plate stand included.

■ Fine Porcelain, 3¼" diam.
800QX410-3, $8.00
Artist: LaDene Votruba

Fifty Years Together

Made of snowy-white bisque porcelain, this bell is adorned with a glazed bas-relief holly design. Captions: "Fifty Years Together" and "Christmas 1986." The glazed porcelain handle is a sculpted number "50."

■ Fine Porcelain, 3¹³⁄₃₂" tall
1000QX400-6, $10.00
Artist: Sharon Pike

Ten Years Together, Twenty-Five Years Together, Fifty Years Together

Loving Memories

This miniature heart-shaped shadow box looks like wood. It holds a brass bell, teddy bear, and Christmas gift, and has room for a tiny memento of your own. The tag on the package carries the date "1986."
▦ Handcrafted, 5¼" tall
900QX409-3, $9.00
Artist: Ed Seale

Timeless Love

A sprig of mistletoe, etched at the top of this heart-shaped acrylic ornament, accents the gold foil-stamped sentiment: "Love... comes not in moments of time, but in timeless moments. Christmas 1986."
▦ Acrylic, 3" tall
600QX379-6, $6.00
Artist: LaDene Votruba

Sweetheart

This ornament is a new caption in the Keepsake line. The detailed gazebo holds a miniature bottle-brush tree decorated with tiny beaded garland. Two signs read, "To My Sweetheart With Love" and "Christmas 1986." The bottom of the ornament has space for personalization.
▦ Handcrafted, 3½" tall
1100QX408-6, $11.00
Artist: Ed Seale

Season of the Heart

An old-fashioned sleigh ride evokes the spirit of the season and the love a family shares. Caption: "Christmas...season of the heart, time of fond remembrance."
▦ Red Glass, 2⅞" diam.
475QX270-6, $4.75
Artist: Joyce Pattee

Friendship Greeting

Contrasting silk-screened fabric patterns were used to create this cheery envelope ornament. The red fabric, with a holly and dot pattern, reverses inside to ivory fabric with a tiny red and green pattern. The enclosed card carries the message: "Friends are forever," and provides space for personalization. Caption on back of envelope reads, "Merry Christmas 1986."
▦ Fabric, 2¼" tall
800QX427-3, $8.00

Joy of Friends

This ice-skating scene, reproduced from stitchery and printed on padded satin, captures the look of American folk art. Framed in chrome, the horizontal oval carries the words: "Friends make the heart warmer, the day merrier, the season more memorable."
▦ Bezeled Satin, 2¾" tall
675QX382-3, $6.75
Artist: Joyce Pattee

Loving Memories, Timeless Love

Sweetheart, Season of the Heart

Friendship Greeting, Joy of Friends

Friendship's Gift, From Our Home To Yours, Gratitude

Friendship's Gift
Fashioned in the shape of a traditional Christmas ornament, this acrylic keepsake carries a message of friendship and an adorable etched mouse playing Santa's helper. Gold foil-stamped is: "Friendship is a gift. Christmas 1986."
■ Acrylic, 3" tall
600QX381-6, $6.00

From Our Home to Yours
Etched onto a teardrop-shaped acrylic ornament is a finely detailed straw basket of fruit—a warm symbol of friendship and welcome. The caption, "From Our Home to Yours Christmas 1986," is stamped in silver foil.
■ Acrylic, 3¼" tall
600QX383-3, $6.00

Gratitude
Inside a wooden embroidery hoop, a vivid cardinal and holly design is silk-screened onto white satin. The caption, "Especially to thank you...especially at Christmas 1986," is printed in a matching shade of green.
■ Satin and Wood, 5" tall
600QX432-6, $6.00
Artist: Sharon Pike

Friends Are Fun
The design on this light blue glass ball is similar to designs in the "Frosty Friends" Collectible Series. A playful pair of Arctic pals riding a sleigh pulled by a team of Husky puppies illustrates the sentiment: "It's fun having friends to go 'round with. Christmas 1986."
■ Light Blue Glass, 2⅞" diam.
475QX272-3, $4.75
Artist: Ken Crow

New Home
A yummy neighborhood of cookie homes and gingerbread people decorate a white, frosted teardrop ball. Designed to look like icing, the caption reads: "Christmas is so special when it's spent in a new home." One of the houses carries the address, "1986."
■ White Glass, 3" diam.
475QX274-6, $4.75
Artist: Ken Crow

Teacher
A little mouse nibbled a star in an apple for his teacher. On the apple on the other side is the caption: "For My Teacher Christmas 1986."
■ White Glass, 2⅞" diam.
475QX275-3, $4.75
Artist: Sue Tague

Friends Are Fun, New Home, Teacher

Baby-Sitter

The word "Baby-Sitter" is absent from the sentiment on this gold teardrop ball to make the ornament suitable for the many different people who take care of children. The design of colorful antique toys evokes memories of childhood. Caption on the toy top: "For being the best friend a child could ever have." Caption on the horse: "Christmas 1986."

■ Gold Glass, 3" diam.
475QX275-6, $4.75

Property Ornaments

The Statue of Liberty

A beautifully etched likeness adorns this acrylic ornament created in honor of the Statue's 100th birthday. The gold foil-stamped caption reads: "The Lady 1886 Centennial 1986."

■ Acrylic, 3⁵⁄₁₆" tall
600QX384-3, $6.00
Artist: Michele Pyda-Sevcik

SNOOPY and WOODSTOCK

SNOOPY and his favorite pal, WOOD-STOCK, enjoy a ride on their saucer-shaped sled called the "Beagle Express."

■ Handcrafted, 1¾" tall
800QX434-6, $8.00
Artist: Bob Siedler

Heathcliff

The little angel watching over Heathcliff reminds this sassy cat to be good. His behavior has been perfect, or so he says in his letter: "Dear Santa, I've been exceptional. Heathcliff."

■ Handcrafted, 3³⁄₃₂" tall
750QX436-3, $7.50
Artist: Ed Seale

Katybeth

Pretty Katybeth is an angel who makes friends with everyone, including a smiling star that passes her way. The ornament is made of fine porcelain and has been painted by hand in pastel colors.

■ Handpainted Fine Porcelain, 2¹⁹⁄₃₂" tall
700QX435-3, $7.00

Paddington™ Bear

A favorite of both young and old, Paddington™ Bear can't imagine a nicer Christmas gift than a fresh jar of honey. His hat says "Paddington," and his jar is decorated with a red fabric bow.

■ Handcrafted, 2⁵⁄₁₆" tall
600QX435-6, $6.00
Artist: Bob Siedler

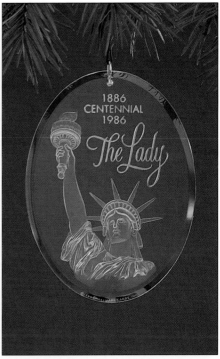

Baby-Sitter   The Statue of Liberty

SNOOPY and WOODSTOCK, Heathcliff, Katybeth, Paddington™ Bear

Norman Rockwell, PEANUTS®, Shirt Tales™ Parade

Norman Rockwell
These three "Christmas Scenes" are owned exclusively by Hallmark. The sentiment and paintings reflect the excitement of the holiday season. Caption: "Christmas time is filled with joy and glad anticipation, and all the loving reasons for a happy celebration."
◼ Green Glass, 2⅛" diam.
475QX276-3, $4.75
Artist: Sharon Pike

PEANUTS®
WOODSTOCK and his friends go ice skating with SNOOPY. They perform pirouettes and etch "Merry Christmas" into the smooth surface. A sign announces it's "1986."
◼ Blue Glass, 3" diam.
475QX276-6, $4.75

Shirt Tales™ Parade
The Shirt Tales™ parade around this gold glass ball. The drum major's shirt reads: "Here Comes Christmas!" The ornament is captioned: "Merriment is all around whenever Christmas comes to town!"
◼ Gold Glass, 2⅛" diam.
475QX277-3, $4.75

Holiday Humor

Santa's Hot Tub
Santa and his reindeer pal recover from their long Christmas Eve journey by spending a leisurely hour in the hot tub. The tub looks like wood, and the shower pipes are made of brass wire. Caption: "Polar Barrel Hot Tub Co."
◼ Handcrafted, 3" tall
1200QX426-3, $12.00
Artist: Ed Seale

Playful Possum
A handcrafted opossum is the clapper inside a clear glass holiday bell. He's upside down and holds a translucent lollipop decorated with a Christmas tree.
◼ Handcrafted, Glass, 3²³⁄₃₂" tall
1100QX425-3, $11.00
Artist: Ken Crow

Treetop Trio
Three bluebirds chirp a carol in a nest made of real straw. The ornament attaches to your tree with a special clip.
◼ Handcrafted, 2" tall
1100QX425-6, $11.00
Artist: Donna Lee

Wynken, Blynken and Nod
Pearly blue waves lap at the boat draped with silver nets. The names, "Wynken, Blynken, and Nod," appear on the stern.
◼ Handcrafted, 2⅛" tall
975QX424-6, $9.75
Artist: Donna Lee

Santa's Hot Tub, Playful Possum, Treetop Trio, Wynken, Blynken and Nod

Acorn Inn

Mr. Squirrel announces the opening of the holiday season at the snowcapped "Acorn Inn" by displaying a festive Christmas wreath.

▥ Handcrafted, 2" tall
  850QX424-3, $8.50
  Artist: Duane Unruh

Touchdown Santa

Santa runs to score a touchdown. His name, "S. Claus," is printed on the back of his red jersey and his number, "86," appears on front and back.

▥ Handcrafted, 2¹⁵⁄₁₆" tall
  800QX423-3, $8.00
  Artist: Peter Dutkin

Snow Buddies

The little mouse gets a big hug from the flocked snowmouse he built for Christmas. The snowmouse's arms were molded from real sticks, and he wears a fabric muffler. His pal has a leather tail.

▥ Handcrafted, 2¼" tall
  800QX423-6, $8.00
  Artist: Peter Dutkin

Open Me First

The box is labeled, "Open Me First 1986," and that's what the child does on Christmas morning. Inside, he finds what he always wanted—a kitten. The tissue inside the box is painted pearly-white, and the ornament attaches to your tree with a clip.

▥ Handcrafted, 2¹⁵⁄₁₆" tall
  725QX422-6, $7.25

Rah Rah Rabbit

Waving a real pompom, the holiday's cheeriest cheerleader inspires her team to victory. Her sweater carries the name of her school, "North Pole High," and her megaphone has the number "86."

▥ Handcrafted, 2½" tall
  700QX421-6, $7.00
  Artist: Ken Crow

Tipping the Scales

Santa's weight of "198.6" on the scale shows that his belly still shakes "like a bowl full of jelly." But he's really just fashionably plump, wearing a robe monogrammed with an "S" and holding his favorite snack—a chocolate-chip cookie.

▥ Handcrafted, 2¹¹⁄₁₆" tall
  675QX418-6, $6.75
  Artist: Peter Dutkin

Li'l Jingler

A chain dotted with brass jingle bells has a hook at each end so this raccoon can dangle between two tree branches. He wears a sporty fabric bow tie.

▥ Handcrafted, 2" tall
  675QX419-3, $6.75
  Artist: Ed Seale

Ski Tripper

Wearing a flocked red jumpsuit, this little skier spends her holidays on the slopes.

▥ Handcrafted, 2⅛" tall
  675QX420-6, $6.75
  Artist: Bob Siedler

Acorn Inn, Touchdown Santa, Snow Buddies

Open Me First, Rah Rah Rabbit, Tipping the Scales

Li'l Jingler, Ski Tripper

Popcorn Mouse, Puppy's Best Friend, Happy Christmas to Owl, Walnut Shell Rider

Heavenly Dreamer, Mouse in the Moon, Merry Koala, Chatty Penguin

Popcorn Mouse

This ornament displays charming touches of authenticity. Real cranberries and popcorn were used to mold the design, and the mouse strings his garland with a metal needle. He has a white leather tail and sits on a spool of red yarn labeled, "Chris-Mouse Sewing Co. Est. 1986."
■ Handcrafted, 2½" tall
675QX421-3, $6.75
Artist: Linda Sickman

Puppy's Best Friend

Man's best friend has his own best friend—a little elf who brings him a Christmas bone.
■ Handcrafted, 2¼" tall
650QX420-3, $6.50
Artist: Duane Unruh

Happy Christmas to Owl

On his perch, an owl reads a classic story to his little friend. The story is familiar with a few variations: "I heard him exclaim, ere he drove out of sight, Happy Christmas to owl, and to owl a good-nite." The book's title: "Christmas Stories."
■ Handcrafted, 3" tall
600QX418-3, $6.00
Artist: Duane Unruh

Walnut Shell Rider

Seated in his walnut shell sled, a merry old elf holds onto cord ropes for a smooth downhill ride. A real walnut was used to mold this design.
■ Handcrafted, 1¼" tall
600QX419-6, $6.00
Artist: Ed Seale

Heavenly Dreamer

This little angel, wearing a brass wire halo, takes a short nap on a frosted acrylic cloud. Stars and holly decorate her billowy bed.
■ Handcrafted, 1⅜" tall
575QX417-3, $5.75
Artist: Donna Lee

Mouse in the Moon

Dressed for the season, this mouse likes what he sees—his own reflection in the mirrored moon. His little leather tail peeps out of his sleepers.
■ Handcrafted, 2¾" tall
550QX416-6, $5.50
Artist: Ed Seale

Merry Koala

When he tried on Santa's knitted red cap, this soft flocked koala discovered that Santa's a big guy!
■ Handcrafted, 2" tall
500QX415-3, $5.00
Artist: Linda Sickman

Chatty Penguin

He's chubby and soft and he speaks! When you shake this plush penguin he makes a squeaking noise. The format was new to the Keepsake line.
■ Plush, 3⅝" tall
575QX417-6, $5.75
Artist: Ken Crow

Special Edition

Jolly St. Nick

In the 1800s, cartoonist Thomas Nast introduced a new style of St. Nicholas to the world—the modernized, grandfatherly Santa we all love today. This Special Edition ornament captures Nast's vision of the "jolly old elf" in fine porcelain that has been carefully painted by hand.
◾ Handpainted Fine Porcelain, 5½" tall
2250QX429-6, $22.50
Artist: Duane Unruh

Special Delivery

Tucked under the penguin's wing is a gift can of "Sardines" for a lucky friend. The can is topped with a red fabric bow.
◾ Handcrafted, 2" tall
500QX415-6, $5.00
Artist: Bob Siedler

Jolly Hiker

Wearing a backpack and a bedroll, Santa hikes up the hill using his candy cane walking stick. Some places, a sleigh and eight reindeer can't go!
◾ Handcrafted, 2" tall
500QX483-2, $5.00
Artist: Bob Siedler

Cookies for Santa

If Santa gets hungry on Christmas Eve, he'll enjoy this plate of cookies. The sign says they're "For Santa," and the frosted star cookie is dated "1986."
◾ Handcrafted, 2¼" diam.
450QX414-6, $4.50
Artist: Diana McGehee

Merry Mouse

This is a reissue from 1985.
(See 1985 Annual Collection.)
◾ Handcrafted, 2½" tall
450QX403-2, $4.50
Artist: Peter Dutkin

Skateboard Raccoon

This is a reissue from 1985.
(See 1985 Annual Collection.)
◾ Handcrafted, 2½" tall
650QX473-2, $6.50
Artist: Peter Dutkin

Beary Smooth Ride

This is a reissue from 1985.
(See 1985 Annual Collection.)
◾ Handcrafted, 1¾" tall
650QX480-5, $6.50
Artist: Linda Sickman

Snow-Pitching Snowman

This is a reissue from 1985.
(See 1985 Annual Collection.)
◾ Handcrafted, 2" tall
450QX470-2, $4.50
Artist: Donna Lee

Kitty Mischief

This is a reissue from 1985.
(See 1985 Annual Collection.)
◾ Handcrafted, 2" tall
500QX474-5, $5.00
Artist: Peter Dutkin

Soccer Beaver

This is a reissue from 1985.
(See 1985 Annual Collection.)
◾ Handcrafted, 2½" tall
650QX477-5, $6.50
Artist: Peter Dutkin

Do Not Disturb Bear

This is a reissue from 1985.
(See 1985 Annual Collection.)
◾ Handcrafted, 3" wide.
775QX481-2, $7.75
Artist: Ed Seale

Special Delivery, Jolly Hiker, Cookies for Santa

Limited Edition

Magical Unicorn

This fine porcelain unicorn has become one of the most sought-after ornaments in the history of the Keepsake line. Handpainted pastel flowers circle the unicorn's neck and are woven through his mane. Matching green and pink fabric ribbons are draped around his body, and his hooves and horn are painted silver. Limited to an edition size of 24,700 pieces, the ornament comes with a wooden display stand.

◾ Handpainted Fine Porcelain, 4½" tall
2750QX429-3, $27.50
Artist: Duane Unruh

Christmas Medley Collection

Joyful Carolers

This design was sculpted to look like handcarved wood. Dressed like Dickens' characters, the carolers are fully dimensional. Caption on front and back: "Joy to the World 1986."

◾ Handcrafted, 3¼" diam.
975QX513-6, $9.75
Artist: Linda Sickman

Festive Treble Clef

A tiny brass bell dangles from a shiny treble clef accented with translucent red and tied with a striped fabric ribbon.

◾ Handcrafted, 3⅞" tall
875QX513-3, $8.75
Artist: Bob Siedler

Favorite Tin Drum

The tin drum is reproduced in miniature, including two tiny drumsticks. A holly design decorates both drumheads, and the bindings are gold cord.

◾ Tin, 2" diam.
850QX514-3, $8.50
Artist: Linda Sickman

Christmas Guitar

Decorated with a green and red holly design, this miniature guitar, dated "1986," hangs from its own guitar strap made of striped fabric ribbon. The tiny frets are accented with gold.

◾ Handcrafted, 3" tall
700QX512-6, $7.00
Artist: Duane Unruh

Holiday Horn

Made of velvety bisque porcelain, this graceful horn is accented with gold and tied with a striped fabric ribbon. The holly design seen on the "Favorite Tin Drum" adorns the ivory surface outside the horn's mouth.

◾ Fine Porcelain, 3" tall
800QX514-6, $8.00
Artist: Duane Unruh

Country Treasures Collection

All of the ornaments in this collection are packaged in a wooden Shaker box.

Country Sleigh

Modeled after an antique sleigh, this ornament evokes memories of an old-fashioned Christmas. Dated "1986," the sleigh holds a plaid fabric blanket.

◾ Handcrafted, 2" tall
1000QX511-3, $10.00
Artist: Linda Sickman

Remembering Christmas

The vivid country quilt pattern recreated on this fine porcelain ornament will appeal to plate and ornament collectors. Dated "1986," the back of the miniature plate says: "Christmas memories are keepsakes of the heart." Plate stand included.

◾ Fine Porcelain, 3¼" diam.
875QX510-6, $8.75

Little Drummers

Motion is the special feature of this unique ornament. The three little drummer boys look like wood. They play their drums when you tap or shake the ornament's platform.

◾ Handcrafted, 4" tall
1250QX511-6, $12.50
Artist: Ken Crow

Welcome, Christmas

Dangling inside a heart-shaped frame, a little angel brings a warm country welcome. The frame, decorated with a delicate stencil-look design of hearts and greenery, carries the caption: "Welcome, Christmas! 1986."

◾ Handcrafted, 2⅝" tall
825QX510-3, $8.25
Artist: Ken Crow

Nutcracker Santa

This Santa's not a real nutcracker, but he looks like one. When you lift the tassel on his cap, his mouth pops open. The design resembles handcarved wood.

◾ Handcrafted, 3⅜" tall
1000QX512-3, $10.00
Artist: Duane Unruh

Joyful Carolers, Festive Treble Clef

Favorite Tin Drum, Christmas Guitar, Holiday Horn

Country Sleigh, Remembering Christmas

Little Drummers; Welcome, Christmas; Nutcracker Santa

Holiday Jingle Bell, Memories to Cherish, Bluebird, Glowing Christmas Tree

Traditional Ornaments

Holiday Jingle Bell

Crafted in the shape of a jingle bell, this French blue and white musical ornament plays a very appropriate melody: "Jingle Bells." Eight tiny bas-relief reindeer race gracefully around a band in the center. Caption: "Merry Christmas 1986."
- Handcrafted, 2¾" diam.
  1600QX404-6, $16.00

Memories to Cherish

A braided ceramic wreath, with a painted bow and holly, is a photoholder for the Christmas tree. Caption: "A memory to cherish. Christmas 1986."
- Ceramic, 3⅛" tall
  750QX427-6, $7.50
  Artist: LaDene Votruba

Bluebird

This red-breasted bluebird, a symbol of happiness, appears to have just landed on a Christmas tree branch. He attaches with a special clip.
- Handpainted Fine Porcelain, 3⁵⁄₁₆" tall
  725QX428-3, $7.25
  Artist: Linda Sickman

Glowing Christmas Tree

A lacy brass Christmas tree, trimmed with colorful stars, is embedded in a teardrop acrylic ornament. The date, "1986," appears on the tree's base.
- Embedded Acrylic, 3¼" diam.
  700QX428-6, $7.00
  Artist: Joyce Pattee

Heirloom Snowflake

Delicate hand-crocheted trim decorates padded lavender-blue satin to create this lacy snowflake.
- Fabric, 4¾" tall
  675QX515-3, $6.75
  Artist: Joyce Pattee

Christmas Beauty

This lacquer-look ornament reflects the spirit of the season. Caption: "Christmas comes gently, touching the world with beauty, filling it with joy."
- Lacquer Look, 2¾" diam.
  600QX322-3, $6.00
  Artist: Joyce Pattee

Star Brighteners

Two charming etched angels polish a star for Christmas. The gold foil-stamped caption, "Joy at Christmas 1986," makes the star glow.
- Acrylic, 2¾" diam.
  600QX322-6, $6.00
  Artist: LaDene Votruba

The Magi

On a gold glass teardrop ball, the Magi come to Christmas once more. Caption: "O come let us adore Him. Christmas 1986."
- Gold Glass, 3" diam.
  475QX272-6, $4.75
  Artist: Sharon Pike

Heirloom Snowflake, Christmas Beauty, Star Brighteners, The Magi

Mary Emmerling:
American Country Collection

Mary Emmerling is a well-known designer and authority on country decor. Her collection of four coordinated glass balls has the speckled look of spatterware and was inspired by popular design motifs found in 19th-century American homes.

■ White-and-Blue Glass, 2⅞" diam.
795QX275-2, $7.95

Collectible Series

Mr. and Mrs. Claus—First Edition

Mrs. Claus starts this series with a holiday kiss for her husband. Standing under the mistletoe she thoughtfully provides, he holds a list dated "1986." Aptly named "Merry Mistletoe Time," the ornament was first in this new 1986 series.

■ Handcrafted, 3⁷⁄₁₆" tall
1300QX402-6, $13.00
Artist: Duane Unruh

Reindeer Champs—First Edition

"Dasher" jogs around Santa's workshop in preparation for his Christmas Eve journey. Wearing a shirt that says "Dasher 86," he's the first in this series of reindeer sports stars.

■ Handcrafted, 2⅞" tall
750QX422-3, $7.50
Artist: Bob Siedler

Betsey Clark:
Home for Christmas—First Edition

The first Betsey Clark ball series ended in 1985, but this new one brings the artist's children back to the Keepsake line. Smaller in diameter, the balls in this second series show Betsey and her friends celebrating Christmas around the home. On the first ornament, they are busy decorating. Caption on wall poster: "May Christmas love fill every little corner of your world." On calendar: "1986."

■ Pink Glass, 2⅞" diam.
500QX277-6, $5.00
Artist: Sharon Pike

Windows of the World—
Second Edition

A Dutch girl peeks over the half-door to her Holland home. Her wooden shoes have been filled with goodies. "Vrolyk Kerstfeest 1986" is the Christmas greeting written above the door.

■ Handcrafted, 3" tall
1000QX408-3, $10.00
Artist: Bob Siedler

Miniature Crèche—Second Edition

This fine porcelain nativity scene is second in a series of crèches in different media. The velvety bisque figures contrast beautifully with the satiny glow of a glazed arch. A brass star shines above.

■ Fine Porcelain, 3¾" tall
900QX407-6, $9.00
Artist: Ed Seale

American Country Collection

Mr. and Mrs. Claus

Reindeer Champs, Betsey Clark: Home for Christmas, Windows of the World, Miniature Crèche

Nostalgic Houses and Shops, Wood Childhood Ornaments, Twelve Days of Christmas

Art Masterpiece, Porcelain Bear, Tin Locomotive

Nostalgic Houses and Shops—Third Edition

This "Christmas Candy Shoppe" ornament has two rooms: one downstairs where the sweets and confections are sold and another upstairs, where the mixing and baking are done. A sign above the door says: "Candies 1986."

■ Handcrafted, 4⁵⁄₁₆" tall
1375QX403-3, $13.75
Artist: Donna Lee

Wood Childhood Ornaments—Third Edition

This "Wooden Reindeer" takes a holiday ride on a wagon with wheels that turn. As he rolls, he makes a galloping motion. The wagon is dated "1986."

■ Handpainted Wood, 2½" tall
750QX407-3, $7.50
Artist: Ken Crow

Twelve Days of Christmas—Third Edition

On the third day of Christmas, three French hens nesting on holly leaves were etched onto a glowing acrylic teardrop. The gold foil-stamped caption reads: "The Twelve Days of Christmas 1986... Three French Hens."

■ Acrylic, 3⅜" tall
650QX378-6, $6.50
Artist: LaDene Votruba

Art Masterpiece—Third and Final Edition

This ornament is the last featuring classic paintings of the Madonna and Child reproduced on padded satin. Bezeled in brass, it carries the caption, "Lorenzo Di Cridi, Madonna and Child with the Infant St. John, The Nelson-Atkins Museum of Art, Kansas City, Missouri (Nelson Fund)."

■ Bezeled Satin, 3¼" tall
675QX350-6, $6.75
Artist: Diana McGehee

Porcelain Bear—Fourth Edition

"Cinnamon Bear" is carrying a brightly wrapped Christmas package behind his back.

■ Handpainted Fine Porcelain, 2¹¹⁄₁₆" tall
775QX405-6, $7.75

Tin Locomotive—Fifth Edition

The stencil-look holly design on the cabin of this pressed "Tin Locomotive" tells us the ornament is the Christmas Express. A mixture of interesting shapes and patterns, the train has wheels that turn as it rolls past your tree. It carries the date "1986."

■ Pressed Tin, 3¹⁷⁄₃₂" tall
1475QX403-6, $14.75
Artist: Linda Sickman

Holiday Wildlife—Fifth Edition

While one Cedar Waxwing samples a berry, another watches. This lifelike portrait is framed in wood. Caption: "Cedar Waxwing (Cedarbird), BOMBYCILLA CEDORUM, Fifth in a series, Wildlife Collection, Christmas 1986."
▓ Wood, 2½" diam.
750QX321-6, $7.50

Clothespin Soldier—Fifth Edition

Dressed in holiday colors and a hat decorated with holly, this French officer has movable arms.
▓ Handcrafted, 1²⁷⁄₃₂" tall
550QX406-3, $5.50
Artist: Linda Sickman

Rocking Horse—Sixth Edition

A golden palomino, with brown-and-blue saddle and trappings, is proud to ride on your tree this Christmas. He stands on seagreen rockers, dated "1986," and has a flowing white yarn tail.
▓ Handcrafted, 4" wide
1075QX401-6, $10.75
Artist: Linda Sickman

Norman Rockwell—Seventh Edition

Santa peers through his telescope to check on all boys and girls before Christmas. Against the red background, the white bas-relief cameo has subtle shadings. Framed in brass, the ornament carries the gold foil-stamped caption on the back: "Checking Up, Seventh in a Series, Christmas 1986, The Norman Rockwell Collection."
▓ Cameo, 3¼" diam.
775QX321-3, $7.75
Artist: Sharon Pike

Frosty Friends—Seventh Edition

This little Eskimo places a wreath around the neck of his new pal—a flocked baby reindeer whose antlers are just beginning to bud. They sit on a clear acrylic ice floe dated "1986."
▓ Handcrafted 2¼" tall
850QX405-3, $8.50
Artist: Bob Siedler

Here Comes Santa—Eighth Edition

A chrome bell announces Santa's arrived with "Kringle's Kool Treats." The freezer advertises "Ice Cream" and "Snow Cones" made by "Kringle's." Fitted with movable wheels, Santa's cart has a license plate dated "1986."
▓ Handcrafted, 3¹⁵⁄₁₆" tall
1400QX404-3, $14.00
Artist: Bob Siedler

Thimble—Ninth Edition

This "Thimble Partridge" is sitting pretty. She has found the perfect nesting place atop a silvery thimble filled with holiday greenery and fruit.
▓ Handcrafted, 1²¹⁄₃₂" tall
575QX406-6, $5.75

Holiday Wildlife, Clothespin Soldier, Rocking Horse

Norman Rockwell, Frosty Friends, Here Comes Santa, Thimble

Baby Locket, Baby's First Christmas: Acrylic

1985

The 1985 Keepsake Ornament line continued Hallmark's attempts to design ornaments that meet collectors' needs. Collectors expressed a definite interest in ornaments that look homemade and are fashioned of natural materials such as wood and fabric. To respond to this demand, Hallmark offered two special coordinated groups of five ornaments each.

The "Country Christmas Collection" included ornaments created of wood or porcelain or fashioned to look like hand-carved wood. The carefully researched designs captured a nostalgic country flavor. The "Heirloom Christmas Collection" used satin, lace, ribbon and intricate crochet work to bring back the romance of another era. These elegant designs were inspired by popular, turn-of-the-century styles, with some even including rose-scented sachets.

Limited Edition and Collectible Series ornaments are also favorites with collectors. The 1985 line featured two new series and the second limited edition Keepsake, a fine porcelain angel called "Heavenly Trumpeter," produced in an edition size of 24,700 pieces. The two new series were "Windows of the World," showing children from all around the globe celebrating Christmas, and "Miniature Crèche," offering a new nativity scene fashioned of different materials each year.

Three properties: "FRAGGLE ROCK™," "Rainbow Brite™," and "Hugga Bunch™" made their debut this year as did an ornament especially designed for "Niece."

Commemoratives

Baby Locket
This textured brass locket has a space for Baby's photo and for personalizing. The caption, "Baby," is decorated with embossed toys.
■ Textured Brass, 2¼" diam.
1600QX401-2, $16.00
Artist: Diana McGehee

Baby's First Christmas
An acrylic baby cup, brimming with toys, is captioned, "Baby's First Christmas 1985," in stamped silver foil.
■ Acrylic, 3¾" tall
575QX370-2, $5.75

Baby's First Christmas
A beautiful embroidered satin baby block, bordered in lace, plays a lullaby for Baby. The ABC, four-sided caption reads, "A Baby's 1st Christmas 1985." Melody: "Schubert's Lullaby."
■ Musical, Fabric, 3¼" tall
1600QX499-5, $16.00

Baby's First Christmas
Baby's out for a ride to deliver a special Christmas gift. This lace-trimmed, rattan-look stroller with real fabric bow and pillow was inspired by a turn-of-the-century mail-order catalog and is built to scale.
Caption: "Baby's First Christmas 1985."
■ Handcrafted, 3¾" tall
1500QX499-2, $15.00
Artist: Donna Lee

Baby's First Christmas: Musical, Handcrafted

Baby's First Christmas: Fabric, Satin Ball; Baby's Second Christmas

Child's Third Christmas, Grandchild's First Christmas: Satin Ball, Handcrafted

Baby's First Christmas

This hand-embroidered tree is just the right size for Baby! It's decorated with ribbon and lace and captioned: "1985 Baby's 1st Christmas."

◼ Embroidered Fabric, 4½" tall
700QX478-2, $7.00

Baby's First Christmas

Dressed in yellow, Baby is delighted by the Christmas toys shown around the center of this green satin ball. The ornament is topped with a handcrafted mouse. Caption: "A Baby keeps the season bright and warms the heart with sweet delight. Baby's First Christmas 1985."

◼ Green Soft-Sheen Satin, 2⅞" diam.
500QX260-2, $5.00
Artist: LaDene Votruba

Baby's Second Christmas

An adorable teddy bear rides a stick pony that has a plush mane and fabric reins. Teddy's shirt is captioned, "Baby's Second Christmas 1985."

◼ Handcrafted, 3½" tall
600QX478-5, $6.00

Child's Third Christmas

A brown flocked teddy bear has found a home in a red and white sneaker laced with a real shoestring. The sneaker is bordered with the caption: "A Child's Third Christmas '85."

◼ Handcrafted, 2¼" tall
600QX475-5, $6.00
Artist: Ed Seale

Grandchild's First Christmas

The elves are busily making Christmas toys on this ecru ball topped with a handcrafted mouse. Sitting on Santa's knee, the adorable little baby can't wait to hug his new teddy bear. The caption reads, "Grandchild's First Christmas 1985."

◼ Ecru Satin, 2⅞" diam.
500QX260-5, $5.00
Artist: LaDene Votruba

Grandchild's First Christmas

A white hand-knitted bootie, trimmed with a red ribbon bow, is filled with toys Baby will love. Caption: "Grandchild's First Christmas 1985."

◼ Handcrafted, 3¼" tall
1100QX495-5, $11.00

Grandparents, Niece, Mother

Mother and Dad, Father, Sister, Daughter

Godchild, Son

Grandmother, Grandson, Granddaughter

Grandparents

A white poinsettia appears against a rich garnet background to create a unique lacquer-look that is new to the Keepsake Ornament line. Framed in brass, the design is accented with gold for an extra-festive touch. Caption: "Grandparents have beautiful ways of adding love to the holidays. Christmas 1985."
▓ Bezeled Lacquer-Look, 2¾"wide
700QX380-5, $7.00
Artist: Sharon Pike

Niece

A new and popular caption is stamped in silver foil on an acrylic teardrop: "A Niece fills hearts with a special kind of love. Christmas 1985."
▓ Acrylic, 3¾" tall
575QX520-5, $5.75

Mother

A clear acrylic raindrop, framed in a golden ring, brings a tribute to Mother. The gold foil-stamped caption reads: "Mother is the heart of our happiest holiday memories. Christmas 1985."
▓ Acrylic, 3⅛" tall
675QX372-2, $6.75
Artist: Sharon Pike

Mother and Dad

This snow-white, fine porcelain bell has a bas-relief paisley design. The trim, caption, tie-cord and tassle are all in soft blue. Caption: "Mother and Dad. Christmas 1985."
▓ Porcelain, 3" tall
775QX509-2, $7.75
Artist: LaDene Votruba

Father

Filled with gifts and a Christmas tree, this old-fashioned sleigh is printed on hardwood with the look of handpainting. Caption: "A Father sees through the eyes of love and listens with his heart. Christmas 1985."
▓ Wood, 3" diam.
650QX376-2, $6.50
Artist: LaDene Votruba

Sister

This white porcelain bell, hanging from a red ribbon, has a cheerful heart and holly design that looks as if it were hand-

First Christmas Together Brass, Love at Christmas, First Christmas Together Acrylic

painted especially for Sister. Caption: "For Sister with love. Christmas 1985."
▓ Porcelain, 2¾" tall
725QX506-5, $7.25
Artist: Joyce Pattee

Daughter

Framed in a wooden embroidery hoop and tied with an embroidered fabric ribbon, this design looks like fine silk-screening. Caption: "A Daughter decorates the holidays with love. Christmas 1985."
▓ Wood, 3¼" diam.
550QX503-2, $5.50

Godchild

This design was reproduced from Hallmark's Antique Greeting Card Collection. The caption on the back is stamped in gold foil. Caption: "A Godchild is a loving gift to treasure through the years. Christmas 1985."
▓ Bezeled Satin, 2¾" diam.
675QX380-2, $6.75
Artist: Diana McGehee

Son

A terrier with a fabric bow at his neck fetches the message: "Merry Christmas, Son 1985."
▓ Handcrafted, 2" tall
550QX502-5, $5.5O
Artist: Bob Siedler

Grandmother

A nostalgic floral design decorates this transparent red, teardrop-shaped ball. The scroll banner bears the caption: "A Grandmother gives the gift of love. Christmas 1985."
▓ Red Glass, 3" diam.
475QX262-5, $4.75
Artist: Joyce Pattee

Grandson

A bright red, green, and yellow antique train chugs around a green glass ball bringing Grandson the Christmas message: "A Grandson makes holiday joys shine even brighter! Christmas 1985."
▓ Green Glass, 2⅞" diam.
475QX262-2, $4.75
Artist: LaDene Votruba

Granddaughter

A contemporary American country look is achieved in the design of the vividly colored animals on the center of this ivory ball. Caption: "There's nothing like a Granddaughter to warm the world at Christmas. 1985."
▓ Ivory Glass, 2⅞" diam.
475QX263-5, $4.75

First Christmas Together

Romantic embossed hearts surround the caption, "First Christmas Together 1985," on the cover of this polished brass locket. With its special hanger, the locket can be displayed closed to show the cover or open to reveal your two photos inside. Locket comes with a special felt storage pouch.
▓ Polished Brass, 2½" tall
1675QX400-5, $16.75
Artist: Ed Seale

Love at Christmas

It's raining romantic red foil hearts on this acrylic heart etched with the caption: "The spirit of Christmas is love."
▓ Acrylic, 3¼" wide
575QX371-5, $5.75
Artist: Diana McGehee

First Christmas Together

On a clear acrylic oval, framed in brass, a graceful pair of etched doves carries a banner bearing the gold foil-stamped caption: "First Christmas Together 1985."
▓ Acrylic, 3½" wide
675QX370-5, $6.75

First Christmas Together

A pale green bisque porcelain bell with scalloped, bas-relief design is a romantic symbol of love. The red porcelain, double-heart clapper bears the caption: "First Christmas Together 1985."

■ Porcelain, 2" tall
1300QX493-5, $13.00
Artist: Linda Sickman

Holiday Heart

Colorful flowers and holiday greenery decorate a white, fine-porcelain puffed heart. The ornament is captioned with the word "Love" in bas-relief and topped with a white fabric tassel.

■ Porcelain 2" tall
800QX498-2, $8.00

First Christmas Together

This design is a unique blend of old-fashioned charm and romance. The red heart is hand-woven inside a wooden frame decorated with a bright red fabric tassel. Caption: "1985 First Christmas Together."

■ Fabric, Wood, 2½" tall
800QX507-2, $8.00

Heart Full of Love

A winter scene of snow-capped trees, accented by brightly colored cardinals and red berries, is printed on padded satin and framed with a chrome ring. Caption: "The world is full of beauty when hearts are full of love. Christmas 1985."

■ Bezeled Satin, 3" tall
675QX378-2, $6.75

First Christmas Together

Heart-shaped frames reveal romantic silhouette vignettes painted in shades of blue, green, and red. Caption: "Love is a gift from heart to heart. First Christmas Together 1985."

■ Light Blue Glass, 2⅞" diam.
475QX261-2, $4.75

Twenty-Five Years Together

This miniature porcelain plate, a new format in 1985, is decorated with a gold, silver and blue holly wreath. The border caption on the front reads: "Twenty-Five Years Together." Back: "Christmas 1985." Plate stand included.

■ Porcelain, 3¼" diam.
800QX500-5, $8.00

First Christmas Together: Porcelain Bell, Holiday Heart, First Christmas Together: Fabric and Wood

Heart Full of Love, First Christmas Together Glass Ball, Twenty-Five Years Together

Friendship: Embroidered, Bezeled Satin; From Our House to Yours, Teacher

Friendship

A new format for 1985, this tasseled container, covered in rich Oriental red satin, is hand-embroidered with a pine and snowflake design. A gift card for personalizing is tucked inside, and the caption reads: "Christmas...a special time for friendship. 1985."
▨ Embroidered Satin, 2" tall
775QX506-2, $7.75
Artist: Joyce Pattee

Friendship

An early American village reflects the warmth of Christmas and friendship. If you look carefully, you'll see Santa standing in the middle of town. The artwork is printed on padded satin and framed with a chrome bezel. Caption: "Christmas...season bright with friendship. 1985."
▨ Bezeled Satin, 3" tall
675QX378-5, $6.75
Artist: Michele Pyda-Sevcik

From Our House to Yours

Holiday decorations in the windows of this handmade needlepoint house tell visiting neighbors that friendship and Christmas cheer are inside. The caption on red satin reads, "A happy home reflects the joy of Christmas all year round. 1985."
▨ Needlepoint Fabric, 4" tall
775QX520-2, $7.75
Artist: Joyce Pattee

Teacher

A wise owl perches on a slate board displaying the lesson "Merry Christmas to a Grade A Teacher!" The owl's book has the title "School Days 1985." There is room for personalization on the back of the slate.
▨ Handcrafted, 3" tall
600QX505-2, $6.00

With Appreciation

Silver and gold appear in this acrylic oval framed in brass. Silver foil-stamped snowflakes surround the gold foil-stamped caption: "Christmas...a time when we think of those who have given us so much. 1985."
▨ Acrylic, 3½" tall
675QX375-2, $6.75

Special Friends

A unique quadrafoil acrylic shape is the setting for this etching of a doll and her "beary" best friend. The silver foil-stamped caption: "Special friends bring special joys to Christmas. 1985."
▨ Acrylic, 3" wide
575QX372-5, $5.75
Artist: Don Palmiter

With Appreciation, Special Friends

New Home

Lovely Victorian homes, decorated with wreaths and Christmas greenery, encircle a blue teardrop ball. Caption: "New Home, new joys, new memories to cherish. Christmas 1985."
- Blue Glass, 3" diam.
  475QX269-5, $4.75
  Artist: Michele Pyda-Sevcik

Babysitter

Pandas prepare for Christmas in their own special ways. The white and black bears, holding red ornaments and red-ribboned packages, are set against a green teardrop ball. Caption: "A Babysitter is a special kind of friend. Christmas 1985."
- Green Glass, 3" diam.
  475QX264-2, $4.75
  Artist: Michele Pyda-Sevcik

Good Friends

On a frosted teardrop ball, penguins frolic in the snow, making patterns and words to commemorate the holiday season. Caption: "Good times with good friends make life's merriest moments. Christmas 1985."
- White Frosted Glass, 3" diam.
  475QX265-2, $4.75

Property Ornaments

SNOOPY and WOODSTOCK

SNOOPY is practicing for the holiday hockey tournament with the help of his star player, WOODSTOCK. They'll skate their way into your Christmas for years.
- Handcrafted, 1¾" tall
  750QX491-5, $7.50
  Artist: Bob Siedler

Muffin the Angel

All dressed up as an angel in a snow-white fabric outfit, Muffin is ready for the Christmas pageant.
- Handcrafted, 2½" tall
  575QX483-5, $5.75
  Artist: Bob Siedler

Kit the Shepherd

Kit is a shepherd dressed in a fabric headdress for the Christmas pageant.
- Handcrafted, 2½" tall
  575QX484-5, $5.75
  Artist: Bob Siedler

Betsey Clark

This little boy is one of Betsey Clark's most charming angels. On bended knee, he gathers a little lamb into his arms.
- Handpainted Porcelain, 2½" tall
  850QX508-5, $8.50

New Home, Babysitter, Good Friends

SNOOPY and WOODSTOCK, Muffin the Angel, Kit the Shepherd, Betsey Clark

Hugga Bunch™, FRAGGLE ROCK™ Holiday, PEANUTS®, Norman Rockwell

Rainbow Brite™ and Friends, A DISNEY Christmas, Merry Shirt Tales™

Hugga Bunch™

Little cuties share hugs and Christmas fun as they make their debut in the Keepsake line. Caption: "Huggy Holidays!"

■ Light Blue Glass, 2⅞" diam.
500QX271-5, $5.00

FRAGGLE ROCK™ Holiday

SPROCKET™ the dog peeks in on the FRAGGLE ROCK™ gang. This was a new property in the Keepsake Ornament line. Caption: "Happy Holidays '85."

■ Light Blue Glass, 3" diam.
475QX265-5, $4.75

PEANUTS®

SNOOPY directs a Christmas chorus starring WOODSTOCK and his friends on a teardrop-shaped ball. Caption: "Sing a song of Christmas joy! 1985."

■ Blue Glass, 3" diam.
475QX266-5, $4.75

Norman Rockwell

Three favorite Rockwell Santa paintings appear. The caption describes the portrayals perfectly: "…He was chubby and plump, a right jolly old elf, and I laughed when I saw him, in spite of myself…C.C. Moore. From the Norman Rockwell Collection 1985."

■ Frosted White Glass, 2⅞" diam.
475QX266-2, $4.75
Artist: Diana McGehee

Rainbow Brite™ and Friends

Rainbow Brite™ and the Sprites make their debut in the Keepsake line amid a rainbow of colorful stars and snowflakes. Visible inside the clear glass ball is a bright gold starburst. Caption: "1985."

■ Clear Glass, 2⅞" diam.
475QX268-2, $4.75

A DISNEY Christmas

Front: It's stocking-hanging time at Mickey Mouse's house. Back: Mickey dons a Santa suit, complete with a pillow for stuffing. The designs on this ornament were printed directly on the glass. Dated "1985."

■ Pearl Blue Glass, 3" diam.
475QX271-2, $4.75

Merry Shirt Tales™

The Shirt Tales™, all bundled up for winter, go skating, skiing, and sledding on a teardrop-shaped ball. Caption: "Every day's a holiday when good friends get together. Christmas 1985."

■ Light Blue Glass, 3" diam.
475QX267-2, $4.75

Porcelain Bird, Sewn Photoholder, Candle Cameo, Santa Pipe

Old-Fashioned Wreath, Peaceful Kingdom, Christmas Treats

Traditional Ornaments

Porcelain Bird

This Tufted Titmouse looks so real you might think he flew into your home to celebrate the holidays. He's made of hand-painted porcelain and perches on your tree with the help of a specially designed clip.
■ Handpainted Porcelain, 2" tall
  650QX479-5, $6.50
  Artist: Linda Sickman

Sewn Photoholder

An array of holiday hearts and Christmas flowers is embroidered on this red fabric photoholder. Caption: "Cherished times that mean the most are kept in memory ever close. Christmas 1985."
■ Embroidered Fabric, 3¼" diam.
  700QX379-5, $7.00
  Artist: Sharon Pike

Candle Cameo

Christmas warmth and cheer are captured with traditional holiday symbols. The gold foil-stamped caption reads: "Christmas…the season that brightens the world. 1985."
■ Bezeled Cameo, 3" tall
  675QX374-2, $6.75
  Artist: Sharon Pike

Santa Pipe

A pipe that looks like carved antique meerschaum displays a bas-relief Santa and reindeer on their Christmas Eve ride.
■ Handcrafted, 4½" tall
  950QX494-2, $9.50
  Artist: Peter Dutkin

Old-Fashioned Wreath

An etched brass wreath of toys is embedded in clear acrylic. The gold foil-stamped caption says: "Christmas 1985."
■ Etched Brass, Acrylic, 3¼" diam.
  750QX373-5, $7.50

Peaceful Kingdom

An etched acrylic lion and lamb symbolize words that are the true meaning of Christmas: "…and peace will reign in the kingdom…Christmas 1985." The caption is stamped in gold foil.
■ Acrylic, 3" wide
  575QX373-2, $5.75
  Artist: Sharon Pike

Christmas Treats

This ornament depicts holiday candies in bright shades of red and green. A lead frame encircles the glass design. This is a new format in the Keepsake line.
■ Bezeled Glass, 3¼" tall
  550QX507-5, $5.50

Special Edition

The Spirit of Santa Claus

Driving a green-and-gold sleigh full of toys and a Christmas tree, Santa holds the reins to a beautiful prancing reindeer. The complexity and detailing of this ornament make it a true work of art. A special wishbone-shaped hanger comes with the ornament.

◼ Handcrafted, 4¼" tall
2250QX498-5, $22.50
Artist: Donna Lee

Nostalgic Sled

This is a reissue from 1984. (See 1984 Annual Collection.)
◼ Handcrafted, 3½" wide
600QX442-4, $6.00
Artist: Linda Sickman

Holiday Humor

Night Before Christmas

This Christmas story is at your fingertips. When you push the button, 30 pages depicting the story flip over before your eyes. This ornament comes with a special stand for off-tree display.
◼ Panorama Ball, 3¼" diam.
1300QX449-4, $13.00
Artist: Ed Seale

Nativity Scene

Birds and bunnies gather 'round, as a group of adorable little angels welcome the Baby. This delicately detailed design illustrates the caption: "O come, all ye faithful…Christmas 1985."
◼ Light Blue Glass, 3" diam.
475QX264-5, $4.75
Artist: Sue Tague

Santa's Ski Trip

Santa waves his hat as he rides to the slopes in the gondola, "Snowflake Mountain No. 1985." The gondola hangs by a pully with a real string "rope."
◼ Handcrafted, 3¼" tall
1200QX496-2, $12.00
Artist: Ed Seale

Night Before Christmas, Nativity Scene, Santa's Ski Trip, Mouse Wagon, Children in the Shoe

Mouse Wagon

Bringing a gift of his favorite cheese, a white mouse rides into Christmas in his red wagon. Dated "1985," the wagon has wheels that turn and a movable handle.
◼ Handcrafted, 2" tall
575QX476-2, $5.75

Children in the Shoe

This ornament depicts the nursery rhyme shoe house with sparkling snow on the roof, a wreath on the door, and children everywhere.
◼ Handcrafted, 3¼" tall
950QX490-5, $9.50
Artist: Ed Seale

Do Not Disturb Bear, Sun and Fun Santa, Bottlecap Fun Bunnies, Lamb in Legwarmers

Candy Apple Mouse, Skateboard Raccoon, Stardust Angel, Soccer Beaver, Beary Smooth Ride

Do Not Disturb Bear
A green stocking and "Do not disturb 'til Christmas" sign hang on a log where a bear is snuggled in a fabric blanket.
■ Handcrafted, 3" wide
775QX481-2, $7.75
Artist: Ed Seale

Sun and Fun Santa
Santa wears a red bathing suit, green flippers, and a reindeer inner tube. His red bathing cap is dated " '85."
■ Handcrafted, 2¾" tall
775QX492-2, $7.75
Artist: Bob Siedler

Bottlecap Fun Bunnies
Mommy bunny, with a real pompom on her hat, gives baby bunny a ride. Her sled is a metal bottle cap from the "Santa Soda, North Pole Bottling Co."
▥ Handcrafted, 2¼" tall
775QX481-5, $7.75
Artist: Bob Siedler

Lamb in Legwarmers
A flocked lamb wears green, red, and white crocheted fabric legwarmers.
■ Handcrafted, 3" tall
700QX480-2, $7.00

Candy Apple Mouse
With his tummy filled, a little white mouse naps on a partially eaten candied red apple at the end of a "1985" stick.
■ Handcrafted, 3¼" tall
650QX470-5, $6.50
Artist: Linda Sickman

Skateboard Raccoon
A flocked raccoon takes a ride on a red skateboard that has green movable wheels.
■ Handcrafted, 2½" tall
650QX473-2, $6.50
Artist: Peter Dutkin

Stardust Angel
An angel brushes the stardust from her star and keeps it in her "Stardust" bag.
■ Handcrafted, 2" tall
575QX475-2, $5.75
Artist: Donna Lee

Soccer Beaver
This energetic beaver, dressed in red, is ready for a holiday game of soccer.
■ Handcrafted, 2½" tall
650QX477-5, $6.50
Artist: Peter Dutkin

Beary Smooth Ride
Teddy enjoys riding his colorful tricycle with wheels that turn.
■ Handcrafted, 1¾" tall
650QX480-5, $6.50
Artist: Linda Sickman

Swinging Angel Bell

Riding on a bright red swing, a little angel is the clapper of this sparkling clear bell.

▓ Handcrafted, Glass, 3¾" tall
1100QX492-5, $11.00
Artist: Bob Siedler

Doggy in a Stocking

This tan terrier snuggles in a crocheted, red-and-green stocking.

▓ Handcrafted, 3" tall
550QX474-2, $5.50

Engineering Mouse

A white mouse engineers a bright red and green train that looks like a wind-up toy.

▓ Handcrafted, 2" tall
550QX473-5, $5.50
Artist: Bob Siedler

Kitty Mischief

A kitten is tangled in a real red yarn ball.

▓ Handcrafted, 2" tall
500QX474-5, $5.00
Artist: Peter Dutkin

Baker Elf

An elf puts green icing on a bell-shaped cookie. "1985" appears in red icing.

▓ Handcrafted, 3" tall
575QX491-2, $5.75
Artist: Ed Seale

Ice Skating Owl

A white owl on ice skates wears a red-and-white hat of real yarn.

▓ Handcrafted, 2" tall
500QX476-5, $5.00
Artist: Bob Siedler

Dapper Penguin

This penguin in a red top hat, gold cane, and green bow tie is ready for a gala.

▓ Handcrafted 2¼" tall
500QX477-2, $5.00
Artist: Ed Seale

Trumpet Panda

A flocked panda practices his holiday music for the Christmas Day parade.

▓ Handcrafted, 2" tall
450QX471-2, $4.50
Artist: Ed Seale

Merry Mouse

Merry mouse wears a hat like Santa's. His tail is fashioned of real leather.

▓ Handcrafted, 2½" tall
450QX403-2, $4.50
Artist: Peter Dutkin

Snow-Pitching Snowman

Winding up to pitch his snowball, this snowman wears a red and green baseball cap.

▓ Handcrafted, 2" tall
450QX470-2, $4.50
Artist: Donna Lee

Swinging Angel Bell, Doggy in a Stocking, Engineering Mouse, Kitty Mischief, Baker Elf

Ice Skating Owl, Dapper Penguin, Trumpet Panda, Merry Mouse, Snow-Pitching Snowman

Three Kittens in a Mitten
This is a reissue from 1984.
(See 1984 Annual Collection.)
■ Handcrafted, 3½" tall
   800QX431-1, $8.00
   Artist: Donna Lee

Roller Skating Rabbit
This is a reissue from 1984.
(See 1984 Annual Collection.)
■ Handcrafted, 2½" wide
   500QX457-1, $5.00
   Artist: Ed Seale

Snowy Seal
This is a reissue from 1984.
(See 1984 Annual Collection.)
■ Handcrafted, 1½" wide
   400QX450-1, $4.00
   Artist: Ed Seale

Country Christmas Collection

Old-Fashioned Doll
A Colonial lady, with handpainted porcelain arms, legs, and head, is dressed in a lace-trimmed holiday costume.
■ Handpainted Porcelain, Fabric, 5½" tall
   1450QX519-5, $14.50

Country Goose
This delicate goose is on natural wood. Caption: "This original design, styled in the American Country Tradition, has been printed on hardwood."
■ Wood, 3" diam.
   775QX518-5, $7.75
   Artist: Michele Pyda-Sevcik

Rocking Horse Memories
The silk-screen applique rocking horse contrasts a holly-patterned background framed in an authentic wooden embroidery hoop. Caption: "Christmas 1985."
■ Wood, Fabric, 3¼" diam.
   1000QX518-2, $10.00
   Artist: LaDene Votruba

Whirligig Santa
A wooden Whirligig Santa with movable arms resembles a popular Colonial toy.
■ Wood, 4" tall
   1250QX519-2, $12.50

Sheep at Christmas
Reminiscent of old carvings, this sheep wears a bell that rings in the holidays. Caption: "Season's Greetings 1985."
■ Handcrafted, 3¼" tall
   825QX517-5, $8.25
   Artist: Linda Sickman

Old-Fashioned Doll, Country Goose, Rocking Horse Memories, Whirligig Santa, Sheep at Christmas

Keepsake Basket, Victorian Lady, Charming Angel, Lacy Heart, Snowflake

Heirloom Christmas Collection

Keepsake Basket
A hand-crocheted basket, trimmed with satin and lace, has a pearl-like button closure that opens to a rose-scented sachet.
■ Fabric, 2½" tall
1500QX514-5, $15.00
Artist: Joyce Pattee

Victorian Lady
This handpainted porcelain doll rests on a burgundy satin, lace-trimmed cone.
■ Handpainted Porcelain, Fabric, 3¾" tall
950QX513-2, $9.50

Charming Angel
A precious angel, with yarn hair and wings of sheer netting, wears a hand-sewn lace dress and holds a satin rose.
■ Fabric, 3¾" tall
975QX512-5, $9.75
Artist: Michele Pyda-Sevcik

Lacy Heart
A padded satin heart is lavishly trimmed with lace and scented with a rose sachet.
■ Fabric, 3" tall
875QX511-2, $8.75

Snowflake
Padded with burgundy satin, this snowflake is hand crocheted.
■ Fabric, 4¼" diam.
650QX510-5, $6.50
Artist: Joyce Pattee

Collectible Series

Windows of the World—First Edition
An adorable Mexican child sits in a brick and stucco archway in this first of a series of worldwide celebrations of Christmas. A "1985" *piñata* and Christmas greeting, "Feliz Navidad," decorate the archway.
■ Handcrafted, 3" tall
975QX490-2, $9.75
Artist: Donna Lee

Miniature Crèche—First Edition
One of a series of nativities, this is made of wood and straw.
■ Wood and Straw
875QX482-5, $8.75
Artist: Ed Seale

Limited Edition

Heavenly Trumpeter
This second limited edition ornament is a handpainted porcelain angel, playing a golden trumpet to announce the joyous tidings of the season. The ornament, limited to an edition size of 24,700, comes with a wooden display stand.
■ Handpainted Porcelain, 5" tall
2750QX405-2, $27.50
Artist: Donna Lee

Windows of the World, Miniature Crèche

Nostalgic Houses and Shops, Art Masterpiece, Wood Childhood Ornaments, Twelve Days of Christmas

Nostalgic Houses and Shops—Second Edition

The town is growing with this second ornament, an "Old-Fashioned Toy Shop." A counter, cash register, dollhouse, and toy truck identify the toy store downstairs, but the owner lives on the fully furnished second floor. The address on the door is "1985."

▩ Handcrafted, 2½" tall
1375QX497-5, $13.75
Artist: Donna Lee

Art Masterpiece—Second Edition

The famous *Madonna of the Pomegranate* is reproduced on padded satin. Caption: "Madonna of the Pomegranate (ca. 1487), The Uffizi Gallery, Florence, Italy."

▩ Bezeled Satin, 2¼" diam.
675QX377-2, $6.75
Artist: Diana McGehee

Wood Childhood Ornaments—Second Edition

The second in this nostalgic series is a handpainted wooden train and log car. Loaded with logs for holiday fireplaces, the train has wheels that turn and a real pull-string.

▩ Handpainted Wood, 3½" wide
700QX472-2, $7.00
Artist: Peter Dutkin

Twelve Days of Christmas—Second Edition

Two turtle doves etched on an acrylic heart represent the second day of the popular Christmas carol. The gold foil-stamped caption reads: "The Twelve Days of Christmas 1985. Two turtle doves…"

▩ Acrylic, 3" tall
650QX371-2, $6.50
Artist: Sharon Pike

Porcelain Bear—Third Edition

The third "Cinnamon Bear" is enjoying his big peppermint candy cane. Every detail is handpainted, including the tiny button on his middle!

▩ Handpainted Porcelain, 2¼" tall
750QX479-2, $7.50
Artist: Peter Dutkin

Tin Locomotive—Fourth Edition

This pressed tin locomotive has wheels that turn and a bell that jingles. The ornament is fashioned after an antique train and carries the date: "1985."

▩ Pressed Tin, 3½" tall
1475QX497-2, $14.75
Artist: Linda Sickman

Holiday Wildlife—Fourth Edition

Two beautiful partridge stand in a field of colorful foliage. The natural wood frame complements the winter scene. Caption: "California Partridge, Lophortyx Californica, Fourth in a Series, Wildlife Collection, Christmas 1985."

▩ Wood, 3" diam.
750QX376-5, $7.50

Porcelain Bear, Tin Locomotive, Holiday Wildlife

Clothespin Soldier—Fourth Edition

The "Scottish Highlander" is dressed in his clan's colorful fabric kilt and has a real pompom on his red tam. His arms are movable.

◾ Handcrafted, 2½" tall
550QX471-5, $5.50
Artist: Linda Sickman

Rocking Horse—Fifth Edition

A brown and white pinto pony rides the range on blue rockers dated "1985." His saddle and trappings are green and red and his flying yarn tail is brown.

◾ Handcrafted, 4" wide
1075QX493-2, $10.75
Artist: Linda Sickman

Norman Rockwell—Sixth Edition

The "Jolly Postman" is making his daily deliveries accompanied by the neighborhood kids who can't wait to see what he's bringing. The white bas-relief design appears against a pale-green background. The caption stamped in silver foil reads: "Jolly Postman, Sixth in a Series, Christmas 1985, The Norman Rockwell Collection."

◾ Cameo, 3" diam.
750QX374-5, $7.50
Artist: Diana McGehee

Here Comes Santa—Seventh Edition

"Santa's Fire Engine" from the "North Pole Fire Department" is the seventh in this series. Wearing fire hat number "85," Santa rides this old-fashioned red and gold fire engine.

◾ Handcrafted, 3" tall
1400QX496-5, $14.00
Artist: Linda Sickman

Frosty Friends—Sixth Edition

These two Arctic pals row a red "1985" kayak into a new holiday season while enjoying their position as number six in the series.

◾ Handcrafted, 2" tall
850QX482-2, $8.50
Artist: Ed Seale

Betsey Clark— Thirteenth and Final Edition

In their final appearance on a series ball ornament, artist Betsey Clark's angelic children are busy playing and dreaming among the clouds and keeping the stars shiny for Christmas. Caption: "Christmas brings a special kind of feeling. 1985."

◾ White Glass, 3¼" diam.
500QX263-2, $5.00
Artist: Sharon Pike

Thimble—Eighth Edition

"Thimble Santa" carries a Christmas tree in his handy thimble backpack. The "rope" holding the thimble is made of real string.

◾ Handcrafted, 2⅜" tall
550QX472-5, $5.50
Artist: Bob Siedler

Clothespin Soldier, Rocking Horse, Norman Rockwell

Here Comes Santa, Frosty Friends, Betsey Clark, Thimble

1984

Baby's First Christmas: Handcrafted

The 1984 Keepsake Ornament Collection expanded to include four new Collectible Series: "The Twelve Days of Christmas," "Art Masterpiece," "Wood Childhood Ornaments," and "Nostalgic Houses and Shops"; two new Friendship captions, "Gratitude" and "Baby-sitter"; timely designs inspired by the 1984 Olympics and the national elections, "Marathon Santa" and "Uncle Sam"; and a new property, "Katybeth." Smaller-sized ball ornaments were introduced, handcrafted juvenile caps appeared on selected satin ornaments, and a new process enabled printing directly onto glass ball ornaments.

The 1984 Christmas season saw the last of "The Bellringers" series and the first musical ornaments in the Keepsake line. "Holiday Magic Lighted Ornaments," a unique Hallmark innovation, and "Classical Angel," the first announced limited edition ornament, also debuted.

Commemoratives

Baby's First Christmas
A finely detailed teddy bear races downhill on an old-fashioned, wood-look sled bearing gifts. Caption: "1984 Baby's First Christmas."
■ Handcrafted, 3½" wide
1400QX438-1, $14.00

Baby's First Christmas—Photoholder
This ornament has a snow-white fabric photoholder with embroidered holly sprigs at the top. The borders are fashioned in ruffled eyelet laced with pale green ribbon. Caption: "Baby's First Christmas. A Baby is a special dream come true. 1984."
■ Fabric, 3¼" diam.
700QX300-1, $7.00

Baby's First Christmas
A holiday parade of animals, led by a baby in a sled, circles the ornament. Caption: "A Baby is...happiness, pleasure, a gift from above...a wonderful, magical treasure of love. Baby's First Christmas 1984." Melody: "Babes in Toyland."
■ Musical, Classic Shape, 4¼" tall
1600QX904-1, $16.00
Artist: Donna Lee

Baby's First Christmas
An etched teddy bear holds a stocking filled with toys. The caption is accented with gold foil-stamping: "1984 Baby's First Christmas."
■ Acrylic, 3¾" tall
600QX340-1, $6.00

Baby's First Christmas: Photoholder

Baby's First Christmas: Musical

Baby's First Christmas: Acrylic

Baby's First Christmas: Boy, Girl; Baby's Second Christmas (Winnie-the-Pooh), Child's Third Christmas

Baby's First Christmas—Boy

A bear drives a train filled with Christmas toys, while a handcrafted mouse stands on top of the ornament. Caption: "A Baby Boy is a bundle of pleasure to fill every day with love beyond measure. Baby's First Christmas 1984."

◼ White Satin, 2⅞" diam.
450QX240-4, $4.50

Baby's First Christmas—Girl

A handcrafted mouse appears atop a festive parade of happy little girls and Christmas toys. Caption: "A Baby Girl is love that grows in the warmth of caring hearts. Baby's First Christmas 1984."

◼ Cream Satin, 2⅞" diam.
450QX240-1, $4.50

Baby's Second Christmas

A golden crown caps the scene of Pooh Bear sharing Christmas with his friends. Caption: "Children and Christmas are joys that go together. Baby's Second Christmas 1984."

◼ White Satin, 2⅞" diam.
450QX241-1, $4.50

Child's Third Christmas

A group of teddy bears decorate for Christmas on this satin ball topped with a handcrafted mouse. Caption: "A Child's Third Christmas. Christmas is a time for fun and wonderful surprises! 1984."

◼ Ecru Satin, 2⅞" diam.
450QX261-1, $4.50

Grandchild's First Christmas

A flocked white lamb with red fabric ribbon around its neck balances on a colorful pull toy. At the lamb's feet are a baby rattle and a ball dated "1984." Caption: "Grandchild's First Christmas."

◼ Handcrafted, 3⅜" tall
1100QX460-1, $11.00

Grandchild's First Christmas

Santa loads toys into his bag. The green satin ornament is capped with a handcrafted mouse. Caption: "A Baby makes Christmas delightfully bright. Grandchild's First Christmas 1984."

◼ Green Satin, 2⅞" diam.
450QX257-4, $4.50

Godchild

Elf-like children paint holly berries red for the holidays. Caption: "Merry Christmas, Godchild 1984."

◼ Gold Glass, 3" diam.
450QX242-1, $4.50

Grandchild's First Christmas: Handcrafted, Satin Ball; Godchild

Father, Mother

Grandson, Granddaughter, Grandparents, Grandmother

The Miracle of Love,
First Christmas Together

Mother and Dad, Sister, Daughter, Son

Father

The wonderful sounds of Christmas are symbolized by holly and musical instruments etched across the top of this ornament. Stamped in gold foil, the caption reads: "A Father has a special gift of giving of himself. Christmas 1984."
◼ Acrylic, 3¼" wide
600QX257-1, $6.00

Mother

Etched fir branches tied with ribbon are accented by a silver foil-stamped caption: "A Mother has a beautiful way of adding love to every day. 1984."
◼ Acrylic, 3¼" wide
600QX343-4, $6.00

Grandson

A polar bear family shares Christmas fun. Caption: "A Grandson has a wonderful way of adding love to every day. Christmas 1984."
◼ Blue Glass, 3" diam.
450QX242-4, $4.50

Granddaughter

A festive holiday sampler is reproduced from original stitchery. Caption: "A Granddaughter is warmth, hope and promise. Christmas 1984."
◼ Green Glass, 2⅞" diam.
450QX243-1, $4.50

Grandparents

A contemporary snow scene, reproduced from original stitchery, provides the perfect setting for the caption: "Grandparents... wherever they are, there is love. Christmas 1984."
◼ French Blue Glass, 2⅞" diam.
450QX256-1, $4.50

Grandmother

Lovely, muted pastel flowers frame a holiday tribute to Grandmother. Caption: "There's a special kind of beauty in a Grandmother's special love. Christmas 1984."
◼ Light Blue Glass, 2⅞" diam.
450QX244-1, $4.50

First Christmas Together: Musical, Brushed Brass, Silver Glass, Cameo

The Miracle of Love

A romantic heart is etched with a festive ribbon and holly design. The caption is gold foil-stamped: "Love...a miracle of the heart. Christmas 1984."
◼ Acrylic, 4" tall
600QX342-4, $6.00

First Christmas Together

Two doves perch on a holly branch. "First Christmas Together 1984" is stamped in silver foil.
◼ Acrylic, 3⅝" diam.
600QX342-1, $6.00

Mother and Dad

Gold highlights the classic Christmas design motifs that adorn this delicate, bone china bell tied with red ribbon. Caption: "Mother and Dad. Christmas 1984."
◼ Bone China, 3" tall
650QX258-1, $6.50

Sister

A bright basket of poinsettias rests against a dark blue background framed in red–all on a delicate bone china bell. Caption: "For a wonderful Sister. Christmas 1984."
◼ Bone China, 3" tall
650QX259-4, $6.50

Daughter

Bright holiday flowers and green and gold colors surround the loving caption: "A Daughter is joy that grows deeper, pride that grows stronger, love that touches your heart every day. Christmas 1984."
◼ Gold Glass, 3" diam.
450QX244-4, $4.50

Son

Holiday designs spell "Merry Christmas." The caption reads: "For a wonderful Son. Christmas 1984."
◼ White Glass, 3" diam.
450QX243-4, $4.50

First Christmas Together

The love of a first Christmas together is captured in this musical ornament with reindeer on a deep blue background. Caption: "First Christmas Together 1984." Melody: "Lara's Theme."
◼ Musical, Classic Shape, 4" tall
1600QX904-4, $16.00
Artist: Diana McGehee

First Christmas Together

A brushed brass oval locket in a felt pouch opens to hold two photos. A hanger allows open or closed display. Engraved on the cover and framed by embossed hearts is the caption: "First Christmas Together 1984."
◼ Brushed Brass, 2½" tall
1500QX436-4, $15.00
Artist: Ed Seale

First Christmas Together

This silvery ball is surrounded by a contemporary pattern of holiday birds, flowers, and greenery. Caption: "Love...a joy for all seasons. First Christmas Together 1984."
◼ Silver Glass, 3" diam.
450QX245-1, $4.50

First Christmas Together

An elegant couple, carved in ivory relief, waltzes across a dark blue background. Caption: "Each moment spent together is a special celebration. First Christmas Together 1984."
◼ Cameo, 3¼" diam.
750QX340-4, $7.50
Artist: Diana McGehee

Heartful of Love

A bone china puffed heart is decorated with a romantic rose design. The date "1984" appears on one side and a banner across the other bears the caption: "Love...the most beautiful treasure of Christmas."

■ Bone China, 3¾" wide
1000QX443-4, $10.00

Love...the Spirit of Christmas

The shiny black band and bright fruit-and-flower Christmas design lend a fine lacquer box appearance to this chrome glass ornament. Caption: "Love, which is the spirit and the heart of Christmas, blossoms all year through. 1984."

■ Chrome Glass, 2⅞" diam.
450QX247-4, $4.50

Love

Classic mimes share thoughts of love against a bright red background. Caption: "Love can say the special things that words alone cannot. Christmas 1984."

■ Chrome Glass, 2⅞" diam.
450QX255-4, $4.50

Ten Years Together

A white bone china bell features a frosty blue winter scene inside an oval. Tied in blue fabric ribbon, the bell is captioned, "Ten Years Together. Christmas 1984."

■ Bone China, 3" tall
650QX258-4, $6.50

Twenty-Five Years Together

A bone china bell, with silver hanging cord, pictures a gold and silver sleigh filled with holiday gifts. Caption: "Twenty-Five Years Together. Christmas 1984."

■ Bone China, 3" tall
650QX259-1, $6.50

Gratitude

An acrylic teardrop shape is etched with a cheery design of ribbon and sleigh bells. Caption is applied with silver foil stamping. Caption: "The spirit of Christmas lives in every heart that gives."

■ Acrylic, 4½" tall
600QX344-4, $6.00

The Fun of Friendship

Scallops decorate the rim of an acrylic bell etched with a charming portrait of two Arctic pals. The silver foil-stamped caption reads: "A friend is a partner in life's merry moments. 1984."

■ Acrylic, 3¾" tall
600QX343-1, $6.00

Heartful of Love, Love...the Spirit of Christmas, Love

Ten Years Together, Twenty-Five Years Together

Gratitude, The Fun of Friendship

Friendship

Carolers sing amidst the gentle fall of snowflakes. Set in a red border, the caption reads: "Let us sing a Christmas song of friendship, joy and cheer. 1984."

◾ Blue Green Glass, 2⅞" diam
450QX248-1, $4.50

A Gift of Friendship

Muffin and her white kitten rest on a light peach glass ball. Caption: "Friendship is the happiest gift of all!"

◾ Peach Glass, 3" diam.
450QX260-4, $4.50

New Home

Pearl blue glass forms the background for a village holiday snow scene. Caption: "Home is where the heart is and a new home always seems the happiest of places, for it is filled with all your dreams. Christmas 1984."

◾ Pearl Blue Glass, 2⅞" diam.
450QX245-4, $4.50

From Our Home to Yours

This sampler design, reproduced from original stitchery, shows an inviting home with a family enjoying the snow. Caption: "The spirit of Christmas adorns a home with love. Christmas 1984."

◾ Green Glass, 2⅞" diam.
450QX248-4, $4.50

Teacher

Whimsical little elves deliver a big red apple to their teacher. Caption: "1984 Merry Christmas, Teacher."

◾ White Glass, 3" diam.
450QX249-1, $4.50

Baby-sitter

A charming group of mice depict the fun of Christmas and the closeness shared by children and their baby-sitters. Caption: "Thank heaven for Baby-sitters like you."

◾ Green Glass, 3" diam.
450QX253-1, $4.50

Friendship, A Gift of Friendship, New Home

From Our House to Yours, Teacher, Baby-sitter

Property Ornaments

Katybeth

Katybeth was a new Hallmark property in the Keepsake line in 1984. Holding a friendly star, this freckle-faced angel wears a golden halo...a little off-center.
- Handpainted Porcelain, 2¼" tall
  900QX463-1, $9.00

DISNEY

The Disney gang—Mickey, Minnie, Donald, Daisy, and Pluto—sends holiday greetings. Caption: "Friends put the merry in Christmas. 1984."
- White Glass, 2⅞" diam.
  450QX250-4, $4.50

Betsey Clark Angel

Betsey Clark's handpainted, fine porcelain angel is clothed in a soft pink dress with a white pinafore. The angel plays a holiday song on her mandolin.
- Handpainted Porcelain, 3½" tall
  900QX462-4, $9.00

PEANUTS®

SNOOPY watches as WOODSTOCK and friends build a gallery of snowmen. SNOOPY's red banner says, "Merry Christmas." Ornament is dated "1984."
- Light Blue Soft-Sheen Satin, 2⅞" diam.
  450QX252-1, $4.50

The MUPPETS™

KERMIT™, framed by a Christmas wreath, dons a Santa cap to wish us, "Hoppy, Hoppy Holidays!" MISS PIGGY™, framed by a heart-shaped wreath, says, "Merry Kissmas!"
- Chrome Glass, 2⅞" diam.
  450QX251-4, $4.50

Norman Rockwell

This gold ball shows three famous paintings from the Hallmark Collection of Norman Rockwell artwork. Each panel depicts the artist's interpretation of Dickens' Christmas characters. Caption: "Good friends, good times, good health, good cheer and happy days throughout the year. From the Norman Rockwell Collection 1984."
- Gold Glass, 2⅞" diam.
  450QX251-1, $4.50
  Artist: Diana McGehee

Currier & Ives

Always a favorite, Currier & Ives artwork is carefully reproduced on white blown glass. Caption: "American Winter Scenes, Evening, Christmas 1984."
- White Glass, 2⅞" diam.
  450QX250-1, $4.50

Katybeth, DISNEY, Betsey Clark, PEANUTS®

MUPPETS™, Norman Rockwell, Currier & Ives, Shirt Tales™

Shirt Tales™

The Shirt Tales™ join in a merry snow-ball fight. The ball ornament is capped with a golden crown. Caption: "Joy in the air, good time to share—Christmas, Christmas everywhere."
▨ Aqua Blue Satin, 2⅞" diam.
450QX252-4, $4.50

SNOOPY and WOODSTOCK

Everyone's favorite beagle takes to the slopes with his pal WOODSTOCK lead-ing the way. But it's cold outside, so SNOOPY wears a warm fabric scarf.
▨ Handcrafted, 4¼" wide
750QX439-1, $7.50
Artist: Ed Seale

Kit

Known for his green cap, Kit brings a candy cane to sweeten your Christmas. Kit and his special friend, Muffin, make a perfect pair on the tree.
▨ Handcrafted, 2¾" tall
550QX453-4, $5.50

Muffin

You'll always know Muffin by her red knitted cap. Here, she's bringing a holiday gift to her friend, Kit.
▨ Handcrafted, 2¾" tall
550QX442-1, $5.50
Artist: Donna Lee

Traditional Ornaments

White Christmas

The hustle and bustle of Christmas time is shown in a wintry town square of yester-year. Caption: "At Christmas time, love shines in every smile, glows in every heart." Melody: "White Christmas."
▨ Musical, Classic Shape, 4½" tall
1600QX905-1, $16.00

Twelve Days of Christmas

This musical ornament was originally part of Hallmark's Musical Decoration line. In 1984, it was reintroduced as a Keepsake Ornament. Melody: "The Twelve Days of Christmas."
▨ Musical, Handcrafted, 3¾" tall
1500QX415-9, $15.00
Artist: Ed Seale

Gift of Music

A colorfully dressed, bearded elf ties a blue gift with red ribbon. The label reads: "Jolly Holidays!" Melody: "Jingle Bells."
▨ Musical, Handcrafted, 3" tall
1500QX451-1, $15.00
Artist: Ed Seale

SNOOPY and WOODSTOCK, Kit, Muffin

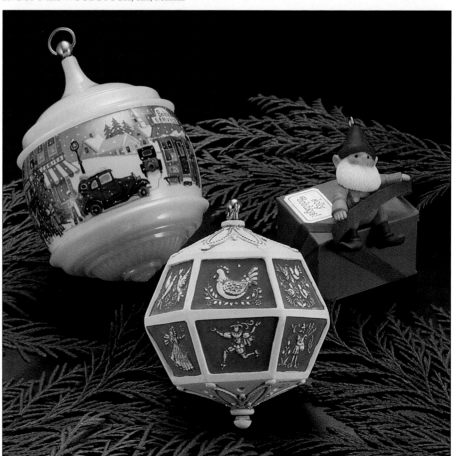

White Christmas, Twelve Days of Christmas, Gift of Music

Amanda

Holiday Jester, Uncle Sam

Amanda
Dressed in a ruffled frock and bonnet of bright green fabric, Amanda is ready for a Christmas party. Her face and hands are handpainted fine porcelain.
■ Fabric, Handpainted Porcelain, 4¾" tall
900QX432-1, $9.00

Holiday Jester
Looking as if he may have played to royal audiences, this jester wears the traditional black and white costume with gold shoes. His arms and legs are movable.
■ Handcrafted, 5¼" tall
1100QX437-4, $11.00
Artist: Linda Sickman

Uncle Sam
A pressed tin Uncle Sam, holding a teddy bear and flags, wears an " '84" badge to remind us it's a presidential election year.
■ Pressed Tin, 5" tall
600QX449-1, $6.00
Artist: Linda Sickman

Chickadee
A handpainted porcelain chickadee brings a cluster of mistletoe to your tree. A metal clip keeps the bird perched on the branch.
■ Handpainted Porcelain, 3¼" wide
600QX451-4, $6.00
Artist: Linda Sickman

Cuckoo Clock
"Merry Christmas" is the "time" etched on the brass face of this intricately detailed clock that comes complete with pinecone pendulums. Santa's face decorates the top, and a reindeer adorns the bottom.
■ Handcrafted, 3¼" tall
1000QX455-1, $10.00
Artist: Donna Lee

Alpine Elf
Holiday messages echo through the Alps when this elf plays his long, carved horn.
■ Handcrafted, 3½" wide
600QX452-1, $6.00
Artist: Ed Seale

Nostalgic Sled
With its real string rope and metal runners, this sled evokes memories of childhood fun. Caption: "Season's Greetings."
■ Handcrafted, 3½" wide
600QX442-4, $6.00
Artist: Linda Sickman

Chickadee, Cuckoo Clock, Alpine Elf, Nostalgic Sled

Santa Sulky Driver, Old Fashioned Rocking Horse, Madonna and Child

Santa Sulky Driver
Santa travels in an etched brass rig that displays a "Season's Greetings" banner.
■ Etched Brass 1¾" tall
  900QX436-1, $9.00

Old Fashioned Rocking Horse
A new look for the Keepsake line, this ornament features a finely etched rocking horse embedded in acrylic.
■ Brass, Acrylic, 3¼" diam.
  750QX346-4, $7.50

Madonna and Child
The Madonna cradles the Holy Child as a dove of peace watches in this loving scene etched in acrylic. The gold foil-stamped caption reads: "All is calm, all is bright..."
■ Acrylic, 4" tall
  600QX344-1, $6.00
  Artist: Don Palmiter

Holiday Friendship
This panorama peek-through ball depicts the friendship shared by a little boy and girl. Both hide gifts as they wave to each other through a frosty window.
■ Peek-Through Ball, 3¼" diam.
  1300QX445-1, $13.00

Peace on Earth
A red oval cameo shows a beautiful old-world angel in ivory relief playing a harp. Caption: "Peace on Earth."
■ Cameo, 3" tall
  750QX341-4, $7.50

A Savior is Born
A nativity scene with holiday flowers brings the most important message of the season: "For unto you is born this day in the City of David a Savior which is Christ the Lord. Luke 2:11."
■ Purple Glass, 2⅞" diam.
  450QX254-1, $4.50

Holiday Starburst
Holiday ribbons wrap around a silver starburst viewed inside this clear glass ball. The caption, printed in gold, reads: "Christmas 1984."
■ Clear Glass, 2⅞" diam.
  500QX253-4, $5.00

Holiday Friendship, Peace on Earth, A Savior is Born, Holiday Starburst

Santa

Santa rides a reindeer over lush green hill-sides, filled with blooming flowers.
- Hand-embroidered Fabric, 4" tall
  750QX458-4, $7.50

Needlepoint Wreath

Needlepoint is beautifully displayed in this handmade wreath of holiday poinsettias.
- Needlepoint Fabric, 3½" diam.
  650QX459-4, $6.50
  Artist: Sharon Pike

Christmas Memories Photoholder

An array of holiday fabrics forms a wreath for a special Christmas photo. Caption: "Christmas is a remembering time 1984."
- Fabric, 3" diam.
  650QX300-4, $6.50

Embroidered Heart

This is a reissue from 1983.
(See 1983 Annual Collection.)
- Hand-embroidered Fabric, 4¾" tall
  650QX421-7, $6.50

Embroidered Stocking

This is a reissue from 1983.
(See 1983 Annual Collection.)
- Hand-embroidered Fabric, 3¼" tall
  650QX479-6, $6.50
  Artist: Linda Sickman

Holiday Humor

Bell Ringer Squirrel

A handcrafted squirrel swings from an acorn, the clapper in this clear glass bell.
- Glass, Handcrafted, 4" tall
  1000QX443-1, $10.00
  Artist: Ed Seale

Raccoon's Christmas

A raccoon peeks out the door of his snow-covered tree house, clutching a candy-cane. Both he and his bird neighbor have hung their Christmas stockings.
- Handcrafted, 2¾" tall
  900QX447-4, $9.00
  Artist: Ed Seale

Three Kittens in a Mitten

Three kittens—black, tan, and gold—play in a knitted red-and-green mitten.
- Handcrafted, 3½" tall
  800QX431-1, $8.00
  Artist: Donna Lee

Marathon Santa

Santa carries a torch dated "1984." He's a gold medalist on December 25!
- Handcrafted, 2¼" tall
  800QX456-4, $8.00
  Artist: Ed Seale

Santa, Needlepoint Wreath, Christmas Memories Photoholder

Bell Ringer Squirrel, Raccoon's Christmas, Three Kittens in a Mitten, Marathon Santa

Santa Star, Snowmobile Santa, Snowshoe Penguin, Christmas Owl

Santa Star
Here's a shining example of Santa, designed in the shape of a five-pointed star.
■ Handcrafted, 3½" tall
550QX450-4, $5.50

Snowmobile Santa
Santa goes out for a ride in his shiny new snowmobile.
■ Handcrafted, 2¾" wide
650QX431-4, $6.50

Snowshoe Penguin
Santa's penguin neighbor dons snowshoes to deliver a Christmas gift himself. His cap has a real pompom.
■ Handcrafted, 3" tall
650QX453-1, $6.50
Artist: Linda Sickman

Christmas Owl
A wise little owl, wearing Santa's hat, watches from a clear acrylic moon. His Christmas stocking, made to fit his foot, hangs from the moon's tip.
■ Handcrafted, Acrylic, 3¼" tall
600QX444-1, $6.00
Artist: Ed Seale

Musical Angel
This little angel has a unique view of Christmas, but even her position won't stop her from playing a heavenly tune. The banner hanging from her brass horn is stamped with the caption: "NOËL."
■ Handcrafted, 1¼" tall
550QX434-4, $5.50
Artist: Donna Lee

Napping Mouse
This little mouse is not "stirring," he's napping in a walnut shell, while holding tightly to his "teddy mouse." The blanket is a red-and-white dotted fabric ribbon.
■ Handcrafted, 1¾" tall
550QX435-1, $5.50

Roller Skating Rabbit
The red wheels on the green and white roller skate shoe actually turn. A white bunny takes a holiday "spin."
■ Handcrafted, 2½" wide
500QX457-1, $5.00
Artist: Ed Seale

Frisbee® Puppy
This playful puppy leaps to catch the "Merry Christmas" Frisbee®. He wears a green fabric bow for the holidays.
■ Handcrafted, 2¾" tall
500QX444-4, $5.00

Musical Angel, Napping Mouse, Roller Skating Rabbit, Frisbee® Puppy

Reindeer Racetrack, A Christmas Prayer, Flights of Fantasy, Polar Bear Drummer

Reindeer Racetrack

The race has started and the reindeer runners are off! Santa encourages his trusty friends with: "On, Comet! On, Cupid! On, Donder! On, Blitzen!"

■ Red Glass, 3" diam.
450QX254-4, $4.50

A Christmas Prayer

Mary Hamilton's charming angels frolic in the clouds, chasing stars. The ball is capped with a golden crown. Caption: "Little prayer be on your way...bless our friends on Christmas Day."

■ Blue Sheen Satin, 2⅞" diam.
450QX246-1, $4.50

Flights of Fantasy

Elves ride on the backs of lovely birds, flying in the moonlight on this fanciful holiday ball. A ribbon banner says, "Christmas 1984."

■ Blue Glass, 2⅞" diam.
450QX256-4, $4.50

Polar Bear Drummer

A white polar bear drums up holiday spirit, staying warm with a plaid fabric scarf.

■ Handcrafted, 2¼" tall
450QX430-1, $4.50
Artist: Ed Seale

Santa Mouse

Mister Mouse dresses as Santa with a jacket and cap and furry plush beard.

■ Handcrafted, 2" tall
450QX433-4, $4.50
Artist: Bob Siedler

Snowy Seal

This softly flocked white seal with dark eyes is dressed for the holidays in a red fabric ribbon.

■ Handcrafted, 1½" wide
400QX450-1, $4.00
Artist: Ed Seale

Fortune Cookie Elf

An elf paints a wish for your holiday fortune cookie. Caption: "May Your Christmas Be Merry."

■ Handcrafted, 2½" tall
450QX452-4, $4.50
Artist: Linda Sickman

Peppermint 1984

The year 1984 is fashioned like peppermint candy. Two birds enjoy the view from atop the number nine.

■ Handcrafted, 2¼" wide
450QX456-1, $4.50
Artist: Donna Lee

Santa Mouse, Snowy Seal, Fortune Cookie Elf, Peppermint 1984

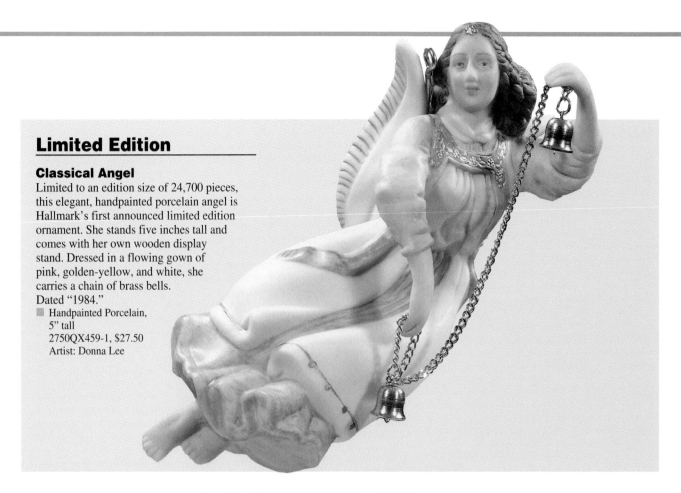

Limited Edition

Classical Angel
Limited to an edition size of 24,700 pieces, this elegant, handpainted porcelain angel is Hallmark's first announced limited edition ornament. She stands five inches tall and comes with her own wooden display stand. Dressed in a flowing gown of pink, golden-yellow, and white, she carries a chain of brass bells. Dated "1984."
◻ Handpainted Porcelain, 5" tall
2750QX459-1, $27.50
Artist: Donna Lee

Mountain Climbing Santa
This is a reissue from 1983. (See 1983 Annual Collection.)
◻ Handcrafted, 2½" tall
650QX407-7, $6.50
Artist: Ed Seale

Collectible Series

Nostalgic Houses and Shops—First Edition
This "Victorian Dollhouse," scaled one-inch to one-foot, suits ornament and dollhouse collectors. The interior is complete with wallpaper, furniture, a Christmas tree, and even a miniature dollhouse.
◻ Handcrafted, 3¼" tall
1300QX448-1, $13.00
Artist: Donna Lee

Wood Childhood Ornaments—First Edition
"Wooden Lamb" evokes memories of Christmas past. Wheels that turn and a red fabric bow at the neck add authentic touches.
◻ Wood, Handcrafted, 2¼" tall
650QX439-4, $6.50

Nostalgic Houses and Shops, Wood Childhood Ornaments

The Twelve Days of Christmas—First Edition

The popular Christmas song is immortalized on scalloped acrylic. An etched partridge and pear tree depict the first of the days, and the gold foil-stamped caption reads: "The Twelve Days of Christmas 1984...and a partridge in a pear tree."

■ Acrylic, 3" tall
   600QX348-4, $6.00

Art Masterpiece—First Edition

This series brings timeless works of art into your home. The first ornament offers a classic oil painting reproduced on padded satin. Caption: "Giuliano Bugiardini, 'Madonna and Child and St. John,' (ca. 1505) The Nelson-Atkins Museum of Art, Kansas City, Missouri, (Nelson Fund)."

■ Bezeled Satin, 2¾" diam.
   650QX349-4, $6.50
   Artist: Diana McGehee

Porcelain Bear— Second Edition

An adorable "Cinnamon Bear," fashioned in handpainted porcelain, holds a gold jingle bell with red bow.

■ Handpainted Porcelain, 2½" tall
   700QX454-1, $7.00

Tin Locomotive—Third Edition

Number three in the pressed "Tin Locomotive Series" is an antique design with movable wheels. The muted colors are red, soft blue, lavender, and steel. Dated "1984."

■ Pressed Tin, 2½" tall
   1400QX440-4, $14.00
   Artist: Linda Sickman

Clothespin Soldier— Third Edition

Red-and-black uniformed Canadian Mountie proudly bears a holiday flag.

■ Handcrafted, 2½" tall
   500QX447-1, $5.00
   Artist: Linda Sickman

Holiday Wildlife—Third Edition

A pair of graceful ring-necked pheasants are pictured against a snow-covered setting on a porcelain-look inset framed in wood. Caption: "Ring-Necked Pheasant, Phasianus Torquatus, Third in a series, Wildlife Collection, Christmas 1984."

■ Handcrafted, 3" diam.
   725QX347-4, $7.25

Twelve Days of Christmas, Art Masterpiece, Porcelain Bear

Tin Locomotive, Clothespin Soldier, Holiday Wildlife

Rocking Horse—
Fourth Edition

Racing into the holiday season is the fourth of the "Rocking Horse" series. The blue and red saddle and rockers provide a colorful contrast to this white-and-black speckled appaloosa with gray mane and flying yarn tail. Dated "1984."

▇ Handcrafted, 4" wide
1000QX435-4, $10.00
Artist: Linda Sickman

Frosty Friends—
Fifth Edition

The little Eskimo has gone ice fishing with his penguin pal. The catch of the day is a Christmas gift, wrapped and dated "1984."

▇ Handcrafted, 2½" tall
800QX437-1, $8.00
Artist: Ed Seale

Norman Rockwell—
Fifth Edition

Rockwell's famous *Caught Napping* is this cameo's subject. Santa peeks from behind a high-backed chair at two pajama-clad children who tried their best to stay awake for his visit. The background is deep blue with white relief. Caption: "Caught Napping, Fifth in a Series, The Norman Rockwell Collection, Christmas 1984."

▇ Cameo, 3" diam.
750QX341-1, $7.50
Artist: Diana McGehee

Here Comes Santa—
Sixth Edition

Santa's "free delivery" service carries a load of Christmas trees as its cargo. Called "Santa's Deliveries," this ornament has wheels that actually turn. License plate: "1984."

▇ Handcrafted, 3¼" tall
1300QX432-4, $13.00
Artist: Linda Sickman

The Bellringers—Sixth
and Final Edition

The "Elfin Artist" swings on the outside of a white, fine porcelain bell. He has painted his message in red: "Christmas 1984."

▇ Porcelain, 3½" tall
1500QX438-4, $15.00

Thimble—
Seventh Edition

This heavenly blue-gowned angel holds a shiny thimble full of sparkling acrylic stars.

▇ Handcrafted 1¾" tall
500QX430-4, $5.00

Betsey Clark—
Twelfth Edition

Betsey Clark waifs decorate for the holidays. Caption: "Days are merry, hearts are light, and all the world's a lovely sight. Christmas 1984."

▇ White Frosted Glass, 3¼" diam.
500QX249-4, $5.00

Rocking Horse, Frosty Friends, Norman Rockwell

Here Comes Santa, The Bellringers, Thimble, Betsey Clark

1983

The Hallmark Keepsake Ornament Collection entered its second decade with a tremendous new look. Commemorative ornaments were introduced in a new ceramic bell format, while Hallmark continued to expand its use of colors on ball ornaments. A variety of new shapes were introduced to supplement the traditional ball-shaped ornaments.

Porcelain ornaments were offered in several original designs, including a new Collectible Series that featured a porcelain teddy bear.

Satin ball ornaments received distinctive new caps in 1983, making them instantly recognizable by their Hallmark "crowns." New commemorative titles included "Grandchild's First Christmas," "Baby's Second Christmas," "Child's Third Christmas," and "Tenth Christmas Together." Two Collectible Series ended in 1983—"Carrousel" (total of six editions) and "SNOOPY and Friends" panoramic ball ornaments (total of five issues).

Commemoratives

Baby's First Christmas
An old-fashioned rocking horse is modeled in ivory on a red background. Stamped in silver foil, the captions are: "Baby's First Christmas 1983" and "A Baby fills each day with joy by filling hearts with love."
◼ Red Cameo, 3¾" wide
750QX301-9, $7.50
Artist: Linda Sickman

Baby's First Christmas
A baby is in a cradle painted in a folk-art Christmas style. A fabric blanket and pillow are trimmed in lace with a real ribbon bow. Captions: "Baby's First Christmas" and "1983."
◼ Handcrafted, 3⁵⁄₃₂"tall
1400QX402-7, $14.00
Artist: Donna Lee

Baby's First Christmas—Girl
This design is a reproduction of original stichery of a red dress with white polka dots, a white apron pinafore, and a matching red bonnet. The pinafore pockets are filled with candy canes. The background is white, bordered in green ribbon with flowers, ABC blocks, a baby's rattle, and diaper pins. Captions: "A Baby Girl is a special gift of love." and "Baby's First Christmas 1983."
◼ White Soft-Sheen Satin, 3¼" diam.
450QX200-7, $4.50

Baby's First Christmas: Cameo, Handcrafted, Girl, Boy, Photoholder

Baby's First Christmas—Boy

This design features six tumbling teddy bears wearing blue sweaters and red scarfs. Captions: "A baby boy is love and joy...and pride that lasts a lifetime" and "Baby's First Christmas 1983."
◻ Light Blue Soft-Sheen Satin, 3¼" diam.
450QX200-9, $4.50

Baby's First Christmas

An open baby book has an area for inserting a picture. Caption: "A Baby is a dream fulfilled, a treasure to hold dear—A Baby is a love that grows more precious every year. Baby's First Christmas 1983."
◻ Acrylic, 3⅛" tall.
700QX302-9, $7.00

Grandchild's First Christmas

This is the first offering of this commemorative in any form. A baby rides in a white wicker-look buggy with red wheels and green trim. A red blanket made of real cloth has white dots and carries the caption: "Grandchild's First Christmas 1983."
◻ Handcrafted, 3¾" long
1400QX430-9, $14.00

Child's Third Christmas

Front: Santa joins "1983." Back: "To Celebrate a Child's Third Christmas. How merry the season, how happy the day When Santa brings Christmas surprises your way." The ball is double-wrapped in textured matt and glossy satin to create a piqué effect—a new texture complementing a new commemorative in the line.
◻ White Satin Piqué, 3¼" diam.
450QX226-9, $4.50

Grandchild's First Christmas

This commemorative ornament was specifically designed to fit the Classic Shape introduced this year. One side has a baby with "A Grandchild is a special reason why Christmas is such a merry season!" The other side has toys and "Grandchild's First Christmas 1983."
◻ Classic Shape, 3¼" diam.
600QX312-9, $6.00

Grandchild's First Christmas Handcrafted, Child's Third Christmas, Grandchild's First Christmas Classic Shape, Baby's Second Christmas

Baby's Second Christmas

The front has a snowman, tree, and the caption: "Baby's Second Christmas 1983." The back shows snowpeople and the caption: "A child knows such special ways to jolly up the holidays!"
◻ White Soft-Sheen Satin, 3¼" diam.
450QX226-7, $4.50

Granddaughter

Three vignettes of artwork from the Hallmark Historical Collection picture three different young girls. A fourth vignette carries the caption and date: "A Granddaughter brings beautiful moments and memories to treasure." and "Christmas 1983."

■ White Porcelain Glass, 3¼" diam.
450QX202-7, $4.50

Grandson

A kitten plays with a red ornament as a puppy looks on. Captions: "Christmas 1983" and "A Grandson, like Christmas, brings joy to the heart."

■ Ecru Soft-Sheen Satin, 3¼" diam.
450QX201-9, $4.50

Son

A little boy, house, Christmas trees, and a snowman riding a snowhorse are depicted. Captions: "A Son brings a bit of Christmas cheer to every day throughout the year" and "1983."

■ Deep Blue Satin, 3¼" diam.
450QX202-9, $4.50

Daughter

In a reproduction based on original stitchery, rows of ruffled lace and velvet, and green and deep red ribbons are intermingled with pearls. The caption is on a card that is circled with pink flowers. Caption: "A Daughter's love makes Christmas beautiful. 1983."

■ Pink Glass, 3¼" diam.
450QX203-7, $4.50

Godchild

This design features an angel and a tiny bird singing a holiday duet. Caption: "To wish a special Godchild a very merry Christmas 1983."

■ White Classical Glass, 3¼" diam.
450QX201-7, $4.50

Grandmother

A snow scene of a fenced-in farmhouse and barn shows a family approaching in a horse-drawn sleigh. Caption: "Over the river and through the woods to Grandmother's house we go...Christmas 1983."

■ White Porcelain Glass, 3¼" diam.
450QX205-7, $4.50

Granddaughter, Grandson, Son, Daughter, Godchild

Grandmother, Mom and Dad, Sister, Grandparents

Mom and Dad

This white ceramic bell has a red fabric ribbon and fired-on decals of poinsettias and holly framing the captions: "Mom and Dad" and "Christmas 1983."
◼ Ceramic, 3" tall
650QX429-7, $6.50
Artist: Sharon Pike

Sister

Candies, cookies, nuts, and a gingerbread man are pictured with flowers, ribbons, bows, a basket, jars, and a wreath. Captions: "A Sister is a forever friend" and "1983."
◼ White Classical Glass, 3¼" diam.
450QX206-9, $4.50

Grandparents

This white ceramic bell has red fabric ribbon and fired-on decals. A wreath on the front encircles: "1983." Back caption: "Grandparents are love."
◼ Ceramic, 3" tall
650QX429-9, $6.50

First Christmas Together

Candy canes form three hearts that surround the caption and the date. The design is printed directly on the surface of the ball. This process was new in 1983. Captions: "First Christmas Together" and "1983."
◼ White Glass, 3¼" diam.
450QX208-9, $4.50
Artist: Linda Sickman

First Christmas Together

A winter forest scene is shown in the newly introduced Classic shape. Captions: "First Christmas Together 1983" and "All the world is beautiful when seen through eyes of love."
◼ Classic Shape, 3¼" diam.
600QX310-7, $6.00

First Christmas Together

In a new oval shape, an ivory relief of a couple in a horse-drawn sleigh is set against a deep blue background. In silver foil stamping, the captions are: "First Christmas Together 1983" and "Love is beauty shared, dreams come true...special memories made by two."
◼ Dark Blue Cameo, 3¼" wide
750QX301-7, $7.50

First Christmas Together: Ball, Classic Shape, Cameo, Brass Heart

Love is A Song, Love Handcrafted, Love Classic Shape, Love Glass Ball

First Christmas Together—Brass Locket

This polished brass locket opens to reveal space for two photos. Caption: "First Christmas Together 1983."
◼ Polished Brass, 2⅜" tall
1500QX432-9, $15.00
Artist: Ed Seale

Love Is a Song

Dickens' characters are silhouetted in red, green, and white on a silver glass bell. Captions: "Christmas is a song of love for every heart to sing" and "1983."
◼ Silver Glass Bell, 2½" tall
450QX223-9, $4.50

Love

A white porcelain heart with embossed design of holly and berries frames a plump red heart hanging in its center which carries the caption lettered in gold. A red satin ribbon is attached for hanging. Caption: "Love 1983."
◼ Porcelain, 3⅛" tall
1300QX422-7, $13.00
Artist: Linda Sickman

Love

Hearts and greenery reproduced from an original needlepoint have a sampler style. This design can be found in the new Classic shape as well. Captions: "Love, the spirit which enhances all the seasons of our lives" and "Christmas 1983."
◼ Classic Shape, 3¼" diam.
600QX310-9, $6.00

Love

A woodland snow scene depicts holiday travelers in a horse-drawn sleigh. Captions: "Love makes each day a joy, each moment a memory" and "Christmas 1983."
◼ Light Green Glass, 3¼" diam.
450QX207-9, $4.50

Twenty-Fifth Christmas Together, Teacher

Friendship, New Home, Tenth Christmas Together

Teacher, Friendship, Mother, First Christmas Together, Love

25th Christmas Together

White lacy snowflakes create a delicate winter wonderland effect on a silver glass bell. Captions: "25th Christmas Together" and "1983."
◻ Silver Glass Bell, 2½" tall
450QX224-7, $4.50

Teacher

A schoolhouse and green and white lettering are bordered with green bands. Captions: "1983" and "For a Special Teacher at Christmas."
◻ Silver Glass Bell, 2½" tall
450QX224-9, $4.50

Friendship

Santa's neighbor, a cute little Eskimo, is shown in Christmas scenes. Captions: "Friendship is a special gift that gives your heart a happy lift" and "Christmas 1983."
◻ White Classic Glass, 3¼" diam.
450QX207-7, $4.50

New Home

This is a snow scene of homes and merry carolers on Christmas Eve. Caption: "Christmas is the perfect way of rounding out each year, for every heart and home's aglow with love and warmth and cheer. 1983."
◻ White Soft-Sheen Satin, 3¼" diam.
450QX210-7, $4.50

Tenth Christmas Together

A new commemorative was introduced in the form of a white ceramic bell. The front is decorated with a golden French horn. The caption on the back reads: "Tenth Christmas Together 1983." The bell is hung from a red fabric ribbon.
◻ Ceramic, 3" tall
650QX430-7 $6.50

Teacher

A smiling raccoon writes "Merry Christmas, Merry Christmas, Merry Christmas, Teacher 1983" in silver foil stamping.
◻ Acrylic, 3¾" tall
600QX304-9, $6.00

Betsey Clark: Handcrafted, Glass Ball, Porcelain

Friendship

Caption: "Friendship grows more beautiful with each passing season. Christmas 1983." The caption is stamped in silver foil.
◻ Acrylic, 5" tall
600QX305-9, $6.00

Mother

This heart-shaped design has the caption stamped in silver foil. Caption: "Mother...always caring, always sharing, always there to love. 1983."
◻ Acrylic, 4" tall
600QX306-7, $6.00

First Christmas Together

The bell-shaped design has the caption stamped in silver foil. Caption: "First Christmas Together 1983."
◻ Acrylic, 4¼" tall
600QX306-9, $6.00

Love

Skaters form the words of the captions in the clear "ice" of the ornament. Captions: "Love" and "Christmas 1983" stamped in silver foil.
◻ Acrylic, 4" tall
600QX305-7, $6.00

Property Ornaments

Betsey Clark

A Betsey Clark child, clad in a white-dotted blue sleeper, is napping peacefully on a yellow flocked moon.
◻ Handcrafted, 3" tall
650QX404-7, $6.50
Artist: Ed Seale

Betsey Clark— Eleventh Edition

Two boys and two girls, dressed for the winter holiday season, ride on a Christmas carousel with their little feathered friends. Caption: "Christmas happiness is found...wherever good friends gather round. 1983."
◻ White Glass, 3¼" diam.
450QX211-9, $4.50

Betsey Clark

A Betsey Clark angel, dressed in blue, sits on a cloud and catches a star with her fishing pole.
◻ Porcelain, 3½" tall
900QX440-1, $9.00

PEANUTS®, DISNEY, SHIRT TAILS™, Mary Hamilton

MISS PIGGY™, MUPPETS™

Norman Rockwell: Cameo, Glass Ball

Currier and Ives, Christmas Joy, Here Comes Santa

PEANUTS®

Comic strip panels show SNOOPY bringing WOODSTOCK and his nest in from the cold. Captions: "May the joy of the season warm every heart" and "Christmas 1983."
◻ White Soft-Sheen Satin, 3¼" diam.
450QX212-7, $4.50

DISNEY

This design shows Mickey Mouse's beaming face framed by a wreath. Caption: "1983."
◻ Chrome Glass, 3¼" diam.
450QX212-9, $4.50

SHIRT TALES™

SHIRT TALES™ make their first appearance in the Keepsake line. They are animals whose shirts bear special messages. This design shows a walrus, a penguin, and a polar bear, each wearing green, red, and yellow shirts. The fronts of their shirts read: "Deck the Halls!" The backs read: "Fa La-La La-La." Captions: "Christmas 1983" and " 'Tis the season to be jolly!"
◻ White Classical Glass, 3½" tall
450QX214-9, $4.50

Mary Hamilton

Forest creatures gather and pray with their friend, a little girl. Caption: "A wee little, warm little Christmastime prayer—may God bless us always with friendships to share. 1983."
◻ White Classical Glass, 3½" tall
450QX213-7, $4.50

MISS PIGGY™

Ever the fashion plate, MISS PIGGY™ cuts a graceful figure on her silver skates. Her skating costume, in soft lavenders, is complete with long gloves, pearl choker, and a silver tiara.
◻ Handcrafted, 4⁹⁄₁₆" tall
1300QX405-7, $13.00

The MUPPETS™

KERMIT™and MISS PIGGY™ are skywriting in a biplane; FOZZIE™ is behind them in a hot air balloon. Captions: "1983" and "Merry Christmas" in skywriting.
◻ Light Blue Satin, 3¼" diam.
450QX214-7, $4.50

Oriental Butterflies, Angels

KERMIT THE FROG™

This is a reissue from 1982. (See 1982 Annual Collection.)
◻ Handcrafted, 1⁹⁄₁₆" tall
1100QX495-6, $11.00
Artist: Donna Lee

Norman Rockwell— Fourth Edition

This circular ornament has a Rockwell painting in ivory relief against a deep blue background. Silver foil stamping highlights the caption: "Dress Rehearsal. Fourth in a series. Christmas 1983. The Norman Rockwell Collection."
◻ Dark Blue Cameo, 3" diam.
750QX300-7, $7.50

Norman Rockwell

In three famous Rockwell scenes, mother and dad decorate the tree, dad gets fitted by mom in his Santa suit, and young son catches Santa (dad) kissing mom. Caption: "Things are humming, Santa's coming, hearts are full of cheer. Lights are gleaming, kids are dreaming...Christmas time is here. From the Norman Rockwell Collection 1983."
◻ Light Green Glass, 3¼" diam.
450QX215-7, $4.50

Decorative Ball Ornaments

Currier & Ives

A favorite print from Currier & Ives is faithfully reproduced on this dated ornament. Caption: "Christmas 1983, Central Park Winter, The Skating Pond, Currier and Ives."
◻ White Porcelain Glass, 3¼" diam.
450QX215-9, $4.50

Christmas Joy

Muffin, a new Hallmark property, is dressed in a green outfit and a red knitted hat. On the front, she is feeding a carrot to a rabbit. Muffin and her dog are pictured on the back. Caption: "May all the joy you give away …return to you on Christmas Day 1983."
◻ Ecru Soft-Sheen Satin, 3¼" diam.
450QX216-9, $4.50

Here Comes Santa

Four views of Santa's face form the design. Caption: "Merry Christmas 1983."
◻ Red Glass, 3¼" diam.
450QX217-7, $4.50

Oriental Butterflies

An array of eight colorful butterflies has been reproduced from original stitchery.
◻ Turquoise Glass, 3¼" diam.
450QX218-7, $4.50

Angels

A gold tinsel starburst sparkles from the inside of this clear glass ball. On the outside are old-world angels in soft pastels, accented in rich gold. One angel is holding a tambourine.
◻ Clear Glass, 3¼" diam.
500QX219-7, $5.00

Seasons Greetings, 1983, The Wise Men

Christmas Wonderland, Old Fashioned Christmas, The Annunciation

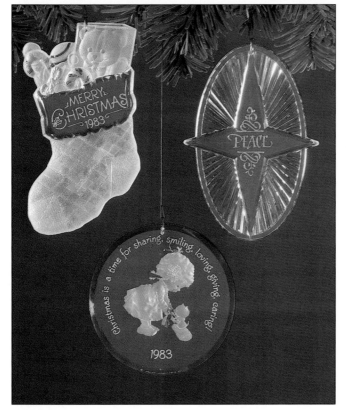

Holiday Highlights: Christmas Stocking, Time For Sharing, Star of Peace

Crown Classics: Memories to Treasure Photoholder, Christmas Wreath, Mother and Child

Season's Greetings

The caption, "Season's Greetings," is in neon-style lettering on this contemporary ornament in chrome glass.

■ Chrome Glass, 3¼" diam.
450QX219-9, $4.50

1983

This contemporary design has the date in gold on a narrow band around the center of the ornament. In raspberry glass, the ornament is trimmed with platinum-colored stripes. Caption: "1983."

■ Raspberry Glass, 3¼" diam.
450QX220-9, $4.50

The Wise Men

Three magnificent kings raise their precious gifts to the star that is leading them to Bethlehem. Two camels and a horse are shown on the back.

■ Gold Glass, 3¼" diam.
450QX220-7, $4.50

Christmas Wonderland

Animals are busy celebrating Christmas in the forest. A "peek-through" section shows another scene inside the clear glass ball.

■ Clear Glass, 3¼" diam.
450QX221-9, $4.50

An Old Fashioned Christmas

Views of Santa's face, roses, Christmas flowers, and children dressed in fashions of yesteryear are printed on a green glass ball. This design is reminiscent of the greeting cards of long ago.

■ Green Porcelain Glass, 3¼" diam.
450QX217-9, $4.50

The Annunciation

This is a beautiful reproduction of "The Annunciation" by Fra Filippo Filippi from the Samuel H. Kress Collection at the National Gallery of Art in Washington, D.C. Caption: "And the Angel said to her, 'The Holy Spirit will come upon you, and the power of the Most High will overshadow you: Therefore the Child to be born will be called Holy, the Son of God...' Luke 1:35 (RSVB)."

■ White Porcelain Glass, 3¼" diam.
450QX216-7, $4.50

Holiday Highlights

Christmas Stocking

An "etched" argyle Christmas stocking is filled to the brim with gifts, animals, toys, and candy. Caption: "Merry Christmas 1983" stamped in silver foil.

■ Acrylic, 4" tall
600QX303-9, $6.00

Time for Sharing

Mary Hamilton created a scene of a kitten sitting on a log as a little girl stoops to tie a scarf around its neck. Caption: "Christmas is a time for sharing, smiling, loving, giving, caring! 1983," stamped in silver foil.

■ Acrylic, 4" tall
600QX307-7, $6.00

Star of Peace

This oval shape is centered with the caption and a four-pointed star that is reflective. Caption: "Peace" in gold foil stamping.

■ Acrylic, 4" tall
600QX304-7, $6.00
Artist: Ed Seale

Crown Classics

Memories to Treasure

This profile of Santa in acrylic has a place to insert a photograph. Caption: "Holiday fun times make memories to treasure. 1983."

■ Acrylic, 4¼" tall
700QX303-7, $7.00

Enameled Christmas Wreath

A colorfully enameled patchwork wreath has a bezel of solid brass. Caption: "Each moment of the season has beauty all its own. Christmas 1983."

■ Enameled, 2¾" tall
900QX311-9, $9.00

Mother and Child

This ornament is an oval-shaped blue-with-ivory Madonna and Child. It's the first Cameo Keepsake with a translucent appearance. Stamped in silver

Holiday Sculpture: Santa, Christmas Heart

foil is the caption: "Come let us celebrate His love for this is the season of rejoicing."

■ Dark Blue Cameo, 3¾" tall
750QX302-7, $7.50

Holiday Sculpture

Santa

This three-dimensional Santa was molded in translucent red acrylic.

■ Acrylic, 2" tall
400QX308-7, $4.00

Heart

This three-dimensional heart was molded in translucent red acrylic.

■ Acrylic, 2" tall
400QX307-9, $4.00
Artist: Linda Sickman

Handcrafted Ornaments

Embroidered Stocking
A quilted red stocking with hand embroidery is lace trimmed and filled with toys.
◾ Fabric, 3¼" tall
650QX479-6, $6.50
Artist: Linda Sickman

Embroidered Heart
Red fabric edged in green cording is hand-embroidered with brightly colored Christmas flowers and greenery.
◾ Fabric, 4¹³⁄₁₆" tall
650QX421-7, $6.50

Scrimshaw Reindeer
Created to look like handcarved ivory scrimshaw accented in brown, a reindeer leaps gracefully into the air.
◾ Handcrafted, 3¾" tall
800QX424-9, $8.00
Artist: Ed Seale

Unicorn
A beautiful prancing unicorn made of porcelain has hand-applied gold trim.
◾ Porcelain, 4" tall
1000QX426-7, $10.00

Jack Frost
Jack Frost "paints" beautiful imagery from his pail of frost on windowpanes that can be viewed from "inside" and "outside."
◾ Handcrafted, 3¾" tall
900QX407-9, $9.00

Porcelain Doll, Diana
Diana's fine porcelain features are hand-painted in the exquisite style of an antique doll. Her burgundy costume is banded and edged in ivory lace, and the matching bonnet is faced in contrasting ivory material.
◾ Porcelain, Fabric, 4¼" tall
900QX423-7, $9.00
Artist: Donna Lee

Brass Santa
Both the front and back views of Santa's head are in polished stamped brass that is protectively coated.
◾ Brass, 4" tall
900QX423-9, $9.00
Artist: Ed Seale

Santa's on His Way
Three-dimensional handpainted scenes show Santa making gifts, packing his sleigh, climbing down the chimney, and standing by the fireplace and Christmas tree.
◾ Handcrafted, 3" tall
1000QX426-9, $10.00

Hand-Embroidered Ornaments: Stocking, Heart

Scrimshaw Reindeer, Unicorn, Jack Frost, Diana

Old-Fashioned Santa

This jointed, realistic interpretation of an old-fashioned Santa wears a knee-length red suit and red-and-white striped hose. His balding head is bare, and he carries a brass bell in one hand and a blue ornament in the other hand. Santa's arms and legs are movable.

■ Handcrafted, 5⁹⁄₆₄" tall
1100QX409-9, $11.00
Artist: Linda Sickman

Cycling Santa

This is a reissue of the popular 1992 Cycling Santa Special Edition. (See 1982 Annual Collection.)
■ Handcrafted, 4⅜" tall
2000QX435-5, $20.00

Santa's Workshop

This miniature version of Santa in his workshop is a reissue from 1982. (See 1982 Annual Collection.)
■ Handcrafted, 3" tall
1000QX450-3, $10.00
Artist: Donna Lee

Ski Lift Santa

Santa waves as he rides a ski lift to the mountain top. A brass bell is the pompom for his hat. Caption: "1983" on his ski lift ticket.
■ Handcrafted, Brass, 3⅞" tall
800QX418-7, $8.00

Mountain Climbing Santa

Santa, the sportsman, is climbing a mountain with a real rope; his backpack is a bag of toys, of course.
■ Handcrafted, 2¹³⁄₃₂" tall
650QX407-7, $6.50
Artist: Ed Seale

Jolly Santa

Merry Santa poses with his pack of toys.
■ Handcrafted, 1¹⁵⁄₁₆'' tall
350QX425-9, $3.50

Hitchhiking Santa

Santa, ready for a vacation from winter, dons sunglasses and summer clothes. He is seated on his suitcase holding a sign that reads "Goin' South," with his right hand making the gesture of hopeful hitchhikers everywhere.
■ Handcrafted, 2²¹⁄₃₂" tall
800QX424-7, $8.00
Artist: Ed Seale

Santa's Many Faces

Six scenes of Santa circle the center of this Classic Shape ornament. Caption: "Merry Christmas 1983."
■ Red Classic Shape, 3¼" diam.
600QX3ll-7, $6.00

Old-Fashioned Santa, Santa's On His Way, Brass Santa

Ski Lift Santa, Mountain Climbing Santa, Jolly Santa, Hitchhiking Santa, Santa's Many Faces

Baroque Angels

Two beautifully rendered angels with white wings are entwined in gilt-trimmed rose banners.

◼ Handcrafted, 2½" tall
1300QX422-9, $13.00
Artist: Donna Lee

Madonna and Child

A white-robed Madonna, wearing a blue and white mantle, is holding the Christ Child. The Infant is wrapped in gold and white swaddling clothes.

◼ Porcelain, 3¹⁄₁₆" tall
1200QX428-7, $12.00

Mouse on Cheese

A mischievous mouse enjoys a large morsel taken from the gift-wrapped cheese on which he is seated.

◼ Handcrafted, 2³⁵⁄₆₄" tall
650QX413-7, $6.50
Artist: Linda Sickman

Skiing Fox

A fox is skiing downhill with his green muffler flying in the wind.

◼ Handcrafted, 2⁵⁄₃₂" tall
800QX420-7, $8.00
Artist: Donna Lee

Peppermint Penguin

A penguin, attired in a red bow-tie and a red and white cap, pedals a "peppermint candy" unicycle.

◼ Handcrafted, 2¼" tall
650QX408-9, $6.50

Skating Rabbit

This skating rabbit has a tail of real cotton and a cleverly designed stocking cap that covers each ear separately.

◼ Handcrafted, 3¼" tall
800QX409-7, $8.00

Mouse in Bell

The clapper of this clear glass bell is a handcrafted mouse with a real leather tail. A brass ring secures his stocking cap by the pompom.

◼ Handcrafted, Glass, 4" tall
1000QX419-7, $10.00

Mailbox Kitten

A fluffy kitten with a stack of letters in his paws is peeking out of a pressed-tin, red and white mailbox. Caption: "1983 Peppermint Lane" on the mailbox.

◼ Handcrafted, 1⁹⁄₁₆" tall
650QX415-7, $6.50

Baroque Angels, Madonna and Child

Mouse on the Cheese, Skiing Fox, Peppermint Penguin, Skating Rabbit, Mouse in Bell

Mailbox Kitten, Tin Rocking Horse, Bell Wreath, Angel Messenger

Holiday Puppy, Rainbow Angel, Sneaker Mouse, Christmas Koala, Caroling Owl

Tin Rocking Horse

Made of lithographed tin, this colorful, three-dimensional rocking horse is a dappled gray. He has been crafted to resemble an Early American nursery toy.

■ Pressed Tin, 3¹¹⁄₆₄" tall
650QX414-9, $6.50
Artist: Linda Sickman

Bell Wreath

A bow-topped holly wreath of solid brass has seven tinkling bells.

■ Brass, 3¹³⁄₁₆" tall
650QX420-9, $6.50
Artist: Linda Sickman

Angel Messenger

A beautiful angel in a blue robe carries a banner of real brass. Caption: "1983."

■ Handcrafted, 2" tall
650QX408-7, $6.50
Artist: Ed Seale

Holiday Puppy

A puppy has red ribbon around his neck.

■ Handcrafted, 1¹⁹⁄₃₂" tall
350QX412-7, $3.50

Rainbow Angel

A playful, brass-haloed angel is depicted sliding down a rainbow. A fleecy cloud guarantees a soft landing.

■ Handcrafted, 2¹⁵⁄₁₆" tall
550QX416-7, $5.50
Artist: Donna Lee

Sneaker Mouse

A white mouse with pink ears has adapted a red and white sneaker with laces of yarn for a bed. His blanket is blue with white polka dots.

■ Handcrafted, 1¹¹⁄₁₆" tall
450QX400-9, $4.50
Artist: Ed Seale

Christmas Koala

A flocked koala bear holds holly berries and a sprig of evergreen.

■ Handcrafted, 2³⁄₁₆" tall
400QX419-9, $4.00
Artist: Ed Seale

Caroling Owl

A small white owl, wearing a real cloth muffler, is perched on a brass ring and holds a Christmas carol book.

■ Handcrafted, 2⁹⁄₃₂" tall
450QX411-7, $4.50
Artist: Ed Seale

Christmas Kitten

This is a reissue from 1982.
(See 1982 Annual Collection.)

■ Handcrafted, 1¼" tall
400QX454-3, $4.00

Collectible Series

The Bellringers—
Fifth Edition

A white porcelain bell with a decal of a star and a holly branch with berries is dated "1983." A brown teddy bear, holding a gold star, rings the bell. This is fifth in The Bellringers Series.

◼ Porcelain, Handcrafted, 2²⁷⁄₃₂" tall
1500QX403-9, $15.00

Holiday Wildlife—
Second Edition

A porcelain-look insert, showing chickadees perched on a berried branch, is framed in natural wood. Captions: "Black-capped Chickadees, Parus Atricapillus" and "Second in a series, Wildlife Collection—Christmas 1983."

◼ Decoform, Wood, 3" diam.
700QX309-9, $7.00

Here Comes Santa—
Fifth Edition

Santa pumps a railroad handcar that carries a teddy bear, a wrapped present, and a ball. The handcar looks like aged wood with green-painted accents. The red wheels actually turn.

◼ Handcrafted, 3⁷⁄₁₆" tall
1300QX403-7, $13.00
Artist: Donna Lee

SNOOPY and
Friends—Fifth and Final
Edition

SNOOPY, dressed as Santa, has delivered a bag of gifts to WOODSTOCK. This is the last design in this series. Dated 1983.

◼ Handcrafted, 3¼" diam.
1300QX416-9, $13.00
Artist: Linda Sickman

Carrousel—Sixth and
Final Edition

Santa leads marching, horn-blowing children around the red, white, and green carrousel titled "Santa and Friends." This is the last design in this series. Caption: "Christmas 1983" circling carrousel top.

◼ Handcrafted, 3³⁄₃₂" tall
1100QX401-9, $11.00
Artist: Linda Sickman

The Bellringers, Holiday Wildlife, Here Comes Santa

SNOOPY and Friends, Carrousel Series

Porcelain Bear—
First Edition

First in a new series, this hand-painted bear made of fine porcelain is named Cinnamon.
▨ Porcelain, 2¹⁵⁄₆₄" tall
700QX428-9, $7.00
Artist: Peter Dutkin

Clothespin Soldier—
Second Edition

This American Revolutionary clothespin soldier is beating his bass drum with arms that actually move.
▨ Handcrafted, 2⁷⁄₁₆" tall
500QX402-9, $5.00
Artist: Linda Sickman

Rocking Horse—
Third Edition

The third "trusty steed" in the series is russet in color, has a blue saddle and bridle of real ecru yarn, and a green rocker dated "1983."
▨ Handcrafted, 2⅞" tall
1000QX417-7, $10.00
Artist: Linda Sickman

Frosty Friends—
Fourth Edition

An Eskimo child and a white baby seal covered with flocking are playing on a clear, free-form block of ice. Caption: "Merry Christmas 1983."
▨ Handcrafted, 1⁵⁹⁄₆₄" tall
800QX400-7, $8.00
Artist: Ed Seale

Thimble—Sixth Edition

A merry elf enjoys a cherry-topped ice cream treat served in a thimble.
▨ Handcrafted, 1¹⁵⁄₁₆" tall
500QX401-7, $5.00

Tin Locomotive—
Second Edition

An early locomotive, lithographed in red and green and trimmed in gold, features wheels that actually turn. Dated 1983.
▨ Pressed Tin, 3" tall
1300QX404-9, $13.00
Artist: Linda Sickman

Porcelain
Bear

Clothespin Soldier, Rocking Horse, Frosty Friends, Thimble Elf, Tin Locomotive

1982

In 1982, Hallmark's Keepsake Ornament Collection introduced three new series of collectible ornaments: "Holiday Wildlife," "Tin Locomotive," and "Clothespin Soldier." Six decorative glass ball ornaments were introduced in a special "Designer Keepsakes" offering that included a clear glass ball ornament with a permanent, fired-on decal. Four new ornament formats were added: cloisonné, hand-embroidered fabric, sculptured acrylic, and dimensional brass ornaments.

The end of the first decade marked a new procedure created to assist Keepsake collectors. Beginning in 1982, all ornaments in the Collector's Series were stamped with an identifying Christmas Tree symbol or the words "—in a series" (which permanently documents which issue the item is in the series). An edition number was also printed in the tree symbol to mark the ornament's issue date. The new identifying symbols made collecting easier and more exciting for the Hallmark Keepsake collectors—a group which represented 65 percent of all Hallmark Keepsake Ornament purchasers in 1982.

Commemoratives

Baby's First Christmas—Photoholder

A red and white Christmas stocking is filled with toys, candy, and gifts. Captions read: "Baby's First Christmas 1982" and "Oh what joy and sweet surprise Christmas brings to little eyes."
▪ Acrylic, 4¼" tall
650QX312-6, $6.50

Baby's First Christmas

A white rattle with a peek-in window shows a baby napping in a crib beside a window. The gold handle has a red ring and a green ribbon. Caption: "Baby's First Christmas 1982."
▪ Handcrafted, 3" tall
1300QX455-3, $13.00
Artist: Ed Seale

Baby's First Christmas—Boy

Most uniquely, this design was actually hand embroidered by an artist and then photographed for this ornament. The baby girl ornament was also created in the same manner. Captions: "Baby's First Christmas 1982" and "A baby boy is a precious gift—a blessing from above."
▪ Light Blue Satin, 3¼" diam.
450QX216-3, $4.50

Baby's First Christmas—Girl

Embroidered toys for a baby girl form a quilt motif. Captions: "Baby's First Christmas 1982" and "A baby girl is the sweetest gift a lifetime can provide."
▪ Light Pink Satin, 3¼" diam.
450QX207-3, $4.50

Baby's First Christmas: Photoholder, Handcrafted, Boy, Girl

Godchild

A little angel stands on a holly bough to reach a snowflake. Caption: "Merry Christmas to a Special Godchild. 1982."
◼ White Glass, 3¼" diam. 450QX222-6, $4.50
Artist: Sue Tague

Grandson

Bunnies sled in the snow. Caption: "A Grandson...makes days bright, hearts light and Christmas time a real delight. Christmas 1982."
◼ White Satin, 3¼" diam . 450QX224-6, $4.50

Granddaughter

Puppies, teddy bears, and bunnies hold a rope of green garland encircling the ornament. This design was reproduced from a three-dimensional soft sculpture. Captions: "A Granddaughter has a special gift for giving special joy" and "Christmas 1982."
◼ White Satin, 3¼" diam . 450QX224-3, $4.50

Son

A marching band dressed in red and teal blue uniforms keeps perfect step on a caramel-colored background. Captions: "A Son is the pride of your heart, the joy of your life" and "Christmas 1982."
◼ Caramel Soft-Sheen Satin, 3¼" diam. 450QX204-3, $4.50

Daughter

Colors of peppermint pink, candy cane red, and soft pastels illustrate a tempting array of Christmas goodies. Caption: "A Daughter's love makes Christmas special. 1982."
◼ Ecru Soft-Sheen Satin, 3¼" diam. 450QX204-6, $4.50

Father

Framed, hand-colored, woodcut-style artwork bands this ornament. Captions: "A Father's love brightens the season" and "Christmas 1982."
◼ Ecru Soft-Sheen Satin, 3¼" diam. 450QX205-6, $4.50
Artist: Linda Sickman

Godchild, Grandson, Granddaughter, Son, Daughter

Father, Mother, Mother and Dad, Sister

Mother

Front: A poinsettia bouquet is tied in pink ribbons. Back: A holly and pine garland surround the caption: "The spirit of Christmas lives in a Mother's loving heart. Christmas 1982."
◼ White Glass, 3¼" diam. 450QX205-3, $4.50

Mother and Dad

Sprays of holly leaves, berries, and evergreens caught with red ribbons form a beautiful contrast against white porcelain glass. Captions: "A Mother and Dad know so many ways to warm a heart with love" and "Christmas 1982."
◼ White Porcelain Glass, 3¼" diam. 450QX222-3, $4.50

Sister

Front: A girl ice skates on a pond with three houses in the background. Back: The girl pets a white bunny. The colors are soft pastels. This is a new introduction of an ornament commemorating Sister. Caption: "A Sister brings the beauty of memories and the warmth of love to Christmas 1982."
◼ White Glass, 3¼" diam . 450QX208-3, $4.50

Grandmother, Grandparents, Grandfather

First Christmas Together: Cameo, Glass Ball, Brass Locket

Grandmother

A patchwork quilt has the look of lace, ribbon, and embroidery. Caption: "A Grandmother is love. Christmas 1982."
■ Dark Pink Satin, 3¼" diam.
450QX200-3, $4.50

Grandparents

Featured are homes on snow-covered hillsides, an ice-skating outing, and an old covered bridge. Captions: "With thoughts of Grandparents come thoughts of days the heart will always treasure" and "Christmas 1982."
■ White Glass, 3¼" diam.
450QX214-6, $4.50

Grandfather

A graceful deer lies amid feathery scrolls. Caption: "Grandfather…in his strength he teaches, in his gentleness he loves. Christmas 1982."
■ Dark Blue Satin, 3¼" diam.
450QX207-6, $4.50

First Christmas Together

Dressed in the style of Charles Dickens' characters, a couple ice skate together. Caption: "Christmas is for sharing with the special one you love. First Christmas Together 1982."
■ Turquoise Cameo, 3⅜" diam.
850QX306-6, $8.50

First Christmas Together

A delicate, frosty background gives a lacy, silvered effect to stark bare trees. A pair of redbirds soaring in the snowy mist symbolize the captions: "Quiet moments together. . . love that lasts forever" and "First Christmas Together 1982."
■ Silver Chrome Glass, 3¼"diam.
450QX211-3, $4.50

First Christmas Together—Locket

A dimensional, hinged, heart-shaped brass locket opens to become two hearts, each with an insert for a photo. Includes a brass hanger. Caption: "First Christmas Together 1982."
■ Polished Brass, 2⅝" tall
1500QX456-3, $15.00
Artist: Ed Seale

Christmas Memories—Photoholder

A square white frame is trimmed in red ribbon and green holly leaves. The outline of a red bow shapes the top with a tab for hanging on the tree. The caption is stamped in raised letters on the back of the design. Captions: "How bright the joys of Christmas, how warm the memories" and "1982."
■ Acrylic, 4⅛ tall
650QX311-6, $6.50
Artist: Linda Sickman

Teacher

Elves in their antics cast shadows that spell "CHRISTMAS 1982." The last elf holds up an apple with the caption on the gift tag. Captions: "To a Special Teacher" and "Christmas 1982."
■ White Glass, 3¼" diam.
450QX214-3, $4.50

Christmas Memories Photoholder, Teacher Glass Ball, New Home, Teacher Photoholder

New Home

It's nighttime in a colorful village with snow-covered homes and hillsides. Caption: "Christmas time fills hearts with love and homes with warmth and joy. 1982."

◼ Dark Blue Satin, 3¼" diam.
450QX212-6, $4.50

Teacher

This snow-covered, red schoolhouse has a bell tower and a Christmas tree at the side. Captions: "Merry Christmas to my Teacher" and "1982."

◼ Acrylic, 3¹⁵⁄₁₆" tall
650QX312-3, $6.50
Artist: Linda Sickman

25th Christmas Together

The warm glow of lighted windows welcomes a frosty, snow-covered night. Captions: "Christmas...as timeless as snowfall, as forever as candleglow, as always as love" and "Twenty-fifth Christmas together 1982."

◼ White Porcelain Glass, 3¼"diam.
450QX211-6, $4.50

50th Christmas Together

A gold-on-gold background has scrolled borders and ornate lettering in burgundy highlighted with white. Captions: "We measure our time, not by years alone, but by the love and joy we've known" and "50th Christmas Together 1982."

◼ Gold Glass, 3¼" diam.
450QX212-3, $4.50

Moments of Love

A stagecoach and galloping horses form a white silhouette against a deep blue sky sprinkled with snowflakes. Captions: "Each moment of love lives forever in memory" and "Christmas 1982."

◼ Blue Soft-Sheen Satin 3¼"diam.
450QX209-3, $4.50

Love

Wreaths of flowers and greenery frame the caption and date: "Christmas...season bright with love" and "Christmas 1982."

◼ Ecru Soft-Sheen Satin, 3¼"diam.
450QX209-6, $4.50

Friendship

Happy animals ice skate merrily. Caption and date: "Hearts are happy when friends are together" and "Christmas 1982."

◼ White Satin, 3¼" diam.
450QX208-6, $4.50

Twenty-Fifth Christmas Together, Fiftieth Christmas Together, Moments of Love, Love, Friendship

MISS PIGGY™ and KERMIT™,
MUPPETS™ Party, KERMIT
the FROG™

Teacher—Apple
A clear acrylic apple with green foil-stamped leaves carries a red foil-stamped caption and etched scrolls. Caption: "To a Special Teacher 1982."
◾ Acrylic, 3½" tall
550QX301-6, $5.50
Artist: Ed Seale

Baby's First Christmas
A teddy bear of frosted acrylic holds a clear acrylic block that contains a stamped caption in silver foil. Caption: "Baby's First Christmas 1982."
◾ Acrylic, 3¹¹⁄₃₂" tall
550QX302-3, $5.50
Artist: Ed Seale

First Christmas Together
A contemporary tailored tree has a caption and date stamped in silver foil. Captions: "1982" and "First Christmas Together."
◾ Acrylic, 4¼" tall
550QX302-6, $5.50
Artist: Ed Seale

Love
This ornament is heart-shaped with etched leaves and scrolls and a caption in gold foil. Caption: "Love is forever between two hearts that share it. 1982."
◾ Acrylic, 4⅛" tall
550QX304-3, $5.50

Friendship
A kitten in a stocking is held by a puppy wearing a knitted Santa cap. The caption is stamped with silver foil. Caption: "Christmas is for friends. 1982."
◾ Acrylic, 3¼" tall
550QX304-6, $5.50

Property Ornaments

MISS PIGGY™ and KERMIT™
Front: MISS PIGGY™ lounges among gifts with a beautiful tree in the background. Back: KERMIT™ hangs Christmas balls on a garland. Caption: "Have yourself a lavish little Christmas" and "Season's Greenings 1982!"
◾ White Satin, 3¼" diam.
450QX218-3, $4.50

MUPPETS™ Party
The whole MUPPETS™ gang is gathered for a Christmas party. There are musicians, carolers, gifts, and MISS PIGGY™ in her finery seated on the piano next to a tall candelabra. Caption: "Merry Christmas 1982."
◾ White Satin, 3¼" diam.
450QX218-6, $4.50

KERMIT the FROG™
KERMIT™ is a real sport, skiing down the slopes of the Christmas tree, wearing a red cap trimmed in white and red skis and poles.
◾ Handcrafted, 3⁵⁄₁₆" tall
1100QX495-6, $11.00
Artist: Donna Lee

THE DIVINE MISS PIGGY™
This is a reissue from 1981. (See 1981 Annual Collection.)
◾ Handcrafted, 4" long
1200QX425-5, $12.00
Artist: John Francis (Collin)

Betsey Clark
A little angel is decorating a Christmas tree while floating on a cloud. Captions: " 'Tis the season for trimming trees and making merry memories" and "Christmas 1982."
◾ Blue Cameo, 3⅜" diam.
850QX305-6, $8.50

Norman Rockwell— Third Edition
Santa laughs at a very tiny stocking he is supposed to fill as he stands in front of a fireplace. The scene is white against a red background. The caption and date are stamped in silver foil on the back. Caption: "Filling the Stockings. Third in a Series. The Norman Rockwell Collection. Christmas 1982."
◾ Red Cameo, 3⅜" diam.
850QX305-3, $8.50

Betsey Clark— Tenth Edition
Three children in their nighties share a bedtime story beside a tiny decorated Christmas tree and wrapped gifts. Captions: "The joys of Christmas are multiplied when shared with those we love" and "Christmas 1982."
◾ White Satin, 3¼" diam.
450QX215-6, $4.50

Teacher, Baby's First Christmas, First Christmas Together, Love, Friendship

Cameos: Betsey Clark, Norman Rockwell; Ball Ornaments: Betsey Clark, Norman Rockwell

Norman Rockwell

A young boy, pictured in three panels, puts on a Santa suit and stuffs a pillow into the front of the pants. Next, he carols enthusiastically in church. Then, he is dressed in a robe and pajamas, holding a candle. Caption: "From the Norman Rockwell Collection 1982. Hearts are light, smiles are bright, child's delight, it's Christmas."

▧ Red Soft-Sheen Satin, 3¼"diam.
450QX202-3, $4.50

PEANUTS®

SNOOPY cycles into the holidays on a tandem bicycle with WOODSTOCK and the flock. Caption: "Christmas 1982."

▧ Light Blue Satin, 3¼" diam.
450QX200-6, $4.50

DISNEY

The Seven Dwarfs carry candy canes, toys, gifts, a wreath, and a tree as they prepare for Christmas. Captions: "Christmas. . . time for surprises—in all shapes and sizes" and "1982."

▧ White Satin, 3½" diam.
450QX217-3, $4.50

Mary Hamilton

Angels are ringing bells, floating on clouds, and perching on musical notes as they sing and play carols. Caption: "Joy to the world. 1982."

▧ Blue Soft-Sheen Satin, 3¼" diam.
450QX217-6, $4.50

Joan Walsh Anglund

Joan Walsh Anglund's children admire a snow-laden tree with a gold star on top. Caption: "Friends make Christmas memories. 1982."

▧ White Satin, 3¼" diam.
450QX219-3, $4.50

PEANUTS®, DISNEY, Mary Hamilton, Joan Walsh Anglund

Designer Keepsakes

Old World Angels

Old world angels hold lighted candles
and float amid stars and streamers.

■ White Porcelain Glass, 3¼" diam.
450QX226-3, $4.50

Patterns of Christmas

Oriental designs of poinsettias and holly
are highlighted in gold. The use of gold
inks adds richness to this elegant design.

■ Gold Glass, 3¼" diam.
450QX226-6, $4.50

Old Fashioned Christmas

Reproductions of antique English cards
from the late 1800s depict children decorating for Christmas. Captions: "Merry
Christmas" and "Happy New Year."

■ White Porcelain Glass, 3¼" diam.
450QX227-6, $4.50

Stained Glass

Styled to depict a leaded, stained-glass
window, this holly and poinsettia design
contrasts nicely against panels of lavender, blue, and green. The use of pearlized inks makes this design shimmer.

■ White Glass, 3¼" diam.
450QX228-3, $4.50

Merry Christmas

This design is the first example of fired-
on decal application to a clear glass
ball. Captions: "Merry Christmas" and
"Happy Holidays."

■ Clear Glass, 3¼" diam.
450QX225-6, $4.50

Twelve Days of Christmas

A painting illustrates the verses of this
favorite old Christmas carol. White pebbled glass captures the look of a snow-
scape realistically. Caption: "The
Twelve Days of Christmas 1982."

■ White Pebbled Glass, 3¼" diam.
450QX203-6, $4.50

Decorative Ball Ornaments

Christmas Angel

An angel on a deep blue background
shelters a candle's flame. Captions:
"From Heaven above the light of love
shines into our hearts at Christmas"
and "1982."

■ Gold Glass, 3¼" diam.
450QX220-6, $4.50

Designer Keepsakes: Old World Angels, Patterns of Christmas, Old Fashioned Christmas

Designer Keepsakes: Stained Glass, Merry Christmas, Twelve Days of Christmas

Christmas Angel, Santa, Currier and Ives, A Season for Caring

Santa

On one side is a close-up of Santa; on the other, Santa smokes his pipe. Captions: "His eyes, how they twinkled, his dimples, how merry" and "Christmas 1982."
◼ White Porcelain Glass, 3¼" diam.
  450QX221-6, $4.50
  Artist: Thomas Blackshear

Currier & Ives

This reproduction of "The Road— Winter" is from an original Currier and Ives print, "registered according to an Act of Congress in 1853." A couple takes an afternoon sleigh ride on a country road. Captions: "Christmas 1982" and "The Road —Winter"; "Currier and Ives."
◼ White Porcelain Glass, 3¼" diam.
  450QX201-3, $4.50

Season for Caring

A beautiful soft blue night scene shows the star over Bethlehem. A little shepherd and his sheep are following the shining star. Captions: "Christmas...Season for caring" and "1982."
◼ Light Blue Soft-Sheen Satin, 3¼" diam.
  450QX221-3, $4.50

Colors of Christmas: Nativity, Santa's Flight

Colors of Christmas

Nativity

A traditional depiction of the Holy Family is portrayed in a leaded, stained-glass-style window.
◼ Acrylic, 4" tall
  450QX308-3, $4.50

Santa's Flight

Looking like stained-glass, this ornament shows Santa aboard a hot air balloon. Caption: "Christmas 1982."
◼ Acrylic, 4¼" tall
  450QX308-6, $4.50

Ice Sculptures

Snowy Seal

A smiling seal is sculpted in clear acrylic.
◼ Clear Acrylic, 1¹⁹⁄₃₂" tall
  400QX300-6, $4.00

Arctic Penguin

A penguin is molded in clear acrylic.
◼ Clear Acrylic, 1½" tall
  400QX300-3, $4.00

Ice Sculptures: Snowy Seal, Arctic Penguin

Holiday Highlights

Christmas Sleigh

A sleigh, bearing gifts and a Christmas tree, has runners and a caption stamped in silver foil. Caption: "Christmas 1982."
◾ Acrylic, 3²³⁄₃₂" tall
550QX309-3, $5.50

Angel

An angel wearing a flowing gown plays a heavenly harp. The caption is stamped in gold foil. Caption: "Rejoice."
◾ Acrylic, 3½" tall
550QX309-6, $5.50

Christmas Magic

An etched design shows a little rabbit admiring an ornament hanging from a bough. This Crown Classic is in the shape of an oval Christmas ornament with scrolling that outlines the cap at the top. Stamped in silver foil is the caption: "Christmas. . . season of magical moments."
◾ Acrylic, 3 ¹³⁄₁₆" tall
550QX311-3, $5.50

Handcrafted Ornaments

Three Kings

On a dark blue background, the Three Kings are depicted traveling to the city of Bethlehem shown in the distance. Captions: "By a star shining brightly, Three Kings set their course and followed the heavenly light to its source" and "1982."
◾ Blue Cameo, 3⅜" diam.
850QX307-3, $8.50
Artist: Thomas Blackshear

Baroque Angel

A beautiful cherub wearing a regal lavender ribbon holds a pole with a tampered brass banner as he flies into Christmas. Caption: "Joyeux Noël."
◾ Brass, Handcrafted, 4⁷⁄₁₆" tall
1500QX456-6, $15.00
Artist: Donna Lee

Holiday Highlights: Christmas Sleigh, Angel, Christmas Magic

Three Kings, Baroque Angel, Cloisonné Angel

Brass Ornaments: Santa and Reindeer, Brass Bell, Santa's Sleigh

Cloisonné Angel

An open heart with a blue enameled leaf border is centered with an angel herald enameled in blue, white, and red. On the reverse of the angel are the words "Peace, Love, Joy" in raised letters.
▣ Cloisonné, 2²³⁄₃₂" tall
1200QX145-4, $12.00

Brass Ornaments

Unique ornaments crafted of polished brass are lacquer-coated to prevent tarnishing. These distinctive ornaments were introduced in 1982.

Santa and Reindeer

Santa flies through the night in a brass-runnered sleigh drawn by four stamped-brass reindeer.
▣ Brass, Handcrafted, 2⁵⁄₃₂" tall
900QX467-6, $9.00
Artist: Linda Sickman

Brass Bell

A stamped design of holly leaves and berries decorates the top and rim of a handsomely paneled bell topped with a red bow and ribbon for hanging.
▣ Polished Brass, 2¹¹⁄₃₂" tall
1200QX460-6, $12.00
Artist: Donna Lee

Santa's Sleigh

This stamped design is of Santa in a sleigh filled with toys.
▣ Polished Brass, 2⅝" tall
900QX478-6, $9.00
Artist: Ed Seale

Handcrafted Ornaments

The Spirit of Christmas

Santa flies around the tree waving at onlookers in a silver-colored, red-trimmed, old-fashioned biplane. Caption: "The Spirit of Christmas 1982."
▣ Handcrafted, 1²⁹⁄₃₂" tall
1000QX452-6, $10.00
Artist: Linda Sickman

Spirit of Christmas, Jogging Santa, Santa Bell, Santa's Workshop, Cycling Santa

Jogging Santa

Dressed in a red and white jogging suit, green shoes, and with a brass bell on his cap, a sporty Santa practices for the great "All Christmas Marathon." His sweater is dated " '82."
▣ Handcrafted, 2²⁷⁄₃₂" tall
800QX457-6, $8.00

Santa Bell

Santa's black boots ring a bell.
▣ Hand-decorated Porcelain, 3¹¹⁄₁₆" tall
1500QX148-7, $15.00

Santa's Workshop

Santa paints a dollhouse in his snow-covered cottage that is all decorated for Christmas. The cottage is open on three sides.
▣ Handcrafted, 3" tall
1000QX450-3, $10.00
Artist: Donna Lee

Cycling Santa

Santa pedals an old "velocipede" with wheels that actually turn. The handlebar basket holds a special present, and his toy-filled pack is safely stowed behind. Three brass bells attached to his pack jingle merrily.
▣ Handcrafted , 4⅜" tall
2000QX435-5, $20.00

Cowboy Snowman, Pinecone Home, Raccoon Surprises, Elfin Artist

Christmas Fantasy
This is a reissue from 1981.
(See 1981 Annual Collection.)
■ Brass, Handcrafted, 3¾" long
1300QX155-4, $13.00

Cowboy Snowman
Dressed in the latest western
fashion, a snowman is ready for
the "Christmas Rodeo." He is
wearing a red cowboy hat with a
green band, red handkerchief
around his neck, rope on his
shoulder, green gloves, a cowboy belt, and red cowboy boots.
■ Handcrafted, 2²⁷⁄₃₂" tall
800QX480-6, $8.00

Pinecone Home
A little mouse in red pajamas
and nightcap peeks out of the
shuttered window of his cozy
pinecone home, and sees his
filled stocking. A red fabric ribbon bow adorns the top.
■ Handcrafted, 2²³⁄₃₂" tall
800QX461-3, $8.00
Artist: Donna Lee

Raccoon Surprises
A racoon stands on a branch to
raid a red, green, and white
argyle Christmas stocking. A red
bird watches from his shoulder.
■ Handcrafted, 3" tall
900QX479-3, $9.00
Artist: Donna Lee

Elfin Artist
A bearded elf hangs onto his
bucket of red paint, while swinging from a bosun's chair and
painting stripes on ribbon candy.
■ Handcrafted, 3" tall
900QX457-3, $9.00
Artist: Linda Sickman

Ice Sculptor
This is a reissue from 1981. (See
1981 Annual Collection)
■ Handcrafted, 3⁵⁄₃₂" tall
800QX432-2, $8.00
Artist: Donna Lee

Tin Soldier
A British soldier in a tall black
hat and a gray, red, and white
uniform stands at attention with
a rifle in his right hand. He sal-
utes with his left hand.
■ Pressed Tin, 4⅞" tall
650QX483-6, $6.50
Artist: Linda Sickman

Peeking Elf
A little elf peeks over the top of
a silver ball ornament that is
diagonally tied in red ribbon.
■ Handcrafted, 3⁵⁄₃₂" tall
650QX419-5, $6.50

Jolly Christmas Tree
A smiling Christmas tree,
dressed in Christmas finery and
a gumdrop "topper," waves a
star as he "flies" into Christmas.
■ Handcrafted, 2¹³⁄₁₆" tall
650QX465-3, $6.50

Embroidered Tree
A dark green fabric tree is decorated with hand-embroidered
red, yellow, blue, orange, and
pink flowers. The base and tree
are trimmed in red braided cord.
■ Fabric, 4⁹⁄₁₆" tall
650QX494-6, $6.50

Little Trimmers

Cookie Mouse
A star-shaped cookie, outlined in
green icing with a dated center
in red, has lost one of its points
to the little white mouse who sits
on top happily munching the
tasty morsel. Caption: "1982."
■ Handcrafted, 2¹⁄₁₆" tall
450QX454-6, $4.50
Artist: Linda Sickman

Merry Moose
A lovable young moose, caught
up in his middle with red leather
strappings, has lost his balance
while ice skating.
■ Handcrafted, 1¾" tall
550QX415-5, $5.50

Musical Angel
A tiny angel dressed in blue with
a brass halo plays a lyre while
floating on a cloud.
■ Handcrafted, 1¹⁵⁄₁₆" tall
550QX459-6, $5.50
Artist: Donna Lee

Dove Love
A white dove swings in the center of a clear red heart in contemporary style.
■ Acrylic, 2¹⁄₁₆" tall
450QX462-3, $4.50
Artist: Linda Sickman

Jingling Teddy
A brown flocked teddy bear
wearing a red fabric ribbon
collar holds a brass bell.
■ Flocked, Brass, 2⅛" tall
400QX477-6, $4.00
Artist: Ed Seale

Christmas Kitten
A brown and white kitten wears
a red fabric ribbon collar with a
brass bell attached.
■ Handcrafted, 1¼" tall
400QX454-3, $4.00

Christmas Owl
This is a reissue from 1980.
(See 1980 Annual Collection.)
■ Handcrafted, 1⅞" tall
450QX131-4, $4.50

Perky Penguin
This is a reissue from 1981.
(See 1981 Annual Collection.)
■ Handcrafted, 1⁵⁄₁₆" tall
400QX409-5, $4.00

Tin Soldier, Peeking Elf, Jolly Christmas Tree, Embroidered Tree

Cookie Mouse, Merry Moose, Musical Angel

Dove Love, Jiggling Teddy, Christmas Kitten

Collectible Series

Holiday Wildlife—First Edition

This round wooden plaque has a white decoform inset that looks like porcelain. The inset has two red cardinals on a pine tree bough. This is the first in this Collectible Series. Caption: "Cardinalis, Cardinalis. First in a series, Wildlife Collection Christmas 1982."
■ Wood, Decoform, 4" diam.
700QX313-3, $7.00

Tin Locomotive—First Edition

This first in the Tin Locomotive series is reminiscent of the "Iron Horse" of early railroad days. Decorated in muted red, blue, and silver, it has a brass bell that hangs in front of the engineer's cab. Caption: "1982."
■ Pressed Tin, 3⅝" tall
1300QX460-3, $13.00
Artist: Linda Sickman

Clothespin Soldier—
First Edition

In a red, white, and blue uniform and a tall black hat, a mustachioed clothespin soldier holds a black baton. Other soldiers of this series follow him year by year.
■ Handcrafted, 3³⁄₃₂" tall
500QX458-3, $5.00
Artist: Linda Sickman

The Bellringers—Fourth Edition

The clapper is a handcrafted red and green wreath with an angel in its center. Caption: "1982" is on a red banner trimmed in gold with sprays of holly.
■ Ceramic, Handcrafted, 2²⁷⁄₃₂" tall
1500QX455-6, $15.00
Artist: Donna Lee

Carrousel Series—Fifth Edition

Skating snowmen hold hockey sticks, brooms, etc. and wear caps and a top hat. Caption: "Merry Christmas 1982."
■ Handcrafted, 3" tall
1000QX478-3, $10.00
Artist: Ed Seale

SNOOPY and
Friends—Fourth Edition

SNOOPY plays Santa on Christmas Eve, flying from a snow-covered rooftop on a sleigh pulled by WOODSTOCK and friends. Caption: "1982" on the red brick chimney.
■ Handcrafted, 3¼" diam.
1300QX480-3, $13.00
Artist: Ed Seale

Holiday Wildlife, Tin Locomotive, Clothespin Soldier

The Bellringers, Carrousel, SNOOPY and Friends, Here Comes Santa

Rocking Horse, Thimble, Frosty Friends

Here Comes Santa— Fourth Edition

Santa wears a conductor's cap as he drives a red, green, and tan trolley. The rolled-up awnings are green and tan. Santa has a passenger. Caption: "1982 Jolly Trolley" in a gold banner across the front.

▦ Handcrafted, 3⅜" tall
1500QX464-3, $15.00
Artist: Linda Sickman

Rocking Horse—Second Edition

This year's rocking horse is in the same style and size as the first rocking horse issued in 1981, except for color. The second issue is a black stallion with a tail of black yarn, a maroon saddle with blue blanket, and a maroon rocker bordered in gold.

▦ Handcrafted, 2" tall
1000QX502-3, $10.00
Artist: Linda Sickman

Thimble—Fifth Edition

A cute white mouse "soldier" with big ears is standing at attention. He is wearing a red jacket, blue shirt, green necktie, and a silver-colored thimble for a hat.

▦ Handcrafted, 2¹¹⁄₃₂" tall
500QX451-3, $5.00

Frosty Friends—Third Edition

The little Eskimo scales an icicle "mountain." His little Husky friend sits at the top next to the dated flag.

▦ Handcrafted, 4⅛" tall
800QX452-3, $8.00
Artist: Ed Seale

Holiday Chimes

Tree Chimes

This lacy, stamped brass tree has five bells and two doves incorporated into its leaf-filled branches.

▦ Stamped Brass, 4⁷⁄₁₆" tall
550QX484-6, $5.50
Artist: Ed Seale

Angel Chimes

Three angels, each holding a holiday poinsettia, are suspended beneath a sparkling snowflake.

▦ Chrome-plated Brass, 4½" tall
550QX502-6, $5.50

Bell Chimes

Three stamped bells, with different snowflake cutouts, hang from a larger snowflake.

▦ Chrome-plated Brass, 3" tall
550QX494-3, $5.50
Artist: Linda Sickman

Holiday Chimes: Tree Chimes, Angel Chimes, Bell Chimes

1981

Two commemorative ball ornaments were introduced in 1981: "Godchild" and "50 Years Together." In addition, new "Baby's First Christmas" ball ornaments, designed specifically for a boy and a girl, were added to the line.

Photoholder ornaments also were introduced this year, and a wooden ornament, "Drummer Boy," with movable arms and legs, was a distinctive addition to the line. Plush, "stuffed animal" ornaments were initiated in 1981, and the first edition of the instantly popular handcrafted "Rocking Horse" series made its debut.

Commemoratives

Baby's First Christmas—Boy

A baby boy holding a stuffed animal is encircled by snowflakes. Snowflakes, toys, and gifts surround the ornament and border the caption on a background of soft blue. Captions: "Baby's First Christmas 1981" and "There's nothing like a baby boy to bring a world of special joy at Christmas."
- White Satin, 3¼" diam.
  450QX601-5, $4.50

Baby's First Christmas—Girl

The pink and white design pictures a baby girl holding a teddy bear. They are centered in a delicate floral ring, and a floral border circles the ornament, framing the caption and scene of toys and gifts. Captions: "Baby's First Christmas 1981" and "There's nothing like a baby girl to cheer and brighten all the world at Christmas."
- White Satin, 3¼" diam.
  450QX600-2, $4.50

Baby's First Christmas—Black

Front: A black baby rests on green gingham cushions with a teddy bear and other toys. Back: The baby plays peekaboo under a comforter. Captions: "Baby's First Christmas 1981" and "A baby is a gift of joy, a gift of love at Christmas."
- Ecru Soft-Sheen Satin, 3¼" diam.
  450QX602-2, $4.50

Baby's First Christmas

A green wreath, decorated with a red bow, baby shoes, rattle, bells, and blocks that spell "BABY," frames the photograph opening. Back: The design repeats and gold and white captions read: "A Baby is the nicest gift of all" and "Baby's First Christmas 1981."
- Acrylic, 4" diam.
  550QX516-2, $5.50

Baby's First Christmas

Front: A cameo design on a soft green background is of a large, gift-wrapped box, a rocking horse on wheels, blocks, stuffed animal, and toys. Back: The caption is circled with a raised design of ribbon and lace. Captions: "Baby's First Christmas 1981" and "A baby adds a special joy to all the joys of Christmas."
- Light Green Cameo, 3⅜" diam.
  850QX513-5, $8.50

Baby's First Christmas

Baby is tucked under a captioned, fabric blanket in an old-fashioned baby carriage, designed to look like wicker. The wheels actually roll, and the top of the carriage is festooned with a red ribbon and a bow. Caption: "Baby's First Christmas, 1981."
- Handcrafted, 3¾" long
  1300QX440-2, $13.00

Godchild

Floating on a cloud, an angel and his puppy are gathering stars from the sky and placing them in a bag. The background is blue. This is the first issue of this commemorative. Captions: "For a special Godchild" and "Christmas 1981."
- White Satin, 3¼" diam.
  450QX603-5, $4.50
  Artist: Sue Tague

Grandson

Santa and a reindeer are busy making and painting toys in his workshop. Captions: "A Grandson makes the 'Holly Days' extra bright and jolly days" and "Christmas 1981."
- White Satin, 3¼" diam.
  450QX604-2, $4.50

Granddaughter

Front: A plump white rocking horse with red, white, and blue ruffled and ribboned saddle is on a yellow background framed in a narrow red border design with blue nosegays at each side. Back: Toys and the caption are framed in a border motif. Captions: "A Granddaughter adds a magical touch to the beauty and joy of Christmas" and "1981."
- White Satin, 3¼" diam
  450QX605-5, $4.50

Daughter

A geometric "wallpaper" design, centered with pink flowers, creates a background Christmas scene of a kitten napping in a wicker chair, a doll, gifts, candy-filled jars, a basket of flowers, and lighted candles. Captions: "A Daughter fills each day with joy by filling hearts with love" and "Christmas 1981."
- Ecru Soft-Sheen Satin, 3¼" diam.
  450QX607 5, $4.50

Son

A christmas tree, Santa, and a variety of toys are shown in multicolored squares. The captions say: "A son puts the merry in Christmas" and "Christmas 1981."
- White Satin, 3¼" diam.
  450QX606-2, $4.50

Mother

Red roses and Christmas greens surround the captions: "In a Mother's heart there is love... the very heart of Christmas." and "Christmas 1981."
- White Satin, 3¼" diam.
  450QX608-2, $4.50

Father

A beautiful male deer pauses briefly in a blue frozen forest. Captions: "Life changes season to season, year to year...but a Father's love is for always" and "Christmas 1981."
- White Satin, 3¼" diam.
  450QX609-5, $4.50

Mother and Dad

Front: The white heart and a red-lettered caption are enhanced by holly and poinsettias on a dark green background. Back: Christmas messages framed in holly and poinsettias say: "For Mother and Dad Christmas 1981" and "The wonderful meaning of Christmas is found in the circle of family love."
- Ecru Soft-Sheen Satin, 3¼" diam.
  450QX700-2, $4.50

Baby's First Christmas: For Boys, Girls, and Black Babies

Baby's First Christmas: Photoholder, Cameo, Handcrafted

Godchild, Grandson, Granddaughter, Daughter, Son

Mother, Father, Mother and Dad

Friendship

The caption is bordered by fruit and flowers in shades of red and green. Captions: "The beauty of friendship never ends" and "Christmas 1981."
▪ White Satin, 3¼" diam.
450QX704-2, $4.50

The Gift of Love

On a deep blue background, gold outlined red roses and holly frame the date and caption, which are printed in gold. Captions: "Love is a precious gift, priceless and perfect, cherished above all life's treasures" and "Christmas 1981."
▪ Gold Glass, 3¼" diam.
450QX705-5, $4.50

Home

A Victorian village is brought to life with Christmas trees, gabled homes, and snow. Captions: "Christmas 1981" and "Love in the home puts joy in the heart."
▪ White Satin, 3¼" diam.
450QX709-5, $4.50

Teacher

A red, green, blue, and yellow stocking in a stitched white circle is filled with red apples for the teacher. A red background surrounds the ornament. Caption: "For a special teacher, Christmas 1981."
▪ White Satin, 3¼" diam.
450QX800-2, $4.50

Grandfather

The captions, in red and gold, are bordered by sprays of holly on a deep brown background. Captions: "Grandfather holds a special place in the heart" and "Christmas 1981."
▪ Gold Glass, 3¼" diam.
450QX701-5, $4.50

Grandparents

A holly-sprigged basket filled with fruit joins a jar of candy canes, Christmas ball ornaments, poinsettias, and a gift. Captions: "Grandparents give the gift of love at Christmas and all year 'round" and "1981."
▪ White Glass, 3¼" diam.
450QX703-5, $4.50

Grandmother

The background is beige with a lacy border and poinsettias. Caption: "A Grandmother is so loving and dear at Christmas and throughout the year" and "Christmas 1981."
▪ Ecru Soft-Sheen Satin, 3¼" diam.
450QX702-2, $4.50

Friendship, Gift of Love, Home, Teacher

Grandfather, Grandparents, Grandmother

First Christmas Together

Dressed in the style of the 1800s, a couple ice skates against a red background sprinkled with golden snowflakes. Hearts, poinsettias, blossoms, and holly, in red, blue, and white, band the ornament and frame a heart shape that encloses a caption on the back. Captions: "First Christmas Together 1981" and "Christmas…the season for sharing the spirit of Love."
■ Chrome Glass, 3¼" diam.
450QX706-2, $4.50

25th Christmas Together

A white heart, wedding bell, and doves rest on a green leaf and red floral background with red ribbons and bows. Captions: "25 Years Together Christmas 1981" and "Christmas season of the heart, time of sweet remembrance."
■ White Glass, 3¼" diam.
450QX707-5, $4.50

50th Christmas

Red poinsettias, holly, and berries surround the captions on the front and back panels of this design. Captions: "Fifty Years Together Christmas 1981" and "A treasure of memories is a very special happiness."
■ Gold Glass, 3¼" diam.
450QX708-2, $4.50

Love

A heart with the caption in its center has a wide border of etched holly and poinsettias. The caption is stamped in silver foil. Caption: "Love…the nicest gift of all. Christmas 1981."
■ Clear Acrylic, 3½" tall
550QX502-2, $5.50

Friendship

A perky squirrel holds a songbook and sings a Christmas duet with his feathered friend. Stamped in silver foil and curving across the top, the captions read: "Friends put the 'Merry' in Christmas" and "1981."
■ Clear Acrylic, 3¼" diam.
550QX503-5, $5.50

First Christmas, Twenty-Fifth Christmas, Fiftieth Christmas

Love, Friendship, First Christmas, Twenty-Fifth Christmas

First Christmas Together

This quadrafoil ornament has the caption, "First Christmas Together 1981," etched on the face and stamped in gold foil.
■ Clear Acrylic, 3" tall
550QX505-5, $5.50

25th Christmas Together

Two molded wedding bells are tied with a bow and holly. The caption is etched and stamped in silver foil. Caption: "25 Years Together, Christmas 1981."
■ Clear Acrylic, 4½" tall
550QX504-2, $5.50

THE DIVINE MISS PIGGY™, KERMIT the FROG™, MUPPETS™

Property Ornaments

THE DIVINE MISS PIGGY™
MISS PIGGY™ poses as an angel with a brass halo and white wings. She is dressed in an aqua evening gown, lavender shoes, and long gloves. Her trademark "diamond" ring is on her pinkie.
■ Handcrafted, 4" long
1200QX425-5, $12.00
Artist: John Francis (Collin)

KERMIT the FROG™
KERMIT™ dons a red and white cap for a coasting adventure on his realistic sled.
■Handcrafted, 3¹¹⁄₃₂" long
900QX424-2, $9.00
Artist: John Francis (Collin)

MUPPETS™
On one side: MISS PIGGY™ lounges in front of the fireplace, awaiting Santa's visit. Her empty "stocking" is a high-heeled, fur-trimmed red boot. On the other side: KERMIT™, dressed as Santa with a bag of toys, is on his way down the chimney. Captions: "Let's hear it for Christmas" and "Let's hear it for Santa" and "1981."
■ White Satin, 3¼" diam.
450QX807-5, $4.50

Betsey Clark
The soft blue background is edged with a raised border of ribbons and flowers. The cameo features a girl petting a fawn. Captions: "Christmas, when hearts reach out to give and receive the gentle gifts of love" and "Christmas 1981."
■ Soft Blue Cameo, 3⅜" diam.
850QX512-2, $8.50

Betsey Clark
A Betsey Clark girl dressed in red and white and an inquisitive fawn are standing in the snow looking at a snow-covered tree, topped with a yellow star.
■ Handcrafted, 3½" tall
900QX423-5, $9.00
Artist: John Francis (Collin)

Betsey Clark—Ninth Edition
Front: A lace-bordered circle surrounds a scene of a girl leaving a gift for her friend. Back: The girl pulls a gift-filled sleigh. The background is red, white, and blue patchwork. This is the ninth design in this Collectible Series. Captions: "Christmas 1981" and "The greatest joy of Christmas day comes from the joy we give away."
■ White Glass, 3¼" diam.
450QX802-2, $4.50

Betsey Clark: Cameo, Handcrafted, Glass Ball

Mary Hamilton, Marty Links™

Mary Hamilton
Little angels are decorating, reading, napping, and playing musical instruments on a heavenly blue background. Captions: "Christmas 1981" and "Christmas decorates the world with wonder."
◻ Gold Glass, 3¼" diam.
450QX806-2, $4.50

Marty Links™
Front: Two Marty Links™ children, carrying a very large candy cane, are followed by their hungry puppy. Back: A laughing little girl holds mistletoe over her head. Captions: "Christmas 1981" and "Happy hearts and good times go hand in hand at Christmas."
◻ White Satin, 3¼" diam.
450QX808-2, $4.50

PEANUTS®
SNOOPY, WOODSTOCK, and his flock sing merrily as they deck the halls. Each bird adds a "la" to the chorus. Caption: "Deck the halls with boughs of holly… Christmas 1981."
◻ White Satin, 3¼" diam.
450QX803-5, $4.50

Joan Walsh Anglund
Front: Three Anglund children are decorating the stair rail. Back: The three are seated on a green couch and reading from a book. The couch is on a braided rug with a decorated tree at one side and a table with a lighted candle at the other. Captions: "'Tis the time of dreams come true. 'Tis the time for merrymaking" and "Christmas 1981."
◻ White Satin, 3¼" diam.
450QX804-2, $4.50

DISNEY
Sorcerer's apprentice Mickey Mouse creates the magic of a decorated, candlelit tree filled with presents and toys against the deep blue of a star-sprinkled sky. Captions: "Christmas 1981" and "Christmas is a time of magic, it's the season of surprise, everything begins to sparkle right before your very eyes."
◻ White Satin, 3¼" diam.
450QX805-5, $4.50

PEANUTS®, Joan Walsh Anglund, DISNEY

Decorative Ball Ornaments

Christmas 1981—Schneeberg

This design, reproduced from a photograph of a Schneeberg collage, has birds, beads, musical instruments, and candy on a white background. A Christmas tree decorated with birds, animals, beads, and candy is the central motif. Santa leaves an array of toys under the tree. Back: A sunburst is made of beads and colored glass ball ornaments with a dated banner. Caption: "1981."
◼ White Satin, 3¼" diam.
   450QX809-5, $4.50

Christmas Magic

A gnome-like Santa and animals are ice skating. Captions: "Christmas 1981" and "It's here, there, everywhere…Christmas magic's in the air."
◼ White Satin, 3¼" diam.
   450QX810-2, $4.50

Traditional (Black Santa)

Front: Santa feeds his animal friends in a snowy forest. Back: Wreath-framed Santa gives a merry wave. Captions: "It's Christmas. It's time for sharing…and dreaming, and caring and merry gift bearing…" and "1981."
◼ White Satin, 3¼" diam.
   450QX801-5, $4.50

Let Us Adore Him

A lovely nativity scene has cherubim adoring the Christ Child in a manger. The background is dark brown. Captions: "Christmas 1981" and "O come let us adore him."
◼ Gold Glass, 3¼" diam.
   450QX811-5, $4.50

Santa's Coming

Front: Santa holds the reins of his toy-filled sleigh while Mrs. Santa wraps his scarf around his neck and the reindeer are poised and ready. Back: Santa and his reindeer are flying through the air on a moonlit night. Captions: "Christmas 1981" and "Hustle, bustle, hurry, scurry, Santa's coming…never worry."
◼ White Satin, 3¼" diam.
   450QX812-2, $4.50

Christmas in the Forest

On a snowy Christmas night, animals and birds admire white blossoms peeking through the snow. Captions: "Christmas 1981" and "Softly…gently…joyfully… Christmas arrives in the heart."
◼ Gold Glass, 3¼" diam.
   450QX813-5, $4.50

Christmas 1981—Schneeberg, Christmas Magic, Traditional (Black Santa), Let Us Adore Him

Santa's Coming, Christmas in the Forest, Merry Christmas, Santa's Surprise

Crown Classics: Angel, Tree Photoholder, Unicorn

Frosted Images: Angel, Mouse, Snowman

Merry Christmas

Front: Gold-accented burgundy diamonds combine with tiny red flowers on a green background centered with "1981." Back: The same design has the colors reversed. Caption: "Merry Christmas 1981."
■ Gold Glass, 3¼" diam.
450QX814-2, $4.50

Santa's Surprise

On a wintry night, Santa plucks the stars from the deep blue sky and uses them to decorate a small evergreen tree in the snow. Captions: "Twinkle, glimmer, sparkle, shimmer…let the Christmas season shine" and "Christmas 1981."
■ White Satin, 3¼" diam.
450QX815-5, $4.50

Crown Classics

Angel

A golden-haired angel with white wings wears a long red-shaded robe with a green sash. The design has a leaded stained-glass look.
■ Acrylic, 3¼" tall
450QX507-5, $4.50

Tree Photoholder

Front: A Christmas tree with multi-colored ornaments has a round opening to hold a photograph. Back: The design repeats, and the caption is in gold. Caption: "Christmas 1981."
■ Acrylic, 3²⁷⁄₃₂" tall
550QX515-5, $5.50

Unicorn

Front: A graceful unicorn in white cameo rests on a soft green background. Back: Raised floral medallions frame the white-lettered caption: "A time of magical moments, dreams come true… Christmas 1981."
■ Light Green Cameo, 3⅛" diam.
850QX516-5, $8.50

Frosted Images

Three frosted, three-dimensional ornaments have the look of etched crystal. Ranging in size from 1¹⁵⁄₃₂" to 1¹⁹⁄₃₂" tall, these ornaments were priced at $4.00.
■ 400QX508-2   Mouse
   Artist: Sue Tague
■ 400QX509-5   Angel
■ 400QX510-2   Snowman

Holiday Highlights

Shepherd Scene

A shepherd with his sheep sees the distant city of Bethlehem glowing by the light of the star. Stamped in silver foil, the caption reads: "Christmas 1981."
- Clear Acrylic, 4" tall
  550QX500-2, $5.50

Christmas Star

A star with a raised, faceted border has emerald shapes tucked between the points. Silver foil-stamping accents the caption. Caption: "Christmas 1981."
- Clear Acrylic, 3½" tall
  550QX501-5, $5.50

Little Trimmers

Puppy Love

A bread-dough look puppy has a red heart on his chest and a cord of real red ribbon around his neck.
- Handcrafted, 1⅝" tall
  350QX406-2, $3.50

Jolly Snowman

This smiling snowman wears a black top hat and a real fabric scarf.
- Handcrafted, 2½" tall
  350QX407-5, $3.50

Perky Penguin

A tiny penguin wears a red cap and red-and-green striped scarf.
- Handcrafted, 1⁵⁄₁₆" tall
  350QX409-5, $3.50
  Artist: Sue Tague

Clothespin Drummer Boy

This drummer boy dressed in a black and brown uniform and a red hat beats a red drum.
- Handcrafted, 2¹³⁄₁₆" tall
  450QX408-2, $4.50

The Stocking Mouse

A white mouse, wearing a blue-and-white polka dot nightcap, peeks out of the top of a green-and-red, real knit stocking.
- Handcrafted, 2¼" tall
  450QX412-2, $4.50
  Artist: Sue Tague

Handcrafted Ornaments

Space Santa

Santa in a space helmet and a silver suit flies while carrying a dated silver star. Caption: "1981."
- Handcrafted, 3" tall
  650QX430-2, $6.50

Holiday Highlights: Shepherd Scene, Christmas Star

Little Trimmers: Puppy Love, Jolly Snowman, Perky Penguin, Clothespin Drummer Boy, The Stocking Mouse

Space Santa, Candyville Express, Ice Fairy, Star Swing

Topsy-Turvy Tunes, A Well-Stocked Stocking, The Friendly Fiddler, The Ice Sculptor

Candyville Express

A locomotive designed with the look of sugar-coated gumdrops has wheels of "cookies" and "licorice candy."
■ Handcrafted, 3" long
750QX418-2, $7.50

Ice Fairy

A lovely white ice fairy with frosted acrylic wings holds a clear acrylic snowflake.
■ Handcrafted, Acrylic, 4⅛" tall
650QX431-5, $6.50
Artist: Donna Lee

Star Swing

A little girl dressed in red, blue, and green swings from a chrome-plated brass star with the date on it.
■ Brass, Handcrafted, 3⅝" tall
550QX421-5, $5.50
Artist: Linda Sickman

A Heavenly Nap

This design is a reissue from 1980. (See 1980 Annual Collection.)
■ Handcrafted, 3¼" tall
650QX139-4, $6.50
Artist: Donna Lee

Dough Angel

This design is a reissue from 1978. (See 1978 Annual Collection.)
■ Handcrafted, 2¹⁵⁄₁₆" tall
550QX139-6, $5.50
Artist: Donna Lee

Topsy-Turvy Tunes

An opossum hangs by his tail from a tree branch, while a red bird perches on the songbook the opossum is holding. On the green book cover is the caption: "Carols."
■ Handcrafted, 3" tall
750QX429-5, $7.50
Artist: Donna Lee

A Well-Stocked Stocking

A real knit, red-and-white stocking is filled to capacity with a doll, jack-in-the-box, candy cane, and other toys.
■ Handcrafted, 4½" tall
900QX154-7, $9.00

The Friendly Fiddler

A rabbit in green and white plays a Christmas tune on a fiddle tucked under his chin.
■ Handcrafted, 3⁵⁄₃₂" tall
800QX434-2, $8.00
Artist: Donna Lee

The Ice Sculptor

A bear in a red smock and green tam sculpts a self-portrait in ice (clear acrylic).
■ Handcrafted, 3½" tall
800QX432-2, $8.00
Artist: Donna Lee

Christmas Dreams

Front: This peek-through design shows a little boy dressed in a blue snowsuit, white scarf, and brown knit cap admiring a teddy bear displayed in a toy shop window.
Back: Take a peek-through view from inside the toy store. Caption: "Toy Shop 1981."
■ Handcrafted, 3¼" diam.
1200QX437-5, $12.00
Artist: Donna Lee

Christmas Fantasy

A graceful white goose with a real brass ribbon in his bill gives a ride to an elf astride his back. The elf is dressed in red and green.
■ Handcrafted, 3¾" long
1300QX155-4, $13.00

Sailing Santa

Santa is sailing in the basket of a red hot air balloon. Christmas stockings are used for weights on the basket. The balloon has gold-painted trim and a white caption and date: "Merry Christmas 1981."
■ Handcrafted, 5" tall
1300QX439-5, $13.00

Love and Joy (Porcelain Chimes)

White bisque chimes are comprised of three white doves suspended from a white heart and bearing an impressed caption and date. Chimes have red fabric ribbon. Caption: "1981."
■ Porcelain, 3¾" tall
900QX425-2, $9.00

Drummer Boy

This handpainted drummer boy is made of real wood and has movable arms and legs.
■ Wood, 3½" tall
250QX148-1, $2.50

St. Nicholas

A traditional European St. Nicholas wears a long coat and holds a lantern that lights his way as he delivers presents from his pack.
■ Pressed Tin, 4⅜" tall
550QX446-2, $5.50
Artist: Linda Sickman

Mr. & Mrs Claus

Mr. & Mrs. Claus are reissued from their introductory year, 1975. Santa has a kitten on his shoulder and Mrs. Claus, wearing a red dress, white bonnet, and apron, holds two kittens in her arms. (See 1975 Annual Collection.)
■ Handcrafted, 3¾" tall
1200QX448-5, 2 in box $12.00

Checking It Twice

This is a reissue from 1980. (See 1980 Annual Collection.)
■ Handcrafted, 5¹⁵⁄₁₆" tall
2250QX158-4, $22.50
Artist: Thomas Blackshear

Christmas Dreams: Top, front view; Bottom, back view

Christmas Fantasy, Sailing Santa

Love and Joy, Drummer Boy, St. Nicholas

Snowman Chimes

Rocking Horse

Holiday Chimes

Snowman Chimes
This new design features the Snowman family. Mr. Snowman holds a straw broom, Mrs. Snowman holds a candle, and the Snowchild holds a cane and gift. They are suspended from a snowflake.
■ Chrome Plate, 4" tall
550QX445-5, $5.50

Santa Mobile
This is a reissue from 1980.
(See 1980 Annual Collection.)
■ 550QX136-1, $5.50

Snowflake Chimes
This is a reissue from 1980.
(See 1980 Annual Collection.)
■ 550QX165-4, $5.50
Artist: Linda Sickman

Collectible Series

Rocking Horse—First Edition
A brown and white palomino horse with a tail of real brown yarn rocks on dated red rockers. Caption: "1981."
■ Handcrafted, 2" tall
900QX422-2, $9.00
Artist: Linda Sickman

The Bellringers—Third Edition

The clapper of this gold-rimmed porcelain bell is a candy cane that has a mouse with a green cap sitting in its curve. This is the third design in this series. "1981" is in the center of the wreath.

■ Ceramic, Handcrafted, 4" tall
1500QX441-5, $15.00

Norman Rockwell— Second Edition

Front: A white cameo on a dark blue background represents Rockwell's "Carolers." Back: The caption in white letters reads: "Carolers, second in a series, the Norman Rockwell Collection Christmas 1981."

■ Dark Blue Cameo, 3⅜" diam.
850QX511-5, $8.50

Here Comes Santa— Third Edition

Santa "drives" over roofs in a vehicle that resembles an old milk truck. The roof of the truck is green. The sign on the side is ornately printed in red, deep yellow, and green. The black-tired wheels have golden spokes. This is the third design in this series. Caption: "S. Claus & Co. Rooftop Deliveries 1981."

■ Handcrafted, 4¹⁄₁₆" tall
1300QX438-2, $13.00

Carrousel—Fourth Edition

Fourth in the series, this ornament features a family ice-skating around a red pole in the center of the carrousel. The carrousel top is handpainted in green, red, and blue with white snowflakes. The date is stamped on the top of the carrousel roof. Caption: "1981."

■ Handcrafted, 2¹⁵⁄₃₂" tall
900QX427-5, $9.00

SNOOPY and Friends— Third Edition

A team of WOODSTOCK and friends pulls SNOOPY past a SNOOPY snowman. The snowman is wearing a black top hat and a green scarf. A sign in the snow is dated. This is the third design in this series. Caption: "1981."

■ Handcrafted, 3¼"diam.
1200QX436-2, $12.00
Artist: John Francis (Collin)

The Bellringers, Norman Rockwell, Here Comes Santa, Carrousel

SNOOPY and Friends, Thimble, Frosty Friends

Sewn Ornaments: Peppermint Mouse, Gingham Dog, Calico Kitty, Cardinal Cutie

Thimble—Fourth Edition
An angel with white wings and a brass halo holds a Christmas tree potted in a thimble. Her pink robe is edged in gold.
■ Handcrafted, 1½" diam.
450QX413-5, $4.50
Artist: Sue Tague

Frosty Friends—
Second Edition
An Eskimo and a Husky puppy are sheltered snugly in an igloo. The date over the entrance is framed with green holly and red berries. This is the second design in this series. Caption: "1981."
■ Handcrafted, 2" tall
800QX433-5, $8.00

Yarn and Fabric Ornaments

Sewn Ornaments
New for 1981, these fabric animals feature ribbon trims and quilting details. All are 3" tall and were priced at $3.00.
■ 300QX401-5   Peppermint Mouse
■ 300QX402-2   Gingham Dog
■ 300QX403-5   Calico Kitty
■ 300QX400-2   Cardinal Cutie

Yarn Ornaments
Four designs were reissued from 1980. (See 1980 Annual Collection.)

Plush Animals

Two charming plush animals were new introductions in 1981 and were individually packaged in gift boxes.

Christmas Teddy
Teddy wears a red knitted stocking cap and perky plaid ribbon bow.
■ Plush, 4" tall
550QX404-2, $5.50

Raccoon Tunes
A merry raccoon caroler clad in a felt vest holds a songbook made of felt.
■ Plush, 4" tall
550QX405-5, $5.50

Plush Ornaments: Christmas Teddy, Raccoon Tunes

1980

In 1980, Hallmark introduced seventy-six new ornament designs, eighteen more than the fifty-eight offered in 1979. Seven commemorative ball ornaments were inaugurated— "Son," "Daughter," "Grandparents," "Dad," "Mother and Dad," "Grandfather," and "Baby's First Christmas" for a black child. New properties included Jim Henson's MUPPETS™ and the drawing of Marty Links.™

"Friendship," "Mother," and "First Christmas Together" captioned ornaments were added to the acrylic line. Pastel-colored, unbreakable "cameo" designs were introduced. Made of acrylic, they feature delicate, milk-white "cameo" reliefs on soft pastel backgrounds. The rims are chrome with a loop for hanging. Other new designs and formats in 1980 included frosted images with the look of softly etched crystal, a flocked ornament, and a pressed tin ornament.

Two new collectible series were issued: "Frosty Friends" (an Eskimo and a polar bear on a dated ice cube) and the first "Norman Rockwell" cameo ornament. Two special edition ornaments also made their first appearance: "Checking It Twice," a very detailed Santa checking his list, and "Heavenly Minstrel," a beautiful blue angel.

By 1980, marketing surveys indicated that 55 percent of all Hallmark ornament purchases were made by collectors adding to their collections.

Commemoratives

Baby's First Christmas
With his bag filled with toys and gifts on his back, Santa talks to a baby who is snuggled under a blanket in a brass baby bed. Caption: "Baby's First Christmas, 1980."
■ White Satin, 3¼" diam. 400QX200-1, $4.00

Black Baby's First Christmas
Another Hallmark first, a black baby dressed in a nightie sits by a decorated Christmas tree that holds nested birds in its branches. Toys surround the tree. Caption: "Baby's First Christmas, 1980."
■ White Satin, 3¼" diam. 400QX229-4, $4.00

Baby's First Christmas: Satin Ball, Satin Ball (Black Baby), Handcrafted

Baby's First Christmas
A wood-look shadow box in the shape of a Christmas tree has five compartments. The compartments hold a silver cup with "Baby" on it, a rubber duck, alphabet blocks, a white ball with a blue star on it, four wood-look rings in red, yellow, and green, and a teddy bear. Captions: "Baby's First Christmas" and "1980."
■ Handcrafted, 3⁵⁄₆₄" tall 12QX156-1, $12.00 Artist: Linda Sickman

Grandson
Front: A jolly snowman rides a sled pulled by raccoons. Back: The snowman adds a candy cane to a decorated tree. Captions: "Grandsons and Christmas are joys that go together. Christmas 1980."
■ White Satin, 3¼" diam. 400QX201-4, $4.00

Granddaughter
A little girl nestled under a patchwork quilt in a brass bed dreams of sweets and toys. Captions: "A Granddaughter is a dream fulfilled, a treasure to hold dear, a joy to warmly cherish, a comfort through the year. Christmas 1980."
■ Ecru Soft-Sheen Satin, 3¼" diam. 400QX202-1, $4.00

Son
A nostalgic scene shows traditional boys' toys. Captions: "A son is…a maker of memories, a source of pride…A son is love." and "Christmas 1980."
■ Gold Glass, 3¼" diam. 400QX211-4, $4.00

Daughter
This was the first year of the Daughter ornament. Front: A white kitten naps next to potted flowers and plants. Back: A kitten plays with ornaments hanging on a potted plant. Caption: "A Daughter is the sweetest gift a lifetime can provide. Christmas 1980."
■ White Glass, 3¼" diam. 400QX212-1, $4.00

Grandson, Granddaughter, Son, Daughter

Dad

Front: The word "DAD" is printed on a red plaid background. Back: A red oval holds the caption that reads: "A Dad is always caring, always sharing, always giving of his love. Christmas 1980."

▨ Gold Glass, 3¼" diam.
400QX214-1, $4.00

Mother

Large poinsettias and Christmas flowers ring the ornament and frame the caption: "A Mother has the special gift of giving of herself. Christmas 1980."

▨ White Satin, 3¼" diam.
400QX203-4, $4.00

Mother and Dad

On a light green background, sprays of holly, lush with red berries, circle the ornament and frame the captions: "When homes are decked with holly and hearts are feeling glad, it's a wonderful time to remember a wonderful Mother and Dad. Christmas 1980."

▨ White Glass, 3¼" diam.
400QX230-1, $4.00

Grandmother

Flowers, birds, and animals frame the caption and date. Captions: "Love and joy and comfort and cheer are gifts a Grandmother gives all year." and "Christmas 1980."

▨ White Glass, 3¼" diam.
400QX204-1, $4.00

Grandfather

Two snow scenes, one of an old covered bridge and the other of a wagon in a barnyard, are pictured. Caption: "A Grandfather is...strong in his wisdom, gentle in his love. Christmas 1980."

▨ White Glass, 3¼" diam.
400QX231-4, $4.00

Grandparents

Reproduced from the Currier & Ives print "Early Winter," this ornament shows a large home nestled in the woods by a pond. Caption: "Grandparents have beautiful ways of giving, of helping, of teaching...especially of loving. 1980."

▨ Gold Glass, 3¼" diam.
400QX213-4, $4.00

Dad, Mother, Mother and Dad

Grandmother, Grandfather, Grandparents

25th Christmas Together, First Christmas Together, Christmas Love

Friendship, Christmas at Home, Teacher

Love, Beauty of Friendship, First Christmas Together, Mother

25th Christmas Together

Applique-style garlands, bells, and ribbons frame the captions. Captions: "The good times of the present blend with memories of the past to make each Christmas season even dearer than the last. 25th Christmas Together. 1980."
▨ White Glass, 3¼" diam.
  400QX206-1, $4.00

First Christmas Together

A couple takes a moonlight sleigh ride in the snow. Caption: "First Christmas Together. Christmas is a love story written in our hearts. 1980."
▨ White Glass, 3¼" diam.
  400QX205-4, $4.00

Christmas Love

This ornament is a reproduction of a Bob Schneeberg collage. The motif in delicate, soft pastels is of hearts trimmed in beads and pearls, a large snowflake, and "LOVE" in ornate lettering. Caption: "Love at Christmas... happy moments spent together, memories to be shared forever. Christmas 1980."
▨ White Glass, 3¼" diam.
  400QX207-4, $4.00

Friendship

White lace, red ribbons, and pretty flowers embellish a muted green background. Caption: "Hold Christmas ever in your heart—For its meaning never ends; Its spirit is the warmth and joy of remembering friends. Christmas 1980."
▨ White Glass, 3¼" diam.
  400QX208-1, $4.00

Christmas at Home

A yule-decorated hearth and brightly burning logs personify the comfort and warmth of home. Caption: "A Home that's filled with Christmas Glows with the joyful light Of the special warmth and happiness That makes the season bright. Christmas 1980."
▨ Gold Glass, 3¼" diam.
  400QX210-1, $4.00'

Betsey Clark: Glass Ball, Cameo, Handcrafted

Teacher

Front: A warmly dressed kitten with a gift walks to school. Back: He places the gift on his teacher's desk. The blackboard has his message to the teacher: "Merry Christmas, Teacher." Caption: "Christmas 1980."
▨ White Satin, 3¼" diam.
  400QX209-4, $4.00

Love

Caption lettering appears cut and etched with the word "LOVE" enhanced by silver foil stamping. A large snowflake in the center of the "O" is the focal point of the ornament. Caption: "Where there is love, there is the spirit of Christmas. 1980."
▨ Acrylic, 4" tall
  400QX302-1, $4.00

Beauty of Friendship

This clear, disc-shaped ornament has a floral garland border and the caption and date stamped in silver foil. Caption: "Friendship brings beauty to our days, joy to our world. Christmas 1980."
▨ Acrylic, 3¼" diam.
  400QX303-4, $4.00

First Christmas Together

Heart-shaped, with floral and ribbon border, this ornament has the caption and date stamped in silver foil. Caption: "First Christmas Together 1980."
▨ Acrylic, 3½" tall
  400QX305-4, $4.00

Mother

A heart with a ribbon-tied floral border has a silver foil-stamped caption and date. Caption: "Mother is another word for Love. Christmas 1980."
▨ Acrylic, 3½" tall
  400QX304-1, $4.00

Property Ornaments

Betsey Clark— Eighth Edition

Betsey Clark's charming children sled past a sign in the snow announcing "Christmas 1980." This is the eighth dated design in the Betsey Clark Series. Caption: "It's joy-in-the-air

time, love-everywhere time, good-fun-to-share time, it's Christmas. Christmas 1980."
▨ White Glass, 3¼" diam.
  400X215-4, $4.00

Betsey Clark

On a soft blue background, a Betsey Clark angel is kneeling in prayer with clasped hands. A banner beneath her carries the date. The angel is surrounded by embossed stars and a holly border, as are the captions on the back of the ornament. Captions: "Love came down at Christmas, Love all lovely, Love divine: Love was born at Christmas, Star and Angels gave the sign" and "Christmas 1980."
▨ Light Blue Cameo, 3⅜" diam.
  650QX307-4, $6.50

Betsey Clark's Christmas

A red shadow box trimmed in a white band with a red ribbon features a Betsey Clark girl in a three-dimensional snow scene. Caption: "1980."
▨ Handcrafted, 4" tall
  750X149-4, $7.50

PEANUTS®

SNOOPY sings as WOOD-STOCK and friends re-enact verses from a traditional Christmas carol. Caption: Four colly birds…three French hens…and a partridge in a pear tree. Christmas 1980."
■ White Satin, 3¼" diam.
400QX216-1, $4.00

Joan Walsh Anglund

The Anglund children are having an ice skating holiday. Caption: "Each and every bright December brings the best times to remember. Christmas 1980."
■ White Satin, 3¼" diam.
400QX217-4, $4.00

DISNEY

Front: Mickey and Minnie Mouse are ice skating. Back: Mickey plays Santa as he approaches a house to make a delivery. Caption: "Merry Christmas 1980."
■ White Satin, 3¼" diam.
400QX218-1, $4.00

Mary Hamilton

Two charming children are reflected in the glow of an old-fashioned candlelit Christmas tree. Caption: "Christmas—the warmest, brightest season of all. Christmas 1980."
■ Gold Glass, 3¼" diam.
400QX219-4, $4.00

Marty Links™

A little girl directs as a little boy and animals carol in the snow. Caption: "We wish you a Merry Christmas and a Happy New Year. Christmas 1980."
■ White Satin, 3¼" diam.
400QX221-4, $4.00

MUPPETS™

Front: KERMIT™ waves a greeting. Back: MUPPETS™ are merrily caroling. This design is the first of Jim Henson's MUPPETS™ to be a Hallmark Keepsake Ornament. Caption: "Merry Christmas 1980."
■ White Satin, 3¼" diam.
400QX220-1, $4.00

PEANUTS®, Joan Walsh Anglund, DISNEY

Mary Hamilton, Marty Links™, MUPPETS™

Decorative Ball Ornaments

Christmas Choir

Front: A country church is depicted. Back: Three black children, dressed in choir robes, sing. One is so small she stands on a stool. Caption: "Go tell it on the mountain…Jesus Christ is born! Christmas 1980."
■ Gold Glass, 3¼" diam.
400QX228-1, $4.00

Christmas Choir, Christmas Time, Nativity

Christmas Time

Front: A stagecoach is rolling along in the snow toward a timbered inn. Back: Depicted are a holly-sprigged top hat, a steaming mug of coffee, and the caption: "These are the days of merry-making, get-togethers, journey-taking, moments of delight and love that last in memory. Christmas 1980."
■ Ecru Soft-Sheen Satin, 3¼" diam. 400QX226-1, $4.00

Nativity

Animals and birds gather beside children kneeling in prayer at the Christ Child's manger. Caption: "Silent night…holy night…Christmas 1980."
■ Gold Glass, 3¼" diam. 400QX225-4, $4.00

Santa's Workshop

Front: Merry Santa wears a warm scarf and his traditional garb. Back: Santa checks his list at his North Pole workshop. Caption: "What merriment is all around when dear old Santa comes to town. Christmas 1980."
■ White Satin, 3¼" diam. 400QX223-4, $4.00

Happy Christmas

Front: A koala bear waters a potted tree. Back: The tree has magically grown into a "pear tree" of Christmas song with a small bird perched at the top. Caption: "Tis the season when hearts are glowing, love is growing, and happiness rounds out the year! Christmas 1980."
■ Ecru Soft-Sheen Satin, 3¼" diam. 400QX222-1, $4.00

Jolly Santa

Ice-skating Santa and reindeer spell out the season's greetings. Caption: "Merry Christmas. Christmas 1980."
■ White Glass, 3¼" diam. 400QX227-4, $4.00

Christmas Cardinals

Two cardinals perch on berry-laden branches of holly. Caption: "Nature at Christmas…a wonderland of wintry art. Christmas 1980."
■ White Glass, 3¼" diam. 400QX224-1, $4.00

Santa's Workshop, Happy Christmas, Jolly Santa, Christmas Cardinals

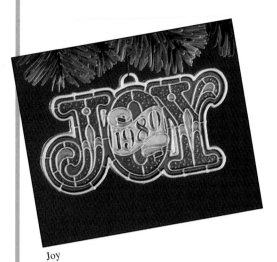

Joy

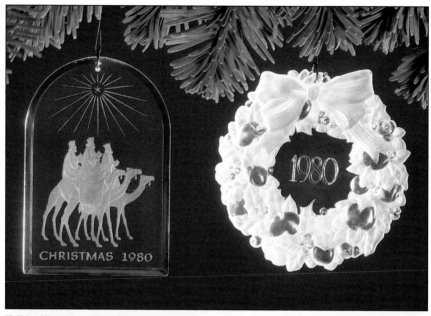

Holiday Highlights: Three Wise Men, Wreath

Colors of Christmas

Joy

Fashioned in rich colors with the look of leaded stained glass, this ornament was molded to spell "JOY." It has the year on a ribbon scroll over the "O." Caption: "Joy 1980."
▪ Acrylic, 4" tall
400QX350-1, $4.00

Holiday Highlights

Three Wise Men

Created with a hand-cut, etched-crystal look, this ornament shows the three wise men following the star to Bethlehem. Intricate detail shows their regal attire and gifts they are bearing. Caption: "Christmas 1980."
▪ Acrylic, 4" tall
400QX300-1, $4.00

Wreath

A wreath topped with a bow features etched-looking leaves and holly. Clear fruit and berries form a pleasing contrast. The date is stamped in silver foil in the center. Caption: "1980."
▪ Acrylic, 3¼" diam.
400QX301-4, $4.00

Frosted Images

Three new frosted images were introduced in the 1980 Collection of Hallmark Keepsake Ornaments. The acrylic ornaments have the

Frosted Images: Santa, Dove, Drummer Boy

appearance of delicate, frosted crystal. They range in size from 1⅞" to 2¼" tall and originally were $4.00 each.

■ 400QX310-1 Santa
    Artist: Sue Tague
■ 400QX309-4 Drummer Boy
    Artist: Sue Tague
■ 400QX308-1 Dove

Little Trimmers

Clothespin Soldier

A proud little soldier in the style of a clothespin is dressed in handpainted blue trousers, a red jacket with white trim, and a red hat.

■ Handcrafted, 2⁵⁄₁₆" tall
    350QX134-1, $3.50

Christmas Teddy

A small brown teddy bear has a smile painted on his face, a black painted outline around his ears and paws, and a red heart painted on his chest. He is made from dough-look material.

■ Handcrafted, 1¼" tall
    250QX135-4, $2.50

Merry Redbird

In a new format, Merry Redbird wears softly flocked "feathers" and carries a sprig of holly in his yellow bill.

■ Handcrafted, 1²⁷⁄₃₂" long
    350QX160-1, $3.50

Swingin' on a Star

A white mouse in a red-and-green striped cap with a brass bell swings on a brass star.

■ Handcrafted, 2⁵⁄₃₂" tall
    400QX130-1, $4.00
    Artist: Sue Tague

Christmas Owl

A Christmas owl cutie wearing a "Santa" cap clutches holly and berries in his beak while perching on a snowy tree stump.

■ Handcrafted, 1²⁷⁄₃₂" tall
    400QX131-4, $4.00

Thimble Series— A Christmas Salute

This is a reissue of the second design in the Thimble Series introduced in 1979. (See 1979 Annual Collection.)

■ Handcrafted, 2¼" tall
    400QX131-9, $4.00

Little Trimmers: Clothespin Soldier, Christmas Teddy, Merry Redbird, Swingin' on a Star, Christmas Owl

Handcrafted Ornaments

The Snowflake Swing

A green-clad angel swings merrily from a dainty star molded of clear acrylic.

■ Handcrafted, 3" tall
400QX133-4, $4.00
Artist: Sue Tague

Santa 1980

A snow-capped chimney represents the "1" in "1980," and Santa is making an entrance to a mouse's house below. A small mouse with an empty stocking awaits Santa's visit. This ornament is fashioned in dough-look material.

■ Handcrafted, 4½" tall
550QX146-1, $5.50
Artist: Sue Tague

Drummer Boy

This bread-dough design drummer boy has textured hair and is dressed in green with brown sandals and a stocking cap. His red drum is accented in gold. Caption: "1980."

■ Handcrafted, 3¾" tall
550QX147-4, $5.50
Artist: Donna Lee

Christmas Is for Children

This little girl in a swing with real motion is a reissue of a popular model introduced in 1979. (See 1979 Annual Collection.)

■ Handcrafted, 4¼" tall
550QX135-9, $5.50

A Christmas Treat

The teddy climbing a large candy cane is a reissue of a favorite in the 1979 line. (See 1979 Annual Collection.)

■ Handcrafted, 4¼" tall
550QX134-7, $5.50

Skating Snowman

Wearing a top hat, a real cloth scarf, and metal skates, this appealing snowman is a reissue of a 1979 ornament. (See 1979 Annual Collection.)

■ Handcrafted, 4¼" tall
550QX139-9, $5.50
Artist: Donna Lee

A Heavenly Nap

An angel dressed in blue is taking a nap on a crescent-shaped moon. There must be a man in the moon, for this frosted acrylic moon seems to be fast asleep in a nightcap with a gold star tassel.

■ Handcrafted, 3½" tall
650QX139-4, $6.50
Artist: Donna Lee

The Snowflake Swing, Santa 1980, Drummer Boy

A Heavenly Nap, Heavenly Sounds, Caroling Bear, Santa's Flight

The Animal's Christmas, A Spot of Christmas Cheer, Elfin Antics, A Christmas Vigil

Heavenly Sounds

Angels dressed in pink and blue produce "heavenly sounds" by ringing a gold metal bell. They twirl about in the center of a wood-look pink ring decorated with green scrolls. Caption: "1980."
- Handcrafted, 3³⁹⁄₆₄" tall
  750QX152-1, $7.50

Caroling Bear

A happy brown bear wearing a green-and-red striped scarf is singing a duet with a red bird perched on his arm. His green songbook carries the caption: "Carols 1980."
- Handcrafted, 3⅓³⁄₃₃" tall
  750QX140-1, $7.50
  Artist: Donna Lee

Santa's Flight

Santa gives up the sleigh and reindeer to make Christmas deliveries in a dirigible of pressed tin. The white dirigible, decorated in blue and gold, is festooned with a green garland tied in red ribbon. Santa rides in the strawlike tin basket. The propeller actually twirls around! Caption: "Merry Christmas 1980."
- Pressed Tin, 4" tall
  550QX138-1, $5.50
  Artist: Linda Sickman

The Animals' Christmas

A brown rabbit and a brown bird are decorating a snow-sprinkled Christmas tree.
- Handcrafted, 2³⁷⁄₆₄" tall
  800QX150-1, $8.00
  Artist: Donna Lee

A Spot of Christmas Cheer

Inside a plump teapot, a chipmunk busily trims a Christmas tree. On the outside, there is a window with shutters and a windowed door that has a golden doorknob and a 1980 "house number." Green garland with a perky red bow decorates this small "home." Caption: "1980."
- Handcrafted, 2⁴⁷⁄₆₄" tall
  800QX153-4, $8.00
  Artist: Donna Lee

Elfin Antics

Dressed in holiday colors, acrobatic elves are tumbling down from the Christmas tree branch and right into Christmas. The bottom elf is ringing a gold metal bell.
- Handcrafted, 4⁵⁄₁₆" tall
  900QX142-1, $9.00

A Christmas Vigil

A pajama-clad little boy and his dog peek out the bedroom window just in time to glimpse Santa and his reindeer flying through the sky on Christmas Eve.
- Handcrafted, 3¹³⁄₁₆" tall
  900QX144-1, $9.00
  Artist: Donna Lee

Special Editions

Heavenly Minstrel

A beautiful old-world angel with widespread wings is wearing a softly flowing blue dress, a beige stole trimmed in gold, and a turquoise ribbon in her hair. She is playing a celestial lute. Intricate details of this design make it exceptionally appealing.
- Handcrafted, 6¼" tall
  15QX156-7, $15.00
  Artist: Donna Lee

Checking It Twice

An elfin Santa with pointed ears is "checking his list" with real names printed on it. He is wearing spectacles of real metal, green elf-type shoes, red-and-white striped stockings, and suspendered red pants that end just below the knee. A ring of keys is caught in his belt loop.
- Handcrafted, 5¹⁵⁄₁₆" tall
  20QX158-4, $20.00
  Artist: Thomas Blackshear

Holiday Chimes

Snowflake Chimes
Three stamped snowflakes revolve as they hang suspended from a fourth snowflake.
▪ Chrome Plate, 1⁵⁹⁄₆₄" diam.
  550QX165-4, $5.50
  Artist: Linda Sickman

Santa Mobile
Santa with his sleigh and reindeer soar over three homes with smoking chimneys.
▪ Chrome Plate, 3⁵⁷⁄₆₄" tall
  550QX136-1, $5.50

Reindeer Chimes
Three reindeer prance as reflections twinkle and snowflakes chime softly. This is a reissue of a 1978 ornament. (See 1978 Annual Collection.)
▪ Chrome Plate, 5½" tall
  550QX320-3, $5.50
  Artist: Linda Sickman

Collectible Series

Norman Rockwell— First Edition
Norman Rockwell's famous "Santa's Visitors" is reproduced in white relief on a soft green background. This is sought by collectors of Norman Rockwell items as well as Christmas ornament collectors. Caption: "Santa's Visitors. The Norman Rockwell Collection, Christmas 1980."
▪ Light Green Cameo, 3⅜" diam.
  650QX306-1, $6.50

Frosty Friends—First Edition
A sweet Eskimo and polar bear are reading books with snowflakes on the covers while sitting on an ice-cube made of clear acrylic and etched with the caption. This is the first issue in the "Frosty Friends" Series. Caption: "Merry Christmas 1980."
▪ Handcrafted, 2⁶⁄₆₄" tall
  650QX137-4, $6.50

SNOOPY and Friends— Second Edition
SNOOPY and WOODSTOCK are on a ski holiday. Wearing a red and green stocking cap, SNOOPY does a slalom. Ahead of him, WOODSTOCK rides the slopes in SNOOPY's feeding bowl. Captions: "1980" and "SNOOPY."
▪ Handcrafted, 3¼" diam.
  900QX154-1, $9.00
  Artist: John Francis (Collin)

Holiday Chimes: Snowflake Chimes, Santa Mobile

Norman Rockwell, Frosty Friends

SNOOPY and Friends, Carousel, Thimble

Here Comes Santa, The Bellringers

Yarn Ornaments: Angel, Santa, Snowman, Soldier

Carrousel—Third Edition

The 1980 Carrousel shows Santa and his reindeer making their "rounds." The carrousel is banded with dots, circles, and flowers in red, white, green, and gold. The caption "Christmas 1980" is on top. This is third in the popular series.
◼ Handcrafted, 3⅛" tall
750QX141-4, $7.50

Thimble—Third Edition

A playful elf dressed in red and green swings on a thimble "bell" that hangs from a golden rope. This is the third design in the Thimble Series.
◼ Handcrafted, 2³¹⁄₃₂" tall
400QX132-1, $4.00
Artist: Sue Tague

Here Comes Santa—Second Edition

Santa steams into Christmas 1980 in an old-fashioned locomotive. In the look of iron, the locomotive is red and black, trimmed in gold. The wheels actually turn. Engineer Santa waves from the cab. This is the second design in this Collectible Series. Caption: "1980."
◼ Handcrafted, 3" tall
12QX143-4, $12.00

The Bellringers—Second Edition

Two blue-gowned angels, suspended from red-ribbon streamers at the top of the bell, ring the white porcelain bell with star "clappers" they are holding. This is the second in The Bellringers Series. Caption: "1980."
◼ Porcelain and Handcrafted, 2⅞₄" tall
15QX157-4, $15.00

Yarn and Fabric Ornaments

Yarn Ornaments

Four exquisitely detailed yarn ornaments were introduced in 1980. With accents of lace and felt, these offerings all are 5" tall and were originally priced at $3.00.
◼ 300QX162-1 Angel
◼ 300QX161-4 Santa
◼ 300QX163-4 Snowman
◼ 300QX164-1 Soldier

Sewn Trimmers

The four versatile family favorites in the 1979 line were reissued in 1980. (See 1979 Annual Collection for photograph and description.)

1979

Baby's First Christmas: Handcrafted

Two new commemorative ball ornaments called "Teacher" and "Special Friend" joined the greatly enlarged Hallmark Keepsake Ornament Collection in 1979.

By then, "Baby's First Christmas" satin ball ornaments had become solid sellers. In response to consumer demand, Hallmark expanded the "Baby's First Christmas" offering to include a handcrafted design in the form of a green-and-white knitted stocking, filled to overflowing with baby toys.

Three new collectible series were inaugurated this year—"The Bellringers," "Here Comes Santa," and "SNOOPY and Friends" panorama ball ornaments.

Ball ornaments were given new packages in 1979, and nearly 60 percent of the ornaments were dated.

Commemoratives

Baby's First Christmas
Front: Gifts for Baby ride a sleigh pulled by animals. Back: Baby's toys surround a Christmas tree being trimmed by birds. Caption: "Baby's First Christmas 1979."
◻ White Satin, 3¼" diam.
350QX208-7, $3.50

Baby's First Christmas
A real, green-and-white knitted stocking is filled with toys for Baby. This was the first handcrafted ornament to commemorate Baby's First Christmas. Caption: "Baby's First Christmas 1979."
◻ Handcrafted, 4" tall
800QX154-7, $8.00

Grandson
A stocking-capped SNOOPY and WOODSTOCK are snow-sledding. Caption: "A Grandson…a special someone whose merry ways bring extra joy to the holidays. Christmas 1979."
◻ White Satin, 3¼" diam.
350QX210-7, $3.50

Granddaughter
A warmly dressed girl feeds red birds, rabbits, and squirrels. Caption: "A Granddaughter fills each day with joy by filling hearts with love. 1979."
◻ White Satin, 3¼" diam.
350QX211-9, $3.50

Mother
White poinsettias and blossoms band this ornament. Caption: "It's love that makes Christmas so special—and Mother who makes us feel loved."
◻ White Glass, 3¼" diam.
350QX251-9, $3.50

Baby's First Christmas: Satin Ball

Grandson, Granddaughter, Mother, Grandmother

Grandmother

Little birds enjoy nectar from a basket of flowers. Captions: "Grandmothers bring happy times—time and time again" and "1979."
■ White Glass, 3¼" diam.
350QX252-7, $3.50

Our First Christmas Together

Golden wedding bells with bows and poinsettias with greenery are shown against a dark green background. Captions: "Our First Christmas Together 1979" and "Christmas and Love are for sharing."
■ Gold Glass, 3¼" diam.
350QX209-9, $3.50

Love

Light scrolling, white snowflakes, and red Gothic printing enhance a white background. Captions: "Love…warm as candleglow, wondrous as snowfall, welcome as Christmas" and "Christmas 1979."
■ White Glass, 3¼" diam.
350QX258-7, $3.50

Our Twenty-Fifth Anniversary

White satin ribbon entwines wedding bells, wedding rings, and a garland of Christmas greenery. Caption: "Year of our Twenty-Fifth Anniversary 1979. Those warm times shared in past Decembers…The mind still sees, the heart remembers."
■ White Glass, 3¼" diam.
350QX250-7. $3.50

Friendship

Front: Friends are skating on a large frozen pond beside an old mill. Back: A sleigh ride along a country road is shown. Captions: "There is no time quite like Christmas for remembering friendships we cherish" and "Christmas 1979."
■ White Glass, 3¼" diam.
350QX203-9, $3.50

New Home

This ornament displays a quaint painting of a snow-covered village, a covered bridge, and ice skaters. Captions: "Christmas…when love fills the heart, when hearts look to home" and "1979."
■ Ecru Soft-Sheen Satin, 3¼" diam.
350QX212-7, $3.50

Teacher

Front: A raccoon writes a message to teacher on a holiday-decorated blackboard. Back: A sleigh with a gift is being drawn toward a Christmas tree with white doves. Captions: "To a Special Teacher" and "Merry Christmas 1979."
■ White Satin, 3¼" diam.
350QX213-9, $3.50

First Christmas Together, Love, Twenty-Fifth Anniversary

Friendship, New Home, Teacher

Property Ornaments

Betsey Clark—Seventh Edition

Front: Miss Clark's children are sitting at home reading. Back: Standing in the snow, they hold a gift and pull a tree-laden sled. This is the seventh ornament in the series. Caption: "Holiday fun times make memories to treasure. 1979."

■ White Satin, 3¼" diam.
350QX201-9, $3.50

PEANUTS® (Time to Trim)

WOODSTOCK and his green-capped flock decorate a tree with candy canes SNOOPY gives them. Caption: "Merry Christmas 1979."

■ White Satin, 3¼" diam.
350QX202-7, $3.50

Spencer® Sparrow, Esq.

Spencer swings on a popcorn and cranberry garland and jauntily tips his hat. Captions: "Christmas time means decorating, spreading cheer and celebrating!" and "1979."

■ Ecru Soft-Sheen Satin 3¼" diam.
350QX200-7, $3.50

Joan Walsh Anglund

Front: The Anglund children hang their stockings on the fireplace. Back: A little girl opens her gift under a candlelit tree, while a little boy rides his new hobby horse. Caption: "The smallest pleasure is big enough to share. 1979."

■ White Satin, 3¼" diam.
350QX205-9, $3.50

Winnie-the-Pooh

Pooh's friends deliver "Hunny" to a very happy bear. This is a Walt Disney design. Caption: "Merry Christmas 1979."

■ White Satin, 3¼" diam.
350QX206-7, $3.50

Mary Hamilton

An angelic choir sings to an audience of forest friends. Captions: "...and heaven and nature sing" and "1979."

■ Ecru Soft-Sheen Satin, 3¼" diam.
350QX254-7, $3.50

Betsey Clark, PEANUTS®, Spencer® Sparrow, Esq.

Joan Walsh Anglund, Winnie-the-Pooh, Mary Hamilton

Night Before Christmas, Christmas Chickadees, Behold the Star

Decorative Ball Ornaments

Night Before Christmas

Front: A Christmas poem is illustrated with Santa preparing to fill "stockings hung by the chimney with care." Back: Santa continues his journey, concluding the poem. Captions: "…I heard him exclaim, ere he drove out of sight, Happy Christmas to all, and to all a good night–C.C. Moore" and "1979."
White Satin, 3¼" diam. 350QX214-7, $3.50

Christmas Chickadees

A pair of chickadees enjoy red berries on a holly branch. Two others frolic on a pine bough. Captions: "Beauty is a gift nature gives every day" and "Christmas 1979."
Gold Glass, 3¼" diam. 350QX204-7, $3.50

Behold the Star

The three wise men and shepherds with their flock follow the star to Bethlehem and the Child in a manger. Caption: "And the light was for all time"; "And the love was for all men."
White Satin, 3¼" diam. 350QX255-9, $3.50

Christmas Traditions

A jar of candy, basket of fruit, lantern with a glowing candle, kitchen scales, wooden toy, and an old mantel clock rest against a wood-paneled wall. Caption: "The old may be replaced with new, traditions rearranged, but the wonder that is Christmas will never ever change. 1979."
Gold Glass, 3¼" diam. 350QX253-9, $3.50
Artist: Linda Sickman

Christmas Collage

Old-fashioned toys and the caption are highlighted on a dark brown and blue, profusely decorated band reproduced from a photograph of a Schneeberg collage. Captions: "Season's Greetings" and "1979."
Gold Glass, 3¼" diam. 350QX257-9 $3.50

Christmas Traditions, Christmas Collage, Black Angel, Light of Christmas

Black Angel

Wearing a red and white robe, a young adult angel is shown in two scenes, utilizing contemporary photographic effects to illustrate the Christmas season's radiance. Caption: "Merry Christmas 1979."
Gold Glass, 3¼" diam. 350QX207-9, $3.50
Artist: Thomas Blackshear

The Light of Christmas

Reminiscent of Art Deco designs in stained glass, this red, orange, and green design encircles the caption on the back and frames three lighted candles and the year on the front. Caption: "There's no light as bright as Christmas to adorn and warm the night. 1979."
Chrome Glass, 3¼" diam. 350QX256-7, $3.50

Angel Delight, A Matchless Christmas

Holiday Highlights: Christmas Cheer, Love

Little Trimmer Collection

Angel Delight
Little angel, with white wings, a golden halo, and a light blue gown, sails in her walnut shell.
◻ Handcrafted, 1¼" tall
300QX130-7, $3.00
Artist: Sue Tague

A Matchless Christmas
A small white mouse has made a comfy bed in a half-opened matchbox. Wearing a red nightcap and lying on a white pillow with red stripes, he sleeps snugly under a blue-and-white checked blanket. This ornament easily clips onto the tree branch.
◻ Handcrafted, 2½" long
400QX132-7, $4.00

Thimble Series—Mouse
First in the Thimble Series introduced in 1978, the popular Thimble Mouse was reissued in 1979. (See 1978 Collection.)
◻ Handcrafted, 1¼" tall
300QX133-6, $3.00
Artist: Sue Tague

Santa
Santa, introduced in 1978, was reissued in 1979. (See 1978 Collection.)
◻ Handcrafted 2¼" tall
300QX135-6, $3.00
Artist: Sue Tague

Note: The Angel, Matchless Christmas, and Thimble also were packaged together as a trio of "Little Trimmers." (Not shown.)
◻ Handcrafted, 3 per box
900QX159-9, $9.00

Holiday Highlights

Christmas Cheer
A plump little bird with berries in its beak perches on a holly bough. Caption: "1979."
◻ Acrylic, 3½" diam.
350QX303-9, $3.50

Love
Beribboned flowers border a heart with a message in flowing script and stamped in silver foil. Caption: "Time of memories and dreams…Time of love. Christmas 1979."
◻ Acrylic, 3½" tall
350QX304-7, $3.50

Christmas Angel
A flying angel with an elegantly "etched" long floral dress, feathery wings, and a halo holds a nosegay. Worn over the shoulder and falling to her side, a ribbon carries the caption: "Christmas 1979."
◻ Acrylic, 4¼" wide
350QX300-7, $3.50

Snowflake
An exquisite snowflake has the date "etched" in the center of a hexagon. Caption: "1979."
◻ Acrylic, 3½" diam.
350QX301-9, $3.50

Christmas Tree
A perfectly shaped, "etched" tree of leaves and flowers highlights a lone dove near the top. On the top, in a halo effect, is "1979." The date is stamped in silver foil.
◻ Acrylic, 4½" tall
350QX302-7, $3.50

Colors of Christmas

Words of Christmas
A message forms a stained-glass look design in red, green, and gold. Caption: "The message of Christmas is love."
◻ Acrylic, 3¼" tall
350QX350-7, $3.50

Holiday Wreath
Decorated with colorfully designed ornaments and topped with a red bow, a wreath frames the red date caption: "1979."
◻ Acrylic, 3½" tall
350QX353-9, $3.50

Partridge in a Pear Tree
A richly colored partridge surrounded by golden pears and green leaves is the central focus of this design. Caption: "1979."
◻ Acrylic, 3¼" diam.
350QX351-9, $3.50

Star Over Bethlehem
Three shepherds and their flock behold the city of Bethlehem in the distance, brilliantly illuminated by the "Star."
◻ Acrylic, 3½" diam.
350QX352-7, $3.50
Artist: Linda Sickman

Holiday Highlights: Christmas Angel, Snowflake, Christmas Tree

Colors of Christmas: Words of Christmas, Holiday Wreath, Partridge in a Pear Tree, Star Over Bethlehem

Handcrafted Ornaments

Holiday Scrimshaw
An ivory angel with wings spread wide and hands clasped has a scrimshaw look. Caption: "Peace-Love-Joy 1979."
▦ Handcrafted, 3½" tall
400QX152-7, $4.00

Christmas Heart
Two doves rotate through the center of this heart-shaped ornament. The design looks like handcarved wood, with a raised floral motif highlighted by handpainting. Caption: "1979."
▦ Handcrafted, 3½" tall
650QX140-7, $6.50
Artist: Linda Sickman

Christmas Eve Surprise
A wood-look shadow box reveals a three-dimensional scene of a toy-laden Santa ready to go down the chimney. Caption: "1979."
▦ Handcrafted, 4¼" tall
650QX157-9, $6.50

Santa's Here
Santa is the center of attention as he twirls inside this snowflake. Caption: "1979."
▦ Handcrafted, 4" diam.
500QX138-7, $5.00
Artist: Linda Sickman

Holiday Scrimshaw, Christmas Heart, Christmas Eve Surprise, Santa's Here

Downhill Run, The Drummer Boy, Outdoor Fun

A Christmas Treat, The Skating Snowman, Christmas is for Children, Ready for Christmas

Raccoon

Mr. Raccoon, on real metal skates, leaves 1978 and goes into the 1979 Hallmark Keepsake Collection. This is a reissue. (See 1978 Annual Collection.)
■ Handcrafted, 2" tall
650QX142-3, $6.50
Artist: Donna Lee

The Downhill Run

Having fun making a fast downhill run on a red toboggan are a red-capped squirrel and a rabbit wearing a blue scarf.
■ Handcrafted, 3" tall
650QX145-9, $6.50
Artist: Donna Lee

The Drummer Boy

A drummer boy plays for a lamb and a duck while standing in the snow near a fence and a tree.
■ Handcrafted, 3¼" diam.
800QX143-9, $8.00

Outdoor Fun

In a snow scene, a young girl swings gently between two Christmas trees.
■ Handcrafted, 3" tall
800QX150-7, $8.00
Artist: Linda Sickman

A Christmas Treat

A teddy bear, wearing a red cap and jacket trimmed in white, tries climbing a large candy cane that hooks over a branch.
■ Handcrafted, 4¾" tall
500QX134-7, $5.00

The Skating Snowman

Wearing a green-and-white real cloth scarf, ice skates of real metal, and a black top hat, this snowman cuts a fancy figure.
■ Handcrafted, 4¼" tall
500QX139-9, $5.00
Artist: Donna Lee

Christmas is for Children

A green-bonneted little girl, clothed in a red dress and red-and-white stockings, swings with a white kitten. All look like handcarved wood.
■ Handcrafted, 4¼" tall
500QX135-9, $5.00

Ready for Christmas

With a sparkling, snow-covered roof and a door festooned in a red-bowed garland, this white birdhouse makes a cozy home for "Mr. and Mrs. Redbird."
■ Handcrafted, 3" tall
650QX133-9, $6.50
Artist: Donna Lee

Thimble, Carrousel

Collectible Series

Thimble— Second Edition

A soldier with epaulets on the shoulders of his red jacket wears blue trousers and a thimble "hat." His salute is left-handed.

- Handcrafted, 2¼" tall
  300QX131-9, $3.00
  Artist: Sue Tague

Carrousel— Second Edition

This second issue in the Carrousel Series has four angel musicians dressed in red, blue, deep-rose, and green revolving on a red, blue, and green carrousel. Caption: "Christmas 1979" twice around the carrousel's top.

- Handcrafted, 3½" tall
  650QX146-7, $6.50

SNOOPY and Friends— First Edition

SNOOPY and WOODSTOCK play ice hockey on a frozen pond. Caption: "1979."

- Handcrafted, 3¼" diam.
  800QX141-9, $8.00

Here Comes Santa— First Edition

Santa is waving his hand as he drives into the holidays in a vintage motorcar. The car is red trimmed in green with a look of real cast metal. The wheels turn, and the tires are black with golden spokes. Santa's green, toy-filled bag rests on the back of the car. Caption: "1979."

- Handcrafted, 3½" tall
  900QX155-9, $9.00

The Bellringers—First Edition

A merry elf swings on the clapper of a white porcelain bell decorated with a fired-on wreath decal. The bell's rim is hand-painted gold. The center of the wreath has the caption: "1979."

- Porcelain, Handcrafted, 4" tall
  10QX147-9 $10.00
  Artist: Sue Tague

SNOOPY and Friends, Here Comes Santa, The Bellringers

Sewn Trimmers: Stuffed Full Stocking, Merry Santa, Rocking Horse, Angel Music

Holiday Chimes: Reindeer Chimes, Star Chimes

Yarn and Fabric Ornaments

Sewn Trimmers

Featuring quilting and stitched edges, four new sewn designs were added in 1979. Ranging from 4" to 5" tall, they were $2.00 each.

▨ 200QX341-9   Stuffed Full Stocking
▨ 200QX342-7   Merry Santa
▨ 200QX340-7   Rocking Horse
▨ 200QX343-9   Angel Music

Yarn Ornaments

Four designs available in 1978 were offered in 1979. (See 1978 Annual Collection for photograph and description.)

Holiday Chimes

Reindeer Chimes

This ornament is a reissue from 1978. (See 1978 Annual Collection.)

▨ Chrome Plate, 5½" tall
450QX320-3, $4.50
Artist: Linda Sickman

Star Chimes

Stars within stars twirl to create dancing reflections. A solid center carries an impressed year date. Caption: "1979."

▨ Chrome Plate, 4" tall
450QX137-9, $4.50
Artist: Linda Sickman

1978

The Hallmark Keepsake Ornament Collection continued to gain popularity as collectibles when the 1978 line was introduced. This year, a design by Joan Walsh Anglund joined the other exclusive properties held by Hallmark.

The popular "Carrousel" collectible series began in 1978 with a dated merry-go-round of children's toys. Chrome-plated chimes were introduced in 1978, and Spencer® Sparrow, Esq. made his debut on ornaments. This was also the initial year of the "25th Christmas Together" ornament and the first year that ecru appeared as a color on soft-sheen satin ball ornaments. The smaller-sized ball ornaments made a final showing in 1978.

PEANUTS® Collection

PEANUTS®
SNOOPY and WOODSTOCK bring home their freshly cut tree and decorate it. Caption: "1978."
◼ White Satin, 2⅝" diam. 250QX204-3, $2.50

PEANUTS®
LINUS holds a dated wreath while the rest of the PEANUTS® gang sings. Caption: "Joy to the World 1978."
◼ White Satin, 3¼" diam. 350QX205-6, $3.50

PEANUTS®
On the front: SNOOPY, WOODSTOCK, and his flock are playing in a toy store. Back: SNOOPY plays Santa as he hangs a filled stocking on the mantel. Caption: "1978."
◼ White Satin, 3¼" diam. 350QX206-3, $3.50

PEANUTS®
WOODSTOCK wraps CHARLIE BROWN in Christmas lights as SNOOPY decorates his doghouse. Caption: "Have a delightful Christmas."
◼ White Satin, 2⅝" diam. 250QX203-6, $2.50

Commemoratives

First Christmas Together
Red hearts, fruits, flowers, greenery, and two red birds combine in a folk art design. Captions: "Sharing is the heart of loving" and "First Christmas Together 1978."
◼ White Satin, 3¼" diam. 350QX218-3, $3.50

25th Christmas Together
Front: Flowers entwine "25th Christmas Together," white doves, wedding bells, and "1953" and "1978." The back caption reads: "Time endears but cannot fade The memories that love has made."
◼ White Glass, 3¼" diam. 350QX269-6, $3.50

Love
Birds hover over a central heart motif, enclosing the year date. Poinsettias and berry-laden boughs complete the design. Captions: "Of life's many treasures, the most beautiful is love" and "1978."
◼ Gold Glass, 3¼" diam. 350QX268-3, $3.50

PEANUTS® Collection: SNOOPY and WOODSTOCK, Joy to the World, SNOOPY as Santa, A Delightful Christmas

First Christmas Together, Twenty-Fifth Christmas Together, Love

Baby's First Christmas, Granddaughter, Grandson

Grandmother, Mother, New Home

Grandmother
Deep red American Beauty roses and holly leaves cover a red background. Caption: "A Grandmother has a special way of bringing joy to every day."
◻ White Satin, 3¼" diam.
350QX267-6, $3.50

Mother
Blue flowers and snowflakes fill a silvery background. Captions: "The wonderful meaning of Christmas is found in a Mother's love" and "Christmas 1978."
◻ White Glass, 3¼" diam.
350QX266-3, $3.50

For Your New Home
A lighted window shows a wreath with a glowing candle. Captions: "Home…where the light of love shines brightest." and "Christmas 1978."
◻ White Satin, 3¼" diam.
350QX217-6, $3.50

Baby's First Christmas
Dressed in yellow, baby is on a blanket playing with a kitten and a stuffed teddy bear. Caption: "Baby's First Christmas 1978."
◻ White Satin, 3¼" diam.
350QX200-3, $3.50

Granddaughter
On a deep red background, an adorable girl decorates her Christmas tree. Caption: "A Granddaughter…never far from thought, ever near in love."
◻ White Satin, 3¼" diam.
350QX216-3, $3.50

Grandson
Raccoons are sledding, ice skating, and building a snowman. Caption: "A Grandson is loved in a special way for the special joy he brings."
◻ White Satin, 3¼" diam.
350QX215-6, $3.50

Property Ornaments

Betsey Clark—Sixth Edition
A little girl is at home wrapping a gift. Then, she is all dressed up and has delivered the present to a friend. This is the first ornament to use the new ecru soft-sheen satin. Captions: "The Christmas spirit seems to bring a cheerful glow to everything" and "1978."
■ Ecru Soft-Sheen Satin, 3¼"diam. 350QX201-6, $3.50

Joan Walsh Anglund
Front: Anglund children are caroling in the snow. Back: They are decorating a snow-covered tree. Caption: "As long as we have love and friends, Christmas never really ends 1978."
■ White Satin, 3¼" diam. 350QX221-6, $3.50

Spencer® Sparrow, Esq.
Front: Spencer® sits in a wreath. Back: Spencer® is pulling a sled loaded with gifts. Captions: "Holly days are jolly days" and "Christmas 1978."
■ Ecru Soft-Sheen Satin, 3¼" diam. 350QX219-6, $3.50

DISNEY
Disney characters ride a wooden train with Mickey Mouse dressed as Santa and ringing a bell. Dated "1978."
■ White Satin, 3¼" diam. 350QX207-6, $3.50

Decorative Ball Ornaments

Merry Christmas (Santa)
Front: Santa and his reindeer soar over rooftops on Christmas Eve. Back: A jolly Santa shoulders his pack. Captions: "Merry Christmas" and "1978."
■ White Satin, 3¼" diam. 350QX202-3, $3.50

Hallmark's Antique Card Collection Design
Bells, holly, and ornate lettering are reproduced from an antique card in Hallmark's Collection. Caption: "Christmas is a special time, a season set apart—a warm and glad remembering time, a season of the heart."
■ Ecru Soft-Sheen Satin, 3¼" diam. 350QX220-3, $3.50

Betsey Clark, Joan Walsh Anglund, Spencer® Sparrow, Esq., DISNEY

Merry Christmas, Antique Card, Yesterday's Toys, Nativity

The Quail, Drummer Boy, Joy

Holiday Highlights: Snowflake, Santa

Holiday Highlights: Dove, Nativity

Yesterday's Toys

Toys of yesterday circle the band of the ornament. Caption: "Every joy of yesterday is a memory for tomorrow. 1978."
■ Gold Glass, 3¼" diam.
350QX250-3, $3.50

Nativity

A beautiful old-world nativity scene is shown on a blue background. Caption: "The joy of heaven is come to earth."
■ White Glass, 3¼" diam.
350QX253-6, $3.50

The Quail

A magnificent quail is depicted in his habitat. Caption: "Nature has a wonderful way of making a wonder-filled world. 1978."
■ Gold Glass, 3¼" diam.
350QX251-6, $3.50

Drummer Boy

A boy kneels and taps his drum for the Christ Child resting in a manger. Sheep and geese sit behind him. Caption: "1978."
■ Gold Glass, 3¼" diam.
350QX252-3, $3.50

Joy

Front: The word "Joy," sprigged with holly, is incorporated in a leaded stained-glass effect oval. Back: A Christmas message is enclosed in a matching oval. Captions: "Joy" and "The beauty of Christmas shines all around us."
■ White Glass, 3¼" diam.
350QX254-3, $3.50

Holiday Highlights

In 1978, the elegant Holiday Highlights group featured four designs that looked like hand-cut crystal. Of unbreakable acrylic, they range from 2¹¹⁄₁₆" to 3⅝" tall and originally were priced at $3.50 each. The snowflake motif is dated.
■ 350QX308-3 Snowflake
■ 350QX307-6 Santa
■ 350QX310-3 Dove
■ 350QX309-6 Nativity
   Artist: Don Palmiter

Colors of Christmas: Merry Christmas, Locomotive, Angel, Candle

Colors of Christmas

Merry Christmas
A luscious oval Christmas ornament is colored red, green, yellow, and white. Caption: "Merry Christmas 1978."
◻ Acrylic, 4⅛" tall
350QX355-6, $3.50
Artist: Don Palmiter

Locomotive
A red train is artfully framed in blue, green, and yellow. Caption: "1978."
◻ Acrylic, 3¼" diam.
350QX356-3, $3.50

Angel
An angel wears a red dress and a golden halo, hair, and wings.
◻ Acrylic, 3⅝" tall
350QX354-3, $3.50

Candle
A lovely red candle with a glowing flame is banked with holly and berries.
◻ Acrylic, 3⅝" tall
350QX357-6, $3.50

Holiday Chimes

Reindeer Chimes
Three prancing reindeer suspended from a large snowflake create a glistening Christmas mobile. This was a new format for 1978.
◻ Chrome-plated Brass, 5½" tall
450QX320-3, $4.50
Artist: Linda Sickman

Handcrafted Ornaments

Dove
A majestic white dove twirls in the center of this white lacy snowflake. Caption: "1978."
◻ Handcrafted, 3⁵⁄₁₆" tall
450QX190-3, $4.50
Artist: Linda Sickman

Holly and Poinsettia Ball
A large ball that looks like an intricate hand-carving is circled with large poinsettias and holiday greenery.
◻ Handcrafted, 3½" diam.
600QX147-6, $6.00
Artist: Linda Sickman

Schneeberg Bell
This is an elegant reproduction of an intricate Schneeberg wood-carving collage. The design used eighty-two decorating processes to achieve a natural wood look. Caption: "Merry Christmas 1978."
◻ Handcrafted, 4" tall
800QX152-3, $8.00

Angels
Angels twirl about, merrily decorating a Christmas tree. Caption: "1978."
◻ Handcrafted, 3⅞" tall
800QX150-3, $8.00

Reindeer Chimes

Dove, Holly and Poinsettia Ball, Schneeberg Bell, Angels

Little Trimmers

Thimble Series—
First Edition

A little white mouse wearing a red cap peeks out of a silver-colored thimble. This was the first edition ornament in the Thimble Series.

■ Handcrafted, 1¾" tall
250QX133-6, $2.50
Artist: Sue Tague

Santa

Santa waves as he holds a gift wrapped in blue and tied in lovely red ribbon.

■ Handcrafted, 2¼" tall
250QX135-6, $2.50

Praying Angel

An angel in a pink gown with lacy cuffs kneels in prayer.

■ Handcrafted, 2" tall
250QX134-3, $2.50
Artist: Donna Lee

Drummer Boy

A drummer boy dressed in red, green, and blue beats his drum.

■ Handcrafted, 2⅟₁₆" tall
250QX136-3, $2.50

Little Trimmer
Collection

Thimble Mouse, Santa, Praying Angel, and Drummer Boy were offered as a boxed set. (Not shown)

■ Handcrafted, 4 per box
900QX132-3, $9.00

Thimble Series, Santa, Praying Angel, Drummer Boy

Carrousel Series

Carrousel Series—
First Edition
Handpainted in red, yellow,
blue, and green, a carrousel has
toys that spin around. Made in
the look of hand-carved wood,
this is the first model in the
Carrousel Series. Caption:
"Christmas 1978" is painted
around the top.
▨ Handcrafted, 3" tall
   600QX146-3, $6.00

Joy
Dressed in blue, a little elfin
boy pops through the center
letter "O" of the word "Joy."
Handpainted "bread dough"
letters are red and trimmed
with white.
▨ Handcrafted, 4¾6" tall
   450QX138-3, $4.50

Angel
Handcrafted, bread-dough look
barefoot angel is dressed in
white and blue and holds a star.
▨ Handcrafted, 2¹⁵⁄₁₆" tall
   450QX139-6, $4.50
   Artist: Donna Lee

Joy, Angel, Calico Mouse, Red Cardinal

Calico Mouse
A smiling red calico mouse with green ears and nose holds a sprig of green holly.
■ Handcrafted, 3¼₆" tall
450QX137-6, $4.50

Red Cardinal
This clip-on cardinal perches realistically on the branches of the Christmas tree.
■ Handcrafted, 4" tall
450QX144-3, $4.50
Artist: Duane Unruh

Panorama Ball
A little boy dressed in red has fallen on the ice after he skated a holiday greeting. In the snow-covered background are a fence and trees. View the scene through the white ornament's peek-through window. Caption: "Merry Christmas 1978" is skate-written on the pond.
■ Handcrafted, 3⅜" diam.
600QX145-6, $6.00

Skating Raccoon
Ice-skating raccoon wears red mittens, a red scarf, and real metal skates.
■ Handcrafted, 2¼" tall
600QX142-3, $6.00
Artist: Donna Lee

Rocking Horse
With a flying, white-yarn mane and red rockers, this handpainted, polka-dot horse has the appearance of hand-carved wood. Caption: "1978."
■ Handcrafted, 3¼₆" tall
600QX148-3, $6.00

Animal Home
A family of mice has taken residence in a little mushroom with red-shuttered windows, a garlanded doorway, and stone steps. Mr. Mouse is in the doorway, and Mrs. Mouse is inside.
■ Handcrafted, 2¼₆" tall
600QX149-6, $6.00
Artist: Donna Lee

Yarn Collection
The collection of four Yarn ornaments for 1978 are all 4½" tall. They were individually packaged and originally priced at $2.00.
■ 200QX125-1   Mrs. Claus
■ 200QX340-3   Mr. Claus
■ 200QX123-1   Green Boy
■ 200QX126-1   Green Girl

Top Photo: Panorama Ball, Skating Raccoon, Rocking Horse, Animal Home

Bottom Photo: Yarn Collection: Mrs. Claus, Mr. Claus, Green Boy, Green Girl

1977

The year 1977 was one of tremendous expansion for the Hallmark Keepsake Ornament Collection. Three new ornament formats—sewn ornaments with silk-screened designs, acrylic ornaments, and ornaments with the look of stained glass—were introduced. A new decorative cap, with a design exclusive to Hallmark, appeared on glass ball ornaments, and two new colors—gold and chrome—appeared for the first time in the glass ball ornament line.

New commemorative ornaments for "Granddaughter," "Grandmother," "Mother," "Love," "Grandson," and "New Home" were offered. This was the only year Hallmark offered die-cast metal snowflakes and ball ornaments with regional scenes .

This year's "Betsey Clark" ball ornament (350QX264-2) is especially hard to find. Initially, Hallmark decided not to offer a Betsey Clark ornament in 1977. Consumer demand was high, however, and the ornament was quickly offered to retailers in August. Due to the delay in production, only a fraction of the normal quantity was distributed.

Grandson
Santa and toys frolic among snowflakes on a deep blue background. Caption: "A Grandson is …a joy bringer…a memory maker…a Grandson is love."
■ White Satin 3½" diam. 350QX209-5, $3.50

Granddaughter
A little girl skates on a pond flanked by trees. Caption: "A Granddaughter is a gift whose worth cannot be measured except by the heart."
■ White Satin, 3¼" diam. 350QX208-2, $3.50

Mother
A motif of pink roses and green holly circle a white glass globe. Caption: "In a Mother's heart, there is love…the very heart of Christmas."
■ White Glass, 3¼" diam. 350QX261-5, $3.50

Grandmother
A bordered band encloses a basket of lovely Christmas flowers. Caption: "Grandmother is another word for love."
■ Gold Glass, 3¼" diam. 350QX260-2, $3.50

Mother

Grandmother

Baby's First Christmas, Grandson, Granddaughter

Commemoratives

Baby's First Christmas
A baby is surrounded by toys and is hugging a stuffed bear. Captions: "Baby's First Christmas" and "1977."
■ White Satin, 3¼" diam. 350QX131-5, $3.50

First Christmas Together, Love, New Home

Currier and Ives, Charmers, Norman Rockwell

First Christmas Together

Front: A beautiful Christmas-red background with a white circle inset shows two cardinals perched on bare branches. Back: The date and caption are printed in gold. Captions: "1977" and "Our First Christmas Together."
■ White Satin, 3¼" diam.
350QX132-2, $3.50

Love

A stained-glass window-look incorporates "Christmas 1977." Caption: "Love is a golden gift…cherished above all life's treasures."
■ Gold Glass, 3¼" diam.
350QX262-2 $3.50

For Your New Home

Front: A holiday-decorated red house has a 1977 "doormat," patchwork flowers, and a checkered border. Back: Patchwork flowers and a large red heart enclose the caption. Caption: "Christmas fills a home with warmth and love…and memories that last forever."
■ Gold Glass, 3¼" diam.
350QX263-5, $3.50

Property Ornaments

Currier & Ives

Shows the Currier & Ives paintings "The Old Grist Mill" and "Trotting Cracks on the Snow." Caption: "1977."
■ White Satin, 3¼" diam.
350QX130-2, $3.50

Charmers

Flowers and greenery surround four little children caroling. Caption: "We wish you a Merry Christmas. 1977."
■ Gold Glass, 3¼" diam.
350QX153-5, $3.50

Norman Rockwell

Four favorite Rockwell designs of Christmas activities are reproduced in separate panels. Caption: "Christmas 1977."
■ White Glass, 3¼" diam.
350QX151-5, $3.50

Betsey Clark

DISNEY: Satin Ball, Set of Two

Betsey Clark—
Fifth Edition

By popular demand, the 1977 Betsey Clark ornament was added to the line at the last minute. This design is particularly scarce due to a limited production run. Front: Three carolers sing from a songbook. Back: A little girl feeds the birds. Captions: "The truest joys of Christmas come from deep inside" and "Christmas 1977."
■ White Glass, 3¼" diam. 350QX264-2, $3.50

DISNEY

Mickey's head, framed by a wreath, is flanked by Donald Duck and Goofy. Caption: "Merry Christmas 1977."
■ White Satin, 3¼" diam. 350QX133-5, $3.50

DISNEY

Design 1: Mickey Mouse in a Santa suit gives Minnie Mouse her Christmas gift. Caption: "Merry Christmas." Design 2: Donald Duck pulls Huey, Luey, and Duey on a present-laden sled. Caption: "Happy Holidays."
■ White Satin, 2¼" diam. 400QX137-5, 2 per box $4.00

PEANUTS® Collection

In 1977, the PEANUTS® gang from Charles Schulz's world-famous cartoon strip was introduced by Hallmark as exclusive additions to the Keepsake Ornament line. Glass and satin ornaments were cleverly packaged in SNOOPY's Christmas-decorated doghouse.

PEANUTS®

Front: CHARLIE BROWN and SALLY watch the empty stockings hanging from the fireplace. Back: SCHROEDER plays the piano as LUCY presents him with a gift. Captions: "A watched stocking never fills" and "Merry Christmas."
■ White Glass, 2⅝'' diam. 250QX162-2, $2.50

PEANUTS®

On one side, SNOOPY is tangled in Christmas tree lights while WOODSTOCK, dressed as Santa, stands on a gift. Both are watching the Christmas tree. On the other side, CHARLIE BROWN and LUCY have built a snowman who holds a snow shovel. Caption: "1977."
■ White Satin, 3¼" diam. 350QX135-5, $3.50

PEANUTS®

Design 1: CHARLIE BROWN, LINUS, WOODSTOCK, SNOOPY, and PEPPERMINT PATTY are building a snowman, having a snowball fight, and ice skating. Design 2: SNOOPY, as Santa, is being pulled in the sleigh by WOODSTOCK and his flock.
■ White Glass, 2¼" diam. 400QX163-5, 2 per box $4.00

Grandma Moses

Two beautiful New England village snow scenes from the Grandma Moses paintings "Sugartime" and "Green Sleigh" are shown. A pamphlet giving the history of Grandma Moses and her beloved paintings was included with each gift-packaged ornament.
■ White Glass, 3¼" diam. 350QX150-2, $3.50

PEANUTS®: Glass Ball, Satin Ball, Set of Two

Grandma Moses (Shown with enclosure card)

Christmas Expressions Collection: Bell, Ornaments, Mandolin, Wreath

The Beauty of America Collection: Mountains, Desert, Seashore, Wharf

Christmas Expressions Collection

Bell
A beautifully decorated bell is blanketed with flowers and festooned with ribbons. Caption: "I heard the bells on Christmas Day/ Their old familiar carols play/ And wild and sweet, the words repeat/ Of peace on earth, good will to men. Henry Wadsworth Longfellow."
◻ White Glass, 3¼" diam.
350QX154-2, $3.50

Ornaments
This banded ornament has a beautiful array of Christmas ornaments with evergreens, ribbons, and bows. Caption: "The spirit of Christmas is peace…the message of Christmas is love. Marjorie Frances Ames."
◻ White Glass, 3¼" diam.
350QX155-5, $3.50

Mandolin
A mandolin and horns are nestled among Christmas greenery. Caption: "Sing a song of seasons; Something bright in all…Robert Louis Stevenson."
◻ White Glass, 3¼" diam.
350QX157-5, $3.50

Wreath
A magnificent green wreath is bedecked with colorful ribbons and bows. Caption: "Christmas is a special time. / A season set apart— / A warm and glad remembering time, / A season of the heart. Thomas Malloy."
◻ White Glass, 3¼" diam.
350QX156-2, $3.50

The Beauty of America Collection

Mountains
Majestic snowcapped mountains surround a valley of snow-covered homes. Caption: "The spirit of Christmas is peace…the message of Christmas is love."
◻ White Glass, 2⅝" diam.
250QX158-2, $2.50

Desert
A desert mission sits below a sky streaked with a golden sunset. Caption: "Ring out Christmas Bells…and let all the world hear your joyful song."
◻ White Glass, 2⅝" diam.
250QX159-5, $2.50

Seashore
Palm trees share a sandy shore with blue skies and a sailboat regatta. Caption: "Christmas is—the company of good friends, the warmth of goodwill, and the memory of good times."
◻ White Glass, 2⅝" diam.
250QX160-2, $2.50

Wharf
Front: Tranquil winter scene shows homes near the wharf. Back: A lighthouse is glimpsed from the oceanside. Caption: "Christmas…when the world stands silent and the spirit of hope touches every heart."
◻ White Glass, 2⅝" diam.
250QX161-5, $2.50

Decorative Ball Ornaments

Rabbit
A rabbit is engrossed with a little bird on a broken tree limb. Caption: "Nature's everchanging beauty brings never-ending joy. Karl Lawrence."
◻ White Satin, 2⅝" diam.
250QX139-5, $2.50

Squirrel
A little squirrel seems to be lucky—he has found food in the snow. A cardinal watches. Caption: "Each moment of the year has its own beauty …Emerson."
◻ White Satin, 2⅝" diam.
250QX138-2, $2.50

Christmas Mouse
On a soft blue background, Mr. and Mrs. Mouse add the finishing touches to their Christmas tree. Caption: "Tinsel and lights make the season so bright."
◻ White Satin, 3¼" diam.
350QX134-2, $3.50

Stained Glass
This sleeve design looks like Art Deco stained glass. The caption reads: "Merry Christmas 1977."
◻ Chrome Glass, 3¼" diam.
350QX152-2, $3.50

Rabbit, Squirrel

Christmas Mouse, Stained Glass

Holiday Highlights Collection

A collection of four unbreakable, clear acrylic ornaments, with a hand-engraved crystal look, feature scenes and messages reflecting traditional Christmas sentiments.

Joy

Letters spell "JOY." The "O" is filled with fruit. The background has delicate scrolling. Caption: "JOY 1977."
◾ Acrylic, 3¼" diam.
350QX310-2, $3.50

Peace on Earth

A snug village scene shows snow-covered houses, pine trees, and a church with its spire reaching for the moonlit sky. Caption: "Peace on earth, good will toward men. 1977."
◾ Acrylic, 3¼" diam.
350QX311-5, $3.50

Drummer Boy

A drummer boy marches as he beats the drum. Caption: "Rumpa-pum-pum" repeated four times around the border.
◾ Acrylic, 3¼" diam.
350QX312-2, $3.50

Star

The star at the top casts etched beams of light that radiate over the ornament's surface. Caption: "Once for a shining hour heaven touched earth."
◾ Acrylic, 3¼" diam.
350QX313-5, $3.50

Colors of Christmas: Bell, Candle, Joy, Wreath

Colors of Christmas

Stained Glass Look

Four designs with the jeweled colors of leaded stained glass were introduced to the line in 1977. Made of acrylic, each measures 3¼" in diameter. Originally, they were priced $3.50 each. Except for the bell, all bear the year date, 1977.
◾ 350QX200-2 Bell
  Artist: Linda Sickman
◾ 350QX203-5 Candle
◾ 350QX201-5 Joy
◾ 350QX202-2 Wreath

Holiday Highlights: Joy, Peace, Drummer Boy, Star

Snowflake Collection

Twirl-About Collection: Snowman, Weather House, Bellringer, Della Robia Wreath

Metal Ornaments

Snowflake Collection

A set of four 2⅛" snowflakes, die-cast in lightweight, chrome-plated zinc, were cleverly packaged in a peek-through gift box accompanied by its own mailing box. This is the only year the snowflake set was offered.

▪ Chrome-plated Zinc, 2⅛" diam.
500QX210-2, 4 per box $5.00
Artist: Linda Sickman

Twirl-About Collection

Snowman

Three-dimensional snowflake has a snowman that rotates in the center. The snowman wears a handpainted rakish hat, a red scarf around his neck, and a happy smile. Caption: "1977."

▪ Handcrafted, 3¾" tall
450QX190-2, $4.50
Artist: Linda Sickman

Weather House

A timbered house with a red-orange roof, double doorways, and shuttered window has a handpainted hearts-and-flowers trim. A Swiss-clad boy and girl pair rotate in and out of the doorways. Caption: "1977."

▪ Handcrafted, 3¹⁵⁄₁₆" tall
600QX191-5, $6.00

Bellringer

A little boy strikes a bell as he rotates inside an arched gate, scrolled at the top and decorated on each side with large red bows. A sleigh full of toys and a dog are outside the gate.

▪ Handcrafted, 3¹¹⁄₁₆" tall
600QX192-2, $6.00

Della Robia Wreath

A little girl, kneeling in prayer, twirls in the center of a traditional Della Robia wreath. Caption: "1977."

▪ Handcrafted, 3³⁄₁₆" tall
450QX193-5, $4.50
Artist: Donna Lee

Nostalgia Collection: Angel, Toys, Antique Car, Nativity

Nostalgia Collection

The Nostalgia Collection is intricately molded and handpainted to create ring-shaped designs with a wooden, antique look. Individual packages included a gift tag.

Angel

A wide outer ring carries a caption, flowers, and symbols. It has a natural hand-carved look. In the center is a flying angel dressed in blue and blowing a horn. Caption: "Peace On Earth" and "Good Will Toward Men"
■ Handcrafted, 3¼" diam.
  500QX182-2, $5.00
  Artist: Donna Lee

Toys

A jack-in-the-box, steaming locomotive, and a toy soldier occupy the center of a red and yellow ring. Caption: "1977."
■ Handcrafted 3¼" diam.
  500QX183-5, $5.00
  Artist: Linda Sickman

Antique Car

A green antique car, trimmed in red and yellow and with a rumble seat filled with gifts, forms the center design. Caption: "Season's Greetings 1977."
■ Handcrafted, 3¼" diam.
  500QX180-2, $5.00
  Artist: Linda Sickman

Nativity

The center of the ring has a star-topped stable, sheltering the Holy Family and animals. Caption: "O Come, Let Us Adore Him."
■ Handcrafted, 3¼" diam.
  500QX181-5, $5.00

Yesteryears Collection

Angel
A smiling angel with arms out-stretched is handpainted in a gay, folk-art style. Caption: "Joy To The World 1977."
▧ Handcrafted, 3½" tall
600QX172-2, $6.00

Jack-in-the-Box
Handpainted in green, blue, and red, Jack springs from a red and pink box. The ornament captures the look of an antique, hand-carved wooden toy. Caption: "Merry Christmas 1977."
▧ Handcrafted, 3¹³⁄₁₆'' tall
600QX171-5, $6.00

House
A handpainted cottage has a red roof and windows with painted shutters. Christmas trees flank a fanlighted door. Caption: "Happy Holidays 1977."
▧ Handcrafted, 3¹¹⁄₁₆'' tall
600QX170-2, $6.00

Reindeer
A reindeer on wheels sports the nostalgic look of a handpainted child's toy. Caption: "1977."
▧ Handcrafted, 4¼" tall
600QX173-5, $6.00

Cloth Doll Ornaments

These two designs were the first to be made from silk-screened cloth. The cloth was stuffed and then quilted.

Angel
A sweet angel has her wings spread. The wings are quilted, and there is lace edging on the bottom of her dress.
▧ Cloth, 4" tall
175QX220-2, $1.75

Santa
Plump and jolly, Santa is "laying a finger beside his nose." A jingle bell is attached to his hat.
▧ Cloth, 4" tall
175QX221-5, $1.75

Yesteryears Collection: Angel, Jack-in-the-Box, House, Reindeer

Cloth Doll Ornaments: Angel, Santa

1976

The first Baby's First Christmas Commemorative

In 1976, Hallmark added a fourth dimension to its handcrafted ornament offerings—movement. Called "Twirl-Abouts," the unique ornaments had a three-dimensional figure in the center that rotated on a brass pin. Three of the four different "Twirl-About" designs were dated.

To mark the bicentennial year, Hallmark also offered a commemorative ornament. The glass ball ornament featured Hallmark "Charmers" characters in 1776 dress. It retailed for $2.50.

Also in 1976, Hallmark introduced the "Baby's First Christmas" ornament. This personalized design grew to be the most popular captioned ornament in the Keepsake line.

First Commemorative Ornament

Baby's First Christmas

The original Baby's First Christmas ornament, designed to commemorate the birth of babies born in 1976, was a record best-seller and introduced a new Christmas tradition to many families. Front: Animals and birds are placing gifts for baby under the decorated tree. Caption: "Baby's First Christmas." Back: Animals and birds visit smiling baby. Caption: "1976."

■ White Satin, 3" diam.
250QX211-1, $2.50

Bicentennial Commemoratives: Bicentennial '76 Commemorative, Bicentennial Charmers; Colonial Children, Set of Two

Bicentennial Commemoratives

Bicentennial '76 Commemorative

Charmers, dressed in the fashions of Christmas 1776, grace the Hallmark Bicentennial special commemorative ornament. Both the ornament and its package are marked "1976 Commemorative."
- White Satin, 3" diam.
  250QX203-1, $2.50

Bicentennial Charmers

Front: Three Charmers in colonial costume admire a Christmas tree in front of their log cabin homes. Back: A girl Charmer gathers holly leaves. Caption: "Merry Christmas 1976."
- White Glass, 3¼" diam.
  300QX198-1, $3.00

Colonial Children

First design, front: A group of colonial children bring home a Christmas tree. Back: "Merry Christmas 1976" is enhanced by a garland, a Christmas tree, and a squirrel. Second design, front: A boy and girl in colonial clothing dress their snowman. Back: A garland, bird, flag, and "Christmas 1976" are featured.
- White Glass, 2¼" diam.
  400QX208-1, 2 per box $4.00

Property Ornaments

Betsey Clark— Fourth Edition

Front: Two little bonnet-clad and dressed-up girls are framed by a circle of flowers and ribbon. Back: Depicted is a wintry scene of snow-covered homes in a countryside setting. Caption: "Christmas 1976." This is the fourth in the Betsey Clark series.
- White Glass, 3¼" diam.
  300QX195-1, $3.00

Betsey Clark: Glass Ball, Satin Ball, Set of Three

Betsey Clark

Front: A little girl warms herself at a potbellied stove. Back: "Christmas 1976."
- White Satin, 3" diam.
  250QX210-1, $2.50

Betsey Clark

The three front designs include a duet of children playing music, a little girl snow skiing, and Santa and a little girl caroling. All are dated on the back.
- White Satin, 2" diam.
  450QX218-1, 3 per box, $4.50

Currier & Ives

Front: A horse-drawn sleigh joins skaters on a pond in front of a snow-covered colonial house. Back: A farmyard in winter is shown. Caption: "To Commemorate Christmas 1976."
- White Satin, 3" diam. 250QX209-1, $2.50

Currier & Ives

Two scenes are named "American Winter Scene" and "Winter Pastime." Caption: "To Commemorate Christmas 1976."
- White Glass, 3¼" diam. 300QX197-1, $3.00

Rudolph and Santa

Front: Rudolph with his "nose so bright" frolics in the snow as Santa watches. Caption: "Rudolph, the Red-Nosed Reindeer." Back: A green garland and "Christmas 1976" are shown.
- White Satin, 2½" diam. 250QX213-1, $2.50

Norman Rockwell

Front: Santa recuperates from his travels; it's "December 25." Back: Santa feeds his reindeer. Caption: "Christmas 1976."
- White Glass, 3¼" diam. 300QX196-1, $3.00

Raggedy Ann™

Front: Raggedy Ann™ is hanging stockings on the decorated mantel of a glowing fireplace. Back: The stockings are filled, toys from Santa surround the fireplace, and "Merry Christmas 1976" is across the top.
- White Satin, 2½" diam. 250X212-1, $2.50

Currier and Ives: Satin Ball, Glass Ball

Rudolph and Santa, Norman Rockwell, Raggedy Ann™

Marty Links™, Happy the Snowman, Charmers

Chickadees, Cardinals

Marty Links™

First design, front: "Stockings are hung by the chimney with care," is written, and a mouse is "sh-sh-ed" quiet. Back: A bow-topped holly wreath has "Noel 1976" in the center. Second design, front: A smiling girl dressed in red places a gift under the tree. Back: A red ball ornament displays "Merry Christmas 1976."

■ White glass, 2½" diam.
   400QX207-1, 2 per box $4.00

Happy the Snowman

First design, front: On a dark green background, Happy the Snowman enjoys the red birds and snowflakes around him. Back: Two Happy Snowmen join the words, "Happy Holidays." Second design, front: There are three snowmen, snowflakes, and holly. Back: One of three Happy Snowmen holds a "Merry Christmas" banner.

■ White Satin, 2½" diam.
   350QX216-1, 2 per box $3.50

Charmers

First design, front: A boy watches his reflection in a pool. Second design, front: A little Charmer prepares holiday food over a glowing campfire. Both are captioned "Christmas 1976."

■ White Satin, 2½" diam.
   350QX215-1, 2 per box $3.50

Decorative Ball Ornaments

Chickadees

Front: Two chickadees are perching on a bough. Back: One bird is perching on a bough. Caption: "Christmas 1976."

■ White Glass, 2⅝" diam.
   225QX204-1, $2.25

Cardinals

Front: Two cardinals nest quiet-ly. Back: One cardinal rests on a spray of evergreen. Caption: "Christmas 1976."

■ White Glass, 2⅝" diam.
   225QX205-1. $2.25

Yesteryears Ornaments: Santa, Partridge, Train, Drummer Boy

Twirl-About Handcrafted Ornaments: Angel, Santa, Partridge, Soldier

Handcrafted Ornaments

Yesteryears

These four, three-dimensional ornaments in "wood-look" designs are intricately hand-painted to enhance their old-world character. Newly designed packaging includes a gift tag with each ornament. Each ornament is dated and was priced originally at $5.00. Sizes vary from 2¾" to 4" tall.

- 500QX182-1   Santa
- 500QX183-1   Partridge
- 500QX181-1   Train
- 500QX184-1   Drummer Boy

Twirl-Abouts

Twirl-Abouts—three-dimensional ornaments centered with rotating figures on a brass pin—were introduced in 1976. Hand-painted, they are highly sought by collectors. Ranging from 3½" to 4" tall, all were priced at $4.50. The angel, partridge, and soldier bear year dates.

- 450QX171-1   Angel
- 450QX172-1   Santa
- 450QX174-1   Partridge
- 450QX173-1   Soldier
  Artist: Linda Sickman (all)

Tree Treats

Tree treats that look good enough to eat were new in 1976. Four ornaments of material resembling baker's dough are another choice for variety and spice in Christmas tree decorations. Tree Treats vary in size from 2¾" to 3⅜" tall. They were priced at $3.00. Shepherd and Santa captions: "Season's Greetings 1976." Angel and Reindeer captions: "Merry Christmas 1976."

- 300QX175-1   Shepherd
- 300QX177-1   Santa
  Artist: Sue Tague
- 300QX176-1   Angel
- 300QX178-1   Reindeer

Tree Treats: Shepherd, Santa, Angel, Reindeer

Nostalgia Ornaments: Drummer Boy, Rocking Horse, Locomotive, Peace On Earth

Nostalgia Ornaments

The four reissues of the extremely popular Nostalgia Ornaments introduced the previous year had slight design modifications. Locomotive and Peace on Earth were captioned: "Christmas 1976."

- 400QX130-1   Drummer Boy
- 400QX128-1   Rocking Horse
- 400QX222-1   Locomotive
- 400QX223-1   Peace on Earth
  Artist: Linda Sickman (all)

Yarn Ornaments

This merry group of six returned in 1976 with very minor changes. All are 4½" tall and were individually packaged and priced at $1.75 . (See 1975 Annual Collection.)

- 175QX123-1   Drummer Boy
- 175QX122-1   Raggedy Andy™
- 175QX121-1   Raggedy Ann™
- 175QX126-1   Caroler
- 175QX124-1   Santa
- 175QX125-1   Mrs. Santa

Hallmark

1975

Betsey Clark: Satin Ball, Glass Ball

In 1975, Hallmark expanded its Christmas ornament line to thirty-two models and introduced two new design formats: decorated satin ball ornaments and handcrafted ornaments. Two handcrafted groupings were offered: figurines called "Adorable Adornments" and "Handcrafted Nostalgia Ornaments."

The new satin ball ornaments featured a decorated band. Both of the handcrafted groups were made of sturdy, molded material and were individually handpainted. The colorful figurines had lively expressions, and the "Nostalgia" collection was distinguished by its antique wood-look. "Raggedy Ann™" and "Raggedy Andy™" were added to the "Yarn Ornaments" collection during this year.

Property Ornaments

Betsey Clark
Four different scenes of Betsey Clark children and the animals and birds associated with Christmas adorn fronts of this set. The ornament backs are dated "Christmas 1975."
◼ White Satin, 2" diam.
450QX168-1, 4 per box $4.50

Betsey Clark
These paired motifs show a stocking-capped little girl on one ornament and two struggling young skaters on the other. On the backs of both, "Christmas 1975" is surrounded by stars.
◼ White Satin, 2½" diam.
350QX167-1, 2 per box $3.50

Betsey Clark
A sweet-looking, pajama-clad toddler, framed by a ring of stars, says bedtime prayers. Caption: "1975."
◼ White Satin, 3" diam.
250QX163-1, $2.50

Betsey Clark— Third Edition
Front: Three little girls dressed in pink, blue, and yellow calico are singing from a songbook they are holding. Back: The front of the book is shown with "Christmas 1975" on the cover. This is the third ornament featured in the Betsey Clark series.
◼ White Glass, 3¼" diam.
300QX133-1, $3.00

Currier & Ives
A panoramic snow scene of a farmhouse and buildings is showcased on white satin.
◼ White Satin, 3" diam.
250QX164-1, $2.50

Currier & Ives
Two Currier & Ives winter scenes are shown on this boxed pair; one of an old mill, the other of a merry group of Victorian ice skaters.
◼ White Glass, 2¼"diam.
400QX137-1, 2 per box $4.00

Betsey Clark: Set of Four, Set of Two

Currier and Ives: Satin Ball, Set of Two

Raggedy Ann™ and Raggedy Andy™ Set of Two, Raggedy Ann™ Satin Ball

Norman Rockwell: Satin Ball, Glass Ball

Charmers, Marty Links™

Raggedy Ann™ and Raggedy Andy™

Front: The colorful pair are seated side-by-side in a green wreath which is tied at the top with a red bow. Back: They hold a "Merry Christmas" banner. On the second ornament, front: They decorate their Christmas tree. Back: A garland of holly leaves circles "Christmas 1975."
◼ White Glass, 2¼" diam.
  400QX138-1, 2 per box $4.00

Raggedy Ann™

Front: Raggedy Ann™ sits in a ring of poinsettias. Caption on the back: "Christmas 1975" is circled by poinsettias.
◼ White Satin, 3" diam.
  250QX165-1, $2.50

Norman Rockwell

Front: Santa writes in the "Good Boys" book while checking on them through a telescope. Back: Santa enters a home, emerging from the fireplace with his bag of toys.
◼ White Satin, 3" diam.
  250QX166-1, $2.50

Norman Rockwell

Front: Two small boys are asleep in a wingback chair as Santa peeks from behind. Back: Youngster kneels at his bed to say a good-night prayer. Caption: "1975."
◼ White Glass, 3¼" diam.
  300QX134-1, $3.00

Charmers

Front: A barefoot girl in a rose-colored dress stands among boughs laden with ornaments. Back: A bough and ornaments surround "1975" written on a large center ornament.
◼ White Glass, 3½" diam.
  300QX135-1, $3.00

Marty Links™

Front: On a beautiful green background, a little girl kisses a shy little boy's hand as he stands under the mistletoe. Back: "Merry Christmas 1975" is written in the center of a festive mistletoe wreath.
◼ White Glass, 3¼" diam.
  300QX136-1, $3.00

Buttons & Bo

In this grouping, Buttons & Bo engage in a variety of Christmas activities. The ornaments are dated on the back.
■ White Glass, 1¾" diam. 500QX139-1, 4 per box $5.00

Little Miracles

This charming set depicts a cherub and his forest friends sharing the joys of Christmas.
■ White Glass, 1¾" diam. 500QX140-1, 4 per box $5.00

Yarn Ornaments

Raggedy Ann™ and Raggedy Andy™ joined this group of yarn characters in 1975. All are 4½" tall. They were individually packaged and originally priced at $1.75.
■ 175QX123-1 Drummer Boy
■ 175QX122-1 Raggedy Andy™
■ 175QX121-1 Raggedy Ann™
■ 175QX126-1 Little Girl
■ 175QX124-1 Santa
■ 175QX125-1 Mrs. Santa

Handcrafted Ornaments

Adorable Adornments

Six handpainted characters of intricate design were another Hallmark first in 1975. Each are 3½" tall and were $2.50.
■ 250QX155-1 Santa
■ 250QX161-1 Drummer Boy
■ 250QX156-1 Mrs. Santa
■ 250QX159-1 RaggedyAnn™
■ 250QX157-1 Betsey Clark
■ 250QX160-1 RaggedyAndy™
Artist: Donna Lee (all)

Nostalgia Ornaments

Nostalgia Ornaments are "rings" crafted of sturdy, molded material and hand painted to resemble antique wood. Motifs evoke memories of Christmas long ago. All are 3¼" in diameter and were priced at $3.50. "Locomotive" and "Peace on Earth" are dated.
■ 350QX130-1 Drummer Boy
■ 350QX131-1 Peace on Earth
■ 350QX132-1 Joy
■ 350QX127-1 Locomotive
■ 350QX128-1 Rocking Horse
■ 350QX129-1 Santa & Sleigh
Artist: Linda Sickman (all)

Buttons and Bo (set of four)

Little Miracles (set of four)

Yarn Ornaments: Drummer Boy, Raggedy Andy™, Raggedy Ann™, Little Girl, Santa, Mrs. Santa

Adorable Adornments: Santa, Drummer Boy, Mrs. Santa

Adorable Adornments: Raggedy Ann™, Betsey Clark, Raggedy Andy™

Nostalgia Ornaments: Drummer Boy, Peace on Earth, Joy, Locomotive, Rocking Horse, Santa and Sleigh

Hallmark

1974

Norman Rockwell (Santa), Norman Rockwell (Postman)

The overwhelming response to Hallmark's 1973 Keepsake Ornaments prompted the company to offer sixteen new designs in 1974. Dating became more common in 1974, and three ornaments, including the second "Betsey Clark" 3¼" ornament, carried a holiday date. In addition, Hallmark offered new packaging and introduced two new sizes—2¼" and 1¾" ball ornaments. The new smaller sizes were offered in sets of two or four, depending upon the design of the ornament.

Norman Rockwell

On one side, Santa is wearing an apron filled with tools. He is napping in a chair while elves, on his lap, shoulder, and all around him, are trying to complete the dollhouse he was building. On the other side, "Santa's Good Boys," shows two pajama-clad children engrossed in Santa's tale.
◼ White Glass, 3¼"
250QX111-1, $2.50

Norman Rockwell

Two Norman Rockwell illustrations grace this ball ornament. One depicts a jolly postman laden with holiday packages and followed by a group of eager children. On the other side, unseen in the photo, a father and son return triumphantly from the woods with that special tree. Caption: "1974."
◼ White Glass, 3¼" diam.
250QX106-1, $2.50

Betsey Clark— Second Edition

An orchestra and a choir of Betsey Clark children are making music. A little girl directs, a boy plays the bass fiddle, a girl plays the banjo, and three children carol. This is the second year-dated design in the Betsey Clark series. Caption: "1974."
◼ White Glass, 3¼" diam.
250QX108-1, $2.50

Charmers

A child decorates a tree, three children are caroling, and a girl seems to be reaching for a little bird perched on a branch. Each scene is circled with a garland. Caption: "1974."
◼ White Glass, 3¼" diam.
250QX109-1, $2.50

Betsey Clark, Charmers

The Snowgoose, Angel

Raggedy Ann™ and Raggedy Andy™ (set of four)   Little Miracles (set of four)

Buttons and Bo (set of two), Currier and Ives (set of two)

Yarn Ornaments: Santa, Angel, Elf, Snowman, Soldier, Mrs. Santa

Snowgoose

A powerful snowgoose flies above white-capped waves with a sailboat in the background. Inspired by Paul Gallico's book, *The Snowgoose*.
▢ White Glass, 3¼" diam.
250QX107-1, $2.50

Angel

A beautiful Renaissance-type angel is featured on this ornament.
▢ White Glass, 3¼" diam.
250QX110-1, $2.50

Raggedy Ann™ and Raggedy Andy™

This famous pair get ready for Christmas by trimming their tree and exchanging gifts with friends. All ornaments are trimmed at the bottom and top with holly garland.
▢ White Glass, 1¾" diam.
450QX114-1, 4 per box $4.50

Little Miracles

An angelic little boy and his rabbit playmate are pictured in four Christmas scenes.
▢ White Glass, 1¾" diam.
450QX115-1, 4 per box $4.50

Buttons & Bo

On one side, Buttons & Bo are entwined in ribbon while wrapping a gift. The other side depicts Buttons & Bo leaning against each other, with Buttons holding a poinsettia blossom.
▢ White Glass, 2¼" diam.
350QX113-1, 2 per box $3.50

Currier & Ives

Two winter scenes picture a snowy farmstead and horse-drawn sleigh passing a colonial home.
▢ White Glass, 2¼" diam.
350QX112-1, 2 per box $3.50

Yarn Ornaments

Six colorfully detailed yarn character ornaments, approximately 4¾" tall, were offered in 1974 at $1.50 each.
▢ 150QX105-1   Santa
▢ 150QX103-1   Angel
▢ 150QX101-1   Elf
▢ 150QX104-1   Snowman
▢ 150QX102-1   Soldier
▢ 150QX100-1   Mrs. Santa

1973

U ntil 1973, Americans had few real choices when decorating their holiday trees. Red, blue, green, silver, and gold glass ball ornaments were standard, and the only way to "dress up" the family tree was to use tinsel, angel hair, flocking, or garlands.

In 1973, however, Hallmark Cards introduced its newest product line—a selection of eighteen specially designed Keepsake Ornaments. Drawing from the talents of its large staff of artists, Hallmark offered six glass ball ornaments with decorative bands and twelve yarn ornaments. More expensive than the basic red, blue, green, silver, and gold balls (and more decorative), Hallmark ornaments were anything but run-of-the-mill. They definitely were destined to become keepsakes. And with this simple beginning, a new holiday tradition of ornament collecting was born.

The 1973 collection included, in the glass ball format, two "Betsey Clark" designs. One was dated and first in the series of "Betsey Clark" ornaments. Another "Betsey Clark" design was not dated. The four remaining ball ornaments included "Manger Scene," "Christmas Is Love," a drawing of elves, and a design of Santa with some of his helpers. The charmingly detailed "Yarn Ornaments," between four and five inches tall, all retailed for $1.25 (except "Soldier" at $1).

Betsey Clark (Musicians), Betsey Clark (First Edition)

Manger Scene, Christmas is Love, Santa with Elves, Elves

Yarn Ornaments: Mr. Santa, Mrs. Santa, Mr. Snowman, Mrs. Snowman, Angel, Elf, Choir Boy, Soldier, Little Girl, Boy Caroler, Green Girl, Blue Girl

Betsey Clark

Five wistful-looking little girls are caroling around a sparse Christmas tree.

▢ White Glass, 3¼" diam.
250XHD100-2, $2.50

Betsey Clark— First Edition

The first Betsey Clark design with a year date features one little girl feeding a deer and the other cuddling a lamb. Caption: "1973."

▢ White Glass, 3¼" diam.
250XHD110-2, $2.50

Manger Scene

An ornately designed scene on a deep red background shows the stable at Bethlehem with the Holy Family and two sheep.

▢ White Glass, 3¼" diam.
250XHD102-2, $2.50

Christmas Is Love

Front: Two angels are playing mandolins in a design executed in shades of green and lavender. Caption: "Christmas is love— Christmas is you."

▢ White Glass, 3¼" diam.
250XHD106-2, $2.50

Santa with Elves

Balding, graying elves are busy with Christmas activities.

▢ White Glass, 3¼" diam.
250XHD101-5, $2.50

Elves

Elves are enjoying the winter sport of ice skating.

▢ White Glass, 3½" diam.
250XHD103-5, $2.50
Artist: Sue Tague

Yarn Ornaments

Each yarn figure measures 4½" tall. The original retail price was $1.25, except for the soldier, which was $1.00.

▢ 125XHD74-5   Mr. Santa
▢ 125XHD75-2   Mrs. Santa
▢ 125XHD76-5   Mr. Snowman
▢ 125XHD77-2   Mrs. Snowman
▢ 125XHD78-5   Angel
▢ 125XHD79-2   Elf
▢ 125XHD80-5   Choir Boy
▢ 100XHD81-2   Soldier
▢ 125XHD82-5   Little Girl
▢ 125XHD83-2   Boy Caroler
▢ 125XHD84-5   Green Girl

THE 1993 KEEPSAKE MAGIC COLLECTION

Radio News Flash

A significant milestone in ornament design occurred in 1984, when Hallmark first introduced its Lighted Ornament Collection. For the first time, collectors could not only decorate their tree with a variety of handcrafted designs, they could actually light their tree with ornaments.

Innovative motion brought the ornaments to life in 1986, eventually earning them the new name of Keepsake Magic Ornaments in 1987. In 1989, the "Baby's First Christmas" and "Joyous Carolers" ornaments introduced the first musical Keepsake Magic Ornaments. By 1992, the ornaments had begun to speak. Talkative designs, such as "Santa's Answering Machine" and "Shuttlecraft Galileo," delighted collectors with holiday messages. Light, motion, music, sound, and voice add enchantment to 1993.

Baby's First Christmas

Our First Christmas Together

Baby's First Christmas

Santa's sleigh goes by outside the window, near where this baby dreams of sugarplums. The ornament is musical and plays "Brahms Lullaby." Above the window, the date announces that "Baby's First Christmas" is "1993." Detail on the back shows a Teddy bear peeking out and the caption: "There's a new little stocking for Santa to fill!"
▪ Handcrafted, 3⅛" tall
  Light and Music
  2200QLX736-5, $22.00
  Artist: John Francis (Collin)

Radio News Flash

A vintage-style desktop radio announces a news bulletin: "We interrupt this program for a holiday news bulletin: Santa's just been spotted overhead! Listen for reindeer on your roof!" A kitty is drawn by the sound and the glowing light of the radio. On the back, the inscription reads "1993" and "Christmas is in the air!"
▪ Handcrafted, 3³⁄₁₆" tall
  Voice, Sound, and Light-On/Off Switch
  2200QLX736-2, $22.00
  Artist: Donna Lee

Our First Christmas Together

The couple on the sofa have love to keep them warm and a glowing fireplace with flickering light. The acrylic window reads: "Our First Christmas Together 1993." Back caption: "Christmas is a magic time of sweet, romantic moments."
▪ Handcrafted, 2¼" tall
  Flickering Light
  2000QLX735-5, $20.00
  Artist: Robert Chad

Home on the Range

Road Runner and Wile E. Coyote™

Winnie the Pooh

Home on the Range
Lassoing a cactus, a cowboy Santa rides to the tune of "Home on the Range." His rocking horse really rocks when the on/off switch is turned. A push button activates the music. One cactus is decorated with a "93"-dated star and glows with light.
▨ Handcrafted, 4⅛" tall
Light, Motion, and Music—On/Off Switch
3200QLX739-5, $32.00
Artist: Linda Sickman

Road Runner and Wile E. Coyote™
This time the coyote's got a sure-fire plan...or does he? Flip on the switch, and these two chase each other through the tunnels and around the realistic-looking, sandy-colored rocks. The date, "1993," is carved into the right side of the mountain, and the inscription on the front says "Have a Dynamite Christmas!"
▨ Handcrafted, 4⅛" tall
Motion—On/Off Switch
3000QLX741-5, $30.00
Artist: Robert Chad

Winnie the Pooh
In this talking ornament, Winnie the Pooh has lost his jar of "hunny" and ponders out loud where it can be. "Think Think Think...If I were a pot of hunny...I would surely find me...in my tummy!" he chuckles. Then he greets the new arrival with: "Oh, Hello. Have you by any chance seen my pot of hunny?" "Oh, Bother!" he finishes. Voice is activated by a push button. The date, "93," is carved into the stump Pooh sits on, and, of course, his "Hunny" jar is right behind him!
▨ Handcrafted, 3⅝" tall
Voice
2400QLX742-2, $24.00
Artist: Bob Siedler

North Pole Merrython
Turn the on/off switch and Santa and his reindeer run a "merrython" around the North Pole, while a polar bear cheers them on. The top of the North Pole glows brightly, and Santa wears the "93" date as his marathon number.
▨ Handcrafted, 4⅛" tall
Light and Motion—On/Off Switch
2500QLX739-2, $25.00
Artist: Ed Seale

Santa's Snow-Getter
This sled's flickering television screen is emblazoned with the headline, "SPORTS," and its headlights and taillights glow. The license plate is dated, "1993," and Santa's flag says "GO TEAM!"
▨ Handcrafted, 3¹/₁₆" tall
Flickering and Glowing Lights
1800QLX735-2, $18.00
Artist: Ken Crow

North Pole Merrython

Santa's Snow-Getter

Santa's Workshop

Song of the Chimes

Santa's Workshop
A spinning top and ball, a helicopter with rotating blade, and a twirling ballerina all revolve around the busy work stations at "Santa's Workshop." Santa, clipboard in hand, is mindful of the "Dec. 23," which is displayed below "1993" on the wall beside his tools. An on/off switch activates the conveyor belt, and a glowing light illuminates the workshop.
▪ Handcrafted, 4¹⁄₁₆" tall
   Light and Motion—
   On/Off Switch
   2800QLX737-5, $28.00
   Artist: Bob Siedler

Song of the Chimes
Golden chimes ring as graceful doves circle above, carrying "1993" streamers past flickering candles. An on/off switch starts or stops the sound and motion, while light flickers continuously. "Peace," "Love," "Joy," and "Hope" appear around the base.
▪ Handcrafted, Brass, 4⅛" tall
   Flickering Light, Motion, and Sound—On/Off Switch
   2500QLX740-5, $25.00
   Artist: Patricia Andrews

Bells Are Ringing
When the bearded elf pulls the real string "rope," he swings up and down as the brass bell rings out holiday joy. "1993" is

inscribed on the base of the quaint, continuously lighted tower that contains an on/off switch for motion and sound.
▪ Handcrafted, 4³⁄₁₆" tall
   Light, Motion, and Sound—
   On/Off Switch
   2800QLX740-2, $28.00
   Artist: Ken Crow

Last-Minute Shopping
Christmas shoppers bustle past a tiny mailbox, then in and out of stores named "Kringle's," "Holiday Bakery" (with its "1993" address) and, of course, "Hallmark." Light shines continuously through shop windows and the translucent green tree, while an on/off switch starts or stops the motion.
▪ Handcrafted, 4⅛" tall
   Light and Motion—
   On/Off Switch
   2800QLX738-5, $28.00
   Artist: LaDene Votruba

Dog's Best Friend
What's a dog to do if he can't find a tree…for Christmas? He decorates a holiday red fire hydrant with a string of tiny yellow lights and a softly shining star! A tag on the dog's collar reads: "93."
▪ Handcrafted, 3" tall
   Glowing Light
   1200QLX717-2, $12.00
   Artist: Julia Lee

Bells Are Ringing

Last-Minute Shopping

Dog's Best Friend

Raiding the Fridge

Dollhouse Dreams

The Lamplighter

Raiding the Fridge

A holly-trimmed note on the refrigerator door tells the jolly old elf, "Cold Milk and Cool Cookies for Santa!" Light glows inside the fridge, and silvery coils on the back form "1993."

⬜ Handcrafted, 3³⁄₁₆" tall
Glowing Light
1600QLX718-5, $16.00
Artist: Anita Marra Rogers

Dollhouse Dreams

A child kneels on a rug to add a Santa to her Victorian dollhouse with a flickering fireplace and lights in the upstairs bedrooms that blink in sequence. "Home Sweet Home" appears on the gable of the dollhouse, and "Noel" decorates a wall-hanging in the living room. "1993" is etched into the back door.

⬜ Handcrafted, 3⅝" tall
Flickering and Sequencing Lights
2200QLX737-2, $22.00
Artist: Ken Crow

The Lamplighter

Bearing glad tidings, this warmly cloaked Victorian lamplighter adds a glow to the holidays. A soft, plush wreath with a red fabric bow decorates the silvery "1993"-dated lamp post, and the cheerful "flame" flickers continuously.

⬜ Handcrafted, 4⅜" tall
Flickering Light
1800QLX719-2, $18.00
Artist: Don Palmiter

Collectible Series

PEANUTS®—
Third Edition

SNOOPY and WOODSTOCK, in warm stocking caps, stand proudly beside the tree they've just finished decorating with blinking lights. Each blinking light has a tiny WOODSTOCK beside it, and the date, "93," is on the star atop the tree.

⬜ Handcrafted, 3½" tall
Blinking Lights
1800QLX715-5, $18.00
Artist: Dill Rhodus

Chris Mouse—
Ninth Edition

Chris Mouse takes flight in a teacup with the aid of a lighted balloon. His red stocking cap matches the balloon. The teacup features a holly design and a golden rim, and the balloon bears the date, "1993," on the back.

⬜ Handcrafted, 4" tall
Glowing Light
1200QLX715-2, $12.00
Artist: Anita Marra Rogers

PEANUTS®

Chris Mouse

Forest Frolics

Forest Frolics—
Fifth Edition
Turn the switch and a raccoon, beaver, rabbit, and skunk circle a glowing Christmas tree with their shiny strands of tinsel garland. A bluebird rides on the tail of the skunk. The bunny and the raccoon wear snowshoes, while the beaver and skunk wear tiny boots. "Merry Christmas 1993" is written on the snow just inside the front of the dome.
◾ Handcrafted, 4⁵⁄₁₆" tall
Light and Motion—
On/Off Switch
2500QLX716-5, $25.00
Artist: Sharon Pike

STAR TREK® THE NEXT GENERATION™

Special Issues

Messages of Christmas
Now anyone can record their own holiday greeting with this new Keepsake Magic recorder ornament. The recorder features the caption: "Starsonic 93 Recorder." A cheery chipmunk wearing headphones listens in—just for fun! Complete instructions are included.
◾ Handcrafted, 4½" tall
Recordable
3500QLX747-6, $35.00
Artist: Bob Siedler

STAR TREK®
THE NEXT GENERATION™
A lighted replica of the *U.S.S. Enterprise*™ from the television program STAR TREK®: THE NEXT GENERATION™ will take your tree where no tree has gone before! The name of the ship and its number, NCC-1701-D, are on top of the saucer section of the ship, and the date, "1993," is on the saucer section just behind the main shuttle bay. The two warp engines glow with light, as does the main deflector dish below.
◾ Handcrafted, 1³⁄₁₆" tall
Blinking and Glowing Lights
2400QLX741-2, $24.00
Artist: Lynn Norton

Messages of Christmas

Baby's First Christmas

Baby's First Christmas

Baby slumbers under a lighted mobile. Adorned with a fabric lace bed ruffle, the intricately designed bed cradles the infant snuggling under a fabric blanket. A bas-relief wreath frames the caption, "Baby's First Christmas 1992," at the foot of the bed. To create sweet dreams for the little one, the music plays "Silent Night."

▪ Handcrafted, 3⁷⁄₁₆" tall
Light and Music
2200QLX728-1, $22.00
Artist: Ken Crow

Our First Christmas Together

These newlyweds enjoy a cozy Christmas together snuggling in front of a flickering fireplace. The hearth room is complete with garland, a Christmas tree, and gifts stowed behind the sofa. Golden letters inscribed on the window of the matte blue ball read, "Our First Christmas Together 1992." Back caption: "Christmas is a magic time of sweet, romantic moments."

▪ Panorama Ball, 3⅝" tall
Flickering Light
2000QLX722-1, $20.00
Artist: Robert Chad

Feathered Friends

To make sure our feathered friends find their way to special treats, this bird feeder is lighted overhead. Cardinals and a junco have found the festive, snow-covered feeder filled with minia-ture "bird seed" that rattles when the feeder is jostled. Dated "1992" under the eve, the feeder has a brass handle serving as the ornament hanger.

▪ Handcrafted, 1¹⁵⁄₁₆" tall
Glowing Light
1400QLX709-1, $14.00
Artist: Linda Sickman

1992 KEEPSAKE MAGIC COLLECTION

Keepsake Magic Ornaments have become increasingly sophisticated as they've progressed from lighted designs to clever creations enlivened with music, motion, and sound.

In 1992, the Keepsake Magic Collection introduced the spoken word. Santa provided excellent "customer service" by leaving us a message on "Santa's Answering Machine." And, Mr. Spock, in his very recognizable voice, greeted us from his "Shuttlecraft Galileo™"!

Feathered Friends

Our First Christmas Together

The Dancing Nutcracker

The Dancing Nutcracker
Enclosed in a handsome red and green book, the nutcracker performs under a spotlight to the Overture to Tchaikovsky's "Nutcracker." The front cover opens so you can see his entire dance. The title, "The Nutcracker," appears in golden letters on the cover, with the date, "1992," on the book's spine.

■ Handcrafted, 3¼" tall
Light, Motion, and Music—On/Off Switch
3000QLX726-1, $30.00
Artist: LaDene Votruba

Enchanted Clock
"When this enchanted clock strikes twelve each starry Christmas Eve, The magic toys will dance and play, if only you believe," reads the caption on the back of the clock. Each toy takes a turn under the front spotlight as they revolve around the spinning candy cane pole in the center. Turn the clock hands to midnight to start the motion, and turn them past midnight to stop it.

■ Handcrafted, 3¹⁵⁄₁₆" tall
Light and Motion—On/Off Switch
3000QLX727-4, $30.00
Artist: Ken Crow

Watch Owls
Watching for Santa, these sculpted, handpainted porcelain owls perch patiently on a tree branch. The larger owl keeps his eyes open. He's warm in a green muffler dated "92." Knowing his partner is standing watch, the little owl rests his eyes.

■ Handpainted Fine Porcelain, 2¼" tall
Glowing Light
1200QLX708-4, $12.00
Artist: John Francis (Collin)

Santa's Answering Machine
The blinking message light on "Santa's Answering Machine 1992" signals there are several messages waiting. Touch the button labeled "PRESS HERE" to hear Santa's voice deliver the outgoing message: "Ho, Ho, Ho! I'm out packing my sleigh now, so be sure to leave your Christmas wishes. Wait for the jingle bells!" A cheerful mouse sits atop the machine.

■ Handcrafted, 1⅞" tall
Voice, Sound, and Blinking Light
2200QLX724-1, $22.00
Artist: Julia Lee

Nut Sweet Nut
A cheerful chipmunk invites guests inside a snow-covered acorn festively decorated for the holidays. The red welcome mat, dated "1992," graces the threshold of a doorway outlined in colorful lights.

■ Handcrafted, 2¹⁄₁₆" tall
Glowing Light
1000QLX708-1, $10.00
Artist: Ken Crow

Enchanted Clock

Watch Owls

Santa's Answering Machine

Nut Sweet Nut

Christmas Parade

Under Construction

Santa Sub

Christmas Parade
A Christmas parade circles the city. Inside each skyscraper, office workers record the scene with their cameras, creating flashing lights with their flash-bulbs. The parade features a sign that says, "Christmas Parade," followed by a giant inflated snowman, reindeer, Santa Claus, and yellow star dated "1992." Light from the center building casts a glow on the parade route.

■ Handcrafted, 3⅜" tall
Light and Motion—
On/Off Switch
3000QLX727-1, $30.00
Artist: Linda Sickman

Under Construction
A construction worker beaver with yellow hard hat strings festive garland on a caution sign in preparation for trimming your tree. A warning light flash-es atop a barricade, warning, "CAUTION TREE-TRIMMING ZONE 1992 BRANCH UNDER CONSTRUCTION."

■ Handcrafted, 3½" tall
Flashing Light
1800QLX732-4, $18.00
Artist: Don Palmiter

Santa Sub
The "USS PEPPERMINT" helps Santa make deliveries to under-water friends. Santa's sub is loaded with presents and is out-fitted with garland and blinking red lights. The front of the sub has a periscope and a glowing red light. A propeller that spins keeps him on track so he reaches his destinations on time. The sub is dated "1992."

■ Handcrafted, 2¼" tall
Blinking Lights
1800QLX732-1, $18.00
Artist: Ken Crow

Lighting the Way
A lovely angel with intricately sculpted wings lights the way to Christmas wonder with a flicker-ing lantern light. Her ivory col-ored robe with golden trim tops a flowing gown that gently swirls around her feet.

■ Handcrafted, 3¹¹⁄₁₆" tall
Flickering Light
1800QLX723-1, $18.00
Artist: Patricia Andrews

Good Sledding Ahead
Happy children enjoy sledding as their puppy scampers behind. They circle a charming Victorian house with lights glowing from within. Lights also adorn the rooftop and the outdoor Christmas tree. The "1992" address appears above the front porch.

■ Handcrafted, 3⁵⁄₁₆" tall
Light and Motion—
On/Off Switch
2800QLX724-4, $28.00
Artist: Don Palmiter

Yuletide Rider
Santa enjoys a ride in his roadster convertible, deliver-ing a bottle-brush Christmas tree. The scenery, roadway, and car wheels revolve, and a light shines on Santa. "Yuletide Ride 1992" is debossed on the top.

■ Handcrafted, 3⅜" tall
Light and Motion—
On/Off Switch
2800QLX731-4, $28.00
Artist: Ed Seale

Lighting the Way

Good Sledding Ahead

Yuletide Rider

Chris Mouse

Special Edition

Santa Special

Artist Ed Seale designed this colorful locomotive to recapture the sights and sounds of an old-fashioned steam engine. This is a reissue from 1991. (See the 1991 Keepsake Magic Collection for design details.)

◼ Handcrafted, 3⅛" tall
Light, Motion, and Sound—On/Off Switch
4000QLX716-7, $40.00
Artist: Ed Seale

Collectible Series

PEANUTS®—
Second Edition

What better place to watch for Santa than atop SNOOPY's house dated "1992"! SNOOPY and WOODSTOCK stay warm, wrapped in a blue blanket on the rooftop. Captioned "Happy Holidays," the doghouse is festively decorated with a holly wreath trimmed with red and green blinking lights.

◼ Handcrafted, 3¹⁵⁄₁₆" tall
Blinking Lights
1800QLX721-4, $18.00
Artist: Dill Rhodus

Chris Mouse—
Eighth Edition

Our little mouse sets up house in a shoe. Framed by green shutters, the white window is dated "1992." Our friend stays toasty under a rooftop book of "Chris Mouse Tales," while a light creates a glow throughout the interior.

◼ Handcrafted, 3⁵⁄₁₆" tall
Glowing Light
1200QLX707-4, $12.00
Artist: Anita Marra Rogers

Forest Frolics—
Fourth Edition

These furry friends gather to frolic in a snow-covered playground, gently rocking back and forth on a seesaw. A raccoon and bunny sit on one side, while a skunk and fox balance the other side. Evergreens decorated with lights illuminate the scene. "Merry Christmas 1992" is inscribed in the snow.

◼ Handcrafted, 4⅛" tall
Light and Motion—
On/Off Switch
2800QLX725-4, $28.00
Artist: Sharon Pike

PEANUTS®

Forest Frolics

Artists' Favorites

Continental Express

This enchanting European village, with its snow-covered rooftops and castle, is "just the kind of place I'd like to visit someday on a train trip," says artist Linda Sickman. Two colorful trains circle the village going in opposite directions. The caboose on the lower train is dated "1992." Linda's signature, "L. Sickman," appears on the blue base.

■ Handcrafted, 3¾" tall
Light and Motion—
On/Off Switch
3200QLX726-4, $32.00
Artist: Linda Sickman

Continental Express

Look! It's Santa

Artist Donna Lee captured childhood memories of staying up late on Christmas Eve, hoping for a glimpse of Santa. "I always fell asleep before he arrived," admits Donna. Two youngsters peek around a spectacular Christmas tree and discover that the light from the tree has cast Santa's shadow on the wall. The date, "1992," appears below the snow-covered rooftop where reindeer tracks are evident. Look underneath the house to find the artist's signature.

■ Handcrafted, 4¹⁄₁₆" tall
Glowing Light
1400QLX709-4, $14.00
Artist: Donna Lee

Look! It's Santa

Special Issue

Shuttlecraft Galileo™ From the Starship Enterprise™

Stardated 1992, this lighted Keepsake Magic Ornament plays a special holiday greeting from Mr. Spock. When the button on the underside is pressed, Spock says: "Shuttlecraft to Enterprise. Shuttlecraft to Enterprise. Spock here. Happy Holidays. Live long and prosper." The ship is based on the shuttlecraft from the original STAR TREK® television series.

■ Handcrafted, 1⅛" tall
Light and Voice
2400QLX733-1, $24.00
Artist: Dill Rhodus

1991
KEEPSAKE MAGIC COLLECTION

In 1991, the Keepsake Magic line offered collectors more than twice as many ornaments as in 1984. This reflected both the growing popularity of Keepsake Magic Ornaments and the wider variety and complexity of designs made possible by technological advances.

Ornaments, such as "Santa Special," brought authentic sounds and on/off switches to control motion, music, or lighting. "PEANUTS®" became a new Collectible Series, and "Starship Enterprise" celebrated the twenty-fifth anniversary of the *Star Trek®* television series.

Chris Mouse

Baby's First Christmas
Santa cuddles and rocks Baby in front of the fire. The ornament plays "Rock-A-Bye Baby," and the words "Rock-a-bye, Baby…" are debossed on the back of the fireplace. A mouse peers around the corner of the fireplace, and a hearthside table holds a snack of milk and cookies, along with a note that reads: "For Santa." Front caption: "Baby's First Christmas 1991."
⬛ Handcrafted, 4½" tall
Flickering Light, Motion, and Music—On/Off Switch
3000QLX724-7, $30.00
Artist: Ed Seale

First Christmas Together
Three graceful swan-shaped cars circle through a nostalgic " Tunnel of Love." Two teddy bears snuggle in one car, and holiday gift packages fill the others. Tiny lights twinkle in garlands above the entrances to the tunnel, and a mirrored floor reflects the light. Front caption: "Our First Christmas Together 1991." Back caption: "Tunnel of Love."
⬛ Handcrafted, 4⅛" tall
Light and Motion—On/Off Switch
2500QLX713-7, $25.00
Artist: Linda Sickman

PEANUTS®—First Edition
Settled next to a cozy, flickering fire, SNOOPY® and WOOD-STOCK wait for Santa. Milk and cookies on the mantel are "For Santa." Stocking caption: "91." Back caption: "The stockings were hung by the chimney with care…" Editions in later years feature the PEANUTS® duo enjoying other holiday activities.
⬛ Handcrafted, 3" tall
Flickering Light
1800QLX722-9, $18.00
Artist: Dill Rhodus

Chris Mouse— Seventh Edition
"Chris Mouse Mail" holds a lighted flashlight to see the message: "JOY." Captions: "Chris Mouse 1991" and "Welcome."
⬛ Handcrafted, 3" tall
1000QLX720-7, $10.00
Artist: Bob Siedler

Baby's First Christmas

First Christmas Together

PEANUTS®

Forest Frolics

Jingle Bears

Bringing Home the Tree

Ski Trip

Friendship Tree

Forest Frolics— Third Edition

A raccoon, skunk, and squirrel give an "ice show" on a mirrored, frozen pond. Their "stage" revolves, so they seem to be skating in a circle as well as turning individually. A rabbit watches from a snowy tree branch, and a lantern illuminates the scene. Caption: "Merry Christmas 1991."

◼ Handcrafted, 4½" tall
Light and Motion—On/Off Switch
2500QLX721-9, $25.00
Artist: Sharon Pike

Jingle Bears

Sheet music says "Jingle Bears"—better known as "Jingle Bells." While the song plays, Papa's hands move up and down over the piano keys, and Mama

sways from side to side. Light glows from the Christmas tree. Caption: "Happy family memories make the season bright."

◼ Handcrafted, 4⅞" tall
Light, Music, and
Motion—On/Off Switch
2500QLX732-3, $25.00
Artist: Julia Lee

Bringing Home the Tree

Carrying a fresh-cut evergreen tree, a man and small child emerge from the forest. The door of their home swings open and they go inside, their little dog trailing behind them. Light glows from within the house when the door opens. Caption: "Merry Christmas 1991."

◼ Handcrafted, 4⅜" tall
Light and Motion—On/Off Switch
2800QLX724-9, $28.00
Artist: Duane Unruh

Ski Trip

Skiers ride the lift to the top of the hill, then glide down the slope at a faster pace. Light shines from the lodge's windows.

◼ Handcrafted, 4¼" tall
Light and Motion—On/Off Switch
2800QLX726-6, $28.00
Artist: Ed Seale

Friendship Tree

It's easy for these best-of-friends to exchange holiday gifts, even in snowy weather, because they have homes in the very same tree. Squirrel holds a package with a gift card that reads, "For Owl," and Owl has a package "For Squirrel." Light glows from within the tree trunk, which carries the carved date "1991."

◼ Handcrafted, 3⅛" tall
1000QLX716-9, $10.00
Artist: Peter Dutkin

Santa's Hot Line

Lights on this old-fashioned switchboard blink. A busy elf is using a quill pen to add requests to his "1991" list: "Sara—train, Paul—puppy." Real cord connectors loop from the plugboard to the console, and from the switchboard to the receiver. The front caption, which has a light in the center of the letter "O," reads: "Santa's Hot Line." Back caption: "North Pole Telephone Company."

▦ Handcrafted, 3⅞" tall
Blinking Lights
1800QLX715-9, $18.00
Artist: Ken Crow

Santa's Hot Line

Kringle's Bumper Cars

Santa, one of his elfin helpers, and a reindeer drive "Kringle's Bumper Cars." They dash about, dodging each other on a blinking track with light that reflects in Santa's goggles, the drivers' helmets, and the cars' antennas.

▦ Handcrafted, 3¼" tall
Blinking Lights and Motion—On/Off Switch
2500QLX711-9, $25.00
Artist: Linda Sickman

Toyland Tower

Marching to and fro on the parapet of a medieval-styled castle, this colorful soldier guards the "Toyland Tower." His teddy bear friend sits at the entrance to the castle, beating a drum.

▦ Handcrafted, 3¹³⁄₁₆" tall
Motion—On/Off Switch
2000QLX712-9, $20.00
Artist: Ken Crow

It's a Wonderful Life

The holiday film classic, *It's a Wonderful Life*, is showing at a nostalgic theater. Blinking marquee lights highlight the film's title and the messages: "Happy Holidays" and "1991." A poster reads: "Coming Soon: A Christmas Carol."

▦ Handcrafted, 3³⁄₁₆" tall
Blinking Lights
2000QLX723-7, $20.00
Artist: Donna Lee

Mole Family Home

The Mole Family celebrates the holidays, with father and child sharing a story in the living room, while mother bakes in the kitchen. Two fires flicker with light in the living room's fireplace and the kitchen's stove. Above ground, light is peeking through the doorway. The home's address is "1991."

▦ Handcrafted, 3⅜" tall
Flickering Lights
2000QLX714-9, $20.00
Artist: Julia Lee

Holiday Glow

Two little friends, a puppy and a kitten, share the special beauty of a home decorated for Christmas. Inside, a light softly fills the room and highlights the red balls decorating the tree. Outside a red bow adorns the lamppost.

▦ Panorama Ball, 3¼" tall
1400QLX717-7, $14.00
Artist: Sharon Pike

Kringle's Bumper Cars

Toyland Tower

Holiday Glow

It's a Wonderful Life

Mole Family Home

Starship Enterprise

Sparkling Angel

Starship Enterprise

The Starship Enterprise™
entered the Keepsake line to
commemorate the twenty-fifth
anniversary of the television
series, *Star Trek*®. The authentically detailed craft says, "U.S.S.
Enterprise" and "NCC-1701" on
top of the saucer section. "NCC-
1701" is repeated beneath the
saucer and on the outside of both
warp engines. Red and green
lights on the saucer's front blink
from left to right, and the dome
light glows. The ship is stardated "1991."
▪ Handcrafted, 1⅝" tall
  Blinking Lights
  2000QLX719-9, $20.00
  Artist: Lynn Norton

Sparkling Angel

Unfurling a long strand of tinsel
garland from a large spool, this
smiling angel adds a golden
touch to your tree. Blinking
lights, set in star-shaped holders,
twinkle along the garland.
▪ Handcrafted, 3¹³⁄₁₆"
  Blinking Lights
  1800QLX715-7, $18.00
  Artist: Robert Chad

Father Christmas

A kindly figure in a long blue
coat trimmed with white, represents the old-world legend of
Father Christmas who walked
through villages and towns
bringing gifts to children. He
holds a lantern with a flickering
light and a small evergreen tree.
Caption: "1991."
▪ Handcrafted, 4" tall
  Flickering Light
  1400QLX714-7, $14.00
  Artist: Duane Unruh

Elfin Engineer

Knowing this red train
will delight a lucky
child on Christmas
morning, a cheerful
elf polishes the toy to
perfection. Light glows from
within the car's windows
and also from the headlight.
▪ Handcrafted, 2¼" tall
  1000QLX720-9, $10.00
  Artist: Robert Chad

Father Christmas

Elfin Engineer

Salvation Army Band

Arctic Dome

Festive Brass Church

Festive Brass Church

With doors ajar, a brass church glows with the light and warmth of the season. This intricately etched design has bells in the steeple and tall arched windows

trimmed with wreaths. It is reminiscent of the 1985 Keepsake lighted ornament, "Christmas Eve Visit."

■ Etched Dimensional Brass, 3⅛" tall
1400QLX717-9, $14.00
Artist: Diana McGehee

Artists' Favorites

Salvation Army Band

Keepsake artist Duane Unruh sculpted this scene just the way he remembered seeing it when he was an 8-year-old. The band stands beneath a lighted lamp on a brick street. Two women are striking their tambourines, and the drummer beats his drum, as the ornament plays "Joy to the World." The scene includes the

familiar tripod with its kettle and sign: "The Salvation Army®, Sharing Is Caring." A portion of the price of this ornament went to The Salvation Army to help them continue their worthwhile endeavors. The artist's signature, "Duane Unruh," appears on the bottom of the ornament. Caption: "Joy to the World."

■ Handcrafted, 4⅜" tall
Light, Motion, and Music—
On/Off Switch
3000QLX727-3, $30.00
Artist: Duane Unruh

Arctic Dome

Artist Ken Crow imagined this friendly holiday football game featuring Santa and his reindeer "North Stars" against a team of polar bear "South Paws." As the reindeer line moves back and

forth across the field, quarter-back Santa and his receiver spin away from the defenders. The artist believes that the fans are such an important part of football fun, he's carefully drawn individual faces and even included the 1987 Keepsake Ornament "Mistletoad." Blinking signs in the stands read: "Cheer" and "Go Santa." The teams' names appear in the end zones, and the scoreboard is dated "1991." "Arctic Dome" is debossed on both sides of the ornament. The artist's signature, "Ken Crow," appears on the bottom.

■ Handcrafted, 2¹⁵⁄₁₆" tall
Blinking Lights and Motion—
On/Off Switch
2500QLX711-7, $25.00
Artist: Ken Crow

Special Edition

Santa Special

Artist Ed Seale set out to design an ornament that would do everything a real train could. The headlight is lighted, and the train whistles and chugs, repeating authentic sounds from period recordings. The wheels and drive rods turn, dramatizing the illusion that the train is running along its section of track as engineer Santa waves from the cab. One switch controls the motion, another controls the sound. The artist's signature, "Ed Seale," is on the back of the cab. This ornament was also available in 1992.

■ Handcrafted, 3⅛" tall
Light, Motion, and Sound—
On/Off Switches
4000QLX716-7, $40.00
Artist: Ed Seale

1990
KEEPSAKE MAGIC
COLLECTION

Responding to requests from collectors, Hallmark introduced an important new feature to seven Keepsake Magic ornaments in 1990. An on/off switch enables collectors to "stop the motion" on these ornaments, while the lighted portion continues to glow. A separate push-button switch initiates one cycle of music on the musical ornament "Song and Dance."

Dancing is a recurring theme in the 1990 Magic line. Reindeer couples square dance, mice twirl on an old-fashioned record player, and gingerbread cookies dance up and down. This year also marked some first appearances in themes: a spacecraft, a computer, and a camera with a blinking light.

The fifth and final edition of the Collectible Series, "Christmas Classics," occurred, and two Artists' Favorites ornaments were issued.

Chris Mouse

Baby's First Christmas

First Christmas Together
A porch light lends a welcoming glow to this charming house with a Swiss chalet look. When the light is on, you see a large front window. When the porch light goes off, a light comes on inside the house, revealing the silhouette of a loving couple in the window. The scene continues to change automatically. Captions: "Our First Christmas Together" and "1990."
▧ Handcrafted, 3⅝" tall
   Light and Changing Scene
   1800QLX725-5, $18.00
   Artist: Donna Lee

Baby's First Christmas
Above village rooftops covered with pearly snow, the stork soars and swoops, carrying his little bundle of joy. Friendly lights shine from the windows of the church and little houses nestled among the evergreens. Caption: "Baby's First Christmas 1990."
▧ Handcrafted, 3¾" tall
   Light and Motion—
   On/Off Switch
   2800QLX724-6, $28.00
   Artist: Don Palmiter

Collectible Series

Chris Mouse—
Sixth Edition
Inside the "Chris Mouse Wreath," the little mouse lights the candle's amber flame with a matchstick. Chris has a tail made of soft leather. Caption: "1990."
▧ Handcrafted, 4½" tall
   1000QLX729-6, $10.00
   Artist: Anita Marra Rogers

First Christmas Together

Forest Frolics

Christmas Classics

Forest Frolics—Second Edition

A raccoon warms his hands over a glowing fire, while a squirrel chins himself on a snowy tree branch. A little skunk moves to push a bunny friend who swings in a tire. Caption: "Merry Christmas 1990."

◾ Handcrafted, 4½" tall
Light and Motion—On/Off Switch
2500QLX723-6, $25.00
Artist: Sharon Pike

Christmas Classics—Fifth and Final Edition

"The Littlest Angel" kneels to watch his gift to the Baby Jesus transform into the Star of Bethlehem. Light shines through the sparkling floor and the little angel's box. Captions: "1990" and "The Littlest Angel."

◾ Handcrafted, 4½" tall
1400QLX730-3, $14.00
Artist: John Francis (Collin)

Santa's Ho-Ho-Hoedown

Four reindeer couples dance and twirl under a shiny light. Each couple turns individually, and the dance floor rotates. Santa's calling the square dance, and his words, "Ho-ho-ho! Doe-see-doe! Grab your partner—And 'round we go!" appear on the base. The caption on the barn reads: "Santa's Ho-Ho-Hoedown."

◾ Handcrafted, 4⅜" tall
Light and Motion—On/Off Switch
2500QLX725-6, $25.00
Artist: Ken Crow

Christmas Memories

In this nostalgic scene, a Clydesdale pulls a sleigh in which a man and two children are bringing home the Christmas tree. The sleigh circles the trees in the center, and the lantern on the sleigh is lighted. Caption: "The joy is in remembering…"

◾ Handcrafted, 4¼" tall
Light and Motion–On/Off Switch
2500QLX727-6, $25.00
Artist: Duane Unruh

Mrs. Santa's Kitchen

Jolly gingerbread cookies dance up and down around Mrs. Santa. A light glows inside the oven of her "1990" stove. Caption: "Christmas cookies dance and play to celebrate the holiday!"

◾ Handcrafted, 4¾" tall
Light and Motion-On/Off Switch
2500QLX726-3, $25.00
Artist: Dill Rhodus

Santa's Ho-Ho-Hoedown

Christmas Memories

Mrs. Santa's Kitchen

Holiday Flash

This elf's camera flash really works, blinking on and off. His bluebird assistant sits on the elf's cap, holding a sign that pictures...cheese!

◼ Handcrafted, 3¹¹⁄₁₆" tall
Blinking Light
1800QLX733-3, $18.00
Artist: Robert Chad

Song and Dance

A mouse couple dances on a revolving record to "Jingle Bells." Turning the crank on the phonograph's side makes the music play. A simulated wood-grain cabinet and a golden horn lend an antique look to the design. The record label reads: "Jingle Bells." Caption: "Love and Christmas...Two reasons to celebrate!"

◼ Handcrafted, 4⅛" tall
Motion and Music
2000QLX725-3, $20.00
Artist: Anita Marra Rogers

Elfin Whittler

This elf with a pearly white beard is busy carving a wooden Santa. A gentle tapping sound is heard as the elf hammers against the chisel. Santa holds a glowing lantern, and a teddy bear is whittled from the same tree stump.

◼ Handcrafted, 3⅛" tall
Light and Motion
2000QLX726-5, $20.00
Artist: Ken Crow

Holiday Flash

Letter to Santa

A child in a red sleeper sends a reminder to Santa on the computer. The screen's lighted message reads: "Dear Santa, I've been very, very, very good!" "Cranberry Computer" appears on the back.

◼ Handcrafted, 2½" tall
1400QLX722-6, $14.00
Artist: Anita Marra Rogers

Elfin Whittler

Song and Dance

Letter to Santa

Starship Christmas

Elf of the Year

This elf holds a lighted "1990" and wears a green cap and coat. The date is bright red with a gold-tone outline.

▨ Handcrafted, 2¹⁵⁄₁₆" tall
1000QLX735-6, $10.00
Artist: Patricia Andrews

Blessings of Love

This manger scene is illuminated by a soft halo of light from above that shines down on the sleeping Baby Jesus. Gathered around are sheep, a donkey, cow, rabbit, and two white doves. Silvery trim and edging decorate the pale blue ball, and on the back is the caption: "His humble birth blessed all the earth with love and joy forever."

▨ Panorama Ball, 4¾" tall
1400QLX736-3, $14.00

Deer Crossing

Red lights flash a warning on the brightly striped "Deer Crossing" signal. As an extra safety measure, a beaver in holiday clothing stands on a mound of pearly snow to display a "STOP" sign.

▨ Handcrafted, 3¹⁵⁄₁₆" tall
Blinking Lights
1800QLX721-3, $18.00
Artist: Bob Siedler

Beary Short Nap

There's not much time for this little Santa bear to nap, since the light of his lamp shows the date to be "Dec. 25 1990." Two other calendar pages, "Dec. 23" and "Dec. 24," are lying on his desk. A special little mouse friend snoozes cozily in a drawer nearby.

▨ Handcrafted, 2⅜" tall
1000QLX732-6, $10.00
Artist: Bob Siedler

Starship Christmas

Santa and a reindeer speed off in their shiny new flying saucer with a bag of toys to deliver. The silvery spacecraft features green and red blinking lights around its perimeter. The ship bears the name "STARSHIP CHRIST-MAS S.S. 1990."

▨ Handcrafted, 2¼" tall
Blinking Lights
1800QLX733-6, $18.00
Artist: Bob Siedler

Beary Short Nap

Elf of the Year

Blessings of Love

Deer Crossing

Starlight Angel

Carrying a bag filled with glowing stars, a cute pearly-winged
angel wears a blue robe and a
shiny brass halo. In her hand she
holds a single, perfect star to
light the Christmas sky.

■ Handcrafted, 2¾" tall
1400QLX730-6, $14.00
Artist: Anita Marra Rogers

Partridges in a Pear

Light adds a warm glow to the
delicate beauty of this dimensional brass pear. Each section
of the ornament features an elegant partridge in an etched and
filigree design. Two separate
pieces of brass, one etched and
one using a pierced design, form
the leaves.

■ Dimensional Brass, 3¼" tall
1400QLX721-2, $14.00
Artist: Joyce Lyle

Starlight Angel

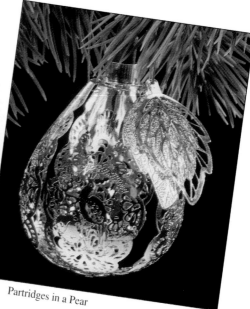

Partridges in a Pear

Artists' Favorites

Children's Express

Memories of weekend train trips
to visit her grandparents inspired
artist Linda Sickman to create
this signed, nostalgic ornament.
The train circles on its track
through a tunnel, while a little
girl sits cross-legged, holding an
extra passenger car. A boy
swings his leg up and down as
the train passes underneath, and
turns his head to watch it go by.
There's a light on the engine,
and light glows in the last car's
windows.

■ Handcrafted, 3¼" tall
Light and Motion—
On/Off Switch
2800QLX724-3, $28.00
Artist: Linda Sickman

Hop 'N Pop Popper

A little bunny waits eagerly with
his bowl on top of the popcorn
popper. "Popcorn and fun seem
to go together," says sculptor
Bob Siedler, whose signature,
"Bob," appears on the back of
the ornament. When the motion
switch is turned on, the popcorn
appears to pop, making a gentle
popping sound. The caption on
the front of the popper reads:
"HOP 'N POP Popping Corn."

■ Handcrafted, 3⁷⁄₁₆" tall
Motion—On/Off Switch
2000QLX735-3, $20.00
Artist: Bob Siedler

Children's Express

Hop 'N Pop Popper

1989
KEEPSAKE MAGIC
COLLECTION

The Keepsake Magic line came alive with the sound of music in 1989! In addition to light and motion, two ornaments offered favorite melodies. Electronic motion became more "magical" and complex, and it appeared in a wide variety of designs: Two mice riding a seesaw spoon, an airplane soaring across the sky, and a cobbler finishing a shoe are just a few. Flickering light was born in 1989, adding realism to the season's romance. And the Collectible Series, "Forest Frolics," featuring woodland animals, debuted.

First Christmas Together

Baby's First Christmas

Forest Frolics

First Christmas Together

The flickering light from the fireplace casts dancing shadows inside a cozy bungalow. Two stockings, hanging from the mantel, and two tiny mugs on the hearth belong to the couple celebrating a special Christmas. The side windows are adorned with curtains molded from real lace. A heart above the fireplace holds the caption, "Our First Christmas Together," and "1989" appears on the front of the house.

■ Handcrafted, 3¾" tall
Flickering Light
1750QLX734-2, $17.50
Artist: Donna Lee

Baby's First Christmas

As Mama mouse rocks in her rocking chair, a touch of her foot makes the cradle rock, too. The mother (or grandmother) mouse reads "Bedtime Tales" by the soft glow of the nursery lamp until Baby is fast asleep. This design is among the first in the Keepsake Magic Collection to feature music. It plays "Brahms' Lullaby." Front

caption: "Baby's First Christmas 1989." Back caption: "Christmas and babies fill a home with love."

■ Handcrafted, 4½" tall
Light, Motion, and Music
3000QLX727-2, $30.00
Artist: Ed Seale

Collectible Series

Forest Frolics—
First Edition

This series, new in 1989, features woodland animals having fun and celebrating the season each year. In this first edition, a raccoon, bunny, squirrel, and skunk ski on the trail that circles the lighted candy cane. A little bluebird perches on a sign that reads, "Merry Christmas! 1989."

■ Handcrafted, 4⁷⁄₁₆" tall
Light and Motion
2450QLX728-2, $24.50
Artist: Sharon Pike

Christmas Classics

Chris Mouse

Tiny Tinker

Christmas Classics—Fourth Edition

Inside the stable, the "Little Drummer Boy" kneels beside the manger, drumming a song for the Baby Jesus. Light shines down from above. The year "1989" appears on the cradle.

▨ Handcrafted, 3¼" tall
1350QLX724-2, $13.50
Artist: Donna Lee

Chris Mouse—Fifth Edition

In "Chris Mouse Cookout," a lantern's light turns a mouse's marshmallow toasty brown. The lantern is decorated with holly and dated "1989."

▨ Handcrafted, 4½" tall
950QLX722-5, $9.50
Artist: Anita Marra Rogers

Tiny Tinker

An elfin cobbler puts the finishing touches on a shoe for one of his friends. The light from his lantern shows him where to hammer every gold-toned nail. His bench, crafted to look like wood, displays his name: "Tiny Tinker." A toy locomotive rests on the back of the bench, waiting for the elf's attention.

▨ Handcrafted, 3" tall
Light and Motion
1950QLX717-4, $19.50
Artist: Ken Crow

Joyous Carolers

This design, the second of two musical ornaments in the 1989 Keepsake Magic line, plays "We Wish You a Merry Christmas." Standing in front of a glowing street light, a trio of Victorian carolers sings favorite tunes to the melody of a violin. The women's heads turn from side to side as if they are moving with the rhythm of the music. The tall gentleman moves as if he is playing the violin.

▨ Handcrafted, 4¹¹⁄₁₆" tall
Light, Motion, and Music
3000QLX729-5, $30.00
Artist: Duane Unruh

Rudolph the Red-Nosed Reindeer®

The most famous reindeer of all is ready to guide Santa on Christmas Eve. His red nose glows to light the way, but Santa has some additional help this year. The sleigh is equipped with blinking lights.

▨ Handcrafted, 2½" tall
Blinking Lights
1950QLX725-2, $19.50
Artist: Robert Chad

Loving Spoonful

Two ingenious mice have created a mouse-sized seesaw out of a spoon and a sugar bowl filled with glowing sugar crystals. The mice, fashioned with leather tails, ride up and down throughout the holiday. Caption: "Sugar."

▨ Handcrafted, 3½" tall
Light and Motion
1950QLX726-2, $19.50
Artist: Bob Siedler

Joyous Carolers

Rudolph the Red-Nosed Reindeer®

Loving Spoonful

Backstage Bear

The Animals Speak

Busy Beaver

Holiday Bell

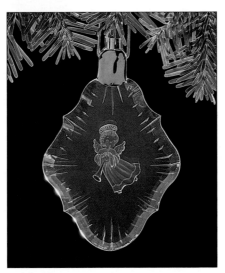

Angel Melody

Busy Beaver
On a frosty night, an enterprising beaver warms his paws over the flickering fire in the barrel. He's selling "Fresh Cut Trees" to his pals in the forest. A bunny is hiding in one of the trees on the back of the design.
■ Handcrafted, 2⅞" tall
 Flickering Light
 1750QLX724-5, $17.50
 Artist: Donna Lee

Backstage Bear
A bear admires his Santa costume in front of a mirror. The mirror reflects the bear's image and is framed by tiny lighted bulbs. Someone has written a

message across the top: "Beary Christmas!" Golden stars on the bear's coffee mug and on the back of the ornament indicate that this fellow has a bright future. His "SCRIPT" is an updated version of a familiar poem: "Beary Christmas to all and to all a good night."
■ Handcrafted, 3⅜" tall
 1350QLX72l-5, $13.50
 Artist: Bob Siedler

The Animals Speak
Inside a lighted panorama ball, an angel listens as the animals speak on the night the Holy Child is born. The town of Bethlehem and the Christmas Star can be seen in the background. The figures are painted in soft colors, and the caption appears in gold: "The animals rejoiced and spoke, the star shone bright above, for on this day a child was born to touch the world with love."
■ Panorama Ball, 3⅝" tall
 1350QLX723-2, $13.50
 Artist: John Francis (Collin)

Holiday Bell
An intricately faceted bell, created in 24-percent lead crystal, sparkles with light. Two lacy snowflakes decorate the sides, and the date "1989" is printed on the front in gold. The shimmery brass cap was designed especially for this ornament.
■ Lead Crystal, 3½" tall
 1750QLX722-2, $17.50

Angel Melody
This baroque-shaped acrylic ornament has been delicately etched and faceted to reflect the light. Wearing a flowing gown, the angel in the center plays her trumpet to herald great tidings of comfort and joy.
■ Acrylic, 5⁷⁄₁₆" tall
 950QLX720-2, $9.50
 Artist: LaDene Votruba

Moonlit Nap
This is a reissue from 1988. (See 1988 Keepsake Magic Collection.)
■ Handcrafted, 2¾" tall
 875QLX713-4, $8.75
 Artist: Robert Chad

Kringle's Toy Shop
This is a reissue from 1988. (See 1988 Added Attractions.)
■ Handcrafted, 3⅝" tall
 Light and Motion
 2450QLX701-7, $24.50
 Artist: Ed Seale

Unicorn Fantasy

Unicorn Fantasy

A gazebo provides the fanciful setting for this beautifully sculpted unicorn. His pearly white coat and silvery hooves and horn shimmer with the light as he brings his magical world to your tree.

▨ Handcrafted, 4½" tall
950QLX723-5, $9.50
Artist: Dill Rhodus

soars over the barn and lighted house. A path in the snow spells, "Merry Christmas!" and the banner behind the plane reads, "Spirit of St. Nick."

▨ Handcrafted, 4" tall
Light and Motion
2450QLX728-5, $24.50
Artist: Ed Seale

Metro Express

Artists' Favorites

Metro Express

It's Christmastime in the city! Two trains, traveling one after the other on two separate levels of track, circle the lighted city. Sculptor Linda Sickman, who created this ornament, says, "The two trains carry commuters to snow-covered skyscrapers and bring shoppers to see the holiday lights." You can see two additional trains in tunnels at the bottom of the design.

▨ Handcrafted, 3½" tall
Light and Motion
2800QLX727-5, $28.00
Artist: Linda Sickman

Spirit of St. Nick

With all of his experience flying every Christmas, Santa would make a terrific barnstormer, says Ed Seale, sculptor of this unique ornament. The scene evokes the early days of aviation. While two people watch from below, Santa's biplane swoops and

Spirit of St. Nick

1988 KEEPSAKE MAGIC COLLECTION

The Keepsake Magic Collection celebrated its fifth year by offering collectors more choices than ever before. The year saw a greater variety of subjects, nearly twice as many designs as in 1984, and twice the number of light-and-motion ornaments as in 1986, when that innovation brightened the line.

In 1988, a second light-and-motion train was offered by Hallmark, and five other new light-and-motion designs joined the line, including the third and final edition of the Collectible Series "Santa and Sparky." This was also the first year that "Baby's First Christmas" featured light and motion. Hallmark artists created ornaments based on personal memories and experiences that many collectors share.

First Christmas Together

Santa and Sparky

Baby's First Christmas

Baby's First Christmas
The carousel goes around, and a tiny light under the blue and white canopy casts a magical glow on four prancing horses. The ornament is handpainted in pearly colors, and the cornice is accented with gold. Caption: "Baby's First Christmas 1988."
▪ Handcrafted, 4" tall
Light and Motion
2400QLX718-4, $24.00
Artist: Ed Seale

First Christmas Together
Two white mice share a holly wreath decorated with colorful handcrafted candies. The sparkly gumdrops glow with light. Back caption: "Our First Christmas Together 1988."
▪ Handcrafted, 3" tall
1200QLX702-7, $12.00
Artist: Linda Sickman

Santa and Sparky—
Third and Final Edition
In the grand finale for the series, Santa and his penguin pal take to the stage with their magical act, titled "On With the Show." As Santa steps forward to wave his wand, Sparky pops up out of the hat. The footlight is lighted and displays the year, "1988."
▪ Handcrafted, 4" tall
Light and Motion
1950QLX719-1, $19.50

Chris Mouse—
Fourth Edition
Wearing a blue nightshirt and red Santa cap, a mouse busily polishes his "Chris Mouse Star." The star is lighted, with "1988" in the center. The mouse has a leather tail.
▪ Handcrafted, 2½" tall
875QLX715-4, $8.75
Artist: Bob Siedler

Christmas Classics—
Third Edition
Santa's in the living room, ready to fill the stockings. He's opened his bag of gifts and pauses to admire the decorated bottle-brush tree. A light shines down from upstairs, where the residents are snug in their beds. Caption: "Night Before Christmas 1988." (Note: The series symbol was inadvertently omitted from this ornament.)
▪ Handcrafted, 4½" tall
1500QLX716-1, $15.00
Artist: Donna Lee

Parade of the Toys
A jack-in-the-box pops up and down, as he rides in a red wagon pulled by a toy soldier. A doll pushes a baby carriage, and three ducks join the happy procession around a lighted Christmas tree.
▪ Handcrafted, 3½" tall
Light and Motion
2450QLX719-4, $24.50
Artist: Linda Sickman

Chris Mouse

Skater's Waltz

Two ice-skating couples glide gracefully around an outdoor rink. They are dressed in Victorian-style clothing and lighted by the glow from a lamppost, amidst a grove of snow-covered evergreen trees.

▨ Handcrafted, 3½" tall
Light and Motion
2450QLX720-1, $24.50
Artist: Duane Unruh

Last-Minute Hug

As Santa comes out one doorway, Mrs. Claus hurries out another. They'll hug, then part, beneath the porch light. Pearly snow decorates the roof of their Swiss chalet-style home.

▨ Handcrafted, 3½" tall
Light and Motion
2200QLX718-1, $22.00
Artist: Duane Unruh

Kitty Capers

This little kitten has made a delightful discovery— a strand of tiny lights that blink on and off. The glow is reflected by handcrafted, pearly white tissue paper in a red box labeled "Christmas Lights." The ornament clips to a branch on your tree.

▨ Handcrafted, 1½" tall
Blinking Lights
1300QLX716-4, $13.00
Artist: Sharon Pike

Christmas Classics

Parade of the Toys

Skater's Waltz

Last-Minute Hug

Kitty Capers

Circling the Globe

Heavenly Glow

Radiant Tree

Festive Feeder

Christmas Is Magic

Bearly Reaching

Circling the Globe

Santa holds the all-time record for on-time delivery. His secret may be this big lighted globe he uses to chart the course for his ambitious Christmas Eve journey.

■ Handcrafted, 2¾" tall
1050QLX712-4, $10.50
Artist: Ken Crow

Heavenly Glow

Holding a Christmas star, this lovely angel symbolizes the hope and joy of the season. The glowing brass ornament combines open-work designs and carefully etched patterns. It is lighted from within.

■ Brass, 3" tall
1175QLX711-4, $11.75
Artist: Michele Pyda-Sevcik

Radiant Tree

Light shimmers through ten triangular panels, which taper upward to form the sides of this richly detailed brass tree. Each panel features cut-out designs of the dove of peace. An unusual brass hanger repeats the shape of a tree. Viewed from above, the ornament is shaped like a star.

■ Brass, 3¼" tall
1175QLX712-1, $11.75
Artist: Joyce Lyle

Festive Feeder

A cardinal, goldfinch, and bluebird enjoy a holiday feast provided by a friendly bird watcher. The lantern-style feeder has a light beneath its roof and colorful Christmas lights on top. Tiny tracks are visible in the snow on the roof.

■ Handcrafted, 3" tall
1150QLX720-4, $11.50
Artist: Linda Sickman

Christmas Is Magic

Santa shows his puppy how to make a reindeer silhouette appear on the window shade. He's using the puppy's Christmas bones and the light from a table lantern. A real lace cloth covers the table. Caption: "Christmas is Magic!"

■ Handcrafted, 3¼" tall
1200QLX717-1, $12.00
Artist: Ken Crow

Bearly Reaching

When it's time to turn out the lights, this little bear is ready to help. He's standing on the candle holder with a candle snuffer in hand. The lighted flame casts a golden glow. Pearly white, handcrafted wax decorates the top of the candle. The ornament clips to a branch of your tree.

▨ Handcrafted, 4" tall
950QLX715-1, $9.50
Artist: Linda Sickman

Moonlit Nap

Who needs a nightlight when you can drift off to sleep on a glowing crescent moon! This little angel wears pearly white wings and a light blue gown. A bright yellow star with a red Christmas stocking swings from the tip of the moon.

▨ Handcrafted, 2¾" tall
875QLX713-4, $8.75
Artist: Robert Chad

Song of Christmas

The cardinal, a favorite songbird, is featured in this elaborate, etched acrylic. The edges of the circular design are beveled and faceted to reflect light. The cardinal perches on a holly branch accented with berries. The caption reads: "Song of Christmas."

▨ Acrylic, 3½" tall
850QLX711-1, $8.50

Tree of Friendship

Light cascades softly down the sides of this shimmering acrylic tree. The beveled edges add depth and sparkle to the design. Delicate snowflakes and

"Friends decorate the holiday with Love" are etched into the clear acrylic.

▨ Acrylic, 4¼" tall
850QLX710-4, $8.50

Christmas Morning

This is a reissue from 1987. (See 1987 Keepsake Magic Collection.)

▨ Handcrafted, 4⁵⁄₁₆" tall
Light and Motion
2450QLX701-3, $24.50
Artist: Ken Crow

Artists' Favorites

Country Express

An engine, boxcar, and little red caboose disappear into a mountain tunnel and then return. The railroad tracks are on top of a trestle, which has the appearance of real wooden timbers. Lighted buildings and a bonfire in the center of town add a warm glow. Artist Linda Sickman says she designed the scene based on memories of visits to old Western towns.

▨ Handcrafted, 3½" tall
Light and Motion
2450QLX721-1, $24.50
Artist: Linda Sickman

Moonlit Nap

Country Express

Tree of Friendship

Song of
Christmas

1987 KEEPSAKE MAGIC COLLECTION

In 1987, the Holiday Magic Lighted Ornament Collection was renamed the Keepsake Magic Ornament Collection. Although the name changed, the Hallmark commitment to innovation and high quality remained the same. A variety of original and commemorative designs were among this first newly renamed group.

Each "light and motion" ornament in the 1987 line displays a different kind of electronic movement: two children sliding down a bannister, Sparky the penguin moving forward to illuminate a sculpture of Santa, then retreating to admire his work, and a man and woman leaving their house to meet face to face, then moving back again. The 1987 "changing scene" ornament, "Angelic Messengers," is truly magical, with shepherds watching their flocks under a sky full of stars that change into angels. Blinking lights and the first lighted photoholder also were introduced.

Santa and Sparky

Baby's First Christmas

Baby's First Christmas
Trimmed with a lacy fabric curtain, this brightly lit window is the perfect place for Teddy to paint his announcement: "Baby's First Christmas." Baby's blocks on the sill show the date "1987."
■ Handcrafted, 3¾" tall
1350QLX704-9, $13.50

First Christmas Together
The igloo glows. with light and love. Holding hands by a bottlebrush tree, the polar bear couple celebrates a special Christmas. A red heart displays the year "1987,"and "First Christmas Together" is etched in the snow at the top.
■ Handcrafted, 2⅝" tall
1150QLX708-7, $11.50

Christmas Classics—Second Edition
The elegantly draped stage is set for Dickens' classic work, identified in gold on the front by, "A Christmas Carol." Illuminated in the center, a happy Scrooge presents gifts to Tiny Tim while Mr. and Mrs. Cratchet look on. Date on back: "1987."
■ Handcrafted, 4⁵⁄₁₆" tall
1600QLX702-9, $16.00

Santa and Sparky—Second Edition
Santa smiles at Sparky's latest work of art. Sparky moves forward and lights the sculpture so Santa can see it's a "Perfect Portrait." The pedestal dates the creation, "1987."
■ Handcrafted, 4¹⁄₁₆" tall
Light and Motion
1950QLX701-9, $19.50

First Christmas Together

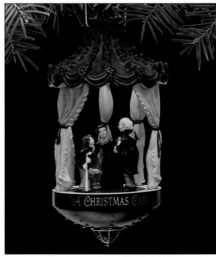
Christmas Classics

Chris Mouse—Third Edition

Designed to look like stained glass, this lamp sheds a lovely "Chris Mouse Glow." The little mouse has a leather tail and wears a cozy nightshirt dated "87."

■ Handcrafted, 4⅛" tall
1100QLX705-7, $11.00
Artist: Bob Siedler

Angelic Messengers

A light shines on the shepherds watching their flocks at night. Suddenly, the sky is aglow and angels appear with joyous tidings of Christmas. Light alternates from the shepherds to the angels, creating the "changing scene" effect. Caption: "Love came down at Christmas, love all lovely, love divine. Love was born at Christmas, star and angels gave the sign."

■ Panorama Ball, 3⅝" tall
Light and Changing Scene
1875QLX711-3, $18.75
Artist: Duane Unruh

Christmas Morning

It's early morning in this cheery Victorian home, and the tree is lit in anticipation of the children's arrival. They slide down the garland-trimmed bannister, eager to open their gifts from Santa.

■ Handcrafted, 4⁵⁄₁₆" tall
Light and Motion
2450QLX701-3, $24.50
Artist: Ken Crow

Loving Holiday

Light glows softly in this ornament sculpted to resemble an old-fashioned glockenspiel. The couple move forward to meet under the clock, then move back and forth again and again. Caption: "Precious times are spent with those we love."

■ Handcrafted, 3⅝" tall
Light and Motion
2200QLX701-6, $22.00
Artist: Ed Seale

Good Cheer Blimp

The blinking lights on the "Good Cheer Blimp" light the way for Santa on Christmas Eve. He leans over the side of the gondola to spot his next stop. This is the first time the "blinking-lights" feature appeared in the Keepsake Magic line.

■ Handcrafted, 3¹⁄₁₆" tall
Blinking Lights
1600QLX704-6, $16.00
Artist: Linda Sickman

Train Station

The "Train Station" lights are on, and the ticket window is open for business. A mother and child sit inside, while the ticket-taker waits for customers. Captions: "Merriville" and "Tickets."

■ Handcrafted, 3³⁄₁₆" tall
1275QLX703-9, $12.75
Artist: Donna Lee

Chris Mouse

Angelic Messengers

Christmas Morning

Loving Holiday

Good Cheer Blimp

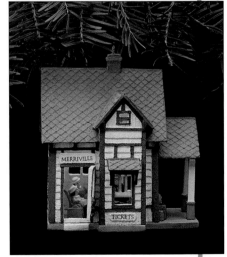
Train Station

Keeping Cozy

Lacy Brass Snowflake

Meowy Christmas!

Memories Are Forever Photoholder

Season for Friendship

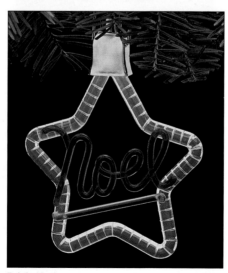

Bright Noel

Keeping Cozy

Dressed in flocked long johns, Santa is warmed by the burning embers inside this potbellied stove. A little mouse is keeping warm, too.

- Handcrafted, 2½" tall
  1175QLX704-7, $11.75
  Artist: Ken Crow

Lacy Brass Snowflake

Fashioned with two interlocking brass snowflakes, this ornament sparkles with light. The back piece is solid, with a delicately etched design. The front piece looks like filigree, with its lacy-etched and cut-out design.

- Brass, 2½" tall
  1150QLX709-7, $11.50

Meowy Christmas!

Two kittens frolic on a glowing, translucent red heart. They're merrily playing with the handcrafted white bow that decorates the ornament.

- Handcrafted, 2½" tall
  1000QLX708-9, $10.00
  Artist: Sharon Pike

Memories Are Forever Photoholder

This is the first-ever photoholder in the Keepsake Magic line. It illuminates one of your cherished photographs in a frame decorated with red and green, bas-relief holly. Back caption: "Memory keeps each Christmas forever warm and bright."

- Handcrafted, 3⅛" tall
  850QLX706-7, $8.50
  Artist: Ed Seale

Season for Friendship

The bevel of this acrylic teardrop has a delicately cut design that reflects light like crystal. Christmas greenery etched at the top of the ornament is accented with gold-foil berries that complement the matching foil caption: "How lovely the season when it's filled with friendship."

- Acrylic, 5⁵⁄₁₆" tall
  850QLX706-9, $8.50

Bright Noel

Within a glowing star, the word "Noel" shines for the holiday. This contemporary acrylic ornament captures the look of neon lighting.

- Acrylic, 5½" tall
  700QLX705-9, $7.00
  Artist: LaDene Votruba

Village Express

This is a reissue from 1986.
(See 1986 Lighted Ornament Collection.)

- Handcrafted, 3½" tall
  Light and Motion
  2450QLX707-2, $24.50

Keep on Glowin'!

This is a reissue from 1986.
(See 1986 Lighted Ornament Collection.)

- Handcrafted, 2⁷⁄₁₆" tall
  1000QLX707-6, $10.00
  Artist: Ken Crow

Chris Mouse

1986
KEEPSAKE LIGHTED ORNAMENT COLLECTION

Lights! Motion! Action! The 1986 Keepsake Lighted Ornaments displayed many technical advances. Designs have lights, electronic motion, scenes that change, and a unique holographic effect. Two of the ornaments feature circular motion, and one has Santa moving forward and backward. The new "hologram" feature premiered inside a panorama ball where Santa appears to be flying over a city.

The "Christmas Classics" and "Santa and Sparky" Collectible Series began, and the commemorative portion of the lighted line increased by three designs in 1986.

Baby's First Christmas

A kitten looks out into the night as Santa and his reindeer appear to deliver a gift for Baby. Light illuminates one scene, then another, creating the "changing scene" effect. Front caption: "Baby's First Christmas 1986." Back: "There's someone new on Santa's list, someone small and dear, someone Santa's sure to love and visit every year!"
- Panorama Ball, 3⅜" tall
  Light and Changing Scene
  1950QLX710-3, $19.50
  Artist: Ken Crow

First Christmas Together

A happy teddy bear couple celebrates their first year with a ride in a brightly lit, hot air balloon captioned: "First Christmas Together." This caption appears for the first time in the Lighted Ornament line. Anchoring the basket is a brass heart etched with the date, "1986."
- Handcrafted 5¼" tall
  1400QLX707-3, $14.00
  Artist: Ed Seale

Santa and Sparky— First Edition

Sparky watches eagerly as Santa moves forward to light the Christmas tree. The excitement of "Lighting the Tree" is just one of the many things Santa shares with his penguin pal each year in this series, which was new in 1986. A gift is tagged "1986."
- Handcrafted, 4¹⁄₁₆" tall
  Light and Motion
  2200QLX703-3, $22.00

Chris Mouse— Second Edition

A nightlight gives this mouse's pinecone bower a cheery glow. His cozy retreat, molded from a real pinecone, is just the right place for "Chris Mouse Dreams." The treetop address is "1986."
- Handcrafted, 3¾" tall
  1300QLX705-6, $13.00
  Artist: Peter Dutkin

Baby's First Christmas

First Christmas Together

Santa and Sparky

Christmas Classics

General Store

Village Express

Christmas Sleigh Ride

Santa's On His Way

Christmas Classics—First Edition

The stage is aglow for the "Sugarplum Fairy." She strikes a classic pose and waits for the "Nutcracker Ballet" to begin. Painted in pearly pastels, the stage carries the caption, "Sugarplum Fairy 1986." This series features scenes from classic Christmas poems, ballets, or stories.

■ Handcrafted, 4½" tall
1750QLX704-3, $17.50

General Store

Warmed by a potbellied stove, this old-fashioned "General Store" is bright and cozy. The woman by the counter may have come in to buy a tree after seeing the sign: "Christmas Trees 50¢."

■ Handcrafted, 2¹¹⁄₁₆" tall
1575QLX705-3, $15.75
Artist: Donna Lee

Village Express

A train circles the peaceful mountain village, chugging over the trestle and through the tunnel, as comforting light from the buildings shines across the newly fallen snow.

■ Handcrafted, 3½" tall
Light and Motion
2450QLX707-2, $24.50
Artist: Linda Sickman

Santa's On His Way

It appears as if Santa and his reindeer are magically flying above a city. A silvery hologram, fashioned through laser photography, creates the three-dimensional effect. Caption: "A time of magical moments and dreams come true…Christmas."

■ Panorama Ball, 3⅝" tall
Light and Hologram
1500QLX711-5, $15.00
Artist: Duane Unruh

Christmas Sleigh Ride

A lamp sheds light on a couple gliding around a park in an old-fashioned sleigh. The dome and bottlebrush trees are sprinkled with snowflakes. Caption: "Love's precious moments shine forever in the heart."

■ Handcrafted, 3¾" tall
Light and Motion
2450QLX701-2, $24.50
Artist: Ed Seale

Santa's Snack

Wearing a striped nightshirt and reindeer slippers, Santa carries a sandwich back to bed. A candle in his hand lights the way.
- Handcrafted, 2¹⁵⁄₁₆" tall
  1000QLX706-6, $10.00
  Artist: Ken Crow

Keep on Glowin'!

One of Santa's elves takes time out for some fun and slides down a glowing icicle.
- Handcrafted, 2⁷⁄₁₆" tall
  1000QLX707-6, $10.00
  Artist: Ken Crow

Gentle Blessings

Animals in the stable gather around the cradle to watch the Baby as He sleeps. Light shines from above, shedding a warm glow on the intricately sculpted scene. Caption: "Baby Jesus, sweetly sleeping, you have blessed our world today."
- Panorama Ball, 3⅝" tall
  1500QLX708-3, $15.00
  Artist: Linda Sickman

Merry Christmas Bell

Bathed in soft light, this acrylic bell is decorated with etched holiday flowers and greenery. "Merry Christmas," the universal message of the season, is etched into the center.
- Acrylic, 5⁵⁄₁₆" tall
  850QLX709-3, $8.50
  Artist: LaDene Votruba

Sharing Friendship

An etched poinsettia provides a festive accent to the gold foil sentiment stamped on this illuminated acrylic teardrop. Caption: "Friendship is a special kind of sharing. 1986."
- Acrylic, 5⁵⁄₁₆" tall
  850QLX706-3, $8.50
  Artist: LaDene Votruba

Mr. and Mrs. Santa

This is a reissue from 1985. (See 1985 Lighted Collection.)
- Handcrafted, 3" tall
  1450QLX705-2, $14.50

Sugarplum Cottage

This is a reissue from 1984. (See 1984 Lighted Collection.)
- Handcrafted, 3" tall
  1100QLX701-1, $11.00

Santa's Snack

Keep on Glowin'!

Gentle Blessings

Merry Christmas Bell

Sharing Friendship

1985 KEEPSAKE LIGHTED ORNAMENT COLLECTION

The 1985 Lighted Ornament line was filled with firsts. It contained the first series, the first commemorative, the first property, and the first dated ornaments to appear in the new lighted format.

A sleepy mouse reading by candlelight was the first edition in the "Chris Mouse" Collectible Series. The first commemorative was "Baby's First Christmas." This caption, the most popular in the Keepsake line, appeared on a handcrafted carousel complete with acrylic ponies. Both the carousel and the ornament called "Swiss Cheese Lane" were dated "1985." Completing the list of firsts in the Lighted Ornament line was the property "Katybeth." This handcrafted angel was seen painting a beautiful acrylic rainbow, shown to wonderful advantage by the addition of light.

Baby's First Christmas

Chris Mouse

Baby's First Christmas
The carousel is aglow with light as two teddy bears ride 'round and 'round on their frosted acrylic ponies. The ornament is trimmed in gold and displays tiny mirrors on the canopy. Caption: "Baby's First Christmas 1985."
▪ Handcrafted, Acrylic, 4" tall
1650QLX700-5, $16.50
Artist: Ed Seale

Chris Mouse— First Edition
Dressed in his blue nightshirt, a little mouse is reading a Christmas story before bedtime. The candle illuminates his book, dated "1985." The ornament attaches to your tree with a specially designed clip.
▪ Handcrafted, 3⅛" tall
1250QLX703-2, $12.50
Artist: Bob Siedler

Katybeth
A rainbow and cloud made of acrylic light up for the angel Katybeth. She is busily painting the rainbow red, gold, and blue, so it will shine for the holidays.
▪ Handcrafted, Acrylic, 3⅝" tall
1075QLX710-2, $10.75

Little Red Schoolhouse
The lights are on and the play is about to begin in this intricately detailed schoolhouse. Inside, three parents watch the children perform in a Christmas pageant.

Wonderful touches of authenticity include a flagpole in the front, a woodpile at the back, a blackboard inside showing a "chalk" rendition of Bethlehem, and a real bell hanging above the front door. A banner announces a "School Play Tonight."
▪ Handcrafted, 2⅝" tall
1575QLX711-2, $15.75
Artist: Donna Lee

Mr. and Mrs. Santa
Mrs. Santa's home is brightly lit as she trims the tree. Santa waves at passersby from the big picture window, inviting them to view the festivities. Inside, pictures cover the wall, and there's a fireplace with a clock on the mantel. The roof is covered with sparkling snow, and the chimney wears a holiday wreath. A sign above the door says, "The Kringles."
▪ Handcrafted, 3" tall
1450QLX705-2, $14.50

Christmas Eve Visit
An intricately etched brass house glows with light to welcome Santa and his reindeer on Christmas Eve.
▪ Etched Brass, 2" tall
1200QLX710-5, $12.00

Love Wreath
A delicate wreath, decorated with hearts and ribbon, is etched in acrylic and softly illuminated. The special message is stamped in gold foil: "Christmas happens in the heart."
▪ Acrylic, 3½" tall
850QLX702-5, $8.50
Artist: LaDene Votruba

Season of Beauty
Blanketed in white, the world reflects the peace and beauty of Christmas. This softly illuminated ornament displays the message: "May joy come into your world as Christmas comes into your heart."
▪ Red-and-Gold Classic Shape, 3¼" diam.
800QLX712-2, $8.00
Artist: Joyce Lyle

Katybeth

Little Red Schoolhouse

Mr. and Mrs. Santa

Christmas Eve Visit

Love Wreath

Season of Beauty

Swiss Cheese Lane

A wedge of Swiss cheese forms an A-frame home for a pair of mice. Through holes in the cheese, you can see the brightly lit interior. One mouse sleeps in a four-poster bed, while the other trims the tree in a living room. Caption: "1985 Swiss Cheese Lane."
▧ Handcrafted, 2⅝" tall
1300QLX706-5, $13.00

Sugarplum Cottage

This is a reissue from 1984. (See 1984 Lighted Ornament Collection.)
▧ Handcrafted, 3" tall
1100QLX701-1, $11.00

Village Church

This is a reissue from 1984. (See 1984 Lighted Collection.)
▧ Handcrafted, 4⅝" tall
1500QLX702-1, $15.00
Artist: Donna Lee

Santa's Workshop

This is a reissue from 1984. (See 1984 Lighted Collection.)
▧ Peek-Through Ball, 3½" diam.
1300QLX700-4, $13.00

Nativity

This is a reissue from 1984. (See 1984 Lighted Collection.)
▧ Panorama Ball, 3½" diam.
1200QLX700-1, $12.00
Artist: Ed Seale

All Are Precious

This is a reissue from 1984. (See 1984 Lighted Collection.)
▧ Acrylic, 4" tall
800QLX704-4, $8.00

Swiss Cheese Lane

1984 KEEPSAKE LIGHTED ORNAMENT COLLECTION

Ornament collectors responded with delight when Lighted Ornaments were introduced by Hallmark in 1984. This marked the first time that the brilliance of Christmas tree lights was added to ornaments. The warm glow they created was truly special.

The care and attention to detail put into the design of Lighted Ornaments was unsurpassed. As one designer told me, "The only difficulty I had was deciding when the design was complete. I kept on wanting to add more details." Indeed, designers have created wonderful new touches for these ornaments, such as real lace trim on the windows of "Santa's Arrival" and the tiny carolers inside the "Village Church."

The beauty of light graced many ornament designs in 1984. Light showed through windows of a handcrafted house in "Santa's Workshop," lit the sky of a panorama ball in "Nativity," and illuminated a traffic signal in "City Lights."

Santa's Workshop

Santa's Workshop
Light shines out the window of Santa's workshop as he offers a toy bunny to his cottontail visitor standing outside.
■ Peek-through Ball, 3½" diam.
1300QLX700-4, $13.00

Sugarplum Cottage
Sugar-coated gumdrops, peppermint candy canes, and lollipops make this brightly lit cottage look good enough to eat!
■ Handcrafted, 3" tall
1100QLX701-1, $11.00

City Lights
To control the flow of forest traffic, Santa and a friendly "traffic squirrel" perch atop the four-way signal that illuminates an animal in each light's surface.
■ Handcrafted, 3½" tall
1000QLX701-4, $10.00
Artist: Bob Siedler

Village Church
A clapboard village church looks like it could have been taken straight from a New England green. The towering spire, topped with a gold cross, rests on a green, shingled roof. Candle-lit windows and an open door reveal the inside decor and holiday carolers.
■ Handcrafted, 4⅝" tall
1500QLX702-1, $15.00
Artist: Donna Lee

Sugarplum Cottage

City Lights

Village Church

Santa's Arrival

'Tis the night before Christmas and a little boy is sleeping soundly, dreaming of holiday toys. Inside the softly lit room, the child's puppy peers out the window and holds up a list of gifts for Santa to read. The window is framed by genuine, white eyelet lace.

◼ Peek-through Ball, 3½" diam.
1300QLX702-4, $13.00
Artist: Donna Lee

Nativity

The dark blue of this panorama ball creates a perfect contrast to the warm glow from inside that illuminates the windows of Bethlehem and the Christmas sky. Caption: "Christmas...light through the darkness...love through the ages."

◼ Panorama Ball, 3½" diam.
1200QLX700-1, $12.00
Artist: Ed Seale

Stained Glass

A colorful, old-fashioned, stained glass design glows like a beautiful window when lit.

◼ Gold Classic Shape, 3⅞" diam.
800QLX703-1, $8.00

Christmas in the Forest

A silver ball evokes a moonlit night in a snowy forest. The design looks almost three-dimensional, with its varying hues of white, gray, and blue, subtly lit from within. Caption: "Christmas...magical, memorable time of year."

◼ Silver Classic Shape, 3⅞" diam.
800QLX703-4, $8.00

Brass Carousel

Lit up and reminiscent of an amusement park merry-go-round, this ornament shows Santa riding in a gift-laden sleigh pulled by reindeer.

◼ Etched Brass, 3" tall
900QLX707-1, $9.00

All Are Precious

A delicately etched shepherd, lamb, and donkey stand in awe of the brilliant star that sends rays of light over the world. The gold foil-stamped caption says: "All are precious in His sight..."

◼ Acrylic, 4" tall
800QLX704-4, $8.00

Santa's Arrival

Nativity

Stained Glass

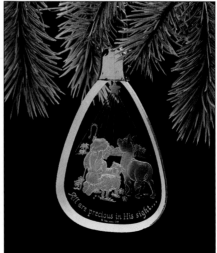

Christmas in the Forest

Brass Carousel

All Are Precious

Hallmark

THE 1993 MINIATURE COLLECTION

Many new treats awaited collectors in the 1993 Keepsake Miniature Collection. The fifth edition of the "Noel R.R." Collectible Series featured a "Flatbed Car" carrying Santa's sleigh—combining the nostalgic appeal of trains with the joys of Christmas. The 1993 collection included the first-ever tin miniature series with the debut of "On the Road," a detailed design by Linda Sickman. "Precious Edition" was expanded to include both a "Cloisonné snowflake" and an exquisite full-lead, gold-plated "Crystal Angel" that delighted both miniature ornament and jewelry enthusiasts.

Baby's First Christmas

Mom

Grandma

Secret Pal

Snuggle Birds

Ears to Pals

Special Friends

Commemoratives

Baby's First Christmas
This happy teddy bear pops out of a jack-in-the-box, which bears the insignia "Baby's 1st Christmas" on the light teal front and "1993" on the back. This jolly jack-in-the-box is appropriate for a boy or a girl.
■ Handcrafted, 1¹⁄₁₆" tall
575QXM514-5, $5.75
Artist: LaDene Votruba

Mom
A tiny mouse carries a poinsettia parasol. The word "Mom" is etched into her dress, and the date, "1993," appears on the back. Her tail peeks around the side of her cheery green skirt.
■ Handcrafted, 1⅛" tall
450QXM515-5, $4.50
Artist: Patricia Andrews

Grandma
Having just discovered "Grandma's Cookie Jar," a sneaky chipmunk helps himself to a cookie in the shape of a Christmas tree. The acorn cookie jar bears the date, "1993," on the back.
■ Handcrafted, 1" tall
450QXM516-2, $4.50
Artist: Ed Seale

Secret Pal
This first-ever Keepsake Miniature secret pal ornament bears the "1993" date on the back. A shy mouse peeks out from the stocking, which carries the inscription, "From Your Secret Pal."
■ Handcrafted, 1" tall
375QXM517-2, $3.75
Artist: Anita Marra Rogers

Snuggle Birds
Two loving birds share a cozy birdhouse and a stocking. Their snow-covered house is trimmed with "gingerbread" detail and garland with a red bow above their peephole door. "93" is etched into the stocking top.
■ Handcrafted, 1⁵⁄₁₆" tall
575QXM518-2, $5.75
Artist: Patricia Andrews

Ears to Pals
With a little bluebird cheerily hitching a ride on his ear, this bunny is delivering a gold-painted gift with a bright red bow and the date, "93," etched on its side.
■ Handcrafted, 1³⁄₁₆" tall
375QXM407-5, $3.75
Artist: Patricia Andrews

Special Friends
A merry moose and cheery cardinal are "Special Friends" at Christmastime. The moose's green blanket, trimmed in white, bears the date "1993" on one side.
■ Handcrafted, 1" tall
450QXM516-5, $4.50
Artist: John Francis (Collin)

Holiday Traditions

Cheese Please

Although he's been nice, this little mouse has to think twice to come up with something to add to his wish list besides "Cheese"! Kneeling on a block of Swiss cheese, he works at his tiny matchbox desk, which bears the date "1993."

▧ Handcrafted, 1¼" tall
375QXM407-2, $3.75
Artist: Bob Siedler

Country Fiddling

This Nashville cat and his cheery bluebird partner are in the country spirit with happy faces and jaunty little hats. The kitten's hat is inscribed with the date, "93."

▧ Handcrafted, 1" tall
375QXM406-2, $3.75
Artist: John Francis (Collin)

I Dream of Santa

A blue-and-green-turbaned Santa rises from this brass-colored lamp to make all your Christmas wishes come true. The ornate lamp, bears the date, "93."

▧ Handcrafted, 1⅛" tall
375QXM405-5, $3.75
Artist: Linda Sickman

Pear-Shaped Tones

This partridge, with his eyes closed, appears to be singing his heart out as he plays his pear-shaped cello. The cello, dated "1993," is topped with a perfectly detailed pair of holly leaves.

▧ Handcrafted, 1" tall
375QXM405-2, $3.75
Artist: Joyce Lyle

North Pole Fire Truck

Incredible detail draws attention to this little red fire truck with silver-tone hubcaps, ladder, windshield, mirrors, lamps, grille, and bumper. The date, "93," is painted on one side below the ladder.

▧ Handcrafted, ⅝" tall
475QXM410-5, $4.75
Artist: Don Palmiter

Refreshing Flight

A detailed Santa rides for refreshment on a nostalgic "Coca-Cola" bottle. Santa's gold-painted buttons and belt buckle, along with the silvery bottle cap, add realistic touches.

▧ Handcrafted, ⅞" tall
575QXM411-2, $5.75
Artist: Robert Chad

Merry Mascot

A cute little Dalmatian pup slides down the pole, wagging his tail. He has a fire hat, painted red and gold and displaying the date, "93," on the front.

▧ Handcrafted, 1⅜" tall
375QXM404-2, $3.75
Artist: Bob Siedler

Pull Out a Plum

The bright-eyed and bushy-tailed raccoon may think he's going to get the most plum pudding, but he may have underestimated the nimble squirrel. Look closely for the date, "93," etched into a holly leaf on the side of the plate.

▧ Handcrafted, ⅝" tall
575QXM409-5, $5.75
Artist: John Francis (Collin)

Visions of Sugarplums

This pewter spoon, with "93" inscribed on the back, is rich with detail. Nestled in the curve of the spoon, a small child sleeps in a four-poster bed, while dreams rise up the handle.

▧ Pewter, 1⅜" tall
725QXM402-2, $7.25
Artist: Don Palmiter

Cheese Please

Country Fiddling

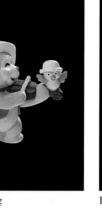

I Dream of Santa

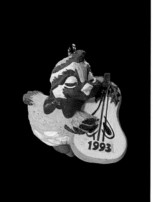

Pear-Shaped Tones

North Pole Fire Truck

Merry Mascot

Refreshing Flight

Pull Out a Plum

Visions of Sugarplums

Trio of Ornaments

Although sold separately, the following three ornaments make a charming trio.

Learning to Skate
This little skater is so confident, he's already holding his mittened hands behind his back. His stocking cap tilts jauntily and his snowy beard blows in the wind.
- Handcrafted, 1⅛" tall
  300QXM412-2, $3.00
  Artist: Robert Chad

Learning to Skate

Lighting a Path
This little lookout holds a lantern in one mittened hand, and with the other, shields his eyes, the better to peer into the drifting snow.
- Handcrafted, 1¹⁄₁₆" tall
  300QXM411-5, $3.00
  Artist: Robert Chad

Lighting a Path

Into the Woods
In stocking cap, fluffy blue coat, blue pants, and boots, the little woodsman is ready for Christmas. His mittened hand holds his golden painted ax, which bears the "93" date on the blade.
- Handcrafted, 1" tall
  375QXM404-5, $3.75
  Artist: Ed Seale

Into the Woods

Monkey Melody
An organ grinder's monkey is holding a bright green package tied with a big golden bow. This nostalgic stringer ornament can be displayed on one branch or two. Santa, the organ grinder, holds an organ box painted with a golden "1993."
- Handcrafted
  Santa, 1" tall
  Monkey, ¹⁵⁄₁₆" tall
  575QXM409-2, $5.75
  Artist: Linda Sickman

Tiny Green Thumbs
Six adorable little mice in this set— or rather, five—are hard at work tending their garden, and the sixth is "Just Resting!" Hope he's not caught by the straw boss in "Here We Grow," who's standing in a flowerpot under a poinsettia, overseeing the work; or the "Li'l Sprinkler," who will no doubt have a good idea how to rouse him. Meanwhile, the merry mouse in "Keep on Hoein' " looks expectantly down the furrows, perhaps preparing a spot for the mouse in "Ever Green" to plant his Christmas tree; and the mouse in "Teeny Clips" struggles manfully with his clippers to prune the holly.
- Here We Grow, 1¼" tall
- Ever Green, ¹³⁄₁₆" tall
- Li'l Sprinkler, ¹³⁄₁₆" tall
- Keep on Hoein', ¹¹⁄₁₆" tall
- Teeny Clips, 1⅛" tall
- Just Resting, ¹¹⁄₁₆" tall
  All Handcrafted
  2900QXM403-2, $29.00
  Artist: Ed Seale

Monkey Melody

Tiny Green Thumbs

Christmas Castle

'Round the Mountain

Crystal Angel

Cloisonné Snowflake

Artists' Favorites

Christmas Castle

Artist Ed Seale became interested in ancient castles when he took a trip to Ireland. This fanciful castle reflects his fascination as well as his eye for detail. The castle's three turrets tower over a green field and a blue moat, where a drawbridge invites travelers to visit. The date, "1993," is displayed on a banner on the red and golden base. Ed's signature is at the base of the castle.
- Handcrafted, 1⅛" tall
575QXM408-5, $5.75
Artist: Ed Seale

'Round the Mountain

A fanciful, snow-covered chalet inside a dome features a tiny brass train that revolves, when the knob is turned, through secret mountain passageways. The artist, Ken Crow, is always intrigued by finding new ways to feature movement in his designs. His signature appears on the side of the mountain. The detail of the mountain hideaway and the evergreens that surround it extends to the back, where the date, "1993," is painted on the mountainside.
- Handcrafted, 1¹¹⁄₁₆" tall
725QXM402-5, $7.25
Artist: Ken Crow

Precious Editions

Crystal Angel

This elegant, full lead crystal angel will catch the lights of any tree or crackling hearth and shine through the holidays. Her gold-plated wings, arms, head, and carol book, dated "93," complement her crystal brilliance.
- Full Lead Crystal, Gold-plated, 1" tall
975QXM401-5, $9.75
Artist: Don Palmiter

Cloisonné Snowflake

With its blue cloisonné and brass snowflake, this elegant ornament adds beauty to any holiday display .
- Cloisonné, Brass, 1" diam.
975QXM401-2, $9.75
Artist: LaDene Votruba

Collectible Series

On the Road— First Edition

Bursting with holiday gifts and happy children, a station wagon heads home. Leading the new series, this pressed tin ornament, marked with incredible detail, bears "1993" on its front and back license plates and features revolving wheels.
- Pressed Tin, ⁷⁄₁₆" tall
575QXM400-2, $5.75
Artist: Linda Sickman

March of the Teddy Bears—First Edition

An adorable drum major in a bright red bow steps into the lead of a new series. Looking enthusiastic, he raises his silver-tone baton and wears "93" smartly on his hat.
- Handcrafted, 1⁷⁄₁₆" tall
450QXM400-5, $4.50
Artist: Duane Unruh

The Bearymores— Second Edition

As the Bearymores sing joyful carols, the littlest Bearymore stands on a mound of pearlized snow to get a better view. The date, "1993," is painted on the front of the red base.
- Handcrafted, 1⅛" tall
575QXM512-5, $5.75
Artist: Anita Marra Rogers

On the Road

March of the Teddy Bears

The Bearymores

The Night Before Christmas

Woodland Babies

Nature's Angels

Thimble Bells

Noel R.R.

The Kringles

Rocking Horse

Old English Village

The Night Before Christmas— Second Edition

Nestled snug in their bed, these children dream of Christmas morning in their house—the Tin Display House created to showcase the series, where a hook is reserved especially for the "93" edition. The date is shown in a patch on their cozy blanket.
◼ Handcrafted, 1⅛" tall
450QXM511-5, $4.50
Artist: Duane Unruh

Woodland Babies— Third and Final Edition

Wearing a diaper and a smile, a sweet baby woodchuck finishes this series. His cute little ears peek out of his nightcap as he climbs a holly bush—more than likely one he's been told to stay out of. The date, "1993," is inscribed on the back of the holly leaves.
◼ Handcrafted, 1⅛" tall
575QXM510-2, $5.75
Artist: John Francis (Collin)

Nature's Angels— Fourth Edition

A shiny brass halo tops this smiling kitten angel, who holds a basket full of silvery stars. Her fluffy tail peeks out from her blue pearlized dress, and her pearly wings add to her angelic appearance.
◼ Handcrafted, 1⅛" tall
450QXM512-2, $4.50
Artist: Patricia Andrews

Thimble Bells—Fourth and Final Edition

A red poinsettia decal is surrounded by holly leaves and berries. The design continues on the back, where "1993" is painted in gold. The clapper is real brass.
◼ Fine Porcelain, 1⅛" tall
575QXM514-2, $5.75
Artist: LaDene Votruba

Noel R.R.—Fifth Edition

Santa's sleigh, bearing a golden "1993" on one side, is hitching a ride on this "Flatbed Car." Toys and other colorful treats, overflow the sleigh. It is decorated with garland on each end, and its tiny red wheels really turn.
◼ Handcrafted, ⅞" tall
700QXM510-5, $7.00
Artist: Linda Sickman

The Kringles— Fifth and Final Edition

Mr. and Mrs. Kringle are ready for the final touch, hanging the Christmas wreath. The nostalgic couple is designed in a fashion that resembles handcarved wood.
◼ Handcrafted, 1" tall
575QXM513-5, $5.75
Artist: Anita Marra Rogers

Rocking Horse— Sixth Edition

This black steed with a black-and-white spotted area on his back is a Blanket Appaloosa. "1993" is painted in golden letters on the red rockers.
◼ Handcrafted, 1⅛" tall
450QXM511-2, $4.50
Artist: Linda Sickman

Old English Village—Sixth Edition

This snow-covered "Toy Shop" bears a tiny wreath on the door, bright cheery windows, and "1993" above the door, just below the glowing porch light.
◼ Handcrafted, Handpainted, 1¹⁄₁₆" tall
700QXM513-2, $7.00
Artist: Julia Lee

Hallmark

Baby's First Christmas

Grandchild's First Christmas

Commemoratives

Baby's First Christmas
Precious baby booties with mint green ties and brass-colored bells attach to a shining brass tag that announces, "Baby's 1st Christmas 1992."
■ Handcrafted, Brass, 1¼" tall
450QXM549-4, $4.50
Artist: Joyce Lyle

Grandchild's First Christmas
This charming revolving carousel celebrates "Grandchild's First Christmas." Little animal friends welcome Baby. "92" appears at the base of the center pole which turns.
■ Handcrafted, 1¼" tall
575QXM550-1, $5.75
Artist: John Francis (Collin)

Friends Are Tops
Two chipmunks spin with delight as they balance on a red and gold top. "Friends Are Tops" is debossed on the top rim, along with the date "92."
■ Handcrafted, 1⅛" tall
450QXM552-1, $4.50
Artist: Ken Crow

Mom
Mom discovers the purrfect bonnet in a lovely Christmas hatbox. The box is captioned "Mom 1992" and is decorated with a golden cord.
■ Handcrafted, 1⁷⁄₁₆" tall
450QXM550-4, $4.50
Artist: Patricia Andrews

Grandma
Grandmas delight in receiving mail from friends and family. This grandma bunny's mailbox is brimming with holiday wishes. Dated "1992," "Grandma" is a new commemorative in the Keepsake Miniature Collection this year.
■ Handcrafted, 1⅛" tall
450QXM551-4, $4.50
Artist: Duane Unruh

A+ Teacher
Teacher earns the highest marks. A raccoon records the message with chalk on a framed blackboard: "A+ TEACHER 1992."
■ Handcrafted, 1⅛" tall
375QXM551-1, $3.75
Artist: Duane Unruh

1992 KEEPSAKE MINIATURE COLLECTION

Keepsake Miniature Ornaments continue to delight collectors. To keep things interesting and new, Hallmark introduced the new "The Night Before Christmas" series inspired by Clement C. Moore's classic poem. This series of five miniature ornaments was introduced in 1992 along with a "Tin Display House." Collectors expressed excitement as they went about adding the "Tin House" and the first in the series ornament, "Rocker with Mouse," to their collections. Each of the next four years introduce another miniature ornament for display in the "Tin Display House."

Friends Are Tops

Mom

Grandma

A+ Teacher

Puppet Show

Wee Three Kings

Hoop It Up

Ski for Two

Christmas Bonus

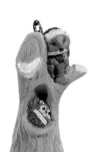

Visions of Acorns

Holiday Traditions

Puppet Show

Ready to bring smiles to his audience with his clever hand puppet, this delightful bear wears a shirt dated "92" and a red Santa cap.

■ Handcrafted, 1" tall
300QXM557-4, $3.00
Artist: Bob Siedler

Wee Three Kings

On their Christmas journey, three brightly dressed kings ride atop a camel. The revolving wheels are attached to a stand dated "1992." The ornament is sculpted to look like carved wood.

■ Handcrafted, 1³⁄₁₆" tall
575QXM553-1, $5.75
Artist: Don Palmiter

Hoop It Up

Enjoying his workout with a flexible red hoop, this elf is outfitted in a green and white coat dated "92." Gently tap the hoop, and both the elf and hoop jiggle.

■ Handcrafted, 1" tall
450QXM583-1, $4.50
Artist: Ken Crow

Ski for Two

Speeding down the slopes on tandem skis, this dog and cat make a dashing pair. The date, "92," appears on the dog's cap.

■ Handcrafted, ¹⁵⁄₁₆" tall
450QXM582-1, $4.50
Artist: Patricia Andrews

Christmas Bonus

To deliver this year's "Christmas Bonus," the smiling bunny climbs out of a festive red envelope, dated "1992" on the back.

■ Handcrafted, 1³⁄₁₆" tall
300QXM581-1, $3.00
Artist: Don Palmiter

Visions of Acorns

When squirrels dream of Christmas surprises, it is of stockings brimming with acorns. This squirrel happily obliges. "92" appears in a heart, carved on the back of the tree.

■ Handcrafted, 1³⁄₁₆" tall
450QXM585-1, $4.50
Artist: Patricia Andrews

Polar Polka

Atop an icy dance floor dated "1992," polar bears enjoy a festive polka. A pair of ice tongs frames this endearing scene and forms a heart at the top, which acts as the ornament hanger.
■ Handcrafted, 1¹³⁄₁₆" tall
450QXM553-4, $4.50
Artist: Ed Seale

Angelic Harpist

You can almost hear the tunes from this angel's harp, as she flies on delicately sculpted angel wings. Her blue gown swirls around her feet.
■ Handcrafted, 1¼" tall
450QXM552-4, $4.50
Artist: Joyce Lyle

Cozy Kayak

Ready for the rapids, this clever turtle has converted his shell into a kayak. The date, "92," appears on the top of the kayak.
■ Handcrafted, ¾" tall
375QXM555-1, $3.75
Artist: Julia Lee

Cool Uncle Sam

With whiskers and goatee like Uncle Sam, our snowman shows a patriotic flair, marking the "92" election year.
■ Handcrafted, 1" tall
300QXM556-1, $3.00
Artist: Julia Lee

Snug Kitty

This kitty found the perfect spot for Christmas Eve dreaming. Snuggled in a dresser drawer, he hangs his stocking, dated "92," on the handle of the drawer.
■ Handcrafted, 1" tall
375QXM555-4, $3.75
Artist: Sharon Pike

Gerbil Inc.

Greeting the workday with a smile and a coffee cup labeled "Joy," a chubby little gerbil holds a "92" clipboard.
■ Handcrafted, ⅞" tall
375QXM592-4, $3.75
Artist: Bob Siedler

Little Town of Bethlehem

A woven wreath frames the town of Bethlehem. A red bow adorns the top, and the date, "1992," appears at the base of the wreath.
■ Handcrafted, 1" diam.
300QXM586-4, $3.00
Artist: Linda Sickman

Polar Polka

Angelic Harpist

Cozy Kayak

Cool Uncle Sam

Snug Kitty

Gerbil Inc.

Little Town of Bethlehem

Friendly Tin Soldier

Minted for Santa

Coca-Cola® Santa

Inside Story

Christmas Copter

Holiday Splash

Friendly Tin Soldier

At attention, a uniformed sentry is posted at the front door of a six-sided guardhouse. Peek in the windows of this pressed tin house, and you'll find a kitten and a colorful poinsettia.

■ Pressed Tin, 1¹⁄₁₆" tall
450QXM587-4, $4.50
Artist: Linda Sickman

Minted for Santa

Santa now has a coin minted just for him. "E PLURIBUS SANTA" appears on the front, along with a bas-relief image of Santa and the date, "1992." The back features the message, "MERRY CHRISTMAS."

■ Antiqued Copper, 1" diam.
375QXM585-4, $3.75
Artist: Duane Unruh

Coca-Cola® Santa

This design of the popular Coca-Cola® Santa Claus is modeled after the illustrations of Haddon Sundblom.

■ Handcrafted, 1³⁄₁₆" tall
575QXM588-4, $5.75
Artist: Duane Unruh

Inside Story

How does Santa and his sleigh full of gifts fit into this tiny, tiny bottle? Only Santa knows for sure. The sleigh is dated "1992."

■ Handcrafted, ¾" tall
725QXM588-1, $7.25
Artist: Ed Seale

Christmas Copter

Dated "1992," this helicopter is ready to deliver holiday cheer. A tiny mouse sits in the cockpit of the colorful copter, complete with candy cane runners and a propeller that spins.

■ Handcrafted, ⅞" tall
575QXM584-4, $5.75
Artist: Julia Lee

Holiday Splash

Outfitted in a red Santa cap is a festive goldfish. The fishbowl, dated "92," houses a coral Christmas tree painted green.

■ Handcrafted, 1" tall
575QXM583-4, $5.75
Artist: John Francis (Collin)

Snowshoe Bunny

With snowshoes securely fastened, this bunny is ready for some cross-country traveling. He's wearing green ear muffs and a colorful red muffler.
- Handcrafted, 1¹⁄₁₆" tall
  375QXM556-4, $3.75
  Artist: LaDene Votruba

Spunky Monkey

Munching on a banana, this spunky fellow has a curly tail that forms the ornament hanger. His red cap is dated "92."
- Handcrafted, 1⅜" tall
  300QXM592-1, $3.00
  Artist: Robert Chad

Bright Stringers

Two bluebirds string colorful lights on a golden wire. The birds can perch on one or two different branches of your tree.
- Handcrafted, 1⅛" tall
  375QXM584-1, $3.75
  Artist: Ed Seale

Perfect Balance

This talented seal balances a gift, dated "92" while he sits atop a colorful red ball ornament. A festive wreath with red bow completes his holiday attire.
- Handcrafted, 1¼" tall
  300QXM557-1, $3.00
  Artist: Anita Marra Rogers

Snowshoe Bunny

Buck-A-Roo

Santa climbs atop this rocking reindeer for a rollicking ride. He's outfitted with cowboy boots and a ten-gallon hat. The rocker is dated "1992."
- Handcrafted, 1⅛" tall
  450QXM581-4, $4.50
  Artist: Ken Crow

Hickory, Dickory, Dock

The date and the title appear on the back of the clock: "Hickory, Dickory, Dock! 1992."
- Handcrafted, 1³⁄₁₆" tall
  375QXM586-1, $3.75
  Artist: Robert Chad

Going Places

These friends snuggle close together, sledding on a silvery saucer dated "92." The puppy sits in front of the child, eager for adventure.
- Handcrafted, 1" tall
  375QXM587-1, $3.75
  Artist: Patricia Andrews

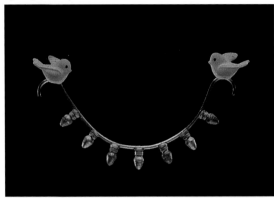

Spunky Monkey

Bright Stringers

Perfect Balance

Buck-A-Roo

Hickory, Dickory, Dock

Going Places

Fast Finish

Feeding Time

Black-Capped Chickadee

Harmony Trio

Sew, Sew Tiny

Fast Finish

Santa hops on his cycle to make deliveries to homes off the reindeer path. On his back, his bundle of surprises is dated "92."
■ Handcrafted, ⅞" tall
375QXM530-1, $3.75
Artist: Dill Rhodus

Harmony Trio

Tux 'n tails is the dapper uniform of this happy trio. Each musician is dated "1992." Harmonizing together are "Fox Violinist," "Horn-Playing Pig," and "Bunny Flutist."
■ Handcrafted, All 1⅛" tall
1175QXM547-1, $11.75
Artist: LaDene Votruba

Sew, Sew Tiny

This set of happy mice is "sew" talented! One mouse discovers a wooden spool of red thread is a handy place to watch the holiday festivities while threading a real needle. Called "Threaded Thru," this design is dated "1992." Another mouse peeks out of a silvery thimble in "Thimble Full." The "Buttoned Up" mouse sews on a button with a real needle. Tiny metal scissors come in handy for clipping real green ribbon in "Cutting Edge." Sticking a pin into a red pin cushion helps the "Pinned On" mouse keep organized. And a sleepy mouse catches a few winks in a basket of green yarn in "Basket Break."
■ Basket Break, 1⅛" tall
■ Pinned On, 1⅛" tall
■ Buttoned Up, ¾" tall
■ Thimble Full, ¹³⁄₁₆" tall
■ Cutting Edge, ⅞" tall
■ Threaded Thru, 1¼" tall
All Handcrafted
2900QXM579-4, $29.00
Artist: Ed Seale

Artists' Favorites

Feeding Time

Artist Ken Crow enjoys creating movement so that "something jiggles or rocks, and the characters come to life" in his designs. When Santa makes the rounds of his reindeer stables at "Feeding Time," the reindeer's head nods in approval. The stall is dated "92," and Ken's signature is on the back.
■ Handcrafted, 1" tall
575QXM548-1, $5.75
Artist: Ken Crow

Black-Capped Chickadee

As a nature lover, artist John Francis (Collin) finds the inspiration for many of his ornament designs perched on one of six bird feeders in his back yard. This "Black-Capped Chickadee" perches on a festive woven wreath adorned with a red bow and dated "92" on the back. You'll find John's middle name, "Collin," on the bird.
■ Handcrafted, 1⅛" tall
300QXM548-4, $3.00
Artist: John Francis (Collin)

The Night Before Christmas

The Bearymores

Collectible Series

The Night Before Christmas—First Edition

With the world's most beloved poem by Clement C. Moore as inspiration, each ornament in this new series will make the story of Santa's visit come to life. A wonderfully detailed tin Display House, which opens like a book, has been created to showcase the series. You'll find the text of "The Night Before Christmas" printed on the inside front cover and continued on the back, so that it can be read and enjoyed every year. The inside right panel highlights interior rooms of the three-story house that features the ornaments. The first edition ornament illustrates the line, "Not a creature was stirring, not even a mouse." A slumbering white mouse curls up on the cushion of a tan rocking chair dated "1992." The chair attaches to the hook you'll place near the grandfather clock in the parlor. The house comes with four additional hooks for future editions.

▨ Tin Display House, 8" tall
   Artist: LaDene Votruba
▨ Handcrafted Mouse, 1⅛" tall
   Artist: Duane Unruh
   1375QXM554-1, $13.75

The Bearymores—First Edition

A new series introduces us to the Bearymores—a merry family of polar bears. Peek inside at these beary friendly bears trimming a Christmas tree. The base of the dome is dated "1992."

▨ Handcrafted, 1⅛" tall
   575QXM554-4, $5.75
   Artist: Anita Marra Rogers

Woodland Babies—Second Edition

With holly berries dancing over his head, this slumbering skunk snuggles under a yellow blanket in a holly leaf cradle that is dated, "1992."

▨ Handcrafted, 1" tall
   600QXM544-4, $6.00
   Artist: Don Palmiter

Thimble Bells—Third Edition

A sweet teddy bear wearing a fluffy bow nestles against a gift-wrapped package. A holly leaf and the date "1992" appear on the back of this porcelain bell with golden clapper.

▨ Fine Porcelain, 1⅛" tall
   600QXM546-1, $6.00
   Artist: Joyce Lyle

Woodland Babies

Thimble Bells

Precious Edition

Holiday Holly

A cherished holiday symbol, holly was once thought to bring good luck to the home. These shimmering 22-karat gold-plated holly leaves are adorned with sparkling red berries. Dated "1992" on the back, the delicately sculpted golden leaves are topped with a red fabric bow.

▨ Plated in 22-Karat Gold, 1⅛" tall
   975QXM536-4, $9.75

Nature's Angels

The Kringles

Old English Village— Fifth Edition

The intricate detail on this carefully sculpted "Church" highlights its Old English charm. The doorway is dated "1992" overhead.

■ Handcrafted, Handpainted, 1⁵⁄₁₆" tall
700QXM538-4, $7.00
Artist: Julia Lee

Old English Village

Nature's Angels— Third Edition

A koala bear joins this band of angels. Designed with pearly blue wings and a brass halo, he carries a Christmas wreath.

■ Handcrafted, 1" tall
450QXM545-1, $4.50
Artist: Sharon Pike

The Kringles— Fourth Edition

Mr. and Mrs. "K" sing holiday carols. The duo is designed to look like handcarved wood.

■ Handcrafted, 1" tall
600QXM538-1, $6.00
Artist: Anita Marra Rogers

Rocking Horse— Fifth Edition

This handsome steed invites you to climb aboard his mint green saddle with red trim. The brown horse stands on green rockers dated "1992."

■ Handcrafted, 1⅛" tall
450QXM545-4, $4.50
Artist: Linda Sickman

Kittens in Toyland— Fifth and Final Edition

This happy kitty bounces into your heart atop a red and silver painted pogo stick.

■ Handcrafted, 1³⁄₁₆" tall
450QXM539-1, $4.50
Artist: Ken Crow

Noel R.R.

Noel R.R.— Fourth Edition

This train car's doors slide open on both sides, revealing tiny toys inside. Dated "1992" on each door panel, the box car has movable wheels.

■ Handcrafted, ¹³⁄₁₆" tall
700QXM544-1, $7.00
Artist: Linda Sickman

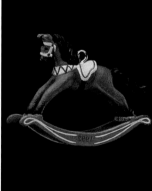

Rocking Horse

Kittens in Toyland

Mom

Baby's First Christmas

1991
KEEPSAKE MINIATURE COLLECTION

The 1991 Keepsake Miniature Ornament line offered the first Keepsake Miniature Ornaments as a set with "Tiny Tea Party." Silver-plating was another miniature first with "Silvery Santa," the second design in the "Precious Edition" category introduced in 1990. A new commemorative caption, "Mom," debuted in 1991, in lieu of the more traditional "Mother." "Love Is Born" became the first fine porcelain collector's plate in miniature, and the holiday wish "Feliz Navidad" made its first appearance.

Collectors also discovered two miniature Ornaments reminiscent of favorite Keepsake and Hallmark designs. "Heavenly Minstrel" is patterned after the 1980 Keepsake Ornament of the same name, and the "Wee Toymaker" shares the styling of the Hallmark figurine series called "The Toymaker." And, for the second year, there were two "Artists' Favorites" designs: "Lulu & Family" and "Ring-A-Ding Elf." Ornaments with movable parts include "Baby's First Christmas," "Busy Bear," and the "Passenger Car" in the "Noel R.R." Collectible Series. The year also saw the debut of the new Collectible Series, "Woodland Babies," and the final edition of "Penguin Pal."

Commemoratives

Mom
There's lots of love in every stitch on a sample made for "Mom 1991." The industrious little chipmunk holds a real needle and thread.
▨ Handcrafted, 1³⁄₁₆" tall
600QXM569-9, $6.00
Artist: Bob Siedler

Baby's First Christmas
A baby mouse sleeps inside a carriage crafted from household objects that resemble a shoebox, nutshell, matchstick, and paper clips. Button-shaped wheels actually turn. Captions: "Baby's 1st Christmas" and "1991."
▨ Handcrafted, 1" tall
600QXM579-9, $6.00
Artist: John Francis (Collin)

Grandchild's First Christmas
This fine porcelain rattle is decorated with holly and a red bow. The hanger is a fabric ribbon. Front: "Grandchild 1991." Back: "1st Christmas."
▨ Handpainted Fine Porcelain, 1¹⁄₁₆" tall
450QXM569-7, $4.50
Artist: Anita Marra Rogers

First Christmas Together
An old-fashioned sleigh ride for two is the perfect way to spend a holiday. This Victorian-style sleigh glides on shiny brass runners. Captions: "First Christmas Together" and "1991."
▨ Handcrafted, Brass, 1⅛" tall
600QXM581-9, $6.00
Artist: Duane Unruh

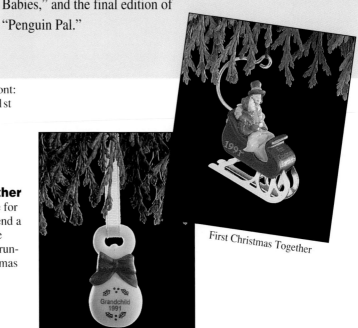

First Christmas Together

Grandchild's First Christmas

Key to Love

Special Friends

Tiny Tea Party Set

These handcrafted mice have come for tea and cookies and stayed to play. A mouse in a blue shirt waves from inside the "Teapot," while another offers a sugar cube from the "Sugar Bowl," and a third stands in the "Creamer" with a spoon in hand. The fourth mouse sits on the "Cookie Plate" and nibbles a cookie. And two more mice have climbed inside teacups—one is resting, and the other has a spoon for stirring. This is the first theme group of Keepsake Miniature Ornaments to be offered only as a set. Fashioned of fine porcelain, the tea set pieces are decorated with a hearts-and-holly pattern and dated "1991."

Fine Porcelain, Handcrafted
■ Cookie Plate, ¹¹⁄₁₆" tall
■ Teacup Lounger, ⅝" tall
■ Teacup Taster, ¹³⁄₁₆" tall
■ Teapot, 1" tall
■ Creamer, 1³⁄₁₆" tall
■ Sugar Bowl, ¹⁵⁄₁₆" tall
2900QXM582-7, $29.00
Artist: Ed Seale

Key to Love

Opening the pretty red heart-shaped lock is easy for this bunny. Someone special has provided a golden key. The caption, "Love 1991," is embossed on the heart.
■ Handcrafted, 1" tall
450QXM568-9, $4.50
Artist: Ken Crow

Special Friends

Inside a real wicker basket, a puppy and kitty settle down for a nap on a red-and-green plaid blanket. A red fabric bow decorates the basket, and the handle has a gift tag that reads "Special Friends" on one side and "1991" on the other.
■ Handcrafted, Wicker, ¹³⁄₁₆" tall
850QXM579-7, $8.50
Artist: Julia Lee

Holiday Traditions

Heavenly Minstrel

The classic styling of this old-world angel is reminiscent of the Special Edition "Heavenly Minstrel" design in the 1980 Keepsake Ornament line. Like her predecessor, she wears a softly flowing blue gown topped with a beige stole, and strums a golden lute.
■ Handcrafted, 1¹³⁄₁₆" tall
975QXM568-7, $9.75
Artist: Donna Lee

Wee Toymaker

Santa is putting the finishing touches on a shiny toy airplane. He's painting the craft a bright metallic silver, and you can see the silver paint on his brush. The jolly old elf sits on a bench dated "1991." This highly detailed ornament is similar in styling to the popular Hallmark figurine series, "The Toymaker."
■ Handcrafted, 1" tall
850QXM596-7, $8.50
Artist: Ron Bishop

Tiny Tea Party Set

Heavenly Minstrel

Wee Toymaker

Treeland Trio

A squirrel, bunny, and mouse dress up in Victorian-era finery to enjoy the old-fashioned fun of going a-caroling. All three have open songbooks, and the bunny's book displays the year date "1991" on the cover.

■ Handcrafted, ⅞" tall
850QXM589-9, $8.50
Artist: Robert Chad

Feliz Navidad

Festively dressed for holiday fun, this little bunny has a real straw *sombrero* that's as big as he is! His *serape* expresses the traditional holiday greeting in Spanish, "Feliz Navidad 1991."

■ Handcrafted, Straw, 1" tall
600QXM588-7, $6.00
Artist: Anita Marra Rogers

Upbeat Bear

Sitting atop a real metal drum, a drum-major bear taps out a lively holiday rhythm. The date, "91," appears on the front of the drum.

■ Handcrafted, Metal, 1¹⁄₁₆" tall
600QXM590-7, $6.00
Artist: John Francis (Collin)

Caring Shepherd

Standing at watchful attention, this appealing little shepherd holds a tiny lamb and carries a staff made of gleaming brass. The ornament has been painted by hand in delicate pastel colors.

■ Handpainted Fine Porcelain, 1¹⁄₁₆" tall
600QXM594-9, $6.00
Artist: John Francis (Collin)

Cardinal Cameo

A beautifully sculpted red cardinal is perched among bas-relief holly branches with red berries. Back caption: "Season's Greetings 1991."

■ Handcrafted, 1¹⁄₁₆" tall
600QXM595-7, $6.00
Artist: Joyce Lyle

Friendly Fawn

Wearing a fluffy wreath collar, this detailed little deer has come for a holiday visit. The sculpted red banner on the collar has a trailing ribbon with "1991."

■ Handcrafted, 1⅛" tall
600QXM594-7, $6.00
Artist: Julia Lee

Top Hatter

A rabbit has created his own magic act. He's popped up out of the magician's shiny hat holding a brightly wrapped gift package. The hat is dated "1991."

■ Handcrafted, 1" tall
600QXM588-9, $6.00
Artist: Ed Seale

Country Sleigh

Brilliant, fired-on enamel colors give this design a special elegance. An antique red sleigh, dated "1991," is carrying a fresh-cut Christmas tree.

■ Enamel, 1" tall
450QXM599-9, $4.50
Artist: LaDene Votruba

Treeland Trio

Feliz Navidad   Upbeat Bear

Caring Shepherd

Cardinal Cameo

Country Sleigh

Top Hatter

Friendly Fawn

Courier Turtle

Fly By

Kitty in a Mitty

Li'l Popper

All Aboard

Cool 'n Sweet

Bright Boxers

Seaside Otter

Courier Turtle

Before heading out on his holiday rounds, a happy turtle puts the finishing touches on his "home" decorations. He's draping a bright red handcrafted bow across his shell and tying it under his chin.

■ Handcrafted, 1⅛" tall
450QXM585-7, $4.50
Artist: Sharon Pike

Fly By

Gliding on a carefully folded "paper" airplane, an elf in a Santa cap holds tight to a gift-wrapped package. The caption, "Merry Christmas," appears on one side of the plane and the date "1991" is on the other.

■ Handcrafted, ⅞" tall
450QXM585-9, $4.50
Artist: Ken Crow

Bright Boxers

Santa's always wanted bright red shorts decorated with green Christmas trees! The outfit includes a T-shirt with the date, "1991," printed in red.

■ Handcrafted, 1" tall
450QXM587-7, $4.50
Artist: Dill Rhodus

Seaside Otter

The first otter ever to appear in the Keepsake line feels right at home, arriving on a sled that was molded from a real seashell. The playful otter is wearing a hand-crafted red scarf.

■ Handcrafted, ⅞" tall
450QXM590-9, $4.50
Artist: Bob Siedler

Li'l Popper

A fun-loving mouse in a red sweater thinks that swinging from a popcorn strand is even more fun than stringing it. This stringer ornament can be placed on one branch or suspended between two branches.

■ Handcrafted, 1¼" tall
450QXM589-7, $4.50
Artist: Linda Sickman

Kitty in a Mitty

Wearing a handcrafted green bow and tucked inside a red mitten (that could be Santa's own), this little kitten could be dreaming of a catnip treat. The back of the mitten says: "1991."

■ Handcrafted, 1" tall
450QXM587-9, $4.50
Artist: Patricia Andrews

Cool 'n Sweet

This rosy-cheeked snowman knows the holidays are here—he's carrying a peppermint-striped candy cane instead of the traditional broom. The date, "1991," appears on his hat.

■ Handpainted Fine Porcelain, 1³⁄₁₆" tall
450QXM586-7, $4.50
Artist: Sharon Pike

All Aboard

Wearing an engineer's cap and riding a green locomotive, a smiling beaver is ready for holiday adventure. The train has a golden cowcatcher and trim, and the date, "1991," appears on the side of the car.

■ Handcrafted, 1" tall
450QXM586-9, $4.50
Artist: Robert Chad

Fancy Wreath

Baby's breath adds a festive touch to this sculpted holly wreath. A handcrafted red bow, with a thin golden border, provides an elegant accent.
▧ Handcrafted, 1¹⁄₁₆" tall
450QXM591-7, $4.50
Artist: Joyce Lyle

Vision of Santa

The look of handcarved wood is especially appropriate for this old-fashioned, wreath-encircled Santa with a striped candy cane. Carved into the back of the ornament is the message: "Happy Holidays 1991."
▧ Handcrafted, 1¹⁄₁₆" tall
450QXM593-7, $4.50
Artist: Robert Chad

Busy Bear

With your help, this lovable teddy moves its arms and legs up and down to earn the name "Busy Bear."
▧ Wood, 1¹⁄₁₆" tall
450QXM593-9, $4.50
Artist: Dill Rhodus

N. Pole Buddy

Softly flocked, a polar bear cub wears a red-and-green stocking cap that's dated "1991."
▧ Handcrafted, 1" tall
450QXM592-7, $4.50
Artist: Don Palmiter

Brass Bells

A pair of gleaming brass bells invites everyone to share the joy of the season. The carefully etched and pierced design includes an intricately ribbed bow and ribbon. "1991" decorates the rim of one bell.
▧ Brass 1¼" tall
300QXM597-7, $3.00
Artist: Patricia Andrews

Holiday Snowflake

The delicate beauty of a single snowflake is captured forever in a clear acrylic teardrop. The date "1991," appears in sparkling blue foil, and the faceted edges are designed to reflect light like fine cut glass.
▧ Acrylic, 1¹⁵⁄₃₂" tall
300QXM599-7, $3.00
Artist: Dill Rhodus

Noel

Shiny red foil forms calligraphy-style letters for the word "Noel," and "1991." The faceted edges of this clear acrylic oval sparkle with the light.
▧ Acrylic, ³⁄₃₂" tall
300QXM598-9, $3.00

Love Is Born

Mary and Joseph kneel beside the crib in the manger. Above them, a bright star radiates golden shafts of light. The front of this fine porcelain plate carries "1991," and the caption on the back reads: "Love is born."
▧ Fine Porcelain, 1¹⁄₁₆" diam.
600QXM595-9, $6.00
Artist: LaDene Votruba

Fancy Wreath

Vision of Santa

Busy Bear

N. Pole Buddy

Brass Bells

Holiday Snowflake

Love Is Born

Noel

Brass Church

Brass Soldier

Ring-A-Ding Elf

Lulu & Family

Woodland Babies

Brass Church

Shimmering in the light, a delicately etched brass church sends its spire skyward, beyond the wreath that encircles the design. The year, "1991," is etched on a banner below the church.
■ Brass, 1¼" tall
300QXM597-9, $3.00

Brass Soldier

A toy soldier proudly stands inside a glowing wreath. The etched and pierced design on his dress uniform sparkles in the light. The date, "1991," is displayed on the crown of the soldier's hat.
■ Brass, 1¼" tall
300QXM598-7, $3.00

Artists' Favorites

Ring-A-Ding Elf

Robert Chad says he loves the music of Christmas and "the fantasy of the elves in Santa's workshop." He especially enjoys sculpting elves in fun situations—such as this one, riding a real brass bell. The front of the bell carries the date, "1991," and the artist's signature, "Chad," is on the back.
■ Handcrafted, Brass, 1¼" tall
850QXM566-9, $8.50
Artist: Robert Chad

Lulu & Family

When basset hound Lulu was a puppy, artist Anita Marra Rogers used her as a model for the 1989 Keepsake Ornament "Thimble

Puppy." Then, when Lulu became a mom, the artist sculpted her and her four playful offspring in their favorite poses. "Lulu was a terrific mom— very patient and proud," says the artist. "There's Fred, the climber, and playful Little Toby, and Junior, and Piggy." Lulu wears a real fabric ribbon around her neck. The artist's signature, "Anita," appears on the bottom of the ornament.
■ Handcrafted, ⅞" tall
600QXM567-7, $6.00
Artist: Anita Marra Rogers

Collectible Series

Woodland Babies— First Edition

Snug in a nutshell cradle, a baby squirrel gently sways from a branch of your tree. In future years, other "Woodland Babies" will arrive in Nature's gifts to join the collection.
■ Handcrafted, 1" tall
600QXM566-7, $6.00
Artist: Ken Crow

Nature's Angels— Second Edition

A puppy, with its mouth open to sing, joins the angelic little creatures in this heavenly series. The puppy has pearly white wings and a shiny brass halo.
■ Handcrafted, Brass, 1⅛" tall
450QXM565-7, $4.50
Artist: Sharon Pike

Precious Edition

Silvery Santa

The first silver-plated ornament in the Keepsake Miniature line is the jolly gentleman who's on everyone's mind at Christmas. This diminutive Santa has lots of toys for good boys and girls. He's holding a teddy bear and carrying a pack of gifts that includes a doll, ball, and candy cane. The date, "1991," is etched on the pack. The gleaming silver-plated ornament has been carefully antiqued to highlight the intricately sculpted design.
■ Silver-Plated, 1⅛" tall
975QXM567-9, $9.75
Artist: Julia Lee

Nature's Angels

Thimble Bells

Thimble Bells—
Second Edition

Holly branches and red berries complement the graceful shape of this ornament dated "1991."
◾ Fine Porcelain, 1⅛" tall
600QXM565-9, $6.00
Artist: Michele Pyda-Sevcik

The Kringles—
Third Edition

Little children know that Santa loves cookies— and so does Mrs. K. "The Kringles" will share this batch before Santa leaves on his rounds.
◾ Handcrafted, 1" tall
600QXM564-7, $6.00
Artist: Anita Marra Rogers

Noel R.R.—Third Edition

Holiday travelers are eagerly waiting inside the "Passenger Car" for their excursion to begin. The wheels on this highly detailed model really turn. Both sides of the car are dated "1991."
◾ Handcrafted, 1³⁄₁₆" tall
850QXM564-9, $8.50
Artist: Linda Sickman

Old English Village—
Fourth Edition

A warm welcome awaits guests at the friendly country "INN," where tiny window panes seem to glow with golden light. The address is "1991."
◾ Handcrafted, 1⅛" tall
850QXM562-7, $8.50
Artist: Julia Lee

Rocking Horse—
Fourth Edition

This dashing grey Arabian steed with a dark gray mane and tail gallops into the holidays on red rockers dated "1991."
◾ Handcrafted, 1⅛" tall
450QXM563-7, $4.50
Artist: Linda Sickman

Kittens in Toyland—
Fourth Edition

A black-and-white kitty pilots a toy airplane.
◾ Handcrafted, ⅞" tall
450QXM563-9, $4.50
Artist: Ken Crow

Penguin Pal—Fourth
and Final Edition

Siding across the ice to join his friends, this little penguin concludes the series.
◾ Handcrafted, ¾" tall
450QXM562-9, $4.50
Artist: Bob Siedler

The Kringles   Noel R.R.

Old English Village

Rocking Horse

Kittens in Toyland, Penguin Pal

1990 KEEPSAKE MINIATURE COLLECTION

Special Friends

There were a number of "firsts" in the 1990 Keepsake Miniature Ornament line. Leading the list was the new category, "Precious Edition," which features a different special material each year. The first edition, "Cloisonné Poinsettia," features an intricate die-cut design in brilliant colors created by the enameling process. "Artists' Favorites" joined the miniature line with "Santa's Streetcar" and "Snow Angel." And two new commemorative captions were added: "Grandchild's First Christmas," and "Teacher." Two new Collectible Series also made their debut— the graceful "Thimble Bells" and the lovable "Nature's Angels."

Keepsakes artists continued to delight collectors with special details on a diminutive scale. The "Wee Nutcracker" opens his mouth, and his arms move. The mobile of tiny bunnies and ducks in "Baby's First Christmas" moves, and the elf in "Stringing Along" holds a flexible strand of beads. Even the attachments to the ornaments are unusual—the little chipmunk in the "Stamp Collector" design is using a real magnifying lens.

Commemoratives

Special Friends
Two kittens ride in a red wagon that says: "Special Friends." Inspiring childhood memories, the wagon has a real string pull.
■ Handcrafted, 1⁵⁄₁₆" tall
600QXM572-6, $6.00
Artist: Sharon Pike

Baby's First Christmas
Baby sleeps in a cradle beneath a mobile of bunnies and ducks. The tiny mobile actually moves, and the caption reads: "Baby's 1st Christmas 1990."
■ Handcrafted, 1⅛" tall
850QXM570-3, $8.50
Artist: John Francis (Collin)

Grandchild's First Christmas
A teddy bear with a white "belly button" snuggles against pink and blue pillows in his rocking chair. Front caption: "Grandchild." Back caption: "1st Christmas 1990."
■ Handcrafted, 1¼" tall
600QXM572-3, $6.00
Artist: Bob Siedler

Mother
White bas-relief flowers on a rose-colored background create a lovely cameo for "Mother." The design is encircled with a brass bezel. Caption: "Wishing you everything beautiful. 1990."
■ Cameo, 1⅛" tall
450QXM571-6, $4.50
Artist: Joyce Lyle

First Christmas Together
Two doves of fine bisque porcelain cuddle in their nest. A sculpted banner reads: "1st Christmas Together 1990."
■ Handpainted Fine Porcelain, 1" tall
600QXM553-6, $6.00
Artist: Patricia Andrews

Baby's First Christmas

Grandchild's First Christmas

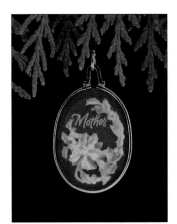

Mother

First Christmas Together

Teacher

An owl carries a bright red pencil that says: "Teacher." The eraser carries the date, "90."
- Handcrafted, ⅞" tall
  450QXM565-3, $4.50
  Artist: Sharon Pike

Loving Hearts

Love adds life to the holidays, just as this faceted ornament adds sparkle to your tree. The gold foil caption reads: "Two Hearts One Love."
- Acrylic, 1¼" tall
  300QXM552-3, $3.00

Holiday Traditions

Stringing Along

Holding a flexible string of golden beads, this rosy-cheeked elf is ready to decorate for Christmas. He's dressed in holiday attire, and has little pointy shoes, cap…and ears!
- Handcrafted, 1⅛" tall
  850QXM560-6, $8.50
  Artist: Ed Seale

Bear Hug

On Christmas Eve this little girl, with her nightgown and bunny slippers on, is ready for bed. She holds a bear with a red bow.
- Handcrafted, ¹⁵⁄₁₆" tall
  600QXM563-3, $6.00
  Artist: Don Palmiter

Santa's Journey

Santa gives a cheery wave as he sets off on his around-the-world journey. His sleigh has shiny brass runners and a "1990" date.
- Handcrafted, 1" tall
  850QXM582-6, $8.50
  Artist: Linda Sickman

Wee Nutcracker

This fellow's arms move, his mouth opens when you lift his coattail, and he has a fluffy white beard and hair. In one hand he holds a horn, in the other, a sheet music with notes on a staff and the date "1990."
- Handcrafted, 1¼" tall
  850QXM584-3, $8.50
  Artist: Bob Siedler

Madonna and Child

Golden halos crown both of the sweet-faced figures, and Baby Jesus is wrapped in a pearly white blanket.
- Handcrafted, 1¼" tall
  600QXM564-3, $6.00
  Artist: Anita Marra Rogers

Loving Hearts

Teacher

Stringing Along

Bear Hug

Santa's Journey

Wee Nutcracker

Madonna and Child

Perfect Fit

Acorn Wreath

Basket Buddy

Puppy Love

Panda's Surprise

Stamp Collector

Christmas Dove

Type of Joy

Basket Buddy

This friendly little spaniel puppy is pretty excited about Christmas. His basket is red woven wicker and is trimmed with a green fabric ribbon bow.

■ Handcrafted, Wicker, ¹³⁄₁₆" tall
600QXM569-6, $6.00
Artist: Anita Marra Rogers

Puppy Love

A boy in drop-seat pajamas gets a kiss from his puppy dog, who's wearing a festive holiday bow.

■ Handcrafted, 1" tall
600QXM566-6, $6.00
Artist: Don Palmiter

Perfect Fit

Santa waves happily as he prepares to slide down the chimney with his bag of toys. The snow on the chimney is pearly white, and the bricks show careful detail in their sculpting. The date, "1990," appears on the back of the chimney.

■ Handcrafted, ¹⁵⁄₁₆" tall
450QXM551-6, $4.50
Artist: Robert Chad

Acorn Wreath

Holding an acorn, the little squirrel actually swings on a red fabric cord. Six more tiny acorns decorate the wreath.

■ Handcrafted, 1¼" tall
600QXM568-6, $6.00
Artist: Ken Crow

Panda's Surprise

A jolly little jack-in-the-box Santa delights his wide-eyed panda pal. The date, "90," appears on the front of the box.

■ Handcrafted, ⅞" tall
450QXM561-6, $4.50
Artist: John Francis (Collin)

Stamp Collector

A chipmunk examines a stamp with a real magnifying lens. The stamp reads "Christmas 90" and features the silhouette of a cardinal on a holly branch.

■ Handcrafted, ⅞" tall
450QXM562-3, $4.50
Artist: Ken Crow

Christmas Dove

With an olive branch in its mouth, this gentle dove brings a wish for peace. The ornament has the appearance of hand-carved wood.

■ Handcrafted, ¹¹⁄₁₆" tall
450QXM563-6, $4.50
Artist: Bob Siedler

Type of Joy

Decked out in a muffler and bright red Santa cap, this mouse is writing holiday memos. He's seated on the keyboard of a typewriter, and has just typed the word "JOY."

■ Handcrafted, ¹¹⁄₁₆" tall
450QXM564-6, $4.50
Artist: Robert Chad

Air Santa

Santa waves from the seat of his jaunty green plane, as he buzzes off on his journey. The plane's propeller is red, and the numerals "90" are printed on the tail.
■ Handcrafted, ½" tall
450QXM565-6, $4.50

Busy Carver

A beaver has been very busy carving himself a Christmas tree. On top of the tree is a golden star, and the date, "90," is carved on the base. The beaver's fur and tail reveal sculpted detail.
■ Handcrafted, ¾" tall
450QXM567-3, $4.50
Artist: Ken Crow

Going Sledding

With a wave of his paw, a little teddy is off on a sledding adventure. His red toboggan lends a Christmasy touch to your tree.
■ Handcrafted, ¹³⁄₁₆" tall
450QXM568-3, $4.50
Artist: Julia Lee

Sweet Slumber

Snug in his matchbox bed, a wee mouse dreams of Christmas morning. A textured strip on each side of the box resembles striking paper, and the top of the box is labeled "Matches."
■ Handcrafted, ⁹⁄₁₆" tall
450QXM566-3, $4.50
Artist: Bob Siedler

Warm Memories

Logs blaze in a fireplace and stockings and candles decorate the mantel. Caption: "Christmas brings warm memories. 1990."
■ Handcrafted, 1⅛" tall
450QXM571-3, $4.50
Artist: Ed Seale

Nativity

Mary and Joseph admire their Child, while a silvery star shines above. Back caption: "O Holy Night 1990."
■ Handcrafted 1⅛" tall
450QXM570-6, $4.50
Artist: Duane Unruh

Lion and Lamb

A lion and lamb sit peacefully together all season long! The wood ornament resembles an old-fashioned pull-toy.
■ Wood, 1⅛" tall
450QXM567-6, $4.50
Artist: Linda Sickman

Country Heart

Real dried flowers add to the natural charm of a heart that looks like a folk-art wheat design. The red-and-green striped fabric ribbon makes a bow, and also serves as the ornament hanger.
■ Handcrafted, 1⅛" tall
450QXM569-3, $4.50
Artist: Anita Marra Rogers

Air Santa

Busy Carver

Going Sledding

Sweet Slumber

Warm Memories

Nativity

Lion and Lamb

Country Heart

Holiday Cardinal

Holiday Cardinal

Perched on an evergreen branch, this cheerful cardinal welcomes the season. The edges of the acrylic teardrop are faceted to catch the light, and the design is etched and frosted.

◼ Acrylic, 1½" tall
300QXM552-6, $3.00
Artist: John Francis (Collin)

Brass Bouquet

An antiqued finish and delicate background texturing highlight the holly bouquet on this brass medallion. The antique look is further enhanced by a graceful scrollwork frame.

◼ Brass, 1¼" tall
600QXM577-6, $6.00
Artist: Joyce Lyle

Brass Bouquet

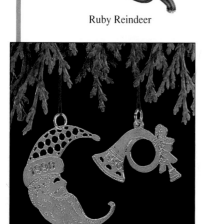

Ruby Reindeer

Brass Peace

Brass Santa, Brass Horn

Brass Year

Ruby Reindeer

Blown glass in a deep, rich red creates a delicate look. The leaping reindeer looks poised to lead the flight on Christmas Eve.

◼ Blown Glass, ¹⁵⁄₁₆" tall
600QXM581-6, $6.00
Artist: Joyce Pattee

Brass Peace

An intricate filigree pattern features the word "Peace" in the center of this gleaming brass design. The Christmas Star shines near the top.

◼ Brass, 1¼" tall
300QXM579-6, $3.00

Brass Santa

Guess who's the man in the moon? Santa himself! His hat has a decorative pierced design and carries the date, "1990."

◼ Brass, 1¼" tall
300QXM578-6, $3.00
Artist: Joyce Pattee

Brass Horn

A shiny hunting horn features an etched and pierced design and an etched bow. The date, "1990," is engraved on the bell of the horn.

◼ Brass, ¾" tall
300QXM579-3, $3.00

Brass Year

"1990" appears on an open scroll of delicate brass filigree. Etched holly leaves add to the festive charm of the design.

◼ Brass, ¾" tall
300QXM583-3, $3.00

These ornaments are reissues from 1989. See the 1989 Miniature Ornament Collection for details.

Happy Bluebird
◼ Handcrafted, ⅞" tall
450QXM566-2, $4.50
Artist: Anita Marra Rogers

Stocking Pal
◼ Handcrafted, 1" tall
450QXM567-2, $4.50
Artist: Julia Lee

Little Soldier
◼ Handcrafted, 1⅜" tall
450QXM567-5, $4.50
Artist: Linda Sickman

Acorn Squirrel
◼ Handcrafted, 1⅜" tall
450QXM568-2, $4.50
Artist: Sharon Pike

Cozy Skater
◼ Handcrafted, 1⅜" tall
450QXM573-5, $4.50
Artist: Joyce Lyle

Old-World Santa
◼ Handcrafted, 1⅜" tall
300QXM569-5, $3.00
Artist: Bob Siedler

Roly—Poly Pig
◼ Handcrafted, ⅞" tall
300QXM571-2, $3.00
Artist: Sharon Pike

Santa's Streetcar

Snow Angel

Thimble Bells

Artists' Favorites

Santa's Streetcar
As a child, artist Donna Lee once saw Santa riding past her house on a streetcar. That memory inspired this Keepsake Miniature Ornament, which shows Santa standing on the platform at one end of a colorful streetcar. The artist's signature, "Donna," appears on Santa's end of the car, and "1990" is on the other end. The ornament hanger is designed to look like the trolley pole which linked the streetcar to the wire overhead.
◼ Handcrafted, 1¼" wide
850QXM576-6, $8.50
Artist: Donna Lee

Snow Angel
Artist Julia Lee remembers making snow angels with her friends. Her design is signed "Julia" on the back, and it shows a smiling pigtailed girl in a snowsuit making an angel.
◼ Handcrafted, 1⅛" tall
600QXM577-3, $6.00
Artist: Julia Lee

Collectible Series

Thimble Bells— First Edition
A winter scene with two bunnies and a fir tree adds special charm to this miniature ornament, the first in the "Thimble Bells" series. Made of fine porcelain,

the bell has a brass clapper and bears the date "1990" on the back. A different design will be featured on the bell every year.
◼ Fine Porcelain, 1⅛" tall
600QXM554-3, $6.00
Artist: Michele Pyda-Sevcik

Nature's Angels— First Edition
This angelic bunny is the first of a series that will offer a different little animal-angel each year. Wearing a pearly white robe and a shiny brass halo, the bunny hovers on pale blue wings.
◼ Handcrafted, 1¼" tall
450QXM573-3, $4.50
Artist: Ed Seale

Nature's Angels

Precious Edition

"Precious Edition" was a new category in the Keepsake Miniature Collection in 1990. Each year, one ornament will be crafted out of a special material, such as cloisonné or silver plate. Unique artistry and detail will make each piece a precious treasure.

Cloisonné Poinsettia
The season's most beloved flower is the perfect subject for the first "Precious Edition." The brilliant colors were achieved through the art of cloisonné enameling. Delicate wires were fused onto the gilded brass surface to form compartments, which were filled with enamels and fired at high temperatures. The shimmering flower design, as well as unique die-cut detailing, appears on both sides of the ornament.
◼ Cloisonné, 1" diam.
1050QXM553-3, $10.50
Artist: LaDene Votruba

Noel R.R.

The Kringles

Old English Village

Penguin Pal

Rocking Horse

Kittens in Toyland

Noel R.R.—
Second Edition
This "Coal Car" has no lumps of coal, but carries instead a load of toys for good little boys and girls. The wheels actually revolve, and the date, "1990," appears on both sides of the car. Because this ornament was produced in two different countries, its series symbol may be found in either of two places—on the end of the car or on the bottom.
■ Handcrafted, ¾" tall
850QXM575-6, $8.50
Artist: Linda Sickman

The Kringles—
Second Edition
Mrs. "K" gives Mr. "K" a parting kiss on Christmas Eve. She holds his hat and he holds the toy bag, ready for his trip. The design looks like carved wood.
■ Handcrafted, 1" tall
600QXM575-3, $6.00
Artist: Anita Marra Rogers

Old English Village—
Third Edition
The schoolhouse is decorated for Christmas, with evergreen garlands and a wreath on the door. Other charming details include a clock tower, a stone chimney in the back, and shrubs all around the building. The word "School" and the date "1990" appear above the door.
■ Handcrafted, 1⅛" tall
850QXM576-3, $8.50
Artist: Julia Lee

Penguin Pal—
Third Edition
This little bird has found a way to fly...on skis! Third in the series of fun-loving penguins, he sports a bright red scarf and Santa hat.
■ Handcrafted, ⅞" tall
450QXM574-6, $4.50

Rocking Horse—
Third Edition
This pretty pinto is on his way to join in the holiday festivities. His turquoise rockers are accented with red and are dated "1990." His saddle and bridle are blue, turquoise, and red.
■ Handcrafted, 1⅛" tall
450QXM574-3, $4.50
Artist: Linda Sickman

Kittens in Toyland—
Third Edition
A kitten in a jaunty striped cap sails merrily along in his tiny boat. The mast is made of brass, and a small paw print decorates the sail.
■ Handcrafted, ¹³⁄₁₆" tall
450QXM573-6, $4.50
Artist: Ken Crow

♔
Hallmark

Mother

Commemoratives

Mother
A serene swan, sculpted in
snowy white, is silhouetted
against a blue background in a
unique cameo design. Bezeled in
chrome, the ornament carries
captions stamped in silver foil.
Front: "Mother." Back: "With
Love at Christmas 1989."
■ Cameo, 1¼" diam.
600QXM564-5, $6.00

Baby's First Christmas
A bunny, a wreath, and a stocking with a teddy bear inside dangle from a frosted acrylic cloud
in this mobile for Baby. The
caption on the cloud reads,
"Baby's 1st Christmas." The
stocking is dated " '89 ."
■ Handcrafted, Acrylic, 1⅛" tall
600QXM573-2, $6.00
Artist: Sharon Pike

First Christmas Together
The snow white bisque finish of
this ceramic ornament empha-
sizes the bas-relief detail of the
delicate design. Inside the

Baby's First Christmas

wreath, the circlet carries the
caption in gold: "Our 1st
Christmas 1989."
■ Ceramic, 1⅜" tall
850QXM564-2, $8.50
Artist: LaDene Votruba

Lovebirds
Two brass birds are framed by a
heart of Christmas greenery and
holly berries in this romantic
Twirl-About ornament. Etched
on both sides, the brass birds can
be rotated inside the wreath.
■ Handcrafted, Brass, 1⅛" tall
600QXM563-5, $6.00
Artist: Sharon Pike

1989
KEEPSAKE MINIATURE
COLLECTION

This year's line offered collectors nearly 40 percent more
Miniature Ornament designs than the 1988 debut offer. A
majority were fashioned in the popular handcrafted format,
but a variety of other formats were represented as well.

The collection included the first cameo design in an ornament for "Mother" and the first dimensional brass design in
an ornament called "Brass Snowflake." Ceramic and porcelain appeared in the "First Christmas Together," "Merry Seal,"
and "Strollin' Snowman" designs. Wood returned in 1989
in "Puppy Cart" and "Kitty Cart," as did acrylic in "Bunny
Hug," "Holiday Deer," and "Rejoice." Three handcrafted
designs are combinations of materials: "Baby's First
Christmas" has an acrylic cloud; "Special Friend" includes
a willow wreath; and "Lovebirds" features two brass birds
that rotate inside a wreath. "Folk Art Bunny" also moves his
front and hind legs as if he were running.

Two new Collectible Series made their premiere in 1989:
"The Kringles" and "Noel R.R." The first miniature Special
Edition ornament, "Santa's Magic Ride," also was offered
in 1989.

First Christmas Together

Lovebirds

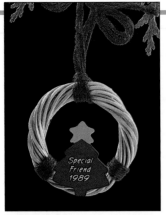

Special Friend

Sharing a Ride

Little Star Bringer

Santa's Roadster

Merry Seal

Starlit Mouse

Little Soldier

Special Friend

A handcrafted Christmas tree, topped with a bright yellow star, carries the caption for this design: "Special Friend 1989." The wreath is made of willow and is tied with a yarn bow.

◼ Handcrafted, Willow, 1⅜" tall
450QXM565-2, $4.50

Holiday Traditions

Sharing a Ride

Safe and secure on the elf's lap, a teddy bear enjoys a ride on the swing. The elf's facial features, including his flowing beard, have been meticulously sculpted and painted.

◼ Handcrafted, 1¼" tall
850QXM576-5, $8.50
Artist: Peter Dutkin

Little Star Bringer

Gowned in shimmery blue, a gentle angel flies on pearly wings to deliver her basket of stars. The star she holds in her hand is dated " '89."

◼ Handcrafted, 1¼" tall
600QXM562-2, $6.00
Artist: Joyce Lyle

Santa's Roadster

Santa's got some snazzy new wheels! The car has a silvery front grill and bumpers, and it carries a personalized license plate: "1989."

◼ Handcrafted, ¹⁵⁄₁₆" tall
600QXM566-5, $6.00
Artist: Ken Crow

Merry Seal

Fashioned in fine porcelain, a white baby seal wears a red bow trimmed with holly for Christmas. The texture of his coat and flippers has been sculpted into the design.

◼ Handpainted Fine Porcelain, ⅞" tall
600QXM575-5, $6.00
Artist: John Francis (Collin)

Starlit Mouse

Sitting on a glowing yellow acrylic star, this cheerful white mouse watches over the world celebrating Christmas. He has a little leather tail.

◼ Handcrafted, 1³⁄₁₆" tall
450QXM565-5, $4.50
Artist: Dill Rhodus

Little Soldier

Wearing his best "dress" blue and white uniform, a rosy-cheeked soldier performs a drum solo in the Christmas parade. His uniform is decorated with touches of gold.

◼ Handcrafted, 1⅜" tall
450QXM567-5, $4.50
Artist: Linda Sickman

Load of Cheer

A golden ball ornament dated, " '89," is as big as the elf carrying it, but that won't prevent him from delivering it to Santa.

◼ Handcrafted, ⅞" tall
600QXM574-5, $6.00
Artist: Dill Rhodus

Slow Motion

Who needs a sleigh and reindeer when you have a turtle to ride! The chipmunk delivers a teeny pack of gifts—perhaps some nuts for his friends. He wears a Santa cap, and his trusty steed wears a red cap with antlers.

◼ Handcrafted, 1" tall
600QXM575-2, $6.00
Artist: Bob Siedler

Load of Cheer, Slow Motion

Happy Bluebird

Carrying holly in his beak and wearing a Santa cap to keep his head warm, a bluebird flies south for Christmas.
- Handcrafted, ⅞" tall
450QXM566-2, $4.50
Artist: Anita Marra Rogers

Stocking Pal

Snug in his rosy stocking, a teddy bear is ready to be somebody's Christmas present. The ornament has been sculpted with careful attention to details, such as the texture of the bear's coat and the folds in the stocking.
- Handcrafted, 1" tall
450QXM567-2, $4.50
Artist: Julia Lee

Acorn Squirrel

An acorn makes a perfect holiday hideaway for a lucky squirrel. He's hanging a wreath outside and telling his friends that a real acorn was used to mold his home.
- Handcrafted, 1⅜" tall
450QXM568-2, $4.50
Artist: Sharon Pike

Scrimshaw Reindeer

Originally created from whalebone or ivory, scrimshaw works of art are prized for their beauty and rarity. This regal reindeer has been designed to look like a scrimshaw sculpture.
- Handcrafted, ¹⁵⁄₁₆" tall
450QXM568-5, $4.50
Artist: LaDene Votruba

Strollin' Snowman

Taking a jaunty stroll in the crisp December air seemed like a good idea to this fine porcelain snowman. He wears a green scarf, matching red boots and cap, and two tiny buttons.
- Handpainted Fine Porcelain, 1¼" tall
450QXM574-2, $4.50
Artist: Bob Siedler

Folk Art Bunny

In the tradition of American folk art, this bunny is sculpted and painted to look like wood. His front and hind legs will move if you want him to run.
- Handcrafted, 1" tall
450QXM569-2, $4.50
Artist: Joyce Pattee

Brass Snowflake

Two shimmering brass snowflakes interlock to form a dimensional, multi-sided ornament. The lacy design has been delicately etched.
- Dimensional Brass, 1⅜" tall
450QXM570-2, $4.50
Artist: Joyce Lyle

Brass Partridge

A beloved symbol of the season, the partridge in a pear tree is interpreted in a glowing filigree design etched in brass.
- Brass, 1¼" diam.
300QXM572-5, $3.00
Artist: Joyce Lyle

Pinecone Basket

Wrapped with an embroidered fabric ribbon, a basket is filled with tiny pinecones. Actual miniature pinecones were used to create the mold for these. The handle is red fabric ribbon.
- Handcrafted, ⅞" tall
450QXM573-4, $4.50
Artist: Dill Rhodus

Happy Bluebird, Stocking Pal

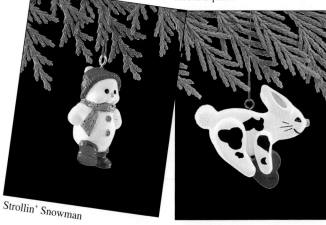

Acorn Squirrel

Scrimshaw Reindeer

Strollin' Snowman

Folk Art Bunny

Brass Snowflake

Brass Partridge

Pinecone Basket

Cozy Skater, Old-World Santa

Cozy Skater

This mouse is wearing a warm green scarf with red trim and matching red mittens. The skates have metal blades.

◾ Handcrafted, 1⅜" tall
450QXM573-5, $4.50
Artist: Joyce Lyle

Old-World Santa

A variety of European collectibles made out of this style of wood were popular in the early 1900s. Santa carries a bottle-brush tree in this ornament, designed to look like wood.

◾ Handcrafted, 1⅜" tall
300QXM569-5, $3.00
Artist: Bob Siedler

Roly-Poly Ram

A whimsical, rounded ram wears a handcrafted green ribbon and red heart. He's warm during the winter because he's been sculpted with a thick curly coat.

◾ Handcrafted, ⅞" tall
300QXM570-5, $3.00

Roly-Poly Pig

This cute little ball of a porker carries a handcrafted golden star. His markings are similar to those of Spotted Poland pigs.

◾ Handcrafted, ⅞" tall
300QXM571-2, $3.00
Artist: Sharon Pike

Puppy Cart

Riding in a custom-designed pull-cart with a brass pull-ring on the front this Dalmatian pup is ready to journey 'cross town.

◾ Wood, 1¼" tall
300QXM571-5, $3.00
Artist: Linda Sickman

Kitty Cart

A black-and-white kitten waits for someone to give her a ride in her specially painted pull-cart. The ornament is fashioned of wood and has a brass pull-ring at the front of the cart.

◾ Wood, 1⅛" tall
300QXM572-2, $3.00
Artist: Joyce Pattee

Holiday Deer

A faceted acrylic teardrop is the setting for this proud stag. The design, etched into the acrylic, looks like elegant cut crystal.

◾ Acrylic, 1½" tall
300QXM577-2, $3.00
Artist: LaDene Votruba

Bunny Hug

It was love at first sight! The child etched onto this faceted acrylic oval gives his bunny friend a warm Christmas hug. The design has been etched to display subtle shadings and nuances of expression.

◾ Acrylic, 1¼" tall
300QXM577-5, $3.00
Artist: LaDene Votruba

Rejoice

This lustrous ornament features the beauty of calligraphy and a caption that expresses the loving message of the season. The caption, "Rejoice," and the holly design are stamped in gold foil and framed by an oval of acrylic facets that sparkle with the light.

◾ Acrylic, 1" tall
300QXM578-2, $3.00
Artist: LaDene Votruba

Holy Family

This is a reissue from 1988. (See 1988 Miniature Ornament Collection.)

◾ Handcrafted, 1¼" tall
850QXM561-1, $8.50
Artist: Duane Unruh

Three Little Kitties

This is a reissue from 1988. (See 1988 Miniature Ornament Collection.)

◾ Handcrafted, 15/16" tall
600QXM569-4, $6.00
Artist: Sharon Pike

Country Wreath

This is a reissue from 1988. (See 1988 Miniature Ornament Collection.)

◾ Handcrafted, 1½" tall
450QXM573-1, $4.50
Artist: Anita Marra Rogers

Roly-Poly Ram, Roly-Poly Pig

Puppy Cart

Kitty Cart

Holiday Deer

Bunny Hug

Rejoice

Collectible Series

Noel R.R.—First Edition

Dated "1989," a special "Locomotive" is on the right track for this new series. Each year, a different type of railroad car will be added to complete the holiday train. The ornament has revolving wheels and is painted with bright colors and touches of gold to accentuate detail.

■ Handcrafted, 1" tall
850QXM576-2, $8.50
Artist: Linda Sickman

The Kringles—First Edition

The season's happiest twosome will make an appearance every year of this new series. In the first edition, Santa hides a green package behind his back for Mrs. Claus. The ornament is sculpted and painted to look like hand-carved wood.

■ Handcrafted, 1⅛" tall
600QXM562-5, $6.00
Artist: Anita Marra Rogers

Old English Village—Second Edition

The shopkeeper stands in the doorway to welcome customers into her "Sweet Shop." Second in the series, this ornament is charmingly detailed with timber trimmings, pearly snow on the roof, and a tiny wreath in the window. A sign on the front advertises "Sweets." The address is "1989."

■ Handcrafted, 1¼" tall
850QXM561-5, $8.50
Artist: Julia Lee

Penguin Pal—Second Edition

The second penguin in the series is lookin' cool and enjoying a tasty candy cane. He wears a dashing green bow-tie and a red Santa cap.

■ Handcrafted, Acrylic, 1⅜" tall
450QXM560-2, $4.50

Rocking Horse—Second Edition

A handsome palomino with flowing white mane and tail prances on blue rockers dated "1989." His saddle and trappings are Christmas green and red with accents of gold.

■ Handcrafted, 1⅛" tall
450QXM560-5, $4.50
Artist: Linda Sickman

Kittens in Toyland—Second Edition

This tan-and-white kitten travels in style. She's put on a blue stocking cap with a white hand-crafted pompom to go for a ride in her brand-new red scooter.

■ Handcrafted, 1" tall
450QXM561-2, $4.50
Artist: Ken Crow

Special Edition

Santa's Magic Ride

Santa races through the forest on a magical unicorn with golden hooves and horn. The sculpted details of this ornament, such as the unicorn's flying tail and Santa's flowing red coat, create a vision of grace and motion. Santa clasps his pack of gifts in one hand and holds onto the unicorn's mane with the other as he takes his wondrous ride.

■ Handcrafted, 1³⁄₁₆" tall
850QXM563-2, $8.50
Artist: Anita Marra Rogers

Noel R.R.

The Kringles

Old English Village

Penguin Pal

Rocking Horse

Kittens in Toyland

Hallmark

1988 KEEPSAKE MINIATURE COLLECTION

Collectors will remember 1988 as the year that Keepsake Miniature Ornaments first appeared in Hallmark retail stores and quickly became cherished collectibles.

The new miniature collection was presented as a complete line, expressed in a wide range of formats, including handcrafted, ball, brass, acrylic, and wood. Three dated, commemorative captions were issued: "Baby's First Christmas," "First Christmas Together," and "Mother."

The first editions of four miniature Collectible Series debuted, introducing a charming "Old English Village," nostalgic "Rocking Horse," friendly "Penguin Pal," and playful "Kittens in Toyland."

Two ornaments were miniature versions of favorite Keepsake designs from years past. They are "Jolly St. Nick" and "Sneaker Mouse." The miniature "Skater's Waltz" was adapted from a popular Keepsake Magic Ornament design.

Commemoratives

Baby's First Christmas
Attached to a pearly white star dated "1988," this nostalgic wood-look swing gives Baby an ideal place to view the holiday festivities. The caption on the blanket confirms that it's "Baby's 1st" Christmas. Baby wears a red handcrafted bow.
▪ Handcrafted, 2½" tall
600QXM574-4, $6.00
Artist: Donna Lee

Mother
A red puffed heart is topped with mistletoe. The inscription reads: "Mother 1988."
▪ Handcrafted, 1¼" tall
300QXM572-4, $3.00
Artist: Sharon Pike

Love Is Forever
A delicate acrylic oval conveys the sentiment: "Love is forever." The caption is stamped in gold foil, and the clear ornament is faceted to reflect the light.
▪ Acrylic, 1" tall
200QXM577-4, $2.00
Artist: Joyce Pattee

First Christmas Together
A country motif is expressed in this straw wreath, wrapped with red-and-green fabric ribbons. The wreath is decorated with dried flowers and a heart made of real wood. Caption: "Our First Christmas 1988."
▪ Wood, Straw, 1¼" tall
400QXM574-1, $4.00
Artist: Diana McGehee

Friends Share Joy
This graceful acrylic is faceted on the front and back. The message, "Friends Share Joy," is stamped in gold foil.
▪ Acrylic, 1¼" tall
200QXM576-4, $2.00
Artist: Joyce Pattee

Baby's First Christmas

Mother

Love Is Forever

First Christmas Together

Friends Share Joy

Holiday Traditions

Skater's Waltz

An elegantly attired couple whirls across the ice on a wintry day. The blades on their skates are painted a silvery color. The design is adapted from a favorite Keepsake Magic Ornament.

◼ Handcrafted, 1⅜" tall
700QXM560-1, $7.00
Artist: Duane Unruh

Holy Family

Feelings of reverance and joy are reflected in the intricate detail of this nativity scene.

◼ Handcrafted, 1¼" tall
850QXM561-1, $8.50
Artist: Duane Unruh

Three Little Kitties

Arriving in a real willow basket with red fabric bows, three kittens will make a special gift.

◼ Handcrafted, Willow, ¹⁵⁄₁₆" tall
600QXM569-4, $6.00
Artist: Sharon Pike

Jolly St. Nick

This miniature ornament is patterned after and carries the same name as the Special Edition in the 1986 Keepsake line. It depicts the jolly old elf in the style popularized by cartoonist Thomas Nast in the 1800s. St. Nick is holding a tiny Christmas stocking, doll, and pull-toy.

◼ Handcrafted, 1⅜" tall
800QXM572-1, $8.00
Artist: Duane Unruh

Happy Santa

The only ball ornament in the Keepsake Miniature line this year, this frosted-glass design is topped with silvery, filigree leaves. Santa carries a bag of toys with a panda peeking out.

◼ Frosted Glass, ¾" diam.
450QXM561-4, $4.50
Artist: Joyce Pattee

Snuggly Skater

A bear snuggles into a white, high-top figure skate laced in red and decorated with a real pom-pom. The silvery blade is carefully crafted to resemble metal.

◼ Handcrafted, 1⅛" tall
450QXM571-4, $4.50
Artist: Bob Siedler

Sweet Dreams

An angel with tiny white wings sits on the lap of a friendly crescent moon. Both are sound asleep, and the pearly golden moon wears a handcrafted stocking cap.

◼ Handcrafted, 1½" tall
700QXM560-4, $7.00

Skater's Waltz

Holy Family

Three Little Kitties

Jolly St. Nick

Happy Santa

Snuggly Skater

Sweet Dreams

Folk Art Reindeer

Little Drummer Boy

Folk Art Reindeer

Reminiscent of an old-fashioned pull-toy, this wooden ornament is carefully handpainted in deep colors. The reindeer has wide green antlers and a decorative saddle to match.
- ◼ Wood, 1⅛" tall
  300QXM568-4, $3.00
  Artist: Joyce Pattee

Little Drummer Boy

The Christmas legend of the little boy who gave the only gift he could offer—a song from his drum—is charmingly captured in this miniature ornament. The rosy-cheeked lad wears a green jacket and a red cap.
- ◼ Handcrafted, 1¼" tall
  450QXM578-4, $4.50
  Artist: Bob Siedler

Sneaker Mouse

Adapted from a favorite 1983 Keepsake Ornament, this mouse may be dreaming of running to meet Santa. He's chosen a red-and-white sneaker, with laces of real cord for his bed.
- ◼ Handcrafted, ½" tall
  400QXM5711, $4.00

Joyous Heart

In this wooden ornament, three blocks twirl about inside a heart-shaped frame. The country-style heart is decorated with green holly leaves and red berries. Red letters on the blocks spell out the caption, "JOY."
- ◼ Wood, 1⅛" tall
  350QXM569-1, $3.50
  Artist: Diana McGehee

Candy Cane Elf

All caught up in holiday fun, the elf is suspended by the hem of his green smock. His red tights match his Santa cap and the stripes on the peppermint cane.
- ◼ Handcrafted, ⅞" tall
  300QXM570-1, $3.00
  Artist: Bob Siedler

Country Wreath

Two bears nestle inside a wreath made of real twigs and decorated with tiny red berries. A red-and-green fabric ribbon forms a bow at the top of the wreath.
- ◼ Handcrafted, 1½" tall
  400QXM573-1, $4.00
  Artist: Anita Marra Rogers

Folk Art Lamb

The scalloped silhouette of this snow white lamb suggests a coat of curly wool. His ears are fashioned of fleecy black fabric, and he rides a colorful pull-cart painted in pink and aqua colors.
- ◼ Wood, 1" tall
  275QXM568-1, $2.75
  Artist: Joyce Pattee

Gentle Angel

A peaceful portrait of an angel kneeling in prayer is featured on a lovely, etched acrylic teardrop. The faceted edges of the ornament sparkle in the light.
- ◼ Acrylic, 1½" tall
  200QXM577-1, $2.00
  Artist: LaDene Votruba

Sneaker Mouse

Joyous Heart

Candy Cane Elf

Country Wreath

Folk Art Lamb

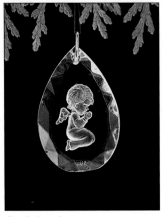

Gentle Angel

Brass Star

Brass Tree

Brass Angel

Kittens in Toyland

Old-English Village

Rocking Horse

Brass Star

Look closely at this lacy silhouette, and discover an intricate series of star-shaped patterns. The elaborate design is etched in shimmering brass.

◾ Brass, 1¼" tall
150QXM566-4, $1.50
Artist: Joyce Lyle

Brass Tree

Light dances on, around, and through this glowing, etched-brass Christmas tree. It is intricately detailed from the ornaments on the branches to a star at the top.

◾ Brass, 1¼" tall
150QXM567-4, $1.50
Artist: Joyce Lyle

Brass Angel

An angel in a flowing gown raises a heavenly trumpet to proclaim the joy of the season. The delicate filigree design is etched in gleaming brass.

◾ Brass, 1¼" tall
150QXM567-1, $1.50
Artist: Joyce Lyle

Collectible Series

Kittens in Toyland—First Edition

Toyland—what a happy place for a playful kitten! This orange and white one has found a green locomotive and climbed aboard for the first adventure of the series. The train is accented with silvery trim.

◾ Handcrafted, ¾" tall
500QXM562-1, $5.00
Artist: Ken Crow

Old-English Village—First Edition

This new series reflects the warmth and charm of a country village at Christmastime. This year's "Family Home" is exquisitely detailed with tiny window-panes, and decorated with wreaths on the bay window and door. Upstairs, the homeowner opens a window. Pearly snow covers the roof, and "1988" appears over the door.

◾ Handcrafted, 1¼" tall
850QXM563-4, $8.50
Artist: Donna Lee

Rocking Horse—First Edition

Adapted from the popular Keepsake Ornament series, this dappled "Rocking Horse" will lead the parade for others to come in this new series. The year date "1988" appears in gold on his red rockers, and his saddle and bridle are painted in bright holiday colors.

◾ Handcrafted, 1⅛" tall
450QXM562-4, $4.50
Artist: Linda Sickman

Penguin Pal—First Edition

This cheerful fellow is the first in the series and the first in his flock to finish his holiday shopping. He's delivering a gift package decorated with a handcrafted red bow. And he's dressed for the occasion in a red Santa hat and green muffler.

◾ Handcrafted, 1" tall
375QXM563-1, $3.75
Artist: Bob Siedler

Penguin Pal

It's in the Mail

SPECIAL DESIGNS FOR MEMBERS OF
THE KEEPSAKE ORNAMENT COLLECTOR'S CLUB

Since its founding in 1987, the Hallmark Keepsake Ornament Collector's Club has offered members a variety of exclusive ornaments. Each of the annual membership kits included an ornament called the "Keepsake of Membership." This design was the Club's special gift to all members. In addition to these ornaments, some members received special Club ornaments in their kits. In 1988, the Keepsake Miniature Ornament, "Hold on Tight," was given to charter members who renewed early or purchased a multi-year membership. Since 1987, every membership kit has included a "Treasury Binder" for cataloguing a collection. In 1991, the Keepsake of Membership Ornament, "Hidden Treasure," was a hinged, handcrafted acorn that when opened, reveals the miniature ornament, "Li'l Keeper," inside.

Club members also have been given the opportunity to purchase a Members Only ornament each year through their Hallmark retailers. The first lighted Members Only ornament, "Beary Artistic," was offered in 1991. Limited Edition ornaments have been offered exclusively to Club members since 1988. Ordered through Hallmark retailers, these designs are among the most beautiful in the Keepsake Collection.

1993

Keepsake of Membership— It's in the Mail
This mailmouse (or is it the Post-mouster himself?) slips a miniature Collector's Courier in the metal "POST" box dated "1993." The back is identified with the Keepsake Ornament Collector's Club logo.
■ Handcrafted, 2⅝" tall
QXC527-2
Artist: Ed Seale

Keepsake of Membership— Keepsake Miniature Ornament— Forty Winks

Nestled all snug in a bottle-cap bed, a mouse naps on a holly leaf with a bright red bow for a pillow. She must be having sweet dreams, because she wears a blissful smile. The caption on the back of the cap reads: "Santa's Club Soda."
■ Handcrafted, 1³⁄₁₆" diam.
QXC529-4
Artist: John Francis (Collin)

Trimmed With Memories

Members Only Keepsake Ornament Anniversary Edition— Trimmed With Memories
A lavishly decorated blue spruce celebrates the twentieth anniversary of Keepsake Ornaments with two dates on the tree stand, "1973" and "1993." Tiny golden replicas of some of the Collectible Series from past years trim the tree, recalling special Christmas memories. The base displays the Keepsake Ornament Collector's Club logo.
■ Handcrafted, 3⅞" tall
1200QXC543-2, $12.00
Artist: Linda Sickman

Limited Editions

Gentle Tidings
Cradling a gray lamb, this delicate angel wears a golden halo. Her feather-textured wings, ruffled crinolines, and ballet slippers are pearly white, and "A Limited Edition Ornament Hand-Painted Fine Porcelain" appears on the bottom of her petticoats. One of an edition of 17,500, she comes with a solid wood display stand.

▪ Fine Porcelain, Handpainted, 4⁹⁄₁₆" tall
2500QXC544-2, $25.00
Artist: Patricia Andrews

Sharing Christmas
Artfully sculpted in bas-relief and encircled by a golden metal frame, this nostalgic pastel scene hangs from a satiny ribbon. The children, clothed in Victorian finery, smile as they unwrap a gift. Bows and holly decorate both sides of the piece, and on the back is written, "Christmas…a beautiful season for sharing" and "A Limited Edition Ornament." The edition size is 16,500. A wood display stand is included.

▪ Handcrafted, Handpainted, 3¼" tall
2000QXC543-5, $20.00
Artist: Joyce Lyle

Rodney Takes Flight

1992

Keepsake of Membership—Rodney Takes Flight

Your holiday imagination will take off in this whimsical stringer ornament designed exclusively for Club members. Rodney pilots a vintage plane dated "1992." The green propeller spins, and the landing wheels turn. The Club logo, "Hallmark Keepsake Ornament Collector's Club," is printed underneath. Trailing behind the plane is a sign inscribed, "RODNEY'S FLIGHT SCHOOL Holiday Special." The other side of the sign reads, "FLY WITH RODNEY Club Members Welcome."
▪ Handcrafted, 1¼" tall
QXC508-1
Artist: Donna Lee

Members Only Keepsake Magic Ornament— Santa's Club List

This raccoon has flickering light from the candle that helps him read "Santa's Club List." "1992" is printed on the back with: "Lorrie, Ed, Rachel, Lee, Tina, Anne, Jack."
▪ Handcrafted, 2⅛" tall
Flickering Light
1500QXC729-1, $15.00
Artist: Ed Seale

Keepsake Miniature Ornament—Chipmunk Parcel Service

A cheerful chipmunk delivers this familiar package to members of the Keepsake Ornament Collector's Club. Our friend carries a parcel dated "1992." This miniature ornament was a special gift exclusively for those Club members who renewed their membership early, as well as multi-year members.
▪ Handcrafted, 1³⁄₁₆" tall
QXC519-4
Artist: Ed Seale

Santa's Club List

Chipmunk Parcel Service

Limited Editions

Keepsake Miniature Ornament Set—Christmas Treasures

Tucked inside this antiqued treasure chest, you'll discover three ornaments. Dated "1992," "Santa-in-the-Box" features a brass crank on the side. "Old Fashioned Skate" has a shiny brass blade and a " '92" date. "Little Horse" sits atop a red stand dated "1992." The Club logo and the caption, "Limited Edition of 15,500 Max.," appear on the bottom panel of the chest. Its lid features a bas-relief scene of Santa and his reindeer soaring over rooftops. The sculpted front panel highlights the words, "Christmas Treasures," and the back panel shows a collection of toys and the date, "1992."

▨ Handcrafted, Hand-antiqued,
Chest, 1³⁄₁₆" tall
Skate, 1¼" tall
Santa, 1³⁄₁₆" tall
Horse, ¹⁵⁄₁₆" tall
2200QXC546-4, $22.00
Artist: Robert Chad

Victorian Skater

Gliding on skates with real metal blades, this "Victorian Skater" captures the nostalgia of holidays past. The ornament's exquisite detail is evident in the sweet expression of her upturned face and in the graceful folds of her holiday outfit. The caption, "A Limited Edition Ornament Handpainted Fine Porcelain," appears underneath her coat. The edition size is 14,700. The ornament can be displayed on a tree or mantel, or on the specially designed wood stand.

▨ Handpainted Fine Porcelain,
3¾" tall
2500QXC406-7, $25.00
Artist: Duane Unruh

Hidden Treasure, Li'l Keeper

Beary Artistic

Five Years Together

1991

Keepsake of Membership— Hidden Treasure & Keepsake Miniature Ornament—Li'l Keeper

There's a surprise inside this homey acorn. Turn the golden key to unlock the hinged lid and discover a separate miniature ornament named "Li'l Keeper." This tiny squirrel in a Santa cap is a bonus gift for members. Oak leaves decorate the acorn's ornate hinge, and a holly wreath trims the inside of the lid. Tiny treasures patterned after some favorite Keepsake Ornaments line the walls. He holds an acorn dated "1991." The Club logo is on both pieces.

■ Handcrafted
Acorn, 2⅛" tall
Squirrel, ⅞" tall
QXC476-9
Artist: Ken Crow

Members Only Keepsake Magic Ornament— Beary Artistic

A bear in a sweater dated " '91" on the back, is creating a holiday ice sculpture. He carves the pale blue acrylic which glows with soft light. The word "JOY" appears in clear letters against a frosted background. The Club logo is printed inside the letter "O." This is the first lighted Members Only ornament.

■ Handcrafted, Acrylic, 2½" tall
1000QXC725-9, $10.00
Artist: Bob Siedler

Charter Member Ornament— Five Years Together

This was a special gift to 1991 members who were founding members. Designed in the classic quadra foil shape, the ornament has the Club logo and the caption: "Charter Member, Five Years Together 1991." It hangs from a golden cord.

■ Acrylic, 3" tall
QXC315-9

Limited Editions

Secrets for Santa

A child snuggles in Santa's lap and whispers a wish in his ear. Santa's beard and the fur trim on his suit are finely textured. There's a sprig of holly on his hat, a candy cane in his hand, and a kind expression on his face. The edition size is 28,700. Caption: "A Limited Edition Ornament." A wood display stand is included.

■ Handpainted, Handcrafted, 3½" tall
2375QXC479-7, $23.75
Artist: Anita Marra Rogers

Galloping Into Christmas

This Santa on horseback reflects the styling of tin pull-toys popular in the 1800s. The horse seems to gallop as it rocks, and the silver-colored metal wheels actually revolve. Copy on the bottom reads: "A Limited Edition of 28,400, Number: (hand-etched number)." Wood display stand included.

■ Pressed Tin, 3" tall
1975QXC477-9, $19.75
Artist: Linda Sickman

Secrets for Santa, Galloping Into Christmas

1990

Keepsake of Membership— Club Hollow

Living in snow-covered "Club Hollow," a wise little owl is reading about "Whoo's Whoo" in the "Courier 1990." He appears to open the door with his wing and holds a bright red ball ornament. Carved on the back of the log is a heart that says: "Collectors Club + Me." The Club logo is on the bottom.

▧ Handcrafted, 1⅞" tall
QXC445-6
Artist: Ken Crow

Members Only Ornament— Armful of Joy

His happy face aglow with the wonder of Christmas, the busy elf balances a stack of brightly wrapped gifts. On top is a box labeled, "1990 Membership Kit." The elf's shopping bag carries the Club logo.

▧ Handcrafted, 2¹³⁄₁₆" tall
975QXC445-3, $9.75
Artist: John Francis (Collin)

Keepsake Miniature Ornament— Crown Prince

A bear wears a golden crown on his head and a Christmasy red-and-green sweater with the Keepsake Ornament Collector's Club logo. The date, "1990," is printed on the back of his sweater, and the Hallmark logo appears on the crown. This ornament was a special bonus included in the 1990 Membership Kit.

▧ Handcrafted, 1⅜" tall
QXC560-3
Artist: Anita Marra Rogers

Limited Editions

Dove of Peace

One of the most beautiful symbols of Christmas—a snow-white dove—carries a brass banner etched with the words "Peace," "Hope," and "Love." The edition is limited to 25,400. Caption: "A Limited Edition Ornament, Fine Porcelain." Wood display stand included.

▧ Handpainted Fine Porcelain, Brass, 2⅜" tall
2475QXC447-6, $24.75
Artist: Linda Sickman

Christmas Limited

This colorful locomotive is made of die-cast metal, a popular material used for toys and collectibles since the 1800s. The name of the train, "Christmas Limited," appears on both sides of the cabin. The wheels of the brass-trimmed engine revolve, and a tiny brass bell announces its arrival. This edition numbers 38,700. Caption on bottom: "A Limited Edition Ornament." Wood display stand included.

▧ Cast Metal, 2⅝" tall
1975QXC476-6, $19.75
Artist: Linda Sickman

Club Hollow

Armful of Joy

Sugar Plum Fairy

Dressed in a pearly white tutu, a fine porcelain ballerina stands en pointe. This ornament is a limited edition of 25,400. Copy on the bottom of the tutu reads: "Sugar Plum Fairy, A Limited Edition Ornament, Hand-Painted Fine Porcelain." Wood display stand included.

▧ Handpainted Fine Porcelain, 5½" tall
2775QXC447-3, $27.75
Artist: Patricia Andrews

Crown Prince

Dove of Peace, Christmas Limited

Sugar Plum Fairy

Visit From Santa, Collect a Dream

Sitting Purrty

1989

Keepsake of Membership—
Visit From Santa
Santa has the entire Collector's Club roster on his special delivery list. He's bringing a sled to every member, personalized with the member's name. A gift inside his bag carries the year date "1989."
◼ Handcrafted, 4" tall
QXC580-2
Artist: Ken Crow

Members Only Ornament—
Collect a Dream
Snug in a leafy hammock, this mouse dreams of Keepsake Ornaments. Club members will recognize his book: "My Keepsake Ornament Treasury 1989." The leaf displays the Club logo, "Hallmark Keepsake Ornament Collector's Club," and is fashioned with hooks at both ends so it can hang between two branches.
◼ Handcrafted, 1¾" tall
900QXC428-5, $9.00
Artist: Sharon Pike

Keepsake Miniature Ornament—
Sitting Purrty
A pretty little kitty, wearing a red stocking cap with a bell at the tip, sits in a custom-made mug. The mug reads: "1989" and "Hallmark Keepsake Ornament Collector's Club." This was a gift for all 1989 members.
◼ Handcrafted, 1¼" tall
QXC581-2
Artist: Peter Dutkin

Limited Editions

Christmas is Peaceful
Two owls perch on a snow-covered branch in this lovely scene created in bone china. A limited edition of 49,900 pieces, the ornament has been painted and individually numbered by hand. A gold cord and golden berries add sparkle to the subtle colors of the design. Caption: "Christmas is peaceful. Bone China, Limited Edition of 49,900 Max., Number: (hand-written number)."
▦ Handpainted Bone China, 2½" tall
1850QXC451-2, $18.50
Artist: Ed Seale

Noelle
This elegant cat is dressed for a Christmas party with Club members. Created in fine porcelain and painted by hand, "Noelle" wears a red bow decorated with a sprig of holly and a real brass jingle bell. The ornament, issued in a limited edition of 49,900, comes with a specially designed wooden display stand.
▦ Handpainted, Fine Porcelain, 3¾" tall
1975QXC448-3, $19.75
Artist: Duane Unruh

Holiday Heirloom—
Third and Final Edition
The melodic tones of the 24-percent lead-crystal bell announce the end of the series. The bell is suspended from a silver-plated design of a Christmas tree and a group of old-fashioned toys. Also plated in silver, the bell clapper is a gift box. The year date, "1989," is debossed on a child's ball on the front of the ornament. The edition size "Limited Edition of 34,600" is embossed on the back.
▦ Lead Crystal, Silver Plating, 2½" tall
2500QXC460-5, $25.00
Artist: Duane Unruh

Christmas is Peaceful, Noelle, Holiday Heirloom

1988

Keepsake of Membership— Our Clubhouse

A mouse opens the clubhouse door to welcome members to the Club's second year. There's a wreath on the door, candles in the windows, and a decorated bottle-brush tree, teddy bear, and gift package inside. Pearly snow covers the roof, and a sign over the door reads: "Club Members Only." "1988" is on the back, and the official Club logo is on the bottom.

■ Handcrafted, 2½" tall
QXC580-4
Artist: Bob Siedler

Members Only Ornament— Sleighful of Dreams

This Members Only ornament resembles an old-fashioned wooden sleigh. Bas-relief designs portray favorite Keepsake Ornaments. A plaid ribbon lap-blanket completes the design, and "1988" is on the front of the sleigh. The official Club logo is engraved in brass on the back.

■ Handcrafted, 2⅛" tall
800QXC580-1, $8.00
Artist: Linda Sickman

Keepsake Miniature Ornament— Hold on Tight

An adventurous mouse with a tiny leaf takes a magic carpet ride. His red-and-white striped cap has a real yarn pompom. This was a gift exclusively for Club members who renewed early or purchased a multi-year membership. The Club's official logo is on the bottom of the leaf.

■ Handcrafted, ⁵⁄₁₆" tall
QXC570-4
Artist: Bob Siedler

Our Clubhouse, Sleighful of Dreams

Hold on Tight

Holiday Heirloom, Angelic Minstrel, Christmas is Sharing

Limited Editions

Holiday Heirloom— Second Edition

Two angels atop a bell hold a silver-plated star. The ornament has "1988" and "Ltd. Ed. 34,600" debossed on the star.

■ Lead Crystal, Silver Plating, 3½" tall
2500QX406-4, $25.00
Artist: Duane Unruh

Angelic Minstrel

Fashioned in fine porcelain, this elegant angel strums a golden lyre. She wears a blue gown, edged and accented with gold, and has a wooden display stand. The edition is limited to 49,900.

■ Handpainted Fine Porcelain, 5" tall
2950QX408-4, $29.50
Artist: Donna Lee

Christmas is Sharing

Finely textured white bone china conveys a subtle impression of two rabbits' furry coats, the pine needles, and bough. Caption: "Christmas is sharing. Bone China, Limited Edition of 49,900 Max., Number: (hand-written number)."

■ Handpainted Bone China, 2¼" tall
1750QX407-1, $17.50
Artist: Ed Seale

Wreath of Memories

Carousel Reindeer

1987

Keepsake of Membership— Wreath of Memories

The Club's first ornament—an elaborate handcrafted wreath—was designed to welcome Charter Members and celebrate the tradition of decorating with Keepsake Ornaments. It marked the first time that tiny reproductions of favorite Keepsake designs from previous years were used on a new ornament. Intricate details help collectors identify "Rocking Horse" and "Clothespin Soldier" among the designs. The year, "1987," appears on the front of the wreath. The caption "1987 Charter Member" appears on the back, along with the official Club logo engraved in brass.

■ Handcrafted, 3⅛" tall
QXC580-9
Artist: Duane Unruh

Members Only Ornament— Carousel Reindeer

This fanciful reindeer prancing inside a hoop symbolizes both the history and the evolution of the Keepsake Ornament line. Although reminiscent of the appealing "Nostalgia" ornaments of the 1970s, the "Carousel Reindeer" is more elegant and contemporary—a reflection of the Hallmark artists' flair for fresh, innovative designs. The caption "1987 Charter Member" appears on the front of the ornament, and the date, "1987," is on the back. The official Club logo is printed in bold on the bottom of the hoop.

■ Handcrafted, 3¾" tall
800QXC581-7, $8.00
Artist: Linda Sickman

You're Always Welcome

Premiere Event Ornament

1993
This ornament was created by artist Ed Seale in 1993 to commemorate the 1993 Keepsake Premiere Event.

You're Always Welcome
A friendly hostess bear puts a "Welcome 1993" mat in front of an open red door. The base carries the artist's signature, the "Tender Touches" logo, and "Keepsake Ornament Premiere."
■ Handcrafted, 2½" tall
975QX569-2, $9.75
Artist: Ed Seale

Special Offer

Santa and His Reindeer Collection

1992
A collection of four pairs of galloping reindeer pulling Santa and his sleigh was offered in 1992 by participating Hallmark stores, during a special five-week promotion. A different pair of reindeer was offered each week and Santa's sleigh was available during the fifth week. The ornaments can be displayed individually or as a collection on your tree, table, or mantel.

Santa and His Reindeer
Each reindeer in this collection wears a festive harness and blanket with his name inscribed in golden letters. "Dasher and Dancer" lead the pack, followed by "Prancer and Vixen," "Comet and Cupid," "Donder and Blitzen," and "Santa Claus," of course. Numbered for its position in the set, each ornament can be attached to the previous one with an interlocking brass hook and eye. When Santa joins the team, they are all linked with a green fabric ribbon rein that Santa holds in his raised hand. Gliding on golden runners, Santa's sleigh is laden with gifts, and a special one is dated "1992."
Handcrafted, Brass
$4.95 each with any
$5.00 purchase.
■ Dasher and Dancer,
3¹/₁₆" tall
495XPR973-5
■ Prancer and Vixen,
3¹/₁₆" tall
495XPR973-6
■ Comet and Cupid,
3" tall
495XPR973-7
■ Donder and Blitzen,
3⁵/₁₆" tall
495XPR973-8
■ Santa Claus, 2⅝" tall
495XPR973-9
Artist: Ken Crow (all)

ADDED ATTRACTIONS

Collectors notice everything. Through the years they have discovered a number of ornaments that were not part of the regular Keepsake Ornament line. These designs were not included in Keepsake Ornament brochures or displayed with the other Keepsake Ornaments. To say the least, collectors have been intrigued.

This section of the Collector's Guide is designed to clear up the mysteries surrounding the precious odds and ends that have been featured in a variety of Hallmark gift and promotional programs. Included are the "Musical Collection" from 1982 and 1983, "Baby Celebrations" commemorative ornaments first introduced in 1989, and special ornaments, including designs that were created for "Open House" and "Premiere" events. The 1989 "Carrousel Horses," 1990 "Little Frosty Friends," 1991 "Claus & Co. R.R.," and 1992 "Santa and His Reindeer" collections were theme groups of ornaments with their own unique displays.

Santa and His Reindeer

Claus & Co. R. R. Collection

Little Frosty, Little Seal, Little Husky, Little Bear

Memory Wreath

Special Offer
Christmas Carousel Horse Collection

1989

A group of four brightly painted carousel horses were offered, one per week, during a special four-week promotion in 1989. Cost was based on a minimum Hallmark purchase. The ornaments can be displayed individually or on their specially designed carousel stand, available during the same period. The stand, dated "1989," has a shiny brass pole festooned with red and green satin ribbons.

Carousel Horses

Each dainty prancing steed is supported by a brass pole which matches the pole on the carousel stand. The name of every horse appears on its saddle and also on the bottom of the ornament, along with the caption "1989, (number) in a Collection of Four." "Snow" is white with a golden mane and tail. "Holly" is gray and wears a festive red, gold, and green saddle. "Star" is dark brown and has four white stockings, and a white mane and tail. "Ginger" is a handsome palomino with a white mane and tail.

Handcrafted, Brass, 3³⁄₁₆" tall
$3.95 each with $10.00 purchase
- 629XPR971-9   Snow
- 629XPR972-2   Holly
- 629XPR972-0   Star
- 629XPR972-1   Ginger
   Artist: Julia Lee (all)

Carousel Display Stand

- Handcrafted, Brass, 4⅝" tall
   629XPR972-3, $1.00
   with any Hallmark purchase

Snow, Holly, Ginger, Star,
Carousel Display Stand

Our First Anniversary

Our Fifth Anniversary

Anniversary Ornaments

1993 and 1992

These handpainted porcelain Anniversary Ornaments were offered in 1992 and 1993 (1992 is shown). All but the "25 Years Together" ornaments are trimmed in 14-karat gold. All are 3¼" tall. Each carries the year.

Our First Anniversary

The caption on the back reads: "Love is the beginning of many happy memories."
- ◼ (1993) 1000AGA786-5, $10.00
- ◼ (1992) 1000AGA731-8, $10.00

Our Fifth Anniversary

The caption on the back reads: "Love is the beginning of many happy memories."
- ◼ (1993) 1000AGA786-6, $10.00
- ◼ (1992) 1000AGA731-9, $10.00

Our Tenth Anniversary

The caption on the back reads: "Love is the beginning of many happy memories."
- ◼ (1993) 1000AGA786-7, $10.00
- ◼ (1992) 1000AGA731-7, $10.00

25 Years Together

The caption on the back reads: "Silver Christmas Memories are Keepsakes of the Heart."
- ◼ (1993) 1000AGA768-6, $10.00
- ◼ (1992) 1000AGA711-3, $10.00

40 Years Together

The caption on the back reads: "Love is the beginning of many happy memories."
- ◼ (1993) 1000AGA786-8, $10.00
- ◼ (1992) 1000AGA731-6, $10.00

50 Years Together

The caption on the back reads: "Golden Christmas Memories are Keepsakes of the Heart."
- ◼ (1993) 1000AGA778-7, $10.00
- ◼ (1992) 1000AGA721-4, $10.00

Anniversary Bells

1993 and 1992

Each of the following bells carries the year and is 3" tall.

25 Years Together

The caption on the back reads: "Silver Christmas Memories are Keepsakes of the Heart."
- ◼ (1993) 800AGA768-7, $8.00
- ◼ (1992) 800AGA713-4, $8.00

50 Years Together

The caption on the back reads: "Golden Christmas Memories are Keepsakes of the Heart."
- ◼ (1993) 800AGA778-8, $8.00
- ◼ (1992) 800AGA723-5, $8.00

Our Tenth Anniversary

25 Years Together

40 Years Together

50 Years Together

25 Years Together

50 Years Together

Musical Ornaments

The 1983 designs were offered in the "Hallmark Musical Collection." The 1982 designs were offered in the "Hallmark Gift Collection." All but the "Twelve Days of Christmas" ornament came packaged with an acrylic display stand.

1983

Twelve Days of Christmas
This French blue and white bas-relief design was included in the 1984 Keepsake Ornament collection. Melody: "Twelve Days of Christmas."
- Musical, Handcrafted, 3¾" tall
  1500QMB415-9, $15.00
  Artist: Ed Seale

Baby's First Christmas
Dressed in Santa sleepers, the babies on this ornament crawl up and down and around candy canes that spell out the caption: "Baby's 1st Christmas 1983." Melody: "Schubert's Lullaby."
- Musical, Classic Shape, 4½" tall
  1600QMB903-9, $16.00

Friendship
Muffin celebrates Christmas with her little friends. Caption: "It's song-in-the-air time, lights-everywhere time, good-fun-to-share time, it's Christmas." Melody: "We Wish You a Merry Christmas."
- Musical, Classic Shape, 4½" tall
  1600QMB904-7, $16.00

Nativity
The Three Kings bring gifts for the Holy Child in this brightly painted nativity scene. Caption: "The star shone bright with a holy light as heaven came to earth that night." Melody: "Silent Night."
- Musical, Classic Shape, 4½" tall
  1600QMB904-9, $16.00

Twelve Days of Christmas, Baby's First Christmas

Friendship, Nativity

1982

Baby's First Christmas

Baby has a merry time with all the new Christmas toys. The blocks spell out the first word in the caption: "Baby's First Christmas 1982." Melody: "Brahms' Lullaby."

▪ Musical, Classic Shape, 4½" tall
1600QMB900-7, $16.00

Love

Pinecones and holiday greenery decorate a festive ornament that offers a loving melody and message of the season. Caption: "Love puts the warmth in Christmas 1982." Melody: "What the Worlds Needs Now Is Love."

▪ Musical, Classic Shape, 4½" tall
1600QMB900-9, $16.00

First Christmas Together

A sleigh ride in the snow is the perfect way to spend your first Christmas. Caption: "First Christmas Together 1982." Melody: "White Christmas."

▪ Musical, Classic Shape, 4½" tall
1600QMB901-9, $16.00

Patriotic Ornament

1991
Flag of Liberty

Patriotism has long been an important value at Hallmark. In 1991, patriotic feelings were stirred by Operation Desert Storm. This ornament, with its yellow ribbon, was created to commemorate the American Armed Forces. With every "Flag of Liberty" purchase, Hallmark contributed $1.00 to the American Red Cross.

▪ Handcrafted, 3½" tall
675QX524-9, $6.75
Artist: Donna Lee

Baby's First Christmas, Love, First Christmas Together

Flag of Liberty

Open House Ornaments

Special Keepsake Ornaments were created for the "Open House" events held by some Hallmark dealers as a festive beginning to the holiday season.

1988
Kringle's Toy Shop

Two elves are busy making Christmas toys in the lighted window of the famous toy shop named "Kringle's." The elves hammer and saw all day long, while passersby, like the two children in the design, watch in fascination.

▪ Handcrafted, 3⅝" tall
Light and Motion
2450QLX701-7, $24.50
Artist: Ed Seale

1987

North Pole
Power & Light

This hard-working elf uses his shiny metal wrench to light your tree for Christmas. Always ready for an emergency, he carries three colorful replacement bulbs in his pack in case a light goes out.

▪ Handcrafted, 3" tall
627XPR933-3, $10.00 value,
$2.95 retail price
Artist: Ken Crow

1986

Santa and His Reindeer

Santa's sleigh is packed, and his reindeer are ready to fly between two branches of your tree, suspended by hooks at both ends of the red cord harness. The ornament can also be displayed on a table or mantel.

▪ Handcrafted, 2" tall, 14" wide
975QX0440-6, $9.75

Coca-Cola® Santa

Reproduced on porcelain white glass, three nostalgic Coca-Cola® paintings show Santa has time for his favorite drink! Caption: "Memories are reflections of the yesterdays we'll always love. Merry Christmas."

▪ Porcelain White Glass, 2⅞" diam.
475QX0279-6, $4.75

Old-Fashioned Santa

Crafted to look like hand-carved wood, this old-world Santa carries a bag filled with intricately sculpted toys. A little kitten rides in his pocket.

▪ Handcrafted, 4½" tall
1275QX0440-3, $12.75
Artist: Linda Sickman

Santa's Panda Pal

This lovable flocked panda dresses just like Santa. His red and white knitted hat is topped with a pompom.

▪ Handcrafted, 2¼" tall
500QX0441-3, $5.00

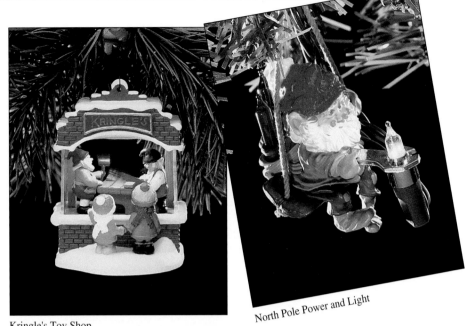

Kringle's Toy Shop

North Pole Power and Light

Santa and His Reindeer

Coca-Cola® Santa, Old-Fashioned Santa, Santa's Panda Pal

Early Promotional Ornament

1982

In 1982, Hallmark offered collectors a specially designed brass ornament for $3.50 with the purchase of Hallmark merchandise. This was the first time an ornament of this quality was offered as a promotion. The packaging did not carry the Keepsake name.

Early Promotional Ornament

Dimensional Ornament

A 24-karat, gold-tone coating adds sparkle to this dimensional brass ornament. In the design, a Victorian couple enjoys a nighttime ride in their one-horse open sleigh. Behind them, a village lies sleeping on Christmas Eve. The back oval features both die-cut shapes and etching. Extending forward from the oval, the cutout sleigh is etched to show detail.
- Dimensional Brass, 2⅜" tall
  No Stock Number, $3.50

SANTA CLAUS — THE MOVIE™ Ornaments

1985

Two Keepsake Ornaments were part of a varied group of Hallmark gifts centering on this film. The "Elfmade" emblem appeared on the back of each design stamped in gold foil.

Santa's Village

The movie's magical portrait of Santa's Village is reproduced in this wintry photograph set in a brass bezel. The caption reads, "Merry, Merry Christmas."
- Lacquer Look, 2¼" tall
  675QX300-2, $6.75

Santa Claus

The sleigh is filled to overflowing with brightly wrapped packages for good girls and boys. Holding the reins, Santa is about to begin his magical journey. Framed in brass, the photograph was taken directly from the movie.
- Lacquer Look, 3½" tall
  675QX300-5, $6.75

Santa's Village, Santa Claus

Gold Crown Ornaments

"Gold Crown" is a special Hallmark promotional program. Groups of exclusive gifts and collectibles are offered at participating stores. A fine porcelain Keepsake Ornament was offered through the 1992, 1991, and 1986 Gold Crown programs.

1992
O Christmas Tree

Created exclusively for the 1992 Keepsake Ornament Premiere events at participating Gold Crown Hallmark stores, this fine porcelain ornament is delicately painted by hand. A festive Christmas tree, complete with a golden star tree topper and packages underneath, forms the handle of the bell. Decorating the border around the rim of the bell is the year in golden letters: "Nineteen Hundred and Ninety-Two." The caption inside the bell reads: "Hallmark Keepsake Ornament Premiere, Gold Crown Exclusive, Hand-Painted Fine Porcelain."

▨ Handpainted Fine Porcelain,
   3¼" tall
   1075QX541-1, $10.75
   Artist: LaDene Votruba

1991
Santa's Premiere

Available for purchase only at the Premiere event held by participating Hallmark Gold Crown stores, this elegant bell is fashioned of fine porcelain and carefully painted by hand. The handle of the bell is Santa himself, dressed in a long red coat and carrying a sack of toys and a tiny doll. The letters in the year date form a decorative border

O Christmas Tree

Santa's Premiere

around the rim of the bell: "Nineteen Hundred and Ninety-One." The caption inside the bell reads: "Hallmark Keepsake Ornament Premiere, Gold Crown Exclusive, Hand-Painted Fine Porcelain."

▨ Handpainted Fine Porcelain,
   3¼" tall
   1075QX523-7, $10.75

1986
On the Right Track

Carefully painted by hand, this fine porcelain Santa puts the finishing touches on a toy train. He wears brass spectacles, and his boot carries the artist's signature, "P. Dutkin."

▨ Handpainted Fine
   Porcelain, 4¼" tall
   1500QSP420-1, $15.00
   Artist: Peter Dutkin

On the Right Track

Granddaughter's First Christmas

Baby's First Christmas (rabbit)

Grandson's First Christmas

Baby's First Christmas (moon)

Baby Ornaments

These baby ornaments display the words "Keepsake Ornament" on their packaging.

1993

Granddaughter's First Christmas

This cradle holds a sleeping baby rabbit and carries the caption, "Granddaughter's First Christmas 1993," on its side.

■ Handcrafted, 1⅞" tall
1400BBY280-2, $14.00

Grandson's First Christmas

Commemorating "Grandson's First Christmas 1993," this cradle holds a baby boy rabbit wrapped in sweet dreams.

■ Handcrafted, 1⅞" tall
1400BBY280-1, $14.00

Baby's First Christmas

Napping on a fluffy-looking cloud, an angelic baby rabbit sleeps blissfully. "Baby's First Christmas 1993" appears on the front of the cloud.

■ Handcrafted, 1½" tall
1200BBY291-8, $12.00

Baby's First Christmas

A baby cuddles happily on a friendly moon, drifting into dreamland. The date, "1993," appears on a star that dangles above the sleeping baby.

■ Handcrafted, 2¾" tall
1400BBY291-9, $14.00

Baby's First Christmas Photoholder

Baby's Christening

Baby's First Christmas Photoholder

This silver-plated, engravable frame ornament holds a photo of Baby. "Baby's First Christmas" and "1993" are engraved on the frame's front.

■ Silver-plated, 2¼" diam.
1000BBY147-0, $10.00

Baby's Christening

An angel rides in on a peaceful dove, carrying the cloud-shaped announcement: "Baby's Christening." The date, "1993," appears on the back of the cloud.

■ Handcrafted, 3¹⁄₁₆" tall
1200BBY291-7, $12.00

Baby's Christening Photoholder

A favorite picture of Baby's Christening can be displayed in this silver-plated frame ornament. Caption: "Baby's Christening 1993."

■ Silver-plated, 2¼" diam.
1000BBY133-5, $10.00

Baby's Christening Photoholder

Baby's First Christmas (bunny)

1992

Baby's First Christmas

Wearing a satiny ribbon and a tag reading, "Baby's First Christmas 1992," a plush pink bunny welcomes the season.
◼ Plush, 3" tall
850BBY155-7, $8.50

Baby's First Christmas

An embroidered, baby-blue rocking horse displays "1992" on its saddle and "Baby's First Christmas" on its rocker.
◼ Fabric, 4" tall
850BBY145-6, $8.50

Baby's Christening

This embroidered fabric heart carries the caption: "Baby's Christening 1992."
◼ Fabric, 4" tall
850BBY133-1, $8.50

Baby's First Christmas (rocking horse)

Baby's Christening

1991: Baby's First Christmas: Bunny, Pony; Baby's Christening

Baby Celebrations

The first baby gifts and shower partyware (including ornaments) from Hallmark were offered year-round in a limited number of Gold Crown stores in 1989.

1991 and 1990

Baby's First Christmas 1991
■ Bunny, 2⅛" tall
1000BBY151-4, $10.00
Artist: Anita Marra Rogers
■ Pony, 2⅝" tall
1000BBY141-6, $10.00
Artist: Nina Aubé

Baby's Christening 1991
■ Lamb, 2¼" tall
1000BBY131-7, $10.00
Artist: Julia Lee

Baby's First Christmas 1990
■ Bunny, 2⅛" tall
1000BBY155-4, $10.00
Artist: Anita Marra Rogers
■ Pony, 2⅝" tall
1000BBY145-4, $10.00
Artist: Nina Aubé

Baby's Christening 1990
■ Lamb, 2¼" tall
1000BBY132-6. $10.00
Artist: Julia Lee

1989

Baby's Christening Keepsake
■ Acrylic, 3¾" tall
700BBY132-5, $7.00

Baby's First Birthday
Captions: "1" and "Baby's 1st Birthday 1989." Acrylic stand included.
■ Acrylic, 4½" tall
550BBY172-9, $5.50

Baby's First Christmas—Baby Girl
This ornament is the same as 475QX272-2. (See 1989 Annual Collection.)
■ Pink Satin, 2⅞" diam.
475BBY155-3, $4.75

Baby's First Christmas—Baby Boy
This ornament is the same as 475QX272-5. (See 1989 Annual Collection.)
■ Blue Satin, 2⅞" diam.
475BBY145-3, $4.75

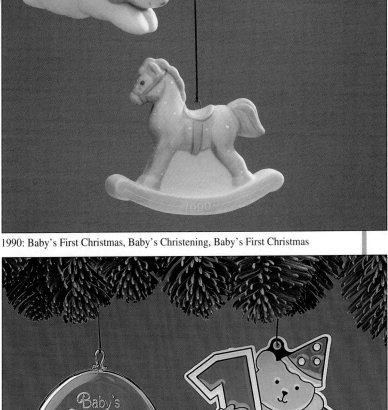

1990: Baby's First Christmas, Baby's Christening, Baby's First Christmas

1989: Baby's Christening Keepsake, Baby's First Birthday

THE 1993 KEEPSAKE EASTER COLLECTION

I n 1993, collectors were invited to start their own special traditions with Keepsake Easter Ornaments. Designs that share the joy of the season or commemorate special events were all a part of this new collection, featuring a somewhat brighter color palette than previous offerings. A new series, "Springtime Bonnets," was introduced, while the "Easter Parade" and "Eggs in Sports" series celebrated their second editions. A "Springtime Topiary" tree offered collectors a new way to display their Keepsake Easter Ornaments.

Grandchild

Grandchild
Headed for a happy Easter with ears flying in the wind, this bunny picks up speed (and a bunch of carrots!) in a lavender wagon captioned: "Grandchild 1993."
■ Handcrafted, 1⅞" tall
675QEO835-2, $6.75
Artist: Bob Siedler

Son
Juggling pearlized pastel eggs, this talented young lamb wears overalls with "Son" on the front pocket and "93" on the back.
■ Handcrafted, 2½" tall
575QEO833-5, $5.75
Artist: Patricia Andrews

Daughter
Sweet little "Daughter" lamb looks pretty as she skips rope wearing a pink jumper and pearly lavender ear-bows. The back pocket is dated "93."
■ Handcrafted, 2½" tall
575QEO834-2, $5.75
Artist: Patricia Andrews

Baby's 1st Easter
Gently pull the string and this little lamb will follow along on wheels that really roll. The flowing yellow bow says: "Baby's 1st Easter 1993."
■ Handcrafted, 1¼" tall
675QEO834-5, $6.75
Artist: Don Palmiter

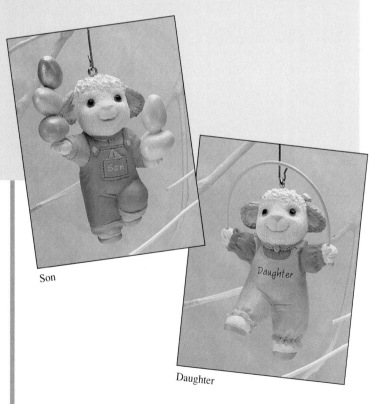

Son

Daughter

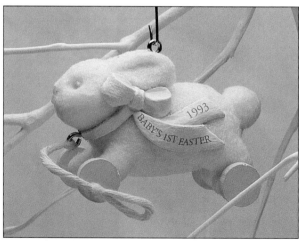

Baby's 1st Easter

Barrow of Giggles

Barrow of Giggles

Playful bunnies have some springtime fun in their "1993" wheelbarrow. One leans over to watch the wheel that really turns, while the other lies back to enjoy the ride.

▧ Handcrafted, 1⅞" tall
875QEO840-2, $8.75
Artist: Patricia Andrews

Backyard Bunny

Bunny finds the perfect place to wait and watch for signs of spring. Bright bas-relief tulips decorate both front and back of the "1993" watering can.

▧ Handcrafted, 2" tall
675QEO840-5, $6.75
Artist: Linda Sickman

Maypole Stroll

In this first-ever Keepsake Easter Ornament set, three jolly friends dance around a striped may-pole with real fabric rib-bons. Pink flowers dot the grassy green base, which has pegs to hold the little pals in place. A basket woven from nat-ural wicker displays the entire group.

▧ 2800QEO839-5, $28.00
Handcrafted Ornaments:
Dollie Duck, 2" tall
Ricky Rabbit, 2½" tall
Chester Chipmunk, 2" tall
Artist: John Francis (Collin)
Handcrafted, Wicker Basket: 4¼" tall
Artist: Robert Chad

Chicks-on-a-Twirl

With a little push, two chicks spin through the openings of their decorative egg-shaped frame. A delicate, bas-relief floral design enhances the front, dated "1993."

▧ Handcrafted, 3" tall
775QEO837-5, $7.75
Artist: Joyce Lyle

Backyard Bunny

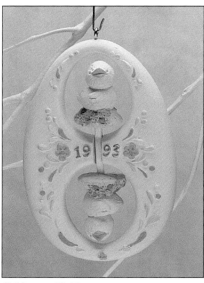
Chicks-on-a-Twirl

Maypole Stroll

Best-Dressed Turtle

Nutty Eggs

Li'l Peeper

Lop-Eared Bunny

Li'l Peeper

Gaily decorated eggs surround the adorable flocked chick who celebrates the season "in the pink" of a textured clip-on basket that contains "real" Easter grass.

◼ Handcrafted, 1⅞" tall
775QEO831-2, $7.75
Artist: Julia Lee

Lop-Eared Bunny

This lop-eared bunny has a classic, handcarved look and a festive lavender bow.

◼ Handcrafted, ⅞" tall
575QEO831-5, $5.75
Artist: Linda Sickman

Radiant Window

When light filters through the acrylic "stained glass" of this lovely window, it adds a soft, warm glow. Bluebirds perch on a flowering branch, which gracefully frames the design with spring blossoms.

◼ Handcrafted, 3¼" tall
775QEO836-5, $7.75
Artist: Duane Unruh

Lovely Lamb

With lavender flowers on her curly head and in her "93"-dated basket, this little lamb is suspended by a satiny pink ribbon. Her ruffled skirt forms a real bell.

◼ Handpainted Fine Porcelain, 3" tall
975QEO837-2, $9.75
Artist: LaDene Votruba

Best-Dressed Turtle

Carrying an Easter lily, this turtle has pastel stripes painted on his shell to look like an Easter egg—just right for a come-as-you-are fashion parade!

◼ Handcrafted, 1⅞" tall
575QE0839-2, $5.75
Artist: Julia Lee

Nutty Eggs

A fluffy-tailed squirrel proudly displays an Easter basket filled with eggs too pretty to hide. But wait, those are decorated acorns!

◼ Handcrafted, 1⅞" tall
675QEO838-2, $6.75
Artist: Julia Lee

Radiant Window

Lovely Lamb

Beautiful Memories Photoholder

Trimmed with colorful spring flowers and a lavender bow in bas-relief, the egg-shaped photoholder holds a treasured picture. The back says: "1993 Beautiful Easter Memories."

■ Handcrafted, 2½" tall
675QEO836-2, $6.75
Artist: Duane Unruh

Time for Easter

This cheery clock is designed with lots of delightful springtime details. Bunnies and a butterfly decorate the top, a tiny bluebird perches above the happy face, and Easter-egg "weights" hang from golden wires. The back, dated "1993," reads: "Time For Happy Easter Fun."

■ Handcrafted, 3½" tall
875QEO838-5, $8.75
Artist: Robert Chad

Collectible Series

Springtime Bonnets— First Edition

First in a new series, this ladylike rabbit smiles shyly beneath her straw-textured hat, trimmed with flowers and ribbon. To complete her fashion ensemble, she carries a handbag dated "1993."

■ Handcrafted, 2¼" tall
775QEO832-2, $7.75
Artist: Donna Lee

Eggs in Sports— Second Edition

Here's an egg that's ready to serve. Second in a series, he looks egg-xactly right with his tennies, headband, and racket. "Tennis Ace 93" is on the back.

■ Handcrafted, 2" tall
675QEO833-2, $6.75
Artist: Bob Siedler

Easter Parade— Second Edition

Second in a series, this band-bunny marches merrily along playing a glockenspiel dated "93." A real pompom forms his fluffy tail.

■ Handcrafted, 2⅞" tall
675QEO832-5, $6.75
Artist: Julia Lee

Beautiful Memories Photoholder

Time for Easter

Springtime Bonnets

Eggs in Sports

Easter Parade

1992
KEEPSAKE EASTER COLLECTION

For the second year of the Keepsake Easter Collection, springtime was heralded by soft pastel colors and delightful characters. More Easter ornaments were available than ever before, with twenty designs to choose from. Included in these were the two first series: "Eggs in Sports" and "Easter Parade." The "CRAYOLA® Bunny" also made his first appearance. To help collectors display their Easter treasures, an "Easter Memory Wreath," "Springtime Trellis," and "Easter Memory Tree" were offered.

Grandchild

Baby's First Easter

Grandchild
Bouncing with energy on a pogo stick shaped like a carrot, this bunny gathers colorful eggs in a lavender Easter basket inscribed: "Grandchild '92."
■ Handcrafted, 3" tall
675QEO927-4, $6.75
Artist: Ken Crow

Baby's First Easter
Joyously bursting from a lavender Easter egg, a newly-hatched chick greets the world. The chick wears part of the egg shell as a hat. "Baby's First Easter 1992" is the inscription on the egg.
■ Handcrafted, 3" tall
675QEO927-1, $6.75
Artist: John Francis (Collin)

Daughter
Ready for Easter, this bunny wears a pink dress and has a purple bow tied around her perky ears. She also has a real string to help her stay attached to a balloon that is decorated with "Daughter 1992."
■ Handcrafted, 3" tall
575QEO928-4, $5.75
Artist: Anita Marra Rogers

Son
An Easter egg-shaped balloon decorated with the words, "Son 1992," helps this bunny reach for the stars. Wearing a blue jacket, he hangs onto the balloon with a real string.
■ Handcrafted, 3" tall
575QEO928-1, $5.75
Artist: Anita Marra Rogers

Daughter

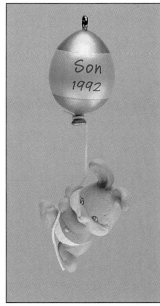

Son

CRAYOLA® Bunny

Somebunny Loves You

Warm Memories Photoholder

Promise of Easter

Springtime Egg

Cultivated Gardener

CRAYOLA® Bunny

The "CRAYOLA® Bunny" decorates Easter eggs with colorful crayons. Wearing a painter's cap bearing the CRAYOLA® logo, he dons spattered overalls and tucks crayons into a back pocket dated "92."

- Handcrafted, 3" tall
  775QEO930-4, $7.75
  Artist: Anita Marra Rogers

Somebunny Loves You

With an enthusiastic hug, this bunny greets a yummy-looking "chocolate" friend who wears a gift tag that reads: "Somebunny Loves You."

- Handcrafted, 3" tall
  675QEO929-4, $6.75
  Artist: John Francis (Collin)

Warm Memories Photoholder

This egg-shaped fabric ornament is embroidered with pastel tulips and dated "1992." A peach fabric bow tops the ornament and serves as its hanger. The back caption reads: "Easter brings warm memories."

- Fabric, 4" tall
  775QEO931-1, $7.75
  Artist: LaDene Votruba

Promise of Easter

A butterfly flutters near a lamb nestling among spring flowers. Scripted on the back of this heart-shaped ornament is the caption: "God's love shines everywhere. 1992." The ornament hangs from a lavender fabric ribbon.

- Handcrafted, Handpainted, 3" tall
  875QEO931-4, $8.75
  Artist: Joyce Lyle

Springtime Egg

This pink Easter egg is decorated with a carefully sculpted bas-relief design. The ornament is dated "1992" and hangs from a pink fabric ribbon.

- Handcrafted, Handpainted, 3" tall
  875QEO932-1, $8.75
  Artist: Julia Lee

Cultivated Gardener

Holding a hoe, this gardener cultivates the soil in preparation for planting the seeds in the packet labeled: "Carrots 92." The bunny wears mint green overalls.

- Handcrafted, 3" tall
  575QEO935-1, $5.75
  Artist: Bob Siedler

Sunny Wisher

Belle Bunny

Eggspert Painter

Belle Bunny
"Belle Bunny" is ready for a springtime waltz. Trimmed in pink, the gown features a lavender bow and a pocket dated "92." This intricately sculpted bell is inscribed on the inside, "Hand-Painted Fine Porcelain."
- Handpainted Fine Porcelain, 3" tall
  975QEO935-4, $9.75
  Artist: LaDene Votruba

Eggspert Painter
This eggspert bunny creates a painter's scaffold from a swing with real string, but uses a little more paint than finesse as he labels his favorite egg "92."
- Handcrafted, 3" tall
  675QEO936-1, $6.75
  Artist: Bob Siedler

Sunny Wisher
This bright little bluebird sings a cheery tune from his "Sunny Easter Wishes" songbook. The supports for his perch serve as the ornament hanger.
- Handcrafted, 3" tall
  575QEO934-4, $5.75
  Artist: Sharon Pike

Joy Bearer
Enjoying her "beary" favorite things, this little bear delivers Easter joy. Intricate detail is evident in her fancy Easter bonnet trimmed with springtime flowers and a pink bow. The real wicker basket is filled with colorful eggs, with the one in front dated "92."
- Handcrafted, Handpainted, 3" tall
  875QEO933-4, $8.75
  Artist: Don Palmiter

Rocking Bunny
This bunny is outfitted with a saddle trimmed with silvery accents. Wearing a decorative purple bow, he sits atop nickel-plated rockers, debossed with the words and date: "Happy Easter" and "1992."
- Handcrafted, Nickel-plated, 3" tall
  975QEO932-4, $9.75
  Artist: LaDene Votruba

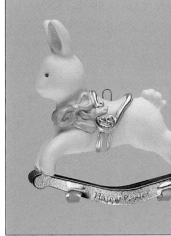
Joy Bearer   Rocking Bunny

Bless You

Cosmic Rabbit

Bless You
Even cuddly rabbits need snuggly toys! Wearing a mint green bow inscribed "Bless You," this rabbit hugs a purple, floppy-eared bunny.
- Handcrafted, 3" tall
  675QEO929-1, $6.75
  Artist: John Francis (Collin)

Cosmic Rabbit
This astronaut goes exploring for Easter eggs in out-of-the-way places. Wearing boots ready for space walking and a clear, domed helmet dated "92," our adventurer collects colorful eggs in a golden basket.
- Handcrafted, 3" tall
  775QEO936-4, $7.75
  Artist: Bob Siedler

Everything's Ducky
This little duck splashes happily in water that's collected in an overturned umbrella. His webbed feet peek just above the surface of the water, and he wears a lavender slicker dated "92."
- Handcrafted, 3" tall
  675QEO933-1, $6.75
  Artist: Sharon Pike

Collectible Series

Eggs in Sports— First Edition
The "egg batter" winds up for the first pitch, as he leads off the lineup of eggstraordinary sports stars in this new Collectible Series, "Eggs in Sports." You'll find the name of this eggstra special team and the date on the back: "GRADE A'S 92."
- Handcrafted, 3" tall
  675QEO934-1, $6.75
  Artist: Bob Siedler

Easter Parade— First Edition
Introducing a new Collectible Series, the "Drum Major" blows a golden whistle and wears a hat adorned with a carrot. His vest is debossed with the date "92," and a real pompom forms the bunny's tail.
- Handcrafted, 3" tall
  675QEO930-1, $6.75
  Artist: Ken Crow

Everything's Ducky

Eggs in Sports

Easter Parade

1991 KEEPSAKE EASTER COLLECTION

During this first year of the Keepsake Easter Collection, four commemorative ornaments were offered: "Baby's First Easter," "Daughter," "Son," and "Grandchild." In addition to these, there's a delicately embroidered, egg-shaped "Easter Memories" photoholder to display a cherished photo of Baby or someone special in Easter finery. Other designs portray playful animals associated with spring, and some celebrate traditions, such as decorating eggs or going for a stroll in the warm sunshine. The porcelain "Lily Egg" as well as all of the handcrafted ornaments in the Keepsake Easter Collection have been carefully painted by hand in pastel colors.

Baby's First Easter
Tucked into a basket, beneath a handpainted quilt, a baby bunny dreams of Easter. Across the quilt is a banner that reads, "Baby's 1st Easter 1991." The basket rocks gently, hanging from lavender ribbons.
■ Handpainted, Handcrafted, 1½" tall
875QEO518-9, $8.75

Daughter
A happy little bunny holds a big carrot with a pearly pink bow. The carrot says "24K Daughter," and the "K" abbreviation stands for "karat," of course!
■ Handpainted, Handcrafted, 1½" tall
575QEO517-9, $5.75

Son
A pearly blue ribbon decorates the carrot in this little bunny's paws. The caption on the carrot reads: "24K Son." Once again, the "K" stands for "karat."
■ Handpainted, Handcrafted, 1½" tall
575QEO518-7, $5.75

Grandchild
A bunny wearing a cowboy outfit with a polka-dot bandana rides a rocking horse with golden hooves. The rockers read: "Grandchild" and "1991."
■ Handpainted, Handcrafted, 2½" tall
675QEO517-7, $6.75

Lily Egg
Pale yellow is a lovely background for the raised design of Easter lilies all around this delicate egg. Gold paint highlights the flowers, and the date "1991" is engraved at the base of the egg. The ornament hangs from a yellow ribbon.
■ Handpainted Fine Porcelain, 2" tall
975QEO513-9, $9.75

Full of Love
A bunny and a chick nestle in a basket of pearly pastel Easter eggs. The mint green egg shows the date "1991." The finishing touch on the Easter basket is a big bow of satiny pink.
■ Handpainted, Handcrafted, 2" tall
775QEO514-9, $7.75

Easter Memories Photoholder
Designed to hold a favorite Easter photo, this egg-shaped ornament is made of fabric and embroidered with delicate flowers and the words, "Easter Memories 1991." The caption on the back reads: "Easter is a joy to remember." A peach fabric bow tops the ornament and serves as its hanger.
■ Fabric, 2½" tall
775QEO513-7, $7.75

Baby's First Easter, Daughter, Son, Grandchild

Li'l Dipper

This bunny had so much fun decorating eggs, he decided to take a dip himself. He sits in a metal egg-dipper, and his tail and bottom are aqua. He wears a turquoise satin ribbon around his neck. The dipper serves as the ornament hanger.

■ Handpainted, Handcrafted,
2½" tall
675QEO514-7, $6.75

Spirit of Easter

Here's a new way to have some high-flying fun delivering eggs! Wearing a shimmery lavender scarf, a pilot is ready for take-off in his airplane, "Easter Bunny." The plane, dated "1991," is pale blue with a light peach propeller.

■ Handpainted, Handcrafted,
2" tall
775QEO516-9, $7.75

Springtime Stroll

A distinguished gentleman bunny is out enjoying the warm spring weather. He carries a walking stick and wears a sporty blue jacket with the date "1991" on the collar. A pink tie and lavender derby complete his dapper attire. This ornament has the appearance of hand-carved wood.

■ Handpainted, Handcrafted,
2½" tall
675QEO516-7, $6.75

Gentle Lamb

A little lamb is all dressed up for Easter in a necklace of dainty pink and blue flowers and a bell dated "91." Realistic fluffy texturing gives his coat the look of soft, curly wool.

■ Handpainted, Handcrafted,
2" tall
675QEO515-9, $6.75

Lily Egg, Full of Love, Easter Memories Photoholder

Li'l Dipper, Spirit of Easter, Springtime Stroll, Gentle Lamb

THE COLLECTIBLE SERIES

KEEPSAKE, KEEPSAKE MAGIC, KEEPSAKE MINIATURE, AND KEEPSAKE EASTER ORNAMENTS

A Collectible Series consists of a group of ornaments that share a specific theme or motif. For example, the "Nostalgic Houses and Shops" series depicts old-fashioned buildings and shops. Series ornaments are issued one per year for a minimum of three years, and they are very popular with collectors.

Two of the longest-running series are "Here Comes Santa" and "Frosty Friends." The fifteenth edition of "Here Comes Santa" was issued in 1993, and "Frosty Friends" celebrated its fourteenth edition the same year.

Beginning with the Collectible Series ornaments offered in 1982, all series editions are identified with the words, "(number) in a series" or a tree-shaped symbol with the edition number inside. The Keepsake Easter ornaments carry an egg-shaped symbol.

Holiday Barbie™, 1993

The PEANUTS® Gang, 1993

Mother Goose, 1993

Special Issue Series

Holiday Barbie™
A superstar for three decades, Barbie™ makes her Keepsake debut as "Holiday Barbie™" in the Collectible Series. The ornament was inspired by Barbie™ dolls offered during the holidays.
- 1993   1475QX572-5

The PEANUTS® Gang
Each year, a different character from Charles Schulz's popular comic strip will be featured in this series.
- 1993   975QX531-5
  PEANUTS®

Mother Goose
The nostalgia of nursery rhymes is the focus of this appealing new series which begins with "Humpty-Dumpty."
- 1993   1375QX528-2
  Humpty-Dumpty

U.S. Christmas Stamps, 1993

U.S. Christmas Stamps
This new series features reproductions of designs selected over the years by the U.S. Postal Service for its commemorative Christmas stamps.
◼ 1993   1075QX529-2

Tobin Fraley Carousel
The magical dreams of childhood are reflected in fanciful carousel horses designed by

Tobin Fraley, a renowned authority on carousels.
◼ 1993   2800QX550-2
◼ 1992   2800QX489-1

Betsey's Country Christmas
This third Betsey Clark ball ornament series is the first ball series that is teardrop-shaped.
◼ 1993   500QX206-2
◼ 1992   500QX210-4

Tobin Fraley Carousel, 1993

Tobin Fraley Carousel, 1992

Betsey's Country Christmas, 1993

Betsey's Country Christmas, 1992

Classic American Cars

A different dream car from the past drives into the "Classic American Car" series each year.

- 1993   1275QX527-5   1956 Thunderbird
- 1992   1275QX428-4   1966 Mustang
- 1991   1275QX431-9   1957 Corvette

Owliver

"Owliver" began this series in 1992 by sharing a story with a perky little rabbit friend. As the years progress, he introduces other forest friends.

- 1993   775QX542-5
- 1992   775QX454-4

Classic American Cars: 1993, 1956 Thunderbird

Classic American Cars: 1992, 1966 Mustang

Classic American Cars: 1991, 1957 Corvette

Owliver, 1993

Owliver, 1992

Merry Olde Santa, 1993

Merry Olde Santa, 1992

Merry Olde Santa

The tradition of a gift-bringing Santa is celebrated by children of many lands. The jolly old gentleman's appearance varies according to local legends and customs. This series presents a different classic Santa each year.

- 1993   1475QX484-2
- 1992   1475QX441-4
- 1991   1475QX435-9
- 1990   1475QX473-6

Puppy Love

A playful cocker spaniel leads the way for a different, lovable puppy each year. Each pup has its own year-dated tag.

- 1993   775QX504-5
- 1992   775QX448-4
- 1991   775QX537-9

Merry Olde Santa: 1990, 1991

Puppy Love, 1991

Puppy Love, 1993

Puppy Love, 1992

Fabulous Decade

This is the first Keepsake Ornament Series designed specifically to commemorate a particular decade. It is considered especially collectible because the large brass numerals are the focal point of the design. A different little animal presents the numerals each year.

- 1993 775QX447-5
- 1992 775QX424-4
- 1991 775QX411-9
- 1990 775QX446-6

Heart of Christmas

Each year, the "Heart of Christmas" heart-shaped shadow-box design opens to reveal a new triptych of intricately detailed holiday scenes. The ornament is styled like a locket with brass hinges and a clasp to display opened or closed.

- 1993 1475QX448-2
- 1992 1375QX441-1
- 1991 1375QX435-7
- 1990 1375QX472-6

Fabulous Decade, 1993

Fabulous Decade, 1992

Fabulous Decade, 1991

Fabulous Decade, 1990

Heart of Christmas, 1993

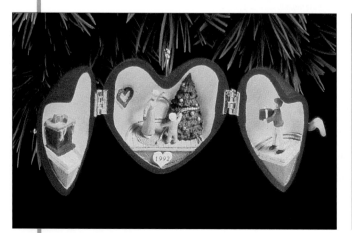
Heart of Christmas, 1992

Heart of Christmas: 1990, 1991

CRAYOLA® Crayon

There's no limit to the ingenuity of the animals in this series. They fashion colorful objects and toys out of CRAYOLA® Crayons and the crayon box!

- 1993 1075QX442-2
  Bright Shining Castle
- 1992 975QX426-4
  Bright Blazing Colors
- 1991 975QX421-9
  Bright Vibrant Colors
- 1990 875QX458-6
  Bright Moving Colors
- 1989 875QX435-2
  Bright Journey

CRAYOLA® Crayon, 1993

CRAYOLA® Crayon, 1992

CRAYOLA® Crayon: 1989, 1990, 1991

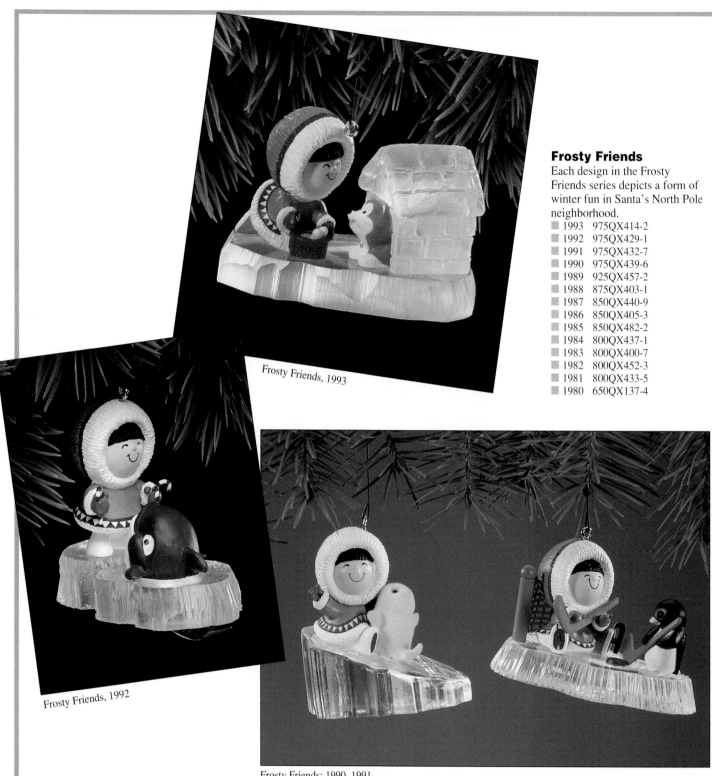

Frosty Friends

Each design in the Frosty Friends series depicts a form of winter fun in Santa's North Pole neighborhood.

- 1993 975QX414-2
- 1992 975QX429-1
- 1991 975QX432-7
- 1990 975QX439-6
- 1989 925QX457-2
- 1988 875QX403-1
- 1987 850QX440-9
- 1986 850QX405-3
- 1985 850QX482-2
- 1984 800QX437-1
- 1983 800QX400-7
- 1982 800QX452-3
- 1981 800QX433-5
- 1980 650QX137-4

Frosty Friends, 1993

Frosty Friends, 1992

Frosty Friends: 1990, 1991

Frosty Friends: 1987, 1988, 1989

Frosty Friends: 1984, 1985, 1986

Frosty Friends: 1980, 1981, 1982, 1983

Nostalgic Houses and Shops

The Nostalgic Houses and Shops series was introduced in 1984. Each piece is carefully researched so that detailing is both authentic and accurate.

- 1993 1475QX417-5
  Cozy Home
- 1992 1475QX425-4
  Five-and-Ten-Cent Store
- 1991 1475QX413-9
  Fire Station
- 1990 1475QX469-6
  Holiday Home
- 1989 1425QX458-2
  U.S. Post Office
- 1988 1450QX401-4
  Hall Bro's Card Shop
- 1987 1400QX483-9
  House on Main St.
- 1986 1375QX403-3
  Christmas Candy Shoppe
- 1985 1375QX497-5
  Old-Fashioned Toy Shop
- 1984 1300QX448-1
  Victorian Dollhouse

Nostalgic Houses and Shops, 1993

Nostalgic Houses and Shops, 1992

Nostalgic Houses and Shops, 1991

Nostalgic Houses and Shops, 1990

Nostalgic Houses and Shops: 1988, 1989

Nostalgic Houses and Shops: 1986, 1987

Nostalgic Houses and Shops: 1984, 1985

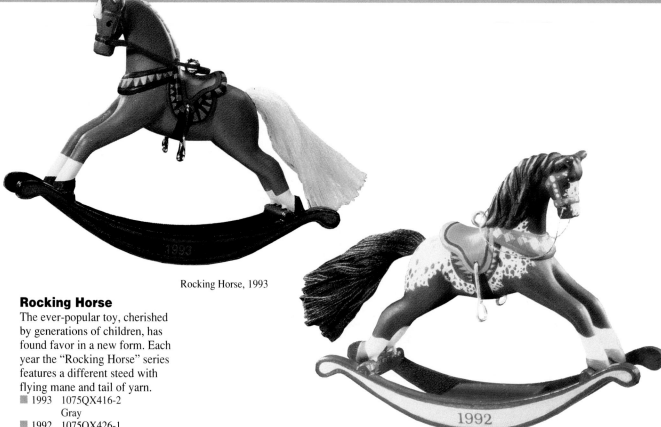

Rocking Horse, 1993

Rocking Horse, 1992

Rocking Horse

The ever-popular toy, cherished by generations of children, has found favor in a new form. Each year the "Rocking Horse" series features a different steed with flying mane and tail of yarn.

- 1993   1075QX416-2
  Gray
- 1992   1075QX426-1
  Spotted Brown
- 1991   1075QX414-7
  Buckskin
- 1990   1075QX464-6
  Appaloosa
- 1989   1075QX462-2
  Bay
- 1988   1075QX402-4
  Dappled Gray
- 1987   1075QX482-9
  White
- 1986   1075QX401-6
  Palomino
- 1985   1075QX493-2
  Pinto
- 1984   1000QX435-4
  Appaloosa
- 1983   1000QX417-7
  Russet
- 1982   1000QX502-3
  Black
- 1981   900QX422-2
  Dappled

Rocking Horse: 1988, 1989, 1990, 1991

Rocking Horse: 1984, 1985, 1986, 1987

Rocking Horse: 1981, 1982, 1983

Here Comes Santa, 1992

Here Comes Santa, 1993

Here Comes Santa, 1991

Here Comes Santa, 1990

Here Comes Santa: 1988, 1989

Here Comes Santa

The "Here Comes Santa" series proves that Santa is capable of using any mode of transportation to make his Christmas Eve deliveries.

▪ 1993   1475QX410-2
       Happy Haul-idays
▪ 1992   1475QX434-1
       Kringle Tours
▪ 1991   1475QX434-9
       Santa's Antique Car
▪ 1990   1475QX492-3
       Festive Surrey
▪ 1989   1475QX458-5
       Christmas Caboose
▪ 1988   1400QX400-1
       Kringle Koach
▪ 1987   1400QX484-7
       Santa's Woody
▪ 1986   1400QX404-3
       Kringle's Kool Treats
▪ 1985   1400QX496-5
       Santa's Fire Engine
▪ 1984   1300QX432-4
       Santa's Deliveries
▪ 1983   1300QX403-7
       Santa Express
▪ 1982   1500QX464-3
       Jolly Trolley
▪ 1981   1300QX438-2
       Rooftop Deliveries
▪ 1980   1200QX143-4
       Santa's Express
▪ 1979   900QX155-9
       Santa's Motorcar

Here Comes Santa: 1986, 1987

Here Comes Santa: 1982, 1983, 1984, 1985

Here Comes Santa: 1979, 1980, 1981

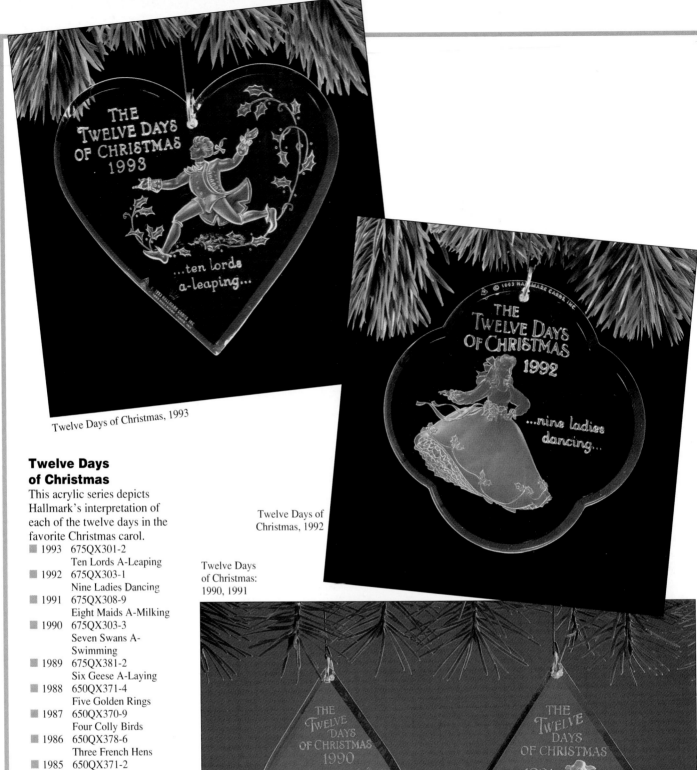

Twelve Days of Christmas, 1993

Twelve Days of
Christmas, 1992

Twelve Days
of Christmas:
1990, 1991

Twelve Days
of Christmas

This acrylic series depicts
Hallmark's interpretation of
each of the twelve days in the
favorite Christmas carol.

- 1993   675QX301-2
         Ten Lords A-Leaping
- 1992   675QX303-1
         Nine Ladies Dancing
- 1991   675QX308-9
         Eight Maids A-Milking
- 1990   675QX303-3
         Seven Swans A-
         Swimming
- 1989   675QX381-2
         Six Geese A-Laying
- 1988   650QX371-4
         Five Golden Rings
- 1987   650QX370-9
         Four Colly Birds
- 1986   650QX378-6
         Three French Hens
- 1985   650QX371-2
         Two Turtle Doves
- 1984   600QX348-4
         Partridge in a Pear Tree

Twelve Days of Christmas: 1988, 1989

Twelve Days of Christmas: 1986, 1987

Twelve Days of Christmas: 1984, 1985

Mr. and Mrs. Claus

Santa and his lovely spouse appear in your home to show how they celebrate Christmas in the Claus household.

- 1993 1475QX420-2
  A Fitting Moment
- 1992 1475QX429-4
  Gift Exchange
- 1991 1375QX433-9
  Checking His List
- 1990 1375QX439-3
  Popcorn Party
- 1989 1325QX457-5
  Holiday Duet
- 1988 1300QX401-1
  Shall We Dance
- 1987 1325QX483-7
  Home Cooking
- 1986 1300QX402-6
  Merry Mistletoe Time

Mr. and Mrs. Claus, 1993

Mr. and Mrs. Claus, 1992

Mr. and Mrs. Claus, 1991

Mr. and Mrs. Claus, 1990

Mr. and Mrs. Claus, 1989

Mr. and Mrs. Claus, 1988

Mr. and Mrs. Claus, 1987

Mr. and Mrs. Claus, 1986

Mary's Angels

The angels in this series are designed by Hallmark artist Mary Hamilton, who is known for her charming depictions of children. Each angel has her own special flower name and appears with an acrylic cloud. The cloud carries the artist's signature, "Mary."

- 1993 675QX428-2 Ivy
- 1992 675QX427-4 Lily
- 1991 675QX427-9 Iris
- 1990 575QX442-3 Rosebud
- 1989 575QX454-5 Bluebell
- 1988 500QX407-4 Buttercup

Retired Collectible Series

Peace on Earth

Children of a different country were featured each year in this series, with the message "Peace on Earth" in both their native language and English. This series ended in 1993.

- 1993 1175QX524-2 Poland
- 1992 1175QX517-4 Spain
- 1991 1175QX512-9 Italy

Mary's Angels, 1993

Mary's Angels, 1992

Mary's Angels: 1988, 1989, 1990, 1991

Peace on Earth, 1993

Peace on Earth, 1992

Peace on Earth, 1991

Heavenly Angels

Sculpted in the elaborate style of old-world masters, a series of graceful angels gathers to celebrate the season. This series was retired in 1993.

- 1993 775QX494-5
- 1992 775QX445-4
- 1991 775QX436-7

Heavenly Angels, 1993

Heavenly Angels, 1992

Heavenly Angels, 1991

Greatest Story

Scenes from the beloved Christmas story were carefully sculpted on fine porcelain medallions, each of which hangs inside a glowing brass snowflake. This series was retired in 1992.

- 1992 1275QX425-1
- 1991 1275QX412-9
- 1990 1275QX465-6

Greatest Story: 1990, 1991

Greatest Story, 1992

Hark! It's Herald, 1992

Hark! It's Herald: 1989, 1990, 1991

Hark! It's Herald

Herald, the talented star of this series, played a different musical instrument every year. The series ended in 1992.

- 1992 775QX446-4
- 1991 675QX437-9
- 1990 675QX446-3
- 1989 675QX455-5

Winter Surprise

The penguins inside the peek-through eggs in this series created a new winter surprise each year. The final edition was 1992.

- 1992 1175QX427-1
- 1991 1075QX427-7
- 1990 1075QX444-3
- 1989 1075QX427-2

Winter Surprise: 1989, 1990, 1991

Winter Surprise, 1992

The Gift Bringers, 1993

The Gift Bringers, 1992

The Gift Bringers

Beloved Christmas legends from around the world are illustrated on the five editions that made up this series. The final edition was released in 1993.

- 1993   500QX206-5 The Magi
- 1992   500QX212-4 Kolyada
- 1991   500QX211-7 Christkindl
- 1990   500QX280-3 St. Lucia
- 1989   500QX279-5 St. Nicholas

The Gift Bringers: 1989, 1990, 1991

Reindeer Champs: 1989 1990, 1991

Reindeer Champs: 1986, 1987, 1988

Reindeer Champs, 1993

Reindeer Champs, 1992

Reindeer Champs

Santa's reindeer champions appear in a series that featured a different sport each year. The final edition was in 1993.

- 1993   875QX433-1 Blitzen
- 1992   875QX528-4 Donder
- 1991   775QX434-7 Cupid
- 1990   775QX443-3 Comet
- 1989   775QX456-2 Vixen
- 1988   750QX405-1 Prancer
- 1987   750QX480-9 Dancer
- 1986   750QX422-3 Dasher

Collector's Plate

The heartwarming artwork on this series of miniature, fine porcelain collector's plates depicts the excitement, joy, and anticipation children experience at Christmas. The series was retired in 1992.

■ 1992 875QX446-1
Sweet Holiday Harmony
■ 1991 875QX436-9
Let It Snow!
■ 1990 875QX443-6
Cookies for Santa
■ 1989 825QX461-2
Morning of Wonder
■ 1988 800QX406-1
Waiting for Santa
■ 1987 800QX481-7
Light Shines at Christmas

Collector's Plate, 1992

Collector's Plate, 1991

Collector's Plate: 1989, 1990

Collector's Plate: 1987, 1988

Windows of the World, 1990

Windows of the World, 1989

Windows of the World, 1988

Windows of the World: 1985, 1986, 1987

Windows of the World

This series depicts international celebrations of Christmas by children, including holiday greetings in a different language each year. The series ended in 1990.

- 1990 1075QX463-6
  Nollaig Shona
- 1989 1075QX462-5
  Fröhliche Weihnachten
- 1988 1000QX402- 1
  Joyeux Noël
- 1987 1000QX482-7
  Mele Kalikimaka
- 1986 1000QX408-3
  Vrolyk Kerstfeest
- 1985 975QX490-2
  Feliz Navidad

Christmas Kitty

It's Christmas...and the kitties in this series love to dress in their holiday best. Every edition offered a different kitty, fashioned in fine porcelain and painted by hand. This series retired in 1991.

- 1991 1475QX437-7
- 1990 1475QX450-6
- 1989 1475QX544-5

Christmas Kitty: 1989, 1990, 1991

Betsey Clark

Starting in 1973 (the year Hallmark introduced its ornaments nationally) and ending with the final Betsey Clark ball ornament in 1985, a total of thirteen ornaments appeared in the "Betsey Clark" series. Other Betsey Clark formats offered have included satin balls, cameo ornaments, handcrafted designs and hand-painted porcelain angels. The series designs shown here are:

- 1985 500QX263-2
Special Kind of Feeling
- 1984 500QX249-4
Days are Merry
- 1983 450QX211-9
Christmas Happiness
- 1982 450QX215-6
Joys of Christmas
- 1981 450QX802-2
Christmas 1981
- 1980 400QX215-4
Joy-in-the-Air
- 1979 350QX201-9
Holiday Fun
- 1978 350QX201-6
Christmas Spirit
- 1977 350QX264-2
Truest Joys of Christmas
- 1976 300QX195-1
Christmas 1976
- 1975 300QX133-1
Caroling Trio
- 1974 250QX108-1
Musicians
- 1973 250XHD110-2
Christmas 1973

Betsey Clark: 1983, 1984, 1985

Betsey Clark: 1980, 1981, 1982

Betsey Clark: 1976, 1977, 1978, 1979

Betsey Clark: 1973, 1974, 1975

Betsey Clark: Home for Christmas

The second Betsey Clark ball series features the artist's lovable children celebrating Christmas around the home. The glass balls are 2⅞" in diameter, smaller than those in the first Betsey Clark series. The "Home for Christmas" collection ended with the 1991 edition, and Hallmark introduced a new Betsy Clark Series in 1992.

1991	500QX210-9
1990	500QX203-3
1989	500QX230-2
1988	500QX271-4
1987	500QX272-7
1986	500QX277-6

Betsey Clark: Home for Christmas: 1989, 1990, 1991

Betsey Clark: Home for Christmas: 1986, 1987, 1988

Porcelain Bear

For teddy bear lovers especially, this series offered an annual porcelain edition of a lovable bear named Cinnamon. Each is hand-painted. The eighth edition, issued in 1990, concluded the series.

■	1990	875QX442-6
■	1989	875QX461-5
■	1988	800QX404-4
■	1987	775QX442-7
■	1986	775QX405-6
■	1985	775QX479-2
■	1984	700QX454-1
		Cinnamon Bear
■	1983	700QX428-9
		Cinnamon Teddy

Porcelain Bear: 1990, 1989, 1988

Holiday Heirloom

This series marked several firsts. It was the first limited edition series and the first to feature lead crystal and a precious metal. It was also the first to have two editions—the second and third—available only through the Hallmark Keepsake Ornament Collector's Club. Each ornament combines an intricately sculpted silver-plated design with a 24-percent lead-crystal bell in an edition limited to 34,600 pieces. The series ended in 1989.

■	1989	2500QXC460-5
■	1988	2500QX406-4
■	1987	2500QX485-7

Porcelain Bear: 1983, 1984, 1985, 1986, 1987

Holiday Heirloom, 1987

Holiday Heirloom: 1988, 1989

The Bellringers: 1982, 1983, 1984

The Bellringers

Holiday bells have a touch of whimsey in this unique series that brought a new interpretation to this traditional design motif. Made of fine porcelain, the bells have different handcrafted clappers for each year. The sixth and last of "The Bellringers" series was produced in 1984.

- 1984 1500QX438-4
  Elfin Artist
- 1983 1500QX403-9
  Teddy Bellringer
- 1982 1500QX455-6
  Angel Bellringer
- 1981 1500QX441-5
  Swingin' Bellringer
- 1980 1500QX157-4
  The Bellringers
- 1979 1000QX147-9
  The Bellswinger

Art Masterpiece

This padded satin series offers reproductions of religious fine art masterpieces from around the world. The series ended in 1986.

- 1986 675QX350-6
  Madonna and Child
  with the Infant St. John
- 1985 675QX377-2
  Madonna of the
  Pomegranate
- 1984 650QX349-4
  Madonna and Child
  and St. John

The Bellringers: 1979, 1980, 1981

Art Masterpiece: 1984, 1985, 1986

Norman Rockwell

The art of Norman Rockwell is known and loved by all, and this delightful series of cameos presents the artist's vision of Christmas in a beautiful dimension. In addition to the cameo series, Rockwell artwork has been featured on glass and satin ball ornaments since 1974. The ninth and final ornament of this series was issued in 1988.

- 1988 775QX370-4
  And to All a Good Night
- 1987 775QX370-7
  The Christmas Dance
- 1986 775QX321-3
  Checking Up
- 1985 750QX374-5
  Postman and Kids
- 1984 750QX341-1
  Caught Napping
- 1983 750QX300-7
  Dress Rehearsal
- 1982 850QX305-3
  Filling the Stockings
- 1981 850QX511-5
  The Carolers
- 1980 650QX306-1
  Santa's Visitors

Norman Rockwell: 1986, 1987, 1988

Norman Rockwell: 1983, 1984, 1985

Norman Rockwell: 1980, 1981, 1982

Wood Childhood Ornaments, 1988

Wood Childhood Ornaments, 1986

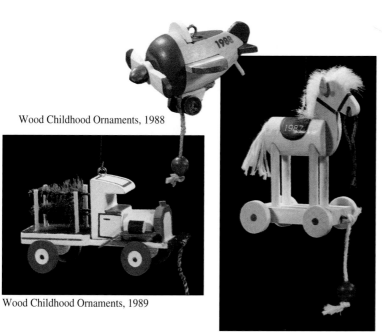

Wood Childhood Ornaments, 1989

Wood Childhood Ornaments, 1987

Wood Childhood Ornaments, 1984

Wood Childhood Ornaments, 1985

Miniature Crèche: 1988, 1989

Miniature Crèche: 1985, 1986, 1987

Wood Childhood Ornaments

These nostalgic wooden ornaments from yesteryear feature special authentic touches such as wheels that turn and bows made of fabric. The 1989 ornament concluded the series.

- 1989 775QX459-5
  Wooden Truck
- 1988 750QX404-1
  Wooden Airplane
- 1987 750QX441-7
  Wooden Horse
- 1986 750QX407-3
  Wooden Reindeer
- 1985 700QX472-2
  Wooden Train
- 1984 650QX439-4
  Wooden Lamb

Miniature Crèche

This series of unique nativities is fashioned in different media, such as wood and porcelain. The last edition, a *retablo*, appeared in 1989.

- 1989 925QX459-2
  Handcrafted
- 1988 850QX403-4
  Acrylic
- 1987 900QX481-9
  Multi-plated Brass
- 1986 900QX407-6
  Fine Porcelain
- 1985 875QX482-5
  Wood and Woven Straw

Tin Locomotive, 1989

Tin Locomotive

Introduced in 1982, the "Tin Locomotive" series is of interest to train, tin, and ornament collectors alike. The series, retired in 1989, depicted eight models of locomotives inspired by trains from the early days of American rail transportation.

- 1989   1475QX460-2
- 1988   1475QX400-4
- 1987   1475QX484-9
- 1986   1475QX403-6
- 1985   1475QX497-2
- 1984   1400QX440-4
- 1983   1300QX404-9
- 1982   1300QX460-3

Tin Locomotive, 1988

Tin Locomotive, 1987

Tin Locomotive, 1986

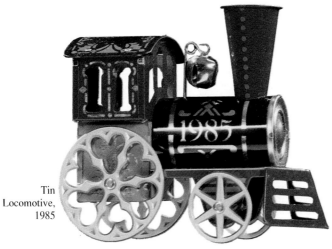

Tin Locomotive, 1985

Tin Locomotive, 1984

Tin Locomotive, 1983

Tin Locomotive, 1982

Holiday Wildlife: 1985, 1986, 1987

Holiday Wildlife, 1988

Holiday Wildlife

The "Holiday Wildlife" series, introduced in 1982, is especially appealing to bird watchers who appreciate skillful and true-to-life artistic representations of beautiful birds. The paintings were reproduced on a white, porcelain-like insert and framed and backed in natural wood. The series was retired in 1988.

- 1988 775QX371-1
       Purple Finch
- 1987 750QX371-7
       Snow Goose
- 1986 750QX321-6
       Cedar Waxwing
- 1985 750QX376-5
       California Quail
- 1984 725QX347-4
       Ring-Necked Pheasant
- 1983 700QX309-9
       Black-Capped
       Chickadees
- 1982 700QX313-3
       Cardinalis Cardinalis

Holiday Wildlife: 1982, 1983, 1984

SNOOPY® and Friends, 1983

SNOOPY® and Friends: 1981, 1982

SNOOPY® and Friends

SNOOPY®, in a three-dimensional format, made his debut in 1979 in an exciting peek-through ball ornament. The "window" in this ornament allows you to peek in on SNOOPY®'s holiday antics. The 1983 edition retired this series.

▦ 1983 1300QX416-9
          Santa SNOOPY®
▦ 1982 1300QX480-3
          SNOOPY® and Friends
▦ 1981 1200QX436-2
          SNOOPY® and Friends
▦ 1980 900QX154-1
          Ski Holiday
▦ 1979 800QX141-9
          Ice-Hockey Holiday

Clothespin Soldier

The "Clothespin Soldier" series features a serviceman wearing a different uniform each year. The final edition was issued in 1987.

▦ 1987 550QX480-7
          Sailor
▦ 1986 550QX406-3
          French Officer
▦ 1985 550QX471-5
          Scottish Highlander
▦ 1984 500QX447-1
          Canadian Mountie
▦ 1983 500QX402-9
          Early American
▦ 1982 500QX458-3
          British

SNOOPY® and Friends: 1979, 1980

Clothespin Soldier: 1982, 1983, 1984, 1985, 1986, 1987

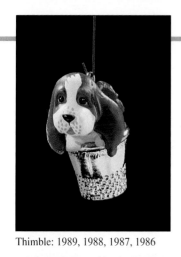

Thimble: 1989, 1988, 1987, 1986

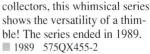

Thimble: 1985, 1984, 1983

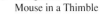

Thimble: 1982, 1981, 1980

Thimble:
1979, 1978

Thimble

Especially popular with thimble collectors, this whimsical series shows the versatility of a thimble! The series ended in 1989.

- 1989 575QX455-2
  Thimble Puppy
- 1988 575QX405-4
  Thimble Snowman
- 1987 575QX441-9
  Thimble Drummer
- 1986 575QX406-6
  Thimble Partridge
- 1985 550QX472-5
  Thimble Santa
- 1984 500QX430-4
  Thimble Angel
- 1983 500QX401-7
  Thimble Elf
- 1982 500QX451-3
  Thimble Mouse
- 1981 450QX413-5
  Thimble Angel
- 1980 400QX132-1
  Thimble Elf
- 1979 300QX131-9
  A Christmas Salute
- 1978 250QX133-6
  Mouse in a Thimble

Carrousel

The "Carrousel" series depicts fun and frolic on a colorful, rotating carrousel. This is one of the series most sought after by collectors. The 1983 design was the final edition.

- 1983 1100QX401-9
  Santa and Friends
- 1982 1000QX478-3
  Snowman Carrousel
- 1981 900QX427-5
  Skaters' Carrousel
- 1980 750QX141-4
  Merry Carrousel
- 1979 650QX146-7
  Christmas Carrousel
- 1978 600QX146-3
  Antique Toys

Carrousel: 1981, 1982, 1983

Carrousel, 1980

Carrousel, 1978

Carrousel, 1979

Chris Mouse, 1991

Chris Mouse, 1990

Keepsake Magic Ornament Series

Chris Mouse

This is the first series to feature light. The little mouse sitting by the candle and the other mice in following years both decorate and light your tree.

- 1993 1200QLX715-2
  Chris Mouse Flight
  (not shown)
- 1992 1200QLX707-4
  Chris Mouse Tales
  (not shown)
- 1991 1000QLX720-7
  Chris Mouse Mail
- 1990 1000QLX729-6
  Chris Mouse Wreath
- 1989 950QLX722-5
  Chris Mouse Cookout
- 1988 875QLX715-4
  Chris Mouse Star
- 1987 1100QLX705-7
  Chris Mouse Glow
- 1986 1300QLX705-6
  Chris Mouse Dreams
- 1985 1250QLX703-2
  Chris Mouse

Chris Mouse, 1989

Chris Mouse, 1988

Chris Mouse, 1987

Chris Mouse, 1986

Chris Mouse, 1985

PEANUTS®, 1993

PEANUTS®, 1992

PEANUTS®, 1991

PEANUTS®

SNOOPY® and his pal WOOD-
STOCK are waiting up for
Santa and looking forward to
enjoying a different holiday
activity each year.
- 1993   1800QLX715-5
- 1992   1800QLX721-4
- 1991   1800QLX722-9

Forest Frolics

Endearing woodland animals
make the forest a merry place.
They play and celebrate the
season in ornaments that feature light and motion.
- 1993   2500QLX716-5
- 1992   2800QLX725-4
- 1991   2500QLX721-9
- 1990   2500QLX723-6
- 1989   2450QLX728-2

Forest Frolics, 1993

Forest Frolics, 1992

Forest Frolics, 1991

Forest Frolics, 1990

Forest Frolics, 1989

Santa and Sparky, 1988

Keepsake Magic Retired Collectible Series

Santa and Sparky
Santa and his penguin pal, Sparky, share the fun of Christmas in this first "light and motion" series. The series ended in 1988.

- 1988   1950QLX719-1
  On With the Show
- 1987   2200QLX701-9
  Perfect Portrait
- 1986   2200QLX703-3
  Lighting the Tree

Santa and Sparky, 1986

Santa and Sparky, 1987

Christmas Classics

This series of lighted three-dimensional scenes illustrates beloved Christmas stories, ballets, books, poems, and songs. The series retired in 1990.

- 1990 1400QLX730-3
  The Littlest Angel
- 1989 1350QLX724-2
  Little Drummer Boy
- 1988 1500QLX716-1
  Night Before Christmas
- 1987 1600QLX702-9
  A Christmas Carol
- 1986 1750QLX704-3
  The Nutcracker Ballet–
  Sugarplum Fairy

Christmas Classics, 1990

Christmas Classics, 1989

Christmas Classics, 1988

Christmas Classics, 1987

Christmas Classics, 1986

Keepsake Miniature Ornament Series

On the Road

A new series of pressed tin vehicles is lead by a family station wagon with an evergreen on top.
■ 1993   575QXM400-2

On the Road, 1993

March of the Teddy Bears, 1993

March of the Teddy Bears

An adorable drum major steps into the lead of this new series of marching teddy bears.
■ 1993   450QXM400-5

The Night Before Christmas

With the world's most beloved poem by Clement C. Moore as inspiration, each ornament in this new series makes the story of Santa's visit come to life. A "Tin Display House" was offered with the first edition ("Rocker with Mouse"). A total of five ornaments will be introduced.
■ 1993   450QXM511-5
■ 1992   1375QXM554-1

The Night Before Christmas, 1993

The Night Before Christmas, 1992

Nature's Angels

Gentle little creatures with pearly wings and gleaming brass halos seem to hover near the branches of the tree. Each year a different animal joins the group in this endearing series.
■ 1993   450QXM512-2
■ 1992   450QXM545-1
■ 1991   450QXM565-7
■ 1990   450QXM573-3

Nature's Angels, 1993

Nature's Angels, 1992

Nature's Angels: 1990, 1991

Noel R.R., 1993

Noel R.R., 1992

Noel R.R.: 1989, 1990, 1991

Old English Village, 1993

Old English Village, 1992

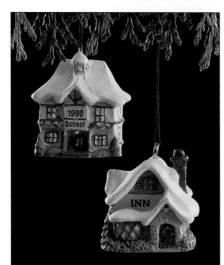

Old English Village: 1990, 1991

Old English Village: 1988, 1989

Noel R.R.

The colorful "Locomotive" was the first car to make a Christmas journey in this series. It picks up a different type of railroad car on every annual trip.

- 1993 700QXM510-5
  Flatbed Car
- 1992 700QXM544-1
  Box Car
- 1991 850QXM564-9
  Passenger Car
- 1990 850QXM575-6
  Coal Car
- 1989 850QXM576-2
  Locomotive

Old English Village

The details and architecture of the houses, buildings, and shops in this series capture the charm of a country village in England.

- 1993 700QXM513-2
  Toy Shop
- 1992 700QXM538-4
  Church
- 1991 850QXM562-7
  Inn
- 1990 850QXM576-3
  School
- 1989 850QXM561-5
  Sweet Shop
- 1988 850QXM563-4
  Family Home

The Bearymores
This series introduces us to the Bearymores—a merry family of polar bears.
- ▨ 1993   575QXM512-5
- ▨ 1992   575QXM554-4

The Bearymores, 1993

The Bearymores, 1992

Rocking Horse
This series of rocking steeds recalls a beloved childhood toy as well as a popular Keepsake Ornament design.
- ▨ 1993   450QXM511-2
- ▨ 1992   450QXM545-4
- ▨ 1991   450QXM563-7
- ▨ 1990   450QXM574-3
- ▨ 1989   450QXM560-5
- ▨ 1988   450QXM562-4

Rocking Horse, 1993

Rocking Horse, 1992

Keepsake Miniature Retired Collectible Series

Woodland Babies
The cutest babies in the forest have come to decorate the tree in this series. The final edition was offered in 1993.
- ▨ 1993   575QXM510-2
- ▨ 1992   600QXM544-4
- ▨ 1991   600QXM566-7

Rocking Horse: 1990, 1991

Rocking Horse: 1988, 1989

Woodland Babies, 1993

Woodland Babies, 1992

Woodland Babies, 1991

Penguin Pal: 1990, 1991

Penguin Pal: 1988, 1989

Penguin Pal

These dapper penguins partake in the holiday's festivities each year. The series ended in 1991.

■ 1991 450QXM562-9
■ 1990 450QXM574-6
■ 1989 450QXM560-2
■ 1988 375QXM563-1

Thimble Bells

Fashioned of fine porcelain and decorated with a different design each year, the ornaments in this series are especially appealing to collectors of thimbles, bells, and ornaments. The final edition was issued in 1993.

■ 1993 575QXM514-2
■ 1992 600QXM546-1
■ 1991 600QXM565-9
■ 1990 600QXM554-3

The Kringles

The most celebrated couple in the North Pole shares the merriment of the season in this series of ornaments. The last edition was issued in 1993.

■ 1993 575QXM513-5
■ 1992 600QXM538-1
■ 1991 600QXM564-7
■ 1990 600QXM575-3
■ 1989 600QXM562-5

Thimble Bells, 1993

Thimble Bells, 1992

Thimble Bells: 1990, 1991

The Kringles, 1993

The Kringles, 1992

The Kringles: 1989, 1991, 1990

Kittens in Toyland

For each year, a different kitten has a fun-filled holiday as he plays with his Christmas gifts. This series retired in 1992.

- 1992 450QXM539-1
- 1991 450QXM563-9
- 1990 450QXM573-6
- 1989 450QXM561-2
- 1988 500QXM562-1

Kittens in Toyland, 1992

Kittens in Toyland: 1990, 1991

Kittens in Toyland: 1988, 1989

Springtime Bonnets, 1993

Keepsake Easter Ornament Series

Springtime Bonnets

This ladylike rabbit smiles shyly beneath her straw textured hat, leading off the "Springtime Bonnets" series.

- 1993 775QEO832-2

Easter Parade

A parade of lovable Easter friends come marching your way in this series.

- 1993 675QEO832-5
- 1992 675QEO930-1

Eggs in Sports

This series features a lineup of "eggstraordinary" sports stars.

- 1993 675QEO833-2
- 1992 675QEO934-1

Easter Parade, 1993

Easter Parade, 1992

Eggs in Sports, 1993

Eggs in Sports, 1992

Index